WILEY
PLUS
+
www.wileyplus.com

ALL THE HELP, RESOURCES, AND PERSONAL SUPPORT YOU AND YOUR STUDENTS NEED!

www.wileyplus.com/resources

2-Minute Tutorials and all of the resources you & your students need to get started.

Student support from an experienced student user.

Collaborate with your colleagues, find a mentor, attend virtual and live events, and view resources.
www.WhereFacultyConnect.com

Pre-loaded, ready-to-use assignments and presentations. Created by subject matter experts.

Technical Support 24/7 FAQs, online chat, and phone support.
www.wileyplus.com/support

Your *WileyPLUS* Account Manager. Personal training and implementation support.

INTRODUCTION TO
INFORMATION SYSTEMS

SUPPORTING AND TRANSFORMING BUSINESS   SECOND CANADIAN EDITION

R. KELLY RAINER, JR.

Auburn University, Auburn, Alabama

CASEY G. CEGIELSKI

Auburn University, Auburn, Alabama

INGRID SPLETTSTOESSER-HOGETERP

York University, Toronto, Ontario

CRISTÓBAL SÁNCHEZ-RODRÍGUEZ

York University, Toronto, Ontario

John Wiley & Sons Canada, Ltd.

Library and Archives Canada Cataloguing in Publication
   Introduction to information systems: supporting and transforming business / R. Kelly Rainer, Jr. . . . [et al.]. — 2nd Canadian ed.
ISBN 978-0-470-67888-6
   1. Information technology—Management—Textbooks.   2. Management information systems—Textbooks.   I. Rainer, R. Kelly (Rex Kelly)
T58.6.I64 2010   658.4'038011   C2010-905742-2
All images are from istock unless otherwise noted.

Production Credits
Acquisitions Editor: Darren Lalonde
Vice President & Publisher: Veronica Visentin
Vice President, Publishing Services: Karen Bryan
Creative Director, Publishing Services: Ian Koo
Marketing Manager: Anne-Marie Seymour
Editorial Manager: Karen Staudinger
Developmental Editor: Daleara Jamasji Hirjikaka
Media Editor: Channade Fenandoe
Editorial Assistant: Laura Hwee
Cover and Interior Design: Mike Chan
Typesetting: Thomson Digital
Printing & Binding: Quad/Graphics

Printed and bound in the United States of America
1 2 3 4 5 QG 15 14 13 12 11

 John Wiley & Sons Canada, Ltd.
6045 Freemont Blvd.
Mississauga, Ontario L5R 4J3
Visit our website at www.wiley.ca

ABOUT THE AUTHORS

R. KELLY RAINER, JR.

R. Kelly Rainer, Jr. is George Phillips Privett Professor of Management Information Systems at Auburn University, Auburn, Alabama. He received his BS degree in Mathematics from Auburn and his Doctor of Dental Medicine (DMD) from the University of Alabama in Birmingham. After practising dentistry for 10 years, Dr. Rainer returned to school and received his Ph.D. at the University of Georgia. He has published numerous articles in leading journals. His research interests include enterprise resource planning (particularly using SAP), business process reengineering, and object-oriented technology.

CASEY G. CEGIELSKI

Casey G. Cegielski is an Assistant Professor of Management Information Systems. His current research interests are in the areas of innovation diffusion, computer facilitated speech recognition, and the strategic use of information technology. His research has appeared in numerous international information technology. Currently, he teaches courses in object-oriented application development and systems analysis and design. Dr. Cegielski earned a doctorate in Business Administration with a concentration in Management Information Systems from the University of Mississippi. Additionally, he holds a master's degree in accountancy as well as a bachelor's degree, both from the University of Alabama.

INGRID SPLETTSTOESSER-HOGETERP

Ingrid Splettstoesser-Hogeterp teaches management information systems, auditing, and information systems auditing using a multidisciplinary approach, at York University in Toronto. Her research and publications are based on real-world cases, involving the documentation and analysis of e-commerce systems. Dr. Splettstoesser-Hogeterp believes in continuing education, as shown by her educational background, which includes mathematics, management sciences, psychology, and forensics. She is also a qualified Chartered Accountant (CA) and Certified Information Systems Auditor (CISA).

CRISTÓBAL SÁNCHEZ-RODRÍGUEZ

Cristóbal Sánchez-Rodríguez is a professor of audit and management information systems at the School of Administrative Studies at York University in Toronto, where he teaches courses in electronic commerce, management of strategic information systems, and business statistics. Dr. Sánchez-Rodríguez has published research papers on a number of operations management and information systems topics. His research has been published in *International Journal of Operations and Production Management*, *International Journal of Production Economics*, and *International Journal of Enterprise Information Management*, among others. Dr. Sánchez-Rodríguez has conducted research with multinational organizations and has provided consulting services to International Data Corporation (IDC) Canada.

PREFACE

WHAT DO INFORMATION SYSTEMS HAVE TO DO WITH BUSINESS?

Rainer, Cegielski, Splettstoesser-Hogeterp, and Sánchez-Rodríguez *Introduction to Information Systems* will answer this question for you. In every chapter, you will see how real global businesses use technology and information systems to increase their profitability, gain market share, improve their customer service, and manage their daily operations. In other words, information systems provide the foundation for business.

Our goal is to teach all business majors, especially undergraduates, how to use IT (information technology) to master their current or future jobs and to help ensure the success of their organization. Our focus is not on merely *learning* the concepts of information technology but rather on *applying* those concepts to facilitate business processes. We concentrate on placing information systems in the context of business, so that students will more readily grasp the concepts presented in the text.

WHAT'S IN IT FOR ME?

The theme of this book is *What's in IT for Me?* This question is asked by all students who take this course. Our book will show you that IT is the backbone of any business, whether you're in Accounting, Finance, Marketing, Human Resources, or Production/Operations Management. We also include information for the Management Information Systems (MIS) major.

NEW TO THIS EDITION

There are many additions and changes in Rainer second Canadian edition. These changes make our book more interesting and readable for students of all majors, while still providing the most current information possible in the rapidly changing field of information systems.

The overall additions are:

- A new chapter on customer relationship management (Chapter 9).
- A new chapter on supply chain management (Chapter 10).
- New and updated chapter openings and closing cases.
- New and updated IT's About Business features in every chapter.
- New examples of real-world applications in every chapter.
- Video clips accompanying Chapters 1 and 2. The videos contain interviews with a Chief Executive Officer concerning issues raised in the first two chapters of the book.
- Video clips accompanying Chapters 3 through 12. The videos contain interviews with practising managers in Accounting, Finance, Marketing, Production/Operations, and Human Resources. In the video clips, each manager responds to questions covering the major topics of the book. For example, in the video clips accompanying Chapter 3, each manager relates how ethical issues, privacy issues, and information security concerns impact their company and its employees.
- New and updated PowerPoint slides incorporating extensive images and video.
- New and updated Test Bank with questions labelled according to difficulty: easy, medium, and hard.

Specific changes include:

Chapter 1 begins with a section on the importance of planning for information technology and contains a new section on business processes, business process reengineering, and business process management.

Chapter 2 describes the importance of IT and its relationship to corporate governance at the beginning of the chapter.

Chapter 4 includes a more detailed discussion on relational database management systems.

Chapter 5 has an expanded discussion of IT-enabled collaboration and collaboration software products.

Chapter 8 includes expanded, in-depth sections on functional area information systems and enterprise resource planning systems.

Chapter 12 adds a section on project management and a section on developing and controlling the acquisition process. The remainder of the chapter has been extensively rewritten, simplified, and shortened for added readability.

Technology Guide 1 has been rearranged for increased readability and impact. Strategic hardware issues are now at the beginning of the technology guide and the more technical material is at the end. The technology guide covers the latest technologies such as server farms, virtualization, and cloud computing. Discussions of these technologies are accompanied by examples.

Technology Guide 2 has been rearranged for increased readability and impact. Recent developments in operating systems such as Windows 7 and open source software have been introduced.

Technology Guide 3 has been updated for current versions of operating systems and browsers.

Technology Guide 4 has been reorganized. It also includes a brief discussion about the new Internet protocol Ipv6.

KEY FEATURES

We have been guided by the following goals that we believe will enhance the teaching and learning experience.

CROSS-FUNCTIONAL APPROACH

We show why IT is important by calling attention in each chapter to how that chapter's IT topic relates to students in each major. Icons (shown below) guide the students to relevant issues for their specific functional area—accounting, finance, marketing, production/operations management, management information systems, and human resources management. In addition, chapters end with a summary of how the concepts relate to each functional area (*What's in IT for Me?*).

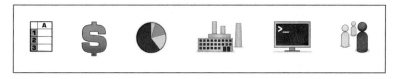

ACTIVE LEARNING

We recognize the need to actively involve students in problem solving, creative thinking, and capitalizing on opportunities. Every chapter includes a variety of hands-on exercises, activities, and mini-cases, including exercises that ask students to use software application tools. Through these activities and an interactive website, we enable students to apply the concepts they learn, such as how to improve a business through IT, configure products, and use spreadsheets to facilitate problem solving.

DIVERSIFIED AND UNIQUE EXAMPLES FROM DIFFERENT INDUSTRIES

Extensive use of vivid examples from large corporations, small businesses, and governments and not-for-profit organizations helps to enliven concepts by showing students the capabilities of IT, its cost and justification, and innovative ways that real corporations are using IT in their operations. Each chapter continually highlights the integral connection between IT and business, and a blend of carefully chosen Canadian examples helps to strengthen this connection for your students. This is especially evident in the *IT's About Business* boxes.

SUCCESSES AND FAILURES

Like other textbooks, we present many examples of IT success. But we also provide examples of IT failures, in the context of lessons that can be learned from such failures. Misuse of IT can be very expensive, as we illustrate.

INNOVATION AND CREATIVITY

In today's rapidly changing environment, businesses must be creative and innovative to operate effectively and profitably. Throughout the book we show how these concepts are facilitated by IT.

GLOBAL FOCUS

Since an understanding of global competition, partnerships, and trading is essential to success in business, we provide a broad selection of international cases and examples. We discuss how IT facilitates export and import, the management of multinational companies, and electronic trading around the globe.

CUTTING-EDGE INFORMATION ON WIRELESS TECHNOLOGIES, E-COMMERCE, AND WEB SERVICES

Mobile and Internet technologies have created a paradigm shift in the way that the world does business. We offer a chapter on electronic commerce (Chapter 6) and a comprehensive chapter on wireless technologies (Chapter 7).

FOCUS ON ETHICS

With corporate scandals in the headlines daily, ethics and ethical questions have come to the forefront of business people's minds. In addition to a chapter that concentrates on ethics and security (Chapter 3), we have included examples and cases that focus on business ethics throughout the chapters.

PEDAGOGICAL STRUCTURE

Other pedagogical features provide a structured learning system that reinforces the concepts through features such as chapter-opening organizers, section reviews, frequent applications, and hands-on exercises and activities.

Chapter Opening organizers include the following pedagogical features:

- The *Learning Objectives* and the *Chapter Preview* together give an overview of the importance of the chapter and the key elements that students should come away with after reading the chapter.
- An opening *Case* identifies a business problem faced by an actual company, describes the IT solution applied to the business problem, with the results of the IT solution being presented and discussed throughout the chapter.

Study Aids are provided throughout each chapter. These include the following:

- *IT's About Business* boxes provide real-world applications, with questions that relate to concepts covered in the text.
- Highlighted *Examples* show the use (and misuse) of IT by real-world organizations and help illustrate the conceptual discussion.
- *Tables* list key points or summarize different concepts.
- End-of-section reviews *(Before You Go On . . .)* prompt students to pause and test their understanding of concepts before moving on to the next section.

End-of-Chapter Study Aids provide extensive opportunity for students to review and actually "do something" with the concepts they have just studied:

- *What's in IT for Me?* is a unique chapter summary that shows the relevance of topics for different functional areas (accounting, finance, marketing, production/operations management, management information systems, and human resources management.)
- The chapter *Summary*, keyed to learning objectives that were listed at the beginning of the chapter, enables students to review the major concepts covered in the chapter.
- *Discussion Questions, Problem-Solving Activities, Web Activities,* and *Team Assignments* provide practice through active learning. These exercises are hands-on opportunities to use the concepts discussed in the chapter.
- A *Case* presents a real-world case organized around a business problem and shows how IT helped to solve it; questions at the end of the case relate it to concepts discussed in the chapter.
- "Interactive Case: Ruby's Club" gives the student an assignment as an intern for Ruby's Club, a downtown music venue that needs hep redesigning its website and overhauling its technological infrastructure, among other things. Students are referred to WileyPLUS or the Student Companion Site for support information and assignments.

ON-LINE SUPPLEMENTS

This book also facilitates the teaching of an Introduction to IT course by providing extensive support materials for instructors and students. Go to www.wiley.com/canada/rainer to access the Student and Instructor websites.

INSTRUCTOR'S MANUAL

The *Instructor's Manual* created by Dana Newton at Eastern Michigan University and Frank Anatol of Wilfrid Laurier University includes a chapter overview, teaching tips and strategies, and answers to all end-of-chapter questions.

TEST BANK

The *Test Bank*, written by Kelly Rainer and Ingrid Splettstoesser-Hogeterp, is a comprehensive resource for test questions. It contains per-chapter short answer and essay questions, along with multiple choice and true/false questions that are labelled according to difficulty: easy, medium, or hard.

POWERPOINT PRESENTATIONS

The media-enriched *PowerPoint Presentations* created by Kelly Rainer and Tony Mao contain slides for each chapter, incorporating key points from the text and text illustrations as appropriate. They include links to relevant websites, videos, and articles to enhance classroom discussion. The PowerPoint presentations make extensive use of images and video clips.

MEDIA RESOURCE LIBRARY

The *Media Resource Library* provides instructors with a wealth of links to websites and videos that can be used in class to help engage students. The library is a compilation of suggestions from the authors as well as many information systems instructors and comes with discussion questions to be used in class after viewing each resource.

IMAGE LIBRARY

All textbook figures are available for download from the website. These figures can easily be added to PowerPoint presentations.

BUSINESS EXTRA SELECT

This feature allows instructors to package the text with software applications, lab manuals, cases, articles, and other real-world content from sources such as INSEAD, Ivey and Harvard Business School cases, *Fortune*, *The Economist*, *The Wall Street Journal*, and much more. You can combine the book with the content you choose to create a fully customized textbook. For additional information, go to www.wiley.com/college/bxs.

ON-LINE QUIZZES

The website includes practice tests for students to help prepare for class tests. Once students have completed a particular quiz, they can submit it electronically and receive feedback regarding any incorrect responses.

COURSE MANAGEMENT

New WebCT and Blackboard courses are available with this text. WebCT and Blackboard are tools that facilitate the organization and delivery of course materials via the Web. It provides powerful communication, loaded content, easy and flexible course administration, sophisticated on-line self-tests and diagnostic systems, and ease-of-use for both students and instructors.

CLICKER QUESTIONS

Clicker questions deliver a variety of multiple choice and true/false questions to use in class in order to assess students' learning throughout the course.

WileyPLUS

www.wiley**plus**.com

WileyPLUS is an innovative, research-based on-line environment for effective teaching and learning.

WileyPLUS builds students' confidence because it takes the guesswork out of studying by providing students with a clear roadmap: what to do, how to do it, if they did it right. This interactive approach focuses on:

DESIGN: Research-based design is based on proven instructional methods. Content is organized into small, more accessible amounts of information, helping students build better time management skills.

ENGAGEMENT: Students can visually track their progress as they move through the material at a pace that is right for them. Engaging in individualized self-quizzes followed by immediate feedback helps to sustain their motivation to learn.

OUTCOMES: Self-assessment lets students know the exact outcome of their effort at any time. Advanced reporting allows instructors to easily spot trends in the usage and performance data of their class in order to make more informed decisions.

With *WileyPLUS*, students take more initiative so you'll have greater impact on their achievement in the classroom and beyond.

What do students receive with *WileyPLUS?*

- Confidence-boosting feedback and proof of progress, 24/7
- Context-sensitive feedback as they work on problems that are linked to relevant sections in the on-line digital textbook
- An easy-to-navigate framework, calendars, visual progress tracking, and self-evaluation tools that help students study more effectively

What do instructors receive with *WileyPLUS?*

- Reliable resources that reinforce course goals inside and outside of the classroom
- Media-rich course materials and assessment content—Instructor's Manual, Test Bank, PowerPoint® Slides, Learning Objectives, Computerized Test Bank, Pre- and Post- Lecture Quizzes, and much more

ACKNOWLEDGEMENTS

Creating, developing, and producing a text for an introductory course to information technology is a formidable undertaking. First of all, we would like to thank our students to whom this book is dedicated. We would like to reiterate our commitment to them and thank them for their feedback in improving this textbook. Also, we would like to extend our thanks to all those instructors who use this textbook in the classroom. You are the reason for the second edition. We are also grateful for the efforts of our supplement reviewer John Kucharczuk of Seneca College, Centennial College, and part-time faculty of York University. Thank you as well to supplement contributors Frank Anatol, Christine Brown, Tony Mao, and Lindsay Silverthorn who contributed so much to the related supplements. Many thanks to our acquisitions editor, Darren Lalonde, and the team at John Wiley & Sons, Canada for all their work and effort. Along the way, we were fortunate to receive continuous evaluation, criticism, and direction from many colleagues who regularly teach this course. Reviewers for this text were:

- James Clark, University of Lethbridge
- Ken Cudeck, York University
- Ernest Johnson, University of Regina
- Leo Kerklaan, McGill University
- Chitu Okoli, Concordia University
- Jennifer Percival, University of Ontario Institute of Technology
- Rob Sorenson, Camosun College
- Haralambie Stirbet, Wilfrid Laurier University
- John H. Walker, Brock University
- Cameron Welsh, University of Calgary

Ingrid Splettstoesser-Hogeterp
Cristóbal Sánchez-Rodríguez
Toronto, Ontario

September 2010

BRIEF CONTENTS

CONTENTS

1

THE MODERN ORGANIZATION IN THE GLOBAL, WEB-BASED ENVIRONMENT

LEARNING OBJECTIVES

1. Link effective information technology planning to business planning.

2. Describe business processes and explain how business process management helps to improve how businesses function.

3. Explain the role of data, information, and knowledge. Differentiate between information technology architecture and information technology infrastructure.

4. Describe the global business environment and how globalization has affected organizations.

5. Discuss the relationships among business pressures, organizational responses, and information systems.

6. Provide examples of the relevance of information systems to individuals and organizations.

7. Describe the plan of this book.

CAN PAYMENT TECHNOLOGY MATCH THE NEEDS OF ORGANIZATIONS AND CONSUMERS?

CASE 1.1

THE BUSINESS PROBLEM

The purchasing world is changing. Newspaper circulation is down, music sales are down, while on-line sales are up. How can organizations sell on-line products for a few cents or a dollar when bank charges often add up to the same amount for each deposit?

Sales are only made if consumers have the money to purchase products and services, right away. For example, Jane is downtown at a new electronics store and would like to buy a laptop computer, but there is not enough money in her chequing account. She heads to the nearest automated teller machine (ATM) to transfer money from her savings account to her chequing account and finds that it is out of service, so the laptop remains in the store.

Or, Sully hears a great song on the radio and decides that it would make a good ring tone, but does not want to order on-line and pay a high bank service charge when the ring tone already costs $2. Half an hour later, when Sully enters a music store to buy the ring tone cheaper, he forgets the name of the song so can't buy the ring tone anymore.

Franci goes out for lunch with her friend, and realizes that she has left her wallet at home. Rather than continuing to owe her friend money for lunch, she would like to pay right away. Since she just has a $5 bill, she only orders a cup of tea and the restaurant loses out.

THE IT SOLUTION

Enter portable banking services and payment methods focused on the cellular telephone. For example, TD Bank launched applications for iPhone and iPod devices on April 14, 2010. In the first two weeks of its service, the bank estimated that it had more than 10,000 downloads per day. TD and the other major Canadian banks now allow most banking activity to be done on a cellular phone (such as checking account balances, paying bills, transferring funds, and sending money to another bank account). The Canadian payment network known as Interac can also be used to complete an e-mail money transfer, perhaps to pay a friend for lunch.

Both the TD Bank application and ING Direct can help users locate the nearest ATM. ING's services function on both BlackBerry and iPhone devices.

In 2009, Amazon.com created a new payment service called PayPhrase. The service requires that the user already have an account with Amazon.com, and a method of payment (such as credit card) established. Then PayPhrase allows the set-up of a payment phrase with a personal identification number (PIN) to create multiple payment profiles. These payment profiles could be for shipments to a specific address, or to set up multiple PayPhrase allowances that can be used by other people. You can use PayPhrase to add additional security to your Amazon account. The Amazon website explains that to give an allowance to another person, you would need to add information in your account that identifies the other person (such as a shipping address, the monthly limit to be used, and how you would pay for their purchases).

WHAT DO YOU THINK?

1. Think about the effect of multiple payment methods. Can every retail organization accept every type of payment method? How does this affect competition?
2. Should all banks and credit unions offer the applications described here? Why or why not?

Sources: Compiled from N. E. Arellano, "New ING Direct App Lets You Do Your Banking from BlackBerry, iPhone," ITbusiness.ca, March 24, 2010; R. Lemos, "Can Amazon's PayPhrase Combine Convenience with Security?", *MIT Technology Review*, November 3, 2009; J. P. Menezes, "TD Bank Customers Have 'App-etite' for iPhone Banking," ITbusiness.ca, April 20, 2010; Amazon website (*www.amazon.com*), accessed May 14, 2010; RBC Financial Group website (*www.rbcroyalbank.com*), accessed May 14, 2010.

Chapter Preview

We are starting on a new journey together—a journey of new words and concepts, of stories and information, of the language of information technology (IT). In this first chapter, you discover why information systems are important, and learn about the building blocks of information technology that are used by individuals and businesses. Together, we explore how systems are put together and how and why businesses use information technology.

Our opening case illustrated the importance of having low-cost electronic payment systems. Depending upon the banking arrangements that organizations make, they could be paying up to $1.98 for each banking deposit. Without the use of new payment methods, organizations cannot accept small payments, known as micropayments. For consumers who are used to accessing the Internet anywhere and anytime, it is a natural progression to also be able to make payments at any time.

The opening case illustrates that IT is having a pervasive effect on payment methods and purchasing methods. We provide other examples of the societal and environmental effects of IT throughout this book. In addition, IT is making our world smaller, enabling more and more people to communicate, collaborate, and compete, thereby levelling the "digital playing field."

Organizational impacts follow from changes in processes such as payment methods. The following points summarize these impacts:

- To succeed in today's environment, it is often necessary to change business models and strategies to respond to changes such as those discussed in our opening case.
- IT enables organizations to survive and thrive in the face of relentless business pressures.
- IT may require a large investment over a long period of time.
- Organizations can use their platforms (discussed in the section on Information Technology Infrastructure below) to develop new web-based applications, products, and services, as well as to provide superb customer service.

These changes also affect you—you are the most connected generation in history. You have grown up on-line. You are, quite literally, never out of touch. You use more information technologies (in the form of digital devices) for more tasks and are bombarded with more information than any generation. The *MIT Technology Review* refers to you as *Homo conexus*. Information technologies are embedded so deeply in your lives that your daily routines would be almost unrecognizable to a university student just 20 years ago.

Essentially, you are practising *continuous computing*, where you are surrounded with a movable information network. Your network is created by constant cooperation between the digital devices you carry (for example, laptops, media players, and smart phones), the wired and wireless networks that you access as you move about, and web-based tools for finding information and communicating and collaborating with other people. Your network enables you to *pull* information about virtually anything from anywhere at any time and *push* your own ideas back to the Web from wherever you are via a mobile device, as well as make large or small payments, as described in our opening case.

So, why study about information systems and information technology when you are already so comfortable using them? The answer is that when you graduate, you either will start your own business or will go to work for an organization, whether it is public-sector, private-sector, for-profit, or not-for-profit. In any case, you and your organization will have to survive and compete in an environment that has been radically changed by information technology. This environment is global, massively interconnected, intensely competitive, available 24/7/365, real-time, rapidly changing, and information-intensive.

In this chapter, we first address the importance of effective information technology planning to business planning, as most organizations now need information technology to function effectively. Then we look at business processes and business process management, because business processes literally constitute what an organization does, and the management of those processes is critical to the success of any organization. In our discussion, we note how information systems enable business process management.

We then discuss the basic concepts of information systems in organizations. Before we do that, we need to distinguish between management information systems, also called **information systems** or **IS**, and information technology. **Management information systems (MIS)** deal with the planning for—and the development, management, and use of—information technology tools to help people perform all of the tasks related to information processing and management. **Information technology (IT)** relates to any computer-based tool that people use to work with information and to support the information and information-processing needs of an organization. Although these are distinct terms, in practice they are typically used interchangeably. For example, organizations refer to their MIS function as the Information Services Department, the Information Systems Department, and the Information Technology Department, among other things. In keeping with common practice, we use these terms interchangeably throughout this book.

After discussing the basic concepts of information systems, we discuss today's global business environment and how businesses use information technologies to survive and prosper in this highly competitive environment. We then turn our attention to considering in greater detail why information systems are important to you. We finish the chapter by presenting the plan of the book.

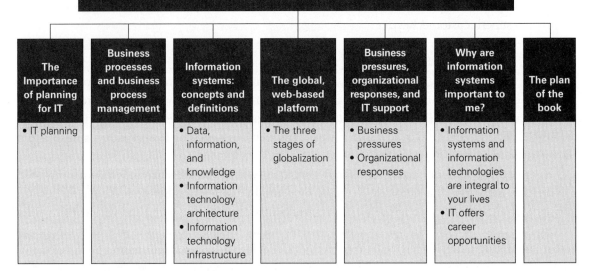

INFORMATION SYSTEMS: CONCEPTS AND MANAGEMENT						
The Importance of planning for IT	Business processes and business process management	Information systems: concepts and definitions	The global, web-based platform	Business pressures, organizational responses, and IT support	Why are information systems important to me?	The plan of the book
• IT planning		• Data, information, and knowledge • Information technology architecture • Information technology infrastructure	• The three stages of globalization	• Business pressures • Organizational responses	• Information systems and information technologies are integral to your lives • IT offers career opportunities	

1.1 The Importance of Planning for IT

Organizations must analyze the need for new information systems and justify these in terms of cost and benefits. The need for information systems is usually related to organizational planning and to the analysis of organizational performance vis-à-vis its competitors. The cost-benefit justification must look at the wisdom of investing in a specific IT system versus spending the funds on alternative projects.

When a company examines its needs and performance, it generates a prioritized list of both existing and potential IT systems. A new information system can apply to the whole organization (for example, the purchase of an enterprise resource planning system, described in Chapter 8) or it can apply to a particular functional or application area of an organization (for example, a sales or payroll transaction processing system, also described further in Chapter 8). New system proposals may be organized and grouped into **application portfolios**. These would be the applications that have to be added, or modified if they already exist.

IT Planning

The planning process for new IT applications begins with analysis of the *organizational strategic plan*, as shown in Figure 1.1. The organization's strategic plan states the firm's overall mission, the goals that follow from that mission, and the broad steps necessary to reach these goals. The strategic planning process modifies the organization's objectives and resources to meet its changing markets and opportunities.

The organizational strategic plan and the existing IT architecture provide the inputs in developing the IT strategic plan. The *IT architecture* delineates the way an organization's information resources should be used to accomplish its mission. It encompasses both the technical and the managerial aspects of information resources. The technical aspects include hardware and operating systems, networking, data management systems, and applications software. The managerial aspects specify how managing the IT department will be accomplished, how the functional area managers will be involved, and how IT decisions will be made.

The **IT strategic plan** is a set of long-range goals that describe the IT infrastructure and identify the major IT initiatives needed to achieve the organization's goals. The IT strategic plan must meet three objectives:

1. It must be aligned with the organization's strategic plan.
2. It must provide for an IT architecture that enables users, applications, and databases to be seamlessly networked and integrated.

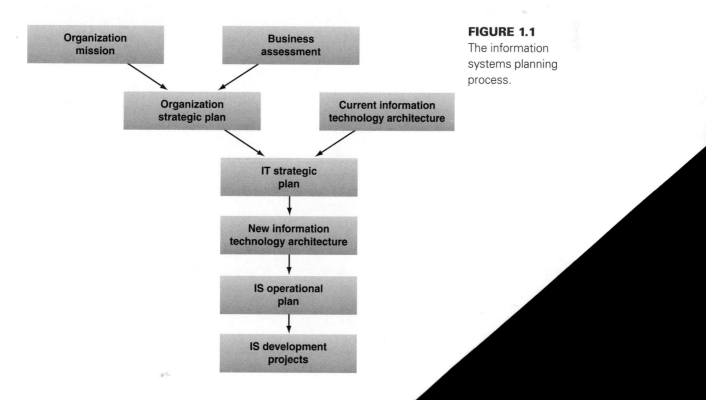

FIGURE 1.1
The information systems planning process.

3. It must efficiently allocate IS development resources among competing projects so the projects can be completed on time and within budget and have the required functionality.

One critical component in developing and implementing the IT strategic plan is the **IT steering committee**. This committee, composed of a group of managers and staff representing various organizational units, is set up to establish IT priorities and to ensure that the MIS function is meeting the enterprise's needs. The committee's major tasks are to link corporate strategy and IT strategy, to approve the allocation of resources for the MIS function, and to establish performance measures for the MIS function and ensure that they are met. The IT steering committee is important to the organization because it ensures that the information systems and applications are acquired so that employees get the resources that they need to do their job. Organizations that do not do effective IT planning run the risk of not having information systems available on time to meet their needs.

After a company has agreed on an IT strategic plan, it next develops the *IS operational plan*. This plan consists of a clear set of projects that the IS department and the functional area managers will execute in support of the IT strategic plan. A typical IS operational plan contains the following elements:

- *Mission* The mission of the IS function (derived from the IT strategy).
- *IS environment* A summary of the information needs of the functional areas and of the organization as a whole.
- *Objectives of the IS function* The best current estimate of the goals of the IS function.
- *Constraints on the IS function* Technological, financial, personnel, and other resource limitations on the IS function.
- *The application portfolio* A prioritized inventory of present applications and a detailed plan of projects to be developed or continued during the current year.
- *Resource allocation and project management* A listing of who is going to do what, how, and when.

IT planning is crucial when developing a new product or service, such as the drug-dispensing kiosks described in IT's About Business 1.1.

IT'S ABOUT BUSINESS 1.1
DRUG-DISPENSING KIOSKS IMPROVE CUSTOMER SERVICE

Sometimes during an emergency, it may not be possible to find a pharmacy that is open 24 hours a day and fill ... at case, why not consider ... ing kiosk that functions in ... ted teller machine? ... ed in Oakville, Ontario, ... enables a customer to ... place an order for a pre- ... anned by the machine, ... motely. Using a screen ... the pharmacist, and a ... consumer can talk to ... n be discussed and ... sumer pays for the ... a dispenser. ... ogy is being used ... (radio frequency

identification) to tag the products, scanning devices and multimedia to interact with the consumer and pharmacist, and data encryption to ensure secure transmission and storage of information. These machines were being tested in medical centres in Ontario over a three-year period starting in 2007.

Sources: N. E. Arellano, "Canadian Company Pushing Pill-dispensing Kiosk," ITbusiness.ca, May 7, 2008; J. Wilkes, "Drug-dispensing Kiosks on the Way," *Toronto Star*, February 1, 2010, p. A2; PCA Services website (*http://pharmatrust.com*), accessed August 12, 2010.

QUESTIONS
1. What might be some of the long-range goals of a new company such as PCA Services Inc.?
2. Explain how the information systems in use at the drug-dispensing kiosks help to support the business requirements of PCA Services Inc.

1.2 Business Processes and Business Process Management

A **business process** is a collection of related activities that produce a product or a service of value to the organization, its business partners, and/or its customers. A process has inputs and outputs, and its activities can be measured. Many processes cross functional areas in an organization, such as product development, which involves design, engineering, manufacturing, marketing, and distribution. Other processes involve only one functional area. Table 1.1 shows examples of business processes in the functional areas of an organization.

An organization's business processes can lead to competitive advantages if they enable the company to innovate or execute better than competitors. Business processes can also be liabilities if they impede organizational responsiveness and efficiency. As an example, consider the airline industry. It has become a competitive necessity for all of the airlines to offer electronic ticket purchases via their websites. At the same time, however, these sites must be highly responsive and have the most current information on flights and prices. A site that provides outdated or inaccurate information will hurt rather than improve business. Figure 1.2 A (*see* p. 9) illustrates the e-ticket purchasing business process.

Business process excellence is widely recognized as the underlying basis for all significant measures of competitive performance in the organization. Consider these measures, for example:

- Customer satisfaction: the result of improving and aligning business processes to fulfill the customer's needs, wants, and desires.
- Cost reduction: the result of having more efficient operations and supplier processes.
- Cycle and fulfillment time: the result of having better manufacturing and product management processes.
- Quality: the result of improving the design, development, and production processes.
- Product differentiation: the result of having effective marketing and innovation processes.
- Productivity: the result of improving each individual's work processes.

The question is: How does an organization ensure business process excellence?

In their book *Reengineering the Corporation*, Michael Hammer and James Champy argued that American businesses needed to radically redesign their business processes to lower costs and increase quality in order to become more competitive. The authors further asserted that information technology was the key enabler of such radical change. This radical redesign, called business process reengineering (BPR), is an approach that improves the efficiency and effectiveness of an organization's business processes. The key to BPR is for enterprises to examine their business processes from a "clean sheet" perspective and then determine how they could best reconstruct those processes to improve their business functions.

TABLE 1.1
EXAMPLES OF BUSINESS PROCESSES

Accounting Business Processes	• Master parts list and files
• Accounts payable	• Packing, storage, and distribution
• Accounts receivable	• Physical inventory procedures
• Bank account reconciliation	• Purchasing procedures
• Cash receipts	• Quality control for finished goods
• Invoice billings	• Quality assurance audit procedure
• Petty cash	• Receiving, inspection, and stocking of parts and materials
• Month-end close	• Shipping and freight claims
• Virtual close	• Vendor selection, files, and inspections
Finance Business Processes	**Human Resources Business Processes**
• Account collection	• Disabilities employment policies
• Bank loan applications	• Employee hiring policies
• Business forecasts	• Employee orientation
• Customer credit approval and credit terms	• Family and medical leave
• Property tax assessments	• Files and records management
• Stock transactions	• Health care benefits
• Financial cash flow reports	• Pay and payroll
Marketing Business Processes	• Performance appraisals and salary adjustments
• After-sale customer follow-up	• Resignations and terminations
• Collection of sales tax	• Training/tuition reimbursement
• Copyrights and trademarks	• Travel and entertainment
• Customer satisfaction surveys	• Workplace rules and guidelines
• Customer service contracts	• Workplace safety
• Customer complaint handling	
• Returned goods from customers	**Management Information Systems Business Processes**
• Sales leads	• Antivirus control programs
• Sales order entry	• Computer security incident reporting
• Sales training	• Computer user/staff training
• Trade shows	• Disaster recovery procedures
• Warranty and service policies	• Electronic mail policy
	• Internet use policy
Production/Operations Management Business Processes	• Service agreements and emergency services
• Bill of materials	• User workstation standards
• Manufacturing change orders	• Use of personal software

Although some enterprises successfully implemented BPR, for many organizations this radical redesign was too difficult, too radical, and too comprehensive. The impact on employees, on facilities, on existing investments in information systems, and even on organizational culture, was overwhelming. Despite the many failures in BPR implementation, however, the process did succeed in convincing businesses to organize work around business processes, rather than tasks. As a result, a less radical, less disruptive, and more incremental approach was developed, called business process management.

To a great degree, an organization's performance depends on how well it manages its business processes. As a result, organizations emphasize **business process management (BPM)**, which is a management technique that includes methods and tools to support the design, analysis, implementation, management, and optimization of business processes.

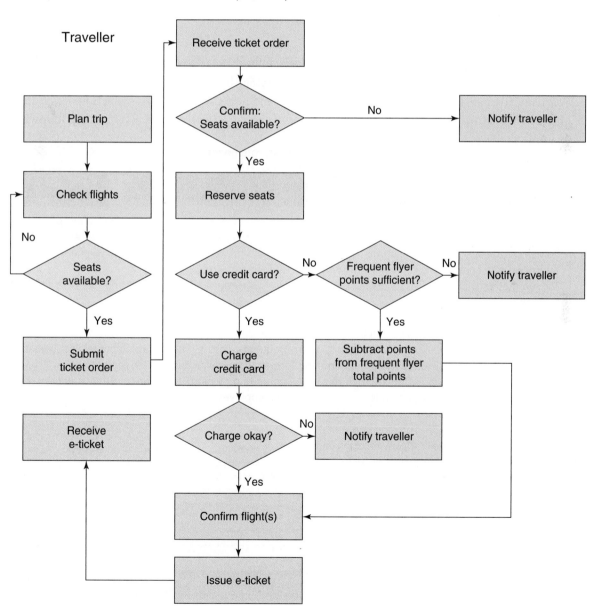

FIGURE 1.2A Business process for ordering an e-ticket from an airline website.

FIGURE 1.2B Customers can now plan and book their vacations on-line.

Initially, BPM helps companies improve profitability by decreasing costs and increasing revenues. Over time, BPM can create a competitive advantage by improving organizational flexibility. For many companies, BPM can provide cost benefits and increase customer satisfaction. Regardless of the benefits from BPM, an organization's strategy should drive the BPM effort, as the following example shows.

EXAMPLE 1.1

Enterprise Rent-A-Car (*www.enterprise.com*) is one of the largest car rental companies in the world. The company's Request Services department processes, approves, and enables the fulfillment of requests for information technology (IT) hardware, software, and services from 65,000 Enterprise employees located in 7,000 locations worldwide. Prior to the BPM effort, the department used multiple manual systems to manage requests, which could not keep up with the growth in IT requests as the company expanded. Enterprise wanted to improve this process and chose to use a BPM product from Appian (*www.appian.com*).

Before starting the BPM project, Enterprise had its strategy in place. The company recognized that the implementation of a new process would cause changes. The people most affected by these changes include the managers who approve IT product and service requests and the employees who fulfill the requests. The Request Services department got

these stakeholders on board early in the project. The company also educated employees about BPM in general, as well as about how to use the new Appian system.

Enterprise eliminated its manual processes entirely, and employees now use the Appian system to request IT products and services. The BPM project resulted in fewer errors and more rapid fulfillment of requests. The new process also contains business rules that provide appropriate restrictions on fulfillment (e.g., what IT hardware, software, or service an employee is entitled to).

Sources: Compiled from B. Violino, "BPM Success at Enterprise," *Baseline Magazine*, March 13, 2009; B. Violino, "BPM: Strategy Before Software," *CIO Insight*, March 13, 2009; D. Byron, "Appian BPM at Enterprise: Can Renting BPM Be Like Renting a Car?" *www.bpminaction.com*, March 24, 2008; "Enterprise Rent-A-Car Goes Live with Appian Enterprise," Appian Press Release, March 24, 2008; Enterprise Rent-A-Car website (*www.enterprise.com*), accessed March 30, 2009; Appian website (*www.appian.com*), accessed March 20, 2009.

BEFORE YOU GO ON ...

1. What is a business process?
2. What is business process management, and why is it so important to organizations?

1.3 Information Systems: Concepts and Definitions

As we will find out in more detail in Chapter 2, an information system (IS) collects, processes, stores, analyzes, and disseminates information for a specific purpose. It has been said that the purpose of information systems is to get the right information to the right people at the right time in the right amount and in the right format. Because information systems are intended to supply useful information, we define information and two closely related terms, data and knowledge. (The term *information technology* is a broader term that includes hardware, software, and information systems.)

An information system is much more than a network of computers. Sending text messages using your cell phone, shopping or paying your bills on-line are all examples of IS in our daily lives.

Data, Information, and Knowledge

One of the primary goals of information systems is to economically process data into information and knowledge. Let's take a closer look at these concepts.

Data items refer to an elementary description of things, events, activities, and transactions that are recorded, classified, and stored but not organized to convey any specific meaning. Data items can be numbers, letters, figures, sounds, or images. Examples of data items are a student grade in a class and the number of hours an employee worked in a certain week, or the price of a ring tone.

Information refers to data that have been organized so that they have meaning and value to the recipient. For example, grade point averages (GPA) are data, but a student's name coupled with his or her GPA is information. Similarly, a list of ring tones sold stating the frequency of sales is also information. The recipient interprets the meaning and draws conclusions and implications from the information.

Knowledge consists of data and/or information that have been organized and processed to convey understanding, experience, accumulated learning, and expertise as they apply to a current business problem. For example, a company recruiting at your school has found over time that students with grade point averages over 3.0 have had the most success in its management program. Based on its experience, that company may decide to interview only those students with GPAs over 3.0. Based on sales of numerous ring tones and past history, a company could decide to market only ring tones that are less than 30 seconds in length. Organizational knowledge, which reflects the experience and expertise of many people, has great value to all employees.

Now that we have a better idea of what information is and how it can be organized to convey knowledge, we shift our focus to the ways that organizations organize and use information. To do this we must look closely at an organization's information technology architecture and information technology infrastructure. These concepts underlie all information systems within the organization.

Information Technology Architecture

An organization's **information technology (IT) architecture** is a high-level map or plan of the information assets in an organization. It is both a guide for current operations and a blueprint for future directions. The IT architecture integrates the entire organization's business needs for information, the IT infrastructure (discussed in the next section), and all applications. The IT architecture is analogous to the architecture of a house. An architectural plan describes how the house is to be constructed, including how the various components of the house, such as the plumbing and electrical systems, are to be integrated. Similarly, as explained earlier, the IT architecture shows how all aspects of information technology in an organization fit together. Figure 1.3 illustrates the IT architecture of an on-line travel agency. For the travel agency, this could include decisions to use packaged software, which operating system platform to use, and how data management is to be handled. We discuss each part of Figure 1.3 in subsequent chapters.

Information Technology Infrastructure

An organization's **information technology (IT) infrastructure** consists of the physical facilities, IT components, IT services, and IT personnel that support the entire organization (see Figure 1.4). Starting from the bottom of Figure 1.4, we see that *IT components* are the computer hardware, software, and communications technologies that provide the foundation for all of an organization's information systems. As we move up the pyramid, we see that *IT personnel* use IT components to produce *IT services*, which include data management, systems development, and security concerns. For example, in a travel organization, the infrastructure could include an internal local area network, an outsourcing organization that maintains the hardware and software, browsing software, and the Internet.

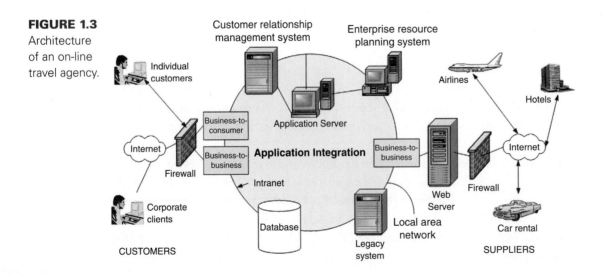

FIGURE 1.3
Architecture of an on-line travel agency.

An organization's IT infrastructure should not be confused with its platform. As we can see in Figure 1.4, a firm's platform consists only of its IT components. Therefore, a platform is a part of an IT infrastructure.

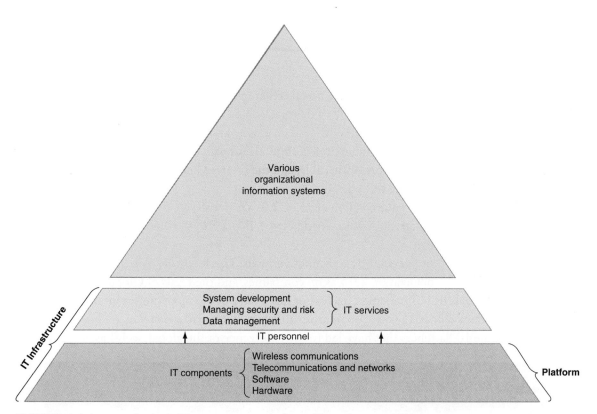

FIGURE 1.4 An organization's IT components, platform, IT services, and IT infrastructure.

IT infrastructures and platforms are critically important to organizations in today's competitive environment. In fact, modern organizations operate within a global, web-based platform, which we discuss in the next section.

BEFORE YOU GO ON ...

1. Provide an example of data items, information, and knowledge.
2. Distinguish between an IT infrastructure and an IT platform.

1.4 The Global, Web-Based Platform

The global, web-based platform that has recently emerged spans the world and is best represented by the Internet and the functionality of the World Wide Web. The platform enables individuals to connect, compute, communicate, collaborate, and compete everywhere and anywhere, anytime and all the time; to access limitless amounts of information, services, and entertainment; to exchange knowledge; and to produce and sell goods and services. It operates without regard to geography, time, distance, or even language barriers. In essence, this platform makes globalization possible. **Globalization** is the integration and interdependence of economic, social, cultural, and ecological facets of life, enabled by rapid advances in information technology. Historically, globalization has occurred in three stages, which we examine in the next section.

The Three Stages of Globalization

In his book *The World Is Flat*, Pulitzer Prize-winning author Thomas Friedman argues that the world is flat in the sense that the global competitive playing field is being levelled. Friedman identifies three eras of globalization. The first era, Globalization 1.0, lasted from 1492 to 1800. During this era, the force behind globalization was how much muscle, horsepower, wind power, or steam power a country had and could deploy.

The second era, Globalization 2.0, lasted from 1800 to 2000. In this era, the force behind globalization was multinational companies; that is, companies that had their headquarters in one country but operated in several countries. In the first half of this era, globalization was driven by falling transportation costs, generated by the development of the steam engine and the railroads. In the second half of this era, globalization was driven by falling telecommunications costs resulting from the telegraph, telephones, computers, satellites, fibre optic cable, and the Internet and World Wide Web. The global economy began appearing during this era.

Around the year 2000, we entered Globalization 3.0, which was driven by the convergence of 10 forces that Friedman calls "flatteners" (discussed below). In era 3.0, the global, web-based platform has emerged.

Each era has been characterized by a distinctive focus. The focus of Globalization 1.0 was on countries, the focus of Globalization 2.0 was on companies, and the focus of Globalization 3.0 is on groups and individuals. This observation makes our discussion all the more important for each of you, because you will be competing with people from all over a flat world when you graduate. Table 1.2 takes a look at the 10 flatteners that have led to the emergence of the global, web-based platform.

TABLE 1.2
FRIEDMAN'S TEN FLATTENERS

1. Fall of the Berlin Wall on November 9, 1989
- Shifted the world toward free-market economies and away from centrally planned economies.
- Led to eventual rise of the European Union and early thinking about the world as a single, global market.

2. Netscape goes public on August 9, 1995
- Popularized the Internet and the World Wide Web.

3. Development of workflow software
- Enabled computer applications to work with one another without human intervention.
- Enabled faster, closer collaboration and coordination among employees, regardless of their location.

4. Uploading
- Empowered everybody to create content and put it on the Web.
- Led the transition from a passive approach to content to an active, participatory, collaborative approach.

5. Outsourcing
- Contracting with an outside company to perform a specific function that your company was doing itself and then integrating their work back into your operation; for example, moving customer call centres to India.

6. Offshoring
- Relocating an entire operation, or just certain tasks, to another country; for example, moving an entire manufacturing operation to China.

7. Supply chaining
- Technological revolution led to the creation of networks composed of companies, their suppliers, and their customers, all of whom could collaborate and share information for increased efficiency.

8. Insourcing
- Delegating operations or jobs within a business to another company that specializes in those operations; for example, Dell hires FedEx to "take over" Dell's logistics process.

9. Informing
- Your ability to search for information, best illustrated by search engines.

10. The steroids (computing, instant messaging and file sharing, wireless technologies, voice over Internet Protocol, video conferencing, and computer graphics)
- Technologies that amplify the other flatteners.
- Enable all forms of computing and collaboration to be digital, mobile, and personal.

In essence, you are entering a flat world that is made possible by the global, web-based platform we have described. This platform has had an enormous impact on many industries, as IT's About Business 1.2 illustrates.

IT'S ABOUT BUSINESS 1.2
ZERO-FOOTPRINT INFORMATION TECHNOLOGY AT STATE STREET

A financial services firm managing $12 billion in equity, State Street (*www.statestreet.com*) processes more than $1 trillion worth of transactions each day, with activities ranging from accounting to cash management, and foreign exchange to securities lending. State Street's customers are largely institutional investors and corporations, served from its offices on four continents.

The overall goal of State Street's IT initiatives is to make the behind-the-scenes technology work so well that the users' experience is seamless, and to provide greater value for customers. The firm processes more than 150,000 trades per day and relies on more than 1,500 core IT applications. To accomplish this huge amount of processing, State Street has concentrated on state-of-the-art technology in its three worldwide data centres and various regional facilities. The firm has developed a business framework that uses a "zero-footprint" IT model to enable the company to react quickly to changing conditions.

For example, in early 2008, State Street used its zero-footprint IT model to establish a new centre in Krakow, Poland, in just two weeks. The centre processes transactions that occur in Europe, including accounting and other administrative services for 150 employees. The centre does all this without a single server on the premises. (A server, which we discuss in Technology Guide 1, is a computer that provides access to various network services, such as data and communications.) Instead, the facility is connected via high-speed to global and regional data centres that have on-site servers, business applications, and data.

State Street uses this zero-footprint model extensively. By centralizing applications, support servers, and secure data centres, the company can set up new offices within a few weeks, meaning that it can respond to business opportunities in new regions almost instantly, since it only has to move people and not IT systems.

State Street further reduces its "carbon footprint" because offices without on-site IT architecture use less heating, cooling, and electrical power. They also require fewer support staff.

The agility and flexibility enabled by IT have positioned the company as an industry leader, even in a deep, global recession. And the bottom line? State Street profits increased by 33 percent from 2005 to 2007. In 2008, the company reported that its revenue increased by 28 percent, despite difficult global economic conditions.

Sources: Compiled from S. Greengard, "State Street Puts Agility in the Fast Lane," *Baseline Magazine*, January 8, 2009; C. Sturdevant, "How Green IT Measures Up," *eWeek*, October 22, 2008; "The Computerworld Honors Program: State Street Corporation," *Computerworld*, 2008; R. Jana, "Green IT: Corporate Strategies," *BusinessWeek*, February 11, 2008; T. Maleshefski, "5 Steps to Green IT," *eWeek*, October 12, 2007; "Virtualization in Financial Services," *Computerworld*, April 11, 2007; State Street website (*www.statestreet.com*), accessed January 30, 2009.

QUESTIONS
1. Discuss the relationship between State Street's zero-footprint IT model and the global, web-based platform.
2. What are potential disadvantages of State Street's zero-footprint IT model?

This book will discuss, explain, and illustrate the characteristics of the dynamic global business environment. Further, we will discuss how you and your organization can use the web-based platform to survive and compete in this environment.

BEFORE YOU GO ON ...
1. What are the characteristics of the modern business environment?
2. Describe the global, web-based platform used by modern organizations.

1.5 Business Pressures, Organizational Responses, and IT Support

Modern organizations must compete in a challenging environment. Companies must react rapidly to problems and opportunities arising from extremely dynamic conditions. In this section we examine some of the major pressures confronting modern organizations, and we discuss how organizations are responding to these pressures.

Business Pressures

The *business environment* is the combination of social, legal, economic, physical, and political factors that affect business activities. Significant changes in any of these factors are likely to create business pressures on organizations. Organizations typically respond to these pressures with activities supported by IT. Figure 1.5 shows the relationships among business pressures, organizational performance and responses, and IT support. We focus on three types of business pressures that organizations face: market, technology, and societal pressures.

Market Pressures

Market pressures are generated by the global economy and strong competition, the changing nature of the workforce, and powerful customers. We'll look at each of these factors in turn.

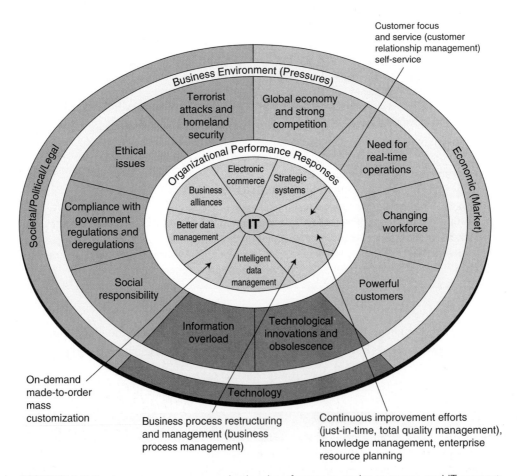

FIGURE 1.5 Business pressures, organizational performance and responses, and IT support.

Global Economy and Strong Competition. The move to a global economy has been facilitated by the emergence of the global, web-based platform. Regional agreements such as the North American Free Trade Agreement (NAFTA), which includes Canada, the United States, and Mexico, and the creation of a unified European market with a single currency, the euro, have contributed to increased world trade. Further, the rise of India and China as economic powerhouses has markedly increased global competition.

One important pressure that exists for businesses in a global market is the cost of labour, which varies widely among countries. In general, labour costs are higher in developed countries like Canada and Japan than in developing countries such as China and El Salvador. Also, developed countries usually offer greater benefits, such as health care, to employees, driving the cost of doing business even higher. Therefore, many labour-intensive industries have moved their operations to countries with low labour costs. IT has made such moves much easier to implement.

The Need for Real-time Operations. Real-time operations provide immediate processing of information. For example, a customer can purchase products at a store or order on-line, knowing that the product is available and will be shipped. Real-time operations are also used to validate credit card payments. Organizations are required to have adequate information systems and technology to provide real-time processing. Organizations lose their competitive edge when they don't have these information systems.

The Changing Nature of the Workforce. The workforce, particularly in developed countries, is becoming more diversified. Increasing numbers of women, single parents, members of visible minorities, and persons with disabilities now work in all types of positions. IT is easing the integration of these employees into the traditional workforce. IT is also enabling people to work from home.

Powerful Customers. Consumer sophistication and expectations increase as customers become more knowledgeable about the availability and quality of products and services. Customers can use the Internet to find detailed information about products and services, compare prices, and purchase items at electronic auctions.

Organizations recognize the importance of customers and have increased their efforts to acquire and retain them. As a result, firms try to know as much as possible about their customers to better anticipate and serve their needs. This process, *customer intimacy*, is an important part of *customer relationship management* (CRM), an organization-wide effort toward maximizing the customer experience. We discuss CRM in Chapter 9.

Technology Pressures

The second category of business pressures consists of those pressures related to technology. Two major technology-related pressures are technological innovation and information overload.

Technological Innovation and Obsolescence. New and improved technologies rapidly create or support substitutes for products, alternative service options, and superb quality. As a result, today's state-of-the-art products may be obsolete tomorrow. For example, how quickly are you replacing your old, standard cell phones with the new smart phones? How quickly are electronic versions of books, magazines, and newspapers replacing traditional hard copy versions? These changes require businesses to keep up with consumer demands.

When TaylorMade Golf's (*www.taylormadegolf.com*) R9 driver appeared in retailers in March 2009, it was the forty-fifth new metal driver the company had produced since 2003. The company's CEO referred to the rapid product rollouts as "relentless innovation." He imported the idea from

Japan where, during a business trip in 2000, he saw how Japanese golf equipment manufacturers were gaining competitive advantage over their North American competitors by turning out products much more often.

In order to successfully compete, TaylorMade changed its product development process. The company spread the responsibility for product development among its nine senior executives and the 40 managers beneath them. These 49 people come up with ideas at a rapid pace and work with each other, oftentimes in conflict, to make the ideas a reality. This process is called creative tension.

The result? In the 2009 Bob Hope Chrysler Classic golf tournament, 13 players put the TaylorMade R9 in play immediately. That is, more players used the R9 than any other driver in the tournament.

Technological innovation drives the production of new products from golf clubs to smart phones.

Information Overload. The amount of information available on the Internet doubles approximately every year, and much of it is free. The Internet and other telecommunications networks are bringing a flood of information to managers. To make decisions effectively and efficiently, managers must be able to access, navigate, and use these vast stores of data, information, and knowledge. Information technologies, such as search engines (discussed in Chapter 5) and data mining (discussed in Chapter 11), provide valuable support in these efforts.

Societal/Political/Legal Pressures

The third category of business pressures includes social responsibility, government regulation and deregulation, spending for social programs, spending to protect against terrorism, and ethics. In this section we consider how all of these elements affect business today.

Social Responsibility. Social issues that affect businesses and individuals range from the state of the physical environment to company and individual philanthropy to education. Some corporations and individuals are willing to spend time and/or money on solving various social problems. These efforts are known as **organizational social responsibility** or **individual social responsibility**.

A major social problem is the state of the physical environment. A growing IT initiative, called *green IT*, is addressing environmental concerns, as the following example shows.

EXAMPLE 1.2

A large number of information technology executives at companies and government organizations are putting their technical expertise to work improving their organizations' bottom lines while improving the environment as well. The executives are using better-designed data centres, virtualization (using a single computer to run multiple programs; see Technology Guide 1), centralized computer management, and computing devices that demand less power and cooling. Let's look at some examples.

In Japan's Kansai region, Osaka Gas (*www. osakagas.co.jp*), with 6.7 million natural gas customers, wanted to move to server virtualization to help protect the environment. It adopted IBM's WebSphere Virtual Enterprise to provide for server virtualization, which has reduced the gas company's electricity costs.

First Light is a Canadian solar energy farm that uses Satcon Technology Company's (*www.satcon. com*) solar converters. Information technology is used

(Continued on next page)

EXAMPLE 1.2 *(Continued)*

to manage the conversion of electricity. Software and hardware are used to invert the power and also to manage the equipment from a distance. This new solar energy farm is expected to produce 9.1 megawatts of electricity on about 35 hectares of land in Stone Mills, Ontario. This is enough electricity for about 1,000 homes.

Ares Management (*www.aresmgmt.com*) manages $20 billion in private equity. The company's electrical system could not keep up with the heat generated from the servers in its data centre. As a result, breakers blew out two or three times every quarter. To deal with that problem, Ares virtualized its data centre. The company's 3.5-tonne air conditioner, previously not powerful enough to cool the data centre, is now more than adequate, with energy savings averaging $8,000 per month.

In Las Vegas, where glittering lights consume plenty of power, the city government is using technology to remotely turn off its unused computers. The city is saving $50,000 per year with this process. This centralized approach to technology also allows the city to monitor and adjust climate controls in city buildings. The city also places servers in its data centre to maximize use of cooling systems. This process has reduced power consumption by 15 percent.

Sources: Compiled from B. Behtash, "Green IT Beyond Virtualization: Storage Matters," *InformationWeek*, November 8, 2008; A. Diana, "The Power of Green," *Baseline Magazine*, July 30, 2008; J. Duffy, "Nortel Sees Green in Virtualization, Down Economy," *Network World*, May 1, 2008; T. Jowitt, "VMWare's 'Green' Virtualization," *PC World*, April 27, 2008; "BancMidwest Services Invests in Green Future with Compellent SAN," Compellent Case Study, *www.compellent.com*, accessed January 30, 2009.

Social problems all over the world may be addressed through corporate and individual philanthropy. In some cases, questions arise as to what percentage of contributions actually go to the worthy causes and persons and what percentage goes to the charity's overhead. Another problem that concerns contributors is that they often do not have a say as to what projects their contributions will support. Two organizations, Kiva and Autism Society Canada, use information technology to help with these questions. IT's About Business 1.3 shows us how these two organizations are supporting a variety of needs.

Still another social problem that affects modern business is the digital divide. The **digital divide** is the wide gap between those who have access to information and communications technology and those who do not. This gap exists both within and among countries.

Many government and international organizations are trying to close the digital divide around the world. As technologies develop and become less expensive, the speed at which the gap can be closed will accelerate. A well-known project is the One Laptop per Child (OLPC, *http://laptop.org/en*) project that originated from MIT's Media Lab. OLPC is a non-profit association dedicated to research and developed a $100 laptop—a technology that is revolutionizing how we educate the world's children. In Chapter 7, we also note how cell phones are helping to close the digital divide in developing nations.

Compliance with Government Regulations and Deregulation. Other business pressures are related to government regulations regarding health, safety, environmental control, and employment equity. Businesses tend to view government regulations as constraints on their activities. Government deregulation can intensify competition. Federal and provincial laws affect basic business operations, such as the calculation of income taxes, payroll or health taxes, and the calculation and collection of sales or excise taxes.

In response to corporate scandals and data privacy risks, Canada and other countries have passed laws and regulations to govern business activities. Canada's equivalent of the U.S. Sarbanes-Oxley Act is the Budget Measures Act, Bill 198, designed to improve investor confidence. Federal privacy legislation called PIPEDA (Personal Information Protection and Electronic Documents Act) became effective in 2004. PIPEDA also applies to health information that crosses provincial boundaries. However, as health care has provincial jurisdiction in Canada, all provinces have separate privacy legislation that may be similar. In Ontario, the health privacy act is called the Personal Health Information Protection Act (PHIPA), and it came into effect on November 1, 2004. The process of becoming and remaining compliant with legislation can be expensive and time-consuming. In almost all cases, organizations rely on IT support to provide the necessary controls and information for compliance.

IT'S ABOUT BUSINESS 1.3
THE INTERNET FACILITATES LINKAGES BETWEEN BORROWERS AND LENDERS

Kiva (*www.kiva.org*), a non-profit enterprise, provides a way to link First World lenders with developing-world entrepreneurs. In Kiva's system, users pledge interest-free loans rather than tax-deductible donations. All of the donations go to loan recipients partly because Kiva receives free payment processing from PayPal. Many charities spend up to 40 percent of their revenues on administrative costs. For its operational costs, Kiva adds on an optional donation of 10 percent of every loan.

As of mid-2009, Kiva had attracted over 250,000 lenders and had disbursed almost $25 million across 40 countries. Kiva donors are evenly distributed between 25 and 60 years of age and between males and females. In addition, almost two-thirds earn more than $50,000 per year. However, Kiva has a cap on individual donations, which encourages younger, older, and less-well-off people to sign up. Lenders may withdraw loans when they are repaid. Significantly, however, 90 percent recirculate their funds, so the amount Kiva has to lend keeps increasing.

Similar to a bank giving a consumer loan, Kiva rates the risk of each borrower. It provides lenders with this risk rating and ongoing information about the loan after they have made the investment. The number of defaults is posted on Kiva's website and is approximately 2.5 percent of all loans—a very small number. The organization also publishes good news about entrepreneurs as well as bad news when it uncovers scams.

One good news story is that of Peter Mukasa, who owns a tiny liquor store in the Ugandan village of Makindye. Just hours after he posted his

funding request on Kiva, 10 lenders pledged $25 each to help Mukasa. As he operates his business, he will begin repaying his loan to his lenders, through Kiva.

Closer to home, more charities are harnessing the power of IT. Autism Society Canada (*www.autismsocietycanada.ca*) uses technology to provide information about autism, as well as to link with provincial autism societies. The society's website provides links to different ways to donate funds. By connecting to the individual provincial link or to the local chapters, you can decide where to provide your money or your time. For example, the Ontario site (*www.autismontario.com*) provides links to 30 chapters in the province, and also enables you to donate your old car rather than donating cash. Donors receive a tax receipt for their old car based upon its market value at the time of donation.

Sources: Compiled from J. Niccolai, "Barrett Says Time Is Right to Close Digital Divide," *Computerworld*, January 15, 2009; "When Small Loans Make a Big Difference," *Forbes*, June 3, 2008; J. O'Brien, "The Only Nonprofit That Matters," *Fortune*, February 26, 2008; "Lending and Philanthropy in the Internet Age," *InformationWeek*, February 2, 2008; Kiva website (*www.kiva.org*), accessed February 5, 2009; Autism Society website (*www.autismsocietycanada.ca*) and Autism Ontario website (*www.autismontario.com*), accessed August 12, 2010.

QUESTIONS
1. Discuss how the Internet facilitates the linkage between borrowers and donors at Kiva and the autism societies.
2. Discuss how Kiva and the autism societies would maintain quality control over their donations.

Ethical Issues. Ethics are general standards of right and wrong. Information ethics specifically are standards of right and wrong in information-processing practices. Ethical issues are very important, because if handled poorly, they can damage an organization's image and destroy its employees' morale. The use of IT raises many ethical issues, ranging from monitoring e-mail to invading the privacy of millions of customers whose data are stored in private and public databases. IT can also be used to improve the methods of processing used by businesses to promote a healthier lifestyle and cleaner environment. Chapter 3 covers ethical issues in detail.

Protection Against Fraud or Terrorist Attacks. Computer systems can be used to create fraudulent or fictitious transactions that are used to steal funds from banks or other organizations, or to engage in identity theft—the use of another person's identity for financial gain. Individuals and organizations need to protect their information to help prevent these actions. This is discussed further in Technology Guide 3. You can learn more about fraud from organizations such as the Association of Certified Fraud Examiners, at *www.acfe.com*.

Since September 11, 2001, organizations have been under increased pressure to protect themselves against terrorist attacks. Canada responded to these attacks in 2001 by passing an Anti-Terrorism Act, which made changes to the Criminal Code, the Official Secrets Act, the Canada Evidence Act, and the National Defence Act. Organizations responsible for Canada's security include the Royal Canadian Mounted Police, Canadian Security Intelligence Service, and the Communications Security Establishment.

Information technology can help protect organizations by providing security systems and possibly identifying patterns of behaviour associated with terrorist activities that will help to prevent attacks, including cyber-attacks (discussed in Chapter 3).

Clearly, then, the pressures on organizations are increasing, and organizations must be prepared to take responsive actions if they are to succeed. We explore these organizational responses in the next section.

Organizational Responses

Organizations are responding to the pressures we just discussed by implementing IT such as strategic systems, customer focus, make-to-order and mass customization, and e-business. The Pippalily.com baby sling case at the end of this chapter illustrates all of these responses. We discuss each type in greater detail in this section.

Strategic Systems

Strategic systems provide organizations with advantages that enable them to increase their market share and/or profits, to better negotiate with suppliers, or to prevent competitors from entering their markets. IT's About Business 1.4 provides two examples of strategic systems. We see that strategic systems require a close alignment between the business and the information technology function.

Customer Focus

Organizational attempts to provide superb customer service can make the difference between attracting and keeping customers on the one hand and losing them to competitors on the other. Numerous IT tools and business processes have been designed to keep customers happy. For example, consider Amazon. When you visit Amazon's website any time after your first visit, the site welcomes you back by name and presents you with information on books that you might like, based on your previous purchases. In another example, Dell guides you through the process of buying a computer by providing information and choices that help you make an informed buying decision.

IT'S ABOUT BUSINESS 1.4
VERIZON COMMUNICATIONS AND DELCAN CORPORATION

Verizon

The telecommunications giant Verizon Communications (*www.verizon.com*) historically was composed of multiple business units, each with its own corporate structure, personnel, and information systems. This structure resulted in unnecessary and redundant departments, redundant tasks, and ineffective communications throughout the corporation. As a result, Verizon divided its operations into three units: residential, wireless, and business. In Canada, Verizon operates as *www.verizonbusiness.com*. There is also a separate website available, *www.verizonwireless.com*.

In the new organizational structure, Verizon's three business units share some centralized functions, including purchasing, accounting, and some information technology (IT) functions. The centralized IT functions include managing Verizon's corporate networks, the help desk, and the data centre. (A corporate data centre is a facility that houses mission-critical information systems—hardware, software, and communications—that serve the entire organization, as well as redundant systems and backup power sources.) However, the IT function is partly decentralized since each business unit has its own IT groups led by IT executives who report to the corporate IT organization. Each unit's IT groups support their unit's strategic business initiatives.

When Verizon technicians call on customers to install products and deliver services, they bring IT staff and executives along to see the technology in action. Verizon believes this process is very effective, because it enables the IT personnel to observe the customer's business problems firsthand.

Verizon's centralized IT department performs several basic but critical roles. First, it is responsible for ensuring that business operations run efficiently and accurately. Second, it works closely with senior executives in the individual business units to help define the company's three- to five-year strategy. To perform this operation, Verizon has given its IT executives access to Verizon's projects, plans, and goals. Finally, IT executives keep up with new technologies and advise business executives on how these technologies might be integrated with the company's existing IT systems.

As a result of the restructuring and the close alignment between IT and the business units, Verizon has saved millions of dollars in operational costs. The company now presents one united front to its vendors and suppliers, and it has developed a portal that provides a single access point for its customers for all their dealings with the company.

Sources: Compiled from "Verizon's Communications and Information Technology Solutions Help Power Retailers," Verizon press release, January 12, 2009; A. Diana, "Verizon: They Can Hear Customers Now," *Baseline Magazine*, September 29, 2008; Verizon website (*www.verizon.com*), accessed April 15, 2009.

Delcan

Delcan Corporation (*www.delcan.com*), with its head office in Markham, Ontario, creates information systems and network solutions for a variety of clients around the globe. Delcan, in business since 1953, has over 700 employees working in 12 offices in Canada, 10 in the United States, and in six more around the globe. Whenever the company contracts for a major development in transportation, water, or information technology, it also establishes a local project office.

Delcan integrates multiple types of technology to provide customized solutions. For example, the company provides traffic control systems, monitoring two highways in Ontario (the 401 and the 407). This expertise, including the installation of other traffic management systems in cities such as Los Angeles and Hong Kong, has enabled the company to assist Beijing in organizing its traffic prior to the summer Olympics that were held there in 2008.

Such traffic management systems use closed circuit television systems and thousands of vehicle detectors that can be buried under the roadway. The information provided by the detectors is used by sophisticated software that uses mathematical calculations to consider where traffic may be delayed. Cameras focus in on problem situations and resolve problems (such as accidents by sending emergency crews). Dealing with accidents more rapidly helps to reduce the size of traffic jams.

The traffic operators also have access to large overhead signs where they can inform drivers about the state of traffic, so that drivers can re-route, also reducing the size of traffic jams due to accidents, volume, or other causes, such as construction.

City officials can decide how much to invest in traffic management, providing information to service providers and the community.

(Continued on next page)

IT'S ABOUT BUSINESS 1.4 *(Continued)*
VERIZON COMMUNICATIONS AND DELCAN CORPORATION

Sources: C. Sorensen, "From the 401 to Beijing: Markham's Delcan Corp. Has Signed on to Help Unsnarl Traffic in the Booming Capital of Beijing," *Toronto Star*, May 28, 2007; Delcan website (*www. delcan.com*), accessed August 12, 2010.

QUESTIONS
1. Consider Verizon and Delcan's customers, such as cities that would like to manage their traffic.

Which comes first: the business strategy, or information technology? Support your answer in both cases.
2. Define business–information technology alignment and discuss how Verizon and Delcan would align their business strategy and information technology function.

Make-to-Order and Mass Customization

Make-to-order is a strategy of producing customized products and services. The business problem is how to manufacture customized goods efficiently and at a reasonably low cost. Part of the solution is to change manufacturing processes from mass production to mass customization. In mass production, a company produces a large quantity of identical items. In **mass customization**, it also produces a large quantity of items, but it customizes them to fit the desires of each customer. Mass customization is simply an attempt to perform make-to-order on a large scale. Bodymetrics (*www.bodymetrics.com*) is an excellent example of mass customization with men's and women's jeans.

EXAMPLE 1.3

Technology has come to the rescue for people on the hunt for well-fitting jeans. A company called Bodymetrics has a "body scanner" in upscale department stores that scans a customer's body, taking more than 150 measurements. Customers can order custom-fit jeans or buy a pair off the rack that matches their body type, and "try on" a pair virtually.

The digital replica of the customer's body is used to create a pattern for their custom-made jeans. It takes three to six weeks for the jeans to be hand-tailored to their exact specifications. Before taking them home, the customers meet with a Bodymetrics tailor to do any final touch-ups.

Customers buying pre-made jeans fall into three body types: straight, semi-curvy, and curvy. Bodymetrics experts help choose the right body-shape jean based on the customer's scan.

Lastly, the scan can be used to help customers "try on" jeans virtually, so they can see how the various styles of jeans would look on their body without going into a dressing room.

Sources: Compiled from Asmita, "Custom-Fit Jeans with Bodymetrics," Styleguru.com, January 18, 2007; R. Young, "Turning Tailoring Over to a Computer," *International Herald Tribune*, January 15, 2007; Bodymetrics website (*www.bodymetrics.com*), accessed March 1, 2009

E-Business and E-Commerce

Doing business electronically is an essential strategy for companies competing in today's business environment. Chapter 6 will focus extensively on this topic. In addition, e-commerce applications appear throughout this book.

We have described the pressures that affect companies in today's business environment and the responses that organizations take to manage these pressures. To plan for the most effective responses, companies formulate strategies. In the new digital economy, these strategies rely heavily on information technology, especially strategic information systems. We discuss corporate strategy and strategic information systems in Chapter 2.

1.6 Why Are Information Systems Important to Me?

Information systems are important to you for a variety of reasons. First, information systems and information technologies are integral to your life. Second, the IS field offers many career opportunities. Finally, all functional areas in an organization use information systems.

Information Systems and Information Technologies Are Integral to Your Lives

There are many examples of the ways in which information systems and technologies are embedded in your lives. For example, think of all you can do on-line:

- Register for classes.
- Take classes, and not just classes from your university.
- Access class syllabi, information, PowerPoint slides, and lectures.
- Research class papers and presentations.
- Conduct banking.
- Pay your bills.
- Research, shop, and buy products from companies or other people.
- Sell your "stuff."
- Search for, and apply for, jobs.
- Make your travel reservations (hotel, airline, rental car).

In addition to all the activities you can perform on-line, there are other examples of how information systems and information technologies are essential to your daily living. For example, you may not use a regular wireline telephone. Rather, you use a smart phone that has a calendar, an address book, a calculator, a digital camera, and several types of software to download music and movies. This phone enables you to seamlessly switch between different wireless modes (Bluetooth, Wi-Fi, cellular, and/or WiMAX) to communicate by voice, e-mail, instant messaging, and text messaging.

Going further, you have your own blog, and you post your own podcasts and videocasts to it. You have your own page on Facebook. You make and upload videos to YouTube. You take, edit, and print your own digital photographs. You "burn" your own custom-music CDs and DVDs. You use RSS feeds to create your personal electronic newspaper. The list goes on. (Note: If a few of these concepts or terms are unfamiliar to you, don't worry. We discuss everything mentioned here in detail later in this book.)

IT Offers Career Opportunities

Becoming knowledgeable about IT can improve your chances of landing a good job. Even though computerization eliminates some jobs, it creates many more. IT also creates many opportunities to work in exciting applications, as you will see in our next IT's About Business.

IT'S ABOUT BUSINESS 1.5
BUILDING THE MOVIES

What would be your dream job? Designing video games or creating a musical script for a new game? How about creating the graphics for top-selling movies? Soho VFX (*www.sohovfx.com*) uses information technology in the movie industry in many different ways. Not only do its employees actually create the three-dimensional graphics used in movies, but they also create customized software to track and render images and build fake fur and fake skin for use on the set. The company can also alter scenery or backgrounds for a movie.

To apply for this type of a position, you are expected to have an understanding of the arts, be able to draw or paint or somehow creatively express yourself in a portfolio, as well as be able to use information technology effectively. There are several world-renowned schools in Canada that offer this type of training. For example, Seneca College, with campuses in the Greater Toronto Area, offers training in visual effects for film and television.

The technology used by Soho VFX has come down dramatically in price. The company uses thousands of servers for its computing, which previously would have run on mid-range computing equipment (we discuss hardware further in Technology Guide 1).

Sources: D. Jemyn, "High Tech Plays Lead Role in Visual Effects Firm," *The Globe and Mail*, November 16, 2009; Seneca College website (*http://myseneca.ca*), accessed August 12, 2010; Soho VFX website (*www.sohovfx.com*), accessed August 12, 2010.

QUESTIONS
1. Describe the types of skills that you would need to create graphics for movies.
2. Can anyone do this type of work? What educational background would you need to apply for these jobs? Support your answer.

Because information technology is vital to the operation of modern businesses, it offers many employment opportunities. The demand for traditional IT staff—programmers, business analysts, systems analysts, and designers—is substantial. In addition, many well-paid jobs exist in emerging areas such as the Internet and e-commerce, mobile commerce, network security, object-oriented programming, telecommunications, and multimedia design. For details about careers in IT, see *www. computerworld.com/careertopics/careers* and *www.monster.com*. In addition, Table 1.3 provides a list of typical IT jobs along with a description of each one.

With the deep recession of 2009, a great deal of misinformation has been communicated concerning careers in information technology. Let's look at four of these myths.

Myth #1: *There are no computing jobs.* Despite the recession, as of May 2010, the IT job market was quite strong. For example, the technology jobs site Dice (*www.dice.com*) listed 69,000 technology jobs that month.

Myth #2: *There will be no IT jobs when I graduate.* In fact, the four fastest-growing jobs that require a bachelor's degree from 2002 through 2012 are IT-related. They are: (1) computer engineers, (2) management/computer information systems staffers, (3) computer and information systems managers, and (4) technical support specialists. Note that numbers (2) and (3) refer to MIS majors in colleges of business.

Myth #3: *All IT-related jobs are moving offshore.* In fact, some IT jobs are offshored (that is, sourced to areas with lower-cost labour), but the more highly skilled IT jobs will typically not be offshored (see IT's About Business 1.5 for examples). In addition, jobs related to a company's core competencies or projects will typically not be offshored, and neither will jobs requiring close business-to-customer contact.

Myth #4: *Computing and IT salaries are low due to cheaper overseas labour.* In fact, graduates who major in management information systems typically command among the highest starting salaries of any business major.

TABLE 1.3
INFORMATION TECHNOLOGY JOBS

POSITION	JOB DESCRIPTION
Chief Information Officer	Highest-ranking IS manager; responsible for strategic planning in the organization
IS Director	Responsible for managing all systems throughout the organization and day-to-day operations of the entire IS organization
Information Centre Manager	Manages IS services such as help desks, hotlines, training, and consulting
Applications Development Manager	Coordinates and manages new systems development projects
Project Manager	Manages a particular new systems development project
Systems Manager	Manages a particular existing system
Operations Manager	Supervises the day-to-day operations of the data and/or computer centre
Programming Manager	Coordinates all applications' programming efforts
Systems Analyst	Interfaces between users and programmers; determines information requirements and technical specifications for new applications
Business Analyst	Focuses on designing solutions for business problems; interfaces closely with users to show how IT can be used innovatively
Systems Programmer	Writes the computer code for developing new systems software or maintaining existing systems software
Applications Programmer	Writes the computer code for developing new applications or maintaining existing applications
Emerging Technologies Manager	Forecasts technology trends and evaluates and experiments with new technologies
Network Manager	Coordinates and manages the organization's voice and data networks
Database Administrator	Manages the organization's databases and oversees the use of database management software
Auditing or Computer Security Manager	Manages ethical and legal use of information systems and evaluates the quality or effectiveness of such systems
Webmaster	Manages the organization's World Wide Web site
Web Designer	Creates World Wide Web sites and pages

IT Is Used by All Departments

Simply put, organizations cannot operate without information technology. For this reason, every manager and professional staff member should learn about IT within his or her specialized field as well as across the entire organization and among organizations.

IT systems are integral to every functional area of an organization. In *finance* and *accounting*, for example, managers use IT systems to forecast revenues and business activity, to determine the best sources and uses of funds, and to perform audits to ensure that the organization is fundamentally sound and that all financial reports and documents are accurate.

In *sales* and *marketing*, managers use information technology to perform the following functions:

- Product analysis: developing new goods and services
- Site analysis: determining the best location for production and distribution facilities
- Promotion analysis: identifying the best advertising channels
- Price analysis: setting product prices to get the highest total revenues

Marketing managers also use IT to manage their relationships with their customers. In *manufacturing*, managers use IT to process customer orders, develop production schedules, control inventory levels, and monitor product quality. They also use IT to design and manufacture products. These processes are called computer-assisted design (CAD) and computer-assisted manufacturing (CAM).

Managers in *human resources* use IT to manage the recruiting process, analyze and screen job applicants, and hire new employees. HR managers use IT to help employees manage their careers, administer performance tests to employees, and monitor employee productivity. These managers also use IT to manage compensation and benefits packages.

These are just a few examples of the roles of information technology in the various functional areas of an organization. We think it is important for students from the different functional areas to see the value of the information systems in their fields.

BEFORE YOU GO ON ...

1. What are the major reasons why it is important for employees in all functional areas to become familiar with IT?
2. Why is it important to become knowledgeable about IT if you are not working as an IT employee?

1.7 The Plan of the Book

A major objective of this book is to help you understand the roles of information technologies in today's organizations. The book is also designed to help you think strategically about information systems. That is, we want you to be able look into the future and see how these information technologies can help you, your organization, and your world. Finally, the book demonstrates how IT supports all of the functional areas of the organization.

This chapter has introduced you to the global business environment and the web-based platform that individuals and organizations use to successfully compete in that environment. Chapter 2 will introduce you to the basic concepts of information technologies in organizations. Chapter 3 addresses three critical and timely topics: ethics, privacy, and security. Corporate scandals at Enron, WorldCom, Nortel, and others, as well as more recent banking, insurance, and housing scandals, emphasize the importance of ethics. The large number of massive data breaches at various institutions (see the opening case of Chapter 3) makes it essential that we keep security in mind at all times. Finally, the miniaturization and spread of surveillance technologies leads many people to wonder if they have any privacy left at all.

The amount of data available to us is increasing exponentially, meaning that we have to find methods and tools to manage the deluge. Chapter 4 discusses how to manage data so that we can use them effectively to make decisions.

Chapter 5 looks at telecommunications and networks, including the Internet. Because the Internet is the foundation of the global business environment, the importance of computer networks cannot be overstated.

Electronic commerce, facilitated by the Internet, has revolutionized how businesses operate today. Chapter 6 covers this important topic. One of the newest technologies to have an impact on organizations is wireless communications. We explore this technology in Chapter 7. Chapter 8 provides a detailed picture of the various types of information systems that are used in organizations today. Chapters 9 and 10, respectively, focus on two fundamental business processes that make extensive use of technology: customer relationship management and supply chain management. Chapter 11 discusses the various information systems that support managerial decision making, and Chapter 12 notes how organizations acquire or develop new applications.

Technology Guides 1 (hardware) and 2 (software) provide a detailed look at the two most fundamental IT components that are the foundation for all information systems. Technology Guide 3 provides information on how to protect your own information assets. Finally, Technology Guide 4 covers the basics of telecommunications.

WHAT'S IN IT FOR ME?

In the previous section, we discussed IT in each of the functional areas. Here we take a brief look at the MIS function.

FOR THE MIS MAJOR

The MIS function directly supports all other functional areas in an organization. That is, the MIS function is responsible for providing the information that each functional area needs in order to make decisions. The overall objective of MIS personnel is to help users improve performance and solve business problems using IT. To accomplish this objective, MIS personnel must understand both the information requirements and the technology associated with each functional area. Given their position, however, they must think "business needs" first and "technology" second.

SUMMARY

1. **Link effective information technology planning to business planning.**

   To help achieve their objectives, organizations develop a business plan. Then, they create an information technology plan. The *IT strategic plan* provides the long-range goals for the information technology infrastructure to accomplish. To be effective, these long-range IT plans must match the organization's business plans.

2. **Describe business processes and explain how business process management helps to improve how businesses function.**

   A business process is a collection of related activities that produce a product or a service of value to the organization, its business partners, and/or its customers. A process has inputs and outputs, and its activities can be measured. Many processes cross functional areas in an organization, such as product development, which involves design, engineering, manufacturing, marketing, and distribution. Other processes involve only one functional area.

   To a great degree, an organization's performance depends on how well it manages its business processes. As a result, organizations emphasize business process management (BPM), a management technique that includes methods and tools to support the design, analysis, implementation, management, and optimization of business processes. As business processes improve, organizations can provide better customer service and more effectively manage their costs.

3. **Explain the role of data, information, and knowledge. Differentiate between information technology architecture and information technology infrastructure.**

   Data items refer to an elementary description of things, events, activities, and transactions that are recorded, classified, and stored, but not organized to convey any specific meaning. Information is data that have been organized so that they have meaning and value to the recipient. Knowledge consists of data and/or information that have been organized and processed to convey understanding, experience, accumulated learning, and expertise as they apply to a current business problem.

   An organization's information technology *architecture* is a high-level map or plan of the information assets in an organization. The IT architecture integrates the information requirements of the overall organization and all individual users, the IT infrastructure, and all applications. An organization's information technology *infrastructure* consists of the physical facilities, IT components, IT services, and IT management that support the entire organization.

4. **Describe the global business environment and how globalization has affected organizations.**

   The global, web-based platform consists of the hardware, software, and communications technologies that form the Internet and the functionality of the World Wide Web. This platform enables individuals to connect, compute, communicate, compete, and collaborate everywhere and anywhere, anytime and all the time. They can access limitless amounts of information, services, and entertainment. This platform operates without regard to geography, time, distance, or even language barriers.

5. **Discuss the relationships among business pressures, organizational responses, and information systems.**
The business environment is the combination of social, legal, economic, physical, and political factors that affect business activities. Significant changes in any of these factors are likely to create business pressures. Organizations typically respond to these pressures with activities supported by IT. These activities include strategic systems, customer focus, make-to-order and mass customization, and e-business.

6. **Provide examples of the relevance of information systems to individuals and organizations.**
As described in our cases and examples in this chapter, information systems help organizations do their jobs, such as provide graphics for movies, or send and receive information and payments. Individuals use information systems to make decisions, and also to send and receive information and payments.

7. **Describe the plan of this book.**
This book addresses the impact of technology on organizations and individuals, considering both the global and national business environment. Technology guides provide additional detail on specific topics.

KEY TERMS

application portfolio, 5
business process, 7
business process management (BPM), 9
data items, 11
digital divide, 19
globalization, 13
individual social responsibility, 18
information, 11
information systems (IS), 4
information technology (IT), 4

information technology (IT) architecture, 12
information technology (IT) infrastructure, 12
information technology (IT) steering
  committee, 6
information technology (IT) strategic plan, 5
knowledge, 11
make-to-order, 23
management information systems (MIS), 4
mass customization, 23
organizational social responsibility, 18

DISCUSSION QUESTIONS

1. List and explain the typical components of an IS operational plan.
2. Why does an organization need both an organizational strategic plan and an IT strategic plan?
3. Describe various business processes in your university.
4. Describe the enabling role of IT in business process management.
5. Describe how IT architecture and IT infrastructure are interrelated.
6. Is the Internet an infrastructure, an architecture, or an application program? Explain your answer. Use your understanding of the components of the Internet to explain its nature.
7. How has the global, web-based platform affected relationships among organizations?
8. Explain why IT is both a business pressure and a business helper that can be used to counteract business pressures.

9. What does a flat world mean to you in your choice of a major? In your choice of a career? Will you have to be a "lifelong learner"? Why or why not?

10. What could the impact of a flat world have on your standard of living?

PROBLEM-SOLVING ACTIVITIES

1. Surf the Internet for information about the federal department called Public Safety Canada. Examine the available information, and comment on the potential role of information technologies in managing national information banks.

2. Access *www.digitalenterprise.org*. Prepare a report regarding the latest electronic commerce developments in the digital age.

3. Enter the website of UPS (*www.ups.com*).
   a. Find out what information is available to customers before they send a package.
   b. Find out about the "package tracking" system and identify the data that it requires.
   c. Calculate the cost of delivering a 10-inch × 20-inch × 15-inch box weighing 40 pounds (note that the UPS Canada site uses inches) from your hometown to Vancouver, British Columbia (or to Halifax, Nova Scotia, if you live in or near Vancouver). Compare the fastest delivery against the least cost.

4. Discuss the impacts of the global, web-based platform on the residential real estate industry. Select examples of local real estate brokers and explain how the broker is using technology to market real estate worldwide. Be specific regarding the websites that you use for examples.

5. Experience customization by designing your own shoes at *www.nike.com*, a car at *www.jaguar.com*, and a CD at *www.easternrecording.com*; find out how to obtain your business card for free at *http://www.vistaprint.ca* and create your own diamond ring at *www.bluenile.com*. Summarize your experiences.

6. Visit some websites that list employment opportunities in IT. Prominent examples are: *www.dice.com*, *www.canada.plusjobs.com*, *www.monster.com*, *www.quintcareers.com*, *www.roberthalftechnology.com*, and *www.workopolis.com*. Compare the IT salaries with salaries offered to accountants, marketing personnel, financial personnel, operations personnel, and human resources personnel. For other information on IT salaries, check *IT World's* salary calculator at *www.itworldcanada.com/salarycalculator*, or a similar calculator at *http://workingcanada.salary.com*. These sites also provide job descriptions for positions listed.

TEAM ASSIGNMENTS

1. a. Create an on-line group for studying IT or a part of it you are interested in. Each member of the group must have a Yahoo! e-mail account (available free). Go to Yahoo! Groups (*http://groups.yahoo.com*) and at the bottom see a section titled "Create Your Own Group."
   Step 1: Click on "Start a Group Now."
   Step 2: Select a category that best describes your group (use the Search Group Categories, or use the Browse Group Categories tool). You must find a category.
   Step 3: Describe the purposes of the group and give it a name.
   Step 4: Set up an e-mail address for sending messages to all group members.
   Step 5: Each member must join the group (select a "profile"); click on "Join this Group."

Step 6: Go to Word Verification Section; follow the instructions.

Step 7: Finish by clicking "Continue."

Step 8: Select a group moderator. Conduct a discussion on-line of at least two topics of interest to the group.

Step 9: Arrange for messages from the members to reach the moderator at least once a week.

Step 10: Find a similar group (use Yahoo!'s "Find a Group" and make a connection). Write a report for your instructor.

b. Now follow the same steps for Google Groups.

c. Compare Yahoo! Groups and Google Groups.

2. Review *The Globe and Mail, National Post, Business Week,* and local newspapers for the last three months to find stories about the use of web-based technologies in organizations. Each group will prepare a report describing five applications. The reports should emphasize the role of the Web and its benefit to the organizations. Cover issues described in this chapter, such as productivity, competitive strategies, and globalization. Present and discuss your work.

PIPPALILY.COM

Courtesy Pippalily.com

THE BUSINESS PROBLEM

Victoria Turner had started a new small business: the production of comfortable baby slings. The slings were customized to the size of the parent and the child, and also had multiple colours available. Victoria was trying to grow the business in such a way that there was no need for large investments in equipment, people, or technology.

As a small business owner, she did not have a lot of funds and wanted to increase her business without a large capital outlay. Using word-of-mouth, Victoria gradually increased sales to friends and local businesses. However, she felt that she lacked the expertise in some areas, such as marketing and fashion design, and many tasks took her long hours. How would she obtain these resources without hiring

expensive contractors or committing to long-term costs?

THE IT SOLUTION

Victoria's company has a website, *www.pippalily.com*, where customers can order different sizes of slings with different types of fabrics. Customers can see what the product looks like in the different colours using graphic images. Payment and order information is received electronically by Victoria's company.

Victoria outsourced her specialized needs to individuals who charge by the hour, doing only the work that she needed. These specialists work from virtual offices, and may not even need to visit Victoria: the telephone and groupware software can facilitate looking at documents together without physical travel time. Individuals who outsource in Victoria's area are available from websites such as *www.craigslist.org*.

THE RESULTS

Since products are manufactured only for confirmed orders, inventory is kept low, as are costs. The use of on-line payment methods helps ensure that products are paid for before they are manufactured, reducing the need to borrow money to finance the production of goods.

Using outsourcing for specialized help reduces costs and means that the company does not need to hire full-time staff, paying only for work that needs to be done. Pippalily.com has been so successful with marketing the idea that other websites, such as *www.lussobaby.ca*, are now selling their slings.

Sources: Compiled from M. Price, "Web Presence Important for Home Business Success," *Toronto Star*, April 21, 2009; Pippalily website (*www.pippalily.com*), accessed May 17, 2010; Lusso Baby website (*www.lussobaby.ca*), accessed May 17, 2010.

QUESTIONS

1. What business pressures affect Pippalily.com? How could Victoria deal with these pressures?
2. What are some additional methods that Pippalily.com could use to market its products using current technology?

CASE 1.2

Web Resources

Student website www.wiley.com/canada/rainer

- Web quizzes
- Lecture slides in PowerPoint

- Author podcasts
- Interactive Case: Ruby's Club assignments

ALL OF THE ABOVE AND

- E-book
- Manager videos
- Vocabulary flash cards

- Pre- and post-lecture quizzes
- Microsoft Office 2007 lab manual and projects

PLANNING A NEW WEBSITE FOR RUBY'S CLUB

Go to the Ruby's Club link at the Student Companion website or WileyPLUS where you will find a description of your internship at Ruby's Club, a downtown music venue, and information for your assignment. Your assignment will include providing input on Ruby's new website design in a memo to the club's managers.

2 INFORMATION SYSTEMS: CONCEPTS AND MANAGEMENT

LEARNING OBJECTIVES

1. Define IT governance and explain why information systems need to be effectively managed.

2. Describe the components, types, and purposes of information systems.

3. Describe Porter's competitive forces model and his value chain model, explaining five strategies companies can use to improve their competitive positions.

4. Explain the importance of information systems to organizations and society and describe how information resources are managed.

ELECTRONIC RECORDS TO TRANSFORM HEALTH CARE

THE IT SOLUTION

A cluster of different technologies serving the medical industry have been developed over the last few years. This includes advanced medical imaging technologies. For example, the University of Toronto has a Department of Medical Imaging that conducts research into medical imaging as well as having an education centre that teaches advanced imaging. These technologies include radiology and nuclear medicine with specific medical technologies that take advantage of advanced computing systems, such as three-dimensional imaging (see *http://medical-imaging.utoronto.ca/cme/aiec.htm*).Some Canadian hospitals, such as the London Health Sciences Centre (*www.lhsc.on.ca*), have shown their own initiative and adopted many different types of technology to process patient and other records. Such hospitals are likely to also have integrated patient information systems to record and track patient information. They will also have information systems to do patient billings, collect funds, manage their inventory, and pay their thousands of employees. For example, Kronos Canadian Systems Inc. (*www.kronos.com/Canada*) provides health care workforce management systems that include payroll processing.

Having automated their own internal operations, hospitals began to build infrastructures to handle the movement of information regarding their patients. The federal government and provincial governments across Canada also established organizations to develop infrastructures so that data about patients could be shared among doctors and medical organizations.

Some jurisdictions are taking a systematic approach to ensure that all publicly run health facilities eventually use electronic patient records, also known as e-health. In 2009, Ontario established a three-year, $2-billion budget for e-health. However, there has been little implementation of an electronic medical records infrastructure in Ontario, with a 2009 special report prepared by the Auditor General of Ontario discovering mismanagement and excessive payments to consultants. As of the time of writing, it was expected to be at least another five years before all of Ontario has e-health records. This is in contrast to Alberta, which was considered the leader in e-health records in 2006. Alberta provided incentives to doctors to purchase equipment that provided networking, printers, voice

THE BUSINESS PROBLEM

There are about 2,000 health-based activities (or "transactions") every minute in Canada. These activities could be a visit to a family doctor, an emergency tooth extraction, taking of x-rays, or many other such activities. These transactions are normally recorded on paper or specialized media (such as special films for x-rays or electronic files for computerized scanning), and are attached to a person's health record at the place where the activity occurred.

How do doctors access a patient's health record if the person has been to many different providers in the last few years? How are records retrieved from remote locations when they are needed rapidly? What if an x-ray negative is sent to a hospital for viewing but is lost or damaged in transit? Who bears the cost of sending all of this information to many different locations? Even within a single hospital, information about a patient can easily be unavailable as the patient moves to different departments for tests and treatment.

Medical information needs to be available to doctors, patients, as well as other service providers on a timely basis. The information needs to be accurate and quickly accessible at low cost. Hospitals are also expected to be cost effective in processing their own records, such as accounting and payroll.

recognition systems, and other technology to transform doctors' habits from using paper to using electronic systems instead.

Sources: Compiled from L. Gregoire, "Alberta Leads Country in E-health Records," CMAJ, May 9, 2006; S. Lysecki, "North York General Puts Software in Charge of Staffing, Payroll," October 31, 2005, itbusiness.ca; Office of the Auditor General of Ontario, "Special Report: Ontario's Electronic Health Records Initiative," October 2009; T. Talaga, "$263M Went into eHealth Amid Scandal," November 3, 2009, *Toronto Star*, pp. A1, A11; J. Shave, "Hospital Information Systems: The Promise and Reality," Presentation at the University of Waterloo, June 24, 2009.

WHAT DO YOU THINK?
1. What are some of the reasons that doctors or hospitals might purchase information systems that do not meet their needs?
2. Describe additional information systems that could be used by doctors or hospitals to meet the needs of their patients or employees.

CASE 2.1

Chapter Preview

Our opening case illustrates the ambitious desire to have electronic records available for the Canadian health care system. Some provinces and hospitals have been able to implement such systems (for example, the province of Alberta and the London Health Services Centre in Ontario), but there have also been financial disasters, such as happened with e-health in Ontario. These problems show why it is important to effectively manage information systems, our first topic in this chapter.

After taking a look at the IT governance process, we introduce you to the basic concepts of information systems in organizations, and we explore how businesses use information systems in every facet of their operations. Information systems collect, process, store, analyze, and disseminate information for a specific purpose.

There are so many different types of information systems. What are they called? What types of information systems do executives use? What about accountants, engineers, or data entry staff? In this chapter we look at different types of systems, talk about who uses them, and how organizations can use information systems to reduce costs, improve profits, or gain customers. The two major determinants of information systems support are the organization's structure and the functions that employees perform within the organization. As this chapter shows, information systems tend to follow the structure of organizations, and they are based on the needs of individuals and groups.

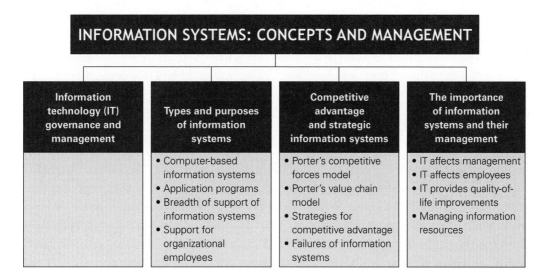

INFORMATION SYSTEMS: CONCEPTS AND MANAGEMENT

Information technology (IT) governance and management	Types and purposes of information systems	Competitive advantage and strategic information systems	The importance of information systems and their management
	• Computer-based information systems • Application programs • Breadth of support of information systems • Support for organizational employees	• Porter's competitive forces model • Porter's value chain model • Strategies for competitive advantage • Failures of information systems	• IT affects management • IT affects employees • IT provides quality-of-life improvements • Managing information resources

We also look at a theoretical framework for examining competitive forces to see the impact that the Internet has had on competition. These concepts will help you to understand the types of changes that organizations make to survive in our global economy. We demonstrate that any information system can be *strategic*, meaning that it can provide a competitive advantage if it is used properly. At the same time, we provide examples of information systems that have failed, often at great cost to the enterprise. We then examine why information systems are important to organizations and society as a whole. Because these systems are so diverse, managing them can be quite difficult. Therefore, we close this chapter by taking a look at how organizations manage their IT systems.

2.1 Information Technology (IT) Governance and Management

Think of some of the largest organizations—multifaceted companies that include manufacturing such as IBM, software companies such as Microsoft, or financial sector organizations such as Canada's large banks. These companies have hundreds of computer systems, thousands of software programs running, and different types of networks that span countries and continents. As described in our first chapter, such organizations have business strategies that then drive the information systems strategies.

These strategies take account of risks or potential problems that could occur and the opportunities that organizations have to serve their customers better or create more value for their stakeholders. Large organizations expect the board of directors and executvives to effectively manage the organization, which is called *corporate governance*.

IT governance, as defined by the Information Systems Audit and Control Association (*www.isaca .org*) is "a structure of relationships and processes to direct and control the enterprise in order to achieve the enterprise's goals by adding value while balancing risk versus return over IT and its processes." We can see that this definition has three parts. First, it talks about relationships and processes; these would be designed by those who lead the organization. These actions are taken to meet the organization's goals. For example, if an organization wants to efficiently process its sales transactions, then systems are needed to capture, store, and organize those sales transactions. The second part of the definition is that these actions should add value; that is, they should make money or bring some kind of intangible benefit to the organization. So any new systems should have a reasonable cost. Finally, there should be a balance between risks and profits; for example, systems should be secure so that they cannot be hacked into and private data exposed.

Chapter 1 talked about an *IT steering committee*. Such a committee is an important part of managing information technology in organizations. However, IT governance is about managing IT throughout the organization. This includes planning, acquisition, implementation, and ongoing support, as well as monitoring and evaluation so that decisions can be made about potential changes.

Without effective IT governance, there are many things that could go wrong. Information systems might not meet organizational business objectives, or systems could be error prone, over budget, or hard to use. If there was poor security, data and programs could be damaged or copied by unauthorized individuals.

Some systems are very detailed and require expert assistance to make sure that they are functioning properly. Even software aimed at consumers can vary in their functionality. Think about one task that you may not like to do every year—prepare your income tax return. The *Toronto Star* (May 15, 2010) evaluated personal tax income tax software and found that there was a difference in the way the various programs handled a caregiver tax credit. Some software provided it for all low-income individuals while other software provided it for only disabled individuals. All organizations must carefully assess their software to make sure that it functions the way it is supposed to, so that taxes are properly calculated and transactions properly recorded.

Companies like CGI (*www.cgi.com*), discussed in our next IT's About Business, help organizations implement their information technology.

IT'S ABOUT BUSINESS 2.1
CGI PROVIDES TECHNOLOGY TO THE LARGE AND THE SMALL

New Community Credit Union is a small credit union located in Saskatoon, Saskatchewan (*www.newcommunitycu.com*) with 10 full-time employees. It is a full-service credit union, handling deposits, loans, and investments, as well as providing electronic services. To provide these services effectively, the credit union needed current information systems comprising software, hardware, and maintenance support.

Rather than handle this using its own employees, the credit union signed a six-year contract with CGI Group, an outsourcing organization. Many small organizations lacking technology expertise outsource their computing development and operations. CGI has software called RFS, which provides Internet-based banking solutions to more than 50 credit unions, banks, or trust companies. CGI provides retail systems that do transaction processing and the company also works with other organizations to provide complete banking systems. Its clients include two other larger Saskatchewan credit unions, Conexus Credit Union and Saskatoon Credit Union, as well as much larger financial institutions, such as the TD Bank Financial Group.

Based in Montreal, CGI has over 31,000 employees in more than 125 offices worldwide and annual revenues over $4.5 billion. To provide continuing services to its customers, CGI has job postings on *www.monster.ca*, with jobs available in most Canadian provinces (*http://www2.monster.ca/media/cgi/search.htm*). The job posting provides a clear description of the types of work that CGI does. CGI follows the information technology cycle from inception: the design of systems, through to development and implementation of systems, and ongoing operations, maintenance, and change. The company serves several specific industry sectors, which include financial services.

Sources: A. Shukla, "CGI Delivers Banking Solution to Canada Credit Union," TMnet.com, December 11, 2009; CGI website (*www.cgi.com*); New Community Credit Union website (*www.newcommunitycu.com*).

QUESTIONS
1. What kind of questions would credit union management ask of a service provider such as CGI before deciding to hire it to provide information systems?
2. Review the industry sectors that CGI services. What kind of software do those industries use?

Implementing effective IT governance involves adopting good controls over the acquisition and ongoing use of information systems, discussed further in Chapter 12. It also involves establishing good security and privacy controls, discussed further in Chapter 3. Chapter 3 also describes the layers of controls that organizations would require to effectively manage their IT resources. Effective IT governance is an organization-wide process, requiring competent management that sets the tone that controls over IT are important, so that employees follow the best practices that are implemented by the organization. These best practices will help the organization select and implement the types of software systems that the organization needs. We discuss examples of these systems and their purposes in the rest of this chapter and throughout this text. Organizations select such systems so that they can thrive and compete.

Smaller businesses implement IT governance by having an aware and knowledgeable owner-manager who actively selects business practices and software.

BEFORE YOU GO ON ...

1. Why is IT governance important?
2. Using the three parts of the IT governance definition, explain why a restaurant would need effective IT governance.

2.2 Types and Purposes of Information Systems

Today organizations employ many different types of information systems. Figure 2.1 illustrates the different types of information systems within organizations, and Figure 2.2 shows the different types of information systems among organizations. In subsequent chapters we describe these systems further. Chapter 8 discusses transaction processing systems, management information systems, and enterprise resource planning systems, Chapter 9 discusses customer relationship management systems, and Chapter 10 discusses supply-chain management systems, electronic data interchange (EDI) systems, and extranets..

Here, we highlight the numerous and diverse types of support that information systems provide, both within a single organization and among organizations.

Computer-Based Information Systems

The IT architecture and IT infrastructure provide the basis for all information systems in the organization. An **information system (IS)** collects, processes, stores, analyzes, and disseminates information for a specific purpose. A **computer-based information system (CBIS)** is an information system that uses computer technology to perform some or all of its intended tasks. Today most information systems are computerized, although not all of them are. For this reason the term "information system" is typically used synonymously with "computer-based information system." The basic components of information systems are listed in Figure 2.1. The terms and concepts will be discussed later.

- **Hardware** is a device such as the processor, monitor, keyboard, and printer. Together these devices accept data and information, process it, and display it.

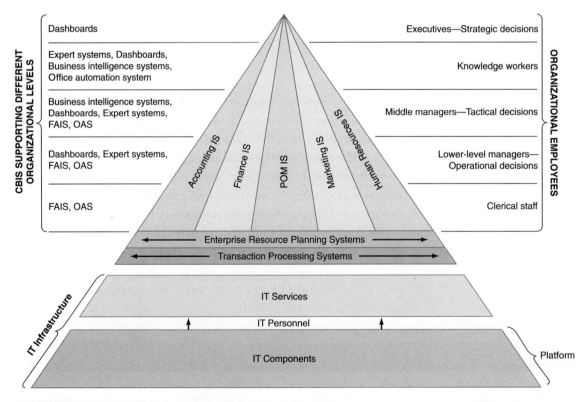

FIGURE 2.1 Information technology inside your organization.

- **Software** is a program or collection of programs that enables the hardware to process data.
- A **database** is a collection of related files or tables containing data.
- A **network** is a connecting system (wireline or wireless) that permits different computers to share resources.
- **Procedures** are the set of instructions about how to combine the above components in order to process information and generate the desired output.
- **People** are those individuals who use the hardware and software, interface with it, or use its output.

Computer-based information systems have many capabilities. Table 2.1 summarizes the most important ones.

TABLE 2.1
MAJOR CAPABILITIES OF INFORMATION SYSTEMS

• Perform high-speed, high-volume numerical computations within and among organizations	• Allow quick and inexpensive access to vast amounts of information worldwide
• Provide fast, accurate communication and collaboration within and among organizations	• Interpret vast amounts of data quickly and efficiently
• Store huge amounts of information in a small, easy-to-access space	• Increase the effectiveness and efficiency of people working in groups in one place or in several locations anywhere
	• Automate both semi-automatic business processes and manual tasks

Application Programs

An **application program** is a computer program designed to support a specific task or business process. Each functional area or department within a business organization uses dozens of application programs. Note that application programs are synonymous with applications. For instance, the human resources department sometimes uses one application for screening job applicants and another for monitoring employee turnover. The collection of application programs in a single department is usually referred to as a departmental information system. For example, the collection of application programs in the human resources area is called the *human resources information system (HRIS)*. We can see in Figure 2.1 that there are collections of application programs—that is, computer-based information systems—in the other functional areas as well, such as accounting and finance. IT's About Business 2.2 shows how a variety of applications enable the National Football League to successfully mount the Super Bowl.

Breadth of Support of Information Systems

Certain information systems support parts of organizations, others support entire organizations, and still others support groups of organizations. We discuss each of these types of systems in this section.

As we have seen, each department or functional area within an organization has its own collection of application programs, or functional information systems. These **functional area information systems (FAIS)** are located at the top of Figure 2.1. Each information system supports a particular functional area in the organization. Examples are accounting IS, finance IS, production/operations management (POM) IS, marketing IS, and human resources IS.

IT'S ABOUT BUSINES 2.2
INFORMATION TECHNOLOGY AND THE NATIONAL FOOTBALL LEAGUE

The National Football League (*www.nfl.com*) is a multi-billion-dollar entertainment business, driven by broadcasts, merchandise sales, box-office revenue, marketing, and event planning and execution. Key information technologies are in place to support the various functions of this popular sport, including global positioning systems (GPS), electronic commerce, wired and wireless networking, voice over Internet protocol (VoIP), data security, storage, and project management. Thanks to these systems, the NFL can better manage logistics and customer relations, and securely store data needed for the teams and the media. Perhaps the most public display of its IT results from work behind the scenes at the Super Bowl.

The Gameday Management Group (*www.game daymanagement.com*) has a great deal of experience with large crowds. In addition to working 10 Super Bowls, Gameday has experience with the Olympics and has overseen such events as Pope Benedict XVI's visit to the United States. The logistics of mounting the Super Bowl mean that Gameday's involvement can result in success or failure for the big event. Everyone getting to the venue by bus and limo—team members and executives, celebrity performers, and other VIPs—needs to arrive exactly on schedule.

Before new IT systems took over, the more than 100 Gameday employees working the Super Bowl tracked all the transportation movements by walkie-talkie. Gameday used to employ radios to communicate with police, entertainment representatives, team officials, and corporate personnel. Now they use a solution from U.S. Fleet Tracking, enabled by information technology from KORE Telematics (*www.koretelematics.com*). The KORE solution combines on-line map technology with GPS sensors, allowing Gameday staff members to receive real-time information on their laptops concerning the location of every key vehicle as it makes its way to and from the stadium. An animated map flashes on each screen, pinpointing every bus and limo en route. This satellite-based technology improves the timeliness and precision of the information flow to Gameday employees.

Gameday staff members now know when the stadium is ready to accept a bus or limo, and they can see how many minutes away each vehicle is from the stadium. They stagger all arrivals to minimize potential confusion, ensuring, for example, that buses for opposing teams do not arrive at the same time.

Thanks to Gameday's use of information technology, the Super Bowl (and other large events) function seamlessly, an operation that no one notices. That is just the way that Gameday wants it.

Sources: Compiled from D. McCafferty, "How the NFL Is Using Business Technology and Information Technology Together," *Baseline Magazine*, August 29, 2008; "Gameday Management Scores NFL Deal for Super Bowl XLI," *Orlando Business Journal*, August 3, 2006; NFL website (*www.nfl.com*), accessed January 28, 2009.

QUESTIONS
1. Identify the various computer-based information systems used by the NFL.
2. What is the NFL's biggest competitive advantage over other major sports, both amateur and professional? Is this advantage related to information systems? Support your answer.
3. Can the NFL sustain its competitive advantage? Why or why not? Hint: What are the barriers to entry for the NFL?

Just below the functional area ISs are two information systems that support the entire organization: enterprise resource planning systems and transaction processing systems. Enterprise resource planning (ERP) systems are designed to correct a lack of communication among the functional area ISs. ERP systems were an important innovation because the various functional area ISs were often developed as stand-alone systems and did not communicate effectively (if at all) with one another. ERP systems resolve this problem by tightly integrating the functional area ISs via a common database. In doing so, they enhance communications among the functional areas of an organization. For this reason, experts credit ERP systems with greatly increasing organizational productivity. Nearly all ERP systems are transaction processing systems (which we discuss next), but transaction processing systems are not all ERP systems.

A **transaction processing system (TPS)** supports the monitoring, collection, storage, and processing of data from the organization's basic business transactions, each of which generates data. For example, when you are checking out of Walmart, each time the cashier swipes an item across the bar code reader, that is one transaction. The TPS collects data continuously, typically in real time—that is, as soon as the data are generated—and provides the input data for the corporate databases. The TPSs are considered critical to the success of any enterprise because they support core operations. We discuss both TPSs and ERP systems in detail in Chapter 8.

Interorganizational information systems (IOSs) are information systems that connect two or more organizations. IOSs support many interorganizational operations; **supply chain** management is the best known. An organization's supply chain describes the flow of materials, information, money, and services from suppliers of raw material through factories and warehouses to the end customers.

Note that the supply chain in Figure 2.2 shows both physical flows, information flows, and financial flows. Information flows, financial flows, and digitizable products (soft products) are represented with dotted lines, and physical products (hard products) as solid lines. Digitizable products are those that can be represented in electronic form, such as music and software. Information flows, financial flows, and digitizable products go through the Internet, whereas physical products are shipped. For example, when you order a computer from *www.dell.ca*, your information goes to Dell via the Internet. When your transaction is processed (that is, your credit card is approved and your order is recorded), Dell ships your computer to you.

Electronic commerce systems are another type of interorganizational information system. These systems enable organizations to conduct transactions, called business-to-business (B2B) electronic commerce, and customers to conduct transactions with businesses, called business-to-consumer (B2C) electronic commerce. They are typically Internet-based. Figure 2.2 illustrates B2B and B2C electronic commerce. Electronic commerce systems are so important that we discuss them in detail in Chapter 6 with additional examples throughout this book.

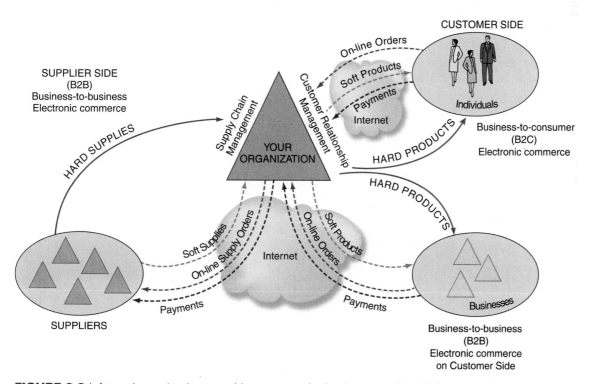

FIGURE 2.2 Information technology outside your organization (your supply chain).

Support for Organizational Employees

So far we have concentrated on information systems that support specific functional areas and operations. We now consider information systems that support particular employees within the organization. The right side of Figure 2.1 identifies these employees. Note that they range from clerical workers all the way up to executives.

Clerical workers, who support managers and work groups at all levels of the organization, include bookkeepers, secretaries, electronic file clerks, and insurance claim processors. Lower-level managers handle the day-to-day operations of the organization, making routine decisions such as assigning tasks to employees and placing purchase orders. *Middle managers* make tactical decisions, which deal with activities such as short-term planning, organizing, and control. **Knowledge workers** are professional employees such as financial and marketing analysts, engineers, lawyers, and accountants. All knowledge workers are experts in a particular subject area. They create information and knowledge, which they integrate into the business. Knowledge workers act as advisors to middle managers and executives, or function in their area of expertise. This includes nurses, doctors, and academic faculty. Finally, *executives* make decisions that deal with situations that can significantly change the manner in which business is done. Examples of executive decisions are introducing a new product line, acquiring other businesses, and relocating operations to a foreign country. IT support for each level of employee appears on the left side of Figure 2.1.

Office automation systems (OASs) typically support the clerical staff, lower and middle managers, and knowledge workers and are often used by other employees, too. Employees use OASs to develop documents (word processing and desktop publishing software), schedule resources (electronic calendars), and communicate (e-mail, voice mail, videoconferencing, and groupware that facilitates multiple individuals working with the same documents).

Functional area information systems summarize data and prepare reports, primarily for middle managers, but sometimes for lower-level managers. Because these reports typically concern a specific functional area, report generators are an important type of functional area IS.

Business intelligence (BI) systems provide computer-based support for complex, non-routine decisions, primarily for middle managers and knowledge workers. (They also support lower-level managers.) These systems are typically used with a data warehouse and allow users to perform their own data analysis. We discuss BI systems further in Chapter 11.

Expert systems (ESs) attempt to duplicate the work of human experts by applying reasoning capabilities, knowledge, and expertise within a specific domain. These systems are primarily designed to support knowledge workers. We discuss ESs in Chapter 11.

Dashboards (also called **digital dashboards**) support all managers of the organization. They provide rapid access to timely information and direct access to structured information in the form of reports. Dashboards that are tailored to the information needs of executives are called executive dashboards. We discuss dashboards in Chapter 11. Table 2.2 provides an overview of the different types of information systems used by organizations

TABLE 2.2
TYPES OF ORGANIZATIONAL INFORMATION SYSTEMS

TYPE OF SYSTEM	FUNCTION	EXAMPLE
Functional area IS	Supports the activities within a specific functional area	System for processing payroll
Transaction processing system	Processes transaction data from business events	Walmart checkout point-of-sale terminal
Enterprise resource planning	Integrates all functional areas of the organization	Oracle, SAP
Office automation system	Supports daily work activities of individuals and groups	Microsoft Office

TABLE 2.2 (*Continued*)		
Management information system	Produces reports summarized from transaction data, usually in one functional area	Report on total sales for each customer
Decision support system	Provides access to data and analysis tools	"What-if " analysis of changes in budget
Expert system	Mimics human expertise in a particular area and makes a decision	Credit card approval analysis
Executive dashboard	Presents structured, summarized information about aspects of business important to executives	Status of sales by product
Supply chain management system	Manages flows of products, services, and information among organizations	Walmart Retail Link system connecting suppliers to Walmart
Electronic commerce system	Enables transactions among organizations and between organizations and customers	*www.dell.ca*

BEFORE YOU GO ON …

1. What is the difference between applications and computer-based information systems?
2. Explain how information systems provide support for knowledge workers.
3. As we move up the organization's hierarchy from clerical workers to executives, how does the type of support provided by information systems change?

2.3 Competitive Advantage and Strategic Information Systems

A competitive strategy is a statement that identifies a business's strategies to compete, its goals, and the plans and policies that will be required to carry out those goals. Through its competitive strategy, an organization seeks a **competitive advantage** in an industry. That is, it seeks to outperform its competitors in some measure such as cost, quality, or speed. Competitive advantage helps a company control a market and generate larger-than-average profits.

Competitive advantage is increasingly important in today's business environment, as we demonstrate throughout the book. In general, the *core business* of companies has remained the same. That is, information technologies simply offer the tools that can increase an organization's success through its traditional sources of competitive advantage, such as low cost, excellent customer service, and superior supply chain management. **Strategic information systems (SISs)** provide a competitive advantage by helping an organization implement its strategic goals and increase its performance and productivity. Any information system that helps an organization gain a competitive advantage *or* reduce a competitive disadvantage is a strategic information system.

FIGURE 2.3
Porter's
competitive
forces model.

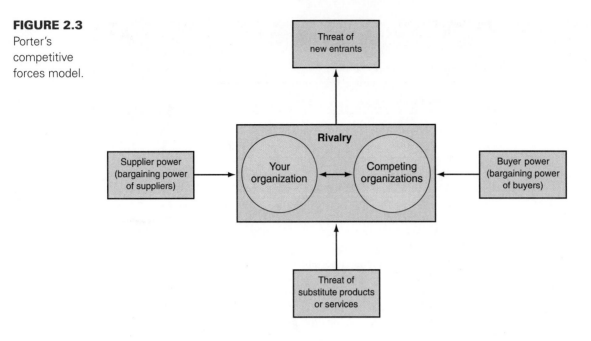

Porter's Competitive Forces Model

The best-known framework for analyzing competitiveness is Michael Porter's **competitive forces model.** Companies use Porter's model to develop strategies to increase their competitive edge. Porter's model also demonstrates how IT can make a company more competitive.

Porter's model identifies five major forces that can endanger or enhance a company's position in a given industry. Figure 2.3 highlights these forces. As we might expect, the Web has changed the nature of competition. Significantly, Porter concludes that the overall impact of the Web is to increase competition, which generally diminishes a firm's profitability. Let's examine Porter's five forces and the ways that the Web influences them.

1. *The threat of entry of new competitors.* The threat that new competitors will enter your market is high when entry is easy and low when significant barriers to entry exist. An **entry barrier** is a product or service feature that customers have learned to expect from organizations in a certain industry. A competing organization must offer this feature in order to survive in the marketplace. For example, suppose you want to open a gasoline station. In order to compete in that industry, you would have to offer pay-at-the-pump service to your customers. Pay-at-the-pump is an IT-based barrier to entering this market because you must offer it free.

   The first gas station that offered this service gained first-move advantage and established barriers to entry. This advantage did not last, however, as competitors quickly offered the same service and thus overcame the barriers to entry.

   For most firms, the Web *increases* the threat that new competitors will enter the market by sharply reducing traditional barriers to entry, such as the need for a sales force or a physical storefront to sell goods and services. Today, competitors frequently need only to set up a website. This threat of increased competition is particularly acute in industries that perform an *intermediation role*, which is a link between buyers and sellers (for example, stockbrokers and travel agents) as well as in industries where the primary product or service is digital (for example, the music industry). In addition, the geographical reach of the Web enables distant competitors to compete more directly with an existing firm.

2. *The bargaining power of suppliers.* Supplier power is high when buyers have few choices from whom to buy and low when buyers have many choices. Therefore, organizations would rather

have more potential suppliers so they will be in a stronger position to negotiate price, quality, and delivery terms.

The Internet's impact on suppliers is mixed. On the one hand, it enables buyers to find alternative suppliers and compare prices more easily, thereby reducing the supplier's bargaining power. On the other hand, as companies use the Internet to integrate their supply chains, participating suppliers prosper by locking in customers.

3. ***The bargaining power of customers (buyers).*** Buyer power is high when buyers have many choices from whom to buy and low when buyers have few choices. For example, in the past, students had few places from which to buy their textbooks (typically, one or two campus bookstores). As a result, students had low buyer power. Today, the Web provides students with access to a multitude of potential suppliers as well as information about textbooks. As a result, student buyer power has greatly increased.

   In contrast, loyalty programs reduce buyer power. As their name suggests, loyalty programs reward customers based on the amount of business they do with a particular organization (for example, airlines, hotels, and rental car companies). Information technology allows companies to track the activities and accounts of millions of customers, thereby reducing buyer power. That is, customers who receive "perks" from loyalty programs are less likely to do business with competitors. (Loyalty programs are associated with customer relationship management, which we discuss in Chapter 9.)

4. ***The threat of substitute products or services.*** If there are many substitutes for an organization's products or services, the threat of substitutes is high. If there are few substitutes, the threat is low. Today new technologies create substitute products very rapidly. For example, today's customers can purchase wireless telephones instead of landline telephones, Internet music services instead of traditional CDs, and ethanol instead of gasoline in cars.

   Information-based industries are in the greatest danger from substitutes. Any industry in which digitized information can replace material goods (for example, music, books, and software) must view the Internet as a threat because the Internet can convey this information efficiently and at low cost and high quality.

   However, companies can create a competitive advantage when there are many substitutes for their products by increasing switching costs. Switching costs are the costs, in money and time, of a decision to buy elsewhere. For example, contracts that you have with your smart phone provider typically have a substantial penalty for switching to another provider until the term of your contract ends (quite often, two years). This switching cost is monetary.

   In addition, as you buy products from Amazon, the company develops a profile of your shopping habits and recommends products targeted to your preferences. If you switch to another bookstore, it will take time for that company to develop a profile on your wants and needs. Thus, the cost of switching is in terms of time.

5. ***The rivalry among existing firms in the industry.*** The threat from rivalry is high when there is intense competition among many firms in an industry. The threat is low when the competition is among fewer firms and is not as intense.

   In the past, proprietary information systems—systems that belong exclusively to a single organization—have provided strategic advantage among firms in highly competitive industries. Today, however, the visibility of Internet applications on the Web makes proprietary systems more difficult to keep secret. In simple terms, when I see my competitor's new system on-line, I will rapidly match its features in order to remain competitive. The result is fewer differences among competitors, which leads to more intense competition in an industry.

   To understand this concept, consider the competitive grocery industry, in which Metro, Loblaws, Walmart, and other companies compete essentially on price. Some of these companies have IT-enabled loyalty programs in which customers receive discounts and the store gains valuable business intelligence on customers' buying preferences. Stores use this business intelligence in their marketing and promotional campaigns. (We discuss business intelligence in Chapter 11.)

Grocery stores are also experimenting with wireless technologies such as radio-frequency identification (RFID, discussed in Chapter 7) to speed the checkout process, track customers through the store, and notify customers of discounts as they pass by certain products. Grocery companies also use IT to tightly integrate their supply chains for maximum efficiency and thus reduce prices for shoppers. (We discuss supply chain management in Chapter 10.)

Competition also is being affected by the extremely low variable cost of digital products. That is, once the product has been developed, the cost of producing additional "units" approaches zero. Consider the music industry as an example. When artists record music, their songs are captured in digital format. Producing physical products, such as CDs or DVDs, with the songs on them for sale in music stores, involves costs. The costs in a physical distribution channel are much higher than the costs involved in delivering the songs over the Internet in digital form.

In fact, in the future companies might give some products away. For example, some analysts predict that commissions for on-line stock trading will approach zero because investors can access the necessary information via the Internet to make their own decisions regarding buying and selling stocks. At that point, consumers will no longer need brokers to give them information that they can obtain themselves for virtually nothing.

Porter's Value Chain Model

Organizations use models such as Porter's competitive forces model to design general strategies. To identify specific activities in which they can use competitive strategies for greatest impact, they can use Porter's **value chain model** (see Figure 2.4). The value chain model also shows points where an organization can use information technology to achieve competitive advantage.

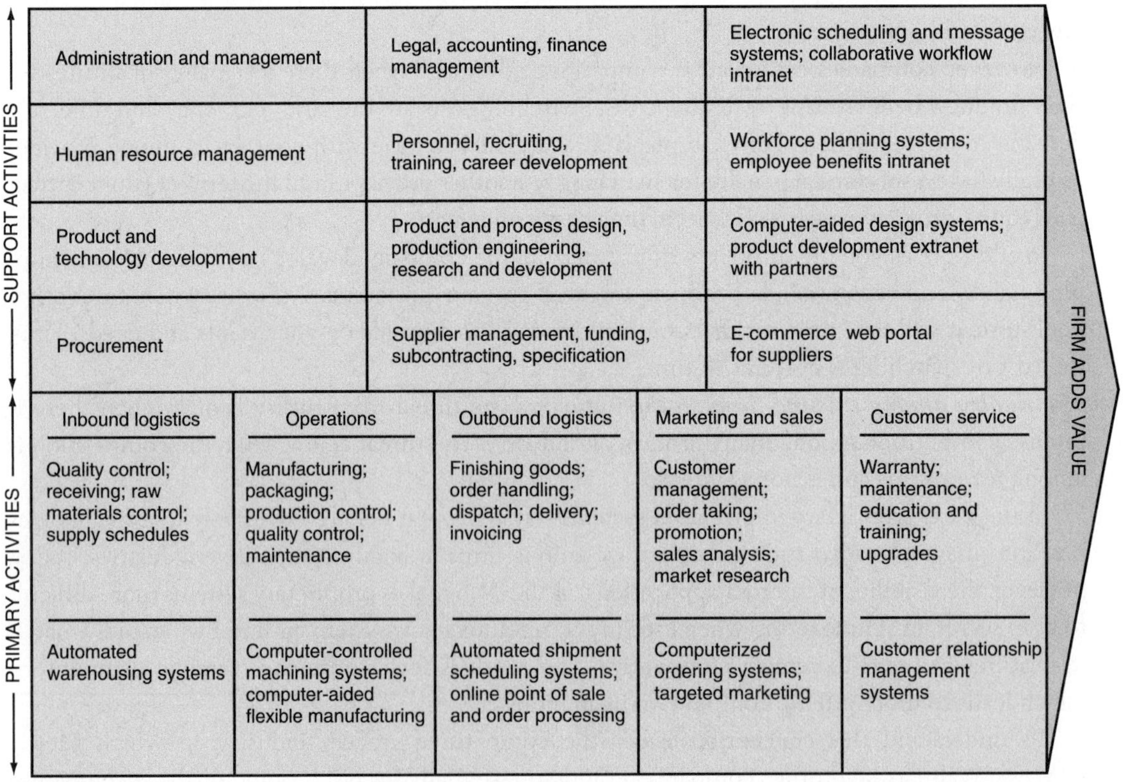

FIGURE 2.4 Porter's value chain model.

According to Porter's value chain model, the activities conducted in any organization can be divided into two categories: primary activities and support activities. The **primary activities** are those business activities that relate to the production and distribution of the firm's products and services, thus creating value for which customers are willing to pay. Primary activities involve purchasing materials, processing materials into products, and delivering products to customers. Typically, there are five primary activities:

1. Inbound logistics (inputs)
2. Operations (manufacturing and testing)
3. Outbound logistics (storage and distribution)
4. Marketing and sales
5. After-sales services

The primary activities usually take place in a sequence from 1 to 5. As work progresses in the sequence, value is added to the product in each activity. Specifically, the incoming materials (1) are processed (in receiving, storage, and so on) in activities called *inbound logistics*. Next, the materials are used in *operations* (2), where value is added by turning raw materials into products. These products then need to be prepared for delivery (packaging, storing, and shipping) in the *outbound logistics activities* (3). Then *marketing and sales* (4) sell the products to customers, increasing product value by creating demand for the company's products. Finally, *after-sales services* (5), such as warranty service or upgrade notification, is performed for the customer, further adding value.

The primary activities are buttressed by support activities. Unlike primary activities, **support activities** do not add value directly to the firm's products or services. Rather, as their name suggests, they contribute to the firm's competitive advantage by supporting the primary activities. Support activities consist of:

1. The firm's infrastructure (accounting, finance, management)
2. Human resources management
3. Product and technology research and development (R & D)
4. Procurement

Each support activity can be applied to any or all of the primary activities. In addition, the support activities can also support one another.

A firm's value chain is part of a larger stream of activities, which Porter calls a value system. A **value system**, or an *industry value chain*, includes the suppliers that provide the inputs necessary to the firm and their value chains. Once the firm creates products, these products pass through the value chains of distributors (which also have their own value chains) all the way to the customers. All parts of these chains are included in the value system. To achieve and sustain a competitive advantage, and to support that advantage with information technologies, a firm must understand every component of this value system.

Strategies for Competitive Advantage

Organizations continually try to develop strategies to counter the five competitive forces identified by Porter. We discuss five of those strategies here.

1. ***Cost leadership strategy.*** Produce products and/or services at the lowest cost in the industry. An example is Walmart's automatic inventory replenishment system, which enables Walmart to reduce inventory storage requirements. As a result, Walmart stores use floor space only to sell products, and not to store them, thereby reducing inventory costs.

2. ***Differentiation strategy.*** Offer different products, services, or product features. WestJet Airlines, for example, has differentiated itself as a low-cost, short-haul, express airline. This has proved to be a winning strategy for competing in the highly competitive airline industry. Also, Dell has differentiated itself in the personal computer market through its mass customization strategy.

3. ***Innovation strategy.*** Introduce new products and services, add new features to existing products and services, or develop new ways to produce them. Research in Motion (RIM) developed an innovative user interface on a wireless PDA (personal digital assistant) called the BlackBerry—with a small, full QWERTY keyboard, which allows users to type messages using two thumbs, and a wheel (now a trackpad) for scrolling menus. Like many innovative products, the RIM BlackBerry changed the nature of competition in the cellular telephone industry. Today, many PDAs come with keyboards, and e-mail has become an important feature of many cellular telephones. Another type of innovation is developing a new product line, as IT's About Business 2.3 illustrates at Under Armour.

4. ***Operational effectiveness strategy.*** Improve the manner in which internal business processes are executed so that a firm performs similar activities better than its rivals. Such improvements increase quality, productivity, and employee and customer satisfaction while decreasing time to

IT'S ABOUT BUSINESS 2.3
UNDER ARMOUR MOVES INTO RUNNING SHOES

Under Armour (*www.underarmour.com*), a rapidly growing sports apparel maker, has great appeal among boys and young men who play team sports. Nevertheless, it remains a niche player in its industry. The company decided to develop a line of footwear with the strategy of broadening its appeal to women, older consumers, and more casual athletes.

Although Under Armour posted more than $850 million in revenue in 2009, the company's executives knew that competing with Nike ($19.2 billion in revenue in 2009) would be very difficult. To accomplish this task, the company turned to information technology.

It's more complicated to make and sell running shoes than clothing. For one thing, shoes don't come in just small, medium, and large. Under Armour would not have been able to even consider entering the running shoe business if it had not implemented SAP's (*www.sap.com*) enterprise resource planning software. The SAP applications allowed Under Armour to keep track of its growing inventory and they even changed the supply chain, allowing the company to ship shoes directly from the factory to distributors. In addition, data management software helps the company figure out how to design shoes that meet profit goals and deadlines.

The move to running shoes depended on other information technologies. For example, Under Armour has a treadmill in the hallway of its headquarters. It records biometric data on what feet, legs, and other body parts look like when in motion. This information allows shoe designers to make sure their products can best support and stabilize feet.

Under Armour's shoe designers have another trick up their sleeves: three-dimensional software. The program can create a mock-up so realistic that managers can make decisions about the design and aesthetics without having to see a physical model. That reduces production time and allows new products to hit store shelves sooner, helping Under Armour get a leg—or foot—up on the competition.

Sources: Compiled from M. Peer, "Under Armour Pierced by Weak Retail," *Forbes*, January 14, 2009; S. Mehta, "Under Armour Reboots," *Fortune*, February 2, 2009; M. McCarthy, "Under Armour Makes a Run at Nike with New Footwear Line," *USA Today*, December 9, 2008; R. Sharrow, "Under Armour Trots Out Product Launch for New Running Shoes," *Washington Business Journal*, December 9, 2008; R. Sharrow, "Under Armour to Unveil a Running Shoe in 2009," *Baltimore Business Journal*, May 29, 2008; Under Armour website (*www.underarmour.com*), accessed January 31, 2009.

QUESTIONS

1. Is Under Armour pursuing a viable strategy in moving into the running shoe business? Analyze Under Armour's risk with this strategy. Discuss the impact of information technology on the level of risk that Under Armour is assuming.

2. Will Under Armour's use of information technology in developing a running shoe line of products lead to a competitive advantage? Why or why not? Support your answer.

market. For example, Petro-Canada replaced its nearly 150 different corporate intranet sites with one portal, which was centrally managed using an Oracle Application Server product. Around the same time, the company replaced its three different retail systems in 700 locations with a single ERP solution. This improved the time it took each location to file its monthly financial information (profit and loss statements) from 20 days to less than seven days, providing more timely information for decision making.

5. **Customer orientation strategy.** Concentrate on making customers happy. Web-based systems are particularly effective in this area because they can provide a personalized, one-to-one relationship with each customer.

Failures of Information Systems

So far, we have introduced you to many success stories. You may wonder, though, "Is IT all success?" The answer is, "Absolutely not." There are many types of failures, and we can learn as much from failures as from successes. A failure can be as simple as a basic error, as the following example shows.

EXAMPLE 2.1

On January 31, 2009, between 6:30 AM and 7:25 AM Pacific Standard Time in the United States, if you had been searching for something using Google, you almost certainly would have received the following warning: "This site may harm your computer." Later that day, the company blog carried a message from a Google vice president apologizing for the mistake, which she attributed to human error.

The VP said that Google keeps a list of websites that are known to install harmful software without a user knowing. Google works with a nonprofit organization, StopBadware.org (*www.stopbadware.org*), to develop the criteria for inclusion on this list. Google periodically updates the list, and the company released an update on the morning in question. Unfortunately, the update contained an error made by a Google programmer.

In addition to apologizing to its users, Google also apologized to owners of the websites that were incorrectly identified as harmful. Google's prominence and the size of its user base magnified the problem. As one analyst noted, "Google on a Saturday morning? You're looking at millions of people."

Although human error is impossible to completely eliminate, Google's on-call website reliability team fixed the error quickly. In addition, the company communicated effectively with Google users about the problem.

Sources: Compiled from N. Eddy, "Human Error Caused Google Glitch," eWeek, February 2, 2009; L. Robbins, "Google Error Sends Warning Worldwide," *The New York Times*, January 31, 2009; "'This Site May Harm Your Computer' on Every Search Result?!?!," The Official Google Blog, January 31, 2009.

BEFORE YOU GO ON ...

1. According to Porter, what are the five forces that could endanger a firm's position in its industry or marketplaces?
2. Describe Porter's value chain model. Differentiate between Porter's competitive forces model and his value chain model.
3. What strategies might companies use to gain competitive advantage?
4. Besides our inability to predict the future, what are other reasons that IT projects might fail?

2.4 The Importance of Information Systems and their Management

Information systems have numerous impacts on organizations and on society as a whole. We discuss some of the more significant impacts in this section.

IT Affects Management

IT Will Reduce the Number of Middle Managers

IT makes managers more productive, and it increases the number of employees who can report to a single manager. In these ways IT ultimately decreases the number of managers and experts. It is reasonable to assume then that fewer managerial levels will exist in many organizations and there will be fewer staff and line managers.

IT Will Change the Manager's Job

One of the most important tasks of managers is making decisions. As we will see in Chapter 11, IT can change the manner in which managers make many of their decisions. In this way IT ultimately can change managers' jobs.

Many managers have reported that IT has finally given them time to get out of the office and into the field. They also have found that they can spend more time planning activities instead of "putting out fires." Managers now can gather information for decision making much more quickly by using search engines and intranets.

Going further, IT tends to reduce the time necessary to complete any step in the decision making process. By using IT properly then, managers today can complete tasks more efficiently and effectively.

Another possible impact on the manager's job is a change in managerial requirements. The use of IT might lead organizations to reconsider what qualities they want in a good manager. For example, much of an employee's work is typically performed on-line and stored electronically. For these employees, electronic or "remote" supervision could become more common. Remote supervision places greater emphasis on completed work and less emphasis on personal contacts and office politics. Managerial supervision becomes particularly difficult when employees work in geographically dispersed locations, including homes, away from their supervisors.

IT Affects Employees

IT Affects Employee Perceptions of Job Security.   One of the major concerns of every employee, part-time or full-time, is job security. Due to difficult economic times, increased global competition, demands

Remote or electronic supervision replaces direct managerial supervision when employees work in geographically dispersed locations, including homes.

for customization, and increased consumer sophistication, many companies have increased their investments in IT. In fact, as computers gain in intelligence and capabilities, the competitive advantage of replacing people with machines is increasing rapidly. For this reason, some people believe that society is heading toward higher unemployment. Others disagree, asserting that IT creates entirely new categories of jobs, in fields such as electronic medical records and nanotechnology, that could lead to lower unemployment.

Other concerns for all employees are outsourcing and offshoring. We introduced these terms in Chapter 1, and we discuss them in detail in Chapter 12.

IT Creates Psychological Effects. Many people have experienced a loss of identity because of computerization, including in the workplace. They feel like "just another number" because computers reduce or eliminate the human element that was present in non-computerized systems.

The Internet threatens to have an even more isolating influence than computers and television. Encouraging people to work and shop from their living rooms could produce some unfortunate psychological effects, such as depression and loneliness.

IT Affects Employees' Health and Safety. Computers and information systems are a part of the environment that may adversely affect individuals' health and safety. To illustrate this point, we will discuss the effects of job stress, video display terminals, and long-term use of the keyboard.

An increase in an employee's workload and/or responsibilities can trigger *job stress*. Although computerization has benefited organizations by increasing productivity, it has also created an ever-expanding workload for some employees. Some workers feel overwhelmed and have become increasingly anxious about their job performance. These feelings of stress and anxiety can diminish workers' productivity and jeopardize their physical and mental health. Management's responsibility is to help alleviate these feelings by providing training, redistributing the workload among workers, or hiring more workers.

Exposure to *video display terminals* (*VDTs*) raises the issue of radiation exposure, which has been linked to cancer and other health-related problems. For example, some experts charge that exposure to VDTs for long periods of time can damage an individual's eyesight.

Finally, the long-term use of keyboards can lead to *repetitive strain injuries* such as backaches and muscle tension in the wrists and fingers. *Carpal tunnel syndrome* is a particularly painful form of repetitive strain injury that affects the wrists and hands.

Designers are aware of the potential problems associated with prolonged use of computers. To address these problems, they have attempted to design a better computing environment. **Ergonomics**, the science of adapting machines and work environments to people, focuses on creating an environment that is safe, well lit, and comfortable. For example, anti-glare screens have helped alleviate problems of fatigued or damaged eyesight. Also, chairs that contour the human body have helped decrease backaches. Figure 2.5 displays some sample ergonomic products.

IT Provides Opportunities for People with Disabilities or Other Impairments. Computers can create new employment opportunities for people with disabilities by integrating speech and vision recognition capabilities. For example, individuals who cannot type are able to use a voice-operated keyboard, and individuals who cannot travel can work at home.

Adaptive equipment for computers permits people with disabilities to perform tasks they would not normally be able to do. For example, Figure 2.6 illustrates a PC for a visually challenged user, a PC for a user with a hearing impairment, and a PC for a user with a motor disability. Our closing case describes a new product, a reader, that is useful for many types of impairments.

FIGURE 2.5
Ergonomic
products protect
computer users.
Source: (a), (b),
and (d) courtesy
of Ergodyne;
(c) courtesy of
3M.com

(a)

(b)   (c)   (d)

(a) Wrist support.
(b) Adjustable foot rest.
(c) Eye-protection filter (optically coated glass).
(d) Back support.

(a)   (b)   (c)

FIGURE 2.6 Enabling people with disabilities to work with computers. (a) A PC for a blind or sight-impaired user, equipped with an Oscar optical scanner and a Braille printer, both by TeleSensory. The optical scanner converts text into ASCII code or into proprietary word processing format. Files saved on disk can then be translated into Braille and sent to the printer. Visually impaired users can also enlarge the text on the screen by loading a TSR software magnification program. (b) The deaf or hearing-impaired user's PC is connected to a telephone via an Ultratec Intele-Modern Baudolt/ASCH Modem. The user is sending and receiving messages to and from someone at a remote site who is using a telecommunications device for deaf people (right). (c) This motor-disabled person is communicating with a PC using a Pointer Systems optical head pointer to access all keyboard functions on a virtual keyboard shown on the PC's display. The user can "strike" a key in one of two ways. He can focus on the desired key for a user-definable time period (which causes the key to be highlighted), or he can click an adapted switch when he chooses the desired key.
(*Source*: J. J. Lazzaro, "Computers for the Disabled," *Byte*, June 1993.)

We should note that the Web and graphical user interfaces often still make life difficult for people with impaired vision. Adding audible screen tips and voice interfaces to deal with this problem is helpful.

Other devices help improve the quality of life for people with disabilities in more routine, useful, ways. Examples are a two-way writing telephone, a robotic page turner, a hair brusher, and a hospital bedside video trip to the zoo or the museum. Several organizations specialize in IT designed for people with disabilities.

IT Provides Quality-of-Life Improvements

On a broader scale, IT has significant implications for our quality of life. The workplace can be expanded from the traditional 9 to 5 job at a central location to 24 hours a day at any location. IT can provide employees with flexibility that can significantly improve the quality of leisure time, even if it doesn't increase the total amount of leisure time. However, IT can also place employees on "constant call" so they are never truly away from the office, even when they are on vacation.

In fact, an Associated Press poll found that 20 percent of respondents took their laptop computers on their most recent vacations and 80 percent took their cell phones. Twenty percent of the respondents did some work while vacationing, and 40 percent checked e-mail.

Robot Revolution

Once restricted largely to science fiction movies, robots that can do practical tasks are becoming more common. In fact, "cyberpooches," nursebots, and other mechanical beings may be our companions before we know it. Around the world, quasi-autonomous devices have become increasingly common on factory floors, in hospital corridors, and in farm fields.

In an example of precision agriculture, Carnegie Mellon University in Pittsburgh, Pennsylvania has developed self-directing tractors that harvest hundreds of acres of crops around the clock in California. These "robot tractors" use global positioning systems combined with video image processing that identifies rows of uncut crops.

Many robotic devices are also being developed for military purposes. For example, the United States Pentagon is researching self-driving vehicles and bee-like swarms of small surveillance robots, each of which would contribute a different view or angle of a combat zone. The Predator, an unmanned aerial vehicle, has been used in Iraq and Afghanistan.

It probably will be a long time before we see robots making decisions by themselves, handling unfamiliar situations, and interacting with people. Nevertheless, robots are extremely helpful in various environments, particularly environments that are repetitive, harsh, or dangerous to humans.

Improvements in Health Care

IT has brought about major improvements in health care delivery. Medical personnel use IT to make better and faster diagnoses and to monitor critically ill patients more accurately. IT also has streamlined the process of researching and developing new drugs. Expert systems now help doctors diagnose diseases, and machine vision is enhancing the work of radiologists. Surgeons use virtual reality to plan complex surgeries. They have also used a surgical robot to perform long-distance surgery by controlling the robot's movements. Finally, doctors discuss complex medical cases via videoconferencing. New computer simulations recreate the sense of touch, allowing doctors-in-training to perform virtual procedures without risking harm to an actual patient.

Of the thousands of other applications related to health care, administrative systems are critically important. These systems range from detecting insurance fraud to nursing scheduling to financial and marketing management.

The Internet contains vast amounts of useful medical information (see *www.webmd.com*, for example). In an interesting study, researchers at the Princess Alexandra Hospital in Brisbane, Australia, identified 26 difficult diagnostic cases published in the *New England Journal of Medicine*. They selected three to five search terms from each case and conducted a Google search. The researchers selected and recorded the three diagnoses that Google ranked most prominently and that appeared to fit the symptoms and signs. They then compared these results with the correct diagnoses as published in the journal. They discovered that their Google searches had found the correct diagnosis in 15 of the 26 cases, a success rate of 57 percent.

The researchers caution, however, against the dangers of self-diagnosis. They maintain that people should use the information gained from Google only to participate in their health care by asking questions of their physician.

Managing Information Resources

Clearly, a modern organization possesses many information resources. *Information resources* is a general term that includes all the hardware, software (information systems and applications), data, and networks in an organization. In addition to the computing resources, numerous applications exist, and new ones are continuously being developed. Applications have enormous strategic value. Firms rely on them so heavily that, in some cases, when they are not working (even for a short time), an organization cannot function. In addition, these information systems are very expensive to acquire, operate, and maintain. Therefore, it is essential to manage them properly.

Our discussion focuses on the IS functions found in a large organization. Smaller firms do not have all these functions or types of jobs. In fact, in smaller firms, one person often handles several functions.

Regardless of the size of the organization, however, it is becoming increasingly difficult to manage an organization's information resources effectively. The reason for this difficulty comes from the evolution of the MIS function in the organization. When businesses first began to use computers in the early 1950s, the *information systems department* (*ISD*) owned the only computing resource in the organization: the mainframe. At that time, end users did not interact directly with the mainframe.

Today, computers are located throughout the organization, and almost all employees use computers in their work. This system is known as *end-user computing*. End-user computing has two components: end-user data entry, reporting, and inquiry (commonly referred to as simply "users"); and end-user development, where users develop usable systems, such as spreadsheets or programs using programming languages or other development tools.

As a result of this decentralization to users, the ISD no longer owns the organization's information resources. Instead, a partnership has developed between the ISD and the end users. The ISD now acts as more of a consultant to end users, viewing them as customers. In fact, the main function of the ISD is to use IT to solve end users' business problems.

Which IT Resources Are Managed and by Whom?

As we just saw, the responsibility for managing information resources is now divided between the ISD and the end users. This arrangement raises several important questions: Which resources are managed by whom? What is the role of the ISD, its structure, and its place within the organization? What is the appropriate relationship between the ISD and the end users? In this section we provide brief answers to these questions.

There are many types of information systems resources. In addition, their components may come from multiple vendors and be of different brands. The major categories of information resources are hardware, software, databases, networks, procedures, security facilities, and physical buildings. These resources are scattered throughout the organization, and some of them change frequently. Therefore, they can be difficult to manage.

To make things more complicated, there is no standard menu for how to divide responsibility for developing and maintaining information resources between the ISD and the end users. Instead, that division depends on many things: the size and nature of the organization, the amount and type of IT resources, the organization's attitudes toward computing, the attitudes of top management toward computing, the maturity level of the technology, the amount and nature of outsourced IT work, and even the country in which the company operates. Generally speaking, the ISD is responsible for corporate-level and shared resources, and the end users are responsible for departmental resources.

It is important that the ISD and the end users work closely together and cooperate regardless of who is doing what. Let's begin by looking at the role of the ISD within the organization (Table 2.3).

The Role of the IS Department

The role of the director of the ISD is changing from a technical manager to a senior executive called the **chief information officer (CIO)**. As Table 2.3 shows, the role of the ISD is also changing from a purely technical one to a more managerial and strategic one. For example, the ISD is now responsible for managing the outsourcing of projects and for creating business alliances with vendors and IS departments in other organizations. Because its role has expanded so much, the ISD now reports directly to a senior vice president of administration or even to the chief executive officer (CEO). (Previously it may have reported to a functional department such as accounting.) In its new role, the ISD must be able to work closely with external organizations such as vendors, business partners, consultants, research institutions, and universities.

Inside the organization, the ISD and the end-user units must be close partners. The ISD is responsible for setting standards for hardware and software purchases, as well as for information security. The

TABLE 2.3
THE CHANGING ROLE OF THE INFORMATION SYSTEMS DEPARTMENT

Traditional Major IS Functions

- Managing systems development and systems project management
- Managing computer operations, including the computer centre
- Staffing, training, and developing IS skills
- Providing technical services
- Infrastructure planning, development, and control

New (Consultative) Major IS Functions

- Initiating and designing specific strategic information systems
- Incorporating the Internet and electronic commerce into the business
- Managing system integration, including the Internet, intranets, and extranets
- Educating the non-IS managers about IT
- Educating the IS staff about the business
- Supporting end-user computing
- Partnering with the executives
- Managing outsourcing
- Proactively using business and technical knowledge to seed innovative ideas about IT
- Creating business alliances with vendors and IS departments in other organizations

ISD also monitors user hardware and software purchases, and it serves as a gatekeeper in regard to software licensing and illegal downloads (for example, music files). IT's About Business 2.4 illustrates how Pitney Bowes manages its information technology function.

IT'S ABOUT BUSINESS 2.4
PITNEY BOWES

The first postage meter approved by the U.S. Post Office was invented by Arthur Pitney and Walter Bowes. From this collaboration, Pitney Bowes (PB, *www.pb.com*) emerged in 1920. Today the company has 33,000 employees in 130 countries and holds approximately 3,500 active patents. The IT department has 200 employees, plus an additional 427 people who work on Pitney Bowes projects through Wipro Technologies (*www.wipro.com*), a services partner based in Bangalore, India, and East Brunswick, New Jersey.

The company began to change the strategic vision of its IT department in 2000. Before that, the IT group demonstrated operational excellence, but did not innovate as well as management wanted. The transformation began when Pitney Bowes gathered all the scattered components of the IT department and created one global IT organization. The new organization was focused on both internal and external customers. Internally, the goal was to use IT to provide reliable and efficient services, and use IT to better solve business problems. Externally, the organization sought ways to use IT to offer more value to customers.

All of Pitney Bowes's IT functions worldwide are the responsibility of the company's CIO. This includes approval of expenditures, systems deployment, technology assessments, IT infrastructure, and partnerships. Each technology area, such as enterprise systems and customer relationship management, and each geographic area has a leader who reports to the CIO.

In every IT project, the IT department builds a business case to show that a new system will support a current or an emerging business need. In order for a new project to be approved, it must either cut costs or improve service without costing more. The IT department knows what internal customers need because they hold monthly meetings to review operations. These meetings include business units and field service technicians around the globe. To determine which projects should be rolled out first, investment priority meetings are held. Once projects are launched, regular project review meetings ensure the systems are doing what they're supposed to and achieving the desired results. In particular, the IT department is concentrating on applications such as enterprise resource planning, customer relationship management, mobile capabilities, and greater use of the Web.

Pitney Bowes also outsources extensively. Most of its software application development and maintenance has been awarded to its partner, Wipro. The partnership with Wipro has saved PB money, given the company access to a larger pool of labour and skills, and provided products of higher quality. The higher quality results in part from Wipro's certification in the Capability Maturity Model Integration (*www.sei.cmu.edu/cmmi*).

Sources: Compiled from "Pitney Bowes MapInfo Integrates GroundView Demographics with AnySite," Reuters, January 5, 2009; "Pitney Bowes Receives 'Strong Positive' Rating in Leading Industry Analyst Firm's MarketScope," *All Business*, December 16, 2008; H. McKeefry, "Pitney Bowes: Stamp of Approval," *Baseline Magazine*, September 29, 2008; Pitney Bowes website (*www.pb.com*), accessed May 22, 2010.

QUESTIONS
1. Describe the role of Pitney Bowes's IT department. Is the IT department of strategic importance to the company? Support your answer.
2. What is the relationship between Pitney Bowes's IT department and Wipro? Is Wipro of strategic importance to Pitney Bowes? What is the role of Pitney Bowes's IT department with regard to Wipro?

BEFORE YOU GO ON ...

1. Describe three examples of how information technology can assist individuals who have visual or auditory impairments.
2. How important are end users to the management of the organization's information resources?
3. Where do you think the IT staff should be located? Should they be decentralized in functional areas? Centralized at corporate level? A combination of the two? Explain your answer.

WHAT'S IN IT FOR ME?

FOR THE ACCOUNTING MAJOR

Data and information are the lifeblood of accounting. Transaction processing systems—which are now web-based—capture, organize, analyze, and disseminate data and information throughout organizations, often through corporate intranets. The Internet has vastly increased the number of transactions (especially global) in which modern businesses engage. Transactions such as billing customers, preparing payrolls, and purchasing and paying for materials provide data that the accounting department must record and track. These transactions, particularly with customers and suppliers, now usually take place on-line through extranets. In addition, accounting information systems must share information with information systems in other parts of a large organization. For example, transactional information from a sales or marketing IS is now input for the accounting system as well.

FOR THE FINANCE MAJOR

The modern financial world turns on speed, volume, and accuracy of information flow. Information systems and networks make these things possible. Finance departments use information systems to monitor world financial markets and to provide quantitative analyses (for example, cash flow projections and forecasting). They use decision support systems to support financial decision making (for example, portfolio management). Financial managers now use business intelligence software to analyze information in data warehouses. Finally, large-scale information systems (for example, enterprise resource planning packages) tightly integrate finance with all other functional areas within a wide-ranging enterprise.

FOR THE MARKETING MAJOR

Marketing now uses customer databases, decision support systems, sales automation, data warehouses, and business intelligence software to perform its functions. The Internet has created an entirely new global channel for marketing from business to business and business to consumer. It also has dramatically increased the amount of information available to customers, who can now compare prices quickly and thoroughly. As a result, shoppers have become more knowledgeable and sophisticated. In turn, marketing managers must work harder to acquire and retain customers. To accomplish this goal, they now use customer relationship management software. The Internet helps here because it provides for much closer contact between the customer and the supplier.

FOR THE PRODUCTION/OPERATIONS MANAGEMENT MAJOR

Organizations are competing on price, quality, time (speed), and customer service—all of which are concerns of production and operations management. Every process in a company's operations that adds value to a product or service (for example, purchasing inventory, quality control, receiving raw materials, and shipping products) can be enhanced by the use of web-based information systems. Further, information systems have enabled the production and operations function to link the organization to other organizations in the firm's supply chain. From computer-aided design and computer-aided manufacturing through web-based ordering systems, information systems support the production and operations function.

FOR THE HUMAN RESOURCES MANAGEMENT MAJOR

Information systems provide valuable support for human resources (HR) management. For example, record keeping has greatly improved in terms of speed, convenience, and accuracy as a result of technology.

Further, disseminating HR information throughout the company via intranets enables employees to receive consistent information and handle much of their personal business (for example, configuring their benefits) themselves, without help from HR personnel. The Internet makes a tremendous amount of information available to the job seeker, increasing the fluidity of the labour market. Finally, many careers require skills in the use of information systems. HR professionals must have an understanding of these systems and skills to support hiring, training, and retention within an organization.

FOR THE MIS MAJOR

Some MIS employees actually write computer programs. More often, however, they act as analysts, interfacing between business users on the one hand and the programmers on the other. For example, if a marketing manager needs to analyze data that are not in the company's data warehouse, he or she would forward the information requirements to an MIS analyst. The analyst would then work with MIS database personnel to obtain the needed data and input them into the data warehouse. MIS employees also maintain and ensure ongoing operations of information systems.

SUMMARY

1. **Define IT governance and explain why information systems need to be effectively managed.**
   IT governance is the structure of relationships and processes used to direct and control organizations in order to achieve the enterprise's goals by adding value while balancing risk versus return over IT and its processes. Without IT governance, errors in information systems or excess costs would be more likely. Also, without IT governance, organizations could implement information systems that do not meet their needs or that do not help them meet their business objectives.

2. **Describe the components, types, and purposes of information systems.**
   A computer-based information system (CBIS) is an information system that uses computer technology to perform some or all of its intended tasks. The basic components of a CBIS are hardware, software, database(s), telecommunications networks, procedures, and people. Hardware is a set of devices that accept data and information, process them, and display them. Software is a set of programs that enable the hardware to process data. A database is a collection of related files, tables, relations, and software, that stores data and the associations among them. A network is a connecting system (wireline or wireless) that permits different computers to share resources. Procedures are the set of instructions about how to combine the above components in order to process information and generate the desired output. People are the individuals who work with the information system, interface with it, or use its output.

   Information systems can be described by breadth of support. The departmental information systems, also known as functional area information systems, each support a particular functional area in the organization. Two major types of information systems support the entire organization: enterprise resource planning (ERP) systems and transaction processing systems (TPSs). ERP systems tightly integrate the functional area IS via a common database, enhancing communications among the functional areas of an organization. A TPS supports the monitoring, collection, storage, and processing of data from the organization's basic business transactions. Information systems that connect two or more organizations are referred to as interorganizational information systems (IOSs). IOSs support many interorganizational operations; supply chain management is the best known. Electronic commerce systems enable organizations to conduct business-to-business (B2B) and business-to-consumer (B2C) electronic commerce. They are generally Internet-based.

   We can also look at major information systems by organizational level or job function. At the clerical level, employees are supported by office automation systems and functional area information systems. At the operational level, managers are supported by office automation systems, functional area information systems, decision support systems, and business intelligence systems. At the managerial level, functional area information systems provide the major support. Middle managers are also supported by office automation systems, decision support systems, and business intelligence systems. At the knowledge-worker level, expert systems, decision support systems, and business intelligence systems provide support. Executives are supported primarily by executive dashboards.

Strategic information systems support or shape a business unit's competitive strategy. An SIS can significantly change the manner in which business is conducted to help the organization gain a competitive advantage or reduce a competitive disadvantage.

3. **Describe Porter's competitive forces model and his value chain model, explaining five strategies companies can use to improve their competitive positions.**

Companies use Porter's competitive forces model to develop strategies to gain a competitive advantage. Porter's model also demonstrates how IT can enhance a company's competitiveness. The model identifies five major forces that can endanger a company's position in a given industry: (1) the threat of new competitors entering the market, (2) the bargaining power of suppliers, (3) the bargaining power of customers (buyers), (4) the threat of substitute products or services, and (5) the rivalries among existing firms in the industry.

Although the Porter competitive forces model is useful for identifying general strategies, organizations use his value chain model to identify specific activities that can use competitive strategies for greatest impact. The value chain model also shows points at which an organization can use information technology to achieve competitive advantage.

According to Porter's value chain model, the activities conducted in any organization can be divided into two categories: primary activities and support activities. The primary activities are those business activities that relate to the production and distribution of the firm's products and services. The primary activities are buttressed by support activities. Unlike primary activities, support activities do not add value directly to the firm's products or services. Rather, as their name suggests, they contribute to the firm's competitive advantage by supporting the primary activities.

The Internet has changed the nature of competition. Porter concludes that the *overall* impact of the Internet is to increase competition, which reduces profitability.

The five strategies that companies can use to achieve competitive advantage in their industries are: (1) *cost leadership strategy*—produce products and/or services at the lowest cost in the industry; (2) *differentiation strategy*—offer different products, services, or product features; (3) *innovation strategy*—introduce new products and services, put new features in existing products and services, or develop new ways to produce them; (4) *operational effectiveness strategy*—improve the manner in which internal business processes are executed so that a firm performs similar activities better than rivals; and (5) *customer orientation strategy*—concentrate on making customers happy.

4. **Explain the importance of information systems to organizations and society and describe how information resources are managed.**

The responsibility for managing information resources is divided between two organizational entities: the information systems department (ISD), which is a corporate entity, and the end users, who are located throughout the organization. Generally speaking, the ISD is responsible for corporate-level and shared information systems resources whereas the end users are responsible for other departmental resources.

KEY TERMS

application program (program), 41

business intelligence (BI) systems, 44

chief information officer (CIO), 57

competitive advantage, 45

competitive forces model, 46

computer-based information
  system (CBIS), 40

dashboards (digital dashboards), 44

database, 41

electronic commerce systems, 43

entry barrier, 46

ergonomics, 53

expert systems (ES), 44

functional area information system (FAIS), 41

hardware, 40

information system (IS), 40

IT governance, 38

knowledge workers, 44

network, 41

office automation systems (OASs), 44

people, 41

primary activities, 49

procedures, 41

software, 41

strategic information systems (SISs), 45

supply chain, 43

support activities, 49

transaction processing system (TPS), 42

value chain model, 48

value system, 49

DISCUSSION QUESTIONS

1. Explain why large organizations need IT governance.
2. Should all organizations have IT governance? Why or why not?
3. Discuss the logic of building information systems in accordance with the organization's structure.
4. Knowledge workers make up the largest segment of the workforce in North American business today. However, many industries need skilled workers who are not knowledge workers. What are some examples of these industries? What (people, machines, or both) might replace these skilled workers? When might our economy need more skilled workers than knowledge workers?
5. Using Figure 2.2 as your guide, draw a model of a supply chain with your university as the central focus. Keep in mind that every university has suppliers and customers.
6. Is IT a strategic weapon or a survival tool? Discuss.
7. Why might it be difficult to justify a strategic information system?
8. Describe the five forces in Porter's competitive forces model and explain how the Internet has affected each one.
9. Describe Porter's value chain model. What is the relationship between the competitive forces model and the value chain model?
10. Why has the Internet been called the creator of new business models?
11. Discuss the idea that an information system by itself can rarely provide a sustainable competitive advantage.
12. Discuss the reasons why some information systems fail.
13. Explain how information systems affect managers and other employees.
14. Describe the functions of a typical information systems department.

PROBLEM-SOLVING ACTIVITIES

1. Access TRUSTe (*www.truste.org*) and find the guidelines that websites displaying its logo must follow. What are the guidelines? Why is it important for websites to be able to display the TRUSTe logo on their sites? How does satisfying the TRUSTe guidelines contribute to effective IT governance?

2. Greenville Hospital is a modern facility that prides itself on having accurate patient information and well-integrated accounting systems. The hospital is always looking for new ways to use computer systems so that its medical staff can spend more time with patients. The hospital has an up-to-date hardware and software infrastructure using wire-based systems. For each of the following information system types, provide a definition and an example system, explaining how the example system could be used by Greenville Hospital.

   TPS – Transaction Processing System
   OAS – Office Automation System (also known as Office System)
   MIS – Management Information System
   DSS – Decision Support System
   SIS – Strategic Information System

3. Characterize each of the following systems as one (or more) of the IT support systems:
   a. A student registration system in a university
   b. A system that advises physicians about which antibiotics to use for a particular infection
   c. A patient-admission system in a hospital
   d. A system that provides a human resources manager with reports regarding employee compensation by years of service
   e. A robotic system that paints cars in a factory

4. Compare and contrast the two companies, Google and Amazon, on their strategies, business models, IT infrastructures, service offerings, and products.

5. Apply Porter's value chain model to Costco (*www.costco.com*). What is Costco's competitive strategy? Who are Costco's major competitors? Describe Costco's business model. Describe the tasks that Costco must accomplish for each primary value chain activity. How would Costco's information systems contribute to Costco's competitive strategy, given the nature of its business?

6. The market for optical copiers is shrinking rapidly. It is estimated that as much as 90 percent of all duplicated documents are done on computer printers. Can a company such as Xerox Corporation survive?
   a. Read about the problems and solutions of Xerox from 2000 to 2010 at *www.fortune.com*, *www.findarticles.com*, and *www.google.com*.
   b. Identify all the business pressures on Xerox.
   c. Find some of Xerox's response strategies (see *www.xerox.com*, *www.yahoo.com*, and *www.google.com*).
   d. Identify the role of IT as a contributor to the business technology pressures (for example, obsolescence).
   e. Identify the role of IT as a facilitator of Xerox's critical response activities.

7. Enter *www.dell.ca*, and find the current information systems used by the company. Explain how the systems' innovations contribute to Dell's success.

8. Enter *www.cio.com* and find recent information on the changing role of the CIO and the ISD. What is the role of the CIO in organizations today?

64

TEAM ASSIGNMENTS

1. Observe your local Walmart checkout counter. Find material on the Web that describes how the scanned code is translated into the price that the customers pay. Hint: Look at *www.howstuffworks.com* and do a search on "bar code."
   a. Identify the following components of the Walmart system: inputs, processes, and outputs.
   b. What kind of a system is the scanner (TPS, DSS, EIS, ES, etc.)? Why did you classify it as you did?
   c. Having the information electronically in the system may provide opportunities for additional managerial uses of that information. Identify such uses.
   d. Checkout systems are now being replaced by self-service checkout kiosks and scanners. Compare the two in terms of speed, ease of use, and problems that may arise (for example, an item that the scanner does not recognize).

2. Assign group members to UPS (*www.ups.com*), FedEx (*www.fedex.com*), Purolator (*www.purolator.com*), and Canada Post (*www.canadapost.ca*). Have each group study the e-commerce strategies of one organization. Then have members present the organization, explaining why it is the best.

3. Divide the class into teams. Each team will select a country government and visit its official website (for example, try Australia, Canada, Denmark, France, Germany, the Netherlands, New Zealand, Norway, Singapore, the United Kingdom, or the United States). The official web portal for Canada is *www.canada.gc.ca* and for the U.S. government is *www.usa.gov*. Review and compare the services offered by each country. How does Canada compare? Are you surprised at the number of services offered by countries through websites? Which country offers the most services? The least?

LETTING THE COMPUTER READ TO YOU ...

THE BUSINESS PROBLEM

As an employer, you would like to be inclusive and hire employees who have special needs, such as difficulty reading. Or, you have an aging workforce that is having trouble reading fine print on documents and regular size print on computer screens. Unfortunately, your most senior executive has experienced macular degeneration (a problem with the back of the eyes that is more common for individuals who have had cataract surgery) that has rendered him almost legally blind. Currently, an executive assistant works full-time with the executive, assisting with reading and writing and resorting to dictation for many documents and memos that are typed up. A second assistant is responsible for reading and transcribing documents so that they can be played by digital players that can readily navigate through large volumes of text.

There is a variety of technology that the company can use, such as increasing the size of text shown on computer screens, but it is rather difficult to take large screens with you to a business meeting, and the volume of material that the executive needs to have accessible has rather frustrated the company, which is considering hiring another assistant to transcribe documents.

THE IT SOLUTION

The *Intel Reader*, available since late 2009, reads text and converts it into the spoken word. According to the product website (*www.intel.com/healthcare/reader*), the reader can hold up to 600 pages if the pages have both images and text, and up to 500,000 pages of text-only. The important aspect of this reader, if it is accurate for technical language, is that text can be scanned in and converted into the spoken word without the need

for a person to read the text and record it (for example into an MP3 file) or the need to take training in speech software (such as DragonSpeak).

The Intel Reader is small (16.5 cm × 13.6 cm × 3.3 cm), with a 10.9 cm LCD screen. It has an automatic focus camera that can focus from a very close distance (10 cm) to about one metre away. Also available is an *Intel Portable Capture Station*, which is a fixed stand to which you attach the reader. The portable stand is used to hold flat documents that are being scanned and to take pictures of full pages at a time.

Software that comes with the reader uses technology that has been proven in managing spoken text: moving around, searching or navigating using small or large blocks of text (for example, words, sentences, page numbers, or other information that is available in the text). Words can be read out loud or spelled, perhaps to clarify pronunciation or meaning.

THE RESULTS

In our hypothetical example above, rather than hiring two assistants to transcribe documents and read aloud, the executive could make do with a single assistant to move large numbers of documents rapidly into machine readable and verbal form. The reader can also be used as a portable device, taken to meetings and other locations to be able to rapidly convert documents on-site. Individuals with borderline visual problems can use the reader to reduce eye strain and help prevent more rapid visual degeneration.

Educators and other users with reading impairments such as dyslexia (where the person literally sees text backwards) can use these readers to improve the teaching of reading. In Canada, one of the suppliers of these readers is Humanware (*www.humanware. com/en-canada*), with offices in Longueuil, Quebec and Toronto, Ontario.

Sources: Compiled from Humanware website (*www.humanware.com/ en-canada/products/blindness/intel_reader/_details/id_156/intel_reader. html*); Intel website (*www.intel.com/healthcare/reader/index.htm*); "Scan and Listen," *Technology Review*, December 17, 2009.

QUESTIONS

1. Is the Intel Reader a strategic information system for the company that employs the visually impaired executive? Why or why not? Support your answer.
2. How would a company like Intel use information technology to develop, produce, and market the Intel Reader? For each use of information technology, identify the type of technology and how it would be used.

Web Resources

Student website www.wiley.com/canada/rainer

- Web quizzes
- Lecture slides in PowerPoint

- Author podcasts
- Interactive Case: Ruby's Club assignments

ALL OF THE ABOVE AND...

- E-book
- Manager videos
- Vocabulary flash cards

- Pre- and post-lecture quizzes
- Microsoft Office 2007 lab manual and projects

SUPPORTING A CUSTOMER-ORIENTED STRATEGY AT RUBY'S CLUB

ruby's club

Go to the Ruby's Club link at the Student Companion website or WileyPLUS for information about your current internship assignment. Your assignment will entail outlining how Ruby's members' site can best support its customer-oriented strategy and creating a presentation for the club's managers.

ETHICS, PRIVACY, AND INFORMATION SECURITY

LEARNING OBJECTIVES

1. Describe and provide examples of the major ethical issues related to information technology, with a focus on privacy.

2. Identify the many threats to information security.

3. Explain methods used to protect information systems, including the role of planning for disaster recovery and IT auditing.

HOW MANY YEARS DOES IT TAKE TO GET PRIVACY "RIGHT"?

THE BUSINESS PROBLEM

With hundreds of millions of users worldwide, the social networking site Facebook generates revenue by selling information about its users. Facebook has encouraged development of applications by providing access to user information to developers, so that the developers can provide more software for its users, continuing to expand the user base, thus continuing to increase revenues. In addition to outsiders, Facebook has also routinely provided information about you to other users (those listed as "friends").

How does Facebook continue to evolve and yet keep users happy? Certainly, not by disclosing or moving information without users' consent. For example, in May 2010 it was noted that Facebook applications were automatically added to user accounts, without their consent, that provided new features and potentially linked users to media such as the *Washington Post*. Also in May 2010, researchers analyzed the type of data that social network sites send to advertisers, and found that Facebook sent real usernames to advertisers, which could readily be used to obtain the real identities of Facebook users, contrary to privacy legislation around the world. There have been other exposures, such as users' dates of birth.

Facebook may have believed that it needed to comply with privacy regulations pertaining only to its home base, in the United States. However, Canadian courts have ruled that organizations that retain data about Canadians are subject to Canadian privacy regulations. This meant that the Canadian privacy commissioner has publicly chastised Facebook and other organizations about their privacy practices, in particular about how information is provided to application developers, how account information is deleted, how non-user information is dealt with, and how the information of those who have died is dealt with.

ATTEMPTS AT A SOLUTION

Lengthy negotiations (spanning more than a year) took place between privacy regulators and Facebook representatives. Facebook developed a new privacy policy, which can be seen at its website *www.facebook.com/privacy/explanation.php*. However, looking at this privacy information in May 2010 identifies many actions that users must take to control their privacy. In fact, some users have stated that there are as many as 150 different settings that must be dealt with to set privacy. Facebook has stated that it will simplify these settings. As of May 2010, Facebook had dealt with the four areas that were identified by the Canadian privacy commissioner as being at issue. For example, Facebook publicized an option that it previously had available, whereby family and friends could inform them about someone who had died, and have access to information posted by that person limited to only family and friends rather than having the dead person continue to be automatically included in the list of suggestions for someone you might want to reconnect with.

For accidental exposures, such as dates of birth or new processes that automatically provide information to friends, Facebook has rapidly altered its programming when users notify it of the problem or state in high numbers that the feature is not desirable. Facebook has also changed its practices so that application developers no longer have access to identifiable user information.

WHAT DO YOU THINK?

1. How should default settings on social networking sites such as Facebook be organized; in other words, what type of information should be shared and how?
2. What type of processes should Facebook have in place to deal with privacy concerns raised by users of the site?

Sources: K. Bardeesy, "Ottawa Takes on Social Media Giant for Violating Canada's Law," *The Globe and Mail*, July 17, 2009; D. Fletcher, "What Happens to Your Facebook after You Die?", Time.com, October 28, 2009; M. Geist, "Standing on Guard for Privacy—Before Facebook," *Toronto Star*, September 14, 2009, p. B4; H. Kelly and N. Mediati, "Facebook Secretly Adding Unsolicited Apps to Your Profile," itbusiness.ca, May 7, 2010; E. Steel and J. E. Vascellaro, "Facebook, MySpace Confront Privacy Loophole," *Wall Street Journal*, May 21, 2010.

Chapter Preview

Privacy legislation clearly requires that personal information be kept private. Yet with a social networking site such as Facebook, there are boundaries between the type of information you share with your social network "friends" and with others. If your employer or relatives are also using the site, then it can be difficult to decide what type of information you would post to the site. Other sites, such as credit agencies and businesses that you work with, also have information about you. How should this information be shared?

The answers to these and other questions are not clear. As we discuss ethics, privacy, and security in the context of information technology, you will acquire a better understanding of these issues, their importance, their relationships, and their trade-offs.

This information systems world we live in is filled with many types of people and organizations. Unfortunately, not all of them are honest. Controls help honest people stay honest and detect potential problems. What type of information systems problems should we protect ourselves and our organizations against? What are the different types of controls and how can information systems auditors help in the control evaluation process? Controls help to manage information systems, while helping organizations use those systems effectively.

Information technologies, properly used, can have enormous benefits for individuals, organizations, and entire societies. In the first two chapters, we discussed the diverse ways in which IT has made businesses more productive, efficient, and responsive to consumers. We also have explored areas such as medicine and philanthropy in which IT has improved people's health and well-being. Unfortunately, information technologies can also be misused, often with devastating consequences. Consider the following:

- Individuals can have their identities stolen.
- Organizations can have customer information stolen, leading to financial losses, erosion of customer confidence, and legal action.
- Countries face the threat of cyber-terrorism and cyber-warfare. Military organizations around the world are training their people in both defence and attack methods that use information technology.

In fact, the misuse of information technologies has come to the forefront of any discussion of IT. For example, the Rotman School of Management at the University of Toronto and TELUS (see *www.rotman.utoronto.ca/securitystudy/*) conducted a survey of 600 Canadian professionals in the field of information security. The researchers concluded that 11.3 percent of organizations had security breaches, which cost those organizations an average of over $834,000 each.

Costs of a data breach include hiring forensic experts, notifying customers, setting up telephone hotlines to field queries from concerned or affected customers, offering free credit-monitoring subscriptions, and offering discounts for future products and services.

According to the study, employee actions caused 33 percent of the data breaches, up from 17 percent the year before. This figure confirms that organizational employees are a weak link in information security. As a result, it is very important for you to learn about information security so that you will be better prepared when you enter the workforce.

Chapters 1 and 2 have acquainted you with the major capabilities of IT. In the next section, we address the complex issues of ethics, privacy, and security.

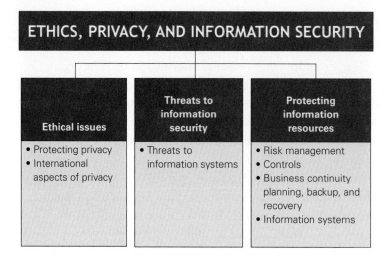

3.1 Ethical Issues

Ethics refers to the principles of right and wrong that individuals use to make choices to guide their behaviours. Deciding what is right or wrong is not always easy or clear-cut. For this reason, many companies and professional organizations develop their own codes of ethics. A **code of ethics** is a collection of principles that is intended to guide decision making by members of the organization. For example, the Association for Computing Machinery (*www.acm.org*), an organization of computing professionals, has a thoughtful code of ethics for its members (see *www.acm.org/about/code-of-ethics*).

Fundamental tenets of ethics include responsibility, accountability, and liability. **Responsibility** means that you accept the consequences of your decisions and actions. **Accountability** refers to determining who is responsible for actions that were taken. **Liability** is a legal concept that gives individuals the right to recover the damages done to them by other individuals, organizations, or systems.

Before we go any further, it is very important that you realize that what is *unethical* is not necessarily *illegal*. In most instances, an individual or organization faced with an ethical decision is not considering whether to break the law. This does not mean, however, that ethical decisions do not have serious consequences for individuals, organizations, or society at large.

Unfortunately, we have seen a large number of extremely poor ethical decisions, not to mention outright criminal behaviour. Three of the most highly publicized fiascos in the United States occurred at Enron Corporation (now Enron Creditors Recovery Corporation), WorldCom (now MCI Inc.), and Tyco International. At each company, executives were convicted of various types of fraud using illegal accounting practices. These illegal acts resulted, at least in part, in the passage of the Sarbanes-Oxley Act in 2002 in the United States. This law requires that public companies implement financial controls and that, to ensure accountability, executives must personally certify financial reports. Similar problems occurred in Canada at companies like Nortel and Southam. In Canada, Bill 198, the Budget Measures Act, imposes similar requirements of management.

More recently, the subprime mortgage crisis in the United States became apparent in 2007, exposing unethical lending practices throughout the mortgage industry and causing worldwide credit problems. The crisis also showed pervasive weaknesses in financial industry regulation and the global financial system and led, at least in part, to a deep recession in the global economy.

Improvements in information technologies are causing an increasing number of ethical problems. Computing processing power doubles about every two years, meaning that organizations are more dependent than ever before on their information systems. Increasing amounts of data can be stored at decreasing cost, meaning that organizations can store more data regarding individuals for longer amounts of time. Computer networks, particularly the Internet, enable organizations to collect, integrate, and distribute enormous amounts of information on individuals, groups, and institutions. As a result, ethical problems are arising about the appropriate use of customer information, personal privacy, and the protection of intellectual property.

All employees have a responsibility to encourage ethical uses of information and information technology. Most, if not all, of the business decisions you will face at work will have an ethical dimension. Consider these decisions you might have to make:

- Should organizations monitor employees' web surfing and e-mail?
- Should organizations sell customer information to other companies?
- Should organizations audit employees' computers for unauthorized software or illegally downloaded music or video files?

The diversity and ever-expanding use of IT applications have created a variety of ethical issues. These issues fall into four general categories: privacy, accuracy, property, and accessibility.

1. *Privacy issues* involve collecting, storing, and disseminating information about individuals.
2. *Accuracy issues* involve the authenticity, integrity, and accuracy of information that is collected and processed.
3. *Property issues* involve the ownership and value of information.
4. *Accessibility issues* revolve around who should have access to information and whether they should have to pay for this access.

Table 3.1 lists representative questions and issues for each of these categories, and our first IT's About Business presents interesting real-life situations that involve ethical and legal questions.

In addition, On-line Appendix W3.1 presents 14 ethics scenarios for you to consider. These scenarios will provide a context in which you can consider situations that involve ethical or non-ethical behaviour. In the next section, we discuss privacy issues in more detail. We cover property issues later in this chapter.

TABLE 3.1
A FRAMEWORK FOR ETHICAL ISSUES

Privacy Issues

- What information about oneself should an individual be required to reveal to others?
- What kind of surveillance can an employer use on its employees?
- What types of personal information can people keep to themselves and not be forced to reveal to others?
- What information about individuals should be kept in databases, and how secure is the information there?

Accuracy Issues

- Who is responsible for the authenticity, integrity, and accuracy of the information collected?
- How can we ensure that the information will be processed properly and presented accurately to users?
- How can we ensure that errors in databases, data transmissions, and data processing are accidental and not intentional?
- Who is to be held accountable for errors in information, and how should the injured parties be compensated?

(Continued on next page)

TABLE 3.1 (Continued)

Property Issues

- Who owns the information?
- What are the just and fair prices for its exchange?
- How should one handle software piracy (copying copyrighted software)?
- Under what circumstances can one use proprietary databases?
- Can corporate computers be used for private purposes?
- How should experts who contribute their knowledge to create expert systems be compensated?
- How should access to information channels be allocated?

Accessibility Issues

- Who is allowed to access information?
- How much should companies charge for permitting accessibility to information?
- How can accessibility to computers be provided for employees with disabilities?
- Who will be provided with equipment needed for accessing information?
- What information does a person or an organization have a right or a privilege to obtain, under what conditions, and with what safeguards?

IT'S ABOUT BUSINESS 3.1
THE INTERNET AS A MULTI-WAY STREET

E-mails sent via the Web can be retrieved and may be stored anywhere—and can be used to convict you. Individuals involved in the development of an e-health system in British Columbia either retired or had their employment terminated when it was found that they had sent e-mails using the words "splitting chickens," and asking about a $10,000 cheque that looked suspicious. The investigators assumed that the reference to chickens was about illegal cash. The RCMP was investigating these e-mails to determine whether charges should be laid about inflated billings or billings for consulting work that had not been completed by the employees and others. Perhaps these individuals should be reminded that anything you send by e-mail is never really private!

In a second example of unwanted disclosure, a Toronto investment dealer called Paradigm Capital Inc. had interviewed the chief executive officer of a start-up company about new technology that could have important consequences to the battery production and development market. This interview was supposed to be confidential, and to be later used to help raise money for the new company for certain investors. Not all potential investors had access to the taped interview. Somehow the confidential interview ended up on YouTube only two weeks later, affecting stock market prices for the target company. Who posted the video? Was it an employee of Paradigm Capital Inc. or one of the investors?

In our third example, consider the sale of e-books by Amazon, to be read on the Kindle e-book reader. Normally, users would download a book, assuming that it is available to read until they decide to delete it. Did you know, though, that Amazon or any other e-book provider can reach into your e-reader and delete books? That is what happened in June 2009 when Amazon removed two books from users (George Orwell's *1984* and *Animal Farm*) when Amazon discovered that it did not have the authorization to distribute these e-books. This illustrates that this type of "e-mistake" on the part of Amazon can be "e-fixed."

Sources: Compiled from P. Brethour and J. Hunter, "RCMP Probe Alleged Fraud of B.C. Health Ministry," *The Globe and Mail*, October 8, 2009; M. Geist, "Amazon, Kindle and an Orewellian Misstep," *Toronto Star*, July 27, 2009; T. Hamilton, "Paradigm Capital Red-faced after Conference Call Posted on Net," *Toronto Star*, August 8, 2009, p. B3.

QUESTIONS

1. Should there be rules against examining employee e-mails? Why or why not? Which information should be considered private?
2. How can organizations prevent having confidential material such as recorded audio from being publicly posted? How can organizations identify which material is more confidential than others?
3. Should organizations like Amazon have the right to remove material from your equipment (such as Kindle)? Who owns this material?

Protecting Privacy

In general, **privacy** is the right to be left alone and to be free of unreasonable personal intrusions. *Information privacy* is the right to determine when, and to what extent, information about yourself can be gathered and/or communicated to others. Privacy rights apply to individuals, groups, and institutions.

The definition of privacy can be interpreted quite broadly. However, court decisions in many countries have followed two rules fairly closely:

1. The right of privacy is not absolute. Privacy must be balanced against the needs of society.
2. The public's right to know supersedes the individual's right to privacy.

These two rules show why it is difficult in some cases to determine and enforce privacy regulations. The right to privacy is recognized today in all Canadian provinces and by the federal government through privacy legislation.

Rapid advances in information technologies have made it much easier to collect, store, and integrate data on individuals in large databases. On an average day, you generate data about yourself in many ways: surveillance cameras on toll roads, in public places, and at work; credit card transactions; telephone calls (landline and cellular); banking transactions; queries to search engines; and government records (including police records). These data can be integrated to produce a **digital dossier**, which is an electronic description of you and your habits. The process of forming a digital dossier is called **profiling**.

Data aggregators in the United States, such as LexisNexis (*www.lexisnexis.com*) and Acxiom Corporation (*www.acxiom.com*), are good examples of profilers. These companies collect public data such as real estate records and published telephone numbers, in addition to non-public information such as U.S. social security numbers (and social insurance numbers in Canada), financial data, and police, criminal, and motor vehicle records. Statistics Canada (*www.statcan. gc.ca*), Canada's national statistics agency, provides aggregated information about businesses and individuals.

Data aggregators integrate these data to form digital dossiers, or profiles, on adults in North America. They sell these dossiers to law enforcement agencies and companies conducting background checks on potential employees. They also sell the dossiers to companies that want to know their customers better, a process called *customer intimacy*.

Electronic Surveillance

Electronic surveillance is rapidly increasing, particularly with the emergence of new technologies. Monitoring is done by employers, the government, and other institutions.

In general, employees have very limited protection against surveillance by employers. The law supports the right of employers to read their employees' e-mail and other electronic documents and to monitor their employees' Internet use. Today, many organizations are monitoring employees' Internet usage. Organizations also use software to block connections to inappropriate websites, a practice called *URL filtering*. Organizations are installing monitoring and filtering software to enhance security by stopping malicious software and to improve employee productivity by discouraging employees from wasting time.

In one organization, before deploying a URL filtering product, the chief information officer (CIO) monitored about 13,000 people for three months to determine the type of traffic they engaged in on the network. He then passed the data to the chief executive officer (CEO) and the heads of the human resources and legal departments. They were shocked at the questionable websites the employees were visiting, as well as the amount of time employees spent on those sites. The executives quickly made the decision to implement the filtering product.

Surveillance is also a concern for private individuals regardless of whether it is conducted by corporations, government bodies, or criminals. As a country, we are still trying to determine the appropriate balance between personal privacy and electronic surveillance, especially where threats to national security are involved.

Personal Information in Databases

Information about individuals is being kept in many databases. Perhaps the most visible locations of such records are credit reporting agencies. Other institutions that store personal information include banks and financial institutions; cable TV, telephone, and utilities companies; employers; mortgage companies; hospitals; schools and universities; retail establishments; government agencies (Canada Revenue Agency, your province, your municipality); and many others.

There are several concerns about the information you provide to these record keepers. Some of the major concerns are:

- Do you know where the records are?
- Are the records accurate?
- Can you change inaccurate data?
- How long will it take to make a change?
- Under what circumstances will personal data be released?
- How are the data used?
- To whom are they given or sold?
- How secure are the data against access by unauthorized people?

Information on Internet Bulletin Boards, Newsgroups, and Social Networking Sites

Every day we see more and more *electronic bulletin boards, newsgroups, electronic discussion sites* such as chat rooms, and *social networking sites* (discussed in Chapter 5). These sites appear on the Internet, within corporate intranets, and on blogs. A blog, short for weblog, is an informal, personal journal that is frequently updated and intended for general public reading. How does society keep owners of bulletin boards from disseminating information that may be offensive to readers or simply untrue? This is a difficult problem because it involves the conflict between freedom of speech on the one hand and privacy on the other.

There is no better illustration of the conflict between free speech and privacy than the Internet. Some websites contain anonymous, derogatory information on individuals who typically have little recourse in the matter.

Privacy Codes and Policies

Privacy policies or **privacy codes** are an organization's guidelines for protecting the privacy of customers, clients, and employees. In many corporations, senior management has begun to understand that when they collect vast amounts of personal information, they must protect it. Many organizations provide opt-out choices for their customers. The **opt-out model** of informed consent permits the company to collect personal information until the customer specifically requests that the data not be collected. Privacy advocates prefer the **opt-in model** of informed consent, in which a business is prohibited from collecting any personal information unless the customer specifically authorizes it.

The Platform for Privacy Preferences (P3P) (see *www.w3.org/TR/P3P/*) was developed by the World Wide Web Consortium, a group that creates standards for the Web. P3P automatically communicates privacy policies between an electronic commerce website and visitors to that site. P3P enables visitors to determine the types of personal data that can be extracted by the websites they visit. It also allows visitors to compare a website's privacy policy with the visitors' preferences or with other standards, such as the Canadian Standards Association (CSA) Model Code for the Protection of Personal Information (see *www.csa.ca/cm/ca/en/privacy-code*) or the European Union Directive on Data Protection.

Canada's privacy legislation is called the Personal Information Protection and Electronic Documents Act (PIPEDA). It became effective January 1, 2004. The legislation applies to businesses and other organizations, such as non-profit organizations. PIPEDA is based upon the principles in the Canadian Standards Association Model Code. As part of the legislation, organizations are required to establish a privacy policy, as well as procedures to ensure that the policy is adhered to.

Table 3.2 provides a sampling of privacy policy guidelines. You can access Google's privacy policy at *www.google.com/privacypolicy.html*. Having a privacy policy in place can help organizations avoid legal problems.

International Aspects of Privacy

As the number of on-line users has increased globally, governments have enacted a large number of inconsistent privacy and security laws. This highly complex global legal framework is causing regulatory problems for companies. Approximately 50 countries have some form of data protection laws.

TABLE 3.2
PRIVACY POLICY GUIDELINES: A SAMPLER

Data Collection

- Data should be collected on individuals only for the purpose of accomplishing a legitimate business objective.
- Data should be adequate, relevant, and not excessive in relation to the business objective.
- Individuals must give their consent before data pertaining to them can be gathered. Such consent may be implied from the individual's actions (e.g., applications for credit, insurance, or employment).

Data Accuracy

- Sensitive data gathered on individuals should be verified before they are entered into the database.
- Data should be kept current where and when it is necessary.
- The file should be made available so the individual can ensure that the data are correct.
- If there is disagreement about the accuracy of the data, the individual's version should be noted and included with any disclosure of the file.

Data Confidentiality

- Computer security procedures should be implemented to ensure against unauthorized disclosure of data. These procedures should include physical, technical, and administrative security measures.
- Third parties should not be given access to data without the individual's knowledge or permission, except as required by law.
- Disclosures of data, other than the most routine sorts of data, should be noted and maintained for as long as the data are maintained.
- Data should not be disclosed for reasons incompatible with the business objective for which they are collected.

Many of these laws conflict with other countries' laws or require specific security measures. Other countries have no privacy laws at all.

The absence of consistent or uniform standards for privacy and security obstructs the flow of information among countries. The European Union (EU), for one, has taken steps to overcome this problem. In 1998, the European Community Commission (ECC) issued guidelines to all its member countries regarding the rights of individuals to access information about themselves. The EU data protection laws are similar to Canadian laws, but stricter than U.S. laws and therefore may create problems for U.S.-based multinational corporations, which may face lawsuits for privacy violation unless they follow the "Safe Harbor" framework that was jointly developed between the United States and the EU (see *www.export.gov/safeharbor*).

The transfer of data in and out of a nation without the knowledge of either the authorities or the individuals involved raises a number of privacy issues. Whose laws have jurisdiction when records are stored in a different country for reprocessing or retransmission purposes? For example, if data are transmitted by a Polish company through a U.S. satellite to a British corporation, which country's privacy laws control the data and when? Questions like these will become more complicated and frequent as time goes on. Governments must make an effort to develop laws and standards to cope with rapidly changing information technologies in order to solve some of these privacy issues.

BEFORE YOU GO ON ...

1. Define ethics and list the four categories of ethics as they apply to IT.
2. Describe the issue of privacy as it is affected by IT.
3. What does a code of ethics contain?
4. Describe the relationship between IT and privacy.

3.2 Threats to Information Security

A number of factors contribute to the increasing vulnerability of organizational information assets. Before we discuss these factors, we list them here.

- Today's interconnected, interdependent, wirelessly networked business environment
- Government legislation
- Smaller, faster, cheaper computers and storage devices
- Decreasing skills necessary to be a computer hacker
- International organized crime taking over cyber-crime
- Downstream liability
- Increased employee use of unmanaged devices
- Lack of management support

The first factor is the evolution of the information technology resource from mainframe only to today's highly complex, interconnected, interdependent, wirelessly networked business environment. The Internet now enables millions of computers and computer networks to freely and seamlessly communicate with one another. Organizations and individuals are exposed to a world of untrusted networks and potential attackers. A *trusted network*, in general, is any network within your organization that is adequately protected. An *untrusted network*, in general, is any network external to your organization. In addition, wireless technologies enable employees to compute, communicate, and access the Internet anywhere and any time. Significantly, wireless technology is an inherently non-secure broadcast communications medium.

The second factor, government legislation, dictates that many types of information must be protected by law. In Canada, PIPEDA applies to customer information that is collected by businesses or non-profit organizations. Each province also has a health privacy act, normally called a Personal Health Information Protection Act, that protects medical records and other individually identifiable health information.

The third factor reflects the fact that modern computers and storage devices (e.g., thumb drives or flash drives) continue to become smaller, faster, cheaper, and more portable, with greater storage capacity. These characteristics make it much easier to steal or lose a computer or storage device that contains huge amounts of sensitive information. Also, far more people are able to afford powerful computers and connect inexpensively to the Internet, thus raising the potential of an attack on information assets.

The fourth factor is that the computing skills necessary to be a hacker are *decreasing*. The reason is that the Internet contains information and computer programs called *scripts* that users with few skills can download and use to attack any information system connected to the Internet. (Security experts can also use these scripts for legitimate purposes, such as testing the security of various systems. The term "scripts" is also used to describe other types of automated processing.)

The fifth factor is that international organized crime is taking over cyber-crime. **Cyber-crime** refers to illegal activities taking place over computer networks, particularly the Internet. For example, *cyberextortion* occurs when individuals attack an organization's website, and then demand money from the website owners to call off the attack.

iDefense (*http://labs.idefense.com*) is a company that specializes in providing security information to governments, financial services firms, and other large companies. The company states that groups of well-organized criminals have taken control of a global billion-dollar crime network. The network, powered by skillful hackers, targets known software security weaknesses. These crimes are typically nonviolent, but quite lucrative. For example, the losses from armed robberies average hundreds of dollars, whereas those from white-collar crimes average tens of thousands of dollars. In contrast, losses from computer crimes average hundreds of thousands of dollars. Also, these crimes can be committed from anywhere in the world, at any time, effectively providing an international safe haven for cyber-criminals. Computer-based crimes cause billions of dollars in damages to businesses each year, including the costs to repair information systems and the costs of lost business.

Security experts at Verizon Business (*www.verizonbusiness.com*), a firm hired by major companies to investigate data breaches, responded to approximately 100 data breaches in 2008 involving some 285 million customer records. This huge number exceeds the combined total of customer records compromised from 2004 to 2007. Verizon investigators found that organized crime groups in Eastern Europe caused more than 50 percent of the 2008 breaches.

The sixth factor is *downstream liability*, which occurs in the following manner. If company A's information systems were compromised by a perpetrator and used to attack company B's systems, then company A could be liable for damages to company B. Note that company B is "downstream" from company A in this attack scenario. A downstream liability lawsuit would put company A's security policies and operations on trial. Under tort law, the plaintiff (injured party or company B) would have to prove that the offending company (company A) had a duty to keep its computers secure and failed to do so, as measured against generally accepted standards and practices.

Legal experts think that it is only a matter of time before victims of computer crime start suing the owners of systems and networks used as launchpads in cyber-attacks. Information security's first downstream liability lawsuit will likely come from a catastrophe. For example, an on-line retailer may be hit with a devastating attack that disrupts its business.

At some point, all companies will have a minimal set of standards that they have to meet when they are operating information systems that connect to the Internet and when accessing or collecting customer information. The models already exist in the form of regulations and laws (such as PIPEDA in Canada). In the United States the Gramm-Leach-Bliley Act mandates the disclosure of security breaches. Legislation about disclosure of security breaches does not exist in Canada.

Verizon, a carrier that provides long distance, data, and Internet services, learned about the importance of due diligence (taking reasonable precautions) in April 2003, when the Maine Public Utilities Commission rejected its request for relief from $62,000 in fees owed to local carriers after the SQL Slammer Worm shut down its networks. Verizon had applied for a steep break on the fees owed under its service agreement, arguing the worm "was an event that was beyond its control" (like a lightning strike). The commission's rejection rested in part on comments submitted by competitors WorldCom (now MCI) and AT&T. They claimed that they handled Slammer with minimal interruption because they did a better job of patching their systems than Verizon did. Why should Verizon, or potentially any company, be an exception?

The seventh factor is increased employee use of unmanaged devices, which are devices outside the control of an organization's IT department. These devices include customer computers, business partners' mobile devices, computers in the business centres of hotels, and many others.

The eighth and final factor is management support. For the entire organization to take security policies and procedures seriously, senior managers must set the tone. Ultimately, however, lower-level managers may be even more important. These managers are in close contact with employees every day and thus are in a better position to determine whether employees are following security procedures.

Before we discuss the many threats to an organization's information resources, we need to look at some key terms. Organizations have many information resources (for example, computers and the information on them, information systems and applications, databases, and so on). These resources are subject to a huge number of threats. A **threat** to an information resource is any danger to which a system may be exposed. The **exposure** of an information resource is the harm, loss, or damage that can result if a threat compromises that resource. A system's **vulnerability** is the possibility that the system will suffer harm by a threat. **Risk** is the likelihood that a threat will occur. **Information systems controls** are the procedures, devices, or software aimed at preventing a compromise to the system. We discuss these controls in Section 3.3.

Information systems are vulnerable to many potential hazards or threats. Figure 3.1 illustrates the major threats to the security of an information system. There are many threats, so the outline should help you follow our discussion.

Threats to Information Systems

Whitman and Mattord in their book *Principles of Information Security* (2003) classified threats into five general categories to help us better understand the complexity of the threat problem. Their categories are:

1. Unintentional acts
2. Natural disasters
3. Technical failures
4. Management failures
5. Deliberate acts

We discuss the five threat categories in the next sections.

Unintentional Acts

Unintentional acts are those acts with no malicious intent. There are three types of unintentional acts: human errors, deviations in the quality of service by service providers, and environmental hazards. Of these three types of acts, human errors represent by far the most serious threats to information security.

FIGURE 3.1
Security
threats.

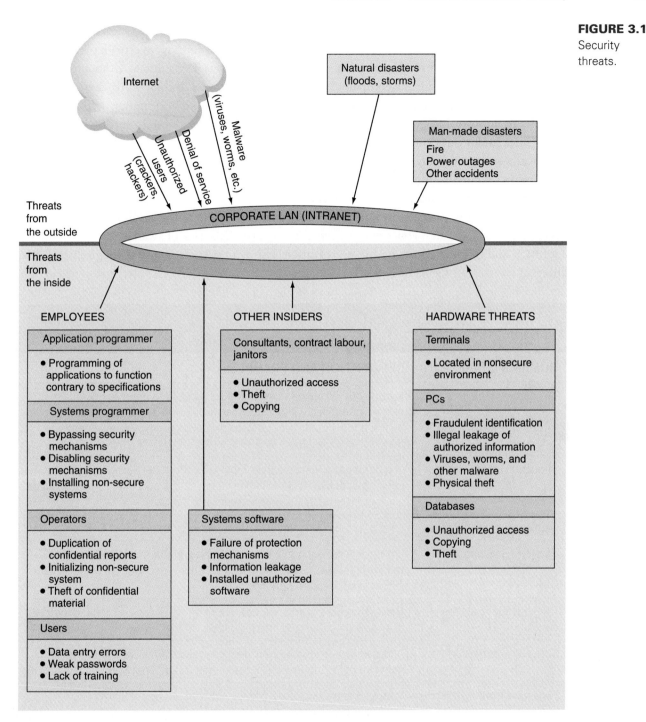

Human Errors. Before we discuss the various types of human errors, we need to consider the different categories of organizational employees. The first category is composed of regular employees who span the breadth and depth of the organization, from mail clerks to the CEO, and in all functional areas. There are two important points to be made about regular employees. First, the higher the level of employee, the greater the threat the employee poses to information security. This situation exists because higher-level employees typically have greater access to corporate data and enjoy greater privileges on organizational information systems. Second, employees in two areas of the organization pose significant threats to information security: human resources and information systems. Human resources employees generally have access to sensitive personal information about all employees. Likewise, information systems employees not only have access to sensitive organizational data, but they often control the means to create, store, transmit, and modify that data.

The second category includes contract labour and consultants. Contract labour, such as temporary hires, may be overlooked in information security. However, these employees often have access to the company's network, information systems, and information assets. Consultants, although technically not employees, do work for the company. Depending on the nature of their work, these people may also have access to the company's network, information systems, and information assets.

Finally, janitors and guards are the most frequently ignored people in information security. Companies might outsource their security and janitorial services and, although these individuals technically are not employees, they do work for the company. Moreover, they are usually present when most—if not all—other employees have gone home. They typically have keys to every office, and nobody questions their presence in even the most sensitive parts of the building.

Human errors or mistakes by employees pose a large problem as the result of laziness, carelessness, or a lack of awareness concerning information security. This lack of awareness comes from poor education and training efforts by the organization. Human mistakes manifest themselves in many different ways, as we see in Table 3.3.

TABLE 3.3
HUMAN MISTAKES IN INFORMATION SECURITY

HUMAN MISTAKE	DESCRIPTION AND EXAMPLES
Tailgating	A technique designed to allow the perpetrator to enter restricted areas that are controlled with locks or card entry. The perpetrator follows closely behind a legitimate employee and, when the employee gains entry, asks them to "hold the door."
Shoulder surfing	The perpetrator watches the employee's computer screen over that person's shoulder. This technique is particularly successful in public areas such as airports, trains, and on airplanes.
Carelessness with laptops	Losing laptops, misplacing laptops, leaving them in taxis, and so on.
Carelessness with portable devices	Losing or misplacing these devices, or using them carelessly so that **malware** (malicious software such as viruses and worms) is introduced into an organization's network.
Opening questionable e-mails	Opening e-mails from someone unknown, or clicking on links embedded in e-mails (see *phishing attacks* in Table 3.4).
Careless Internet surfing	Accessing questionable websites; can result in malware and/or alien software being introduced into the organization's network.
Poor **password** selection and use	Choosing and using weak passwords (see *strong passwords* in the section Access Controls below).
Carelessness with one's office	Leaving unlocked desks and filing cabinets when employees go home at night; not logging off the company network when gone from the office for an extended period of time.
Carelessness using unmanaged devices	Unmanaged devices are those outside the control of an organization's IT department and company security procedures. These devices include computers belonging to customers and business partners, computers in the business centres of hotels, and computers in coffee shops, restaurants, or other public areas.
Carelessness with discarded equipment	Discarding old computer hardware and devices without completely wiping the memory; includes computers, cell phones, smart phones, digital copiers, and printers.

The human errors that we have just discussed are unintentional on the part of the employee. However, employees can also make mistakes as a result of deliberate actions by an attacker. Such deliberate actions fall into three categories: social engineering, reverse social engineering, and social data mining.

Social Engineering, Reverse Social Engineering, and Social Data Mining. Social engineering is an attack in which the perpetrator uses social skills to trick or manipulate a legitimate employee into providing confidential company information such as passwords. The most common example of social engineering occurs when the attacker impersonates someone else on the telephone, such as a company manager or information systems employee. The attacker claims he forgot his password and asks the legitimate employee to give him a password to use. Other common exploits include posing as an exterminator, an air conditioning technician, or a fire marshal. Examples of social engineering abound.

In one company, a perpetrator entered a company building wearing a company ID card that looked legitimate. He walked around and put up signs on bulletin boards saying, "The help desk telephone number has been changed. The new number is 555-1234." He then exited the building and began receiving calls from legitimate employees thinking they were calling the company help desk. Naturally, the first thing the perpetrator asked for was user name and password. He now had the information necessary to access the company's information systems.

In another company, an attacker loaded a Trojan horse program (discussed later in this chapter) on 20 thumb drives (USB keys). The Trojan horse was designed to collect passwords and login information from an employee's computer and then e-mail the information to the attacker. Early one morning, he scattered the thumb drives in the parking lots, designated smoking areas, and near walkways of the target company. Employees found 15 of the drives and plugged them into company computers without first scanning them with security software. The Trojan horse software transmitted their user names and passwords to the attacker and enabled him to compromise additional systems in the company.

In social engineering, the attacker approaches legitimate employees. In **reverse social engineering**, the employees approach the attacker. For example, the attacker gains employment at a company and, in informal conversations with his co-workers, lets it be known that he is "good with computers." As is often the case, they ask him for help with their computer problems. While he is helping them, he loads Trojan horses on their computers that e-mail him their passwords and information about their machines.

Social data mining, also called *buddy mining*, occurs when attackers seek to learn who knows whom in an organization and how. If attackers have an understanding of the trusted relationships within an organization, they can exploit that knowledge to plant malware and acquire sensitive data.

How can an attacker obtain the organizational charts of a company he wants to target? There are many ways. For example, consider the simple Google query: "at site: *linkedin.com*." This will return a list of public LinkedIn profiles to be returned, and each result will specify the name of the person working in the specified company, his or her position, and maybe even a list of his or her colleagues. An attacker who knows the e-mail address formatting conventions within a company would automatically know the e-mail addresses of many potential victims.

Deviations in the Quality of Service by Service Providers. This category consists of situations in which a product or service is not delivered to the organization as expected. There are many examples of such deviations in quality of service. For example, heavy equipment at a construction site cuts a fibre-optic line to your building or your Internet service provider has availability problems. Organizations may also experience service disruptions from various providers, such as communications, electricity, telephone, water, wastewater, garbage pickup, cable, and natural gas.

Environmental Hazards. Environmental hazards include dirt, dust, humidity, and static electricity. These hazards are harmful to the safe operation of computing equipment.

Natural Disasters

Natural disasters include floods, earthquakes, hurricanes, tornadoes, lightning, and in some cases, fires. In many cases, these disasters—sometimes referred to as acts of God—can cause catastrophic losses of systems and data. To avoid such losses, companies must engage in proper planning for backup and recovery of information systems and data, a topic we discuss later in this chapter.

Technical Failures

Technical failures include problems with hardware and software. The most common hardware problem is a crash of a hard disk drive. A notable hardware problem occurred when Intel released a Pentium chip with a defect that caused the chip to perform some mathematical calculations incorrectly.

The most common software problem is errors—called bugs—in computer programs. Software bugs are so common that entire websites are dedicated to documenting them. For example, see *www. bug-track.com* and *www.bugaware.com*.

Management Failures

Management failures involve a lack of funding for information security efforts and a lack of interest in those efforts. Such lack of leadership will cause the information security of the organization to suffer.

Deliberate Acts

Deliberate acts by organizational employees (i.e., insiders) account for a large number of information security breaches. There are so many types of deliberate acts that we provide just a brief list here to guide our discussion.

- Espionage or trespass
- Information extortion
- Sabotage or vandalism
- Theft of equipment or information
- Identity theft
- Compromises to intellectual property
- Software attacks
- Supervisory control and data acquisition (SCADA) attacks
- Cyber-terrorism and cyber-warfare

Espionage or Trespass. Espionage or trespass occurs when an unauthorized individual attempts to gain illegal access to organizational information. When we discuss trespass, it is important that we distinguish between competitive intelligence and industrial espionage. Competitive intelligence consists of legal information-gathering techniques, such as studying a company's website and press releases, attending trade shows, and so on. In contrast, industrial espionage crosses the legal boundary.

Information Extortion. Information extortion occurs when an attacker either threatens to steal, or actually steals, information from a company. The perpetrator demands payment for not stealing the information, for returning stolen information, or for agreeing not to disclose the information.

Sabotage or Vandalism. Sabotage and vandalism are deliberate acts that involve defacing an organization's website, possibly causing the organization to lose its image and experience a loss of confidence by its customers. For example, MySpace (*www.myspace.com*) has had problems with cyber-vandals (known as trolls) who attack a number of MySpace groups with offensive comments and photographs.

Targeted groups include those dedicated to such interests as home beer brewing, animal welfare, and gay rights issues.

These trolls are taking advantage of vulnerabilities on the MySpace website. One vulnerability allows trolls to post comments on a group when they are not approved members. This problem leads to a troll attack called bombing, where dozens of empty comments can be posted in a group's discussion area using a computer program. The empty boxes create hundreds of empty comment pages, pushing down the real comments from group members and ruining the conversation.

Another form of on-line vandalism is a hacktivist or cyber-activist operation. These are cases of high-tech civil disobedience to protest the operations, policies, or actions of an organization or government agency.

Theft of Equipment and Information. Computing devices and storage devices are becoming smaller yet more powerful with vastly increased storage (for example, laptops, netbooks, BlackBerrys, personal digital assistants, smart phones, digital cameras, thumb drives, and iPods). As a result, these devices are becoming easier to steal and easier for attackers to use to steal information.

Table 3.3 points out that one type of human mistake is carelessness with laptops. In fact, such carelessness often leads to a laptop being stolen. The Ponemon Institute (*www.ponemon.org*) found that 10 percent of all laptops are stolen and 88 percent of these stolen laptops are never recovered. Further, the average cost of a stolen laptop to an organization is approximately $50,000. This total includes the loss of data (80 percent of the cost), the loss of intellectual property (11 percent), laptop replacement, legal and regulatory costs, investigation fees, and loss of productivity.

The uncontrolled proliferation of portable devices in companies has led to a type of attack called pod slurping. In *pod slurping*, perpetrators plug portable devices into a USB port on a computer and download huge amounts of information very quickly and easily. An iPod, for example, contains 60 gigabytes of storage and can download most of a computer's hard drive in a matter of minutes.

Another form of theft, known as *dumpster diving*, involves the practice of rummaging through commercial or residential garbage to find information that has been discarded. Paper files, letters, memos, photographs, IDs, passwords, credit cards, and other forms of information can be found in dumpsters. Unfortunately, many people never consider that the sensitive items they throw in the garbage may be recovered. Such information, when recovered, can be used for fraudulent purposes.

Dumpster diving is not necessarily theft, because the legality of this act varies. Because dumpsters are usually located on private premises, dumpster diving is illegal in some parts of the country, although these laws are enforced with varying degrees of rigour.

Copying data on a thumb drive from the server

Identity Theft. **Identity theft** is the deliberate assumption of another person's identity, usually to gain access to their financial information or to frame them for a crime. Techniques for obtaining information include:

- Stealing mail or dumpster diving
- Stealing personal information in computer databases
- Infiltrating organizations that store large amounts of personal information (e.g., data aggregators such as Acxiom) (*www.acxiom.com*)
- Impersonating a trusted organization in an electronic communication (phishing)

The Office of the Privacy Commissioner of Canada provides instructions for businesses and individuals to help reduce their risk of identity theft (see *www.privcom.gc.ca/id/business_e.cfm*). Additional information and articles are also available at the Better Business Bureau website (*www. bbb.org/canada*).

Recovering from identity theft is costly, time consuming, and difficult. A survey by the Identity Theft Resource Center (*www.idtheftcenter.org*) found that victims spent an average of 330 hours repairing the damage. Victims also reported difficulties in obtaining credit and obtaining or holding a job, as well as adverse effects on insurance or credit rates. In addition, victims stated that it was difficult to remove negative information from their records, such as their credit reports.

Your personal information can be compromised in other ways. For example, in 2006 AOL released detailed keyword search data for approximately 658,000 anonymous users. AOL claimed that the release of the data, which amounted to about 20 million search queries, was an innocent attempt to help academic researchers interested in search queries. The data, which were mirrored on multiple websites, represented a random selection of searches conducted over a three-month period. They included user ID, the actual query, the time of the search, and the destination domain visited. In some cases, the data included personal names, addresses, and U.S. social security numbers.

Although AOL apologized for the error and withdrew the site, the damage was done. The ability to analyze all searches by a single user can enable a criminal to identify who the user is and what he is doing. As just one example, *The New York Times* tracked down a particular person based solely on her AOL searches.

Compromises to Intellectual Property. Protecting intellectual property is a vital issue for people who make their livelihood in knowledge fields. **Intellectual property** is the property created by individuals or corporations that is protected under *trade secret*, *patent*, and *copyright laws*.

A **trade secret** is an intellectual work, such as a business plan, that is a company secret and is not based on public information. An example is a corporate strategic plan. A **patent** is a document that grants the holder exclusive rights on an invention or process for 20 years. **Copyright** is a statutory grant that provides the creators of intellectual property with ownership of the property for the life of the creator plus 50 years. Owners are entitled to collect fees from anyone who wants to copy the property.

The most common intellectual property related to IT deals with software. In Canada, the Canadian Copyright Act protects a variety of intellectual property, including written work. A computer program is considered to be a written work, as it is written instructions for the computer system to perform specific functions. However, copyright law does not protect similar concepts, functions, and general features such as pull-down menus, colours, and icons. Under copyright law, copying a software program—including giving a disk to a friend to install on his or her computer—without making payment to the owner is a copyright violation. Not surprisingly, this practice, called **piracy**, is a major problem for software vendors. The global trade in pirated software amounts to hundreds of billions of dollars.

The Canadian Alliance Against Software Theft (CAAST, see *www.caast.org*) is an organization representing the commercial software industry that promotes legal software and conducts research on software piracy in an attempt to eliminate it. CAAST is affiliated with the Business Software

Alliance (BSA, see *www.bsa.org*), which identifies Vietnam, China, Indonesia, Ukraine, and Russia as the countries with the highest percentage of illegal software compared with legal software. In those countries, more than 85 percent of the software used consists of illegal copies. The BSA estimated that 32 percent of personal computer software in Canada in 2009 was pirated, which they estimated as representing about US$943 million in software sales.

Software Attacks. Software attacks have evolved from the outbreak era, when malicious software tried to infect as many computers worldwide as possible, to the profit-driven, web-based attacks of today. Cyber-criminals are heavily involved with malware attacks to make money, and they use sophisticated, blended attacks typically via the Web. Table 3.4 shows a variety of software attacks, and IT's About Business 3.2 provides examples of such an attack.

TABLE 3.4
TYPES OF SOFTWARE ATTACKS

SOFTWARE ATTACK	DESCRIPTION
Virus	Segment of computer code that performs malicious actions by attaching to another computer program
Worm	Segment of computer code that performs malicious actions and will replicate, or spread, by itself (without requiring another computer program)
Trojan Horse	Software programs that hide in other computer programs and reveal their designed behaviour only when they are activated
Back Door	Typically a password, known only to the attacker, that allows him to access a computer system at will, without having to go through any security procedures (also called **trap door**)
Blended Attack	An attack using multiple delivery methods (e.g., e-mail and web), and combines multiple components, such as phishing, spam, worms, and Trojans in one attack
Logic Bomb	Segment of computer code that is embedded with an organization's existing computer programs and is designed to activate and perform a destructive action at a certain time or date
Password Attacks	
Dictionary Attack	Attack that tries combinations of letters and numbers that are most likely to succeed, such as all words from a dictionary
Brute Force Attack	Attack that uses massive computing resources to try every possible combination of password options to uncover a password
Denial-of-Service Attack	An attack in which the attacker sends so many information requests to a target computer system that the target cannot handle them successfully and typically crashes (ceases to function)
Distributed Denial-of-Service Attack	An attack in which the attacker first takes over many computers (called zombies or bots), typically by using malicious software. The attacker uses these bots (which form a botnet) to deliver a coordinated stream of information requests to a target computer, causing it to crash.
Phishing Attack	An attack involving deception to acquire sensitive personal information by masquerading as official-looking e-mails or instant messages

(Continued on next page)

TABLE 3.4 *(Continued)*

Spear Phishing Attack	An attack in which the perpetrators find out as much information about an individual as possible to improve their chances that phishing techniques will be able to obtain sensitive personal information. Contrast with *phishing attacks,* which target large groups of people.
Zero-day Attack	An attack that takes advantage of a newly discovered, previously unknown vulnerability in a software product. Perpetrators attack the vulnerability before the software vendor can prepare a patch for the vulnerability.

IT'S ABOUT BUSINESS 3.2
COMPUTER INFECTION AFFECTS MANY PEOPLE

A botnet code named "Mariposa" is one cause of a computer infection. In the spring of 2010, a group of security and computer intelligence organizations around the world shut down a group that it estimated had infected over 15 million computers. It is possible to purchase botnet kits on the Internet that will help people to infect other computers, so that they can then steal passwords and access codes.

Defence Intelligence (*http://defintel.com*) is an information security firm based in Ottawa. It worked with Canadian, U.S., and Spanish police to divert the traffic from the botnet to secure systems, which enabled them to ultimately track down and arrest the creators of the botnet. Defence Intelligence estimated that thousands of organizations and government agencies, as well as millions of home computers, were infected with the virus that created this botnet. This means that the creators of the botnet likely stole millions of user access codes using the botnet system, because the botnet was designed to send information to the originators. They could also have used the botnet to enable denial of service attacks. This is why banks and financial institutions that had been infected were told about their infection when Defence Intelligence detected it.

In a separate incident, Toronto Hydro admitted that its electronic billing system had been hacked into, and close to 180,000 customers' data were accessed. Such information could be used to contact customers and then phishing tactics could obtain further customer details, potentially leading to identity theft. To prevent this from occurring, the utility sent warning e-mails to all of its customers. It also sent letters to the customers (imagine the costs of processing and sending letters to about 685,000 people or organizations!) telling them about the breach and warning them about not responding to phishing e-mails or other requests for personal information. This intrusion caused some people to question whether a new Toronto Hydro initiative—"smart" meters for recording and tracking electricity—was appropriate, wondering whether ultimately even the electricity usage records could be tampered with.

Sources: O. El Akkad, "Canadian Firm Helps Disable Massive Botnet," *The Globe and Mail*, March 12, 2010; J. Sidhu, "Toronto Hydro Admits Customer Data Breach," *Toronto Star*, July 28, 2009; T. Hamilton, "Smart Grid Saves Power, but Can it Thwart Hackers?" *Toronto Star*, August 3, 2009.

QUESTIONS
1. Who is responsible when an organization's computers are infected by a botnet and data such as e-mails are used to target phishing attacks? Who is responsible when a user responds to the phishing attack and believes it is a legitimate request?
2. Should organizations limit their implementation of e-commerce–based services due to the threat of botnet attacks or other types of unauthorized access?

Alien Software. Many personal computers have alien software (also called *pestware*) running on them that the owners do not know about. **Alien software** is clandestine software that is installed on your computer through duplicitous methods. Alien software is typically not as malicious as viruses, worms, or Trojan horses, but it does use up valuable system resources. In addition, it can report on your web surfing habits and other personal behaviour.

One clear indication that software is pestware is that it does not come with an uninstaller program. An *uninstaller* is an automated program that removes a particular software package systematically and entirely. The different types of alien software include adware, spyware, spamware, and cookies.

The vast majority of pestware is **adware**—software that is designed to help pop-up advertisements appear on your screen. The reason adware is so common is that it works. According to advertising agencies, for every 100 people who delete such an ad, three click on it. This "hit rate" is extremely high for Internet advertising.

Spyware is software that collects personal information about users without their consent. We discuss two types of spyware here: keystroke loggers and screen scrapers.

Keystroke loggers (also called **keyloggers**) record your keystrokes and record your web browsing history. The purposes range from criminal (for example, theft of passwords and sensitive personal information such as credit card numbers) to annoying (for example, recording your Internet search history for targeted advertising).

Companies have attempted to counter keystroke loggers by switching to other forms of input for authentication. For example, all of us have been forced to look at wavy, distorted letters and type them correctly into a box. That string of letters is called a CAPTCHA, and it is a test. The point of CAPTCHA is that reading those distorted letters is something that computers cannot do accurately (yet). The fact that you can transcribe them means that you are probably not a software program run by an unauthorized person, such as a spammer. As a result, attackers have turned to **screen scrapers** (or **screen grabbers**). This software records a continuous "movie" of a screen's contents rather than simply recording keystrokes.

Spamware is pestware that is designed to use your computer as a launchpad for spammers. **Spam** is unsolicited e-mail, usually for the purpose of advertising for products and services. When your computer is used this way, e-mails from spammers appear to come from you. Even worse, spam will be sent to everyone in your e-mail address book.

Not only is spam a nuisance, but it wastes time and money. Spam costs companies billions of dollars per year. These costs come from productivity losses, clogged e-mail systems, additional storage, user support, and anti-spam software. Spam can also carry viruses and worms, making it even more dangerous.

Cookies are small amounts of information that websites store on your computer, temporarily or more or less permanently. In many cases, cookies are useful and innocuous. For example, some cookies are passwords and user IDs that you do not have to retype every time you load a new page at the website that issued the cookie. Cookies are also necessary if you want to shop on-line because they are used for your shopping carts at various on-line merchants.

Tracking cookies, however, can be used to track your path through a website, the time you spend there, what links you click on, and other details that the company wants to record, usually for marketing purposes. Tracking cookies can also combine this information with your name, purchases, credit card information, and other personal data, to develop an intrusive profile of your spending habits.

Most cookies can be read only by the party that created them. However, some companies that manage on-line banner advertising are, in essence, cookie-sharing rings. These companies can track information such as which pages you load and which ads you click on. They then share this information with their client websites (which may number in the thousands). For a cookie demonstration, see *http://privacy.net/track*.

Supervisory Control and Data Acquisition (SCADA) Attacks. SCADA refers to a large-scale, distributed measurement and control system. SCADA systems are used to monitor or to control chemical, physical, or transport processes such as oil refineries, water and sewage treatment plants, electrical generators, and nuclear power plants.

SCADA systems consist of multiple sensors, a master computer, and communications infrastructure. The sensors connect to physical equipment. They read status data such as the open/closed status of a switch or a valve, as well as measurements such as pressure, flow, voltage, and current. By sending signals to equipment, sensors control that equipment, such as opening or closing a switch or valve or setting the speed of a pump.

The sensors are connected in a network, and each sensor typically has an Internet (Internet protocol, or IP) address. (We discuss IP addresses in Technology Guide 4.) If an attacker can gain access to the network, he can disrupt the power grid over a large area or disrupt the operations of a large chemical plant. Such actions could have catastrophic results, as we see in IT's About Business 3.3.

Cyber-terrorism and Cyber-warfare

With both **cyber-terrorism** and **cyber-warfare**, attackers use a target's computer systems, particularly via the Internet, to cause physical, real-world harm or severe disruption, usually to carry out a political agenda. Cyber-terrorism and cyber-warfare range from gathering data to attacking critical infrastructure (via SCADA systems). We discuss the two types of attacks synonymously here, even though cyber-terrorism typically is carried out by individuals or groups, whereas cyber-warfare involves nations. Here we examine cyber-attacks against Estonia and the Republic of Georgia.

IT'S ABOUT BUSINESS 3.3
VULNERABILITIES IN SUPERVISORY CONTROL AND DATA ACQUISITION SYSTEMS

Supervisory Control and Data Acquisition (SCADA) Systems are vulnerable to computer system errors and cyber-attacks. Consider the following examples.

In August 2006, at a nuclear plant in Athens, Alabama, an overflow of data on the computer system controlling parts of one unit caused two water recirculation pumps to lock up, and the unit shut down.

In March 2008, at a nuclear power plant near Baxley, Georgia, a contract engineer updated the software on a single computer on the plant's business network. The update was meant to synchronize data from the chemical and diagnostic monitoring systems. After the update was installed, the computer was rebooted, and it reset the data on the control system, which thought there had been a drop in the level of water reservoirs used to cool radioactive fuel rods. The safety system automatically kicked in and shut the plant down for 48 hours.

In 2008, the Central Intelligence Agency reported that cyber-attackers used the Internet to hack into the computer systems of utility companies outside the United States, causing a power outage in several cities. All the cyber-attacks were for purposes of extortion. The CIA declined to disclose the location of the attacks.

As described in IT's About Business 3.2, Toronto Hydro's systems were hacked in July 2009, resulting in unauthorized access to customer data. It is possible that the smart meters Toronto Hydro has installed for customers in the area could be infected with viruses. Then, damage could be caused by shutting down the meters, or by otherwise affecting the measurement of electricity, perhaps even cutting power to hundreds of thousands of locations.

Why are SCADA systems so vulnerable to computer system errors and attacks, and what can be done about this problem? The problem begins with the fact that utility control systems were originally developed as proprietary closed systems with no connection to systems outside the organization. Further, these control systems were developed with no security considerations. Therefore, these systems operated with "security through obscurity." Today, however, organizations are connecting their control systems to SCADA systems that are accessible via corporate networks and the Internet. The use of SCADA systems is a double-edged sword. While the systems allow employees to operate equipment remotely, they are also vulnerable to outside attack. The examples above show the vulnerabilities that occur when business information technology systems interconnect with industrial control systems without adequate design considerations.

Sources: Compiled from T. Hamilton, August 3, 2009, "Smart Grid Saves Power, but Can it Thwart Hackers?" *Toronto Star*, p. B1, B3; B. Krebs, "Cyber Incident Blamed for Nuclear Power Plant Shutdown," *Washington Post*, June 5, 2008; B. Krebs, "TVA Power Plants Vulnerable to Cyber Attacks, GAO Finds," *Washington Post*, May 21, 2008; T. Greene, "Experts Hack Power Grid in No Time," *Network World*, April 9, 2008; R. McMillan, "CIA Says Hackers Have Cut Power Grid," *PC World*, January 19, 2008; "Paller: Government Cybersecurity Gets an F: SCADA Attacks Are Latest Proof of Vulnerable Infrastructure," *InfoWorld*, September 11, 2006; *www.irawinkler.com*, accessed January 15, 2009.

QUESTIONS

1. Could legislation be used to strengthen SCADA defences against cyber-attacks? Support your answer. If not, what do you think utility companies should do to protect their SCADA systems?
2. Discuss the trade-offs for utility companies between having their control systems connected to their business systems or not.

In 2007, a three-week wave of massive **distributed denial-of-service (DDoS)** cyber-attacks against the Baltic country of Estonia disabled the websites of government ministries, political parties, newspapers, banks, and companies. One of the most wired societies in Europe, Estonia is a pioneer of e-government. As a result, the country is highly vulnerable to cyber-attack. In the early phase of the DDoS attack, some perpetrators were identified by their Internet protocol addresses. Many of these addresses were Russian, and some of them were from Russian state institutions.

In August 2008, Russian troops entered the Republic of Georgia's province of South Ossetia to crush a Georgian attempt to control a breakaway by that region. DDoS attacks on Georgian websites were apparently synchronized with the Russian invasion. The cyber-attack shut down the website of the Georgian president, Mikheil Saakashvilli, for 24 hours, and defaced the Georgian parliament website with images of Adolph Hitler. Saakashvilli blamed Russia for the attacks, but the Russian government denied the charges.

Terrorist groups around the world have expanded their activities on the Internet, increasing the sophistication and volume of their videos and messages, in an effort to recruit new members and raise money. In response, the U.S. military is expanding its training of its members with respect to cyberwar tactics. Cadets who are information systems majors compete annually in cyberwar games. The *New York Times* reported in May 2009 that there were teams from different divisions (Navy, Air Force, Marines) competing (see C. Kilgannon and N. Cohen, "Cadets Trade the Trenches for Firewalls," *New York Times*, May 10, 2009).

What Companies Are Doing

Why is it so difficult to stop cyber-criminals? One reason is that the on-line commerce industry is not particularly willing to install safeguards that would make it harder to complete transactions. It would be possible, for example, to demand passwords or personal identification numbers for all credit card transactions. However, these requirements might discourage people from shopping on-line. Also, there is little incentive for companies to share leads on criminal activity either with one another or with the RCMP. For credit card companies, it is cheaper to block a stolen credit card and move on than to invest time and money on a prosecution.

Despite these difficulties, the information security industry is battling back. Companies are developing software and services that deliver early warnings of trouble on the Internet. Unlike traditional antivirus software, which is reactive, early warning systems are proactive, scanning the Web for new viruses and alerting companies to the danger.

The new systems are emerging in response to ever more effective virus writers. As virus writers become more expert, the gap between the time when they learn of vulnerabilities and when they exploit them is closing quickly. Hackers are now producing new viruses and worms in a matter of hours (see zero-day attacks).

Technicians at Symantec (*www.symantec.com*) are working around the clock to monitor web traffic. Symantec's team taps into 20,000 sensors placed at Internet hubs in 180 countries to spot e-mail and other data packets that seem to be carrying viruses.

In addition, many companies realize that information systems security is important and are allocating funds to have appropriate hardware and software protection. The company may also hire information security experts to attack their own systems. These surprise attacks are called penetration tests or *white hacking*. A **penetration test** is a method of evaluating the security of an information system by simulating an attack by a malicious perpetrator. The idea is to proactively discover weaknesses before real attackers exploit them.

Despite the difficulties involved in defending against attacks, organizations spend a great deal of time and money protecting their information resources. We discuss these methods of protection in the next section.

3.3 Protecting Information Resources

Before spending money to apply controls, organizations must perform risk management. Effective risk management is done by an organization's management and includes risks pertaining to IT. As we discussed earlier in the chapter, a risk is the probability that a threat will affect an information resource. The goal of **risk management** is to identify, control, and minimize the impact of threats. In other words, risk management seeks to reduce risk to acceptable levels. There are three processes in risk management: risk analysis, risk mitigation, and controls evaluation. We consider each one below.

Risk Management

Risk analysis is the process by which an organization assesses the value of each asset being protected, estimates the probability that each asset will be compromised, and compares the probable costs of the asset's being compromised with the costs of protecting that asset. Organizations perform risk analysis to ensure that their information systems' security programs are cost effective. The risk analysis process prioritizes the assets to be protected based on each asset's value, its probability of being compromised, and the estimated cost of its protection. The organization then considers how to mitigate the risk.

In **risk mitigation**, the organization takes concrete actions against risks. Risk mitigation has two functions: (1) implementing controls to prevent identified threats from occurring; and (2) developing a means of recovery should the threat become a reality. There are several risk mitigation strategies that organizations may adopt. The three most common are risk acceptance, risk limitation, and risk transference.

- **Risk acceptance:** Accept the potential risk, continue operating with no controls, and absorb any damages that occur.
- **Risk limitation:** Limit the risk by implementing controls that minimize the impact of the threat.
- **Risk transference:** Transfer the risk by using other means to compensate for the loss, such as by purchasing insurance.

In **controls evaluation**, the organization identifies security deficiencies and calculates the costs of implementing adequate control measures. If the costs of implementing a control are greater than the value of the asset being protected, control is not cost effective.

For example, an organization's mainframe computers are too valuable for risk acceptance. As a result, organizations limit the risk to mainframes through controls, such as access controls. Organizations also use risk transference for their mainframes by purchasing insurance and having off-site backups.

Controls

The purpose of **controls** is to safeguard assets, optimize the use of the organization's resources, and prevent or detect errors or fraud. Organizations protect their systems using "layers" of control systems. First comes the control environment, and then general controls, followed by application controls. The **control environment** encompasses management attitudes toward controls, as evidenced

TABLE 3.5
THE DIFFICULTIES IN PROTECTING INFORMATION RESOURCES

- Hundreds of potential threats exist.
- Computing resources may be situated in many locations.
- Many individuals control information assets.
- Computer networks can be located outside the organization and may be difficult to protect.
- Rapid technological changes make some controls obsolete as soon as they are installed.
- Many computer crimes are undetected for a long period of time so it is difficult to learn from experience.
- People tend to violate security procedures because the procedures are inconvenient.
- The amount of computer knowledge necessary to commit computer crimes is usually minimal. As a matter of fact, one can learn hacking for free on the Internet.
- The cost of preventing hazards can be very high. Therefore, most organizations simply cannot afford to protect against all possible hazards.
- It is difficult to conduct a cost-benefit justification for controls before an attack occurs because it is difficult to assess the value of a hypothetical attack.

by management actions, as well as by stated policies and procedures that address ethical issues and the quality of supervision. **General controls** apply to more than one functional area. For example, passwords are general controls. Controls specific to one application, such as payroll, are **application controls**. A typical payroll application control would be the approval of payroll wage rates.

Information systems security encompasses all of the types of controls, as organizations need to have security policies and procedures, to protect all applications using physical and software controls such as antivirus or firewalls, and to protect individual applications with controls over how information is entered and managed.

Because it is so important to the entire enterprise, organizing an appropriate defence system is one of the major activities of any prudent CIO and of the functional managers who control information resources. As a matter of fact, IT security is the business of *everyone* in an organization. Table 3.5 lists the major difficulties involved in protecting information.

Controls that protect information assets are called defence mechanisms or *countermeasures*. *Security controls* are designed to protect all of the components of an information system, including data, software, hardware, and networks.

Controls are intended to prevent accidental hazards, deter intentional acts, detect problems as early as possible, enhance damage recovery, and correct problems. Before we discuss controls in more detail, we emphasize that the most effective control is user education and training, leading to increased awareness of the vital importance of information security on the part of every organizational employee.

We will look at three categories of general controls: physical controls, access controls, and communications controls. Figure 3.2 illustrates these controls. Then, we will look at examples of application controls.

Physical Controls

Physical controls prevent unauthorized individuals from gaining access to a company's facilities. Common physical controls include walls, doors, fencing, gates, locks, badges, guards, and alarm systems. More sophisticated physical controls include pressure sensors, temperature sensors, and motion detectors. One weakness of physical controls is that they can be inconvenient to employees.

Guards deserve special mention because they have very difficult jobs for at least two reasons. First, their jobs are boring and repetitive and generally do not pay well. Second, if they do their jobs

FIGURE 3.2
Where defence
mechanisms
are located.

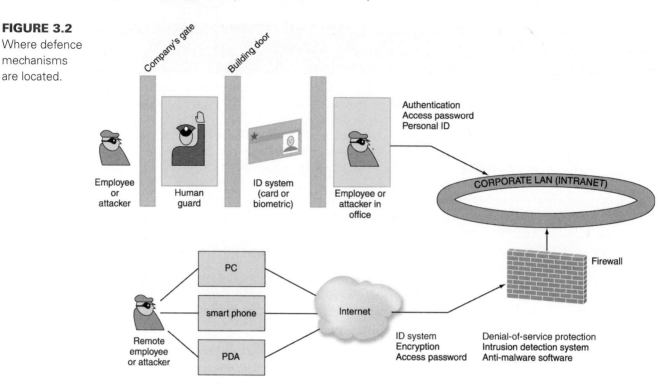

thoroughly, other employees may harass them, particularly if their being conscientious slows up the process of entering a facility.

Access Controls

Access controls restrict unauthorized individuals from using information resources. Access controls can be physical controls or logical controls. Both types restrict unauthorized individuals from using information resources. **Logical controls** are implemented by software. For example, access control programs limit users to acceptable login times and acceptable login locations. These controls can limit the number of unsuccessful login attempts and they require everyone to log off their computers when they leave for the day. In addition, computers are set to automatically log the user off after a certain period of disuse.

Access controls involve two major functions: authentication and authorization. **Authentication** determines the identity of the person requiring access. In contrast, **authorization** determines which actions, rights, or privileges the person has based on verified identity. Organizations use many methods to identify authorized personnel (i.e., authenticate someone). These methods include something the user is, something the user has, something the user does, and something the user knows.

Something the User Is. Also known as **biometrics**, these authentication methods examine a person's innate physical characteristics. Common biometric applications are fingerprint scans, palm scans, retina scans, iris recognition, and facial recognition. Of these, fingerprints, retina scans, and iris recognition provide the most definitive identification.

Something the User Has. These authentication mechanisms include regular identification (ID) cards, smart ID cards, and tokens. **Regular ID cards**, or *dumb cards*, typically have the person's picture, and often his or her signature. **Smart ID cards** have a chip embedded in them with pertinent information about the user. (Smart ID cards used for identification differ from smart cards used in electronic commerce [see Chapter 6]. Both types of card have embedded chips, but they are used for different purposes). **Tokens** have embedded chips and a digital display that presents a login number that the employees use to access the organization's network. The number changes with each login.

Something the User Does. These authentication mechanisms include voice and signature recognition. In **voice recognition**, the user speaks a phrase (e.g., her name and department) that has been previously recorded under controlled, monitored conditions. The voice recognition system matches the two voice signals.

In **signature recognition**, the user signs his name, and the system matches this signature with one previously recorded under controlled, monitored conditions. Signature recognition systems also match the speed of the signature and the pressure of the signature.

Something the User Knows. These authentication mechanisms include passwords and pass phrases. Passwords present a huge information security problem in all organizations. All users should use strong passwords so that the password cannot be broken by a password attack, which we discussed earlier. **Strong passwords** have the following characteristics:

- They should be difficult to guess.
- They should be long rather than short.
- They should have uppercase letters, lowercase letters, numbers, and special characters.
- They should not be a recognizable word.
- They should not be the name of anything or anyone familiar, such as family names or names of pets.
- They should not be a recognizable string of numbers, such as a social insurance number or birthday.

Unfortunately, strong passwords are irritating. If the organization mandates longer (stronger) passwords and/or frequent password changes, they become more difficult to remember, causing employees to write them down. What is needed is a way for a user to create a strong password that is easy to remember. A pass phrase can help, either by being a password itself or by helping you create a strong password.

A **pass phrase** is a series of characters that is longer than a password but can be memorized easily. Examples of pass phrases include "maytheforcebewithyoualways," "heshootshescores," "livelongand-prosper," and "aman'sgottoknowhislimitations." A user can turn a pass phrase into a strong password in this manner. Start with the last pass phrase above, and use the first letter of each word. You will have amgtkhl. Then capitalize every other letter, to have AmGtKhL. Then add special characters and numbers, to have 9AmGtKhL//*. Now you have a strong password that you can remember.

Multifactor Authentication. Many organizations are using multifactor authentication to more efficiently and effectively identify authorized users. This type of authentication is particularly important when users are logging in from remote locations.

Single-factor authentication, which is notoriously weak, commonly consists simply of a password. Two-factor authentication consists of a password plus one type of biometric identification (e.g., a fingerprint). Three-factor authentication is any combination of three authentication methods. We should keep in mind that stronger authentication is more expensive and can be irritating to users as well.

Once users have been properly authenticated, the rights and privileges that they have on the organization's systems are established, a process called authorization. Companies use the principle of least privilege for authorization purposes. A **privilege** is a collection of related computer system operations that can be performed by users of the system. **Least privilege** is a principle that users be granted the privilege for some activity only if there is a justifiable need to grant this authorization. This means that employees would have access to only those functions they need to complete their job effectively. The accounts payable data entry clerk, for example, would be unable to access wage rates.

As IT's About Business 3.4 shows, granting least privilege is important for preventing plunder of bank accounts.

IT'S ABOUT BUSINESS 3.4
USING YOUR OWN PASSWORD TO STEAL CASH!

As described earlier in this chapter, computer viruses called Trojan horses can be used to capture information about the passwords that are in use on your computer system. If an organization uses on-line banking to pay suppliers or employees, the on-line banking password could also be captured by the virus, and then transmitted to unauthorized individuals, who can then set up fictitious employees and pay these employees over and over again. The unauthorized person could also initiate a bank transfer that empties the organization's bank account. The U.S. Federal Deposit Insurance Corporation disclosed in March 2010 that in the final three months of 2009, over US$150 million had been stolen from small businesses this way (earlier reports had estimated the losses at $120 million for that period).

Two companies in the United States, Hillary Machinery Inc. (which lost more than $800,000) and Expert Metal Inc. (which lost about $560,000) were suing their banks to try to recover some of their cash after their bank accounts had been emptied by hackers. The banks did not want to pay, because the banks stated that the companies should have had better control over their passwords. The banks only returned money to the companies that the banks were able to recover from the thieves.

Organizations can protect themselves by requiring two passwords from two different users on different machines, and by preventing after-hours access to their equipment, notifying the bank in writing that transactions after business hours should not be accepted by the financial institution. They can also limit the number of individuals who have access to the on-line banking password, and restrict the use of on-line banking to a single machine. They should also make sure that they have current antivirus software that is run regularly on all of their machines. Combining logical controls (such as passwords) with physical controls (such as fingerprint scanning) substantially improves controls at relatively low cost.

Service providers that provide electronic commerce transactions are also vulnerable. In one example, a company called PayChoice Inc., located in Moorestown, New Jersey, which provides payroll processing services to over 25,000 clients, was shut down due to security violations twice in October 2009. The cause of one of the violations was not explained, but the second violation involved the trapping of passwords, and fictitious employees were added to some customer accounts. PayChoice responded by changing the login identification codes of all of its customers—likely a costly process.

Sources: Compiled from R. McMillan, "Cyber Scammers Stole $120 million in 3 Months from Small Firms," itbusiness.ca, March 10, 2010; J. Vijayan, "Furor over Plunder of SMB Online Bank Accounts," itbusiness.ca, March 12, 2010; J. Vijayan, "Security Breach Shuts Down Payroll Service Yet Again," itbusiness.ca, October 20, 2009.

QUESTIONS
1. Why is it so important for organizations to provide least privilege to employees, both to prevent theft of cash, but also access to other assets?
2. What are possible disadvantages of least privilege?

Communications Controls

Communications (network) controls secure the movement of data across networks. Communications controls consist of firewalls, anti-malware systems, whitelisting and blacklisting, intrusion detection systems, encryption, virtual private networking (VPN), secure socket layer (SSL), vulnerability management systems, and employee monitoring systems. Each of these controls is described below.

Firewalls. A **firewall** is a system that prevents a specific type of information from moving between untrusted networks, such as the Internet, and private networks, such as a company's network. Put simply, firewalls prevent unauthorized Internet users from accessing private networks. Firewalls can consist of hardware, software, or a combination of both. All messages entering or leaving a company's network pass through a firewall. The firewall examines each message and blocks those that do not meet specified security rules.

Firewalls range from simple versions for home use to very complex versions for organizational use. Figure 3.3a shows a basic firewall for a home computer. In this case, the firewall is implemented as software on the home computer. Figure 3.3b shows an organization that has implemented an external firewall, which faces the Internet, and an internal firewall, which faces the company network. A **demilitarized zone (DMZ)** is located between the two firewalls. Messages from the Internet must first pass through the external firewall. If they conform to the defined security rules, they are sent to company servers located in the DMZ. These servers typically handle web page requests and e-mail. Any messages designated for the company's internal network (for example, its intranet) must pass through the internal firewall, again with its own defined security rules, to gain access to the company's private network.

The danger from viruses and worms is so severe that many organizations are placing firewalls at strategic points *inside* their private networks. In this way, if a virus or worm does get through both the external and internal firewalls, the internal damage may be contained.

Anti-malware Systems. **Anti-malware systems**, also called AV or **antivirus software**, are software packages that attempt to identify and eliminate viruses, worms, and other malicious software. This software is implemented at the organizational level by the information systems department. There are currently hundreds of AV software packages available. Among the best known are Norton Antivirus (*www.symantec.com*), McAfee Virusscan (*www.mcafee.com*), and Trend Micro PC-cillin (*www.trendmicro.com*).

Anti-malware systems are generally reactive. They work by creating definitions, or signatures, of various types of malware, and then updating these signatures in their products. The anti-malware software then examines suspicious computer code to see if it matches a known signature. If it does, the anti-malware software will remove it. This is the reason that organizations update their malware definitions so often.

Because malware is such a serious problem, the leading vendors are rapidly developing anti-malware systems that function proactively as well as reactively. These systems evaluate behaviour rather than rely on signature matching. In theory, therefore, it is possible to catch malware before it can infect systems. Cisco, for example, has released a product called Cisco Security Agent. This product functions proactively by analyzing computer code to see if it functions like malware (see *www.cisilion.com*). Prevx is another vendor offering this type of proactive malware system (*www.prevx.com*).

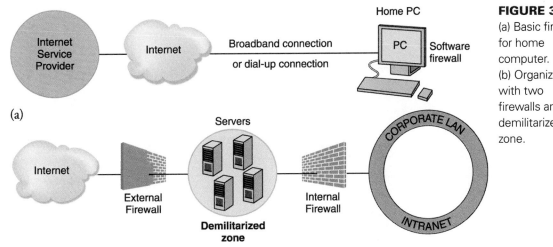

FIGURE 3.3
(a) Basic firewall for home computer.
(b) Organization with two firewalls and demilitarized zone.

Whitelisting and Blacklisting. A report by the Yankee Group (*www.yankeegroup.com*), a technology research and consulting firm, stated that 99 percent of organizations had anti-malware systems installed, but 62 percent of companies still suffered successful malware attacks. As we have discussed, anti-malware systems are usually reactive, and malware continues to infect companies.

One solution to this problem is **whitelisting**. Whitelisting is a process in which a company identifies the software that it will allow to run and does not try to recognize malware. Whitelisting permits acceptable software to run and either prevents anything else from running or lets new software run in a quarantined environment until the company can verify its validity.

Whereas whitelisting allows nothing to run unless it is on the whitelist, blacklisting allows everything to run unless it is on the blacklist. A **blacklist** then includes certain types of software that are not allowed to run in the company environment. For example, a company might blacklist peer-to-peer file sharing on its systems. In addition to software, people, devices, and websites can also be whitelisted and blacklisted.

Intrusion Detection Systems. **Intrusion detection systems** are designed to detect all types of malicious network traffic and computer usage that cannot be detected by a firewall. These systems capture all network traffic flows and examine the contents of each packet for malicious traffic. An example of this type of malicious traffic is a denial-of-service attack (discussed earlier).

Encryption. When organizations do not have a secure channel for sending information, they use encryption to stop unauthorized eavesdroppers. **Encryption** is the process of converting an original message into a form that cannot be read by anyone except the intended receiver.

FIGURE 3.4
How public-key encryption works. (*Source*: Omnisec AG.)

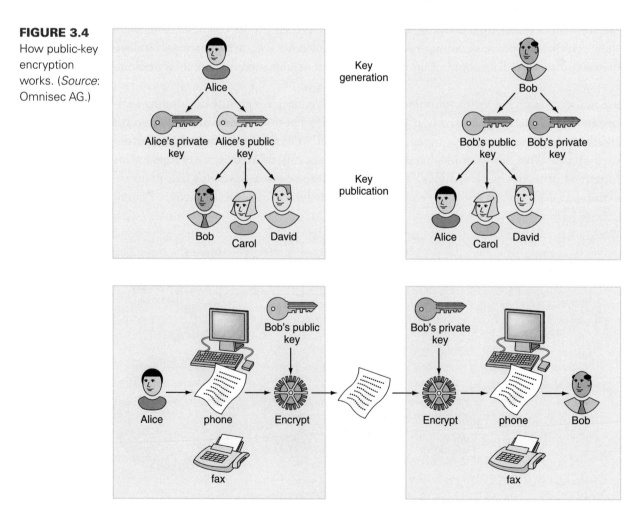

All encryption systems use a key, which is the code that scrambles and then decodes the messages. The majority of encryption systems use public-key encryption. **Public-key encryption**—also known as *asymmetric encryption*—uses two different keys: a public key and a private key (see Figure 3.4). The public key and the private key are created simultaneously using the same mathematical formula or algorithm. Because the two keys are mathematically related, the data encrypted with one key can be decrypted by using the other key. The public key is publicly available in a directory that all parties can access. The private key is kept secret, never shared with anyone, and never sent across the Internet. In this system, if Alice wants to send a message to Bob, she first obtains Bob's public key, which she uses to encrypt (scramble) her message. When Bob receives Alice's message, he uses his private key to decrypt (unscramble) it.

Public key systems also show that a message is authentic. That is, if you encrypt a message using your private key, you have electronically "signed" it. A recipient can verify that the message came from you by using your public key to decrypt it.

Although this system is adequate for personal information, organizations doing business over the Internet require a more complex system. In such cases, a third party, called a **certificate authority**, acts as a trusted intermediary between companies. As such, the certificate authority issues digital certificates and verifies the worth and integrity of the certificates. A **digital certificate** is an electronic document attached to a file certifying that the file is from the organization it claims to be from and has not been modified from its original format. As you can see in Figure 3.5, Sony requests a digital certificate from VeriSign, a certificate authority, and uses this certificate when doing business with Dell. Note that the digital certificate contains an identification number, the issuer, validity dates, and the requester's public key. For examples of certificate authorities, see *www.entrust.com*, *www.verisign.com*, *www.secude.com*, and *www.thawte.com*.

Virtual Private Networking. A **virtual private network (VPN)** is a private network that uses a public network (usually the Internet) to connect users. As such, VPNs integrate the global connectivity of the Internet with the security of a private network and thereby extend the reach of the organization's networks.

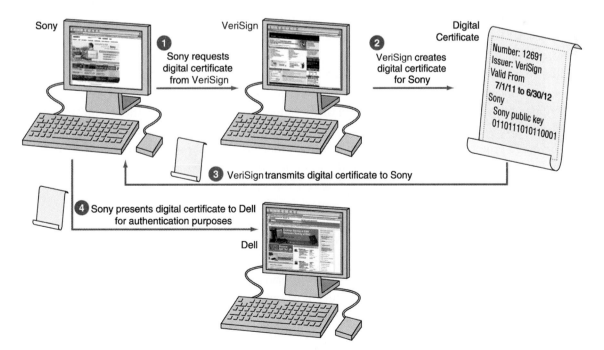

FIGURE 3.5 How digital certificates work. Sony and Dell, business partners, use a digital certificate from VeriSign for authentication.

FIGURE 3.6
Virtual private
network and
tunnelling.

VPNs are labelled "virtual" because the connections (among organizations, among remote sites of one organization, or between an organization and its off-site employees) are created when a transmission needs to be made and then terminated after the transmission has been sent. VPNs are handled by common carriers (i.e., telephone service providers).

VPNs have several advantages. First, they allow remote users to access the company network. Second, they allow flexibility. That is, mobile users can access the organization's network from properly configured remote devices. Third, organizations can impose their security policies through VPNs. For example, an organization may dictate that only corporate e-mail applications are available to users when they connect from unmanaged devices.

To provide secure transmissions, VPNs use a process called tunnelling. **Tunnelling** encrypts each data packet to be sent and places each encrypted packet inside another packet. In this manner, the packet can travel across the Internet with confidentiality, authentication, and integrity. Figure 3.6 illustrates a VPN and tunnelling.

Secure Socket Layer (SSL). Secure socket layer, now called **transport layer security (TLS)**, is an encryption standard used for secure transactions such as credit card purchases and on-line banking. TLS is indicated by a URL that begins with "https" rather than "http," and it often has a small padlock icon in the browser's status bar. TLS encrypts and decrypts data between a web server and a browser end to end.

Vulnerability Management Systems. Users may need access to their organization's network from any location and at any time. To accommodate these needs, **vulnerability management systems**, also called security on demand, extend the security perimeter that exists for the organization's managed devices. That is, vulnerability management systems handle security vulnerabilities on unmanaged remote devices. Recall that we discussed the dangers inherent in using unmanaged devices earlier. Vendors of vulnerability management software include Symantec (*www.symantec.com*), Trend Micro (*www.trendmicro.com*), McAfee (*www.mcafee.com*), and Genetec (*www.genetec.com*).

Vulnerability management systems scan the remote system and decide whether to allow the user to access it. These systems allow the user to download anti-malware software to the remote computer for the user's protection. The systems will also implement virtual user sessions on the remote computer. These sessions separate and encrypt data, applications, and networks from the main system of the unmanaged computer. After the user is finished, the vulnerability management system cleans the unmanaged computer's browser cache and temporary files.

Employee Monitoring Systems. Many companies are taking a proactive approach to protecting their networks from what they view as one of their major security threats, namely employee mistakes. These companies are implementing **employee monitoring systems**, which monitor their employees' computers, e-mail activities, and Internet surfing activities. These products are useful to identify employees who spend too much time surfing on the Internet for personal reasons, who visit questionable websites, or who download music illegally. Vendors that provide monitoring software include SpectorSoft (*www.spectorsoft.com*) and Websense (*www.websense.com*).

Application Controls

Application controls, as their name suggests, are security countermeasures that protect specific applications. Application controls fall into three major categories: input controls, processing controls, and output controls.

Input controls are programmed routines that edit input data for errors before they are processed. For example, social insurance numbers should not contain any alphabetical characters.

Processing controls are programmed routines that perform actions that are part of the record-keeping of the organization, reconcile and check transactions, or monitor the operation of applications. Processing controls, for example, might match entered quantities of goods received in the shipping area to amounts ordered on authorized purchase orders. Processing controls also balance the total number of transactions processed with the total number of transactions input or output.

Finally, output controls are programmed routines that edit output data for errors, or help to ensure that output is provided only to authorized individuals. An example of output controls is documentation specifying that authorized recipients have received their reports, paycheques, or other critical documents.

Business Continuity Planning, Backup, and Recovery

An important strategy for organizations is to be prepared for any eventuality. A critical element in any security system is a business continuity plan, also known as a disaster recovery plan.

Business continuity is the chain of events linking planning to protection and recovery. The purpose of the business continuity plan is to keep the business operating after a disaster occurs. The plan prepares for, reacts to, and recovers from events that affect the security of information assets, and the subsequent restoration to normal business operations. The plan ensures that critical business functions continue.

In the event of a major disaster, organizations can employ several strategies for business continuity. These strategies include hot sites, warm sites, cold sites, and off-site data storage. A **hot site** is a fully configured computer facility, with all services, communications links, and physical plant operations. A hot site duplicates computing resources, peripherals, telephone systems, applications, and work stations. A **warm site** provides many of the same services and options as the hot site. However, a warm site typically does not include the actual applications the company needs. A warm site does include computing equipment such as servers, but it often does not include user work stations. A **cold site** provides only rudimentary services and facilities, such as a building or room with heating, air conditioning, and humidity control. This type of site provides no computer hardware or user work stations. Hot sites reduce risk to the greatest extent, but they are the most expensive option. Conversely, cold sites reduce risk the least, but they are the least expensive option. In addition to hot, warm, and cold sites, organizations also use off-site data storage services. **Off-site data storage** is a service that allows companies to store valuable data in a secure location geographically distant from the company's data centre.

Information Systems Auditing

Companies implement security controls to ensure that information systems work properly. These controls can be installed in the original system, or they can be added after a system is in operation. Installing controls is necessary but not sufficient to provide adequate security. In addition, people responsible for security need to answer questions such as:

- Are all controls installed as intended?
- Are the controls effective?

- Has any breach of security occurred?
- If so, what actions are required to prevent future breaches?

These questions must be answered by independent and unbiased observers. Such observers perform the task of *information systems auditing*. An audit involves the accumulation and evaluation of evidence that is used to prepare a report about the information or controls that are being examined, using established criteria and standards. In an IS environment, an **audit** is an examination of information systems, their inputs, outputs, and processing.

Types of Auditors and Audits

There are several types of auditors. External auditors, also referred to as independent auditors, work at a public accounting firm, auditing primarily financial statements. Government auditors work for the provincial or federal auditors general offices. Canada Revenue Agency auditors audit compliance with tax legislation. Internal auditors work for specific organizations, and may have the Certified Internal Auditor (CIA) designation. Specialist auditors can be from a variety of fields. Information systems auditors, for example, may work for any of the above organizations, and may have a Certified Information Systems Auditor (CISA) designation.

IS auditing is usually conducted as part of the controls evaluation for the financial statement audit or as part of *internal auditing*, which looks at the efficiency or effectiveness of systems.

IS auditing is a broad topic, so we present only its essentials here. Auditing focuses on topics such as operations, data integrity, software applications, security and privacy, budgets and expenditures, cost control, and productivity. Guidelines are available to assist auditors in their jobs, such as those from the Institute of Internal Auditors (*www.theiia.org*) or the Information Systems Audit and Control Association (*www.isaca.org*).

How Does the Auditor Decide on Audits?

IS auditors conduct their work using a risk-based approach. They consider the likelihood of errors or fraud, or the risk of organizations not following their procedures. Then, they design procedures to test compliance or the percentages of errors. Information systems audits could be part of the evaluation of controls for a financial statement audit, which are required by statute for organizations that sell shares to the public, or for publicly accountable organizations such as registered charities.

Internal auditors conduct their audits based on a plan approved by management. This plan may look at areas where there are high risks of theft, such as an electronic commerce system, or at new systems development projects where there is an elevated potential for error, such as a new point-of-sale system. Where legislation is relatively new, such as privacy legislation, auditors could conduct a privacy audit to evaluate whether the organization is in compliance with the legislation.

Auditors could use computers in the actual conduct of their audit, by using software to create reports or by creating test data that is run through systems to evaluate their functioning.

BEFORE YOU GO ON ...

1. Describe the major types of controls for information systems.
2. What is information system auditing?
3. What is the purpose of a disaster recovery plan?

WHAT'S IN IT FOR ME?

FOR THE ACCOUNTING MAJOR

Public companies, their accountants, and their auditors now have significant information security responsibilities. Accountants are now being held professionally responsible for reducing risk, assuring compliance, reducing the risk of fraud, and increasing the transparency of transactions according to generally accepted accounting principles (GAAP). Regulatory agencies require information security, fraud prevention and detection, and internal controls over financial reporting and the privacy of information. Forensic accounting, a combination of accounting and information security, is one of the most rapidly growing areas in accounting today.

FOR THE FINANCE MAJOR

Because information security is essential to the success of organizations today, it is no longer just the concern of the CIO. As a result of global regulatory requirements, responsibility for information security lies with the CEO and Chief Financial Officer (CFO). Consequently, all aspects of the security audit, including the security of information and information systems, are a key concern for financial managers.

In addition, CFOs and treasurers are increasingly involved with investments in information technology. They know that a security breach of any kind can have devastating financial effects on a company. Banking and financial institutions are prime targets for computer criminals. A related problem is fraud involving stocks and bonds that are sold over the Internet. Finance personnel must be aware of both the hazards and the available controls associated with these activities.

FOR THE MARKETING MAJOR

Marketing professionals have new opportunities to collect data on their customers; for example, through business-to-consumer electronic commerce. Business ethics clearly state that these data should only be used internally in the company and should not be sold to anyone else. Marketers clearly do not want to be sued for invasion of privacy concerning data collected for the marketing database.

Customers expect their data to be properly secured. However, profit-motivated criminals want that data. Therefore, marketing managers must analyze the risk of their operations. Failure to protect corporate and customer data will cause significant public relations problems and make customers very angry, causing them to go elsewhere. Customer relationship management operations and tracking customers' on-line buying habits can expose data to misuse (if the data are not encrypted) or result in privacy violations.

FOR THE PRODUCTION/OPERATIONS MANAGEMENT (POM) MAJOR

Every process in a company's operations—inventory purchasing, receiving, quality control, production, and shipping—can be disrupted by an information technology security breach or an IT security breach at a business partner. Any weak link in supply chain management or enterprise resource management systems puts the entire chain at risk. Companies may be held liable for IT security failures that affect other companies.

Production operations management professionals decide whether to outsource (or offshore) manufacturing operations. In some cases, these operations are sent overseas to countries that do not have strict labour laws. This situation raises serious ethical questions. For example, is it ethical to hire people as employees in countries with poor working conditions in order to reduce labour costs? POM managers must answer other difficult questions: To what extent do security efforts reduce productivity? Are incremental improvements in security worth the additional costs?

FOR THE HUMAN RESOURCES (HR) MANAGEMENT MAJOR

Ethics is critically important to HR managers. HR policies describe the appropriate use of information technologies in the workplace. Questions arise such as: Can employees use the Internet, e-mail, or chat systems for personal purposes while at work? Is it ethical to monitor employees? If so, how? How much? How often? HR managers must formulate and enforce such policies and at the same time maintain trusting relationships between employees and management.

HR managers also have responsibilities to secure confidential employee data and provide a non-hostile work environment. In addition, they must ensure that all employees explicitly verify that they understand the company's information security policies and procedures.

FOR THE MANAGEMENT INFORMATION SYSTEMS (MIS) MAJOR

Ethics might be more important for MIS personnel than for anyone else in the organization because they have control of the information assets. They also have control over a huge amount of personal information on all employees. As a result, the MIS function must be held to the highest ethical standards.

The MIS function provides the security infrastructure that protects the organization's information assets. This function is critical to the success of the organization, even though it is almost invisible until an attack succeeds. All application development, network deployment, and introduction of new information technologies have to be guided by IT security considerations. MIS personnel must customize the risk exposure security model to help the company identify security risks and prepare responses to security incidents and disasters.

Senior executives look to the MIS function for help in meeting Sarbanes-Oxley requirements, particularly in detecting "significant deficiencies" or "material weaknesses" in internal controls and remediating them. Other functional areas also look to the MIS function to help them meet their security responsibilities.

SUMMARY

1. **Describe and provide examples of the major ethical issues related to information technology, with a focus on privacy.**

   The major ethical issues related to IT are privacy, accuracy, property (including intellectual property), and accessibility to information. Privacy may be violated when data are held in databases or transmitted over networks. Privacy policies that address issues of data collection, data accuracy, and data confidentiality can help organizations avoid legal problems. Intellectual property is the intangible property created by individuals or corporations that is protected under trade secret, patent, and copyright laws. The most common intellectual property concerns related to IT deals with software. Copying software without paying the owner is a copyright violation, and it is a major problem for software vendors.

2. **Identify the many threats to information security.**

   There are numerous threats to information security, which fall into the general categories of unintentional and intentional. Unintentional threats include human errors, environmental hazards, and computer system failures. Intentional threats include espionage, extortion, vandalism, theft, software attacks, and compromises to intellectual property. Software attacks include viruses, worms, Trojan horses, logic bombs, back doors, denial-of-service, alien software, and phishing. A growing threat is cyber-crime, which includes identity theft and phishing attacks.

3. **Explain methods used to protect information systems, including the role of planning for disaster recovery and IT auditing.**

Information systems are protected with a wide variety of controls such as security procedures, physical guards, and detection software. Management is responsible for the control environment, the attitudes, and the policies used as a framework to establish controls. General controls include controls for the prevention, deterrence, detection, damage control, recovery, and correction of information systems. The major types of general controls include physical controls, access controls, administrative controls, and communications controls. Application controls include input, processing, and output controls.

Preparation for disaster recovery specifically addresses how to avoid, plan for, and quickly recover from a disaster. Information systems auditing is a specialization that helps financial, internal, government, or tax auditors evaluate or assess controls or compliance with procedures or legislation. A detailed internal and external IT audit may involve hundreds of issues and can be supported by both software and checklists.

KEY TERMS

access controls, 92

accountability, 70

adware, 87

alien software, 86

anti-malware systems (antivirus software), 95

application controls, 91

audit, 100

authentication, 92

authorization, 92

back door (trap door), 85

biometrics, 92

blacklisting, 96

brute force attack, 85

certificate authority, 97

code of ethics, 70

cold site, 99

communications controls (network controls), 94

control environment, 90

controls, 90

controls evaluation, 90

cookies, 87

copyright, 84

cyber-crime, 77

cyber-terrorism, 88

cyber-warfare, 88

demilitarized zone (DMZ), 95

denial-of-service attack, 85

dictionary attack, 85

digital certificate, 97

digital dossier, 73

distributed denial-of-service (DDoS), 89

electronic surveillance, 73

employee monitoring systems, 98

encryption, 96

ethics, 70

exposure, 78

firewall, 94

general controls, 91

hot site, 99

identity theft, 84

information systems controls, 78

intellectual property, 84

intrusion detection system, 96

keystroke loggers (keyloggers), 87

least privilege, 93

logical controls, 92

liability, 70

logic bomb, 85

malware, 80

network controls (communications controls), 94

off-site data storage, 99

opt-in model, 74

opt-out model, 74

pass phrase, 93

password, 80

password attack, 85

patent, 84

penetration test, 89

phishing attack, 85

physical controls, 91

piracy, 84

privacy, 73

privacy codes, 74

privacy policies, 74

privilege, 93

profiling, 73

public-key encryption, 97

DISCUSSION QUESTIONS

1. Access the Computer Ethics Institute's website at *www.cpsr.org/issues/ethics/cei*. The site offers the "Ten Commandments of Computer Ethics." Should any others be added?
2. What would you do if you purchased a computer that had confidential information about individuals stored on it?
3. Why are computer systems so vulnerable?
4. Why should information security be of prime concern to management?
5. Compare information security in an organization with insuring a house.
6. Why are authentication and authorization important to e-commerce?
7. Why is cross-border cyber-crime expanding rapidly? Discuss possible solutions.
8. Discuss why the Sarbanes-Oxley Act and its Canadian equivalent, Bill 198, the Budget Measures Act, are having an impact on information security.
9. What types of user authentication are used at your university and/or place of work? Do these authentication measures seem to be effective? What if a higher level of authentication were implemented? Would it be worth it, or would it decrease productivity?

PROBLEM-SOLVING ACTIVITIES

1. Complete the computer ethics quiz at *http://web.cs.bgsu.edu/maner/xxicee/html/welcome.htm*.

2. An information security manager routinely monitored the web surfing among her company's employees. She discovered that many employees were visiting the "sinful six" websites. (Note: The sinful six are websites with material related to pornography, gambling, hate, illegal activities, tastelessness, and violence). She then prepared a list of the employees and their surfing histories and gave the list to management. Some managers punished their employees. Some employees, in turn, objected to the monitoring, claiming that they should have a right to privacy.
   a. Is monitoring of web surfing by managers ethical? (It is legal.) Support your answer.
   b. Is employee web surfing on the "sinful six" ethical? Support your answer.

c. Is the security manager's submission of the list of abusers to management ethical? Why or why not?

d. Is punishing the abusers ethical? Why or why not? If yes, then what types of punishment are acceptable?

e. What should the company do in order to rectify the situation?

3. Frank Abignale, the criminal played by Leonardo di Caprio in the motion picture *Catch Me If You Can*, ended up in prison. However, when he left prison, he went to work as a consultant to many companies on matters of fraud.

a. Why do so many companies not report computer crimes?

b. Why do these companies hire the perpetrators (if caught) as consultants? Is this a good idea?

c. You are the CEO of a company. Discuss the ethical implications of hiring Frank Abignale as a consultant to your company.

4. Assume that the daily probability of a tornado in Brampton, Ontario, is .07 percent. The chance of your computer centre being damaged during such a tornado is 5.0 percent. If the centre is damaged, the average estimated damage will be $4.0 million.

a. Calculate the expected loss in dollars.

b. An insurance agent is willing to insure your facility for an annual fee of $25,000. Analyze the offer and discuss whether to accept it.

5. A critical problem is assessing how far a company is legally obligated to go in order to secure personal data. Because there is no such thing as perfect security (i.e., there is always more that you can do), resolving this question can significantly affect cost.

a. When are security measures that a company implements sufficient to comply with its obligations?

b. Is there any way for a company to know if its security measures are sufficient? Can you devise a method for any organization to determine if its security measures are sufficient?

6. A company receives 50,000 messages each year. Currently, the organization has no firewalls. On average, there are two successful hackings each year. Each successful hacking results in a loss to the company of about $150,000. A firewall is proposed at an initial cost of $75,000 and an annual maintenance fee of $6,000. The estimated useful life is three years. The chance that an intruder will break through this firewall is 0.00002 percent. In such a case, there is a 30 percent chance that the damage will total $100,000, a 50 percent chance that the damage will total $200,000, and a 20 percent chance that there will be no damage at all.

a. Should management buy this firewall?

b. An improved firewall that is 99.9988 percent effective and that costs $90,000, with a useful life of three years and an annual maintenance cost of $18,000, is available. Should the company purchase this firewall instead of the first one?

7. Enter *www.scambusters.org*. Find out what the organization does. Learn about e-mail scams and website scams. Report your findings.

8. Visit *www.rcmp-grc.gc.ca/qc/services/gict-itcu/accueil-gict-itcu-home-eng.htm* (the RCMP Integrated Technological Crime Unit) and find out about the types of information technology crime that the RCMP investigates. Prepare a report for your class.

9. Enter *www.alltrustnetworks.com* and search for other vendors of biometrics. Describe the devices they make that can be used to control access to information systems. Prepare a list of products and major capabilities of each.

10. Software piracy is a global problem. Access the following websites: *www.bsa.org* and *www.microsoft.com/piracy*. What can organizations do to mitigate this problem? Are some organizations dealing with the problem better than others?

11. Go to *http://crazedmonkey.com/toronto-transit-map/*. This map was created by combining data from other sources. Is it legal? Why or why not?

TEAM ASSIGNMENTS

1. Access *www.fcac-acfc.gc.ca* to learn more about how financial organizations would work together to improve security over credit cards. Search the Internet to look for statistics about credit card fraud. Provide a report for your class.

2. Read the article: "The Security Tools You Need" at *www.pcworld.com/downloads/collection/collid,1525/files.html*. Each team should download a security product and discuss its pros and cons for the class. Be sure to take a look at all the comments posted about this article.

INFORMATION SECURITY AT THE INTERNATIONAL FUND FOR ANIMAL WELFARE

THE BUSINESS PROBLEM

The International Fund for Animal Welfare (*www. ifaw.org*) is the world's leading international animal welfare organization. The nonprofit organization contends that "the fate and future of all animals on Earth are inextricably linked to mankind." IFAW has approximately 375 experienced campaigners, legal and political experts, and internationally acclaimed scientists working from offices in 15 countries. The organization targets everything from baby seal hunts in Canada to the illegal trade in elephant tusks and rhinoceros horns in Africa.

IFAW has three characteristics that impact the organization's information security. First, as an extremely dispersed organization, IFAW must deal with information security on a large international scale. Second, IFAW's mobile users carry laptops that must be protected for use outside IFAW's network yet remain safe enough to return to the network without causing damage when the user returns from trips out in the field. Third, IFAW is a controversial force in conservation and therefore finds itself targeted by individuals, organizations, and even governments that object to the organization's activities.

In one instance, during the Canadian baby seal hunt, IFAW experienced probing attacks against its users' laptops when they attended the watch observation mission on Prince Edward Island. In another case, IFAW encountered denial-of-service attacks from dozens of Japanese servers because IFAW operatives were performing DNA analysis of whale meat found in a Tokyo fishmonger's shop in support of the organization's anti-whaling position. IFAW has also been targeted by custom-built malicious software designed to attack the organization. The malware was delivered from some governments specifically for the purposes of spying on IFAW's operations.

THE SOLUTION

Because IFAW has been the target of custom attacks, the organization is aware of the problems associated with relying exclusively on anti-malware software to protect its computers. Unfortunately, anti-malware software offers little protection against unknown malware because it relies on the digital signatures of known malware discovered by security researchers. If these researchers do not uncover a particular malware, they cannot record a digital signature and cannot protect the customer.

To protect its information assets, IFAW still uses commercial anti-malware software, despite its limitations. However, IFAW also uses intrusion detection software from SourceFire (*www.sourcefire.com*) and has installed network access control software called Procurve from Hewlett-Packard (*www.procurve.com*). IFAW's most effective defence, though, has been whitelisting technology. Rather than blocking out known malware and missing all unknown malware, whitelisting allows only known "good" software programs to run while preventing all other programs from running. IFAW selected Check Point Endpoint Security (*www. checkpoint.com*) to implement whitelisting.

THE RESULTS

Using the Check Point software, IFAW implemented very restrictive controls on the software programs it allows to run on its hardware. For the whitelisting software to work, the organization had to decide on every application that needed to be run on any of its computers. If a program is not whitelisted, it will not run until someone in IFAW's IT department allows it to run.

One unexpected result was that IFAW was able to use the whitelisting system to identify and segregate unknown malware—malware that was not recognized by IFAW's anti-malware software. The whitelisting system immediately reduced the number of infections and exploitations of security vulnerabilities on the organization's computers. In fact, security incidents dropped by some 75 percent. In addition, the whitelisting system enabled IFAW to improve its software licensing compliance because the organization now knew exactly what software was running on its computers.

One problem remained. Even though IFAW had success with its various defences, the organization still had to manage computers that it did not own. Many users who belong to partner organizations need to connect to IFAW's network. As a result, IFAW policies balance network access with security. IFAW now gives its partners bare minimum necessary access to its network and closely monitors users from its partner organizations.

Sources: Compiled from M. Cobb, "The Value of Application Whitelists," *www.searchsecurity.com*, November 12, 2008; E. Chickowski, "Wildlife Organization Tames Security Endpoints," *Baseline Magazine*, June 18, 2008; "IFAW Captures Total Security with Check Point Endpoint Security," Check Point Case Study, *www.checkpoint.com*; M. Hamblen, "Survey: eBay Auctions Allow Elephant Ivory Trading," *Computerworld*, May 17, 2007; *www.ifaw.org*, accessed January 15, 2009.

QUESTIONS
1. Does the whitelisting process place more of a burden on the IT group at IFAW? Why or why not? Support your answer.
2. Analyze the risk involved in IFAW's allowing users from its partner organizations to access the IFAW network.

Web Resources

Student website www.wiley.com/canada/rainer

- Web quizzes
- Lecture slides in PowerPoint

- Author podcasts
- Interactive Case: Ruby's Club assignments

ALL OF THE ABOVE AND...

- E-book
- Manager videos
- Vocabulary flash cards

- Pre- and post-lecture quizzes
- Microsoft Office 2007 lab manual and projects

DEVELOPING INFORMATION SECURITY MEASURES FOR RUBY'S CLUB

Go to the Ruby's Club link at the Student Companion website or WileyPLUS for information about your current internship assignment. You will investigate security policies at other clubs, make suggestions for Ruby's information security system, and build security measures into the spreadsheet that currently maintains member information.

4 DATA, INFORMATION, AND KNOWLEDGE MANAGEMENT

LEARNING OBJECTIVES

1. Recognize the importance of data, the issues involved in managing them and understand the data life cycle.

2. Explain the advantages of the database approach.

3. Describe the main characteristics of the relational database model.

4. Explain how a data warehouse operates and how it supports decision making.

5. Define data governance and explain how it helps produce high-quality data.

6. Define knowledge, and differentiate between explicit and tacit knowledge.

CASE 4.1

COFCO CHINA FOODS LIMITED ADOPTS A NEW DATABASE MANAGEMENT SYSTEM

THE BUSINESS PROBLEM

COFCO Group is one of China's largest enterprises, with over 100,000 employees, and it specializes in importing and exporting food products. One of its subsidiaries, China Foods Ltd. is the market leader in the food industry, selling wines, oils, confectionery, and other food products. Its brands are among the most widely known among Chinese consumers: Great Wall wine, Fu Lin Men oil, Le Conte chocolate, and Huang Zhong Huang Shaoxing rice wine are but some examples. China Foods Limited is also the official partner of Coca-Cola, producing and distributing its products all across China.

China Foods Ltd. grew rapidly through a number of mergers and acquisitions. This created a number of problems, especially with regards to integrating the information systems of the newly acquired subsidiaries. Data errors, duplication, and data inconsistencies across subsidiaries became everyday problems. Data arrived at headquarters in different formats, and times

to report was not standardized, so one business unit could report sales data at the beginning of one month and another subsidiary at the end of the same month. This made it very difficult for managers to know exactly what was happening in the business at that time. At the end of the fiscal year, problems were even more excruciating as managers at China Foods Ltd. could not access the original source data of figures that had been already consolidated centrally.

As an illustration, employees in the finance department used to enter most of their daily data manually, a repetitive task that was very error prone. In another example, because of a lack of unified information systems across subsidiaries, purchasing agents could not take advantage of aggregating purchases and negotiation power.

THE IT SOLUTION

China Foods Limited quickly realized that the problems could only be fixed by integrating the systems from all of its factories, subsidiaries, and headquarters. To accomplish this task, the company decided to invest in a new ERP system supported by a centralized database management system. The new database management system had to be able to perform data analysis quickly and with minimal requirements in terms of database administration workload. As a result, China Foods Ltd. selected IBM's DB2 technology as the core database.

Sources: Compiled from "COFCO China Foods Ltd. Enters a New Era in Data Management and Business Intelligence," IBM Case Study, January 14, 2010; "COFCO Food Sales & Distribution Company Limited Selected as One of the Leading Top 500 Informatized Enterprises in China for 2007," news release, March 22, 2008 (*www.chinafoodsltd.com*), accessed April 28, 2010; SAP website (*www.sap.com/china/*), accessed April 26, 2010.

WHAT DO YOU THINK?

1. Why has data management become so important for today's organizations?
2. What are the potential benefits of investing in database management technology?
3. What are the technological and managerial challenges of managing a large database management system such as the one implemented at COFCO China Foods Ltd.?

Chapter Preview

The case of COFCO's China Foods Ltd. represents the very real problems that almost every business faces as it grows, regarding one of its most valuable resources: data. Data problems become even more pronounced when we consider the incredibly rapid increase in the amount of data that organizations capture and store. The opportunity for errors in the data is increasing exponentially as businesses expand. Increasingly, more and more businesses, like COFCO, are investing in database technology to manage their valuable data so that they can better support their business processes and ultimately improve profitability.

But why should you learn about data management? The reason is that you will have an important role in the development of database applications. The structure and content of your organization's database depends on how the users look at their business activities. For example, when database developers in a firm's MIS group build a database, they use a tool called entity-relationship (ER) modelling. This tool creates a model of how users view a business activity. You must understand how to interpret an ER model so you can examine whether the developers have captured your business activity correctly.

We begin this chapter by discussing the multiple problems involved in managing data and the database approach that organizations use to solve those problems. We then show how database management systems enable organizations to access and use the data in databases. We will also discuss how businesses manage historical data by using data warehouses and the importance of data governance in ensuring the correct functioning of databases. We close the chapter with a look at knowledge management.

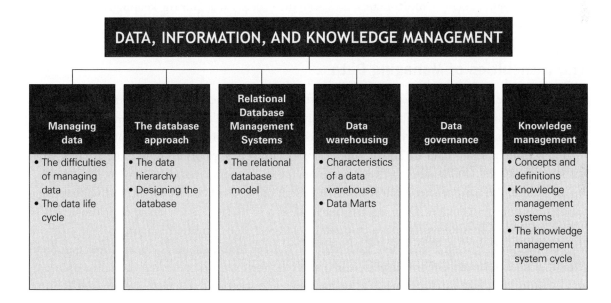

4.1 Managing Data

Between 2006 and 2010, the amount of digital information created, captured, and replicated each year will add about 18 million times as much information as currently exists in all the books ever written. Images captured by more than a billion devices around the world, from digital cameras and camera phones to medical scanners and security cameras, make up the largest component of this digital information.

We are accumulating data and information at a frenzied pace from such diverse sources as company documents, e-mails, web pages, credit card swipes, phone messages, stock trades, memos, address books, and radiology scans. New sources of data and information include blogs, podcasts, videocasts (think of YouTube), digital video surveillance, and radio frequency identification (RFID) tags and other wireless sensors (discussed in Chapter 7). We are awash in data, and we have to manage them and make sense of them. To deal with the growth and the diverse nature of digital data, organizations must employ sophisticated techniques for information management.

Information technologies and systems support organizations in managing—that is, acquiring, organizing, storing, accessing, analyzing, and interpreting—data. As we discussed in Chapter 1, when these data are managed properly, they first become *information* and then *knowledge*. As we have seen, information and knowledge are valuable organizational resources that can provide a competitive advantage. In this chapter, we explore the process whereby data are transformed first into information and then into knowledge.

Few business professionals are comfortable making or justifying business decisions that are not based on solid information. This is especially true today, when modern information systems make access to that information quick and easy. For example, we have technology that puts data in a form that managers and analysts can easily understand. These professionals can then access the data themselves and analyze them according to their needs using a variety of tools, thereby producing information. They can then apply their experience to use this information to address a business problem, thus producing knowledge. Knowledge management, enabled by information technology, captures and stores knowledge in forms that all organizational employees can access and apply, creating the flexible, powerful "learning organization."

The first requisite to providing sound information that is useful to managers and staff is that data need to be of high quality, meaning that they should be accurate, complete, timely, consistent, accessible, relevant, and concise. Unfortunately, however, the process of acquiring, keeping, and managing data is becoming increasingly difficult. Let's see the reasons why.

The Difficulties of Managing Data

Because data are processed in several stages and often in several places, they are frequently subject to problems and difficulties. Managing data in organizations is difficult for many reasons.

First, the amount of data increases exponentially with time. Much historical data must be kept for a long time, and new data are added rapidly. For example, to support millions of customers, large firms such as COFCO China Foods Ltd. have to manage many terabytes (1 trillion bytes) of data.

In addition, data are scattered throughout organizations and collected by many individuals using various methods and devices. Data are frequently stored in numerous servers and locations and in different computing systems, databases, formats, and human and computer languages.

Another problem is that data come from multiple sources: internal sources (for example, corporate databases and company documents), personal sources (for example, personal thoughts, opinions, and experiences), and external sources (for example, commercial databases, government reports, and corporate websites). Data also come from the Web, in the form of clickstream data. **Clickstream data** are data that visitors and customers produce when they visit a website and click on hyperlinks. Clickstream data provide a trail of the users' activities in the website, including user behaviour and browsing patterns.

Adding to these problems is the fact that new sources of data, such as blogs, podcasts, videocasts, and RFID tags and other wireless sensors, are constantly being developed. Many of these new data are unstructured, meaning that their content cannot be truly represented in a traditional computer record. Examples of unstructured data are digital images, digital video, voice packets, and musical notes in an MP3 or iPod file.

Another issue with data is that data degrade over time. For example, customers move to new addresses or change their names, companies go out of business or are bought, new products are developed, employees are hired or fired, companies expand into new countries, and so on.

Data are also subject to *data rot*. Data rot refers primarily to problems with the media on which the data are stored. Over time, temperature, humidity, and exposure to light can cause physical problems with storage media and thus make it difficult to access the data. The second aspect of data rot is that finding the machines needed to access the data can be difficult. For example, nowadays it is difficult to find PCs with a floppy disk reader.

Another problem in managing data is data errors—information that is out of date, inaccurate, or technically corrupt. IT's About Business 4.1 illustrates the case of Mediatech Corp. and its efforts to reduce data errors.

IT'S ABOUT BUSINESS 4.1
MEDIATECH DIRECT WORKS TO REMOVE DATA ERRORS

Your *data shadow* is the collection of traceable data that are left behind after you use technologies such as credit cards, debit cards, toll booths, smart phones, and the Internet. As you use these technologies over time, your data shadow constantly increases. For example, when you visit a popular website such as Amazon and make a purchase using a credit card, several pieces of data regarding your transaction are captured, stored, and remain as a digital record of the activity. The data that are preserved may be used for any number of related business purposes.

For Mediatech Direct (*www.mediatechdirect. co.uk*), a direct mail fulfillment company, the most common use of its customers' data shadows involves direct mail marketing. Therefore, the most important data in the Mediatech systems involve customer contact information—addresses, phone numbers, and e-mail addresses. Mediatech uses these contact data to establish points of contact with its customers. These data constitute the vital link that provides sales opportunities, and ultimately revenue, for the company. Clearly, then, maintaining accurate data is critical to Mediatech's success.

In 2008, Mediatech dramatically expanded its capabilities and scope of operations. Although this expansion created new profit potential, it also contributed to widespread data errors. The company discovered that much of its customer data had become degraded; that is, the data were either incomplete or obsolete. In many cases, the Mediatech data warehouse contained multiple entries for the same customer, with different addresses, phone numbers, and e-mail contacts. In other cases, customer contacts were incomplete, lacked postal street addresses, or contained only partial e-mail addresses. In all cases, the results were the same, namely a lost point of contact and thus a lost sales opportunity. An analysis of the Mediatech data warehouse estimated that almost 5 percent of those data degraded each month. If that rate of error was left unchecked, within one

year approximately half of all of customer contact information would be fully deteriorated.

Mediatech chose to address its data errors by outsourcing to Capscan (*www.capscan.com*), an international data integrity service. Capscan applied a comprehensive data-scanning and data-matching service to Mediatech's data warehouse. The Capscan system identified redundant, fragmented, and incorrect data and cleaned them from the data warehouse.

In the first round of data cleaning, Capscan reconciled more than 3,000 customer records in just one customer data file. Each record that was reconciled had contained either incomplete or incorrect customer contact information. Mediatech estimated that reconciling the data in this single file would save the company more than $250,000 annually. It projects similar cost savings in each of its other 12 customer data files. In fact, the company estimates that overall cost savings through the elimination of data errors could approach $3 million per year.

Sources: Compiled from J. Buchanan, "Mediatech Direct," *Direct Response*, July/August, 2007; "Data Quality," BCS website (*www.bcs.org*), August 2007; R. Whiting, "Hamstrung by Defective Data," *InformationWeek*, May 8, 2006; "Poor Quality Data Biggest CIO Headache," *BusinessWeek*, May 4, 2006; S. Stahl, "Data Quality Is Everyone's Problem," *InformationWeek*, August 30, 2004; "Mediatech Direct," Capscan Customer Case Study, Capscan website (*www.capscan.com*), accessed March 11, 2009; "IBM Cognos Data Quality Rapid Assessment Service," *www.cognos.com*, accessed March 19, 2009.

QUESTIONS

1. How important are accurate data for on-line businesses?
2. Is technology sufficient to guarantee that data errors will not occur? If not, then what other factors should a business need to consider?
3. Provide examples of cost savings that can be achieved by reducing data errors.

Data security, quality, and integrity are critical, yet easily jeopardized and make the process of managing data more difficult. In addition, legal requirements relating to data differ among countries and industries, and they change periodically.

Because of these problems, data are difficult to manage. As a result, organizations are using databases and data warehouses to manage their data more efficiently and effectively in a process that is referred to as the data life cycle, which we discuss next.

The Data Life Cycle

Businesses run on data that have been processed into information and knowledge. Managers then apply this knowledge to business problems and opportunities. Businesses transform data into knowledge and solutions in several ways. The general process is illustrated in Figure 4.1 and is referred to as the data life cycle. It shows how organizations process and manage data to make decisions, generate knowledge, and use them in a variety of applications. It starts with the collection of data from various sources.

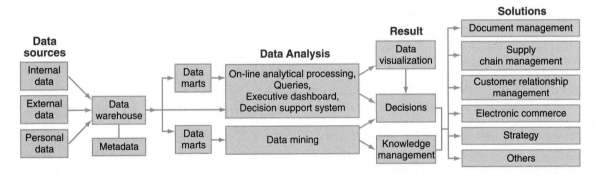

FIGURE 4.1 Data life cycle.

These sources can be internal data (e.g., employee names, social insurance numbers), external data (e.g., data from Statistics Canada, the Bank of Canada, newspapers), and personal data (e.g., opinions, sales estimates from employees). External and internal data can be collected manually or by the assistance of technology. For example, grocery stores use point-of-sale systems with scan technology to enter sales data.

The data are stored in one or more databases. Selected data from the organization's databases are then processed to fit the format of a data warehouse or data mart. Users then access the data in the warehouse or data mart for analysis. Then, as we will see in Chapter 11, the analysis is performed with data-analysis tools, which look for patterns, and with intelligent systems, which support data interpretation.

These activities ultimately generate knowledge that can be used to support decision making. Therefore, both the data (at various times during the process) and the knowledge (derived at the end of the process) must be presented to users. This presentation can be accomplished by using different visualization tools. The created knowledge can also be stored in an organizational knowledge base and then used, together with decision support tools, to provide solutions to organizational problems. The remaining sections of this chapter will examine the elements and the process shown in Figure 4.1 in greater detail starting with the database approach.

BEFORE YOU GO ON...

1. Describe the data life cycle.
2. What are the various sources for data?

4.2 The Database Approach

A **database management system (DBMS)** is a set of programs that provides users with tools to add, delete, access, and analyze data stored in one location. An organization can access the data by using query and reporting tools that are part of the DBMS or by using application programs specifically written to access the data. DBMSs also provide the mechanisms for maintaining the integrity of stored data, managing security and user access, and recovering information if the system fails. Because databases and DBMSs are essential to all areas of business, they must be carefully managed.

Figure 4.2 illustrates a university database. Note that university applications from the registrar's office, the accounting department, and the athletics department access data through the database management system.

Using databases eliminates many problems that arose from previous methods of storing and accessing data. For example, in our opening case, after the adoption of the new database management system, China Foods Ltd. staff no longer had to input data manually, which resulted in significant time savings and reduction of data errors. Warehouse and inventory data are now accurate and up-to-date. Purchasing data are now shared and unified across all business units, allowing China Foods Ltd. to take advantage of increased bargaining power and forecast production levels with more accuracy. In addition, the new database system provides China Foods Ltd. with consolidated sales data that can be examined by product, customer, region, or factory, allowing managers to compare performance between locations and identify areas of improvement across the business.

In general, database management systems contribute to minimize the following problems:

- *Data redundancy:* The same data are stored in many places.
- *Data isolation:* Applications cannot access data associated with other applications.
- *Data inconsistency:* Various copies of the data do not agree.

In addition, database systems maximize the following issues:

- *Data security:* Because data are essential to organizations, databases have extremely high security measures in place to deter mistakes and attacks (recall our discussion in Chapter 3).
- *Data integrity:* Data meet certain constraints, such as no alphabetic characters in a social insurance number field.
- *Data independence:* Applications and data are independent of one another (that is, applications and data are not linked to each other, meaning that applications can be designed to access the same data).

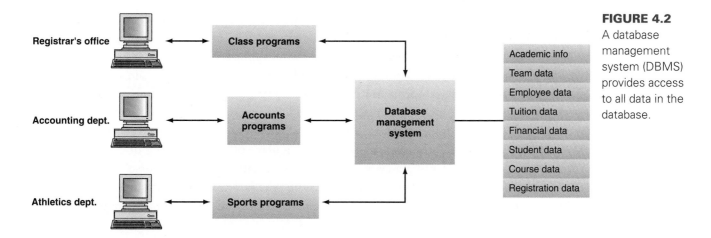

FIGURE 4.2
A database management system (DBMS) provides access to all data in the database.

IT's About Business 4.2 illustrates the example of using the database approach at one of Canada's largest hospitals in order to manage patient's records.

IT'S ABOUT BUSINESS 4.2
SUNNYBROOK HOSPITAL TURNS TO ELECTRONIC MEDICAL RECORDS

Sunnybrook Health Sciences Centre is one of the largest health institutions in Canada. With over 10,000 staff and volunteers, it serves more than one million patients each year across its three campuses. Originally a war veteran hospital, Sunnybrook has become known for its excellence in patient care, education, and research.

Sunnybrook recently announced that it will begin to offer physicians, nurses, social workers, therapists, and support personnel access to a new electronic medical records (EMR) system in an effort to reduce costs and improve the quality of care. The potential benefits are very promising if one considers that retrieving a paper chart can take up to 48 hours and can only be accessed by one user. In contrast, the new EMR system will provide immediate electronic access to multiple users.

Experts also claim that EMRs can help eliminate duplicate medical tests and incorrect or lost information, while reducing administrative costs and helping to prevent numerous serious illnesses or deaths that result from prescription or other medical errors each year. Under the manual system, tests or X-rays had to be repeated when the original results were lost or misplaced.

The project is scheduled to start with the Women and Babies unit and will continue with the rest of the hospital in subsequent years. The total cost of implementation has been estimated at $2.2 million.

Sources: Compiled from "CGI Selected by Sunnybrook Health Sciences Centre for Health Enterprise Content Management," CGI new release, February 23, 2010; K. Lau, "Sunnybrook Digitizes Patient Records," *ComputerWorld Canada*, February 25, 2010; Sunnybrook website (*www.sunnybrook.ca*), accessed April 28, 2010.

QUESTIONS
1. What additional advantages result from storing your health records in a database? Give examples.
2. What are the disadvantages of storing your health records in a database? Give examples.
3. Why is it difficult to build a nationwide electronic medical record system?

The Data Hierarchy

Data in databases are arranged in a hierarchy in order to make them more understandable and useful. This hierarchy that begins with bits and proceeds all the way to databases (see Figure 4.3). A **bit** (*bi*nary dig*it*) represents the smallest unit of data a computer can process. The term "binary" means that a bit can consist only of a 0 or a 1. A group of eight bits, called a **byte**, represents a single character. A byte can be a letter, a number, or a symbol.

As we move to larger components of the hierarchy, there are two sets of terms that have developed and are in common usage. In addition to the terms we describe next, there are additional labels that have evolved from the use of entity-relationship modelling, described later in this chapter.

A logical grouping of characters into a word, a small group of words, or an identification number is called a **field**. For example, a student's name in a university's computer files would appear in the "name" field, and her or his social insurance number would appear in the "Social Insurance Number" field. Fields can also contain data other than text and numbers. A field can contain an image, or any other type of media. For example, a motor vehicle department's licensing database could contain a person's photograph. A logical grouping of related fields, such as the student's name, the courses taken, the date, and the grade, compose a **record**. A logical grouping of related records is called a **file** or **table**. For example, the records from a particular course, consisting of course number, professor's name, and students' grades, would constitute a data file for that course. A logical grouping of related tables would constitute a **database**. Using the same example, the student course table could be grouped with tables on students' personal histories and financial backgrounds to create a student database.

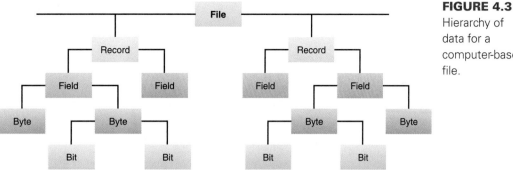

FIGURE 4.3
Hierarchy of data for a computer-based file.

Users play a critical role in the development of new databases, especially in the design stage. As such, we now turn our attention to database design.

Designing The Database

To be valuable, a database must be organized so that users can retrieve, analyze, and understand the data they need. A key to designing an effective database is the data model. A **data model** is a diagram that represents entities in the database and their relationships. Data modelling resulted in new terminology being used to describe what had previously been known as a field or a record, as the concept of information organization changed. An **entity** (previously known as a record) is a person, place, thing, or event—such as a customer, an employee, or a product—about which information is maintained. Entities can typically be identified in the user's work environment. A record generally describes an entity. Each characteristic or quality of a particular entity (previously called a field) is called an **attribute** in the context of data modelling. For example, if our entities were a customer, an employee, and a product, entity attributes would include customer name, employee number, and product colour.

Every record in a table must contain at least one attribute/field that uniquely identifies that record so that it can be retrieved, updated, and sorted. This identifier is called the **primary key**. For example, a student record at a Canadian college or university would probably use the student's ID number as its primary key. In some cases, locating a particular record requires the use of secondary keys. **Secondary keys** are other fields that have some identifying information but typically do not identify the record or entity with complete accuracy. For example, the student's major might be a secondary key if a user wanted to find all students in a particular major field of study. It should not be the primary key, however, because many students can have the same major.

Entity-Relationship Modelling

Designers plan and develop the database through a process called **entity-relationship (ER) modelling**, using an **entity-relationship (ER) diagram**. Users are likely to be asked to review an ER diagram to make sure it includes all the data they need in order to obtain the information they need to perform their job. ER diagrams consist of entities, attributes, and relationships. Entities are pictured in boxes, and relationships are shown in diamonds. The attributes for each entity are listed next to the entity, and the primary key is underlined. Figures 4.4a and 4.4b show an entity-relationship diagram.

As defined earlier, an *entity* is something that can be identified in the users' work environment. For example, consider student registration at a university. Students register for courses and register their cars for parking permits. In this example, STUDENT, PARKING PERMIT, CLASS, and PROFESSOR are entities, as shown in Figure 4.4.

Entities of a given type are grouped in **entity classes**. In our example, STUDENT, PARKING PERMIT, CLASS, and PROFESSOR are entity classes. An **instance** of an entity class is the representation

FIGURE 4.4
Entity-
relationship
diagram model.

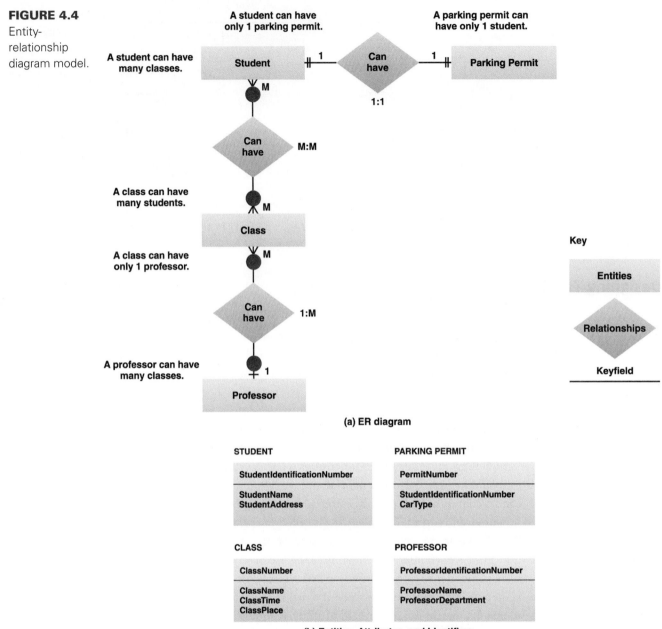

(a) ER diagram

(b) Entities, Attributes, and Identifiers

of one particular entity. Therefore, a particular STUDENT (Lihang Zhong, 145-89-7123) is an instance of the STUDENT entity class; a particular parking permit (91778) is an instance of the PARKING PERMIT entity class; a particular class (76890) is an instance of the CLASS entity class; and a particular professor (Hélène Lavoie, 115-65-7632) is an instance of the PROFESSOR entity class.

Entity instances have **identifiers**, which is another name for the primary key, attributes (or fields) that are unique to that entity instance. For example, STUDENT instances can be identified with StudentIdentificationNumber; PARKING PERMIT instances can be identified with PermitNumber; CLASS instances can be identified with ClassNumber; and PROFESSOR instances can be identified with ProfessorIdentificationNumber. These identifiers are underlined on ER diagrams, as in part (b) of Figure 4.4.

Entities have attributes, or properties, that describe the entity's characteristics. In our example, examples of attributes (i.e., fields) for STUDENT are StudentName and StudentAddress. Examples of attributes for PARKING PERMIT are StudentIdentificationNumber and CarType. Examples of attributes for CLASS are ClassName, ClassTime, and ClassPlace. Examples of attributes for

PROFESSOR are ProfessorName and ProfessorDepartment. (Note that each course at this university has one professor—there is no team teaching.)

Why is StudentIdentificationNumber an attribute of both the STUDENT and PARKING PERMIT entity classes? That is, why do we need the PARKING PERMIT entity class? If you consider all inter-linked university systems, the PARKING PERMIT entity class is needed for other applications, such as fee payments and parking tickets.

Entities are associated with one another in relationships, which can include many entities. (Remember that relationships are noted by diamonds on ER diagrams.) The number of entities in a relationship is the degree of the relationship. Relationships between two items are called *binary relationships*. There are three types of binary relationships: one-to-one, one-to-many, and many-to-many. We discuss each one below.

In a *one-to-one* (1:1) relationship, a single-entity instance of one type is related to a single-entity instance of another type. Figure 4.4 shows STUDENT–PARKING PERMIT as a 1:1 relationship that relates a single STUDENT with a single PARKING PERMIT. That is, no student has more than one parking permit, and no parking permit is issued for more than one student.

The second type of relationship, *one-to-many* (1:M), is represented by the CLASS–PROFESSOR relationship in Figure 4.4. This relationship means that a professor can have many classes, but each class can have only one professor.

The third type of relationship, *many-to-many* (M:M), is represented by the STUDENT–CLASS relationship. This M:M relationship means that a student can have many classes, and a class can have many students.

Entity-relationship modelling is valuable because it allows database designers to talk with users throughout the organization to ensure that all entities and the relationships among them are represented. This process underscores the importance of taking all users into account when designing organizational databases. Notice that all entities and relationships in our example are labelled in terms that users can understand. Now that we understand how a database is designed, we turn our attention to relational database management systems.

BEFORE YOU GO ON...

1. What is a data model?
2. What is a primary key? A secondary key?
3. What is an entity? A relationship?

4.3 Relational Database Management Systems

There are a number of different database architectures, but we focus on the relational database model because it is the most widely used. Other database models are also available such as the hierarchical, network, and object-oriented models. Popular examples of relational databases are Microsoft Access, Oracle 11g, and IBM DB2. In our opening case, COFCO China Foods Ltd. had implemented the DB2 relational database management system from IBM.

The Relational Database Model

Most business data—especially accounting and financial data—traditionally were organized into simple tables consisting of columns and rows. Tables allow people to compare information quickly by row or column. In addition, items are easy to retrieve by finding the point of intersection of a particular row and column.

The **relational database model** is based on the concept of two-dimensional tables. A relational database generally is not one big table—usually called a *flat file*—that contains all of the records and

FIGURE 4.5
Student database example.

Student Name	Student ID	Major	GPA	Graduation Date
Sally Adams	111-12-4321	Finance	2.94	5/12/2011
John Jones	420-33-9834	Accounting	3.45	12/5/2011
Jane Lee	241-35-7432	MIS	3.17	5/12/2011
Kevin Durham	021-79-6679	Economics	2.77	5/12/2011
Juan Rodriguez	335-77-5124	Marketing	3.52	12/5/2011
Stella Zubnicki	408-99-5798	Operations Man	3.37	8/5/2011
Ben Jones	422-89-0011	Finance	3.11	5/12/2011

attributes. Such a design would entail far too much data redundancy. Instead, a relational database is usually designed with a number of related tables. Each of these tables contains entities (as records listed in rows) and attributes (as fields listed in columns).

These related tables can be joined when they contain common columns. The uniqueness of the primary key tells the DBMS which records are joined with others in related tables. This feature allows users great flexibility in the variety of queries they can make. Despite these features, however, this model has some disadvantages. Because large-scale databases can be composed of many interrelated tables, the overall design can be complex and therefore have slow search and access times.

Consider the relational database example about students shown in Figure 4.5. The table contains data about the entity called students. Attributes of the entity are student name, undergraduate major, grade point average, and graduation date. The rows are the records on Sally Adams, John Jones, Jane Lee, Kevin Durham, Juan Rodriguez, Stella Zubnicki, and Ben Jones. Of course, your university keeps much more data on you than our example shows. In fact, your university's student database probably keeps hundreds of attributes on each student.

Query Languages

Requesting information from a database is the most commonly performed operation. **Structured query language (SQL)** is the most popular query language used to request information. SQL allows people to perform complicated searches by using relatively simple statements or key words. Typical key words are SELECT (to specify a desired attribute), FROM (to specify the table to be used), and WHERE (to specify conditions to apply in the query).

To understand how SQL works, imagine that a university wants to know the names of students who will graduate with honours in May 2011. The university IS staff would query the student relational database with an SQL statement such as: SELECT Student Name, FROM Student Database, WHERE Grade Point Average > 3.40 and Grade Point Average < 3.59. The SQL query would return: John Jones and Juan Rodriguez.

Another way to find information in a database is to use **query by example (QBE)**. In QBE, the user fills out a grid or template (also known as a *form*) to construct a sample or description of the data he or she wants. Users can construct a query quickly and easily by using drag-and-drop features in a DBMS such as Microsoft Access. Conducting queries in this manner is simpler than keying in SQL commands.

Data Dictionary

When a relational model is created, the **data dictionary** defines the format necessary to enter the data into the database. The data dictionary provides information on each attribute, such as its name, whether it is a key or part of a key, the type of data expected (alphanumeric, numeric, dates, and so on), and valid values. Data dictionaries can also provide information on how often the attribute should be updated, why it is needed in the database, and which business functions, applications, forms, and reports use the attribute.

Data dictionaries provide many advantages to the organization. Because they provide names and standard definitions for all attributes, they reduce the chances that the same attribute will be used in different applications but with a different name. In addition, data dictionaries enable programmers to develop programs more quickly because they don't have to create new data names.

Normalization

In order to use a relational database management system effectively, the data must be analyzed to eliminate redundant data elements. **Normalization** is a method for analyzing and reducing a relational database to its most streamlined form for minimum redundancy, maximum data integrity, and best processing performance. When data are *normalized*, attributes in the table depend only on the primary key.

As an example of normalization, consider an automotive repair garage. This business takes orders from customers who want to have their cars repaired. In this example, ORDER, PART, SUPPLIER, and CUSTOMER are entities. For this garage, there can be many PARTS in an ORDER, but each PART can come from only one SUPPLIER. In a non-normalized table (see Figure 4.6), each order would have to

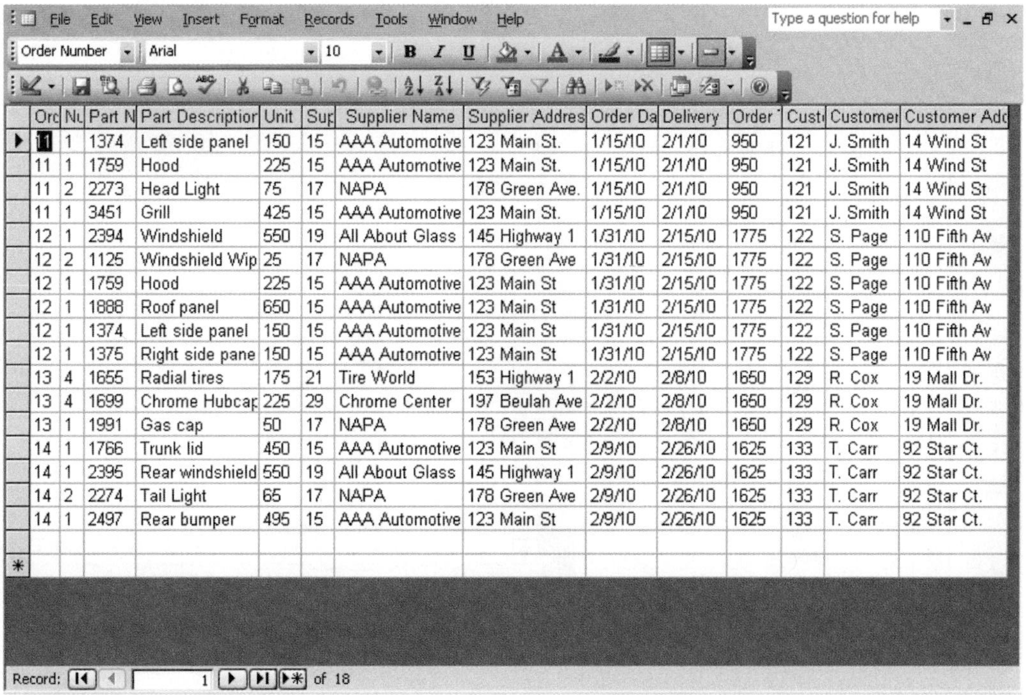

Orc	Nu	Part N	Part Descriptior	Unit	Sup	Supplier Name	Supplier Addres	Order Da	Delivery	Order T	Custo	Customer	Customer Add
11	1	1374	Left side panel	150	15	AAA Automotive	123 Main St.	1/15/10	2/1/10	950	121	J. Smith	14 Wind St
11	1	1759	Hood	225	15	AAA Automotive	123 Main St.	1/15/10	2/1/10	950	121	J. Smith	14 Wind St
11	2	2273	Head Light	75	17	NAPA	178 Green Ave.	1/15/10	2/1/10	950	121	J. Smith	14 Wind St
11	1	3451	Grill	425	15	AAA Automotive	123 Main St.	1/15/10	2/1/10	950	121	J. Smith	14 Wind St
12	1	2394	Windshield	550	19	All About Glass	145 Highway 1	1/31/10	2/15/10	1775	122	S. Page	110 Fifth Av
12	2	1125	Windshield Wip	25	17	NAPA	178 Green Ave	1/31/10	2/15/10	1775	122	S. Page	110 Fifth Av
12	1	1759	Hood	225	15	AAA Automotive	123 Main St	1/31/10	2/15/10	1775	122	S. Page	110 Fifth Av
12	1	1888	Roof panel	650	15	AAA Automotive	123 Main St	1/31/10	2/15/10	1775	122	S. Page	110 Fifth Av
12	1	1374	Left side panel	150	15	AAA Automotive	123 Main St	1/31/10	2/15/10	1775	122	S. Page	110 Fifth Av
12	1	1375	Right side pane	150	15	AAA Automotive	123 Main St	1/31/10	2/15/10	1775	122	S. Page	110 Fifth Av
13	4	1655	Radial tires	175	21	Tire World	153 Highway 1	2/2/10	2/8/10	1650	129	R. Cox	19 Mall Dr.
13	4	1699	Chrome Hubcap	225	29	Chrome Center	197 Beulah Ave	2/2/10	2/8/10	1650	129	R. Cox	19 Mall Dr.
13	1	1991	Gas cap	50	17	NAPA	178 Green Ave	2/2/10	2/8/10	1650	129	R. Cox	19 Mall Dr.
14	1	1766	Trunk lid	450	15	AAA Automotive	123 Main St	2/9/10	2/26/10	1625	133	T. Carr	92 Star Ct.
14	1	2395	Rear windshield	550	19	All About Glass	145 Highway 1	2/9/10	2/26/10	1625	133	T. Carr	92 Star Ct.
14	2	2274	Tail Light	65	17	NAPA	178 Green Ave	2/9/10	2/26/10	1625	133	T. Carr	92 Star Ct.
14	1	2497	Rear bumper	495	15	AAA Automotive	123 Main St	2/9/10	2/26/10	1625	133	T. Carr	92 Star Ct.

FIGURE 4.6 Non-normalized table.

repeat the name, description, and price of each part needed to complete the order, as well as the name and address of each supplier. This relation contains repeating groups and describes multiple entities.

The normalization process, illustrated in Figure 4.7, breaks down the non-normalized table into smaller tables: ORDER, SUPPLIER, and CUSTOMER (Figure 4.7a), ORDERED-PARTS and PART (Figure 4.7b). Each of these tables describes a single entity. This process is conceptually simpler, and it eliminates repeating data.

FIGURE 4.7 Smaller relationships broken down from the non-normal relations.

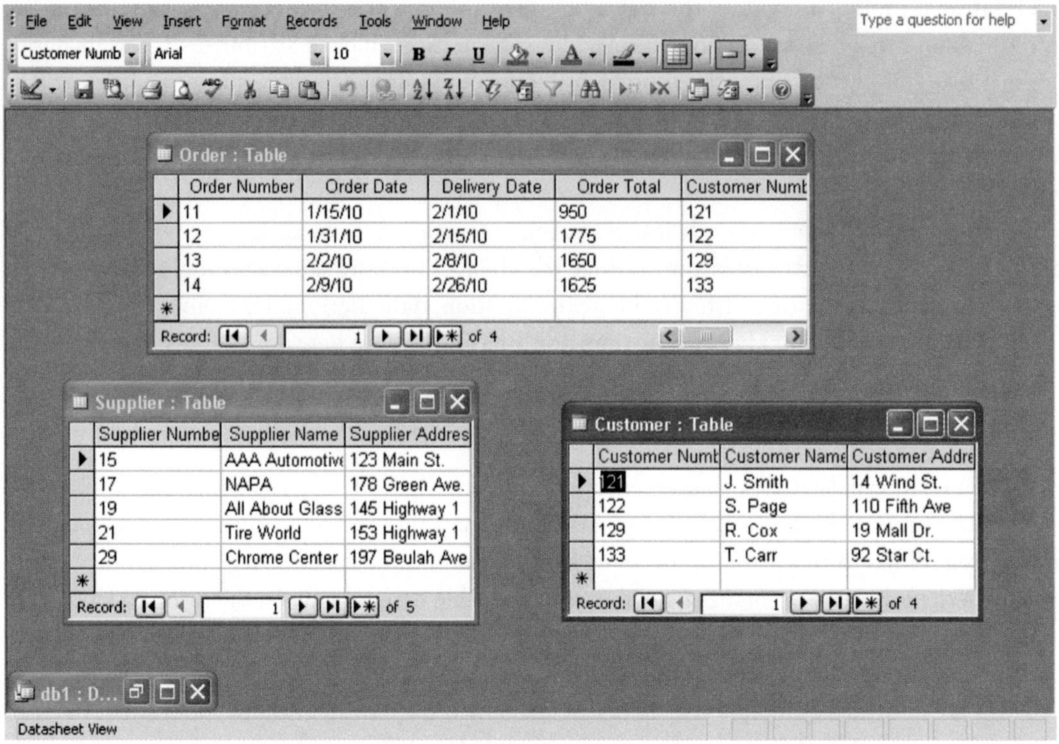

Order : Table

Order Number	Order Date	Delivery Date	Order Total	Customer Numb
11	1/15/10	2/1/10	950	121
12	1/31/10	2/15/10	1775	122
13	2/2/10	2/8/10	1650	129
14	2/9/10	2/26/10	1625	133

Supplier : Table

Supplier Numbe	Supplier Name	Supplier Addres
15	AAA Automotiv	123 Main St.
17	NAPA	178 Green Ave.
19	All About Glass	145 Highway 1
21	Tire World	153 Highway 1
29	Chrome Center	197 Beulah Ave

Customer : Table

Customer Numb	Customer Name	Customer Addre
121	J. Smith	14 Wind St.
122	S. Page	110 Fifth Ave
129	R. Cox	19 Mall Dr.
133	T. Carr	92 Star Ct.

(a)

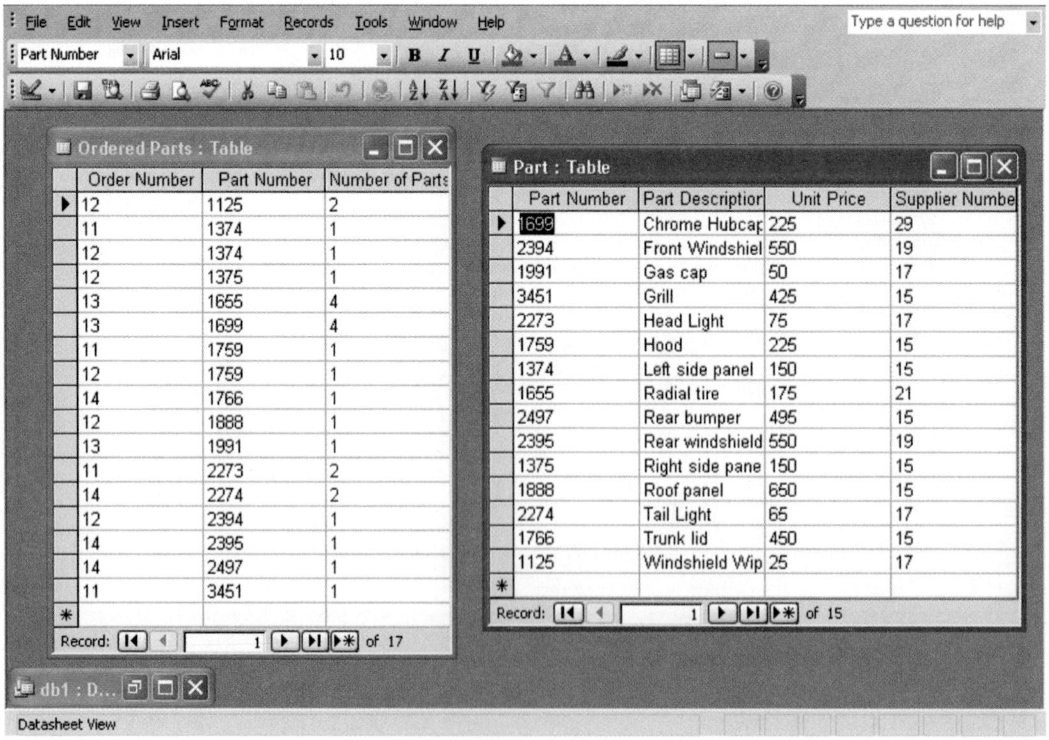

Ordered Parts : Table

Order Number	Part Number	Number of Parts
12	1125	2
11	1374	1
12	1374	1
12	1375	1
13	1655	4
13	1699	4
11	1759	1
12	1759	1
14	1766	1
12	1888	1
13	1991	1
11	2273	2
14	2274	2
12	2394	1
14	2395	1
14	2497	1
11	3451	1

Part : Table

Part Number	Part Descriptior	Unit Price	Supplier Numbe
1699	Chrome Hubcap	225	29
2394	Front Windshiel	550	19
1991	Gas cap	50	17
3451	Grill	425	15
2273	Head Light	75	17
1759	Hood	225	15
1374	Left side panel	150	15
1655	Radial tire	175	21
2497	Rear bumper	495	15
2395	Rear windshield	550	19
1375	Right side pane	150	15
1888	Roof panel	650	15
2274	Tail Light	65	17
1766	Trunk lid	450	15
1125	Windshield Wip	25	17

(b)

BEFORE YOU GO ON...
1. What are the advantages and disadvantages of relational databases?
2. What are the benefits of data dictionaries?
3. Describe how structured query language works.

4.4 Data Warehousing

Today, the most successful organizations are those that can respond quickly and flexibly to market changes and opportunities. As we saw in the opening case of COFCO China Foods Ltd., a key to this response is the effective and efficient use of data and information by managers and employees.

Access to corporate data is of vital importance for managers so they can analyze them and lead the firm in the right direction. Let's look at an example. If the manager of a local bookstore wanted to know the profit margin on used books at her store, she could find out from her database, using SQL or QBE. However, if she needed to know the trend in the profit margins on used books over the last 10 years, she would have a very difficult query to construct in SQL or QBE.

This example illustrates two reasons why organizations are building data warehouses. First, the bookstore's databases have the necessary information to answer the manager's query, but this information is not organized in a way that makes it easy for her to find what she needs. Second, the organization's databases are designed to process millions of transactions per day. Therefore, complicated queries might take a long time to answer and also might degrade the performance of the databases. As a result of these problems, companies are using data warehousing to make it easier and faster for users to access and query data.

Characteristics of a Data Warehouse

A **data warehouse** is a repository of historical data organized by subject to support decision makers in the organization. Data warehouses facilitate the analysis of data through the use of business intelligence tools such as data mining and decision support, which we will discuss in Chapter 11. The basic characteristics of a data warehouse are described below.

- *Organized by business dimension or subject.* Data are organized by subject (for example, by customer, vendor, product, price level, and region) and contain information relevant for decision support and data analysis.
- *Consistent.* Data in different databases may be encoded differently. For example, gender data may be encoded 0 and 1 in one operational system and "m" and "f" in another. In the data warehouse, though, all data must be coded in a consistent manner.
- *Historical.* The data are kept for many years so they can be used for trends, forecasting, and making comparisons over time.
- *Non-volatile.* Data do not change after they are entered into the warehouse.
- *Has the ability to use on-line analytical processing.* On-line analytical processing (OLAP) is the process of performing complex, multi-dimensional analyses of data stored in a database or data warehouse. Typically, organizational databases are oriented toward handling transactions. That is, databases use **on-line transaction processing (OLTP)**, where business transactions are processed on-line as soon as they occur. The objectives are speed and efficiency, which are critical to a successful Internet-based business operation. Data warehouses, which are not designed

to support OLTP but to support decision makers, provide better support for on-line analytical processing.

- *Multi-dimensional.* Typically the data warehouse uses a multi-dimensional data structure. Recall that relational databases store data in two-dimensional tables. In contrast, data warehouses store data in more than two dimensions. For this reason, the data are said to be stored in a **multi-dimensional structure**. A common representation for this multi-dimensional structure is the *data cube* (see Figure 4.10.)

  The data in the data warehouse are organized by *business dimensions*, which are the edges of the data cube and are subjects such as product, geographic area, and time period. Figure 4.10 provides an example of a data cube where the product dimension is composed of nuts, screws, bolts, and washers; the geographic area dimension is composed of east, west, and central; and the time period dimension is composed of 2008, 2009, and 2010. Users can view and analyze data from the perspective of these business dimensions. This analysis is intuitive because the dimensions are in business terms, easily understood by users.

- *Relationship with relational databases.* The data in data warehouses come from the company's operational databases, which can be relational databases. Figure 4.8 illustrates the process of building and using a data warehouse. The organization's data are stored in operational database management systems (left side of the figure). Using special software called extract, transform, and load (ETL), the system processes data and then stores them in a data warehouse. Not all data are necessarily transferred to the data warehouse. Frequently only a summary of the data is transferred. Within the warehouse the data are organized in a form that is easy for end users to access.

To differentiate between relational and multi-dimensional databases, suppose your company has four products (nuts, screws, bolts, and washers), which have been sold in three territories (East, West, and Central) for the previous three years (2008, 2009, and 2010). In a relational database, these sales data would look like Figures 4.9a, b, and c. In a multi-dimensional database, the data would be represented by a three-dimensional matrix (or data cube), as shown in Figure 4.10.

We would say that this matrix represents sales *dimensioned by* products and regions and year. Notice that in Figure 4.10a we can see only sales for 2010. Therefore, sales for 2009 and 2008 are

FIGURE 4.8

Data warehouse framework and views.

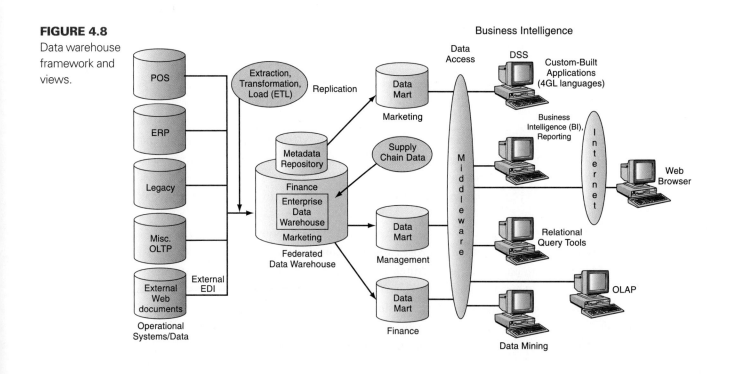

FIGURE 4.9
Relational
databases.

(a) 2008

Product	Region	Sales
Nuts	East	50
Nuts	West	60
Nuts	Central	100
Screws	East	40
Screws	West	70
Screws	Central	80
Bolts	East	90
Bolts	West	120
Bolts	Central	140
Washers	East	20
Washers	West	10
Washers	Central	30

(b) 2009

Product	Region	Sales
Nuts	East	60
Nuts	West	70
Nuts	Central	110
Screws	East	50
Screws	West	80
Screws	Central	90
Bolts	East	100
Bolts	West	130
Bolts	Central	150
Washers	East	30
Washers	West	20
Washers	Central	40

(c) 2010

Product	Region	Sales
Nuts	East	70
Nuts	West	80
Nuts	Central	120
Screws	East	60
Screws	West	90
Screws	Central	100
Bolts	East	110
Bolts	West	140
Bolts	Central	160
Washers	East	40
Washers	West	30
Washers	Central	50

presented in Figures 4.10b and 4.10c, respectively. Figure 4.11 shows the equivalence between these relational and multi-dimensional databases.

Companies have reported hundreds of successful data-warehousing applications. For example, you can read client success stories and case studies at the websites of vendors such as NCR Corporation (*www.ncr.com*) and Oracle Corp. (*www.oracle.com*). For a more detailed discussion visit The Data Warehousing Institute (*www.tdwi.org*). Some of the benefits of data warehousing include:

- End users can access needed data quickly and easily via web browsers because the data are located in one place.
- End users can conduct extensive analysis with data in ways that may not have been possible before.
- End users can obtain a consolidated view of organizational data.

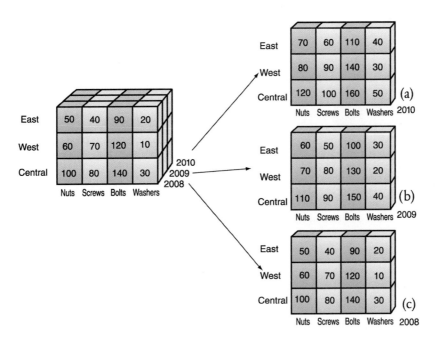

FIGURE 4.10 Multi-dimensional database.

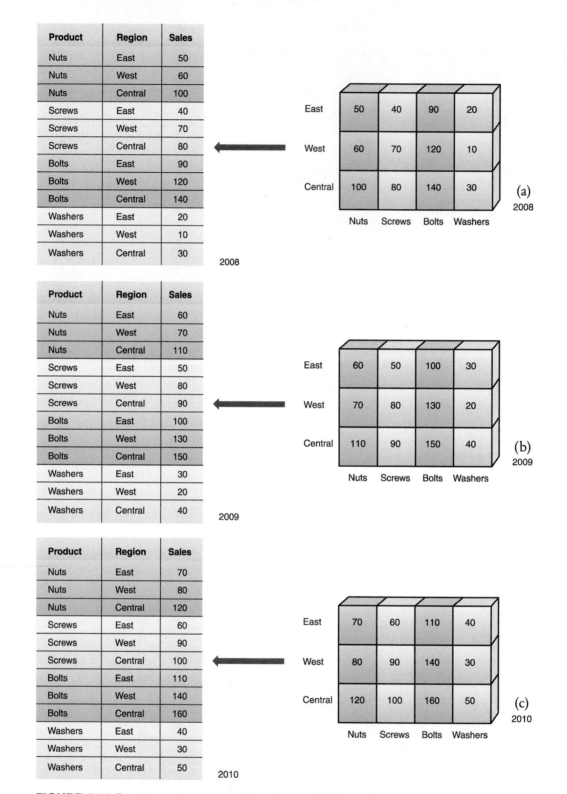

FIGURE 4.11 Equivalence between relational and multi-dimensional databases.

These benefits can improve business knowledge, provide competitive advantage, enhance customer service and satisfaction, facilitate decision making, and streamline business processes. IT's About Business 4.3 demonstrates the benefits of data warehousing and business intelligence systems at the Hudson's Bay Company.

IT'S ABOUT BUSINESS 4.3
DATA WAREHOUSING AT THE HUDSON'S BAY COMPANY

The Hudson's Bay Company (HBC), once the oldest and largest fur trading company in the world, owns and operates a chain of over 500 retail stores across Canada employing more than 70,000 people. Among its most familiar brands are The Bay, Zellers, Home Outfitters, and Fields.

It was back in the 1990s when HBC implemented its first data warehousing solution with 250GB storage capacity. At that time the data warehouse was operated by two people and worked as a peripheral system rather than a central resource for decision makers. The problem with the old data warehouse was that users, mainly store managers, buyers, and merchandisers, still had to access operational systems to complete their reports because merchandising information was spread across several operational systems. That meant that custom reports used to take up to a week to generate and contained incomplete and sometimes misleading information. One example was weekly sales reports. One system would produce sales figures that were from Monday to Sunday while another system would produce sales from Saturday to Tuesday. As a result, store managers, buyers, and merchandisers made crucial decisions based on their instinct rather than careful analysis of the situation.

In order to respond to these problems, HBC recently expanded its data warehouse to a 10TB (terabyte) Teradata database. The data warehouse stores all of HBC's point-of-sale (POS) data, detailed sales summaries, and inventory data. All these data are refreshed daily with different frequency depending on the type of data; a few hundred thousand times a day in the case of POS data, and nightly in the case of sales summaries and inventory. The data warehouse is accessed by more than 3,000 HBC users and over 700 suppliers and generates between 2,500 and 6,000 reports daily, reaching 9,000 on peak days.

The information generated by the new Teradata warehouse helps with making decisions such as what products to advertise, how much inventory to keep, and what products to keep in what stores. It also helps in evaluating sales performance. The new data warehouse provides HBC with greater flexibility to extract the information users need when they need it and in the format they need it.

Sources: Compiled from "Driving Insights and Decisions: Data Warehousing at Hudson's Bay Company," TDWI Case Study, February 2007; "Hudson Bay Company Expands Its Investment in Teradata as Innovative Data Management Strategy Proves Successful," *Business Wire*, January 17, 2008; "Hudson's Bay Company Taps QuantiSense to Improve Retail Analytics, Transition to Cost Method of Inventory Accounting," Dashboard Insight, November 10, 2009; Teradata website (*www.teradata.com*), accessed April 29, 2010.

QUESTIONS
1. Why was it necessary for HBC to develop a data warehouse?
2. What are the challenges of having a data warehouse? What could management do to overcome those challenges?
3. Provide examples of how different areas of the Hudson's Bay Company (finance, accounting, marketing, operations, MIS) could benefit from the use of the data warehouse.

Despite their many benefits, data warehouses do have problems. They can be very expensive to build and to maintain. Also, incorporating data from obsolete mainframe systems can be difficult and expensive. Third, people in one department might be reluctant to share data with other departments. Finally, because data are transferred from other systems, they may go through a cleansing process that changes the information, meaning that the data are not the historical record and do not fully represent the actual accounting systems.

Data Marts

Because data warehouses are so expensive, they are used primarily by large companies. Many other firms employ a lower-cost, scaled-down version of a data warehouse called a data mart. A **data mart** is a small data warehouse that is designed for the end user's needs in a strategic business unit (SBU) or a department.

As previously stated, data marts are far less costly than data warehouses. A typical data mart costs less than $100,000, compared with $1 million or more for a data warehouse. Also, data marts can be implemented more quickly, often in less than 90 days. Further, because they contain less information than a data warehouse, they have a more rapid response and are easier to learn and navigate. Finally, they support local rather than central control by conferring power on the user group.

Thus far, we have discussed databases, data warehouses, and data marts as systems for managing organizational data. However, companies are finding that, even with these tools, their data have developed problems over time. To address these problems, companies must develop an enterprise-wide approach to managing their data. This approach, which we discuss in the next section, is called data governance.

BEFORE YOU GO ON...

1. What are the characteristics of a data warehouse?
2. Differentiate between relational and multi-dimensional databases.
3. What is a data mart?

4.5 Data Governance

At the beginning of this chapter, we discussed the many reasons why managing data is so difficult. Another problem arises from the fact that over time organizations have developed information systems for specific business processes, such as transaction processing, supply chain management, customer relationship management, and other processes. Information systems that specifically support these processes impose unique requirements on data, which result in repetition and conflicts across an organization. For example, the marketing function might maintain information on customers, sales territories, and markets, which duplicates data within the billing or customer service functions. This situation produces inconsistent data in the enterprise. Inconsistent data prevent a company from developing a unified view of core business information—data concerning customers, products, finances, and so on—across the organization and its information systems.

Two other factors complicate data management. First, government regulations (for example, the Sarbanes-Oxley Act in the United States, and Canada's Personal Information Protection and Electronic Documents Act and Ontario's Bill 198, which regulates securities issued in the province) have made it a top priority for companies to better account for how information is being managed within their organizations. Sarbanes-Oxley and Bill 198 require that (1) public companies and companies with public accountability evaluate and disclose the effectiveness of their internal financial controls, and (2) independent auditors for these companies agree to this disclosure. The law also holds CEOs and CFOs personally responsible for such disclosure. If their companies lack satisfactory data management policies, and fraud or a security breach occurs, they could be held personally responsible and face prosecution.

Second, companies are drowning in data, much of them unstructured. As we have seen, the amount of data is increasing exponentially. In order to be profitable, companies must develop a strategy for managing these data effectively.

For these reasons, organizations are turning to data governance. **Data governance** is an approach to managing information across an entire organization. It involves a formal set of business processes and policies that are designed to ensure that data are handled in a certain, well-defined fashion. That is, the organization follows unambiguous rules for creating, collecting, handling, and protecting its information. The objective is to make information available, transparent, and useful for the people authorized to access it, from the moment it enters an organization, until it is outdated and deleted.

One strategy for implementing data governance is master data management. But first, let's look at master data. **Master data** are a set of core data, such as customer, product, employee, vendor, geographic location, and so on, that span the enterprise information systems and it is important to distinguish them from transaction data. *Transaction data*, which are generated and captured by operational systems, describe the activities, or transactions, of the business. In contrast, master data are applied to multiple transactions and used to categorize, aggregate, and evaluate the transaction data.

Let's look at an example of a transaction. The transaction is: You (Andrea Sakic) purchase one Samsung 42-inch plasma television, part number 6345, from Bill Tsai at The Bay, for $2,000, on April 20, 2010. In this example, the master data items are "product sold," "vendor," "salesperson," "store," "part number," "purchase price," and "date." When specific values are applied to the master data, then a transaction is represented. Therefore, transaction data would be, respectively, "42-inch plasma television," "Samsung," "Bill Tsai," "The Bay," "6345," "$2000," and "April 20, 2010."

Master data management is a process that spans all organizational business processes and applications. It provides companies with the ability to store, maintain, exchange, and synchronize a consistent, accurate, and timely "single version of the truth" for the company's core master data. IT's About Business 4.4 shows the example of Panasonic and the implementation of master data management.

IT'S ABOUT BUSINESS 4.4
MASTER DATA MANAGEMENT AT PANASONIC

Panasonic (*www.panasonic.com*), one of the world's leading electronics manufacturers, makes plasma TVs, DVD players, mobile phones, and many other products. Panasonic can gather and manipulate data about a multitude of products, customers, and suppliers. But in processing all these data, the company noted that it did not have a "single view" of what this information meant. Further, it had developed numerous duplicate, inconsistent, and incomplete records stored in multiple isolated databases across the enterprise.

Its data were often contradictory and incorrect, causing Panasonic to bungle shipments, make mistakes in invoices, and turn customers away. It also prevented the company from making timely decisions, which diminished the company's flexibility and agility. Product launches were delayed and customer satisfaction and service declined. In essence, poor information was costing Panasonic a great deal of money.

Consider the introduction of a single product at Panasonic. With multiple sales subsidiaries, manufacturing facilities, research and development centres, and administrative centres, the task of procuring the right materials—photos, product specifications, manuals, pricing, and point-of-sale marketing information—from the right sources and getting them into the right hands and in the right language had become incredibly complex. In addition, the amount of time required to modify product materials for regional or national purposes had made it almost impossible for Panasonic to have a simultaneous product launch in one of its regions, much less across the world. This problem made Panasonic more vulnerable to its competitors, who could enter markets before Panasonic could. This "timeliness" problem is particularly acute in the electronics industry, where being first to market with new products is absolutely essential.

Panasonic set the goal of vastly improving its data management, the "single version of the truth," by implementing a master data management process using IBM's master-data-management software.

Before the data management overhaul, company employees in marketing and sales had to ask for information, from product details to photographs. With the new system, information is updated and automatically sent to those who need it. Necessary information, from product introduction to product phase-out, is delivered to retail partners, electronic commerce systems (for example, direct-to-consumer Internet sales), and Panasonic employees, when and where they need it.

The master-data-management system enabled Panasonic to save millions of dollars each year. Perhaps most significantly, the system improved Panasonic's time to market. It reduced the time required to bring a product to market from six months to one month. It similarly reduced the amount of time required for creating and maintaining product information by 50 percent.

Sources: Compiled from D. McDonald, "Panasonic Searches the Master Data for a Single Version of the Truth," *CIO Insight*, May 22, 2006; D. Bartholomew, "Master Data Management: How Mentor Graphics Mastered the Data Monster," *Baseline Magazine*, September 8, 2006; S. Schwartz, "Out of Many, One," *DB2 Magazine*, May 2006; Panasonic website (*www.panasonic.com*), accessed June 7, 2010.

QUESTIONS
1. Provide specific examples of master data at Panasonic.
2. What are the challenges of master data management?

BEFORE YOU GO ON...

1. Describe data governance.
2. What is the difference between transaction data and master data?
3. Describe master data management.

4.6 Knowledge Management

As we have discussed, data and information are critically important organizational assets. Knowledge is a vital asset as well. Successful managers have always used intellectual assets and recognized their value. But these efforts were not systematic, and they did not ensure that knowledge was shared and dispersed in a way that benefited the overall organization. Moreover, industry analysts estimate that most of a company's knowledge assets are not housed in relational databases. Instead, they are dispersed in e-mail, Word documents, spreadsheets, and presentations on individual computers. This arrangement makes it extremely difficult for companies to access and integrate their knowledge. Frequently, the result is less-effective decision making. Consequently, more and more businesses are investing in knowledge management systems as a way to capture, analyze, and disseminate knowledge that resides within the organization. In order to better understand how this technology works and what it can do for organizations, let's first describe some important concepts.

Concepts and Definitions

Knowledge management (KM) is a process that helps organizations manipulate important knowledge that is part of the organization's memory, usually in an unstructured format. For an organization to be successful, knowledge, as a form of capital, must exist in a format that can be exchanged among people. In addition, it must be able to grow.

Knowledge

In the information technology context, knowledge is distinct from data and information. As we discussed in Chapter 1, data are a collection of facts, measurements, and statistics; information is organized or processed data that are timely and accurate. Knowledge is information that is *contextual*, *relevant*, and *actionable*. Simply put, knowledge is *information in action*. Intellectual capital (or intellectual assets) is another term for knowledge.

To illustrate with an example, a bulletin listing all the courses offered by your university during one semester would be considered data. When you register, you process the data from the bulletin to create your schedule for the semester. Your schedule would be considered information. Your work schedule, your major, and your desired social schedule are criteria that you would use to develop your own study schedule, as use of your own knowledge. When your instructors comment on your term papers and provide you with constructive feedback, their knowledge helps you refine the way you study and take your exams. Thus, knowledge requires the use of criteria and experience to develop new materials. The implication is that knowledge has strong experiential and reflective elements that distinguish it from information in a given context. Unlike information, knowledge can be exercised to solve a problem.

There are numerous theories and models that classify different types of knowledge. Here we focus on the distinction between explicit knowledge and tacit knowledge.

Explicit and Tacit Knowledge

Explicit knowledge deals with more objective, rational, and technical knowledge. In an organization, explicit knowledge consists of the policies, procedural guides, reports, products, strategies, goals, and core competencies of the enterprise. In other words, explicit knowledge is the knowledge that has been codified (documented) in a form that can be distributed to others or transformed into a process or strategy. A description of how to process a job application that is documented in a firm's human resources policy manual is an example of explicit knowledge.

In contrast, **tacit knowledge** is the cumulative store of subjective or experiential learning. In an organization, tacit knowledge consists of an organization's experiences, insights, expertise, know-how, trade secrets, skill sets, understanding, and learning. It also includes the organizational culture, which reflects the past and present experiences of the organization's people and processes, as well as the prevailing values. Tacit knowledge is generally imprecise, and costly to transfer. It is also highly personal and because it is unstructured, it is difficult to formalize or codify in contrast to explicit knowledge. A salesperson who has worked with particular customers over time and has come to know their needs quite well would possess extensive tacit knowledge. This knowledge is typically not recorded, and in fact, it might be difficult for the salesperson to put into writing.

Knowledge Management Systems

The goal of knowledge management is to help an organization make the most effective use of the knowledge it has. Historically, management information systems have focused on capturing, storing, managing, and reporting explicit knowledge. Organizations now realize they need to integrate both explicit and tacit knowledge in formal information systems. **Knowledge management systems (KMSs)** refer to the use of modern information technologies—the Internet, intranets, extranets, groupware, data warehouses—to systematize, enhance, and expedite intrafirm and interfirm knowledge management. KMSs are intended to help an organization cope with turnover, rapid change, and downsizing by making the expertise of the organization's human capital widely accessible. IT's About Business 4.5 describes a knowledge management system used by the insurance company CNA.

Organizations can realize many benefits with KMSs. Most importantly, they make **best practices**, which are the most effective and efficient ways of doing things, readily available to a wide range of employees. Enhanced access to best-practice knowledge improves overall organizational performance. For example, account managers can now make available their tacit knowledge about how best to handle large accounts. This knowledge can then be used to train new account managers. Other benefits include improved customer service, more efficient product development, and improved employee morale and retention.

At the same time, however, there are challenges to implementing effective KMSs. First, employees must be willing to share their personal tacit knowledge. To encourage this behaviour, organizations must create a "knowledge management" culture that rewards employees who add their expertise to the knowledge base. Second, the knowledge base must be continually maintained and updated. New knowledge must be added, and old, outdated knowledge must be deleted. Companies must be willing to invest in the resources needed to carry out these operations. Let's now turn our attention to how a knowledge management system works.

IT'S ABOUT BUSINESS 4.5
KNOWLEDGE MANAGEMENT TRANSFORMS CNA

CNA (*www.cna.com*) is one of the world's largest insurance companies, with more than 50 brand name insurance products and 19,000 employees in 175 locations in Canada and the United States. Because a company of this size is very difficult to manage, CNA is organized into 35 separate strategic business units (SBUs), which function independently. Each SBU has its own systems, processes, and financial statements, and tailors its operations according to the market demands for its products. Historically, the SBUs did not communicate and share knowledge effectively. However, corporate executives wanted to gather the expertise from the SBUs and make it available to the entire organization so that the company could capitalize on the opportunity to cross-sell products. As a result, CNA embarked on a new corporate strategy: "Transform the organization from a collection of companies to a portfolio of expertise."

The challenge would not be easy. With so many SBUs, it was almost impossible for employees to share information among the units. This meant that a customer with questions regarding a variety of types of insurance might need to speak to representatives in several departments.

CNA knew it wouldn't be satisfied with just a database of information. It wanted its information system to connect employees and allow them to share their expertise with colleagues in other SBUs. The company knew it had to expand the knowledge of its employees—many of whom were specialized—to include all of CNA's products.

To accomplish these goals, CNA employed AskMe (now AskMe-Realcom, *www.realcom-inc. com*), a company that specializes in knowledge management and knowledge-sharing strategies, to develop a knowledge-based system. For the new system to be effective, each employee had to add his or her specialized product and market expertise to the company's knowledge base.

The new system, called the Knowledge Network, uses software to connect employees with an expert in any field in the company. The system builds on existing knowledge by adding the results of inquiries to its knowledge base for employees to search the next time such a question comes up. Not only is this knowledge base searchable, but it can generate reports and analyses of the information stored within.

CNA deployed the Knowledge Network throughout the company. The system is now being actively used by 4,000 employees. The system identifies employees with expert knowledge as knowledge sources.

Since policy underwriting can be a major cost in an insurance company, it's expected that the new system will save money as it can enable the underwriting to be done faster and at a higher quality. However, CNA finds it difficult to measure the financial impact of the new system. The CEO asserted that the new system is a "soft, person-based idea"; therefore, it is difficult to quantify its benefits.

Sources: Compiled from M. Santosus, "How CNA Insurance Created a KM Culture," *CIO*, September 1, 2002; C. Pryer, "Show Me the Knowledge: CNA Employs Hi-Tech Knowledge Sharing Solution," *OutSourcing Center*, March 2002; CNA website (*www.cna.com*), accessed March 29, 2009; former AskMe website (*www.askme. com*), accessed March 28, 2009.

QUESTIONS
1. What aspects of corporate culture are particularly important for the successful implementation of a knowledge management program like the one at CNA?
2. If it is difficult to quantify the benefits of the new KMS at CNA, what other measures could the company use to measure its benefits?

The Knowledge Management System Cycle

A functioning KMS follows a cycle that consists of six steps (see Figure 4.12). The reason the system is cyclical is that knowledge is dynamically refined over time. The knowledge in an effective KMS is never finalized because the environment changes over time, and knowledge must be updated to reflect these changes. The cycle works as follows:

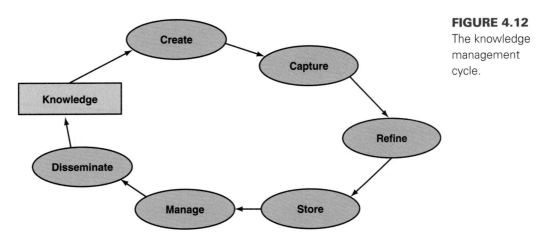

FIGURE 4.12
The knowledge management cycle.

1. ***Create knowledge.*** Knowledge is created as people determine new ways of doing things or develop know-how. Sometimes external knowledge is brought in.
2. ***Capture knowledge.*** New knowledge must be identified as valuable and be represented in a reasonable way.
3. ***Refine knowledge.*** New knowledge must be placed in context so that it is actionable. This is where tacit qualities (human insights) must be captured along with explicit facts.
4. ***Store knowledge.*** Useful knowledge must then be stored in a reasonable format in a knowledge repository so that others in the organization can access it.
5. ***Manage knowledge.*** Like a library, the knowledge must be kept current. It must be reviewed regularly to verify that it is relevant and accurate.
6. ***Disseminate knowledge.*** Knowledge must be made available in a useful format to anyone in the organization who needs it, anywhere and anytime.

BEFORE YOU GO ON...

1. What is knowledge management?
2. What is the difference between tacit knowledge and explicit knowledge?
3. Describe the knowledge management system cycle.

WHAT'S IN IT FOR ME?

FOR THE ACCOUNTING MAJOR

The accounting function is intimately concerned with keeping track of the transactions and internal controls of an organization. Modern data warehouses enable accountants to perform these functions more effectively. Data warehouses help accountants manage the flood of data in today's organizations so they can keep their firms in compliance with new standards.

Accountants also play a role in cost-justifying the creation of a knowledge base and then auditing its cost-effectiveness. In addition, if you work for a large public accounting company that provides management services or sells knowledge, you will most likely use some of your company's best practices that are stored in a knowledge base.

FOR THE FINANCE MAJOR

Financial managers make extensive use of computerized databases or repositories that are external to the organization, such as Compustat, Dow Jones, or the System for Electronic Document Analysis and Retrieval (SEDAR), to obtain financial data on organizations in their industry. They can use these data to determine if their organization meets industry benchmarks in return-on-investment, cash management, and other financial ratios.

Financial managers, who produce the organization's financial status reports, are also closely involved with regulatory compliance. Data warehouses help these managers comply with the law.

FOR THE MARKETING MAJOR

Data warehouses help marketing managers access data from the organization's marketing transactions (for example, customer purchases) to plan targeted marketing campaigns and to evaluate the success of previous campaigns. Knowledge about customers can make the difference between success and failure. In many data warehouses and knowledge bases, the vast majority of information and knowledge concerns customers, products, sales, and marketing. Marketing managers regularly use an organization's knowledge base and they often participate in its creation.

FOR THE PRODUCTION/OPERATIONS MANAGEMENT MAJOR

Production/operations personnel access organizational data to determine optimum inventory levels for parts in a production process. Past production data enable POM personnel to determine the optimum configuration for assembly lines. Firms also keep quality data that inform them not only about the quality of finished products but also about quality issues with incoming raw materials, production irregularities, shipping and logistics, and after-sale use and maintenance of the product.

Knowledge management is extremely important for running complex operations. The accumulated knowledge regarding scheduling, logistics, maintenance, and other functions is very valuable. Innovative ideas are necessary for improving operations and can be supported by knowledge management.

FOR THE HUMAN RESOURCES MANAGEMENT MAJOR

Organizations keep extensive data on employees, including gender, age, race, current and past job descriptions, and performance evaluations. Human resources personnel access these data to provide reports to government agencies regarding compliance with legislation and guidelines, such as employment equity. HR managers also use the data to evaluate hiring practices, evaluate salary structures, and manage any discrimination grievances or lawsuits brought against the firm.

Data warehouses help HR managers provide assistance to all employees as companies turn over more and more decisions about health care and retirement planning to the employees themselves.

The employees can use the data warehouses for help in selecting the optimal mix among these critical choices.

Human resources managers also need to use a knowledge base frequently to find out how past cases were handled. Consistency in how employees are treated is not only important, but it protects the company against legal actions. Also, training for building, maintaining, and using the knowledge system is sometimes the responsibility of the HR department. Finally, the HR department could be responsible for compensating employees who contribute their knowledge to the knowledge base.

FOR THE MIS MAJOR

The MIS function manages the organization's data as well as the databases, data warehouses, and data marts where they are stored. MIS database administrators standardize data names by using the data dictionary. This process ensures that all users understand what data are in the database. Database personnel also provide reports from the data warehouse to help users access needed data. MIS personnel—and users as well—can now generate reports with query tools much more quickly than was possible using old computer systems.

SUMMARY

1. **Recognize the importance of data, the issues involved in managing them and understand the importance of the data life cycle.**

   IT applications cannot be performed without using data. Data should be accurate, complete, timely, consistent, accessible, relevant, and concise. Managing data in organizations is difficult for various reasons: (1) the amount of data increases with time; (2) data are stored in various systems, databases, formats, and languages; and (3) data security, quality, and integrity are often compromised. The data life cycle starts with data collection. Then data are stored in a database(s) and then they may be processed to fit the format of a data warehouse or data mart. Users then access data from the warehouse or data mart for analysis. The result of all these activities is the generation of decision support and knowledge.

2. **Explain the advantages of the database approach.**

   In a database, which is a group of logically related files, data are integrated and related so that one set of software programs provides access to all the data. Therefore, data redundancy, data isolation, and data inconsistency are minimized, and data can be shared among all users. In addition, data security and data integrity are increased, and applications and data are independent of each other.

3. **Describe the main characteristics of the relational database model.**

   A database management system (DBMS) is a set of programs that provides users with tools to add, delete, access, and analyze data stored in one location. Among the different database architectures the relational database model is the most widely used among businesses. Relational databases are usually designed with a number of related tables, and each one contains entities and attributes.

4. **Explain how a data warehouse operates and how it supports decision making.**

   A data warehouse is a repository of subject-oriented historical data that are organized to be accessible in a form readily acceptable for analytical processing activities. End users can access needed data in a data warehouse quickly and easily via web browsers. They can conduct extensive analysis with data and can develop a consolidated view of organizational data. These benefits can improve business knowledge, provide competitive advantage, enhance customer service and satisfaction, facilitate decision making, and help streamline business processes.

5. **Define data governance and explain how it helps produce high-quality data.**

Data governance is an approach to managing information across an entire organization. It ensures that data are handled in a certain, well-defined fashion. That is, the organization follows unambiguous rules for creating, collecting, handling, and protecting information.

6. **Define knowledge, and differentiate between explicit and tacit knowledge.**

Knowledge is information that is contextual, relevant, and actionable. Explicit knowledge deals with more objective, rational, and technical knowledge. Tacit knowledge is usually in the domain of subjective, cognitive, and experiential learning. It is highly personal and difficult to formalize and communicate to others.

KEY TERMS

attribute, 117
best practice, 131
bit, 116
byte, 116
clickstream data, 112
database, 116
database management system (DBMS), 115
data dictionary, 121
data governance, 128
data mart, 127
data model, 117
data warehouse, 123
entity, 117
entity-relationship (ER) diagram, 117
entity-relationship (ER) modelling, 117
entity class, 117
explicit knowledge, 131
field, 116
file, 116
identifier, 118

instance, 117
intellectual capital (intellectual asset), 130
knowledge, 130
knowledge management (KM), 130
knowledge management system (KMS), 131
master data, 128
master data management, 129
multi-dimensional structure, 124
normalization, 121
on-line analytical processing (OLAP), 123
on-line transaction processing (OLTP), 123
primary key, 117
query by example (QBE), 121
record, 116
relational database model, 119
secondary key, 117
structured query language (SQL), 120
table, 116
tacit knowledge, 131

DISCUSSION QUESTIONS

1. Explain the difficulties involved in managing data.
2. What are the problems associated with poor quality data?
3. What is master data management? What does it have to do with high-quality data?
4. Describe the advantages of relational databases.
5. Discuss the benefits of data warehousing to end users.
6. What is the relationship between a company's databases and its data warehouse?
7. Distinguish between data warehouses and data marts.
8. Explain why master data management is so important in companies that have multiple data sources.
9. Explain why it is important to capture and manage knowledge.
10. Compare and contrast tacit knowledge and explicit knowledge.

PROBLEM-SOLVING ACTIVITIES

1. Access various employment websites (for example, *www.canada.plusjobs.com*, *www.monster.ca*, and *www.dice.com*) and find several job descriptions for a database administrator. Are the job descriptions similar? What are the salaries offered in these positions?

2. Access the websites of several real estate companies. Find the sites that take you through a step-by-step process for buying a home, that provide virtual reality tours of homes in your price range and location, that provide mortgage and interest rate calculators, and that offer financing for your home. Analyze the website and build a table indicating for each feature available on the website the data that needs to be collected and its source.

3. It is possible to find many websites that provide demographic information. Access several of these sites and see what they offer. Do the sites differ in the types of demographic information they offer? If so, how? Do the sites require a fee for the information they offer? Would demographic information be useful to you if you wanted to start a new business? If so, how and why?

4. The Internet contains many websites that provide information on financial aid resources for students. Access several of these sites. Think about all the data that needs to be collected and how it would appear in a relational database. Draw some examples of tables and their relationships.

5. Draw an entity-relationship diagram for a small retail store. You wish to keep track of the product name, description, unit price, and number of items of that product sold to each customer. You also wish to record customer name, mailing address, and billing address. You must track each transaction (sale) as to date, product purchased, unit price, number of units, tax, and total amount of the sale.

6. Access the websites of IBM (*www.ibm.com*), Sybase (*www.sybase.com*), and Oracle (*www.oracle.com*) and trace the capabilities of their latest database management systems.

7. Access the websites of two of the major data warehouse vendors, such as NCR (*www.ncr.com*) and SAS (*www.sas.com*). Describe their products and how they are related to the Web.

8. Enter the website of Gartner, Inc. (*www.gartner.com*). Examine its research studies pertaining to data management and data warehousing. Prepare a report on the state of the art.

9. Calculate your personal digital footprint at *www.emc.com/digital_universe/downloads/web/personal-ticker.htm*.

10. Access *http://academicprograms.teradata.com/tun/* and sign in under the student registration option. Choose one of the topics related to database and data warehouse that are available on the website and prepare a short presentation for your class.

TEAM ASSIGNMENTS

1. Each team will select an on-line database to explore, such as AOL Music (*http://music.aol.com*), or the Internet Movie Database (*www.imdb.com*). Explore these websites to see what information they provide for you. List the entities and the attributes that the websites must track in their databases. Diagram the relationship between the entities you have identified.

2. In groups, create a data model for a pet store to include:
   - customer data
   - product data
   - employee data
   - financial data
   - vendor data
   - sales data
   - inventory data
   - building data
   - other data (specify)

Create attributes (four or more) for each entity. Create relationships between the entities, name the relationships, and create an entity-relationship diagram for the pet store.

DOCUMENT MANAGEMENT AT PROCTER & GAMBLE

THE BUSINESS PROBLEM

The consumer goods giant Procter & Gamble (P&G, www.pg.com) is a huge firm with reported sales of US$79 billion in 2009. Its portfolio includes Crest, Tide, Gillette, Pampers, and Charmin. Even though it used advanced IT and business processes, P&G faced problems managing the vast amounts of paper required for a company that develops drugs and over-the-counter medications. Regulatory issues, research and development (R&D), and potential litigation generate even more paper documents and files. As a result, P&G wanted to gain control of its company documents, reduce administrative oversight of its paper documents, reduce costs, accelerate R&D initiatives, and improve tracking and signature compliance. The strategy it adopted to achieve these goals was to transition from paper-based to electronic document management. A document management system consists of hardware and software that converts paper documents into electronic documents, manages and archives those electronic documents, and then indexes and stores them according to company policy.

While information systems can automate processes, the transition from a paper to an electronic system can require huge changes in workflow and how the company can get new products approved. Any delay in bringing a product to market can be costly; for example, sales of a successful over-the-counter drug can be more than $1 million daily.

During the approval process, documents are sent back and forth between researchers, quality-control personnel, clinicians, marketing specialists, and external partners. Under the manual system, P&G would produce microfiche (flat pieces of photographic film) versions of the documents and store them in rented warehouses, producing indexes to find the information in the correct microfiche file. Unfortunately, the indexes were not always accurate. Adding to this problem, manually searching for a particular document and associated documents required far too much time. The company also used third-party providers to store its documents off-site. Hundreds of boxes of P&G paper records were lost in a fire at a London warehouse where the company was storing them through a service provider.

Moving to an electronic system was not without its challenges. For one thing, the daily workflow had to include ways to archive electronic material. Also, signatures had to be digitally reproduced and authenticated and company lawyers wanted a set of legally binding signatures. Therefore, P&G adopted the pharmaceutical industry's Signatures and Authentication for Everyone (SAFE) BioPharma Association standard, which was created to help companies producing pharmaceuticals that need to do business digitally with regulatory authorities around the world. P&G's initiative focused on managing and authenticating digital signatures. The company's IT and legal departments verified that the SAFE-BioPharma digital signature standard met its risk policy and business needs.

THE IT SOLUTIONS

P&G chose Adobe LiveCycle Reader Extensions and Adobe LiveCycle PDF Generator (www.adobe.com), which were implemented by IT integrator Cardinal Solutions (www.cardinalsolutions.com). The software was integrated with P&G's existing eLab Notebook program. The Adobe products can take massive amounts of R&D files in many formats, including Microsoft Word, Excel, and PowerPoint, and turn them into documents that can be reviewed, approved, and signed electronically.

The manual way of preparing documents for regulatory approval was cumbersome. Researchers had to record data from experiments in paper notebooks, number and sign each page, and have a witness sign each page. With the new document management system, experiment notes and other documentation are recorded using a variety of software programs and file formats and then turned into PDF documents by the LiveCycle PDF Generator. The system prompts the user to create a digital signature with a USB token for authentication. LiveCycle Reader Extensions takes over at this point and embeds usage rights within the document, locking out any user who does not have a SAFE-BioPharma digital signature certificate.

THE RESULTS

Today, once a digital signature is added to a file, an auditor can immediately view the document and all activity related to the document. The auditor right-clicks on the signature and views the entire audit trail. The signature can also be appended as a last page of the file so that it can be shared externally when necessary, such as in a court of law.

The electronic document management system is estimated to save each employee an average of 30 minutes of signing and archiving time per week. That doesn't seem like much, but in a huge company like P&G, it is expected to add up to a savings of tens of millions of dollars in productivity gains. The system also saves time, as P&G can access vast amounts of data at its fingertips that may be asked for by government regulators or business partners.

The R&D department is not the only one singing the praises of electronic documents. P&G's German operations now use digital signatures for its marketing department to approve instructions to retailers on how its products should be displayed in stores.

The most significant problem that P&G has encountered has been to convince its employees to accept the new system and learn how to use the eLab Notebook application. To address this problem, P&G is providing training to overcome any employee's reluctance to use the new technology.

Sources: Compiled from M. Vizard, "Balancing Document Management," *eWeek*, April 2, 2009; "Adobe Success Story: Procter & Gamble," Adobe website (*www.adobe.com*), accessed March 12, 2009; J. deJong, "The Case for Online Document Management," *Forbes*, December 22, 2008; S. Greengard, "A Document Management Case Study: Procter and Gamble," *Baseline Magazine*, August 29, 2008; T. Weiss, "Law Firm Turns to Software to Streamline Case Data Searches," *Computerworld*, September 22, 2006; R. Mitchell, "Record Risks," *Computerworld*, May 30, 2005; H. Havenstein, "Rules Prompt Pfizer to Consolidate Content Management Systems," *Computerworld*, May 23, 2005; Procter & Gamble website (*www.pg.com*), accessed June 28, 2010; SAFE-BioPharma website (*www.safe-biopharma.org*), accessed March 12, 2009.

QUESTIONS

1. Company documents are one type of data that companies must manage. Compare the benefits of P&G's document management system with the benefits of database technology. Do you notice any differences? Support your answer.
2. This case has described numerous advantages of P&G's move to electronic documents. Describe the disadvantages of electronic documents.

CASE 4.2

Web Resources

Student website www.wiley.com/canada/rainer

- Web quizzes
- Lecture slides in PowerPoint

- Author podcasts
- Interactive Case: Ruby's Club assignments

ALL OF THE ABOVE AND...

- E-book
- Manager videos
- Vocabulary flash cards

- Pre- and post-lecture quizzes
- Microsoft Office 2007 lab manual and projects

ANALYZING CUSTOMER DATA FOR RUBY'S CLUB

ruby's
club

Go to the Ruby's Club link at the Student Companion website or WileyPLUS for information about your current internship assignment. Your assignment will include working with customer data in a spreadsheet and preparing them for use within a database.

5

NETWORK APPLICATIONS

LEARNING OBJECTIVES

1. Describe the three major applications of computer networks.

2. Discuss the various technologies, applications, and websites that fall under the umbrella of Web 2.0.

3. Differentiate between e-learning and distance learning.

4. Understand the advantages and disadvantages of telecommuting for employers and employees.

EFFECTIVE MARKETING AT DEL MONTE WITH SOCIAL NETWORKS

THE BUSINESS PROBLEM

Del Monte (*www.delmonte.com*) is a worldwide conglomerate known for canned fruits and vegetables. In Canada it operates under its CanGro foods subsidiary (*www.cangrofoods.ca*) and markets its products under the Del Monte and Aylmer brands. Other major retail brands include College Inn, Contadina, and Starkist in the canned fruit and vegetable market; and pet products such as 9 Lives, Gravy Train, Milk-Bone, and Meow Mix. Del Monte faces fierce competition from other food conglomerates. The company realizes that understanding the modern fast-moving marketplace is critical. Unfortunately, its sophisticated database and analytics tools were no longer capable of addressing that challenge on their own. The company, therefore, turned to social networking to better understand its customer base.

THE IT SOLUTION

As the popularity of social networking has exploded, websites such as MySpace and Facebook are attracting more and more users. However, companies are just beginning to use social networking to achieve substantial business gains. Del Monte is capitalizing on social networking as a marketing tool to help the company get closer to its customers (a process called *customer intimacy*), create the kind of products consumers want, and gain competitive advantage.

Del Monte introduced three initiatives to use the power of social networking. The first two, "I Love My Dog" and "I Love My Cat," offer one community for dog owners and another for cat owners, where each group can interact and share ideas. The third, "Moms Online Community," lets mothers exchange ideas and information.

When Del Monte executives decided to pursue these initiatives, they recognized that the company did not have the information technology (IT) expertise to ensure success. Therefore, they turned to MarketTools (*www.markettools.com*) to develop and host the Del Monte social networking sites. MarketTools collected and analyzed the data and implemented the technology to make the websites operate effectively. Del Monte also turned to Drupal (*http://drupal.org*), the open-source content management system. Drupal offers a wide range of features, including polls, threaded discussions, and blogging. In a threaded discussion, messages are grouped visually in a hierarchy by topic. A set of messages grouped in this manner is called a topic thread or simply a thread.

When MarketTools began working on the "I Love My Dog" initiative, it gathered data from roughly 50 million blogs, forums, and message boards over a period of months in order to identify key themes in the marketplace. It then built a data warehouse and developed themes and discussion points for the community. The website allows dog owners to discuss issues, chat, participate in surveys, share photos and videos, and locate resources. Consumers use the password-protected site, which is accessible only by invitation. The "I Love My Cat" site essentially functions the same way.

Del Monte uses these two sites to gather data to help shape its marketing decisions. The private networks guide decision making about products, test market campaigns, provide data on buying preferences, and generate discussion about new products and product changes.

The third site, "Moms Online Community," helps Del Monte gather information about the preferences and buying habits of mothers. The site has approximately 10,000 participants and uses a community manager to moderate discussions and facilitate day-to-day communication. It features tips, forums, recipes, subscriptions for topics of interest, and profiles of moms who are participating in the community. The company periodically provides topics for discussion and conducts polls to gather feedback on ideas, products, and trends.

Del Monte sends out products for the moms to sample, and it collects detailed feedback on their responses. The company often sends out different iterations of a product and asks moms to post their comments on-line. It also conducts web surveys that quickly tabulate responses to help formulate a new strategy or alter an existing one.

Sources: Compiled from E. Feretic, "The Business of Being Social," *Baseline Magazine*, July 20, 2008; S. Greengard, "Del Monte Gets Social," *Baseline Magazine*, July 30, 2008; E. Steele, "The New Focus Groups: Online Networks," *The Wall Street Journal*, January 14, 2008; M. Estrin, "Social Networks Are the New Focus Groups," *www.imediaconnection.com*, January 14, 2008; P. Kim, "Case Study: Del Monte Listens with Customer-Centric Technology," Forrester, June 19, 2007; "Del Monte Foods Gains Online Social Networking Insight with MarketTools," *DMNews.com*, August 4, 2006; Del Monte website (*www.delmonte.com*), MarketTools website (*www.markettools.com*), Drupal website (*http://drupal.org*), accessed January 30, 2009.

WHAT DO YOU THINK?

1. What are the business reasons for a company to adopt social network technologies?
2. In which areas of a business would it be beneficial to use social network technologies? Give a specific example of how Del Monte could use them and what would be the benefit.
3. How would the adoption of social network technologies across the firm affect employees and management? What implications would it have on them?

CASE 5.1

Chapter Preview

The opening case about Del Monte illustrates three fundamental points about network computing. First, computers do not work in isolation in modern organizations. Rather, they constantly exchange data with one another. Second, this exchange of data—facilitated by telecommunications technologies—provides companies with a number of very significant advantages. Third, this exchange can take place over any distance and over networks of any size. In essence, Del Monte and its customers form an extended network with advantages to each. Del Monte becomes closer to its customers and gains extremely valuable knowledge from them. The company's customers provide meaningful feedback to Del Monte and can see many of their ideas put into practice.

Without networks, the computer on your desk would be merely another productivity enhancement tool, just as the typewriter once was. The power of networks, however, turns your computer into an amazingly effective tool for accessing information from thousands of sources, thereby making both you and your organization more productive. Regardless of the type of organization (profit/not-for-profit, large/small, global/local) or industry (manufacturing, financial services, health care), networks in general, and the Internet in particular, have transformed—and will continue to transform—the way we do business.

In this chapter, we discuss network applications; that is, what networks help us to do. We then explore the variety of network applications that fall under the umbrella of Web 2.0. We conclude the chapter with a brief look at e-learning and telecommuting. Network infrastructure and Internet technology are covered in Technology Guide 4.

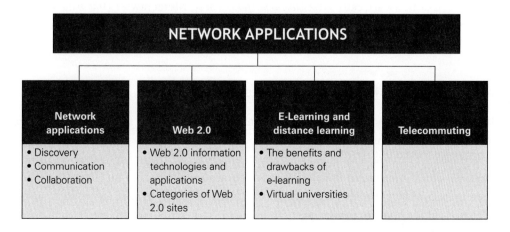

5.1 Network Applications

Stated in general terms, networks support businesses and other organizations in all areas of the business and for three main usages or applications: discovery, communication, and collaboration. We discuss these three main applications and the Internet-related technologies that support them in the following subsections.

Discovery

The Internet enables users to access information located in databases all over the world. By browsing and searching data sources on the Web, users can apply the Internet's discovery capability to areas ranging from education to government services to entertainment and commerce. Although having access to all this information is a great benefit, it is critically important to know that there is no quality assurance applied to information on the Web. The Web is truly democratic in that *anyone* can post information to it. For example, as we see later in this chapter, anyone can edit a Wikipedia page (with some exceptions in controversial areas). Therefore, the fundamental rule about information on the Web is: user beware!

In addition, the Web's major strength—the vast stores of information it contains—also presents a major challenge. The amount of information on the Web can be overwhelming, and it doubles approximately each year. As a result, navigating through the Web and gaining access to necessary information are becoming more and more difficult. To accomplish these tasks, people increasingly are using search engines, directories, and portals.

Search Engines and Metasearch Engines

A **search engine** is a computer program that searches for specific information, by keywords, and reports the results. A search engine maintains an index of billions of web pages. It uses that index to find pages that match a set of user-specified keywords. Such indexes are created and updated by *webcrawlers*, which are computer programs that browse the Web and create a copy of all visited pages. Search engines then index these pages to provide fast searches.

People use four main search engines for almost all of their searches: Google (*www.google.ca*), Yahoo! (*www.yahoo.ca*), Sympatico, (*www.sympatico.ca)*, and Ask (*www.ask.com*). However, there are an incredible number of other search engines that are quite useful, with many providing very specific searches (see *www.readwriteweb.com/archives/top_100_alternative_search_engines.php*).

For an even more thorough search, you can use a metasearch engine. **Metasearch engines** search several engines at once and integrate the findings of the various search engines to answer queries posted by users. Examples are Surf Wax (*www.surfwax.com*), Metacrawler (*www.metacrawler.com*), Mamma (*www.mamma.ca*), and Dogpile (*www.dogpile.com*). Figure 5.1 shows the home page of one of these sites.

Publication of Material in Foreign Languages

Not only is there a huge amount of information on the Internet, but it is written in many different languages. How, then, do you access this information? The answer is that you use an *automatic translation* of web pages. Such translation is available, to and from all major languages, and its quality is improving with time. Some major translation products are Yahoo! Babel Fish (*http://babelfish.yahoo. com/*) (see Figure 5.2) and Google (*www.google.com/language_tools*) as well as products and services available at SDL/Trados (*www.trados.com*).

FIGURE 5.1. The Dogpile home page, *www.dogpile.com*.

Should companies care about providing their websites in multiple languages? The answer is, absolutely. In fact, multilingual websites are now a competitive necessity because of the global nature of the business environment, discussed in Chapter 1. Companies are increasingly looking outside their home markets to grow revenues and attract new customers. When companies are disseminating

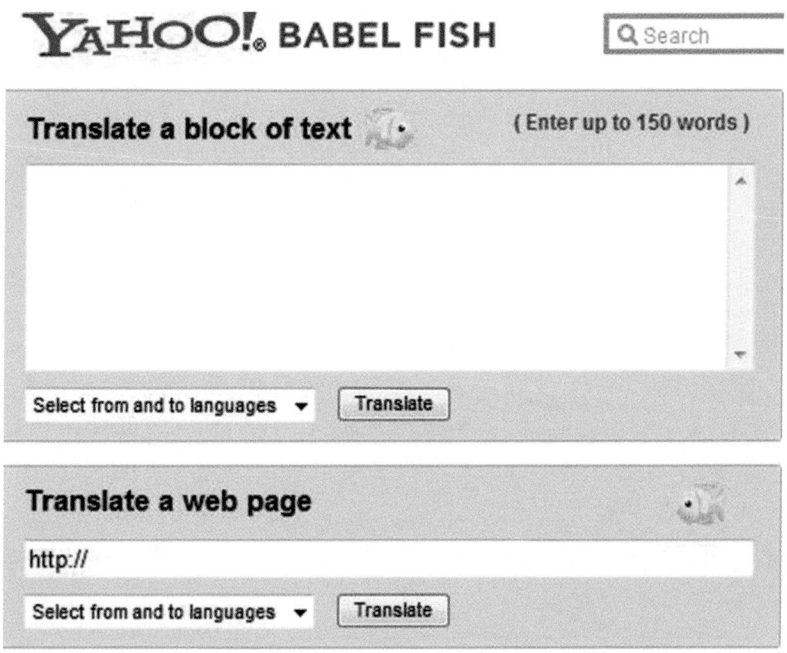

FIGURE 5.2
Yahoo!
translator.

information around the world, getting that information correct is essential. It is not enough for companies to translate web content. They must also localize that content and be sensitive to the needs of the people in local markets.

To reach 80 percent of the world's Internet users, a website needs to support a minimum of 10 languages: English, Chinese, Spanish, Japanese, German, Korean, French, Italian, Russian, and Portuguese. At 20 cents or more per word, translation services are expensive. Companies supporting 10 languages can spend $200,000 a year to localize information and another $50,000 to maintain their websites. Translation budgets for big multinational companies can run into the millions of dollars. Therefore, many large companies use software, such as SYSTRAN (*www.systransoft.com*), for their translations.

Portals

Most organizations and their managers encounter information overload. Information is scattered across numerous documents, e-mail messages, and databases at different locations and in different systems. Finding relevant and accurate information is often time-consuming and may require users to access multiple systems. IT's About Business 5.1 offers the example of the Centre for Addiction and Mental Health (CAMH) and how it dealt with this problem.

One solution to this problem is to use portals. A **portal** is a web-based, personalized gateway to information and knowledge that provides relevant information from different IT systems and the

---

IT'S ABOUT BUSINESS 5.1
CENTRE FOR ADDICTION AND MENTAL HEALTH PORTAL

The Centre for Addiction and Mental Health (CAMH) is the largest mental health and addiction organization in Canada. CAMH's main goal is to provide clinical programs, support, and rehabilitation services to individuals who suffer from mental illness or to those who are diagnosed with an addiction.

As a research institute, CAMH publishes numerous scientific documents throughout the year, making it one of the most prominent institutions in the creation of knowledge in the mental health field. CAMH's dissemination of knowledge is of crucial importance in order to provide mental health care professionals with the latest research, technologies, initiatives, and best practices in the field.

CAMH turned to technology in order to support this role by creating a new a web portal called KnowledgeX (*http://knowledgex.camh.net/*). KnowledgeX, which stands for "knowledge exchange," is an on-line tool to enable collaboration and sharing of best practices based on the expertise and experience of mental health professionals. The resources in the new portal include videos, podcasts, toolkits, research papers, conference presentations, and collaboration tools such as blogs, discussion boards, and wikis.

The new portal allows health professionals, whether they're specialists or primary care service providers, and whether they work in health promotion or education, to share information and resources to keep up with best practices and provide the best kind of care for patients with mental health problems.

For example, the KnowledgeX portal helps primary care health professionals on the frontlines by providing them with on-line access to brochures, resource materials, and training programs that help to educate the general public.

Sources: Compiled from "CAMH Launches KnowledgeX Portal: A New Frontier of CAMH's Role as Expert Resource for Professionals," news release, February 25, 2010; CAMH Knowledge Exchange website (*http://knowledgex.camh.net*), accessed May 25, 2010.

QUESTIONS
1. What type of portal is KnowledgeX?
2. How do mental health professionals benefit from using this portal? ?
3. What challenges can KnowledgeX pose for CAMH?

FIGURE 5.3 York University alumni portal, *www.yorku.ca/alumni.*

Internet using advanced search and indexing techniques. We distinguish among four types of portals: commercial, affinity, corporate, and industry-wide.

Commercial (public) portals are the most popular portals on the Internet. They are intended for broad and diverse audiences, and they offer fairly routine content, some in real time (for example, a stock ticker). Examples are Lycos Canada (*www.lycos.ca/*) and Sympatico (*www.sympatico.ca*).

In contrast, **affinity portals** offer a single point of entry to an entire community of people with affiliated interests, such as hobby groups or a political party. Your university most likely has an affinity portal for its alumni. Figure 5.3 shows the affinity portal for the alumni association at York University. Other examples of affinity portals are *www.techweb.com* and *www.zdnet.com.*

As their name suggests, **corporate portals** offer a personalized, single point of access through a web browser to critical business information located inside and outside of an organization. These portals are also known as *enterprise portals*, *information portals*, or *enterprise information portals*. In addition to making it easier to find needed information, corporate portals can offer employees, customers, and suppliers self-service opportunities. Figure 5.4 provides a framework for corporate portals. Some businesses have automated the business processes involved in purchasing products between a single buyer and multiple suppliers through their corporate portal. For example, Boeing has deployed such a type of procurement portal called the Boeing Supplier Portal through which it conducts business with its suppliers. Other corporate portals automate the business processes involved in selling or distributing products from a single supplier to multiple buyers; these are known as distribution portals. For example, Dell services its business customers through its distribution portal at *http://premier.dell.com.*

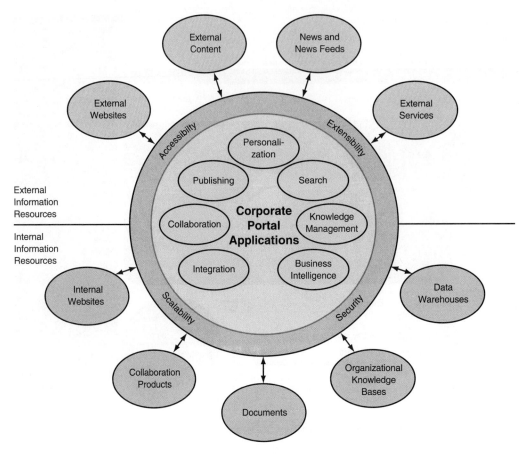

FIGURE 5.4 A corporate portal framework.
Sources: Compiled from A. Aneja et al., "Corporate Portal Framework for Transforming Content Chaos on Intranets," *Intel Technology Journal*, Q1, 2000, and from T. Kounandis, "How to Pick the Best Portal," *e-Business Advisor*, August 2000.

Whereas corporate portals are associated with a single company, **industry-wide portals** serve entire industries. An example is TruckNet (*www.truck.net*), which is the portal for the trucking industry and the trucking community, including professional drivers, owner/operators, and trucking companies. TruckNet provides drivers with personalized web-based e-mail, access to applications to leading trucking companies in Canada and the United States, and access to the Drivers RoundTable, a forum where drivers can discuss issues of interest. The portal also provides a large database of trucking jobs and general information related to the trucking industry.

These four portals are differentiated by the audiences they serve. Another type of portal, the mobile portal, is distinguished by its technology. **Mobile portals** are portals that are accessible from mobile devices. Significantly, any of the four portals we just discussed can be accessed by mobile devices. Mobile devices are typically wireless, so we discuss them in detail in Chapter 7.

Communication

The second major category of network applications is communication. There are many types of communication, including e-mail, call centres, chat rooms, voice, and unified communications. We discuss each one in this section. We consider another type of communication, blogging, in the section on Web 2.0.

Electronic Mail

Electronic mail (e-mail) is the largest-volume application running over the Internet. Studies have found that almost 90 percent of companies conduct business transactions via e-mail, and nearly

70 percent confirm that e-mail is tied to their means of generating revenue. In fact, for many users, e-mail has all but replaced the telephone.

Web-Based Call Centres

Effective personalized customer contact is becoming an important aspect of web-based customer support. Such service is provided through *web-based call centres,* also known as *customer care centres.* For example, if you need to contact a software vendor for technical support, you will usually be communicating with the vendor's web-based call centre, using e-mail, a telephone conversation, or a simultaneous voice/web session. Web-based call centres are sometimes located in foreign countries such as India or the Philippines. Such *offshoring* is an important issue for Canadian companies.

Electronic Chat Rooms

Electronic chat refers to an arrangement in which participants exchange conversational messages in real time. A **chat room** is a virtual meeting place where groups of regulars come to "gab." Chat programs allow you to send messages to people who are connected to the same channel of communication at the same time. Anyone can join in the on-line conversation. Messages are displayed on your screen as they arrive, even if you are in the middle of typing a message.

There are two major types of chat programs. The first type is a web-based chat program, which allows you to send messages to Internet users by using a web browser and visiting a web chat site (for example, *http://ca.messenger.yahoo.com*). The second type is an e-mail-based (text-only) program called *Internet Relay Chat (IRC).* A business can use IRC to interact with customers, provide experts' answers to questions, and so on.

Voice Communication

When people need to communicate with one another from a distance, they use the telephone more frequently than any other communication device. With the "plain old telephone service," every call opened up a dedicated circuit for the duration of the call. (A dedicated circuit connects you to the person you are talking with and is devoted only to your call.) In contrast, as we discuss in Technology Guide 4, the Internet divides data into packets, which traverse the Internet in random order and are reassembled at their destination.

With **Internet telephony,** also known as **voice-over Internet protocol** or **VoIP,** phone calls are treated as just another kind of data. That is, your analogue voice signals are digitized, sectioned into packets, and then sent over the Internet. VoIP significantly reduces your monthly phone bills. In the past, VoIP required a computer with a sound card and a microphone. Today, however, you do not need special phones or headsets for your computer.

Skype (*www.skype.com*) provides several free voice-over IP services: voice and video calls to users who also have Skype, instant messaging, short message service, voice mail, one-to-one and group chats, and conference calls with up to nine people (see Figure 5.5). In February 2009, Skype released Skype 4.0 for Windows, which offers full-screen video calling, improved quality of calls, and improved ease of use. Skype offers other functions for which users pay. SkypeOut allows you to make calls to landline phones and mobile phones. SkypeIn is a number that your friends can call from any phone and you pick up the call in Skype. Other functions include Skype Voicemail and Skype Short Message Service (SMS).

Unified Communications

In the past, organizational networks for wired and wireless data, voice communications, and video-conferencing operated independently, and the IT department managed each separately. This situation led to higher costs and lower productivity.

FIGURE 5.5 Skype interface, *www.skype.com. Sources:* Jochen Tack/Alamy.

Unified communications (UC) simplifies and integrates all forms of communications—voice, voice mail, fax, chat, e-mail, instant messaging, short message service, presence (location) services, and videoconferencing—on a common hardware and software platform. Presence services enable users to know where their intended recipients are and if they are available in real time.

UC unifies all forms of human and computer communications into a common user experience. For example, UC allows an individual to receive a voice mail message and then read it in his e-mail inbox. In another example, UC enables users to seamlessly collaborate with another person on a project, regardless of where the users are located. One user could quickly locate the other user by accessing an interactive directory, determine if that user were available, engage in a text messaging session, and then escalate the session to a voice call or even a video call, all in real time.

Collaboration

The third major category of network applications is collaboration. An important feature of modern organizations is that people collaborate to perform work. **Collaboration** refers to efforts by two or more entities (that is, individuals, teams, groups, or organizations) who work together to accomplish certain tasks. The term **work group** refers specifically to two or more individuals who act together to perform some task.

Workflow is the movement of information as it flows through the sequence of steps that makes up an organization's work procedures. Workflow management makes it possible to pass documents, information, and tasks from one participant to another in a way that is governed by the organization's rules or procedures. Workflow systems are tools for automating business processes. If group members are in different locations, they constitute a **virtual group (team)**.

Virtual groups conduct *virtual meetings*; that is, they "meet" electronically. **Virtual collaboration** (or *e-collaboration*) refers to the use of digital technologies that enable organizations or individuals to collaboratively plan, design, develop, manage, and research products, services, and innovative applications. Organizational employees may collaborate virtually, but organizations also collaborate virtually with customers, suppliers, and other business partners to improve productivity and competitiveness.

One type of collaboration is *crowdsourcing*, which refers to outsourcing a task to an undefined, generally large group of people in the form of an open call. IT's About Business 5.2 shows how one entrepreneur used crowdsourcing to start a restaurant.

Collaboration can be *synchronous*, meaning that all team members meet at the same time. Teams may also collaborate *asynchronously* when team members cannot meet at the same time. Virtual teams, whose members are located throughout the world, typically must collaborate asynchronously.

IT'S ABOUT BUSINESS 5.2
STARTING A RESTAURANT WITH THE HELP OF A FEW FRIENDS

Three enterprising entrepreneurs wanted to open a restaurant in Washington, D.C., that caters to vegetarian/raw-food diets. These diets are restricted to fruits, vegetables, nuts, seeds, and sprouts, none of which has been heated above 45 °C. For about a year, one of the owners has attended meetings and shared her ideas on a community website to persuade others of the virtues of a vegetarian diet.

The owners have not, however, had to contribute cash because the model for the restaurant, Elements, is crowdsourcing. That is, the restaurant was conceived and developed by an open-source community of experts and interested parties. Crowdsourcing outsources a task to a group, uses the group's collective intelligence to come up with the best ideas, and then distributes operational tasks to the group members who are best suited to perform them. In short, crowdsourcing puts the wisdom of crowds to work.

Almost 400 Elements community members have helped develop the concept (a sustainable vegetarian/raw-foods restaurant), the look (a comfortable gathering space with an open kitchen), the logo (a bouquet of colourful leaves), and even the name. Most businesses begin with an idea that is taken to the public to see if they like it. Elements takes the opposite approach: It finds out what the public wants and then does it.

The Elements project began in February 2007 when the founders of the restaurant established an electronic community, *http://elements.collectivex. com*. One month later, the group held its first meeting, which attracted 14 people. Over the next several months, the group grew to include architecture buffs, food lovers, designers, potential chefs and servers, and a not-for-profit organization called Live Green (*www.livegreen.net*), whose purpose is to help establish affordable, environmentally sound businesses.

The restaurant concept expanded over time. The original plan called for a 140-square-metre (1,500-square-foot) café, but the group wanted something more. The café expanded to a 325-square-metre (3,500-square-foot), green-certified restaurant. The kitchen would be sustainable, using food from local farms as well as growing some ingredients on a green roof.

Group members earn points for attending meetings and for performing tasks such as referring a new member to the community. Any member who amasses at least 1 percent of the total points is eligible for a share of the 10 percent profit (if there is one) that has been allocated to community members.

As one member observed, "It is not about the money. It's the community. What is rewarding is coming together to create a place in the city that's beneficial to the community and you and your friends."

Sources: Compiled from N. Gelinas, "Crowdsourcing," *New York Post*, August 24, 2008; "Crowdsourced Restaurant Taps Local Community," *Springwise.com*, August 12, 2008; J. Black, "Online, a Community Gathers to Concoct a Neighborhood Eatery," *Washington Post*, July 27, 2008; "Crowdsourcing a Restaurant: Good Luck with That," Joelogon blog (*www.joelogon.com/ blog/2008/07/crowdsourcing-restaurantgood-luck-with.html*), July 27, 2008; M. Brandel, "Should Your Company Crowdsource Its Next Project?" *Computerworld*, December 6, 2007; P. Boutin, "Crowdsourcing: Consumers as Creators," *BusinessWeek*, July 13, 2006; Elements website (*http://elements.collectivex.com/*), accessed February 11, 2009.

QUESTIONS

1. In planning for and developing the Elements restaurant, what are the advantages of crowdsourcing? The disadvantages?
2. Can the Elements restaurant be successful if "it's not about the money, it's the community?" Why or why not? Support your answer.

Collaboration Software

A variety of software products are available to support all types of collaboration. These products include Microsoft SharePoint Workspace, Google Docs, IBM Lotus Quickr, and Jive. In general, these products provide on-line collaboration capabilities, work-group e-mail, distributed databases, bulletin whiteboards, electronic text editing, document management, workflow capabilities, instant virtual meetings, application sharing, instant messaging, consensus building, voting, ranking, and various application development tools. We discuss each of these in turn.

Google Docs, Microsoft SharePoint Workspace, and Jive provide for shared content with *version management*, whereas Microsoft SharePoint and IBM Lotus Quickr provide for shared content with *version control*. Products that provide version management track changes to documents and provide features to accommodate concurrent work. Version control systems give each team member an account with a set of permissions. Shared documents are located in shared directories. Document directories are often set up so that users must check out documents before they can edit them. When a document is checked out, no other team member can access it. Once the document has been checked in, it becomes available to other members.

Microsoft SharePoint Workspace. Microsoft SharePoint Workspace (*http://office.microsoft.com/en-ca/sharepoint-workspace/*) is a collaboration product that provides shared content with version management. SharePoint Workspace's core concept is the shared workspace, which consists of a set of files to be shared plus tools to help in group collaboration. SharePoint Workspace users create workspaces, add documents, and invite other members to a workspace. A user who responds to an invitation is made an active member of that workspace.

Team members interact and collaborate in the common workspace. SharePoint Workspace tracks all changes, which are sent to all members. When multiple users try to edit one document at the same time, the software disallows one of them until the other is finished. SharePoint Workspace provides many tools, some of which include document repositories, discussion forums, to-do lists, calendars, meeting agendas, and others.

Google Docs. Google Docs (*http://docs.google.com*) is a free, web-based word processor, spreadsheet, and presentation application. It allows users to create and edit documents on-line while collaborating with other users. In contrast to Microsoft SharePoint Workspace, Google Docs allows multiple users to open, share, and edit documents at the same time.

IBM Lotus Quickr. IBM's Lotus Quickr (*www.ibm.com/lotus/quickr*) product provides shared content with version control in the form of document directories with check-in and check-out features based on user privileges. Quickr provides on-line team spaces where members can share and collaborate by using team calendars, discussion forums, blogs, wikis, and other collaboration tools for managing projects and other content.

Compagnie d'Enterprises (CFE), one of Belgium's largest construction companies, has put the collaboration tools of Quickr to good use. In construction projects many parties must collaborate effectively. When these projects are conducted on a global scale and the parties are scattered throughout the world, the projects become incredibly complex. CFE needed to tap its best resources for its projects, regardless of where those resources were located. The company was using e-mail to share documents with suppliers and clients, but this process resulted in version control errors and security vulnerabilities. To eliminate these problems, CFE deployed Quickr with its centralized document libraries and version control. The software reduced both the volume of large attachments sent through e-mail and the impact of those e-mails on the system. As a result, project teams were able to work more efficiently.

Jive. Jive's (*www.jivesoftware.com*) newest product, Clearspace, uses web collaboration and communication tools such as forums, wikis, and blogs to allow people to share content with version management via discussion rooms, calendars, and to-do lists. For example, Nike originally used Clearspace Community to run a technical support forum on Nike Plus (*www.nike.com/nikeplus*), a website where runners track their distance run and calories burned using a sensor in their shoes. Soon the company noticed that runners were also using the forum to meet other athletes and challenge them to races. In response to this development, Nike expanded its forum to include a section enabling runners to meet and challenge each other. Since that time, 40 percent of visitors to the site who did not own the Nike Plus sensor ended up buying the product.

We then turn our attention to electronic teleconferencing and videoconferencing, which are tools that support collaboration. Wikis are also a type of collaboration, and we discuss them in detail in the section on Web 2.0.

Electronic Teleconferencing

Teleconferencing is the use of electronic communication that allows two or more people at different locations to hold a simultaneous conference. There are several types of teleconferencing. The oldest and simplest is a telephone conference call, in which several people talk to one another from multiple locations. The biggest disadvantage of conference calls is that they do not allow the participants to communicate face-to-face. In addition, participants in one location cannot see graphs, charts, and pictures at other locations.

To overcome these shortcomings, organizations are increasingly turning to video teleconferencing, or videoconferencing. In a **videoconference**, participants in one location can see participants' documents and presentations at other locations. The latest version of videoconferencing, called telepresence, enables participants to seamlessly share data, voice, pictures, graphics, and animation by electronic means. Conferees can also transmit data along with voice and video, which allows them to work on documents together and to exchange computer files.

Several companies offer high-end telepresence systems. Hewlett-Packard's Halo system (*www. hp.ca*), Cisco's TelePresence 3000 (*www.cisco.com*), and Polycom's HDX (*www.polycom.com*) use massive high-definition screens up to two-and-a-half metres wide to show people sitting around conference tables (see Figure 5.6). Telepresence systems also have advanced audio capabilities that let everyone talk at once without cancelling out any voices. Telepresence systems can cost up to $400,000 for a room, with network management fees ranging up to $18,000 per month. Financial and consulting firms are

FIGURE 5.6
Telepresence.
Sources: © 2009
Polycom, Inc/
Newscom. All
rights reserved.

quickly adopting telepresence systems. For example, the Blackstone Group (*www.blackstone.com*), a private equity firm, has 40 telepresence rooms around the world, and Deloitte & Touche is installing 12 telepresence rooms.

Google

We mention Google in its own section because the company is developing and deploying applications that span discovery, communications, and collaboration. The company's applications fall into five categories: (1) search applications, which allow users to search web pages (Google Web), news, books (Google Books), maps (Google Maps), pictures (Google Images), and videos (Google Video), among others; (2) "communicate, show, and share" applications, which allow users to create and share their documents on-line and access them remotely (Google Docs), to create mailing lists and discussion groups (Google Groups), and to communicate with other users over the Internet (Google Talk); (3) mobile applications, which consist of search (Google Web Search, and Google Maps) and communication products (Google SMS) specifically adapted for mobile devices; (4) applications to "make your computer work better" such as Google Pack and Google Web Accelerator; and (5) applications to "explore and innovate," which includes a number of tools for application developers (Google Code), tools to build custom searches on the Web (Google Custom Search), and a list of potential Google products that are under development (Google Labs), such as Google Mars, which provides views of maps of Mars created by NASA scientists, or Google Accessible Search, which consists of a web search engine for the visually impaired. The following link provides more information about all of Google's applications: *www.google.com/intl/en/options/*.

BEFORE YOU GO ON...

1. Describe the three network applications that were discussed in this section and the tools and technologies that support each one.
2. Identify the business conditions that have made videoconferencing more important.

5.2 Web 2.0

Web 1.0 was the first generation of the World Wide Web, in which users had minimal interaction and the technology was mainly used as a means to provide information about products, events, people, and so on. For the most part, Web 1.0 allowed for the creation of websites and the commercialization of the Web.

Web 2.0 is a popular term that is proving difficult to define. According to Tim O'Reilly, a noted blogger (see *www.oreillynet.com/lpt/a/6228*), Web 2.0 is a loose collection of information technologies and applications, and the websites that use them. These websites enrich the user experience by encouraging user participation, social interaction, and collaboration. Unlike Web 1.0 sites, Web 2.0 sites are not so much on-line places to visit as services to get something done, usually with other people. Web 2.0 sites harness collective intelligence (for example, wikis); deliver functionality as services, rather than packaged software; and feature remixable applications and data (for example, mashups).

We begin our exploration of Web 2.0 by examining the various Web 2.0 information technologies and applications. We then look at the categories of Web 2.0 sites and we provide examples for each category.

Web 2.0 Information Technologies And Applications

Information technologies and applications used by Web 2.0 sites include XML, AJAX, tagging, blogs, wikis, really simple syndication (RSS), podcasting, and videocasting. Before we take a closer look at each of these technologies, we provide an example of a company that uses Web 2.0 tools to build its brand in IT's About Business 5.3.

IT'S ABOUT BUSINESS 5.3
HOW DOES A SMALL VINEYARD BUILD ITS BRAND?

An adage posits that it takes a large fortune to make a small fortune in the wine business. Stormhoek (meaning "stormy corner" in Afrikaans) is trying to buck that trend. Stormhoek Vineyards (*www. stormhoek.com*), a small South African winery, produces 10 types of red and white wine ranging in price from $10 to $15 per bottle. With a staff of about 20, including farm workers, Stormhoek has built its brand from scratch with a marketing budget of only $50,000 in 2006 and $100,000 in 2007.

Stormhoek measures success according to a few metrics. Some of the metrics are quantifiable, such as revenue growth and the number of bottles sold per wine store. Other metrics are not as quantifiable. One such metric is being mentioned in the trade press. Significantly, Stormhoek was mentioned about 100 times in the first half of 2006 and about 200 times in the second half. Another metric involves winning tasting awards. Stormhoek's pinotage, a signature South African red wine, was named the best pinotage of 2006 by the International Wine and Spirit competition.

Clearly then Stormhoek was offering a high-quality product. The company's major business problem was simple. How could it increase market share with a very limited budget?

To accomplish this goal, Stormhoek decided to use a variety of Web 2.0 tools, including blogs and wikis. For example, the company uses a blog as its corporate website. When visitors go to the site, they are presented with the latest posting from a Stormhoek employee. The blog supports video links (Stormhoek bloggers can cut and paste embedded links to YouTube videos directly into an entry); an RSS feed that sends new posts to subscribers; and an e-commerce component that allows visitors to purchase promotional items, such as Stormhoek-branded posters and underwear.

Stormhoek used its blog to launch a public relations campaign called "100 Geek Dinners in 100 Days." The goal was to have a different person host a wine-tasting party each night for 100 nights, with Stormhoek supplying the wine.

To plan the dinners, Stormhoek employees did absolutely nothing except blog about the parties and ship one case of wine to each of the 100 hosts across the United States and Great Britain. The volunteer hosts, who included well-known bloggers and wine enthusiasts, as well as people who simply wanted to throw a party, organized the dinners by contributing contact and location information to a wiki. The hosts and their guests posted more than 150 photos of the events on Flickr (*www.flickr.com*). In all, about 4,500 people attended the dinners.

Integrated into the wiki is an interactive map of the United States. The mashup allowed dinner hosts to display their geographic location graphically. When visitors clicked on an event on the map, represented by a coloured dot, they could sign up to attend the dinner, send a message to the host, and view photos of him or her.

How successful was this strategy? Stormhoek's sales tripled from 2005 to 2009, a gain executives attribute entirely to a marketing push that exploits Web 2.0 technologies.

Sources: Compiled from "Stormhoek Scoops Marketing Excellence Award," *BizCommunity.com*, November 19, 2007; T. McNichol, "How a Small Winery Found Internet Fame," *Business 2.0 Magazine*, August 8, 2007; E. Bennett, "Web 2.0: Turning Browsers into Buyers," *Baseline Magazine*, June 14, 2007; Stormhoek website (*www.stormhoek.com*), accessed January 30, 2009.

QUESTIONS
1. Visit Stormhoek's website at *www.stormhoek. com*. Discuss the advantages and disadvantages of Stormhoek's having a blog for a website.
2. Should Stormhoek use traditional marketing methods to go along with its Web 2.0 marketing efforts? How? Why? Support your answer.

Ajax

AJAX (Asynchronous Java Script and XML) is a web development technique that allows portions of web pages to reload with fresh data instead of requiring the entire web page to reload. This process speeds up response time and increases user satisfaction.

Tagging

A **tag** is a keyword or term that describes a piece of information (for example, a blog, a picture, an article, or a video clip). Users typically choose tags that are meaningful to them. Tagging allows users to place information in multiple, overlapping associations rather than in rigid categories. For example, a photo of a car might be tagged with "Corvette," "sports car," and "Chevrolet." Tagging is the basis of *folksonomies*, which are user-generated classifications that use tags to categorize and retrieve web pages, photos, videos, and other web content.

As one example, the website Delicious (*http://delicious.com*) provides a system for organizing not just information for individuals but for the entire Web. Delicious is basically a tagging system, or a place to store all those links that do not fit in a "Favorites" folder. It not only collects your links in one place, but it organizes them as well. The website has no rules governing how its users create and use tags. Instead, each person makes her own. However, the product of all those individual decisions is well organized. That is, if we conduct a search on Delicious for all the pages that are tagged with a particular word, you will likely come up with a very good selection of related web sources.

Blogs and Blogging

A **weblog** (**blog** for short) is a personal website, open to the public, in which the site creator expresses his feelings or opinions. *Bloggers*—people who create and maintain blogs—write stories, tell news, and provide links to other articles and websites that are of interest to them. The simplest method to create a blog is to sign up with a blogging service provider, such as *www.blogger.com* (now owned by Google, see Figure 5.7), *http://wordpress.com*, and *www.sixapart.com*. The **blogosphere** is the term for the millions of blogs on the Web.

Companies are using blogs in different ways. Some companies listen to the blogosphere for marketing purposes. Others open themselves up to the public for input into their processes and products.

Many companies are listening to consumers in the blogosphere who are expressing their views on products. In marketing, these views are called consumer-generated media. Two companies, Cymfony (*www.cymfony.com*) and Nielsen Online (*www.nielsen-online.com*), "mine" the blogosphere for their clients to provide information in several areas. For example, they help their clients find ways to serve potential markets, from broad-based to niche markets. They also help their clients detect false rumours before they appear in the mainstream press, and they gauge the potency of a marketing push or the popularity of a new product.

Wikis

A **wiki** is a website on which anyone can post material and make changes to other material. Wikis have an "edit" link on each page that allows anyone to add, change, or delete material, fostering easy collaboration.

Wikis harness the collective intelligence of Internet users, meaning that the collective input of many individuals can produce outstanding results. Consider this example. Amazon.ca and chapters-indigo.ca sell the same products, and they receive the same product descriptions and editorial content from their vendors. However, Amazon.ca has led all bookstores in soliciting user input in the form of

FIGURE 5.7
Blogger, *www. blogger.com.*

File   Edit   View   Favorites   Tools   Help

Back   Search   Favorites

Address   http://www.blogger.com/start   Go   Lin

Blogger

Already have an account? Sign in:
Username: Password: ?

SIGN IN   ☐ Remember me (?)

What's a **blog**?   TAKE A QUICK TOUR

Publish   **Get**   **Find**   **And**
thoughts   feedback   people   more...

A **blog** is your easy-to-use web site, where you can quickly post thoughts, interact with people, and more. All for **FREE**.

Create a **blog** in 3 easy steps:

① Create an account
② Name your blog
③ Choose a template

CREATE YOUR BLOG NOW

user editorial reviews. As a result, most Amazon.ca users go directly to the user reviews when they are deciding whether to buy a book.

Wikipedia (*www.wikipedia.org*), the on-line encyclopedia, is the largest wiki in existence (see Figure 5.8). It contains almost two million articles in English, which are viewed almost 400 million times every day. Wikipedia's volunteer administrators enforce a neutral point of view and encourage users to delete copy displaying clear bias. However, the question is: How reliable and accurate are the articles? Many educators do not allow students to cite references from Wikipedia because content can be provided by anyone at any time. This process leads to questions about the authenticity of the content.

FIGURE 5.8 Wikipedia, *www.wikipedia.org.*

WIKIPEDIA
The Free Encyclopedia

The reliability of content on Wikipedia, compared with encyclopedias and more specialized sources, is assessed in several ways, including statistically, by comparative review, and by analysis of the strengths and weaknesses inherent in the Wikipedia process. For example, in 2005 the British journal *Nature* suggested that for scientific articles, Wikipedia came close to the level of accuracy of the *Encyclopedia Britannica* and had a similar rate for "serious errors." Not surprisingly, the *Britannica* disputes the *Nature* article's findings.

Organizations use wikis in several ways. In project management, for example, wikis provide a central repository for capturing constantly updated product features and specifications, tracking issues, and resolving problems, and maintaining project histories. In addition, wikis enable companies to collaborate with customers, suppliers, and other business partners on projects. Wikis are also useful in knowledge management. For example, companies use wikis to keep enterprise-wide documents, such as guidelines and frequently asked questions, accurate and current.

Really Simple Syndication

Really simple syndication (RSS) allows users to receive the information they want (customized information), when they want it, without having to surf thousands of websites. RSS allows anyone to syndicate (publish) his or her blog, or any other content, to anyone who has an interest in subscribing. When changes to the content are made, subscribers receive a notification of the changes and an idea of what the new content contains. Subscribers can click on a link that will take them to the full text of the new content. You can find thousands of websites that offer RSS feeds at Syndic8 (*www.syndic8.com*) and NewsIsFree (*www.newsisfree.com*). Figure 5.9 shows an example of how RSS feeds can be located.

To start using RSS, you need a special news reader that displays RSS content feeds from websites you select. There are many such readers available, several of which are free. Examples of readers are AmphetaDesk (*www.disobey.com/amphetadesk*) and Pluck (*www.pluck.com*). For an excellent tutorial of RSS, visit *www.mnot.net/rss/tutorial*.

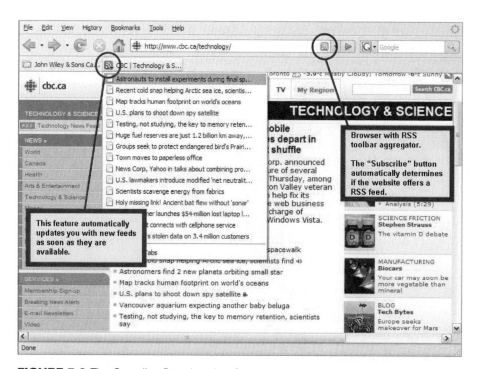

FIGURE 5.9 The Canadian Broadcasting Corporation (CBC) website (*www.cbc.ca*) with RSS toolbar aggregator.

Podcasts and Videocasts

A podcast is a digital audio file that is distributed over the Web using RSS for playback on portable media players and personal computers. A videocast is the same as a podcast, except that it is a digital video file.

Categories of Web 2.0 Sites

Web 2.0 sites that use some or all of the technologies and applications we have just discussed can be grouped into three major categories: social media, aggregators, and mashups. In this section, we discuss these categories, and we examine the various ways in which business uses them.

Social Networking

Social networking websites allow users to upload their content to the Web in the form of text (for example, blogs), voice (for example, podcasts), images, and videos (for example, videocasts). Social networking sites provide an easy, interactive way to communicate and collaborate with others on the Web. These sites can be a useful way to find like-minded people on-line, either to pursue an interest or a goal or just to help establish a sense of community among people who may never meet in the real world. In addition, many organizations are finding useful ways to employ social networks to pursue strategic objectives.

In our opening case, when Del Monte began exploring a new breakfast treat for dogs, the company surveyed members of its network to find out what they thought. Based on this feedback, it created a vitamin- and mineral-enriched treat called Snausages Breakfast Bites. The Snausages Bites project took six months, shorter than a typical product development cycle. During that time, the company regularly interacted with members of the dog lovers' group. This interactive process helped Del Monte formulate the product and also guided the packaging and marketing strategies by giving the company a better idea of what to expect in the marketplace. For example, when research indicated that buyers were more likely to be small-dog owners, the company produced a smaller treat. As a bonus, marketing the smaller-size dog treat trimmed costs.

Clearly then, social networking tools allowed Del Monte to get much closer to consumers. The company is able to identify its customers' most pressing issues and understand important matters that influence their buying decisions. The company can also explore concepts, including the development of new products.

Some well-known social networking sites are listed below:

- MySpace (*www.myspace.com*) and Facebook (*www.facebook.com*) are popular social networking websites.
- YouTube (*www.youtube.com*) is a social networking site for video uploads.
- Flickr (*www.flickr.com*) is a photo-sharing website, widely used by bloggers as a photo repository.
- Last.fm (*www.last.fm*) is a personalized streaming web-based radio station based on a profile of your musical tastes.
- LinkedIn (*www.linkedin.com*) is a business-oriented social networking site that is valuable for recruiting, sales, and investment. The company makes money from advertising and services. People—mainly the site's 60,000 recruiters—pay an average of $3,600 per year for premium features such as sending messages to LinkedIn members outside their own networks. Corporate members pay fees of up to six figures for access to the network.
- Tagworld (*www.tagworld.com*) is a website that people use for sharing blogs, photos, and music, as well as for on-line dating. All of the site's content can be tagged for easy searching.

- Twitter (*http://twitter.com*) allows users to post short updates (called "tweets") on their lives (no more than 140 characters) via the website, instant messaging, or mobile devices. With some 14 million users, in mid-2009 Twitter was the third largest social networking site, behind Facebook and MySpace. IT's About Business 5.4 illustrates how Twitter is a useful tool for solving problems and providing insights into public sentiment.

IT'S ABOUT BUSINESS 5.4
TWITTER BECOMES SURPRISINGLY USEFUL

Your first reaction to Twitter may be confusion. Why would anyone want to read anything so banal? However, Twitter is becoming surprisingly useful in a number of ways.

Customer reactions to products and services: Researchers have found that, taken collectively, the stream of messages from Twitter users can provide the immediate reactions of a company's customers to a product. Companies such as Starbucks and Dell can see what their customers are thinking as they use a product and adjust their marketing efforts accordingly. At Starbucks, customers used to complain by leaving notes in suggestion boxes. Now they can also post their complaints or suggestions on Twitter where the company keeps track of what people are saying about Starbucks on-line.

Dell noticed that customers complained on Twitter that the apostrophe and return keys were too close together on the Dell Mini 9 Laptop. As a result, Dell fixed the problem on the Dell Mini 10.

In an example of the main challenges that companies face with new social networking technologies, Nissan Canada in 2009 launched a social media campaign to give away 50 free Cube cars. It was a good idea but it was not long before Catherine Green, marketing manager of Nissan Canada, realized that the corporate 9-to-5 world does not fit the profile of Twitter, which is active 24/7. In addition, the company does not control the conversation and Twitter users expect you to listen and answer right away. Participants quickly started complaining about how long the company was taking to answer their tweets. Finally, Nissan Canada decided to stop using Twitter and direct the communications via e-mail.

Government: Government institutions are also learning how important it is becoming to have an on-line presence as an economical and quick way to inform their constituents. For example the federal Department of Finance started using Twitter (*www.twitter.com/financecanada*) to deliver information about the 2010 federal budget, adding links to relevant portions of the budget that were tweeted in real time. "Using social media will bring our message to

Canadians in a new, cost-effective and convenient way," said Finance Minister Jim Flaherty in a news release.

Police: Police forces across the country, including in Toronto, Calgary, and Vancouver, and the RCMP, have also created Twitter accounts in an effort to improve their communication links with the communities they serve. The Ontario Provincial Police force is the latest police agency to join the social media movement by opening a Twitter account (*www.twitter.com/OPP_News*), which includes news releases and other messages.

Fundraising: When Twitter first appeared in 2006, few realized its potential to rapidly spread awareness about a cause, and virtually no one even thought of using it to raise funds. On September 21, 2008, Canadian Internet executive Jordan Banks launched "A Million Tweets to Remember" with the main goal of remembering a million people who have suffered from Alzheimer's disease and to raise funds to support research. Participants came from 74 countries. The project helped to raise even more funds for research and treatment as an anonymous donor contributed up to a maximum of $50,000 to match every dollar donated through A Million Tweets. Apart from Twitter, the project took full advantage of other social networking sites, including Facebook.

Disaster relief: In early January 2010, a terrible earthquake shook Haiti, devastating homes, public infrastructure, and killing thousands of people. As help poured in from all over the world, the challenge was to distribute this help to those parts of the country that most needed it, especially in Haiti's capital, Port-au-Prince. From that day, Rachelle Houde from Montreal worked with Twitter and GPS location software called Ushahidi to coordinate the delivery of material help sent to Haiti. Using her contacts with Oxfam and World Water Relief officials on the ground in Haiti and the support from Twitter and Ushahidi technology, she managed to coordinate the delivery of water bottles donated by an American Baptist mission to two

(Continued on next page)

IT'S ABOUT BUSINESS 5.4 (*Continued*)
TWITTER BECOMES SURPRISINGLY USEFUL

orphanages in Port-au-Prince. Ushahidi software is an international platform originally developed by a Kenyan lawyer in 2008 to track ethnic violence in that country. Now Ushahidi and a host of social networking tools such as Twitter and Facebook are combining to confront the crisis in Haiti, wielded by an untold number of unlikely freelance volunteers, including Houde.

Tracking epidemics: If Twitter grows enough to collect a more representative sample of what the world is thinking, it could enable researchers to track epidemics. To make this process easier, Twitter has added a search box to its home page so users can search for terms such as "flu" and receive any tweets about those topics in their Twitter feeds.

Sources: Compiled from C. Miller, "Putting Twitter's World to Use," *The New York Times*, April 14, 2009; L. Bourgon, "Tweeting Them Where it Hurts," *Canadian Business*, November 2009; "OPP Joins Twitter," *Canadian Press*, January 26, 2010; J. P. Menezes, "How to Turn a Million Tweets into a Million Bucks," *IT World*, February 12, 2010; K. Kidd, "Twitter Spells Remote-control Relief via Montreal," *The Globe and Mail*, January 20, 2010; K. Kanji, "1 Million Tweets to Remember: A Case Study," Techvibes.com, February 7, 2010; "Hey There! The Department of Finance Is Using Twitter," news release, February 24, 2010.

QUESTIONS
1. What other challenges could businesses face when using Twitter?
2. How could your university benefit from the use of Twitter? Provide specific examples.

Aggregators

Aggregators are websites that provide collections of content from the Web. Well-known aggregator websites include:

- Bloglines (*www.bloglines.com*) collects blogs and news from all over the Web and presents it in one, consistent, updated format.
- Digg (*http://digg.com*) is a news aggregator that is part news site, part blog, and part forum. Users suggest and rate news stories, which are then ranked based on this feedback.
- Simply Hired (*www.simplyhired.com*) searches some 4.5 million listings on job and corporate websites and contacts subscribers via an RSS feed or an e-mail alert when a job that meets their parameters is listed.
- Technorati (*http://technorati.com*) contains information on all blogs in the blogosphere. It shows how many other blogs link to a particular blog, and it ranks blogs by topic.

Mashups

Mashup means to "mix and match" content from various parts of the Web. A **mashup** is a website that takes different content from a number of other websites and mixes them together to create a new kind of content. The launch of Google Maps is credited with providing the start for mashups. Anyone can take a map from Google, add their own data, and then display a map mashup on their website that plots crime scenes, cars for sale, or virtually any other item.

New tools are emerging to build location mashups. For example, Pipes from Yahoo! (*http://pipes.yahoo.com*) is a service that lets users visually remix data feeds and create mashups, using drag-and-drop features to connect multiple web data sources.

BEFORE YOU GO ON...

1. Describe the underlying technologies that support Web 2.0.
2. What are the main categories of Web 2.0 sites?

5.3 E-Learning and Distance Learning

E-learning and distance learning are not the same thing, but they do overlap. **E-learning** refers to learning supported by the Web. It can take place inside classrooms as a support to conventional teaching, such as when students work on the Web during class. It also can take place in virtual classrooms, in which all coursework is done on-line and classes do not meet face-to-face. In these cases, e-learning is a part of distance learning. **Distance learning (DL)** refers to any learning situation in which teachers and students do not meet face-to-face.

Today, the Web provides a multimedia interactive environment for self-study. Web-enabled systems make knowledge accessible to those who need it, when they need it, any time, anywhere. For this reason, e-learning and DL can be useful both for formal education and for corporate training.

For example, Gap (*www.gap.com*) used a combination of classroom and e-learning instruction to school its information technology managers in leadership skills. Gap employed an interactive e-learning course to help its leaders develop management and coaching tools they need to assess and enhance their employees' skills and competencies. The company placed the e-learning course between an in-person, three-hour kickoff program that included a demonstration of the software and a two-day classroom course designed to reinforce the material presented in the e-learning program.

Using simulation and interactive scenarios, the course instructs students on how to assess staffers' skills and competencies, identify the best management approach in assisting and directing people based on their competencies, and partner with individuals to help them be more productive and self-sufficient.

The Benefits and Drawbacks of E-Learning

There are many benefits to e-learning. For example, on-line materials can deliver very current content that is high quality (created by content experts) and consistent (presented the same way every time). It also gives students the flexibility to learn anywhere, at any time, and at their own pace. In corporate training centres that use e-learning, learning time generally is shorter, which means that more people can be trained within a given timeframe. This system reduces training costs as well as the expense of renting facility space.

Despite these benefits, e-learning has some drawbacks. To begin with, students must be computer literate. Also, they may miss the face-to-face interaction with instructors. Finally, assessing students' work can be problematic because instructors really do not know who completed the assignments.

E-learning does not usually replace the classroom setting. Rather, it enhances it by taking advantage of new content and delivery technologies. Advanced e-learning support environments, such as Blackboard (*www.blackboard.com*), add value to traditional learning in higher education.

Virtual Universities

Virtual universities are on-line universities that students use to take classes from home or at an off-site location, via the Internet. A large number of existing universities offer on-line education of some form. Some universities, such as Athabasca University (*www.athabascau.ca*), the University of Manitoba (*http://umanitoba.ca*), Thompson Rivers University (*www.tru.ca*), and TÉLUQ (*www.teluq.uquebec.ca*), offer hundreds of courses and dozens of degrees to students, all on-line. Other universities offer limited on-line courses and degrees but use innovative teaching methods and multimedia support in the traditional classroom. IT's About Business 5.5 shows how the University of British Columbia has taken on-line learning even further.

IT'S ABOUT BUSINESS 5.5
E-LEARNING REAL ESTATE AT UBC

An increasing number of universities in Canada are going on-line, allowing their students to take courses on-line. As an example of how to blend technology and education, the University of British Columbia (UBC) Real Estate Division (RED) has recently added live on-line instruction, or "webinars," to its suite of distance education offerings.

On-line instruction was a suitable solution for students taking Appraisal Institute of Canada courses. Most of the educational centres don't have sufficient number of students to run a full in-class session. Therefore, on-line delivery appeared as a viable and effective way of delivering these courses. Currently, students can attend live on-line classroom presentations and work on class materials at their pace. RED also provides webinars for continuing professional development short courses.

In order to deliver these courses, UBC's E-Learning Centre selected Horizon Wimba because it is simple to set up, easy to learn, and has minimal computer and network requirements. For example, students living in rural areas can still connect to Wimba using a simple dial-up access.

The Wimba system allows students to listen to their instructor, watch the PowerPoint presentation the instructor is using, and interact with their instructor by means of raising their hands virtually through the use of icons, instant messaging, or by directly using their computer microphone. The technology even allows students more informal forms of interaction such as applause or laughing at a joke. Wimba also offers instructors the possibility to conduct real-time on-line quizzes with immediate feedback to the class.

One of the main benefits of using on-line instruction is that it provides a face-to-face classroom experience without the need to be physically present, avoiding travel time and expenses. However, e-learning does not come without its drawbacks. A recent study by the U.S. Department of Education found that while on-line learners do better on average than those in a traditional class environment, combining face-to-face with on-line instruction results in greater learning overall. The report also found that the effectiveness of on-line learning differs depending on the type of subject being taught and the type of student. Some students like learning in a class because they can interact with others and get immediate feedback from the teacher. Motivation and determination also differ from student to student and has critical impact on the success of on-line learners.

Sources: Compiled from: "Online EMBAs: Get a Global Focus," *Canadian Business*, November 2009; J. Bridal, "UBC Webinars Bring the Classroom to You," *Canadian Property Valuation* 53(1), 2009; N. Keung, "English Classes for Immigrants Aren't Old School," *The Toronto Star*, January 18, 2010.

QUESTIONS
1. What factors need to be taken into consideration by an organization when considering entering into e-learning?
2. What reasons lead the RED at UBC to choose its system to deliver on-line instruction?
3. What challenges do students face when taking a course on-line?

BEFORE YOU GO ON...

1. Differentiate between e-learning and distance learning.
2. Describe virtual universities.

5.4 Telecommuting

Knowledge workers are being called the distributed workforce. This group of highly prized workers is now able to work anywhere and at any time by using a process called **telecommuting**. Distributed workers have no permanent office at their companies, preferring to work in home offices, airport lounges, or client conference rooms. The growth of the distributed workforce is driven by globalization, extremely long commutes to work, rising gasoline prices, ubiquitous broadband communications links (wireline and wireless), and powerful laptop computers and computing devices.

Currently, about 10 percent of the Canadian workforce qualifies as distributed, according to recent data from Statistics Canada. Forty percent of IBM's workforce has no office at the company; at AT&T, more than 30 percent of its managers are distributed; and at Sun Microsystems, nearly 50 percent of employees are distributed, saving the company $300 million in real estate costs. Sun also notes that its distributed workers are 15 percent more productive than their co-workers in offices.

Telecommuting has a number of potential advantages for employees, employers, and society. For employees, the benefits include reduced stress and improved family life. In addition, telecommuting offers employment opportunities for housebound people such as single parents and persons with disabilities. Employer benefits include increased productivity, the ability to retain skilled employees, and the ability to attract employees who don't live within commuting distance.

However, telecommuting also has some potential disadvantages. For employees, the major disadvantages are increased feelings of isolation, possible loss of fringe benefits, lower pay (in some cases), no workplace visibility, the potential for slower promotions, and lack of socialization. The major disadvantages to employers are difficulties in supervising work, potential data security problems, and training costs.

BEFORE YOU GO ON...

1. What is telecommuting? Do you think you would like to telecommute?
2. What are the advantages and disadvantages of telecommuting from the viewpoint of the employee? From the viewpoint of the organization?

WHAT'S IN IT FOR ME?

FOR THE ACCOUNTING MAJOR

Accounting personnel use corporate intranets and portals to consolidate transaction data from legacy systems to provide an overall view of internal projects. This view contains the current costs charged to each project, the number of hours spent on each project by individual employees, and a comparison of actual costs with projected costs. Finally, accounting personnel use Internet access to government and professional websites to stay informed on legal and other changes affecting their profession.

FOR THE FINANCE MAJOR

Corporate intranets and portals can provide a model to evaluate the risks of a project or an investment. Financial analysts use two types of data in the model: historical transaction data from corporate databases via the intranet, and industry data obtained via the Internet. In addition, financial services firms can use the Web for marketing and to provide services.

FOR THE MARKETING MAJOR

Marketing managers use corporate intranets and portals to coordinate the activities of the sales force. Sales personnel access corporate portals via the intranet to discover updates on pricing, promotion, rebates, customer information, and information about competitors. Sales staff can also download and customize presentations for their customers. The Internet, and particularly the Web, provides a new marketing channel for many industries. Just how advertising, purchasing, and information dispensation should occur appears to vary from industry to industry, product to product, and service to service.

FOR THE PRODUCTION/OPERATIONS MANAGEMENT MAJOR

Companies are using intranets and portals to speed product development by providing the development team with three-dimensional models and animation. Team members can access the models for faster exploration of ideas and enhanced feedback. Corporate portals, accessed via intranets, enable managers to supervise their inventories as well as real-time production on assembly lines. Extranets are also valuable as communication formats for joint research and design efforts among companies. The Internet is also a great source of cutting-edge information for production/operations managers.

FOR THE HUMAN RESOURCES MANAGEMENT MAJOR

Human resources personnel use portals and intranets to publish corporate policy manuals, job postings, company telephone directories, and training classes. Many companies deliver on-line training obtained from the Internet to employees through their intranets. Human resources departments use intranets to offer employees healthcare, savings, and benefit plans, as well as the opportunity to take competency tests on-line. The Internet supports worldwide recruiting efforts, and it can also be the communications platform for supporting geographically dispersed work teams.

FOR THE MIS MAJOR

As important as the networking technology infrastructure is, it is invisible to users (unless something goes wrong). The MIS function is responsible for keeping all organizational networks up and running all the time. MIS personnel, therefore, provide all users with an "eye to the world" and the ability to compute, communicate, and collaborate anytime, anywhere. For example, organizations have access to experts at remote locations without having to duplicate that expertise in multiple areas of the firm. Virtual teaming allows experts physically located in different cities to work on projects as though they were in the same office.

SUMMARY

1. **Describe the three major applications of computer networks.**
   Networks support discovery, communication, and collaboration. Discovery involves browsing and information retrieval, and allows users to view information in databases, download it, and/ or process it. Discovery tools include search engines, directories, and portals. Networks provide fast, inexpensive communications, via e-mail, call centres, chat rooms, voice communications, and blogs. Collaboration refers to mutual efforts by two or more entities (individuals, groups, or companies) who work together to accomplish tasks. Collaboration is enabled by workflow systems and collaboration software.

2. **Discuss the various technologies, applications, and websites that fall under the umbrella of Web 2.0.**
   Information technologies and applications used by Web 2.0 sites include XML, AJAX, tagging, blogs, wikis, really simple syndication (RSS), podcasting, and videocasting. AJAX is a web development technique that allows portions of web pages to reload with fresh data instead of requiring the entire web page to reload. This process speeds up response time and increases user satisfaction. A tag is a keyword or term that describes a piece of information. Users typically choose tags that are meaningful to them. A weblog (blog for short) is a personal website, open to the public, in which the site creator expresses his or her feelings or opinions. A wiki is a website on which anyone can post material and make changes to other material.

   Really simple syndication (RSS) allows anyone to syndicate (publish) a blog, or any other content, to anyone who has an interest in subscribing. Subscribers get a notification of content changes and an idea of what the new content contains. Subscribers can click on a link that will take them to the full text of the new content.

   A podcast is a digital audio file that is distributed over the Web using RSS for playback on media players or computers. A videocast is similar, except that it is a digital video file.

   Web 2.0 websites use some or all of these technologies and applications and may be grouped into several categories: social media, aggregators, and mashups. Social networking websites allow users to upload their content to the Web in the form of text (e.g., blogs), voice (e.g., podcasts), images, and videos (e.g., videocasts). Social networking sites provide an easy, interactive way to communicate and collaborate with others on the Web. Aggregators are websites that provide collections of content from the Web. A mashup is a website that takes content from a number of other websites and mixes it together to create a new kind of content.

3. **Differentiate between e-learning and distance learning.**
   E-learning refers to learning supported by the Web. It can take place inside classrooms as a support to conventional teaching. It can also take place in *virtual classrooms*, in which coursework is done on-line and classes do not meet face-to-face. In these cases, e-learning is a part of distance learning. Distance learning refers to any learning situation in which teachers and students do not meet face-to-face.

4. **Understand the advantages and disadvantages of telecommuting for employers and employees.**
   The benefits of telecommuting for employees include less stress, improved family life, and employment opportunities for housebound people. Telecommuting can provide the organization with increased productivity, the ability to retain skilled employees, and the ability to tap the remote labour pool.

   The disadvantages for employees are feelings of isolation, possible loss of fringe benefits, lower pay (in some cases), no workplace visibility, slower promotions, and lack of socialization. The major disadvantages to employers are difficulties in supervising work, potential data security problems, training costs, and the cost of equipping and maintaining telecommuters' homes.

KEY TERMS

affinity portal, 147
aggregator, 161
AJAX, 156
blog, 156
blogosphere, 156
chat room, 149
collaboration, 150
commercial (public) portal, 147
corporate portal, 147
distance learning (DL), 162
e-learning, 162
industry-wide portal, 148
Internet telephony, 149

mashup, 161
metasearch engine, 144
mobile portal, 148
podcast, 159
portal, 146
really simple syndication
   (RSS), 158
search engine, 144
social networking, 159
tag, 156
telecommuting, 163
teleconferencing, 153
unified communications, 150

videocast, 159
videoconference, 153
virtual collaboration, 150
virtual group
   (team), 150
virtual university, 162
voice-over Internet protocol
   (VoIP), 149
Web 2.0, 154
weblog, 156
wiki, 156
work group, 150
workflow, 150

DISCUSSION QUESTIONS

1. How would you describe Web 2.0 to someone who has not taken a course in information systems?
2. If you were the CEO of a company, would you pay any attention to blogs about your company? Why or why not? If yes, would you consider some blogs to be more important or reliable than others? If so, which ones? How would you find blogs relating to your company?
3. Is it a good idea for a business major to join LinkedIn (*www.linkedin.com*) as a student? Discuss.
4. How are the network applications of communication and collaboration related? Do communication tools also support collaboration? Give examples.
5. Access this article from *The Atlantic*: "Is Google Making Us Stupid?" (*www.theatlantic.com/doc/200807/google*). Do you think Google is making us stupid? Support your answer.
6. Search Google for recent news about telecommuting in Canada. Identify obstacles to telecommuting and report on why firms don't use telecommuting more often? Are these factors the same for every province in Canada? Are they the same for every country?

PROBLEM-SOLVING ACTIVITIES

1. You plan to take a two-week vacation in Australia this year. Using the Internet, find information that will help you plan the trip. Such information includes, *but is not limited to*, the following:
   a. geographical location and weather conditions at the time of your trip;
   b. major tourist attractions and recreational facilities;
   c. travel arrangements (airlines, approximate fares);
   d. car rental and local tours;
   e. alternatives for accommodation (within a moderate budget) and food;
   f. estimated cost of the vacation (travel, lodging, food, recreation, shopping, etc.);
   g. country regulations regarding the entrance of your dog, which you would like to take with you;
   h. shopping;
   i. passport information (either to obtain one or to renew one); and
   j. information on the country's language and culture.
   k. What else do you think you should research before going to Australia?

2. From your own experience or from the vendor's information, list the major capabilities of Lotus Notes/Domino. Do the same for Microsoft Exchange. Compare and contrast the products. Explain how the products can be used to support knowledge workers and managers.

3. Visit websites of companies that manufacture telepresence products for the Internet. Prepare a report. Differentiate between telepresence products and videoconferencing products.

4. Access Google videos and search for "Cisco Magic." This video shows Cisco's next-generation telepresence system. Compare and contrast it with current telepresence systems.

5. Access the website of your university. Does the website provide high-quality information (right amount, clear, accurate, etc.)? Do you think a high school student who is thinking of attending your university would feel the same way?

6. Enter *www.programmableweb.com* and study the various services that the website offers. Learn about how to create mashups and then propose a mashup of your own. Present your mashup to the class.

7. Compare and contrast Google Sites (*www.google.com/sites*) and Microsoft Office Live (*www.liveoffice.com*). Which site would you use to create your own website? Explain your choice.

8. Research the companies involved in Internet telephony (voice-over IP). Compare their offerings as to price, necessary technologies, ease of installation, etc. Which company is the most attractive to you? Which company might be the most attractive for a large business looking to use VoIP?

9. Access some of the alternative search engines at *www.readwriteweb.com/archives/top_100_alternative_search_engines.php*. Search for the same terms on several of the alternative search engines and on Google. Compare the results on breadth (number of results found) and precision (results are what you were looking for).

10. Second Life (*www.secondlife.com*) is a three-dimensional, on-line world built and owned by its residents. Residents of Second Life are avatars created by real-world people. Access Second Life, learn about it, and create your own avatar to explore this world. Make a presentation to your class as to how it could be used as a learning tool in this course or any other course in your major.

11. Access the Boeing Supplier Portal information page at *www.boeingsuppliers.com/*. Describe some of the many services offered there for Boeing's suppliers.

12. Surf the Web to find a procurement (sourcing) portal and a distribution portal. (Other than the examples in this chapter.) List the features they have in common and those features that are unique.

TEAM ASSIGNMENTS

1. Assign each group member to an integrated group support tool kit (e.g., SharePoint Workspace, Jive, Google Docs, SharePoint, or Quickr). Have each member visit the website of the commercial developer and obtain information about this product. As a group, prepare a comparative table of the major similarities and differences among the kits.

2. Have each team download a free trial of SharePoint Workspace from *http://sharepoint.microsoft.com/en-us/Pages/Try-It.aspx*. Install the software on the members' PCs and arrange collaborative sessions. What can the free software do for you? What are its limitations?

3. Each team should pick a subject that needs aggregation. Set up the plans for an aggregator website to accomplish this mission. Present to the class.

4. Each team will pick one of the following: Art in Canada (*www.artincanada.com/*) CanadianArt (*www.canadianart.ca/*) and Canada Council for the Arts (*www.canadacouncil.ca/*). Compare and contrast these sites as to features and ease of use. Present each product to the class. Each group will collaborate on writing a report on its product using Google Docs.

5. Enter *www.podcasting-tools.com*. Explain how to record a podcast and make it available on the Web. Each team will create a podcast on some idea in this course and make it available on-line.

CANADIAN FIRM HELPS BUILD SOCIAL NETWORKS

THE BUSINESS PROBLEM

More and more businesses are looking at social networking technologies for different purposes and in very different ways: to attract new customers, keep existing ones, get feedback from customers, and to advertise and create awareness. Twitter and Facebook are among the most popular social networking websites for businesses to promote their products. However, firms looking for more personalized interactive contact with their customers need other technology tools that provide them with the flexibility to change content and allow customers to personalize their interaction.

THE IT SOLUTION

A Toronto firm that started in 2005 is doing just this for many Canadian firms. Filemobile provides the technical tools and consulting services for firms to create their own mini social network site. The software also allows these companies to connect to their Facebook or Twitter sites and can be used as a back end for these sites. However, it provides much more functionality than the generic Facebook or Twitter, by allowing users to upload videos and send comments. Many companies include these two websites as integral parts of their marketing campaigns.

THE RESULTS

Using Filemobile, MSN launched a website that tracked the Olympic torch relay across Canada leading up to the 2010 Winter Games in Vancouver. In addition to mapping the trek, the site allowed users to share their own relay stories.

The CBC ran a campaign to find a song for its popular show Hockey Night in Canada. The CBC used the Filemobile platform to create a website that allowed users to upload their songs. The campaign received over 20,000 submissions, making it, according to Filemobile, the most successful user-generated contest in Canadian history.

Hasbro, the company behind the popular board game Monopoly, set up an on-line version of the game, attracting five million participants. Monopoly City Streets used a mashup of the game and Google Maps to allow users to virtually buy and build on millions of streets around the globe. Players bought nine million streets and built 175 million structures.

In another example, Mars, the company that makes Skittles candy, has made use of social networks in order to increase its brand awareness. Most recently, it set up a website, Skittle Skuffle, where visitors could create their own personalized Skittle avatars. Different characters could be created by choosing a different head, glasses, facial hair, limbs, and weapons. The ultimate aim is to gain points by winning "Skuffles," getting fans to support your Skittler, and being liked by other site visitors. Previously Skittles had created a homepage containing a series of Twitter posts from anyone who included the word "Skittles" in their post.

Sources: Compiled from O. El Akkad, "Filemobile Capitalizes on Active Marketing," *The Globe and Mail*, February 16, 2010; Filemobile website (*www.filemobile.com*), accessed April 12, 2010.

QUESTIONS

1. What is different about Filemobile and traditional social networking websites such as Facebook or Twitter?
2. Provide examples of how your university could take advantage of social networking technology using Filemobile.

Web Resources

Student website www.wiley.com/canada/rainer

- Web quizzes
- Lecture slides in PowerPoint

- Author podcasts
- Interactive Case: Ruby's Club assignments

ALL OF THE ABOVE AND...

- E-book
- Manager videos
- Vocabulary flash cards

- Pre- and post-lecture quizzes
- Microsoft Office 2007 lab manual and projects

ANALYZING NETWORK OPPORTUNITIES FOR RUBY'S CLUB

ruby's club

Go to the Ruby's Club link at the Student Companion website or WileyPLUS for information about your current internship assignment. Your assignment will entail working with data about how Ruby's network can create a better experience for its customers.

E-BUSINESS AND E-COMMERCE

CAN FACEBOOK GENERATE REVENUE WITH ADVERTISING?

THE BUSINESS PROBLEM

The social networking website Facebook (*www.facebook.com*) helps people communicate more effectively with friends, family, and coworkers. It does so by allowing anyone to sign up in a trusted environment and interact with people they know. Users can easily build networks of friends to share news and photos, join groups, and search for acquaintances from school or work. The website also provides tools such as instant messaging and e-mail.

Facebook is attracting users from other social networking websites by mimicking some of their features. One feature allows you to type in your school name and graduation date and see fellow classmates, a challenge to Classmates (*www.classmates.com*) and similar sites. Similarly, why use Evite (*www.evite.com*) to announce an event when you can contact your friends via Facebook? Facebook's ultimate goal is to build a global website where you can just type in anyone's name, find that person, and communicate with him or her.

Currently, Facebook has more than 500 million active users and is growing at the amazing rate of 5 million users per week. At this growth rate, by early 2011 Facebook will have 600 million active users, and in the next three to five years Mark Zuckerberg, the co-founder of Facebook, estimates that it will have one billion users. The fastest-growing age group is individuals over the age of 55, and the next-fastest-growing age group is individuals between the ages of 45 and 54. In addition, the average Facebook user spends 169 minutes per month on the website. Visitors to the *New York Times*, for comparison, spend an average of only 10 minutes per month on the site.

Ironically, however, it seems that everyone but Facebook is capitalizing on the site. For example, accounting firm Ernst & Young goes to Facebook when it's looking to hire new recruits, as does Dell. Interestingly, Microsoft's Windows 7 operating system contains many features adopted directly from Facebook.

Given Facebook's dazzling usage statistics, it is not surprising that marketers want to place advertising on the website. However, brand advertising on Facebook has been less than successful. In the past, many companies have unsuccessfully attempted to use traditional banner advertisements, which consist only of a brief text or graphical message. (We discuss banner ads in Section 6.2.) However, Facebook users have largely ignored these efforts. Other marketing campaigns have relied on promotional giveaways and contests, but these techniques, too, have produced disappointing results.

This lack of advertising success is a real concern for Facebook executives. In fact, despite the site's exploding popularity, as of mid-2009, Facebook was not yet profitable. Accordingly, Facebook wants to develop a revenue stream from advertising on its website.

POTENTIAL IT SOLUTIONS

Facebook managers realize that their company is a natural and valuable medium for marketing efforts. The extensive amount of data that Facebook gathers on its users provides the company with a huge competitive advantage. This information would enable companies that advertise on Facebook to target very specific groups of people.

In an initial test, Facebook and Proctor and Gamble (P&G, *www.pg.com*) set up a promotion for Crest Whitestrips. They created a Facebook page for the tooth-whitening product and invited Facebook users at 20 universities to join up as "fans." Additionally, Facebook created a feature called "Connect," letting members use their Facebook logins to sign on to corporate websites. When a user logs on to a company's site using Connect, it shows up on their friends' news feeds. In turn, these friends might interpret this news as a de facto endorsement of the company's products or services. Connect also helps connect users' friends to sites for other companies. For example, Starbucks (*www.starbucks.com*) has a Pledge5 (*http://pledge5.starbucks.com*) site, which encourages people to volunteer for at least five hours on a community project. The site uses Connect, which means that if you sign in using a Facebook account, a new screen, a hybrid of Facebook and the Pledge5 home page, appears with information on local volunteer opportunities.

At first glance the P&G Crest Whitestrips advertising campaign appeared to attract 14,000 fans. In fact, Crest provided so many additional enticements—thousands of free movie screenings, as well as sponsored Def Jam concerts—that the results of the campaign were called into question. As of mid-2009, more than 4,000 of the one-time 14,000 Facebook fans of Crest Whitestrips had left the fan club.

Sources: Compiled from M. Brush, "Is Facebook the New Wal-Mart?" *MSN Money*, April 7, 2009; J. Hempel, "How Facebook Is Taking Over Our Lives," *Fortune*, March 11, 2009; R. Stross, "Advertisers Face Hurdles on Social Networking Sites," *The New York Times*, December 14, 2008; M. Arrington, "Interview With Facebook CEO Mark Zuckerberg: Products, Funding, Competition," *Tech Crunch*, December 7, 2008; M. Arrington, "Facebook May Be Growing Too Fast, and Hitting the Capital Markets Again," *Tech Crunch*, October 31, 2008; T. Barjarin, "Why Will Facebook Continue to Grow," *PCMag*, October 11, 2010; Facebook website (*www.facebook.com*), accessed April 5, 2009 and July 22, 2010.

WHAT DO YOU THINK?

1. What type of e-commerce business model would Facebook, and social network websites in general, fit into?
2. What challenges do social network websites face as a profitable business model?
3. Could electronic payment methods add value to social network websites?
4. What are the potential ethical concerns of using social networks to conduct e-commerce?

Chapter Preview

Electronic commerce (e-commerce) offers two very important advantages to companies. First, it increases an organization's reach, defined as the number of potential customers to whom the company can market its products. This advantage extends to both large and small businesses. Facebook is an excellent example of increased reach, as we saw in the opening case. Second, electronic commerce removes many of the barriers that previously impeded entrepreneurs who start businesses. Facebook provides a cautionary story here. Even though the company effectively used electronic commerce to grow rapidly, its future is unclear because its revenue model has, so far, not been as effective. The important point here is that a company using electronic commerce, despite all its advantages, still must have a viable method for generating revenue, or the company will fail.

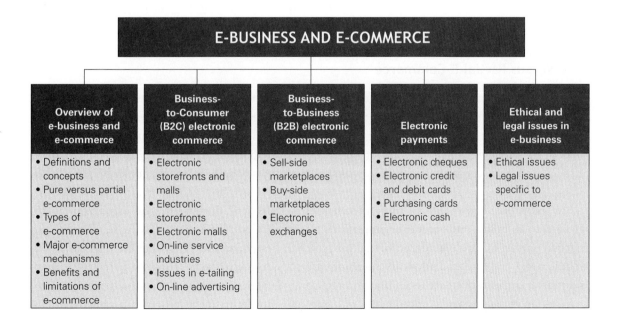

E-BUSINESS AND E-COMMERCE				
Overview of e-business and e-commerce	**Business-to-Consumer (B2C) electronic commerce**	**Business-to-Business (B2B) electronic commerce**	**Electronic payments**	**Ethical and legal issues in e-business**
• Definitions and concepts • Pure versus partial e-commerce • Types of e-commerce • Major e-commerce mechanisms • Benefits and limitations of e-commerce	• Electronic storefronts and malls • Electronic storefronts • Electronic malls • On-line service industries • Issues in e-tailing • On-line advertising	• Sell-side marketplaces • Buy-side marketplaces • Electronic exchanges	• Electronic cheques • Electronic credit and debit cards • Purchasing cards • Electronic cash	• Ethical issues • Legal issues specific to e-commerce

We begin this chapter with a general overview of e-commerce and e-business. We then look at two of the major types of electronic commerce: business-to-consumer (B2C) e-commerce and business-to-business (B2B) e-commerce. We continue with an examination of the major electronic payment methods in e-commerce. We conclude by examining several legal and ethical issues that have arisen as a result of the rapid growth of e-commerce. Before we examine these specifics, however, we begin with a general overview of e-commerce and e-business.

6.1   Overview of E-Business and E-Commerce

One of the most profound changes in the modern world of business is the emergence of electronic commerce, also known as e-commerce (EC). E-commerce is changing all business functional areas and their important tasks, from advertising to paying bills. Its impact is so widespread that it is affecting almost every organization. In addition, it is drastically changing the nature of competition, due to the development of new on-line companies, new business models, and the diversity of EC-related products and services. E-commerce provides unparalleled opportunities for companies to expand worldwide at a small cost, to increase market share, and to reduce costs. In fact, by using electronic commerce, many small businesses can now operate and compete in market spaces once dominated by larger companies. E-commerce also offers amazing opportunities for you to open your own business by developing an e-commerce website.

This section examines the basics of e-business and e-commerce. We begin by defining these two concepts and then discussing pure and partial electronic commerce. We then take a look at the various types of electronic commerce. Next, we focus on e-commerce mechanisms, which are the ways in which businesses and people buy and sell over the Internet. We conclude this section by considering the benefits and limitations of e-commerce.

Definitions and Concepts

Electronic commerce (**EC** or **e-commerce**) describes the process of buying, selling, transferring, or exchanging products, services, or information via computer networks, including the Internet. **E-business** is a somewhat broader concept. In addition to the buying and selling of goods and services, e-business also refers to servicing customers, collaborating with business partners, and performing electronic transactions within an organization. However, because e-commerce and e-business are so similar, we use the two terms interchangeably throughout the book.

Pure Versus Partial E-Commerce

Electronic commerce can take several forms depending on the degree of digitization involved. The *degree of digitization* refers to the extent to which the commerce has been transformed from physical to digital. It can relate to: (1) the product or service being sold, (2) the process by which the product or service is produced, or (3) the delivery agent or intermediary. In other words, the product can be physical or digital, the process can be physical or digital, and the delivery agent can be physical or digital.

In traditional commerce all three dimensions are physical. Purely physical organizations are referred to as **bricks-and-mortar organizations**. In *pure EC* all dimensions are digital. Companies engaged only in EC are considered **virtual** (or *pure-play*) **organizations**. All other combinations that include a mix of digital and physical dimensions are considered *partial* EC (but not pure EC). **Clicks-and-mortar organizations** are those that conduct some e-commerce activities, yet their primary business is done in the physical world. Therefore, clicks-and-mortar organizations are examples of partial

EC. E-commerce is now so well established that people increasingly expect companies to offer this service in some form.

For example, buying a shirt from Walmart on-line or a book from Amazon.ca is *partial EC*, because the merchandise is physically delivered by FedEx or UPS. However, buying an e-book from Amazon.ca or a software product from Buy.com is pure EC, because the product as well as its delivery, payment, and transfer are all conducted on-line. In this book we use the term EC to denote either pure or partial EC. IT's About Business 6.1 illustrates how a partial EC apparel retailer with a unique corporate culture uses Twitter to engage its customers.

IT'S ABOUT BUSINESS 6.1
ZAPPOS AND TWITTER

The social networking and micro-blogging service Twitter (*www.twitter.com*) has become the preferred method of streaming real-time activity updates to millions of subscribers on the World Wide Web. The activity updates or *tweets* are text-based posts of up to 140 characters in length. Tweets are delivered to any user who has signed up to receive them from a particular sender. Users can send and receive updates via the Twitter website or through other websites that use Tweeter software on their sites. Additionally, the service is accessible on smart phones via short message service (SMS).

Twitter symbolizes the rapid, short, synchronous, and public conversations that are very much a part of the lives of people who use Facebook, MySpace, or other social networking tools. In the few brief years since Twitter was introduced, it has attained extensive global visibility and popularity, making it attractive as a business application for opening a new and unrestricted consumer channel for electronic marketing.

Zappos (*www.zappos.com*), an on-line retailer of shoes and clothing, employs Twitter as an e-commerce tool. Twitter functionality fits perfectly with Zappos' corporate value structure and beliefs. As described on the company home page, the company's core values are:

1. Deliver WOW through Service
2. Embrace and Drive Change
3. Create Fun and a Little Weirdness
4. Be Adventurous, Creative, and Open-Minded
5. Pursue Growth and Learning
6. Build Open and Honest Relationships with Communication
7. Build a Positive Team and Family Spirit
8. Do More with Less
9. Be Passionate and Determined
10. Be Humble

So what has Zappos been able to accomplish through its use of Twitter? First, it added a link to a separate Twitter page (*http://twitter.zappos.com*) on every page of its website. If you click on "What are Zappos employees doing right now?," you can read the latest tweets from employees about what they're doing at work and interesting finds both on the Zappos site and elsewhere in cyberspace. Additionally, the tweets contain links to the various shoes and clothes that Zappos sells.

Another application of Twitter is the Employee Leader Board, tallying the number of tweets and followers and who's tweeting at any given time. Zappos' popular CEO, Tony Hsieh, is usually on top of the leader board, gaining five times as many followers as anyone else. Under Tony's leadership, Zappos has increased gross merchandise sales from $1.6 million in 2000 to more than $1 billion in 2008. Tony believes that the Zappos success story begins and ends with a relentless focus on customer service. To this end, Twitter is another opportunity for Zappos to drive core value # 6—"Build open and honest relationships with communication."

Sources: Compiled from S. Gaudin, "Web 2.0 Tools Like Twitter, Facebook Can Foster Growth in Hard Times," *Computerworld*, March 13, 2009; "Extreme Customer Service: Zappos CEO and UPS Step In," *BusinessWeek*, February 19, 2009; H. Coster, "A Step Ahead," *Forbes*, June 2, 2008; M. Kirkpatrick, "Zappos Shows How Social Media Is Done," *ReadWriteWeb*, April 30, 2008; S. Durst, "Zappos Has Become the No. 1 Footwear Retailer on the Web By Making Customer Service a Competitive Weapon," *Business 2.0*, March 15, 2007; Zappos website (*www.zappos.com*), accessed April 4, 2009.

QUESTIONS

1. If you were shopping for shoes, would a text message update from the CEO of Zappos influence your purchase decision? Why or why not?
2. Many e-marketers are championing the use of technologies like Twitter as an electronic form of word-of-mouth marketing. In your opinion, will this strategy be effective? Why or why not?

Types of E-Commerce

E-commerce can be conducted between and among various parties. In this section, we identify the six common types of e-commerce and we discuss three of them—C2C, B2E, and e-government—in detail. We then devote a separate section to B2C and one to B2B because of their importance for businesses. Mobile commerce (m-commerce) will be covered in Chapter 7.

- **Business-to-consumer (B2C):** In B2C, the sellers are organizations, and the buyers are individuals. We discuss B2C electronic commerce in Section 6.2. Recall that Figure 2.2 (see p. 63) illustrated B2C electronic commerce.
- **Business-to-business (B2B):** In B2B transactions, both the sellers and the buyers are business organizations. The vast majority of EC volume is of this type. We discuss B2B electronic commerce in Section 6.3. Figure 2.2 also illustrates B2B electronic commerce.
- **Consumer-to-consumer (C2C):** In C2C, an individual sells products or services to other individuals. (You also will see the term C2C explained as "customer-to-customer." The terms are interchangeable, and we use both in this book.) The major strategies for conducting C2C on the Internet are auctions and classified ads.

In dozens of countries, C2C selling and buying on auction sites is exploding. Most auctions are conducted by intermediaries, like eBay (*www.ebay.ca*). Consumers can select general sites such as *www.auctionanything.com*. In addition, many individuals are conducting their own auctions. For example, *www.greatshop.com* provides software to create on-line C2C reverse auction communities. (We discuss reverse auctions, in which buyers solicit bids from sellers, later in this section.)

The major categories of on-line classified ads are similar to those found in print ads: vehicles, real estate, employment, pets, tickets, and travel. Classified ads are available through most Internet service providers (Rogers, MSN/Sympatico, etc.), at some portals (Yahoo!, etc.), and from Internet directories and on-line newspapers. Many of these sites contain search engines that help shoppers narrow their searches.

Internet-based classified ads have one big advantage over traditional types of classified ads: they provide access to an international, rather than a local, audience. This wider audience greatly increases both the supply of goods and services, and the number of potential buyers.

- **Business-to-employee (B2E):** In B2E, an organization uses EC internally to provide information and services to its employees. Companies allow employees to manage their benefits and to take training classes electronically. In addition, employees can buy discounted insurance, travel packages, and tickets to events on the corporate intranet. They also can order supplies and materials electronically. Finally, many companies have electronic corporate stores that sell the company's products to their employees, usually at a discount.
- **E-government:** E-government is the use of Internet technology in general and e-commerce in particular to deliver information and public services to citizens (called government-to-citizen or G2C EC), and business partners and suppliers (called government-to-business or G2B EC). It is also an efficient way of conducting business transactions with citizens and businesses and within the governments themselves. E-government makes government more efficient and effective, especially in the delivery of public services. An example of G2C e-commerce is electronic benefits transfer, in which governments transfer benefits, such as employment insurance or Canada Pension Plan payments, directly to recipients' bank accounts.
- **Mobile commerce (m-commerce):** The term *m-commerce* refers to e-commerce that is conducted entirely in a wireless environment. An example is using cell phones to shop over the Internet. We discuss m-commerce in Chapter 7.

Each of the above types of EC is executed in one or more business models. A **business model** is the method by which a company generates revenue to sustain itself. Table 6.1 summarizes the major EC business models. Other classifications of EC business models include Michael Rappa's Business Models on the Web (*http://digitalenterprise.org/models*) and Thomas Eisenmann's book *Internet Business Models: Text and Cases* (2002).

Facebook is a good example of how difficult it can be to find a viable e-commerce business model. Facebook is a privately held company, so it does not have to release its revenue figures. Therefore, quantifying the success of advertising on its website is not possible. However, Facebook CEO Mark

TABLE 6.1
E-COMMERCE BUSINESS MODELS

EC MODEL	DESCRIPTION AND EXAMPLES
On-line direct marketing	Manufacturers or retailers sell directly to customers. Very efficient for digital products and services. Can allow for product or service customization. (*www.dell.ca*)
Electronic tendering system	Businesses request quotes from suppliers. Uses B2B with a reverse auction mechanism.
Name-your-own-price	Customers decide how much they are willing to pay. An intermediary (for example, *www.priceline.com*) tries to match a provider.
Find-the-best-price	Customers specify a need; an intermediary (for example, *www.hotwire.com*) compares providers and shows the lowest price. Customers must accept the offer in a short time or may lose the deal.
Affiliate marketing	Vendors ask partners to place logos (or banners) on partner's site. If customers click on logo, go to vendor's site, and buy, then vendor pays commissions to partners.
Viral marketing	Receivers send information about your product to their friends.
Group purchasing (e-coops)	Small buyers aggregate demand to get a large volume; then the group conducts tendering or negotiates a low price.
On-line auctions	Companies run auctions of various types on the Internet. Very popular in C2C, but gaining ground in other types of EC. (*www.ebay.ca*)
Product customization	Customers use the Internet to self-configure products or services. Sellers then price them and fulfill them quickly (build-to-order). (*www.jaguar.com*)
Electronic marketplaces and exchanges	Transactions are conducted efficiently (more information to buyers and sellers, lower transaction costs) in electronic marketplaces (private or public).
Bartering on-line	Intermediary administers on-line exchange of surplus products and/or company receives "points" for its contribution, and the points can be used to purchase other needed items. (*www.bbu.com*)
Deep discounters	Company (for example, *www.half.com*) offers deep price discounts. Appeals to customers who consider only price in their purchasing decisions.
Membership	Only members can use the services provided, including access to certain information, conducting trades, etc. (*www.egreetings.com*)

Zuckerberg did assert that advertising revenue has increased substantially. The evolution of the Facebook website and the refinements of the systems that facilitate advertising have generated more than $50 million in revenue for the company.

If Facebook wants to take advantage of social advertising—which means extending a commercial message to users' friends—the company will face real resistance. Members are understandably reluctant to become walking advertisements for products. Analysts at SocialMedia Networks (*www.socialmedia. com*) somewhat humorously describe the advertising cycle in social networks in this way: "Advertisers distract users; users ignore advertisers; advertisers distract better; users ignore better." The bottom line is that advertisers on Facebook can try one of two approaches: They can make their ads more intrusive, or they can create genuinely entertaining commercials. Unfortunately, neither approach promises to be very successful. Intrusive ads will not generate positive outcomes, and entertaining ads are too expensive to produce.

Financial analysts estimate that Facebook's overhead (salaries, utilities, network bandwidth, hardware, software, etc.) is $300 million per year. eMarketer (*www.emarketer.com*), the digital marketing and media research firm, estimates $265 million in revenue for Facebook in 2008. Further, analysts assert that, with Facebook's rapid growth in users, its overhead will increase faster than its revenues. These figures do not paint a pretty picture going forward for Facebook.

All websites that rely on ads struggle to convert traffic, even high traffic, into meaningful revenue. Ads that run on Google and other search engines are a profitable exception because their visitors are often in a "buying mood." Other kinds of sites, however, cannot deliver similar types of visitors to advertisers. Google's own YouTube, which, like Facebook, relies heavily on user-generated content, remains a costly experiment in the high-traffic, low-revenue marketing business.

Major E-Commerce Mechanisms

There are a number of mechanisms through which businesses and customers can buy and sell on the Internet. The most widely used ones are electronic catalogues, electronic auctions, e-storefronts, e-malls, and e-marketplaces.

Catalogues have been printed on paper for generations. Today, however, they are available on CD-ROM and the Internet. Electronic catalogues consist of a product database, directory and search capabilities, and a presentation function. They are the backbone of most e-commerce sites.

An **auction** is a competitive process in which either a seller solicits consecutive bids from buyers or a buyer solicits bids from sellers. The primary characteristic of auctions is that prices are determined dynamically by competitive bidding. Electronic auctions (e-auctions) generally increase revenues for sellers by broadening the customer base and shortening the cycle time of the auction. Buyers generally benefit from e-auctions because they can bargain for lower prices. In addition, they don't have to travel to an auction at a physical location.

The Internet provides an efficient infrastructure for conducting auctions at lower administrative costs and with many more involved sellers and buyers. Individual consumers and corporations alike can participate in auctions. There are two major types of auctions: forward and reverse.

Forward auctions are auctions that sellers use as a channel to many potential buyers. Usually, sellers place items at sites for auction, and buyers bid continuously for them. The highest bidder wins the items. Both sellers and buyers can be individuals or businesses. The popular auction site eBay.ca is a forward auction.

In **reverse auctions**, one buyer, usually an organization, wants to buy a product or a service. The buyer posts a request for quotation (RFQ) on its website or on a third-party website. The RFQ provides detailed information on the desired purchase. The suppliers study the RFQ and then submit bids electronically. Everything else being equal, the lowest-price bidder wins the auction. The buyer notifies the winning supplier electronically. The reverse auction is the most common auction model for large purchases (in terms of either quantities or price). Governments and large corporations frequently use this approach, which may provide considerable savings for the buyer.

Auctions can be conducted from the seller's site, the buyer's site, or a third party's site. For example, eBay, the best-known third-party site, offers hundreds of thousands of different items in several types of auctions. Overall, more than 300 major companies, including Amazon.ca and Dell (*www.dellauction.com*), offer on-line auctions.

An *electronic storefront* is a website on the Internet that represents a single store. An *electronic mall*, also known as a *cybermall* or *e-mall*, is a collection of individual shops under one Internet address. Electronic storefronts and electronic malls are closely associated with B2C electronic commerce. We discuss each one in more detail in Section 6.2.

An **electronic marketplace** (e-marketplace) is a central, virtual market space on the Web where many buyers and many sellers can conduct electronic commerce and electronic business activities. Electronic marketplaces are associated with B2B electronic commerce. We discuss this topic in Section 6.3.

Benefits and Limitations of E-Commerce

Few innovations in human history have provided as many benefits to organizations, individuals, and society as has e-commerce. E-commerce benefits organizations by making national and international markets more accessible and by lowering the costs of processing, distributing, and retrieving information. Customers benefit by being able to access a vast number of products and services, around the clock. The major benefit to society is the ability to easily and conveniently deliver information, services, and products to people in cities, rural areas, and developing countries. Despite all these benefits, EC has some limitations, both technological and non-technological, that have slowed its growth and acceptance. Technological limitations include the lack of universally accepted security standards, insufficient telecommunications bandwidth, and expensive accessibility. Non-technological limitations include the perceptions that EC is insecure, has unresolved legal issues, and lacks a critical mass of sellers and buyers. As time passes, the limitations, especially the technological ones, will lessen or be overcome.

BEFORE YOU GO ON...

1. Define e-commerce, and distinguish it from e-business.
2. Differentiate among B2C, B2B, C2C, and B2E electronic commerce.
3. Define e-government.
4. Describe forward and reverse auctions.
5. List some benefits and limitations of e-commerce.

6.2 Business-to-Consumer (B2C) Electronic Commerce

B2B EC is much larger than B2C EC by volume, but B2C EC is more complex. The reason for this complexity is that B2C involves a large number of buyers making millions of diverse transactions per day with a relatively small number of sellers. As an illustration, consider Amazon, an on-line retailer (e-tailer) that offers thousands of products to its customers. Each customer purchase is relatively small, but Amazon must manage each transaction as if that customer were its most important. Each order must be processed quickly and efficiently, and the products must be shipped to the customer in a timely manner. In addition, returns must be managed. Multiply this simple example by millions, and you get an idea of the complexity of B2C EC.

This section addresses the more important issues in B2C EC. We begin by discussing the two basic mechanisms for customers to access companies on the Web: electronic storefronts and electronic malls. In addition to purchasing products over the Web, customers also access on-line services. Our next section covers several on-line services, such as banking, securities trading, job search, travel, and real estate. The complexity of B2C EC creates two major challenges for sellers: channel conflict and order fulfillment. We examine these two topics in detail. Finally, companies engaged in B2C EC must "get the word out" to prospective customers. Therefore, we conclude this section with a look at on-line advertising.

Electronic Storefronts and Malls

For several generations, home shopping from catalogues, and later from television shopping channels, has attracted millions of customers. Today, shopping on-line offers an alternative to catalogue and television shopping. **Electronic retailing (e-tailing)** is the direct sale of products and services through electronic storefronts or electronic malls, usually designed around an electronic catalogue format and/or auctions.

Like any mail-order shopping experience, e-commerce enables you to buy from home and to do so 24 hours a day, seven days a week. However, EC offers a wider variety of products and services, including the most number of unique items, often at lower prices. Furthermore, within seconds, shoppers can access very detailed supplementary information on products. In addition, they can easily locate and compare products and prices. Finally, buyers can find hundreds of thousands of sellers. Two popular on-line shopping mechanisms are electronic storefronts and electronic malls.

Electronic Storefronts

An **electronic storefront** is a website that represents a single store. Hundreds of thousands of electronic storefronts can be found on the Internet. Each one has its own Internet address, or uniform resource locator (URL), at which buyers can place orders. Some electronic storefronts are extensions of physical stores such as Future Shop, Chapters, and Sears. Others are new businesses started by entrepreneurs who saw a niche on the Web. Examples are Tigerdirect.ca and Booksforschools.ca. Manufacturers (for example, *www.dell.ca*) as well as retailers (for example, *www.staples.ca*) also use storefronts.

Electronic Malls

Whereas an electronic storefront represents a single store, an **electronic mall**, also known as a cyber-mall or e-mall, is a collection of individual shops under a single Internet address. The basic idea of an electronic mall is the same as that of a regular shopping mall—to provide a one-stop shopping place that offers many products and services. Each cybermall may include thousands of vendors. In most cyber malls you cannot buy anything but, instead, you are transferred from the mall to a participating storefront. This is why they are also known *referral malls* (for example, *http://yahoo.shoptoit.ca*, *http://shopping.ca.msn.com/*) (see Figure 6.1).

On-Line Service Industries

In addition to purchasing products, customers can also access needed services via the Web. Selling books, toys, computers, and most other products on the Internet can reduce vendors' selling costs by 20 to 40 percent. Further reduction is difficult to achieve because the products must be delivered physically. Only a few products (such as software or music) can be digitized to be delivered on-line for additional savings. In contrast, services, such as buying an airline ticket or purchasing stocks or

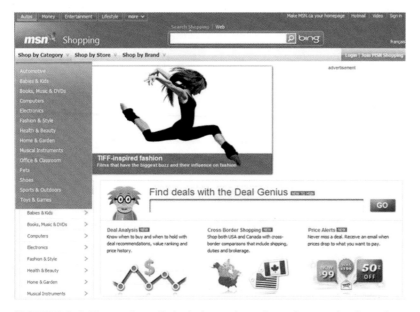

FIGURE 6.1 Electronic malls include products from thousands of vendors, *http://shopping.ca.msn.com/*.

insurance, can be delivered entirely through e-commerce, often with considerable cost reduction. Not surprisingly, then, on-line delivery of services is growing very rapidly, with millions of new customers being added each year.

One of the most pressing EC issues relating to on-line services (as well as in marketing tangible products) is disintermediation. Intermediaries, also known as middlemen, have two functions: (1) They provide information, and (2) they perform value-added services such as consulting. The first function can be fully automated and will most likely be assumed by e-marketplaces and portals that provide information for free. When this occurs, the intermediaries who perform only (or mainly) this function are likely to be eliminated. This process is called **disintermediation**.

In contrast, performing value-added services requires expertise. Unlike the information function, then, it can be only partially automated. Thus, intermediaries who provide value-added services not only are likely to survive, but they may actually prosper. The Web helps these service providers in two situations: (1) when the number of participants is enormous, as with job searches, and (2) when the information that must be exchanged is complex.

In this section, we examine some leading on-line service industries: banking, trading of securities (stocks, bonds), job matching, and travel services.

Cyberbanking

Electronic banking, also known as **cyberbanking**, involves conducting various banking activities from home, at a place of business, or on the road instead of at a physical bank location. Electronic banking has capabilities ranging from paying bills to applying for a loan. For customers, it saves time and is convenient. For banks, it offers an inexpensive alternative to branch banking (for example, a cost of about two cents per transaction versus $1.07 at a physical branch). It also enables banks to attract remote customers. In addition to regular banks with added on-line services, we are seeing the emergence of **virtual banks**, which are dedicated solely to Internet transactions. An example of a virtual bank is Virtual One Credit Union Limited (see Figure 6.2).

International banking and the ability to handle trading in multiple currencies are critical for international trade. Transfers of electronic funds and electronic letters of credit are important services in international banking. An example of support for EC global trade is provided by TradeCard Inc., in

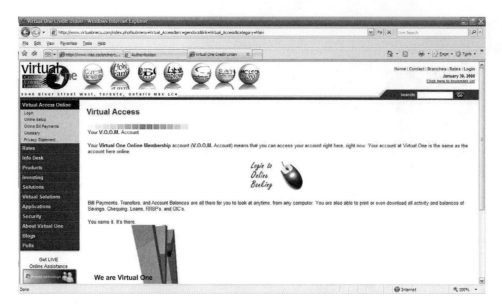

FIGURE 6.2 Virtual banks are devoted to on-line transactions, *www.virtualonecu.com.*

conjunction with MasterCard. TradeCard is an international company that provides a secure method for buyers and sellers to make digital payments anywhere on the globe (see the Procure-to-Pay demonstration at *www.tradecard.com*). In another example, banks and companies such as Oanda (*www. oanda.com*) provide conversions of more than 160 currencies.

On-Line Securities Trading

Many Canadians use computers to trade stocks, bonds, and other financial instruments. In Korea, more than half of stock traders are already using the Internet for that purpose. Why? Because it is cheaper than a full-service or discount broker. On the Web, investors can find a considerable amount of information regarding specific companies or mutual funds in which to invest (for example, *www. questrade.com* and *www.bloomberg.com*).

For example, let's say you have an account with an on-line broker. You access the broker's website from your personal computer or your Internet-enabled mobile device, enter your account number and password to access your personalized web page, and then click on "stock trading." Using a menu, you enter the details of your order (buy or sell, margin or cash, price limit, market order, and so on). The computer tells you the current "ask" and "bid" prices, much as a broker would do over the telephone. You can then approve or reject the transaction. Some well-known Canadian companies that offer only on-line trading are iTrade (*www.scotiaitrade.com*), the Bank of Montreal's Investorline (*www. bmoinvestorline.com*), and RBC Direct Investing (*www.rbcdirectinvesting.com*).

The On-Line Job Market

The Internet offers a promising new environment for job seekers and for companies searching for hard-to-find employees. Thousands of companies and government agencies advertise available positions, accept resumés, and take applications via the Internet.

Job seekers use the on-line job market to reply on-line to employment ads, to place resumés on various sites, and to use recruiting firms (for example, *www.monster.ca* and *www.workopolis.com*). Companies that have jobs to offer advertise openings on their websites, and they search the bulletin boards of recruiting firms. In many countries, governments must advertise public service job openings on the Internet.

Travel Services

The Internet is an ideal place to plan, explore, and arrange almost any trip economically. On-line travel services allow you to purchase airline tickets, reserve hotel rooms, and rent cars. Most sites also offer a fare-tracker feature that sends you e-mail messages about low-cost flights. Examples of comprehensive on-line travel services are Expedia.ca, Travelocity.ca, and itravel2000.com. On-line services are also provided by all major airline vacation services, large conventional travel agencies, car rental agencies, hotels (for example, *www.hotels.ca*), and tour companies. In a variation of this process, Priceline.com allows you to set a price you are willing to pay for an airline ticket or hotel accommodations. It then attempts to find a vendor that will match your price.

An interesting problem that e-commerce can cause is "mistake fares" in the airline industry. For example, over the weekend of May 4–6, 2007, United Airlines offered a $1,221 fare for a United States-to-New Zealand round trip in business class. This price was incorrect; the actual price was much higher. By the time United noticed the mistake and pulled the fare, however, hundreds of tickets had been sold, thanks in part to on-line travel discussion groups.

Issues in E-Tailing

Despite e-tailing's increasing popularity, many e-tailers continue to face serious issues that can restrict their growth. Perhaps the two major issues are channel conflict and order fulfillment.

Clicks-and-mortar companies may face a conflict with their regular distributors when they sell directly to customers on-line. This situation, known as **channel conflict**, can alienate the distributors. Channel conflict has forced some companies (for example, Ford Motor Company) to avoid direct on-line sales. An alternative approach for Ford allows customers to configure a car on-line but requires them to pick up the car from a dealer, where they arrange financing, warranties, and service.

Channel conflict can arise in areas such as pricing of products and services and resource allocation (for example, how much to spend on advertising). Another potential source of conflict involves logistics services provided by the off-line activities to the on-line activities. For example, how should a company handle returns of items bought on-line? Some companies have completely separated the "clicks" (the on-line portion of the organization) from the "mortar" or "bricks" (the traditional bricks-and-mortar part of the organization). However, this approach can increase expenses and reduce the synergy between the two organizational channels. As a result, many companies are integrating their on-line and off-line channels, a process known as **multi-channelling**.

The second major issue is order fulfillment, which can also be a source of problems for e-tailers. Any time a company sells directly to customers, it is involved in various order-fulfillment activities. It must perform the following activities: quickly find the products to be shipped; pack them; arrange for the packages to be delivered speedily to the customer's door; collect the money from every customer, either in advance, or by individual bill; and handle the return of unwanted or defective products.

It is very difficult to accomplish these activities both effectively and efficiently in B2C, because a company has to ship small packages to many customers and do it quickly. For this reason, companies involved in B2C activities often have difficulties in their supply chains.

In addition to providing customers with the products they ordered and doing it on time, order fulfillment also provides all related customer services. For example, the customer must receive assembly and operation instructions for a new appliance. In addition, if the customer is not happy with a product, an exchange or return must be arranged. (Visit *www.fedex.ca* to see how returns are handled via FedEx.)

In the late 1990s, e-tailers faced continuous problems in order fulfillment, especially during the holiday season. These problems included late deliveries, delivering wrong items, high delivery costs,

IT'S ABOUT BUSINESS 6.2
CANADIAN TIRE CLOSES ITS ON-LINE STORE

In a time where more and more businesses are looking for ways to sell their products on-line, one large Canadian retailer has decided to close its on-line store operations. Canadian Tire Corp. stopped selling on-line as of January 29, 2010.

The reasons given by the company for getting out of e-tailing included cost savings and focusing on its core businesses. The website was mostly used by customers as a research tool where they could search and compare products and read the specifications. However, customers still prefer to come to the stores and touch the merchandise before buying, so the website was not making enough money to keep it open. High shipping costs were also to blame for the decision, as some of the merchandise available were large bulky items such as patio sets, which are very expensive to ship.

Canadian Tire is not the only large retailer that does not sell on-line. Walmart Canada and the Hudson's Bay Company, for example, also have no on-line store.

However, Canadian Tire is not abandoning its on-line strategy completely as it will continue to operate its informational website and sell gift cards on-line. Also, the company has announced that in 2011 it will test a new service in selected markets allowing shoppers to buy merchandise on-line and pick the items up at a store. Canadian Tire CEO Stephen Wetmore indicated that the goal for the future will be to reinstate an e-commerce site.

Sources: Compiled from H. Shaw, "Canadian Tire Stops Selling Online," *Financial Post*, January 19, 2009; M. Strauss, "Canadian Tire Going Back to Basics," *The Globe and Mail*, April 7, 2010.

QUESTIONS
1. What reasons led Canadian Tire to stop its on-line operations?
2. What future implications (positive or negative) could this decision have for Canadian Tire? Discuss the opportunities and threats derived from this decision.
3. What characteristics make a product suitable for on-line shopping?

---

and compensation to unhappy customers. For e-tailers, taking orders over the Internet is the easy part of B2C e-commerce. Delivering orders to customers' doors is the hard part. Businesses today still face the same problems as it can be seen in the recent case of Canadian Tire Corp., which decided to stop selling merchandise on its website (see IT's About Business 6.2). In contrast, order fulfillment is less complicated in B2B. These transactions are much larger, but they are fewer in number. In addition, these companies have had order fulfillment mechanisms in place for many years.

On-Line Advertising

Advertising is the practice of disseminating information in an attempt to influence a buyer–seller transaction. Traditional advertising on TV or in newspapers is impersonal, one-way mass communication. Direct-response marketing, or telemarketing, contacts individuals by direct mail or telephone and requires them to respond in order to make a purchase. The direct-response approach personalizes advertising and marketing, but it can be expensive, slow, and ineffective. It can also be extremely annoying to the consumer.

Internet advertising redefines the advertising process, making it media-rich, dynamic, and interactive. It improves on traditional forms of advertising in a number of ways. First, Internet ads can be updated any time at minimal cost and therefore be kept current. In addition, these ads can reach very large numbers of potential buyers all over the world. Further, they are generally cheaper than radio, television, and print ads. Finally, Internet ads can be interactive and targeted to specific interest groups and/or individuals. Despite all these advantages, it is difficult to measure the effectiveness of on-line ads. For this reason, there are no concrete standards to evaluate whether the results of Internet ads justify their costs.

Advertising Methods

The most common on-line advertising methods are banners, pop-ups, and e-mail. **Banners** are simply electronic billboards. Typically, a banner contains a short text or graphical message to promote a product or a vendor. It may even contain video clips and sound. When customers click on a banner, they are transferred to the advertiser's home page. Banner advertising is the most commonly used form of advertising on the Internet (see Figure 6.3).

A major advantage of banners is that they can be customized to the target audience. If the computer system knows who you are or what your profile is, you may be sent a banner that is supposed to match your interests. A major disadvantage of banners is that they can convey only limited information due to their small size. Another drawback is that many viewers simply ignore them.

Pop-up and pop-under ads are contained in a new browser window that is automatically launched when you enter or exit a website. A **pop-up ad** appears in front of the current browser window. A **pop-under ad** appears underneath the active window: when users close the active window, they see the ad. Many users strongly object to these ads, which they consider intrusive. Modern browsers let users block pop-up ads, but this feature must be used with caution because some websites depend on pop-ups to function correctly.

E-mail is emerging as an Internet advertising and marketing channel. It is generally cost-effective to implement, and it provides a better and quicker response rate than other advertising channels. Marketers develop or purchase a list of e-mail addresses, place them in a customer database, and then send advertisements via e-mail. A list of e-mail addresses can be a very powerful tool because the marketer can target a group of people or even individuals.

As you have probably concluded by now, there is a potential for misuse of e-mail advertising. In fact, some consumers receive a flood of unsolicited e-mail, or *spam*. **Spamming** is the indiscriminate distribution of electronic ads without the permission of the receiver. Unfortunately, spamming is becoming worse over time.

Two important responses to spamming are permission marketing and viral marketing. **Permission marketing** asks consumers to give their permission to voluntarily accept on-line advertising and e-mail. Typically, consumers are asked to complete an electronic form that asks what they are interested in and requests permission to send related marketing information. Sometimes, consumers are offered incentives to receive advertising.

Permission marketing is the basis of many Internet marketing strategies. For example, millions of users receive e-mails periodically from airlines such as WestJet and Air Canada. Users of this marketing service can ask to be notified of low fares from their hometown or to their favourite destinations. Significantly, they can easily unsubscribe at any time. Permission marketing is also extremely important for market research (for example, see Media Metrix at *www.comscore.com*). In one particularly interesting form of permission marketing, companies such as ExpressPaidSurveys.com and CashSurfers.com

FIGURE 6.3 When customers click on a banner ad, they are transferred to the vendor's homepage, *http://ca.travel.yahoo.com*.

have built customer lists of millions of people who are happy to receive advertising messages whenever they are on the Web. These customers are paid $0.25 to $0.50 an hour to view messages while they do their normal surfing.

Viral marketing refers to on-line "word-of-mouth" marketing. The strategy behind viral marketing is to have people forward messages to friends, family members, and other acquaintances suggesting that they "check this out." For example, a marketer can distribute a small game program embedded with a sponsor's e-mail that is easy to forward. The marketer releases only a few thousand copies, with the expectation that the recipients in turn will forward the program to many more thousands of potential customers. In this way, viral marketing allows companies to build brand awareness at a minimal cost.

Social networking websites rely mainly on viral marketing and banner ads as their main advertising methods and as a way of generating revenue. In our opening case, at first glance the P&G Crest Whitestrips advertising campaign appeared to be a great success, attracting 14,000 fans. In fact, Crest provided so many additional enticements—thousands of free movie screenings, as well as sponsored Def Jam concerts—that the results of the campaign were called into question. As of mid-2009, more than 4,000 of the one-time 14,000 Facebook fans of Crest Whitestrips had left the fan club.

Web advertising is just one part of the puzzle of selling goods and services electronically. If a website is not appealing to potential buyers it would be very unlikely that they would visit the website and place an order, no matter how superior the company's products might be compared with their competitors'. Therefore, web design is one of the most important elements to consider in electronic commerce. Web analytics is another important and recent development in electronic commerce. Web analytics allow firms to collect and analyze data from their websites to better understand the behaviour of website users. This information can then be used by the firm to develop marketing campaigns specifically targeted to groups of users according to their web behaviours.

BEFORE YOU GO ON...

1. Describe electronic storefronts and malls.
2. Discuss various types of on-line services (for example, cyberbanking, securities trading, job searches, travel services).
3. List the major issues relating to e-tailing.
4. Describe on-line advertising, its methods, and its benefits.
5. What are spamming, permission marketing, and viral marketing?

6.3 Business-to-Business (B2B) Electronic Commerce

In *business to business* (B2B) e-commerce, the buyers and sellers are business organizations. B2B makes up about 85 percent of EC volume. It covers a broad spectrum of applications that enable an enterprise to form electronic relationships with its distributors, resellers, suppliers, customers, and other partners. Organizations can use B2B to restructure their supply chains and their partner relationships, as we can see in the example of Google's new on-line marketplace in IT's About Business 6.3.

There are several types of B2B electronic commerce. The major ones are sell-side marketplaces, buy-side marketplaces, and electronic exchanges.

Sell-Side Marketplaces

In the **sell-side marketplace** model, organizations attempt to sell their products or services to other organizations electronically from their own private e-marketplace website and/or from a third-party

IT'S ABOUT BUSINESS 6.3
GOOGLE OPENS APPS ON-LINE MARKETPLACE

In 2010, Google celebrated reaching 25 million users and 2 million businesses that now are using Google applications, like its popular Gmail e-mail service and its Google calendar application. In an effort to develop its appeal to enterprises, Google has unveiled an on-line store where users can buy cloud-based applications (that is, apps that are hosted on Google's servers instead of a user's hard drive; details on cloud computing are in Technology Guide 1). These apps, largely from third parties, are designed to work with Google's own apps.

Until recently, Google allowed third-party developers to advertise applications based on Google technology through its Marketplace Solutions website. However, this website didn't have e-commerce capabilities, meaning that customers interested in purchasing the products and services had to contact the vendors by going to their websites or calling them on the phone.

This new Google Apps Marketplace website features applications and professional services from third-party developers that complement Google apps and other Google enterprise products. Some of the applications available in the marketplace include Intuit's on-line payroll application, Manymoon's

project management application, and accounting, image management, and e-mail newsletter management applications. All apps are specifically designed to work with Google's own applications and are mainly geared to businesses.

The new on-line marketplace will benefit both Google and its community of third-party developers. It will allow these developers to display and market their applications to a wider audience and potentially increase their sales. And it will allow Google to tap into new sources of revenue in addition to its core on-line search advertising business. Google will collect 20 percent of the revenue from all sales transactions on the marketplace site.

Sources: J.C. Perez, "Google to Open App Store for Business Users," IDG News Service, February 2, 2010; S. Gaudin, "Google Opens Marketplace for Cloud Apps," *Computerworld*, March 10, 2010.

QUESTIONS
1. What type of B2B electronic commerce would the new Google on-line marketplace fit into?
2. Would an electronic auction (forward or reverse) be appropriate for the Google on-line application marketplace? Why or why not?

---

website. This model is similar to the B2C e-storefront model in which the buyer is expected to come to the seller's site, view catalogues, and place an order. In the B2B sell-side marketplace, however, the buyer is an organization.

The key mechanisms in the sell-side model are electronic catalogues, which can be customized for each large buyer, and forward auctions. Sellers such as Dell Computer (*www.dellauction.com*) use auctions extensively. In addition to auctions from their own websites, organizations can use third-party auction sites, such as eBay, to liquidate items. Companies such as Ariba, Inc. (*www.ariba.com*) are helping organizations to auction old assets and inventories.

The sell-side model is used by hundreds of thousands of companies. It is especially powerful for companies with superb reputations. The seller can be either a manufacturer (for example, Dell, IBM), a distributor (for example, *www.avnet.com*), or a retailer (for example, *www.staples.ca*). The seller uses EC to increase sales, reduce selling and advertising expenditures, increase delivery speed, and reduce administrative costs. The sell-side model is especially suitable to customization. Many companies allow their business customers to configure their orders on-line. For example, at Dell (*www.dell.ca*), corporate clients can determine the exact type of computer they want. They can choose the type of chip (for example, Intel Core i5), the size of the hard drive (for example, 300 gigabytes), the type of monitor (for example, 21-inch flat screen), and so on. Similarly, the Jaguar website (*www.jaguar.com*) allows business clients to customize the Jaguar they want. Self-customization generates fewer misunderstandings about what customers want, and it encourages businesses to fill orders more quickly.

Buy-Side Marketplaces

The **buy-side marketplace** is a model in which organizations attempt to buy needed products or services from other organizations electronically. A major method of buying goods and services in the buy-side model is the reverse auction.

The buy-side model uses EC technology to streamline the purchasing process. The goal is to reduce both the costs of items purchased and the administrative expenses involved in purchasing them. In addition, EC technology can shorten the purchasing cycle time. Procurement includes purchasing goods and materials as well as sourcing, negotiating with suppliers, paying for goods, and making delivery arrangements. Organizations now use the Internet to accomplish all of these functions.

Purchasing by using electronic support is referred to as **e-procurement**. E-procurement uses reverse auctions, particularly group purchasing. In **group purchasing**, multiple buyers combine their orders so that they constitute a large volume and therefore attract more seller attention. In addition, when buyers place their combined orders on a reverse auction, they can negotiate a volume discount. Typically, the orders of small buyers are aggregated by a third-party vendor, such as the United Sourcing Alliance (*www.usa-llc.com*).

Electronic Exchanges

Private exchanges have one buyer and many sellers. E-marketplaces, in which there are many sellers and many buyers, are called **public exchanges**, or just **exchanges**. Public exchanges are open to all business organizations. They frequently are owned and operated by a third party. Public exchange managers provide all the necessary information systems to the participants. Thus, buyers and sellers merely have to "plug in" in order to trade. B2B public exchanges are often the initial point for contacts between business partners. Once they make contact, the partners may move to a private exchange or to the private trading rooms provided by many public exchanges to conduct their subsequent trading activities.

Some electronic exchanges are for direct materials, and some are for indirect materials. *Direct materials* are inputs to the manufacturing process, such as safety glass used in automobile windshields and windows. *Indirect materials* are those items, such as office supplies, that are needed for maintenance, repairs, and operations (MRO). There are three basic types of public exchanges: vertical, horizontal, and functional.

Vertical exchanges connect buyers and sellers in a given industry. Examples of vertical exchanges are *www.plasticsnet.com* in the plastics industry, *www.papersite.com* in the paper industry, *www. chemconnect.com* in the chemical industry, and *www.isteelasia.com* in the steel industry.

Horizontal exchanges connect buyers and sellers across many industries and are used mainly for MRO materials. Examples of horizontal exchanges are ECeurope (*www.eceurope.com*), Globalsources (*www.globalsources.com*), and Alibaba (*www.alibaba.com*).

In **functional exchanges**, services such as temporary help or extra office space are traded on an "as-needed" basis. For example, ADP Employease (*www.employease.com*) can find temporary labour using employers in its Employease Network.

All types of exchanges offer diversified support services, ranging from payments to logistics. Vertical exchanges are frequently owned and managed by a *consortium*, a term for a group of big players in an industry. For example, Marriott and Hyatt own a procurement consortium for the hotel industry, and ChevronTexaco owns an energy e-marketplace. The vertical e-marketplaces offer services that are particularly suited to the community they serve.

BEFORE YOU GO ON...

1. Briefly differentiate between the sell-side marketplace and the buy-side marketplace.
2. Briefly differentiate among vertical exchanges, horizontal exchanges, and functional exchanges.

6.4 Electronic Payments

Implementing EC typically requires electronic payments. **Electronic payment systems** enable you to pay for goods and services electronically, rather than writing a cheque or using cash. Electronic payment systems include electronic cheques, electronic credit cards, purchasing cards, and electronic cash. Payments are an integral part of doing business, whether in the traditional manner or on-line. Traditional payment systems have typically involved cash and/or cheques. In most cases, traditional payment systems are not effective for EC, especially for B2B. Cash cannot be used because there is no face-to-face contact between buyer and seller. Not everyone accepts credit cards or cheques, and some buyers do not have credit cards or chequing accounts. Finally, contrary to what many people believe, it may be less secure for the buyer to use the telephone or mail to arrange or send payments, especially from another country, than to complete a secured transaction on a computer. For all of these reasons, a better way is needed to pay for goods and services in cyberspace. This better method is electronic payment systems. We now take a closer look at four types of electronic payment: electronic cheques, electronic credit cards, purchasing cards, and electronic cash.

Electronic Cheques

Electronic cheques (e-cheques) are similar to regular paper cheques. They are used mostly in B2B. A customer who wishes to use e-cheques must first establish a chequing account with a bank. Then, when the customer buys a product or a service, he or she e-mails an encrypted electronic cheque to the seller. The seller deposits the cheque in a bank account, and funds are transferred from the buyer's account into the seller's account.

Like regular cheques, e-cheques carry a signature (in digital form) that can be verified (see *www.authorize.net*). Properly signed and endorsed e-cheques are exchanged between financial institutions through electronic clearinghouses. (See *www.cdnpay.ca* for details.)

Electronic Credit and Debit Cards

Electronic credit (e-credit) and *electronic debit (e-debit)* cards allow customers to charge on-line payments to their credit card account (see Figure 6.4).

Here is how a credit card works when used for on-line electronic transactions. Electronic debit cards work in a similar fashion.

- Step 1: When you buy a book from Amazon, for example, your credit card information and purchase amount are encrypted in your browser. This way the information is safe while it is "travelling" on the Internet to Amazon.
- Step 2: When your information arrives at Amazon, it is not opened. Rather, it is transferred automatically (in encrypted form) to a clearinghouse, where the information is decrypted for verification and authorization.
- Step 3: The clearinghouse asks the bank that issued you your credit card (the card issuer bank) to verify your credit card information.
- Step 4: Your card issuer bank verifies your credit card information and reports this to the clearinghouse.
- Step 5: The clearinghouse reports the result of the verification of your credit card to Amazon.
- Step 6: Amazon reports a successful purchase and amount to you.
- Step 7: Your card issuer bank sends funds in the amount of the purchase to Amazon's bank.

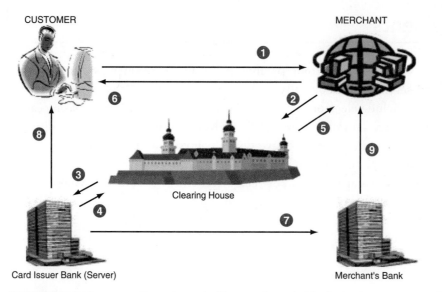

FIGURE 6.4 How e-credit cards work. (The numbers 1–9 indicate the sequence of activities.)
Source: Drawn by E. Turban.

- Step 8: Your card issuer bank notifies you (either electronically or in your monthly statement) of the debit on your credit card.
- Step 9: Amazon's bank notifies Amazon of the funds credited to its account.

The complete process of how e-credit cards work is shown in Figure 6.4. Electronic credit cards are used primarily in B2C and in shopping by small-to-medium enterprises (SMEs).

FIGURE 6.5
Example of a virtual credit card.

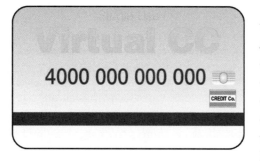

Several major credit card issuers are offering customers the option of shopping on-line with *virtual, single-use credit card numbers*. The goal is to thwart criminals by using a different, random card number every time you shop on-line. A virtual number is good only on the website where you make your purchase. An on-line purchase made with a virtual card number shows up on a customer's bill just like any other purchase. Figure 6.5 shows a sample of a virtual credit card.

PrivaSys (*www.privasys.com*) offers an interesting credit card that gives the user additional security features. This card contains a calculator-style keypad, a small LCD screen, a very thin battery, a special magnetic stripe, and a chip (microprocessor), all in a plastic card the same size as a traditional credit card. The card's chip holds all your credit and debit card numbers. When you make a purchase, you enter your four-digit PIN using the card's keypad. The card then produces a unique authorization number for that particular transaction.

Purchasing Cards

The B2B equivalent of electronic credit cards is *purchasing cards*. In some countries, companies pay other companies primarily by means of purchasing cards rather than by paper cheques. Unlike credit cards, where credit is provided for 30 to 60 days (for free) before payment is made to the merchant, payments made with purchasing cards are settled within a week.

Purchasing cards typically are used for unplanned B2B purchases, and corporations generally limit the amount per purchase (usually $1,000 to $2,000). Purchasing cards can be used on the Internet, much like regular credit cards.

Electronic Cash

Despite the growth of credit and debit cards, cash remains the most common mode of payment in off-line transactions. However, many EC sellers, and some buyers, prefer electronic cash. *Electronic cash (e-cash)* appears in four major forms: stored-value money cards, smart cards, person-to-person payments, and digital wallets.

Stored-Value Money Cards

Although they resemble credit cards, **stored-value money cards** actually are a form of e-cash. The cards you use to pay for photocopies in your library, for transportation, and for telephone calls are stored-value money cards. They are called "stored-value" because they allow you to store a fixed amount of prepaid money and then spend it as necessary. Each time you use the card, the amount is reduced by the amount you spent. Several Canadian universities provide their students with this type of card, which students can use to buy their meals and pay for photocopies at selected stores across campus. (See the York University card at *www.yorku.ca/yucard/*.)

Smart Cards

Although some people refer to stored-value money cards as "smart cards," they are not really the same. True **smart cards** contain a chip that can store a considerable amount of information (more than 100 times that of a stored-value money card). Smart cards are frequently *multi-purpose*; that is, you can use them as a credit card, a debit card, or a stored-value money card. In addition, when you use a smart card in department store chains as a *loyalty card*, it may contain your purchasing information.

Advanced smart cards can help customers transfer funds, pay bills, and purchase items from vending machines. Consumers can also use them to pay for services such as those offered on television or personal computers. For example, the Multos smart card (see Figure 6.6) allows you to buy goods or services at participating gas stations, fast-food outlets, pay phones, discount stores, post offices, convenience stores, coffee shops, and even movie theatres. You can load money values onto advanced smart cards at ATMs and kiosks as well as from your personal computer. Smart cards are ideal for *micropayments*, which are small payments of a few dollars or less.

FIGURE 6.6
Smart cards are frequently multi-purpose.

However, smart cards have additional functions. For example, Ottawa and some cities in the Greater Toronto Area (GTA) have a transportation card called Presto that is a stored-value money card that can be used for public transit.

Person-to-Person Payments

A **person-to-person payment** is a form of e-cash that enables two individuals or an individual and a business to transfer funds without using a credit card. They are one of the newest and fastest-growing payment mechanisms. Person-to-person payments can be used for a variety of purposes, such as sending money to students at university, paying for an item purchased at an on-line auction, or sending a gift to a family member.

One of the first companies to offer this service was PayPal (an eBay company). Today, 2Checkout and Authorize.Net compete with PayPal.

Virtually all of these person-to-person payment services work in a similar way. First, you select a service and open up an account. Basically, this process entails creating a user name, selecting a password, and providing the service with a credit card or bank account number. Next, you transfer funds from your credit card or bank account to your new account. Now you're ready to send money to someone over the Internet. You access the service (for example, PayPal) with your user name and password, and you specify the e-mail address of the person to receive the money, along with the dollar amount that you want to send. The service then sends an e-mail to the payee's e-mail address. The e-mail will contain a link back to the service's website. When the recipient clicks on the link, he or she will be taken to the service. The recipient will be asked to set up an account to which the money that you sent will be credited. The recipient can then credit the money from this account to either a credit card or a bank account. The service charges the payer a small amount, generally around $1 per transaction.

In addition, an attractive security feature of PayPal is that you have to put only enough money in the account to cover any upcoming transactions. Therefore, if anyone should gain access to your account, they will not have access to all of your money.

Digital Wallets

Digital wallets (or **e-wallets**) are software mechanisms that provide security measures, combined with convenience, to EC purchasing. The wallet stores the financial information of the buyer, such as credit card number, shipping information, and so on. Thus, the buyer does not need to re-enter sensitive information for each purchase. In addition, if the wallet is stored at the vendor's website, then it does not have to travel on the Internet for each purchase, making the information more secure.

The major shortcoming of this system is that you need to set up a separate e-wallet with each merchant. One solution to this problem is to install a wallet on your computer (for example, MasterCard Wallet). In that case, though, you cannot use the e-wallet to make a purchase from another computer. An alternative would be to use a web e-wallet such as Yahoo! Wallet or Google Checkout. Convenience is the main advantage of digital wallets; however, they are not totally secured systems. IT's About Business 6.4 provides an example of how Google's digital wallet could be used to pay for news on-line. This case reflects the interconnectedness between business decisions and technology, specifically the need to have a viable on-line business model supported by and supporting on-line payment technology.

IT'S ABOUT BUSINESS 6.4
CAN THE NEW GOOGLE MICROPAYMENT SYSTEM SAVE THE NEWSPAPER INDUSTRY?

Since the early days of e-commerce, the newspaper industry has been struggling to find a way to keep its doors open and turn its news into cash. The use of search engines and aggregators has become a common way for newspaper readers to get access to daily news, supplanting the traditional reading of printed newspaper. Just as an example, in 2009 the U.S. newspaper industry had the lowest total circulation in about six decades (selling 44 million copies a day). In turn, newspaper advertisers have been losing to on-line advertising, where campaigns are less expensive and more targeted. As such, profits for newspaper companies have been continuously declining.

With this bleak outlook in the horizon, the Newspaper Association of America issued a call for proposals to find new innovative ways to turn on-line news into cash. Eleven companies responded to the call, including Google, IBM, Microsoft, and Oracle.

As part of its solution to boost revenues, Google proposed a micropayment option as part of its Checkout on-line payment system. This micropayment system would combine small payments of a few cents to a few dollars where newspaper users would be able to buy one of several subscriptions to a newspaper or other publication. The system would also let users pay for individual stories in what has been termed "payment à la carte." This solution would be similar to what Apple did when it introduced its iTunes on-line store, giving users the option to buy digital songs for $1.

(Continued on next page)

IT'S ABOUT BUSINESS 6.4 *(Continued)*
CAN THE NEW GOOGLE MICROPAYMENT SYSTEM SAVE THE NEWSPAPER INDUSTRY?

Along with the development of new on-line payment systems, recent innovations in consumer electronics, such as tablet or slate computers, could also help to reverse the fate of the newspaper industry.

Sources: Compiled from M. Hartley, "Google Could Make Good with Publishers," *Financial Post*, September 11, 2009; J. Kirk, "Google Plans Micropayments Service to Media Owners," IDG News Service, September 10, 2009; T. Hamilton, "Can the Web Save Newspapers?", *Toronto Star*, January 23, 2010.

QUESTIONS
1. Discuss the advantages and disadvantages of Google's proposed micropayment system for the newspaper industry.
2. What type of content would on-line users be willing to pay for using Google's proposed micropayment system?
3. What other on-line business models could the newspaper industry adopt in order to survive?

BEFORE YOU GO ON...

1. List the various electronic payment mechanisms. Which of these mechanisms are most often used for B2B payments?
2. What are micropayments?

6.5 Ethical and Legal Issues in E-Business

Technological innovation often forces a society to re-examine and modify its ethical standards. In many cases the new standards are incorporated into law. In this section, we discuss two important ethical issues: privacy and job loss. We then turn our attention to various legal issues arising from the practice of e-business.

Ethical Issues

Many of the ethical and global issues related to IT also apply to e-business. Here we consider two basic issues: privacy and job loss.

By making it easier to store and transfer personal information, e-business presents some threats to privacy. To begin with, most electronic payment systems know who the buyers are. It may be necessary, then, to protect the buyers' identities. Businesses frequently use encryption to provide this protection.

Another major privacy issue is tracking. For example, individuals' activities on the Internet can be tracked by cookies, discussed in Chapter 3. Programs such as cookies raise privacy concerns. Cookies store your tracking history on your personal computer's hard drive, and any time you revisit a certain website, the computer knows it. In response, some users install programs to exercise some control over cookies and thus restore their on-line privacy.

In addition to compromising employees' privacy, the use of EC may eliminate the need for some of a company's employees, as well as brokers and agents. The manner in which these unneeded workers, especially employees, are treated can raise ethical issues: How should the company handle the layoffs? Should companies be required to retrain employees for new positions? If not, how should the company compensate or otherwise assist the displaced workers?

Legal Issues Specific to E-Commerce

Many legal issues are related specifically to e-commerce. When buyers and sellers do not know one another and cannot even see one another, there is a chance that dishonest people will commit fraud and other crimes. During the first few years of EC, the public witnessed many such crimes. These illegal actions ranged from creating a virtual bank that disappeared along with the investors' deposits to manipulating stock prices on the Internet. Unfortunately, fraudulent activities on the Internet are increasing. In the following section we examine some of the major legal issues that are specific to e-commerce.

Fraud on the Internet

Internet fraud has grown even faster than the Internet use itself. In one case, stock promoters falsely spread positive rumours about the prospects of the companies they touted in order to boost the stock price. In other cases the information provided might have been true, but the promoters did not disclose that they were paid to talk up the companies. Stock promoters specifically target small investors who are lured by the promise of fast profits. Stocks are only one of many areas where swindlers are active. Auctions are especially conducive to fraud, by both sellers and buyers. Other types of fraud include selling bogus investments and setting up phantom business opportunities. Because of the growing use of e-mail, financial criminals now have access to many more potential victims. The Royal Canadian Mounted Police (RCMP) regularly publishes examples of scams that are most likely to be spread via e-mail or to be found on the Web (*www.rcmp-grc.gc.ca/scams-fraudes/index-eng.htm*). Later in this section we discuss some ways in which consumers and sellers can protect themselves from on-line fraud.

Domain Names

Another legal issue is the competition over domain names. Domain names are assigned by central non-profit organizations that check for conflicts and the possible infringement of trademarks. Obviously, companies that sell goods and services over the Internet want customers to be able to find them easily. In general, the closer the domain name matches the company's name, the easier it is to locate.

Problems arise when several companies with similar names compete over a domain name. Several cases of disputed names are already in court. IT's About Business 6.5 provides an example of legal, but perhaps unethical, use of domain names.

Cybersquatting refers to the practice of registering or using domain names for the purpose of profiting from the goodwill or trademark belonging to someone else.

However, some practices that could be considered cybersquatting are not illegal, although they may well be unethical. Perhaps the more common of these practices is domain tasting. Domain tasting lets registrars profit from the complex money trail of pay-per-click advertising. The practice can be traced back to the policies of the organization responsible for regulating web names, the Internet Corporation for Assigned Names and Numbers (ICANN) (*www.icann.org*). In 2000, ICANN established the "create grace period," a five-day period when a company or person can claim a domain name and then return it for a full refund of the $6 registry fee. ICANN implemented this policy to allow someone who mistyped a domain to return it without cost.

"Domain tasters" exploit this policy by claiming Internet domains for five days at no cost. These domain names frequently resemble those of prominent companies and organizations. The tasters then jam these domains full of advertisements that come from Google and Yahoo. Because this process involves zero risk and 100 percent profit margins, domain tasters register millions of domain names every day—some of them over and over again. Experts estimate that registrants ultimately purchase less than 2 percent of the sites they sample. In the vast majority of cases, they use the domain names for only a few days to generate quick profits.

A domain name is considered to be legal when the person or business who owns the name has had a legitimate business under that name for some period of time. Companies such as Christian

Dior, Nike, Deutsche Bank, and even Microsoft have had to fight or pay to get the domain name that corresponds to their company's name away from cybersquatters.

Not all disputes over domain names involve cybersquatting, however. As one example, Delta Air Lines originally could not obtain the Internet domain name Delta.com because Delta Faucet had purchased it first. Delta Faucet, in business under that name since 1954, had a legitimate business interest in it. Delta Air Lines had to settle for Delta-airlines.com until it bought the domain name from Delta Faucet. Delta Faucet is now at Deltafaucet.com. Several cases of disputed domain names are already in court. IT's About Business 6.5 provides an example of a recent legal judgement on the use of domain names.

Taxes and Other Fees

In off-line sales, most provinces and localities tax business transactions that are conducted within their jurisdiction. The most obvious example is sales taxes. Federal, provincial, and local authorities now are scrambling to create some type of taxation policy for e-business. This problem is particularly complex for interprovincial and international e-commerce. For example, some people claim that the province in which the *seller* is located deserves the entire sales tax (or in some countries, value-added

IT'S ABOUT BUSINESS 6.5
TORONTO RAPTORS PLAYER WINS A CYBERSQUATTING VERDICT

It is clear that cybersquatting is most commonly used with business names; however, individuals can also become victims of cybersquatters. This was the case of Toronto Raptors forward Chris Bosh. The power forward, one of the athletes most involved with the Web and social media, had sued a company owned by Luis Zavala, Hoopology.com, over its use of the name chrisbosh.com.

In a legal brief, Chris Bosh accused Luis Zavala of registering at least 800 domain names confusingly similar to his name such as chrisbosh.com. The list of domain names, which is available for download at *www.winston.com/siteFiles/Domain_Name_List.pdf*, also includes names of other NBA stars, and names of close relatives of famous celebrities such as Britney Spears's son, Rob Zombie's wife, and Jennifer Lopez and Marc Anthony's twin sons. Significantly, none of these sites has anything to do with Chris Bosh or any of the celebrities listed.

In addition to the monetary judgement, $120,000, Luis Zavala was ordered to remit to Chris Bosh all the domain names that it had registered and to cease and desist from any further registration of Chris Bosh. "I am thrilled that I am able to offer the return of these domain names to a host of other athletes and celebrities whose names were cybersquatted," Bosh said in a statement.

Although there is a legal remedy available to address the issue of cybersquatting, a tremendous amount of time and money is required to fight the unethical practice. Further complicating the matter, many cybersquatting cases involve individuals or companies based outside the jurisdiction of the Canadian legal system, such as the example above where the charges had to be filed in a U.S. court.

Executives at domain registry companies argue that they provide a business service and they themselves should not be held responsible for policing all the domains that are registered daily. The organization that is ultimately responsible for regulating web names is the Internet Corporation for Assigned Names and Numbers (ICANN) (*www.icann.org*). Many businesses have pressured ICANN to revise its policies to limit the abuses inherent in the current system.

Sources: Compiled from D. Smith, "Bosh Wins Back Rights to Online Identities," *Toronto Star*, October 15, 2009; H. Beck, "Bosh's Win Over Cybersquatter Frees 800 Domain Names," *New York Times*, October 14, 2009; ICANN website (*www.icann.org*), accessed April 20, 2010.

QUESTIONS
1. Should cybersquatting be outlawed? Why or why not?
2. If your name were David Sony and you want to register www.davidsony.com, should you be prohibited from doing so because Sony is also the name of a major international company? Access *www.digest.com/Big_Story.php* and build your case.

tax, VAT). Others contend that the province in which the *server* is located also should receive some of the tax revenues.

In addition to the sales tax, there is a question about where (and in some cases, whether) electronic sellers should pay business licence taxes, franchise fees, gross-receipts taxes, excise taxes, privilege taxes, and utility taxes. Furthermore, how should tax collection be controlled? Legislative efforts to impose taxes on e-commerce are opposed by an organization named the Internet Freedom Fighters. So far, their efforts have been successful.

Copyright

Recall from Chapter 3 that intellectual property is protected by copyright laws and cannot be used freely. This point is significant because many people mistakenly believe that once they purchase a piece of software, they have the right to share it with others. In fact, what they have bought is the right to use the software, not the right to *distribute* it. That right remains with the copyright holder. Similarly, copying material from websites without permission is a violation of copyright laws. Protecting intellectual property in e-commerce is very difficult, however, because it involves hundreds of millions of people in some 200 countries with differing copyright laws having access to billions of web pages.

BEFORE YOU GO ON...

1. List some ethical issues in EC.
2. List the major legal issues of EC.

WHAT'S IN IT FOR ME?

FOR THE ACCOUNTING MAJOR

Accounting personnel are involved in several EC activities. Designing the ordering system and its relationship with inventory management requires accounting attention. Billing and payments are also accounting activities, as are determining cost and profit allocation. Replacing paper documents by electronic means will affect many of the accountant's tasks, especially the auditing of EC activities and systems. Finally, building a cost-benefit and cost-justification system of which products and services to take on-line and creating a chargeback system are critical to the success of EC.

FOR THE FINANCE MAJOR

The worlds of banking, securities and commodities, and other financial services are being reengineered due to EC. On-line securities trading and its supporting infrastructure are growing more rapidly than any other EC activity. Many innovations already in place are changing the rules of economic and financial incentives for financial analysts and managers. Public financial information is now accessible in seconds. These innovations will dramatically change the manner in which finance personnel operate.

FOR THE MARKETING MAJOR

A major revolution in marketing and sales is taking place due to EC. Perhaps its most obvious feature is the transition from a physical to a virtual marketplace. Equally important, though, is the radical transformation to one-on-one advertising and sales and to customized and interactive marketing. Marketing channels are being combined, eliminated, or recreated. The EC revolution is creating new products and markets and significantly altering others. The digitization of products and services also has implications for marketing and sales. The direct producer-to-consumer channel is expanding rapidly and is fundamentally changing the nature of customer service. As the battle for customers intensifies, marketing and sales personnel are becoming the most critical success factor in many organizations. On-line marketing can be a blessing to one company and a curse to another.

FOR THE PRODUCTION/OPERATIONS MANAGEMENT MAJOR

EC is changing the manufacturing system from product-push mass production to order-pull mass customization. This change requires a robust supply chain, information support, and reengineering of processes that involve suppliers and other business partners. Using extranets, suppliers can monitor and replenish inventories without the need for constant reorders. In addition, the Internet and intranets help reduce cycle times. Many production/operations problems that have persisted for years, such as complex scheduling and excess inventories, are being solved rapidly with the use of web technologies. Companies can now use external and internal networks to find and manage manufacturing operations in other countries much more easily. Also, the Web is reengineering procurement by helping companies conduct electronic bids for parts and subassemblies, thus reducing cost. All in all, the job of the progressive production/operations manager is closely tied in with e-commerce.

FOR THE HUMAN RESOURCES MANAGEMENT MAJOR

HR majors need to understand the new labour markets and the impacts of EC on old labour markets. Also, the HRM department may use EC tools for such functions as procuring office supplies. Also, becoming knowledgeable about new government on-line initiatives and on-line training is critical. Finally, HR personnel must be familiar with the major legal issues related to EC and employment.

FOR THE MIS MAJOR

The MIS function is responsible for providing the information technology infrastructure necessary for electronic commerce to function. In particular, this infrastructure includes the company's networks, intranets, and extranets. The MIS function is also responsible for ensuring that electronic commerce transactions are secure.

SUMMARY

1. **Describe the different types of electronic commerce, its mechanisms, and its limitations.**
   E-commerce can be conducted on the Web and on other networks. It is divided into the following major types: business-to-consumer, business-to-business, consumer-to-consumer, business-to-employee, and government-to-citizen. E-commerce offers many benefits to organizations, consumers, and society, but it also has limitations (technological and non-technological).

2. **Describe B2C electronic commerce, e-tailing, and on-line advertising.**
   B2C (e-tailing) can be pure or part of a clicks-and-mortar organization. Direct marketing is done via e-storefronts, e-malls, via electronic catalogues, or by using electronic auctions. The leading on-line B2C service industries are banking, securities trading, job markets, travel, and real estate. Order fulfillment is especially difficult and expensive in B2C because of the need to ship relatively small orders to many customers.

3. **Describe the main types of B2B electronic commerce.**
   The major B2B applications are selling from e-catalogues and by forward e-auctions (the sell-side marketplace), buying in e-reverse auctions and in group and desktop purchasing (the buy-side marketplace), and trading in electronic exchanges and hubs.

4. **Explain the main types of on-line electronic payment methods.**
   New electronic payment systems are needed to complete transactions on the Internet. Electronic payments can be made using e-cheques, e-credit cards, purchasing cards, e-cash, stored-value money cards, smart cards, and person-to-person payments.

5. **Explain the main ethical and legal issues relating to e-commerce.**
   There is increasing fraud and unethical behaviour on the Internet, including invasion of privacy by sellers and misuse of domain names. The value of domain names, taxation of on-line business, and legal issues in a multi-country environment are major concerns. Protection of customers, sellers, and intellectual property is also important.

KEY TERMS

auction, 178

banner, 185

bricks-and-mortar organization, 174

business-to-business electronic
   commerce (B2B), 176

business-to-consumer electronic commerce
   (B2C), 176

business-to-employee electronic commerce
   (B2E), 176

business model, 177

buy-side marketplace, 188

channel conflict, 183

clicks-and-mortar organization, 174

consumer-to-consumer electronic commerce
   (C2C), 176

cyberbanking, 181

cybersquatting, 194

digital wallet, 192

disintermediation, 181

e-business, 174

DISCUSSION QUESTIONS

1. Discuss the major limitations of e-commerce. Which of these limitations are likely to disappear? Why?
2. Discuss the reasons for having multiple EC business models.
3. Distinguish between business-to-business forward auctions and buyers' bids for requests for quotation.
4. Discuss the benefits to sellers and buyers of a B2B exchange.
5. What are the major benefits of G2C electronic commerce?
6. Discuss the various ways to pay on-line in B2C. Which one(s) would you prefer and why?
7. Why is order fulfillment in B2C considered difficult?
8. Discuss the reasons for EC failures.
9. Should Mr. Coffee sell coffee makers on-line? Hint: Take a look at the discussion of channel conflict in this chapter.

PROBLEM-SOLVING ACTIVITIES

1. Assume you are interested in buying a car. You can find information about cars at numerous websites. Access five of them for information about new and used cars, financing, and insurance. Decide what car you want to buy. Configure your car by going to the car manufacturer's website. Finally, try to find the car from *www.autobytel.com*. What information is most supportive of your decision making process? Write a report about your experience.

2. Compare the various electronic payment methods. Specifically, collect information from the vendors cited in the chapter and find more using Google. Pay attention to security level, speed, cost, and convenience.

3. Conduct a study on selling diamonds and gems on-line. Access such sites as *www.bluenile.com*, *www.diamond.com*, *www.thaigem.com*, *www.tiffany.com*, and *www.jewelryexchange.com*.
    a. What features are used in these sites to educate buyers about gemstones?
    b. How do these sites attract buyers?

   c. How do these sites increase trust for on-line purchasing?

   d. What customer service features do these sites provide?

4. Access *www.nacha.org*. What is NACHA? What is its role? What is the ACH? Who are the key participants in an ACH e-payment? Describe the "pilot" projects currently underway at ACH.

5. Access *www.theshoppingnetwork.com*. What are the different ways in which it generates revenue?

6. Access *www.queendom.com*. Examine its offerings and try some of them. What type of electronic commerce is this? How does this website generate revenue?

7. Access *www.ediets.com*. Prepare a list of all the services the company provides. Identify its revenue model.

8. Access *www.theknot.com*. Identify its revenue sources.

9. Access *www.mint.com*. Identify its revenue model. What are the risks of giving this website your credit and debit card numbers, as well as your bank account number?

10. Access *www.bytheowner.com*. Prepare a list of services available on this site. Then prepare a list of advantages derived by the users and advantages to realtors. Are there any disadvantages? To whom?

11. Enter *www.alibaba.com*. Identify the site's capabilities. Look at the site's private trading room. Write a report. How can such a site help a person who is making a purchase?

12. Enter *www.campusfood.com*. Explore the site. Why is the site so successful? Could you start a competing one? Why or why not?

13. Enter *www.dell.ca*, go to "desktops," and configure a system. Register to "my cart" (no obligation). What calculators are used there? What are the advantages of this process as compared with buying a computer in a physical store? What are the disadvantages?

14. Enter *http://www.checkfree.fiserv.com/index.html* and *www.lmlpayment.com* and find their services. Prepare a report.

15. Access various travel sites such as *www.travelocity.ca*, *www.orbitz.com*, *www.expedia.ca*, and *www.sidestep.com*. Compare these websites for ease of use and usefulness. Note differences among the sites. If you ask each site for the itinerary, which one gives you the best information and the best deals?

16. Access *www.outofservice.com* and answer the musical taste and personality survey. When you have finished, click on Results and see what your musical tastes say about your personality. How accurate are the findings about you?

TEAM ASSIGNMENTS

1. Have each team study a major bank or credit union with an extensive EC strategy. For examples, look at ING Direct (*www.ingdirect.ca*), Desjardins (*www.desjardins.com*), Scotiabank (*www.scotiabank.ca*), and HSBC (*www.hsbc.ca*). Each team should attempt to convince the class that its e-bank activities are the best.

2. Assign each team to one industry vertical. An industry vertical is a group of industries in the same business, such as financial services, insurance, healthcare, manufacturing, telecommunications, pharmaceuticals, chemicals, and so on. Each team will find five real-world applications of the major business-to-business models listed in the chapter. (Try success stories of vendors and EC-related magazines.) Examine the problems they solve or the opportunities they exploit.

3. Have teams investigate how B2B payments are made in global trade. Consider instruments such as electronic letters of credit and e-cheques. Visit *www.tradecard.com* and examine its services to small and medium size enterprises (SMEs). Also, investigate what Visa and MasterCard are offering. Finally, check Citicorp and some German and Japanese banks.

SALES GROWTH AT THE HEART OF SEARS CANADA'S NEW E-COMMERCE WEBSITE

THE BUSINESS PROBLEM

Sears Canada, one of the largest retail store chains in the country, has been trying to get customers back into shopping. Without closing any of its stores, sales decreased by 6.3 percent in a recent year, totalling $5.7 billion in annual revenue. On-line sales have also slowed down to single-digit growth and now represent 10 percent of total sales.

Pressed by the same outlook, some of Sears's direct competitors, such as the Hudson's Bay Co. (owner of the Bay and Zellers) and Canadian Tire Corp., decided to close their on-line stores in an effort to reduce costs and concentrate on their core business. But other firms are entering the e-commerce space. Sporting goods retailer Sport Chek, athletic clothing chain Lululemon Athletica, and the men's upscale clothier Harry Rosen are some recent examples of new virtual stores in direct competition with Sears Canada. Even fashion giant Gap Inc. plans to open a virtual store in the near future.

As competition intensifies, the pressure for Sears Canada to improve its on-line operations has increased. Sears, whose e-commerce website was run by e-tailing giant Amazon, needed to improve its customer experience on-line as its platform was not flexible enough to respond to customer inquiries in a timely and effective manner. For example, not all products available in the retail and catalogue channels were available on-line, and the only way for on-line customers to contact Sears was through e-mail.

THE IT SOLUTION

Sears Canada responded by launching a project to update its e-commerce website. For the next eight months a team of 80 members worked together to develop a new on-line strategy and redesign its on-line store (*www. sears.ca*). The new website, launched in late 2009, has several interactive features, such as on-line chats, demo videos, and even connections with Facebook and Twitter. The new website is now able to carry every item that is in the retail stores and catalogues, offering the customer a wide variety of merchandise.

Appealing to younger buyers, the e-commerce website is continuously updated with new products such as sports collectibles (for example, a $1,300 autographed Wayne Gretzky jersey), eco-clothing, and other items that are not carried in Sears's stores or catalogues. The customer experience is further improved by the site's automatic search technique that suggests related products and services when a shopper looks for an item.

THE RESULTS

The new e-commerce website has provided Sears with the flexibility to respond to customers' questions in an interactive way. When a customer asked how a treadmill for sale could be folded, an e-commerce team member videotaped himself doing it and posted the video on YouTube and on the Sears.ca website.

Sears also saves on inventory costs since suppliers carry the merchandise and ship it directly to customers. But one of the greatest benefits of the new website is the almost endless range of products that it carries: about 350,000 items are available on the Sears.ca website, more than twice the number in one of its typical department stores, and the number is planned to increase.

The new e-commerce team is also expected to grow to 100 members, in order to implement a number of additional web initiatives, such as mobile phone applications, and an application for drive-through purchase pickups dubbed MyGofer. The company is even considering an e-marketplace where other businesses could sell their wares at Sears.ca, paying the retailer a commission of up to 20 percent.

As on-line sales for 2010 in the United States were expected to increase by nine percent, growing faster than in bricks-and-mortar stores, the new Sears.ca e-commerce website should help Sears Canada achieve its most important business goal: sales growth.

Sources: Compiled from M. Strauss, "Sears Canada Turns to Web for 'Endless Aisle'," *The Globe and Mail,* February 12, 2010; M. Semansky, "Sears Exec Puts E-commerce in Perspective at CMA Conference," *Marketing Magazine,* March 5, 2010; M. Strauss, "What Investors Should Know: Sears Canada Faces Mounting Cyber-competition," *The Globe and Mail,* March 6, 2010.

QUESTIONS

1. Why was Sears Canada so focused on improving the customer experience in its new e-commerce website?
2. What role do new social media tools play in on-line stores such as Sears.ca? What are the benefits? What are the disadvantages?
3. Visit Sears Canada's website and evaluate its website. How appealing is it for the younger shoppers? How could Sears Canada make its website more appealing to this market segment?
4. Identify any other on-line business models that Sears Canada could benefit from.
5. What are the main obstacles Sears Canada faces with its new e-commerce strategy?
6. Is channel conflict a problem for Sears Canada? Explain why or why not.

TIPS FOR SAFE ELECTRONIC SHOPPING

- Look for reliable brand names at sites like Amazon.ca, Dell.ca, and AirMilesShops.ca. Before purchasing, make sure that the site is authentic by entering the site directly and not from an unverified link.
- Search any unfamiliar-sounding site for the company's address and phone and fax numbers. Call up and quiz the employees about the seller.
- Check out the vendor with the local Chamber of Commerce or Better Business Bureau (*www.bbb.org/canada*). Look for seals of authenticity such as TRUSTe.
- Investigate how secure the seller's site is by examining the security procedures and by reading the posted privacy policy.
- Examine the money-back guarantees, warranties, and service agreements.
- Compare prices with those in regular stores. Too-low prices are too good to be true, and some catch is probably involved.
- Ask friends what they know. Find testimonials and endorsements in community sites and well-known bulletin boards.
- Find out what your rights are in case of a dispute. Consult consumer protection agencies and the National Fraud Information Center (*www.fraud.org*) for general advice on fraud.
- Check *http://consumerworld.org* for a listing of useful resources.

CASE 6.2

Web Resources

Student website www.wiley.com/canada/rainer

- Web quizzes
- Lecture slides in PowerPoint
- Author podcasts
- Interactive Case: Ruby's Club assignments

ALL OF THE ABOVE AND...

- E-book
- Manager videos
- Vocabulary flash cards
- Pre- and post-lecture quizzes
- Microsoft Office 2007 lab manual and projects

PLANNING E-COMMERCE APPLICATIONS FOR RUBY'S CLUB

Go to the Ruby's Club link at the Student Companion website or WileyPLUS for information about your current internship assignment. You will evaluate opportunities for e-commerce at Ruby's and build a spreadsheet application that will help Ruby's managers make decisions about e-commerce options.

7

WIRELESS, MOBILE COMPUTING, AND MOBILE COMMERCE

LEARNING OBJECTIVES

1. Discuss today's wireless devices and wireless transmission media.

2. Describe wireless networks according to their effective distance.

3. Define mobile computing and mobile commerce and describe m-commerce applications.

4. Define pervasive computing and its underlying technologies.

5. Examine threats to wireless networks.

WIRELESS IN THE DEVELOPING WORLD

Courtesy Digicel

THE BUSINESS PROBLEM
Neither corruption nor coups nor kidnappings can prevent Denis O'Brien from expanding his cell phone business, Digicel (*www.digicelgroup.com*), in the developing world. Digicel does business in 27 countries and territories, and it dominates the mobile business in many of them. O'Brien is savvy in business and politics. In a world where stores are sloppy and staff are rude, Digicel's clean and friendly retail outlets are a welcome sight. The company spends millions on its network and yet cuts other costs so that it can offer deep discounts to customers—charging up to 80 percent less than competitors for the phones and 50 percent for calls. O'Brien's business model is worth studying. How does Digicel successfully start and grow mobile telephone businesses in such dangerous places?

THE IT AND POLITICAL SOLUTIONS
You could call O'Brien something of a renegade. Capitalizing on the desire of people in developing countries to have any kind of phone service for the first time, he erects cell towers quickly—sometimes even before he has government authority to do so. From day one, he prices his phones and services so low that he quickly builds a loyal customer base he's betting will go to bat for his service if the government opposes it. He often ends up being able to keep his business in a country that is otherwise corrupt and violent instead of having to sell his assets for next to nothing, which often happens to other Western firms doing business with these governments.

But that doesn't mean that Digicel has not had any close calls. One potential disaster was averted in Papua New Guinea, where the company won a licence to operate in 2006 and spent $120 million building 130 cell towers. Soon after, the country's telecommunications minister, the son of the prime minister, overturned the licence because his family had a vested interest in the state-owned monopoly that offered cell phone service. Digicel held on to its licence after a lawsuit, but then the government threatened to seize the towers and nationalize the company. That plan was defeated after intense lobbying by Digicel.

Things got even nastier. The telecommunications minister ordered that the cell towers could not transmit signals, but Digicel fought back by selling phones for just $6—only one fifth of what the state monopoly charged. As a further salvo, Digicel gave customers with a state phone a chip that allowed them to operate on Digicel's network. All these moves gained Digicel 350,000 customers within five months—more than twice those of the state enterprise. When faced with the threat that Digicel might close, customers wrote letters to newspapers across Papua New Guinea and the government acquiesced.

In addition to corruption, Digicel has faced coups and kidnappings. Its cell towers went silent for a time after a coup in Haiti, and five Digicel workers were kidnapped in Haiti. This, despite the fact that Haitians seem to love their cell phones, calling Digicel the "company of the people," which is likely why a mob in Port-au-Prince once spared the Digicel stores from its rioting.

Customers in developing nations have good reason to embrace cell phone operators. Merchants are able to earn a lot more because they can call suppliers and customers instead of leaving their stalls. In Papua New Guinea, a nut seller can call wholesalers to see if new shipments have arrived, saving him nearly a half-day's work. A mango exporter sells 150,000 more mangoes each year because his truck drivers can call for help when they break down and the fruit doesn't rot. Likewise, a fisherman in Samoa increased his income four-fold with his cell phone because he can call the fish markets to see which ones want his product instead of walking to each one while the fish spoil.

The government of Papua New Guinea eventually came around to Digicel's point of view, admitting that the cell phone competition the company created accounted for 0.7 percentage points of the country's 6.2 percent economic growth from 2006 to 2008. That figure stands up to a study by the London Business School, which found that gross domestic product rises on average by half a percentage point for each 10 percent of the population that gets a cell phone.

Investing heavily in the developing world has paid off handsomely for Digicel, which saw its profits double in 2007 from the year before to $505 million, on total revenue of $2 billion.

Sources: Compiled from B. Condon, "Babble Rouser," *Forbes*, August 11, 2008; B. Rodgers, "Instant Communication Changes Customs, Politics, in Developing World," *Wireless Innovator*, May 19, 2008; "Mobile Phones and a Brighter Future for the Third World," Dialaphone.com, April 30, 2008; "Digicel Wins Mobile Bid in Fiji," Digicel Barbados, February 27, 2008; M. Reardon, "Emerging Markets Fuel Cell Phone Growth," *CNET News*, February 14, 2007; "M. Foster, "Cell phones Fuel Growth in Developing World," *USA Today*, January 26, 2007;

"Denis O'Brien's Digicel Group Expands to Papua New Guinea in South Pacific," *FinFacts Ireland*, September 11, 2006; I. Elwood, "Wireless Pioneers Bring the Internet to the Developing World," *VoIP News*, May 11, 2006; "Digicel Sharpens Focus on Corporate Clients," *News Blaze*, 2005; Digicel website (*www.digicelgroup.com*), accessed January 23, 2009.

WHAT DO YOU THINK?

1. Is it appropriate for organizations such as Digicel to establish infrastructures for communication systems without local regulatory approval? Why or why not?
2. Provide additional examples of how use of wireless technology could improve the quality of life of residents of Papua New Guinea or Haiti.

CASE 7.1

Chapter Preview

Wireless is a term that is used to describe telecommunications in which electromagnetic waves, rather than some form of wire or cable, carry the signal between communicating devices (for example, computers, personal digital assistants, cell phones, and so on). The opening case describes the huge impacts that one wireless technology, cellular telephones, can have on people's lives.

Before we continue, we must distinguish between the terms "wireless" and "mobile," as they can mean two different things. The term *wireless* means exactly what it says: without wires. The term *mobile* refers to something that changes its location over time. Wireless networks can be mobile or fixed. For example, microwave towers form fixed wireless networks.

In many situations, the traditional working environment that requires users to come to a wired computer is either ineffective or inefficient. In these situations, the solution is to build computers small enough to carry or wear that can communicate via wireless networks. The ability to communicate anytime and anywhere provides organizations with a strategic advantage by increasing productivity and speed and improving customer service.

Wireless technologies enable mobile computing, mobile commerce, and pervasive computing. We define these terms here and then discuss each one in more detail later in the chapter. **Mobile computing** refers to a real-time, wireless connection between a mobile device and other computing environments, such as the Internet or an intranet. **Mobile commerce**—also known as **m-commerce**—refers to e-commerce (EC) transactions that are conducted in a wireless environment, especially via the Internet. **Pervasive computing**, also called **ubiquitous computing**, means that virtually every object has processing power with wireless or wired connections to a global network.

Wireless technologies and mobile commerce are spreading rapidly, replacing or supplementing wired computing. In fact, Cisco (*www.cisco.com*) predicts that mobile web traffic volume will double every year until 2013. As we saw in the opening case, wireless technologies are allowing countries to build a communications infrastructure from scratch. Another example of the effects of wireless technologies involves the use of Wi-Fi. In India's Orissa state, a nongovernmental organization is providing bus-powered Wi-Fi service. The buses use short-range radio to pick up electronic messages three or four times per day from Wi-Fi–enabled computers placed in kiosks. This combination of wireless technology and old-fashioned "bus technology" makes communications affordable to people who had no previous access to the Internet.

The wireless infrastructure upon which mobile computing is built may reshape the entire IT field. The technologies, applications, and limitations of mobile computing and mobile commerce are the main focus of this chapter. We begin the chapter with a discussion of wireless devices and wireless transmission media. We continue by examining wireless computer networks and wireless Internet access. We then look at mobile computing and mobile commerce, which are made possible by wireless technologies. Next we turn our attention to pervasive computing, and we conclude the chapter by discussing wireless security.

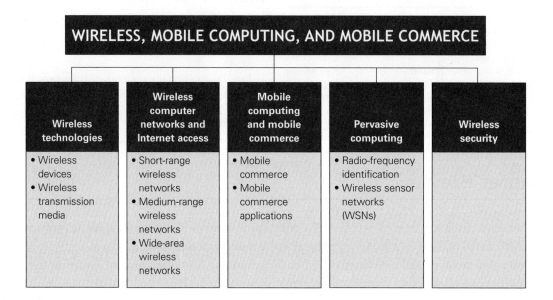

7.1 Wireless Technologies

Wireless technologies include both wireless devices, such as smart phones, and wireless transmission media, such as microwave, satellite, and radio. These technologies are fundamentally changing the ways organizations operate and do business.

Wireless Devices

Individuals are finding it convenient and productive to use wireless devices for several reasons. First, they can make productive use of time that was formerly wasted (for example, while commuting to work on public transportation). Second, because they can take these devices with them, their work locations are becoming much more flexible. Third, wireless technology enables them to allocate their working time around personal and professional obligations.

The **wireless application protocol (WAP)** is the standard that enables wireless devices to access web-based information and services. Older WAP-compliant devices contain **microbrowsers**, which are Internet browsers with a small file size that can work within the confines of small screen sizes on wireless devices and the relatively low bandwidths of wireless networks. Figure 7.1A shows the full-function browser on msn's web page, and Figure 7.1B shows a microbrowser on the screen of a cell phone accessing a news website. As wireless devices have become increasingly powerful, they now have full-function browsers. For example, the Apple iPhone (*www.apple.com/iphone*) runs the Safari browser.

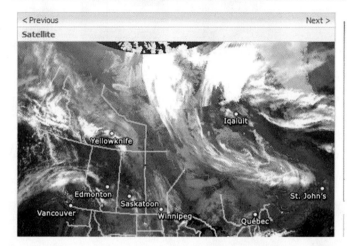

FIGURE 7.1A
msn web page browser, *www. msn.com.*

Wireless devices are small enough to easily carry or wear, have sufficient computing power to perform productive tasks, and can communicate wirelessly with the Internet and other devices. In the past, we have discussed these devices in separate categories, such as pagers, e-mail hand-helds, personal digital assistants (PDAs), and cellular telephones. Today, however, new devices, generally called *smart phones*, combine the functions of these devices. The capabilities of these new devices include cellular telephony, Bluetooth,

FIGURE 7.1B
Cell phone microbrowser. *Source:* Alex Segre/Alamy.

Wi-Fi, a digital camera, a global positioning system (GPS), an organizer, a scheduler, an address book, a calculator, access to e-mail, and **short message service (SMS)** (sending and receiving text messages up to 160 characters in length), instant messaging, text messaging, an MP3 music player, a video player, Internet access with a full-function browser, and a QWERTY keyboard. Not all of these new devices have all of these capabilities, but they are heading rapidly in that direction. Examples of new devices include (see Figure 7.2):

- The BlackBerry Curve 8900 and BlackBerry Bold (*www.blackberry.com*)
- The Palm Pre, Centro, Treo Pro, and Treo 800W (*www.palm.com*)
- The Motozine ZN5 (*www.motorola.com*)
- The Apple iPhone (*www.apple.com/iphone*)
- The Sony Mylo (*www.sony.com/mylo*)

One downside of smart phones is that people can use them to copy and pass on confidential information. For example, if you were an executive at Intel, would you want workers snapping pictures of their colleagues with your secret new technology in the background? Unfortunately, managers think of these devices as phones, not as digital cameras that can transmit wirelessly. Many cell phone

FIGURE 7.2
Examples of smart phones.
Source: Jessica Griffin/ Philadelphia Daily News/MCT/ NewsCom.

jamming devices are now available (*www.phonejammer.com*), developed to counter this threat and also to jam cell phones at locations where it would be inconvenient to have noise, such as during a religious service. These devices jam signals from phones when they enter specific locations. Regardless of any disadvantages, cell phones, and particularly smart phones, have far greater impact on human society than most of us realize (see Table .7.1).

TABLE 7.1
DO NOT UNDERESTIMATE THE POWER OF CELL PHONES!

- In January 1982, Washington, D.C.'s first 100 hand-held cell phones, each weighing one kilogram, were put into service. By mid-2009, there was one cell phone for every two humans on earth. This is the fastest global diffusion of any technology in human history. Cell phones have transformed the world faster than electricity, automobiles, refrigeration, credit cards, or television.
- Cell phones have made a bigger difference faster in underdeveloped areas where landlines have been scarce. As we saw in the opening case, cell phones have become the driving force behind many modernizing economies. Cell phones are the first telecommunications technology in history to have more users in the developing world—60 percent of all users—than in the developed nations. In just one example, cell phone usage in Africa has been growing at 50 percent annually, faster than in any other region.
- Cell phones can heavily influence politics. For example, in 2001 the people of the Philippines overthrew a dictator with their cell phones. Joseph Estrada, accused of massive corruption, was driven out of power by activists, who brought hundreds of thousands of protestors into the streets in minutes through text messaging.
- Your cell phone now can be your wallet. There is almost nothing in your wallet that you cannot put in your cell phone; for example, pictures of spouses and children, credit card access codes, bus payments, and many other items. In fact, cell phones can now be used for contactless payment rather than using a credit card. The user simply waves the cell phone at a reader, and the credit card is debited.
- Around Cambridge, England, bicycle couriers carry cell phones equipped with global positioning systems to monitor air pollution.
- Scientists at Purdue University want to network the United States with millions of cell phones equipped with radiation sensors to detect terrorists trying to assemble dirty bombs.
- In the San Francisco Bay area, cell phones are being used to transmit real-time traffic information, such as speeds of automobiles, the extent of traffic jams, and travel time.
- And there is more to come! Even with all their power, cell phones do have problems such as haphazard sound quality, dropped calls, slow downloads, and annoying delays between speaking and being heard. To help solve these problems, a company called picoChip (*www.picochip.com*) is marketing miniature cellular base stations, called femtocells, for placement in the home or office that wants better reception. Femtocells work with any cell phone, and they relieve congestion on cell towers and cellular frequencies by creating extra capacity at very small cost. The transmitter is cheap, the broadband connection is free (most houses and offices have existing idle broadband connections), and the low-power signal does not interfere with other frequencies.

Wireless Transmission Media

Wireless media, or broadcast media, transmit signals without wires over the air or in space. The major types of wireless media are microwave, satellite, radio, and infrared. Let's examine each type more closely. Table 7.2 lists the advantages and disadvantages of each of the major types.

TABLE 7.2		
ADVANTAGES AND DISADVANTAGES OF WIRELESS MEDIA		
CHANNEL	**ADVANTAGES**	**DISADVANTAGES**
Microwave	High bandwidth Relatively inexpensive	Must have unobstructed line of sight Susceptible to environmental interference
Satellite	High bandwidth Large coverage area	Expensive Must have unobstructed line of sight Signals experience propagation delay Must use encryption for security
Radio	High bandwidth Signals pass through walls Inexpensive and easy to install	Creates electrical interference problems Susceptible to snooping unless encrypted
Infrared	Low to medium bandwidth Used only for short distances	Must have unobstructed line of sight

Microwave

Microwave transmission systems are widely used for high-volume, long-distance, line-of-sight communication. Line-of-sight means that the transmitter and receiver must be in view of each other. This requirement creates problems because the earth's surface is curved, not flat. For this reason, microwave towers usually cannot be spaced more than 50 kilometres apart.

Clearly, then, microwave transmissions offer only a limited solution to data communications needs, especially over very long distances. Additionally, microwave transmissions are susceptible to environmental interference during severe weather, such as heavy rain or snowstorms. Although long-distance microwave data communication systems are still widely used, they are being replaced by satellite communication systems.

Satellite

Satellite transmission systems make use of communication satellites. Currently, there are three types of satellites around the earth: geostationary (GEO), medium earth orbit (MEO), and low earth orbit (LEO). Each type has a different orbit, with the GEO being farthest from the earth and the LEO the closest. In this section, we examine the three types of satellites. We then look at two major satellite applications: global positioning systems and Internet transmission via satellites. Table 7.3 compares and contrasts the three types of satellites.

As with microwave transmission, satellites must receive and transmit data via line of sight. However, the enormous *footprint*—the area of the earth's surface reached by a satellite's transmission––overcomes the limitations of microwave data relay stations. The most basic rule governing footprint size is simple:

TABLE 7.3
THREE BASIC TYPES OF TELECOMMUNICATIONS SATELLITES

TYPE	CHARACTERISTICS	ORBIT	NUMBER	USE
GEO	• Satellites remain stationary relative to point on earth • Few satellites needed for global coverage • Transmission delay (approximately .25 second) • Most expensive to build and launch • Longest orbital life (many years)	35,900 kilometres	8	TV signal
MEO	• Satellites move relative to point on earth • Moderate number needed for global coverage • Requires medium-powered transmitters • Negligible transmission delay • Less expensive to build and launch • Moderate orbital life (6 to 12 years)	10,354 kilometres	10 to 12	GPS
LEO	• Satellites move rapidly relative to point on earth • Large number needed for global coverage • Requires only low-power transmitters • Negligible transmission delay • Least expensive to build and launch • Shortest orbital life (as low as 5 years)	640 to 1,125 kilometres	Many	Telephone

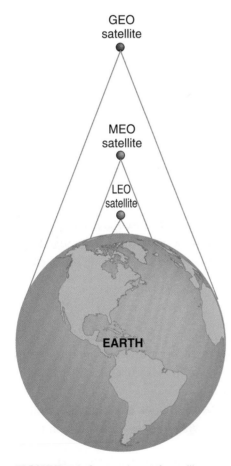

FIGURE 7.3 Comparison of satellite footprints.
Source: Drawn by Kelly Rainer.

The higher a satellite orbits, the larger its footprint. Thus, middle earth orbit satellites have a smaller footprint than geostationary satellites, and low earth orbit satellites have the smallest footprint of all. Figure 7.3 compares the footprints of the three types of satellite.

In contrast to line-of-sight transmission with microwave, satellites use *broadcast* transmission, which sends signals to many receivers at one time. Even though satellites are line-of-sight like microwave, they are high enough for broadcast transmission, thus overcoming the limitations of microwave.

Types of Orbits. *Geostationary earth orbit (GEO)* satellites orbit 35,900 kilometres directly above the equator. These satellites maintain a fixed position above the earth's surface because at their altitude, their orbital period matches the 24-hour rotational period of the earth. For this reason, receivers on the earth do not have to track GEO satellites. GEO satellites are excellent for sending television programs to cable operators and broadcasting directly to homes.

One major limitation of GEO satellites is that their transmissions take a quarter of a second to send and return. This brief pause, called **propagation delay**, makes two-way telephone conversations difficult. Also, GEO satellites are large, expensive, and require large amounts of power to launch.

Medium earth orbit (MEO) satellites are located about 10,000 kilometres above the earth's surface. MEO orbits require more satellites to cover the earth than GEO orbits because MEO footprints are smaller. MEO satellites have two advantages over GEO satellites: They are less expensive, and they do not have an appreciable propagation delay. However, because MEO satellites move with respect to a point on the earth's surface, receivers must track these satellites. (Think of a satellite dish slowly turning to remain oriented to a MEO satellite).

Low earth orbit (LEO) satellites are located 640 to 1,125 kilometres above the earth's surface. Because LEO satellites are much closer to the earth, they have little, if any, propagation delay. Like MEO satellites, however, LEO satellites move with respect to a point on the earth's surface and therefore must be tracked by receivers. Tracking LEO satellites is more difficult than tracking MEO satellites because LEO satellites move much more quickly than MEO satellites relative to a point on the earth.

Unlike GEO and MEO satellites, LEO satellites can pick up signals from weak transmitters. This characteristic makes it possible for satellite telephones to operate via LEO satellites because they can operate with less power and smaller batteries. Another advantage of LEO satellites is that they consume less power and cost less to launch than GEO and MEO satellites.

At the same time, however, the footprints of LEO satellites are small, which means that many of them are required to cover the earth. For this reason, a single organization often produces multiple LEO satellites, known as *LEO constellations*. Two examples are Iridium and Globalstar.

Iridium (*www.iridium.com*) has placed a LEO constellation in orbit that consists of 66 satellites and 12 in-orbit spare satellites. The company maintains that it provides complete satellite communication coverage of the earth's surface, including the polar regions. Globalstar (*www.globalstar.com*) also has a LEO constellation in orbit.

Global Positioning Systems. The **global positioning system (GPS)** is a wireless system that uses satellites to enable users to determine their position anywhere on earth. GPS is supported by 24 MEO satellites that are shared worldwide. The exact position of each satellite is always known because the satellite continuously broadcasts its position along with a time signal. By using the known speed of the signals and the distance from three satellites (for two-dimensional location) or four satellites (for three-dimensional location), it is possible to find the location of any receiving station or user within a range of three metres. GPS software can also convert the user's latitude and longitude to an electronic map.

For example, GPSs in automobiles "talk" to drivers when giving directions. Figure 7.4 shows a GPS system in an automobile.

Commercial use of GPS has become widespread. Its uses include navigation, mapping, and surveying, particularly in remote areas. Cell phones in many parts of Canada now must have a GPS

FIGURE 7.4
Dashboard GPS in car.
Source: Michael Ventura/Alamy.

embedded in them so that the location of a person making an emergency call (for example, 911) can be detected immediately. For a GPS tutorial, see *www.trimble.com/gps*.

Three other global positioning systems are either planned or operational. The Russian GPS, called *GLONASS*, was completed in 1995. However, the system fell into disrepair with the collapse of the Soviet economy. Russia is now restoring the system, with the government of India as a partner. The European Union GPS called *Galileo* has an expected completion date of 2013. Finally, China expects to complete its GPS called *Beidou* by 2015.

Internet over Satellite (IoS). In many regions of the world, *Internet over Satellite* (IoS) is the only option available for Internet connections because installing the necessary cables is either too expensive or is physically impossible. IoS enables users to access the Internet via GEO satellites from a dish mounted on the side of their homes. Although IoS makes the Internet available to many people who otherwise could not access it, it has its drawbacks. As we have seen, GEO satellite transmissions entail a propagation delay, and they can be disrupted by environmental influences such as thunderstorms.

Radio

Radio transmission uses radio-wave frequencies to send data directly between transmitters and receivers. Radio transmission has several advantages. To begin with, radio waves travel easily through normal office walls. In addition, radio devices are fairly inexpensive and easy to install. Finally, radio waves can transmit data at high speeds. For these reasons, radio increasingly is being used to connect computers to both peripheral equipment and local area networks (LANs, discussed in Technology Guide 4).

As with other technologies, however, radio transmission also has its drawbacks. First, radio media can create electrical interference problems. Also, radio transmissions are susceptible to snooping by anyone who has similar equipment that operates on the same frequency.

Satellite Radio. One problem with radio transmission is that when you travel too far away from the source station, the signal breaks up and fades into static. Most radio signals can travel only about 50 or 65 kilometres from their source. However, **satellite radio**, also called **digital radio**, overcomes this problem. Satellite radio offers uninterrupted, near CD-quality music that is beamed to your radio, either at home or in your car, from space. In addition, satellite radio offers a broad spectrum of stations, types of music, news, and talk.

XM Satellite Radio (*www.xmradio.com*) and Sirius Satellite Radio (*www.sirius.com*) were competitors that launched satellite radio services. XM broadcast its signals from GEO satellites, and Sirius used MEO satellites. The two companies merged in July 2008 to form Sirius XM in the United States, though both services operate separately in Canada. Listeners subscribe to the service for a monthly fee.

Infrared Transmission. The final type of wireless transmission is infrared transmission. **Infrared** light is red light that is not commonly visible to human eyes. Common applications of infrared light are in remote control units for televisions, VCRs, DVDs, and CD players. In addition, like radio transmission, infrared transceivers are used for short-distance connections between computers and peripheral equipment and local area networks. A *transceiver* is a device that can transmit and receive signals. Many portable PCs have infrared ports, which are handy when cable connections with a piece of peripheral equipment (such as a printer or modem) are not practical.

BEFORE YOU GO ON ...

1. Describe today's wireless devices.
2. Describe the various types of transmission media.

7.2 Wireless Computer Networks and Internet Access

We have discussed various wireless devices and how these devices transmit wireless signals. These devices typically form wireless computer networks, and they provide wireless Internet access. We organize our discussion of wireless networks by their effective distance: short-range, medium-range, and wide-area.

Short-Range Wireless Networks

Short-range wireless networks simplify the task of connecting one device to another, eliminating wires and enabling users to move around while they use the devices. In general, short-range wireless networks have a range of 30 metres or less. In this section, we consider three basic short-range networks: Bluetooth, ultra-wideband (UWB), and near-field communications (NFC).

Bluetooth Networks

Bluetooth (*www.bluetooth.com*) is an industry specification used to create small personal area networks. A **personal area network** is a computer network used for communication among computer devices (for example, telephones, personal digital assistants, and smart phones) close to one person. Bluetooth 1.0 can link up to eight devices within a 10-metre area with a bandwidth of 700 Kbps (kilobits per second) using low-power, radio-based communication. Bluetooth 2.0 can transmit up to 2.1 Mbps (megabits per second) and at greater power can transmit up to 100 metres. Ericsson, the Scandinavian mobile handset company that developed this standard, named it after the tenth-century Danish king Harald Blatan, who was known as Bluetooth.

Common applications for Bluetooth are wireless handsets for cell phones and portable music players. Other novel applications include the use of Bluetooth in toys, such as the Lego Mindstorms NXT systems where you can build your own Lego robot (*http://mindstorms.lego.com*). Advantages of Bluetooth include low power consumption and the fact that it uses omnidirectional radio waves (that is, waves coming from many different directions). This means that you do not have to point one Bluetooth device at another for a connection to occur.

Ultra-Wideband Networks

Ultra-wideband (UWB) is a high-bandwidth wireless technology with transmission speeds in excess of 100 Mbps. This very high speed makes UWB a good choice for applications such as streaming multimedia from, say, a personal computer to a television.

Time Domain (*www.timedomain.com*), a pioneer in ultra-wideband technology, has developed many UWB applications. One interesting application is the PLUS Real-Time Location System (RTLS). Using PLUS, an organization can accurately locate multiple people and assets simultaneously. Employees, customers, and/or visitors wear the PLUS Badge Tag. PLUS Asset Tags are placed on equipment and products. PLUS is extremely valuable for health-care environments, in which real-time location of caregivers (e.g., doctors, nurses, technicians) and mobile equipment (e.g., laptops, monitors) is critically important.

Near-Field Communications Networks

Near-field communications (NFC) has the smallest range of any short-range wireless networks. It is designed to be embedded in mobile devices such as cell phones and credit cards. For example, using NFC, you can swipe your device or card within a few centimetres of point-of-sale terminals to pay for items.

Medium-Range Wireless Networks

Medium-range wireless networks are the familiar wireless local area networks (WLANs). The most common type of medium-range wireless network is wireless fidelity or Wi-Fi. WLANs are useful in a variety of settings, and some of these may be challenging, as IT's About Business 7.1 illustrates.

Wireless Fidelity (Wi-Fi)

Wireless fidelity (or Wi-Fi) is a medium-range **wireless local area network (WLAN)**, which is basically a wired LAN but without the cables. In a typical configuration, a transmitter with an antenna, called a **wireless access point**, connects to a wired LAN or to satellite dishes that provide an Internet connection. Figure 7.5 shows a wireless access point. A wireless access point provides service to a number of users within a small geographical perimeter (up to about 60 metres), known as a **hotspot**. To support a larger number of users across a larger geographical area, several wireless access points are needed. To communicate wirelessly, mobile devices, such as laptop PCs, typically have a built-in **wireless network interface card (NIC)**.

IT'S ABOUT BUSINESS 7.1
"SCI-FI" WIRELESS COMMUNICATIONS COMES TO TORONTO EAST GENERAL HOSPITAL

Deploying a wireless local area network (WLAN) in a health-care environment with its many regulations and security requirements is extremely complicated. Caregivers are highly mobile, their job duties are time-critical and impact people's lives, and numerous regulations exist to ensure patient safety and security. To address these challenges, hospitals are increasingly deploying WLANs.

The large Toronto East General Hospital (*www.tegh.on.ca*), located in downtown Toronto, has space of over 93,000 square metres (one million square feet). It required almost 300 wireless stations (wireless access points) to be located in the hospital, particularly since it is primarily built in concrete block.

The hospital wanted to improve employee communication and thus also improve patient care. Nurses or doctors could be in a surgery or in a highly infectious area, yet need contact with outsiders rapidly. A cellular telephone is not suitable in such situations if the nurse or doctor needs both hands to work with patients or equipment.

Enter a communications system developed by Vocera (*www.vocera.com*). It uses a wireless local area network with voice over Internet protocol and voice recognition to provide employees with almost hands-free communication. Employees wear a communication device around their neck, reminiscent of science fiction TV shows. They simply tap the device quickly to start it, then can do the rest hands-free. For example, a nurse can call for a doctor's help, or a broadcast message about an emergency can be sent to a group of people. With close to 3,000 employees, about 800 will be enabled with the Vocera devices.

The hospital communications network can also be used with other systems. For example, a Vocera voice command can be used to ring through to a cellular telephone, or to send text messages using voice recognition systems. It has also improved employee safety, since employees can call for security by double-tapping an emergency button on the Vocera device, which is also being used to indicate a patient crisis that requires immediate assistance.

Sources: Compiled from T. Burgmann, "A New Badge of Honour," *Toronto Star*, November 16, 2009, pp. B1 and B4; Toronto East General Hospital, "Vocera—Highlighting TEGH's Commitment to Workplace Safety," *In General*, September 1, 2008; Vocera website (*www.vocera.com*), accessed June 13, 2010.

QUESTIONS

1. Discuss the reasons that it is more difficult to implement a WLAN in a hospital than in another type of organization.
2. There are a large variety of end users in a hospital, including physicians, nurses, pharmacists, and laboratory technicians on the clinical side, as well as executives, managers, and other personnel on the business side. Discuss how you would gather end-user requirements for a WLAN from these diverse groups. Would you expect to encounter conflicting requirements? If so, how would you manage the user requirements process?
3. Describe ways that physicians, nurses, pharmacists, or laboratory technicians could use the Vocera system to improve productivity or workplace safety.

FIGURE 7.5
Wireless access point.
Source: Courtesy
D-Link systems.

FIGURE 7.6 A customer using Wi-Fi at a coffee shop.
Source: Courtesy Tamara Capar

Wi-Fi provides fast and easy Internet or intranet broadband access from public hotspots located at airports, hotels, Internet cafés, coffee shops, universities, conference centres, offices, and homes (see Figure 7.6). Users can access the Internet while walking across the campus, to their office, or throughout their homes. Users can access Wi-Fi with their laptops, desktops, or PDAs through a wireless network card. Most PC and laptop manufacturers incorporate these cards directly in their PCs.

The Institute of Electrical and Electronics Engineers (IEEE) has established a set of standards for wireless computer networks. The IEEE standard for Wi-Fi is the 802.11 family. There are four standards in this family: 802.11a, 802.11b, 802.11g, and 802.11n.

Today, most WLANs use the 802.11g standard, which can transmit up to 54 Mbps and has a range of about 100 metres. The 802.11n standard, still under development, is designed to have wireless transmission speeds up to 600 Mbps and a range double that of 802.11g, or some 200 metres. Although the standard remains in development, vendors already offer 802.11n products. One example is D-Link's (*www.dlink.ca*) DWL-8600AP Unified Wireless N Access Point.

The major benefits of Wi-Fi are its low cost and its ability to provide simple Internet access. It is the greatest facilitator of the *wireless Internet*; that is, the ability to connect to the Internet wirelessly. Many laptop PCs are equipped with chips that can send and receive Wi-Fi signals.

Corporations are integrating Wi-Fi into their strategy. For example, Starbucks, McDonalds, and Chapters are offering customers Wi-Fi in many of their stores, primarily for Internet access. IT's About Business 7.2 illustrates how Starbucks uses Wi-Fi to promote its corporate strategy of being everyone's "third place" after home and the office.

Although Wi-Fi has become extremely popular, it is not without problems. Three factors are preventing the commercial Wi-Fi market from expanding even further: roaming, security, and cost. Regarding the first factor, at this time users cannot roam from hotspot to hotspot if the hotspots use different Wi-Fi network services. Unless the service is free, users have to log on to separate accounts and pay a separate fee for each service. Keep in mind that some Wi-Fi hotspots offer free service, whereas others charge a fee.

Security is the second barrier to greater acceptance of Wi-Fi. Because Wi-Fi uses radio waves, it is difficult to shield from intruders. We discuss Wi-Fi security in the last section of this chapter.

The final limitation to greater Wi-Fi expansion is cost. Even though Wi-Fi services are relatively inexpensive, many experts question whether commercial Wi-Fi services can survive when so many free hotspots are available to users.

In some places, Wi-Fi Internet hubs are marked by symbols on sidewalks and walls. This practice is called *war chalking*. Certain war chalking symbols indicate that there is an accessible Wi-Fi hotspot

IT'S ABOUT BUSINESS 7.2
STARBUCKS' "THIRD PLACE" STRATEGY

Starbucks want to be in "third place." It wants to be number one in the coffee business, naturally, but it wants its customers to think of their stores as the third place they go after home and the office to get a coffee and relax.

Everything about a Starbucks location is carefully considered to optimize the customer experience, and offering Wi-Fi is a big part of that strategy. In 2002, Starbucks was considered a pioneer when it launched its wireless hotspots, and sceptics wondered if people really wanted to surf the Internet over coffee. Others predicted that customers would want to do just that and in fact would overstay their welcome, which would deny access to other customers and thus reduce profits.

The market has shown that customers are very interested in surfing the Net while they drink coffee. While people started out lingering over their laptops, many now surf on their smart phones, and Starbucks was there to foster that trend. The chain even encourages customers to stay, unlike in a fast-food restaurant, where quick service and consumption is the norm. The company says it offers Wi-Fi and its specialized music and other content to enhance the customer experience.

Sources: Compiled from D. Berthiaume, "Sometimes Less Is More," *eWeek,* July 28, 2008; N. Gohring, "Starbucks Can't Handle Demand for Free Wi-Fi," *Network World,* June 4, 2008; G. Fleishman, "T-Mobile Loses Starbucks," *Wi-Fi Net News,* February 11, 2008; M. Turner, "Starbucks, AT&T Brew Up Wireless Service," *Sacramento Business Journal,* February 11, 2008; Starbucks website (*www. starbucks.com*), accessed February 22, 2009.

QUESTIONS
1. Compare the strategies of Starbucks and McDonalds. How does making Wi-Fi available in their outlets affect each strategy?
2. Discuss possible security problems for Starbucks customers as they use a public Wi-Fi hotspot. Hint: We discuss wireless security in Section 7.5.

in the vicinity of a building. Therefore, if your laptop has a wireless network interface card (NIC), you can access the Internet free. You could also access the wireless network of a company located in the building. Other symbols indicate that the Wi-Fi hotspot around the building is closed. You can access it only if you are authorized.

Wireless Mesh Networks

Mesh networks use multiple Wi-Fi access points to create a wide area network that can be quite large. Mesh are essentially a series of interconnected local area networks. For example, Moncton, New Brunswick established a free Wi-Fi network in 2008 for the downtown core, which is also used by the municipal government.

Wide-Area Wireless Networks

Wide-area wireless networks connect users to the Internet over geographically dispersed territory. These networks typically operate over the licensed spectrum. That is, they use portions of the wireless spectrum that are regulated by the government. In contrast, Bluetooth and Wi-Fi operate over the unlicensed spectrum and are therefore more prone to interference and security problems. In general, wide-area wireless network technologies fall into two categories: cellular radio and wireless broadband. We discuss both technologies in this section.

Cellular Radio

Cellular telephones (cell phones) use radio waves to provide two-way communication. The cell phone communicates with radio antennas (towers) placed within adjacent geographic areas called *cells* (see Figure 7.7). A telephone message is transmitted to the local cell (antenna) by the cell phone and then is passed from cell to cell until it reaches the cell of its destination. At this final cell, the

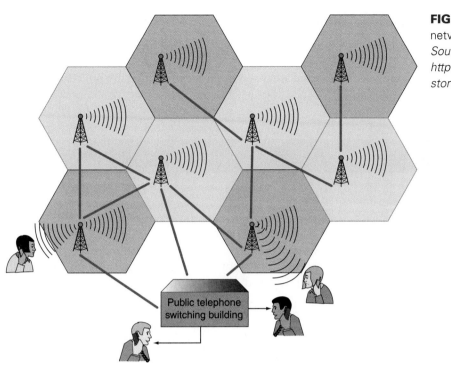

FIGURE 7.7 Cellular network.
Source: Adapted from *http://people.bu.edu/ storo/iml.gif*

message is either transmitted to the receiving cell phone or is transferred to the public switched telephone system to be transmitted to a wireline telephone. This is why you can use a cell phone to call both other cell phones and standard wireline phones.

Cellular technology is quickly evolving, moving toward higher transmission speeds and richer features. The technology has progressed through several stages. *First generation (1G)* cellular used analog signals and had low bandwidth (capacity). *Second generation (2G)* uses digital signals primarily for voice communication; it provides data communication up to 10 Kbps. 2.5G uses digital signals and provides voice and data communication up to 144 Kbps.

Third generation (3G) uses digital signals and can transmit voice and data up to 384 Kbps when the device is moving at a walking pace, 128 Kbps when moving in a car, and up to 2 Mbps when the device is in a fixed location. 3G supports video, web browsing, and instant messaging.

Fourth generation (4G) is still under development and does not fall under one defined technology or standard. The Wireless World Research Forum defines 4G as a network that operates on Internet technology, combines this technology with other applications and technologies such as Wi-Fi and WiMAX (discussed next), and operates at speeds ranging from 100 Mbps in cell phone networks to 1 Gbps in local Wi-Fi networks.

Third-generation cellular service does have disadvantages. Perhaps the most fundamental problem is that cellular companies in North America use two separate technologies: Code Division Multiple Access (CDMA) and Global System for Mobile Communications (GSM). CDMA companies are currently using *Evolution-Data Optimized (EV-DO)* technology, which is a wireless broadband cellular radio standard.

In addition, 3G is relatively expensive, and most carriers limit how much you can download and what the service can be used for. For instance, some carriers prohibit downloading or streaming audio or video. If you go beyond the limits, the carriers reserve the right to cut off your service.

Wireless Broadband or WiMAX

Worldwide Interoperability for Microwave Access, popularly known as WiMAX, is the name for IEEE Standard 802.16. WiMAX has a wireless access range of up to 50 kilometres, compared with 100 metres for Wi-Fi. WiMAX also has a data transfer rate of up to 75 Mbps. It is a secure system, and it offers features such as voice and video. WiMAX antennas can transmit broadband Internet connections to antennas on homes and businesses kilometres away. The technology can therefore provide long-distance broadband wireless access to rural areas and other locations that are not currently being served, as the following example shows.

EXAMPLE 7.1

Argentina implemented the first WiMAX network in Latin America in 2004, providing Internet and data transmission services along with voice over Internet protocol (VoIP).

The network was launched by Ertach, which created more than 1,500 Internet access points. Access is available in schools, public hospitals, and state agencies such as vehicle licensing offices. In all, some 40 percent of the province of Buenos Aires has WiMAX coverage.

Then, in August 2006, Ertach launched the first mobile broadband network in Latin America with WiMAX technology. This network covered the city of Carlos Casares and surrounding rural and remote communities, extending coverage to one of the largest agro-business companies in Argentina.

Ertech (now part of Telmex—*www.telmex. com/mx*) had a presence in more than 160 cities in Argentina in mid-2009 and was still expanding rapidly.

Sources: Compiled from C. Garza, "Ertach's WiMAX Experience in Argentina," WiMAX.com, accessed February 2, 2009; "Ertach Sale to Telemex Approved," *WiMAX Day*, June 27, 2007; "Ertach Completes Patagonian WiMAX Deployment," news release, January 16, 2007; Ertach website (*www.ertach.com*), accessed February 2, 2009.

BEFORE YOU GO ON ...

1. What is Bluetooth? What is a WLAN?
2. Describe Wi-Fi, cellular service, and WiMAX.

7.3 Mobile Computing and Mobile Commerce

In the traditional computing environment, users come to a computer, which is connected with wires to other computers and to networks. The need to be linked by wires makes it difficult or impossible for people on the move to use them. In particular, salespeople, repair people, service employees, law enforcement agents, and utility workers can be more effective if they can use IT while they are in the field or in transit. Thus, mobile computing was designed for workers who travel outside the boundaries of their organizations as well as for anyone travelling outside the home.

Recall that mobile computing refers to a real-time wireless connection between a mobile device and other computing environments, such as the Internet or an intranet. This innovation is revolutionizing how people use computers. It is spreading at work and at home; in education, health care, and entertainment; and in many other areas.

Mobile computing has two major characteristics that differentiate it from other forms of computing: mobility and broad reach. *Mobility* means that users carry a device with them and can initiate a real-time contact with other systems from wherever they happen to be. *Broad reach* refers to the fact that when users carry an open mobile device, they can be reached instantly, even across great distances.

These two characteristics, mobility and broad reach, create five value-added attributes that break the barriers of geography and time: ubiquity, convenience, instant connectivity, personalization, and localization of products and services. A mobile device can provide information and communication regardless of the user's location (*ubiquity*). With an Internet-enabled mobile device, you can access the Web, intranets, and other mobile devices quickly and easily without booting up a PC or placing a call via a modem (*convenience* and *instant connectivity*). A company can customize information and send it to individual consumers as an SMS (*customization*). Finally, knowing a user's physical location helps a company advertise its products and services (*localization*). Mobile computing provides the foundation for mobile commerce (m-commerce), which we discuss next.

Mobile Commerce

In addition to affecting our everyday lives, mobile computing is also transforming the way we conduct business by allowing businesses and individuals to engage in mobile commerce. As we saw at the beginning of the chapter, mobile commerce (or m-commerce) refers to e-commerce (EC) transactions that are conducted in a wireless environment, especially via the Internet. Like regular EC applications, m-commerce can be transacted via the Internet, private communication lines, smart cards, and other infrastructures. M-commerce creates opportunities for businesses to deliver new services to existing customers and to attract new customers. To see how m-commerce applications are classified by industry, see *www.mobiforum.org*.

The development of m-commerce is driven by the following factors:

- *Widespread availability of mobile devices.* By mid-2009, over 3 billion cell phones were in use throughout the world. Experts estimate that within a few years about 70 percent of cell phones in developed countries will have Internet access. Thus, a potential mass market is developing for mobile computing and m-commerce. Going further, as we discussed earlier in this chapter, cell phones are spreading even more quickly in developing countries.
- *No need for a PC.* Because users can access the Internet via a smart phone or other wireless device, they do not need a PC to go on-line. Even though the cost of a PC that is used primarily for Internet access can be less than $300, that amount is still a major expense for the vast majority of people in the world, particularly in developing countries.
- *The "cell phone culture."* The widespread use of cell phones is a social phenomenon, especially among young people. The use of SMS and instant messaging has increased enormously in European and Asian countries. The members of the "cell phone culture" will constitute a major force of on-line buyers once they begin to make and spend more money.
- *Declining prices.* The price of wireless devices is declining and will continue to decline.
- *Bandwidth improvement.* To properly conduct m-commerce, you need sufficient bandwidth for transmitting text, voice, video, and multimedia. Wi-Fi, 3G cellular technology, and WiMAX provide the necessary bandwidth.

Mobile computing and m-commerce include many applications. These applications result from the capabilities of various technologies. We examine these applications and their impact on business activities in the next section.

Mobile Commerce Applications

There are a large variety of mobile commerce applications. The most popular applications include financial services, intrabusiness applications, information accessing, location-based applications, telemedicine, and telemetry. We devote the rest of this section to examining these various applications and their effects on the ways we live and do business.

Financial Services

Mobile financial applications include banking, wireless payments and micropayments, money transfers, wireless wallets, and bill payment services. The bottom line for mobile financial applications is to make it more convenient for customers to transact business regardless of where they are or what time it is. Harried customers are demanding such convenience, as the following example illustrates.

EXAMPLE 7.2

First Data (*www.firstdata.com*) is in the business of authorizing credit card and debit card transactions for banks and retailers. Thinking strategically, however, the company decided to be a pioneer in the next wave of electronic commerce, namely mobile commerce.

At the U.S. Democratic National Convention in Denver, Colorado in 2008, First Data demonstrated its GO-Tag by distributing small buttons to 5,000 journalists and delegates. When they tapped the buttons on electronic sensors at concession stands in the convention centre, they received free snacks and drinks. These peanut-sized chips, each with a radio transmitter inside, can be stuck on a cell phone or an ID badge to make paying for purchases fast and easy. The transactions are handled on the networks that First Data uses for traditional debit and credit cards. First Data has signed up several major customers, including Blockbuster in

the United States. Completing a sale with prepaid GO-Tag takes about one second, which is much faster than using either a traditional credit card or cash. Blockbuster claims its goal is to eliminate the need for cash in its stores. As it does with its core business, First Data makes money with GO-Tag by collecting transaction fees.

Similar devices are already in wide use in Japan and Korea. After a slow start in North America, this mobile commerce technology is reaching critical mass because merchants see it as a much needed way to trim costs and boost sales.

Sources: Compiled from S. Hamm, "Will GO-Tags Make Your Wallet Obsolete?" *BusinessWeek*, September 8, 2008; "First Data's GO-Tags—The First Step Toward Mobile Commerce?", *Mobile Industry Review*, August 21, 2008; "First Data GO-Tag Contactless Prepaid Sticker Consumer Survey," *www.firstdata.com*, January 2008; "Mobile Commerce and the M-Wallet: A Market Brief," *www.firstdata.com*, 2007.

Mobile Banking. In many countries, banks increasingly offer mobile access to financial and account information. For example, banks could alert customers on their digital cell phones about changes in account information.

Wireless Electronic Payment Systems. Wireless payment systems transform mobile phones into secure, self-contained purchasing tools capable of instantly authorizing payments over the cellular network. As described in Chapter 1, the major banks in Canada allow people to transfer money instantly to other individuals and make payments to businesses anywhere in the world with any wireline or mobile phone.

Contactless payment is common for gasoline stations and many grocery stores—simply wave your credit card (or enabled telephone) at the payment station. This process speeds up customer flow and frees up workers to help other customers.

Micropayments. If you took a taxi ride in Frankfurt, Germany, you could use your cell phone to pay the taxi driver. Electronic payments for small-purchase amounts (generally less than $10) are called micropayments.

Web shoppers have historically preferred to pay with credit cards. But because credit card companies may charge fees on transactions, credit cards are an inefficient way of making very small purchases. The growth of relatively inexpensive digital content such as music (for example, iTunes), ring tones, and downloadable games, is driving the growth of micropayments because customers want to avoid credit card fees on small transactions.

The success of micropayment applications, however, ultimately depends on the costs of the transactions. Transaction costs will be small only when the volume of transactions is large. One technology that can increase the volume of transactions is wireless m-wallets.

Mobile (Wireless) Wallets. Various companies offer **mobile wallet** (m-wallet, also known as *wireless wallet*) technologies that enable cardholders to make purchases with a single click from their mobile devices. One example is the Nokia wallet. This application securely stores information (such as credit card numbers) in the customer's Nokia phone for use in making mobile payments. People can also use this information to authenticate transactions by signing them digitally. Microsoft also offers an m-wallet, Passport, for use in a wireless environment.

Wireless Bill Payments. A number of companies are now providing their customers with the option of paying their bills directly from a cell phone. For example, HDFC Bank of India (*www.hdfcbank.com*) allows customers to pay their utility bills through SMS.

In China, SmartPay allows consumers to use their mobile phones to pay their phone bills and utility bills, buy lottery tickets and airline tickets, and make other purchases. SmartPay launched 172. com (see *www.172.com/web/websit/english/english/index.html*), a portal that centralizes the company's mobile, telephone, and Internet-based payment services for consumers. The portal is designed to provide a convenient, centralized source of information for all these transactions.

Intrabusiness Applications

Although B2C m-commerce gets considerable publicity, most of today's m-commerce applications actually are used *within* organizations. In this section, we will look at how companies use mobile computing to support their employees.

Mobile devices increasingly are becoming an integral part of workflow applications. For example, companies can use non-voice mobile services to assist in dispatch functions; that is, to assign jobs to mobile employees, along with detailed information about the job. Target areas for mobile delivery and dispatch services include transportation (delivery of food, oil, newspapers, cargo, courier services, tow trucks, and taxis), utilities (gas, electricity, phone, water), field service (computer, office equipment, home repair), health care (visiting nurses, doctors, social services), and security (patrols, alarm installation). The following example illustrates an exciting intrabusiness application, telematics, that is being used at UPS.

EXAMPLE 7.3

UPS (*www.ups.com*) was a pioneer in adopting information technology. It currently has an annual IT budget of $1 billion. For the past 20 years, its trucks have been equipped with telematics. *Telematics* refers to the wireless communication of location-based information and control messages to and from vehicles and other mobile assets. The courier company's equipment gathers large amounts of data, and in 2009 it launched a major program to collect and use even more information. The global positioning systems in its trucks can take more than 200 engine measurements—from the number of starts to oil pressure. Analyzing these data can help improve fuel efficiency, safety, and maintenance.

With this information, the company can help recreate what a driver does in a day and look for ways to be more efficient. Changing driver behaviour can save time and money and reduce the risk of accidents. For example, analysis of data from the engines' gears reduced the use of the reverse gear by 25 percent, which increases safety. Daily idling by drivers was cut by 15 minutes, reducing emissions and gasoline use. (Idling consumes 3.8 litres of gas per hour and spews 20 percent more pollution than a truck going at 50 kilometres an hour.) Maintenance costs are also reduced, because mechanics only repair or replace items when they're actually used, rather than according to a schedule based on averages.

Sources: Compiled from C. Murphy, "UPS: Positioned for the Long Haul," *InformationWeek*, January 17, 2009; UPS website (*www. ups.com*), accessed February 5, 2009.

Accessing Information

Mobile portals and voice portals are designed to aggregate and deliver content in a form that will work with the limited space available on mobile devices. These portals provide information anywhere and at any time to users.

Mobile Portals. A mobile portal aggregates and provides content and services for mobile users. These services include news, sports, and e-mail; entertainment, travel, and restaurant information; community services; and stock trading.

The field of mobile portals is increasingly being dominated by a few big companies. The world's best-known mobile portal—i-mode from NTT DoCoMo—has more than 40 million subscribers, primarily in Japan. Major players in Europe are Vodafone, O2, and T-Mobile. Some traditional portals—for example, Yahoo, AOL, and MSN—have mobile portals as well.

Voice Portals. A voice portal is a website with an audio interface. Voice portals are not websites in the normal sense because they can also be accessed through a standard phone or a cell phone. A certain phone number connects you to a website, where you can request information verbally. The system finds the information, translates it into a computer-generated voice reply, and tells you what you want to know. Most airlines provide real-time information on flight status this way.

An example of a voice portal is the voice-activated 511 travel information line developed by Tellme. com. It enables callers to inquire about weather, local restaurants, current traffic, and other handy information. In addition to retrieving information, some sites provide true interaction. For example, iPing (*www.iping.com*) is a reminder and notification service that allows users to enter information via the Web and receive reminder calls. This service can even call a group of people to notify them of a meeting or conference call.

Location-based Applications

As in e-commerce, m-commerce B2C applications are concentrated in three major areas: retail shopping, advertising, and customer service. Location-based mobile commerce is called **location-based commerce** or **L-commerce**.

Shopping from Wireless Devices. An increasing number of on-line vendors allow customers to shop from wireless devices. For example, customers who use Internet-ready cell phones can shop at certain sites such as *http://mobile.yahoo.com* and *www.amazon.com*.

Cell phone users can also participate in on-line auctions. For example, eBay offers "anywhere wireless" services. Account holders at eBay can access their accounts, browse, search, bid, and rebid on items from any Internet-enabled phone or PDA. The same is true for participants in Amazon. com auctions.

Location-based Services. Location-based services provide information specific to a location. For example, a mobile user can request the nearest business or service, such as an ATM or restaurant; can receive alerts, such as warnings of a traffic jam or accident; or can find a friend. Wireless carriers can provide location-based services such as locating taxis, service personnel, doctors, and rental equipment; scheduling fleets; tracking objects such as packages and train boxcars; finding information such as navigation, weather, traffic, and room schedules; targeting advertising; and automating airport check-ins.

Location-based Advertising. One type of location-based service is location-based advertising. When marketers know the current locations and preferences of mobile users, they can send user-specific advertising messages to wireless devices about nearby shops, malls, and restaurants. The following example shows how Sense Networks is developing location-based advertising.

EXAMPLE 7.4

Marketers have dreamed of having deep knowledge of shopper preferences in addition to knowing their location in real-time. In that way, they can zero in on shoppers, whether in a mall or a competitor's store, and send them targeted ads or coupons.

A company called Sense Networks (*www.sensenetworks.com*) is analyzing data on the movements of smart phone users gathered from global positioning systems, cell towers, and Wi-Fi networks. Phone companies and advertisers provide Sense with raw data on people's movements and behaviour. Sense's mission is to transform vast amounts of data into actionable customer intelligence.

Much of this is possible because of Apple's App Store, which offers more than 8,000 programs to iPhone users, including some that provide local information based on the user's position. Every time a customer clicks on an application to find a nearby restaurant or store, the time and place of the event is captured by the company selling the service.

In addition to cellular service, many smart phones, including the iPhone, have Wi-Fi capability. When you pass by Wi-Fi access points in public places, such as stores in a mall, they pick up your presence via your smart phone. Companies offering mobile services can hire a company such as Skyhook Wireless (*www.skyhookwireless.com*) to track their customers on the move. Skyhook keeps tabs on users through 100 million Wi-Fi access points around the globe.

For Sense, the data on users show up as dots on maps. After monitoring a dot for a few weeks, Sense can place it in a tribe, which is a group of people with common behaviours. Patterns can emerge to show typical movements, such as patrons flocking to a popular restaurant, business travellers hitting the same spots in a city, or newly unemployed people moving more randomly.

If this all sounds like invasion of privacy, consider this. In the summer of 2008, Sense deployed a consumer application, called CitySense, in San Francisco. It works on the premise that some people want to be tracked and grouped with like-minded people. The users agreed to download the software to their smart phones and be placed in a tribe. Spotting the marketing opportunities, Kinetics (*www.kineticww.com*), the outdoor advertising unit of WPP (*www.wpp.com*), analyzed the dots in San Francisco and saw that one tribe hung around an area of the city where bars were offering a beer promotion. Kinetics informed the brewery, which extended the promotion to other areas of the city where similar tribes hung out. The campaign was a success.

And the downsides to this type of customer analysis? The consensus among marketers is that consumers will not stand for targeted ads on their phones unless they have asked for them. Users must also give permission for provision of any type of identifying information to marketers. Privacy laws and regulations vary country by country (discussed in Chapter 3), which would make this type of tracking prohibited in some countries, such as Canada.

Sources: Compiled from S. Baker, "The Next Net," *BusinessWeek*, March 9, 2009; N. Davey, "Mapping Out the Future of Location-Based Advertising?," MyCustomer.com, June 20, 2008; O. Malik, "Are You Ready for Location-Based Advertising?," gigaOM.com, February 6, 2008; Sense Networks website (*www.sensenetworks.com*), accessed March 28, 2009; Kinetic website (*www.kineticww.com*), accessed March 30, 2009.

Wireless Telemedicine

Telemedicine is the use of modern telecommunications and information technologies to provide clinical care to individuals located at a distance and to transmit the information that clinicians need in order to provide that care. There are three different kinds of technology that are used for telemedicine applications. The first type involves storing digital images and then transferring them from one location to another. The second allows a patient in one location to consult with a medical specialist in another location in real-time through videoconferencing. The third uses robots to perform remote surgery. In most of these applications, the patient is in a rural area, and the specialist is in an urban location.

Another valuable application involves emergency situations that arise during airplane flights. Inflight medical emergencies occur more frequently than you might think. Alaska Airlines, for example, deals with about 10 medical emergencies every day. Many companies now use mobile communications to attend to these situations. For example, MedLink, a service of MedAire (*www.medaire.com*), provides around-the-clock access to board-certified physicians. These mobile services can also remotely control medical equipment such as defibrillators that are located on the plane.

Telemetry Applications

Telemetry is the wireless transmission and receipt of data gathered from remote sensors. Telemetry has numerous mobile computing applications. For example, technicians can use telemetry to identify maintenance problems in equipment. Also, as we just saw, doctors can monitor patients and control medical equipment from a distance.

Car manufacturers use telemetry applications for remote vehicle diagnosis and preventive maintenance. For instance, drivers of many General Motors cars use its OnStar system (*www.onstar.com*) in numerous ways. As one example, OnStar automatically alerts an OnStar operator when an air bag deploys. In another example, drivers can call OnStar with questions about a warning light that appears on their dashboard.

BEFORE YOU GO ON ...

1. What are the major drivers of mobile computing?
2. Describe mobile portals and voice portals.
3. Describe wireless financial services.
4. List some of the major intrabusiness wireless applications.

7.4 Pervasive Computing

A world in which virtually every object has processing power with wireless or wired connections to a global network is the world of *pervasive computing*, also called *ubiquitous computing*. Pervasive computing is invisible "everywhere computing" that is embedded in the objects around us—the floor, the lights, our cars, the washing machine, our cell phones, our clothes, and so on.

For example, in a *smart home*, your home computer, television, lighting and heating controls, home security system, and many appliances can communicate with one another via a home network. These linked systems can be controlled through various devices, including your pager, cellular phone, television, home computer, PDA, or even your automobile. One of the key elements of a smart home is the *smart appliance*, an Internet-ready appliance that can be controlled by a small hand-held device or a desktop computer via a home network (wireline or wireless). Two technologies provide the infrastructure for pervasive computing: radio-frequency identification (RFID) and wireless sensor networks (WSNs).

Radio-frequency Identification

Radio-frequency identification (RFID) technology allows manufacturers to attach tags with antennas and computer chips on goods and then track their movement through radio signals. RFID was developed to replace bar codes.

A typical bar code, known as the *Universal Product Code (UPC)*, is made up of 12 digits in various groups. The first digit identifies the item type, the next five digits identify the manufacturer, and the next five identify the product. The last digit is a check digit for error detection. Bar codes have worked well, but they have limitations. First, they require line of sight to the scanning device. This is fine in a store, but it can pose substantial problems in a manufacturing plant or a warehouse or on a shipping/receiving dock. Second, because bar codes are printed on paper, they can be ripped, soiled, or lost. Third, the bar code identifies the manufacturer and product but not the actual item.

RFID systems use tags with embedded microchips, which contain data, and antennas to transmit radio signals over a short distance to RFID readers. The readers pass the data over a network to a computer for processing. The chip in the RFID tag is programmed with information that uniquely identifies an item. It also contains information about the item such as its location and where and when it was made. Figure 7.8 shows an RFID reader and an RFID tag on a pallet.

FIGURE 7.8
Small RFID reader and RFID tag.

There are two basic types of RFID tag: active and passive. *Active RFID tags* use internal batteries for power, and they broadcast radio waves to a reader. Because active tags contain batteries, they are more expensive than passive RFID tags and can be read over greater distances. Active tags, therefore, are used for more expensive items. *Passive RFID tags* rely entirely on readers for their power. They are less expensive than active tags and can be read only up to 6 metres. They are generally applied to less expensive merchandise.

One problem with RFID has been the expense. To try to alleviate this problem, Staples (*www.staples.com*) is testing reusable RFID tags, described in the following example.

EXAMPLE 7.5

Tired of inaccurate inventory counts, Staples tried out reusable RFID tags by selectively tagging about 2,000 items. The tags cost Staples between $5 and $8 each. Staples used the tags in its stores to not only obtain an accurate inventory, but to precisely locate each item in the store. When Staples relied on its old manual system, inventory was rarely, if ever, accurate. Now, these items have an active RFID tag, and inventory is 100 percent accurate. In addition, the tags retain the entire movement history of the item to and through the store up to the actual sale.

The bottom line: Staples is seeing labour savings because the retailer does not have to manually count these items. The tag cost seems steep, but they are reused repeatedly and removed at the cash register. Staples expects each tag to function for five years, reducing the cost per use to about three cents if a tag is used 200 times.

Sources: Compiled from "Staples to Expand Reusable RFID Tag Test," *RetailWire*, December 19, 2007; "Staples Goes Reusable with RFID Tags," *FierceMobileIT*, June 10, 2007; E. Schuman, "Staples Tries Reusable RFID Tags," *eWeek*, June 9, 2007; Staples website (*www.staples.com*), accessed February 3, 2009.

Another problem with RFID has been the comparatively large size of the tags. However, this problem may have been solved. Hitachi's mu chip was 0.4 mm by 0.4 mm, but the company now has released its "RFID powder" chips, which are 0.05 mm by 0.05 mm, some 60 times smaller than the mu chips.

The Beijing Olympics successfully deployed RFID technology. IT's About Business 7.3 shows how the technology proved invaluable for the 2008 Olympic Games.

IT'S ABOUT BUSINESS 7.3
RADIO-FREQUENCY IDENTIFICATION AT THE BEIJING OLYMPICS

The 2008 Olympics in Beijing (*http://en.beijing2008.cn/*) represented one of the largest radio-frequency identification (RFID) deployments in history. The scope of the Olympics is vast. During the 2008 Games, China hosted 280,000 athletes, referees, journalists, and other workers from more than 200 countries. Approximately 5 million overseas tourists and more than 120 million domestic travellers visited

Beijing in 2008, and 7 million spectators watched the games at the various venues.

Not only must Olympic coordinators create game schedules and make certain that media coverage is flawless, but they also must protect against counterfeit tickets, arrange food and beverage transportation, and even ensure the safety of food for athletes by tracking the path of all food from farm

(Continued on next page)

IT'S ABOUT BUSINESS 7.3 *(Continued)*
RADIO-FREQUENCY IDENTIFICATION AT THE BEIJING OLYMPICS

to plate. All these processes were facilitated by the RFID vendors at the Games, who created more than 16 million RFID-enabled tickets, along with systems that protected the production, processing, and transport of food and beverage products to coaches and athletes.

The Olympics' use of RFID differed from other large-scale projects. Other projects were in controlled environments such as toll roads or access control and security. ASK TongFang (*www.askthtf.com*), a joint venture between French and Chinese companies, manufactured contactless inlays for 16 million tickets, including gate readers, software, and service. Anti-counterfeiting printed security features were provided by China Bank Note for added security.

The amount of food and beverages moving into and around the Games is immense. For the food applications, the RFID system was paired with sensor technology, which recorded the temperature of the shipment at every moment. For a product such as a case of sports drinks, this process might not have been so important, but for highly perishable foods such as beef or pork, the information was invaluable, given that the food was offered to thousands of athletes and coaches, as well as millions of spectators. The RFID and sensor systems allowed officials with readers to determine whether a food had been subjected to temperatures outside a specified range, rather than just reading a bar code to determine that the correct food was in the correct box.

The Olympic Games' success with RFID-enabled tickets changed how ticketing would be done at other large-scale events. For example, the technology was used for the 2010 World Expo in Shanghai where it was placed into nearly 70 million tickets.

Sources: Compiled from P. Wong, "RFID Goes Prime Time in Beijing Olympics," CNET.com, August 7, 2008; "Beijing Olympics Will Use 16 Million Tickets with Embedded RFID," *RFID News*, May 15, 2008; E. Millard, "Beijing Olympics: Going for the Gold with RFID," *Baseline Magazine*, March 3, 2008; S. Zheng, "Beijing Olympic Games Prompts RFID Development in China," *Network World*, September 3, 2007; ASK TongFang website (*www.askthtf.com/en/index.aspx*), accessed February 1, 2009.

QUESTIONS
1. Describe the advantages of using RFID and sensors for food and beverage tracking versus using bar codes.
2. The RFID-enabled tickets were much more expensive than an ordinary printed ticket (particularly when you add in the readers). Discuss the advantages of the RFID-enabled tickets that outweighed the extra costs.

RuBee, a wireless networking protocol that relies on magnetic rather than electrical energy, gives retailers and manufacturers an alternative to RFID for some applications. RuBee works in harsh environments, near metal and water, and in the presence of electromagnetic noise. Environments such as these have been a major impediment to the widespread, cost-effective deployment of RFID. RuBee is an alternative to, not a replacement for, RFID. RuBee technology is being used in smart shelf environments, where specially designed shelves can read RuBee transmissions. The shelves alert store employees when inventory of a product is running low.

As opposed to RuBee, which is an alternative to RFID, the Memory Spot by Hewlett-Packard is a competitor to RFID. The Memory Spot, the size of a tomato seed, stores up to 4 megabits of data and has a transfer rate of 10 Mbps.

Wireless Sensor Networks (WSNs)

Wireless sensor networks (WSNs) are networks of interconnected, battery-powered, wireless sensors called *motes* (analogous to nodes) that are placed into the physical environment. The motes collect data from many points over an extended space. Each mote contains processing, storage, and radio-frequency sensors and antennas. Each mote "wakes up" or activates for a fraction of a second when it has data to transmit and then relays that data to its nearest neighbour. So, instead of every mote transmitting its information to a remote computer at a base station, the data are moved mote by mote until they reach a central computer where they can be stored and analyzed. An advantage of a wireless sensor network is that, if one mote fails, another one can pick up the data. This process makes WSNs very efficient and reliable. Also, if more bandwidth is needed, it is easy to boost performance by placing new motes when and where they are required.

The motes provide information that enables a central computer to integrate reports of the same activity from different angles within the network. Therefore, the network can determine with much greater accuracy information such as the direction in which a person is moving, the weight of a vehicle, or the amount of rainfall over a field of crops.

One kind of wireless sensor network is ZigBee (*www.ZigBee.org*). ZigBee is a set of wireless communications protocols that target applications requiring low data transmission rates and low power consumption. ZigBee can handle hundreds of devices at once. Its current focus is to wirelessly link sensors that are embedded into industrial controls, medical devices, smoke and intruder alarms, and building and home automation.

A promising application of ZigBee is reading meters for utilities, such as electricity. ZigBee sensors embedded in these meters would send wireless signals that could be picked up by utility employees driving by your house. The employees would not even have to get out of their trucks to read your meter. Wireless sensor networks can also be used to add intelligence to electrical grids.

BEFORE YOU GO ON ...

1. Define pervasive computing, RFID, and wireless sensor networks.
2. Differentiate between RFID and RuBee and describe the benefits of each.

7.5 Wireless Security

Clearly wireless networks provide numerous benefits for businesses. However, they also present a huge challenge to management, namely, their inherent lack of security. Wireless is a broadcast medium, and transmissions can be intercepted by anyone who is close enough and has access to the appropriate equipment. Also, due to their broad reach, those with unauthorized access could play havoc with the data, as illustrated in IT's About Business 7.4. There are four major threats unique to wireless networks: rogue access points, war driving, eavesdropping, and RF (radio frequency) jamming.

A *rogue access point* is an unauthorized access point to a wireless network. The rogue could be someone in your organization who sets up an access point meaning no harm but fails to tell the IT department. In more serious cases, the rogue is an "evil twin," someone who wishes to access a wireless network for malicious purposes.

In an evil twin attack, the attacker is in the vicinity with a Wi-Fi–enabled computer and a separate connection to the Internet. Using a hotspotter—a device that detects wireless networks and provides information on them (see *http://www.canarywireless.com*)—the attacker simulates a wireless access point with the same wireless network name, or SSID, as the one that authorized users expect. If the signal is strong enough, users will connect to the attacker's system instead of the real access point. The attacker can then serve them a web page asking for them to provide confidential information such as user names, passwords, and account numbers. In other cases, the attacker simply captures wireless transmissions. These attacks are more effective with public hotspots (for example, at McDonald's or Starbucks) than in corporate networks.

War driving is the act of locating WLANs while driving (or walking) around a city or elsewhere (see *www.wardriving.com*). To war drive or walk, you simply need a Wi-Fi detector and a wirelessly enabled computer. If a WLAN has a range that extends beyond the building in which it is located,

IT'S ABOUT BUSINESS 7.4
WIRELESS COMMON SENSE

An important practice that should occur when an employee leaves an organization is to remove their ability to access the corporate network, and to change any master or supervisory passwords that the former employee might know about. A car dealership in Austin, Texas had its clients harassed by a former employee, using a wireless system. The former employee disabled cars so that they would not start, or caused the client vehicles to honk; the only way to stop the honking was to remove the vehicle's battery. How was this possible?

The car dealer had a system that is used to encourage clients to pay for their cars. If payments are late, the car can actually be disabled so that it will not start, or the horn will honk. Such features would be stopped when the customer pays up any overdue amounts. About 100 vehicles were disabled by the former car dealership employee before he was tracked down using Internet tracing methods.

In another incident, BlackBerry users who were customers of Etisalet (a cellular service organization in the United Arab Emirates) were informed that a software update was required for their phone. Once they loaded the update, which was spyware, information about their location (using GPS software) as well as actual copies of their text messages were sent to a server. This activity drained power, causing BlackBerrys to drain their batteries faster than

normal. These users complained to RIM (Research in Motion), the manufacturer of the BlackBerry, which tracked down the cause and sent broadcast messages to BlackBerry users, warning them to not load this software.

These and other types of problems with wireless systems described in this section may be one reason why some organizations are refusing to go wireless. For example, Lakehead University in Thunder Bay, Ontario decided in 2006 that it would not implement wireless systems on its campus.

Sources: Compiled from P. Ling, "U. A. E. Mobile Carrier Sends Spyware to BlackBerry Users," *Ottawa Citizen*, July 23, 2009; M. Mittelstaedt, "Lakehead Says No Way to Wireless," *Globe and Mail*, February 24, 2006; I. Paul, "Ex-employee Wirelessly Disables Customer Cars, Causes Others to Honk Endlessly," itbusiness. ca, March 19, 2010.

QUESTIONS
1. Describe controls that should be present over wireless networks that can prevent unauthorized access.
2. What are some good practices that users of smart phones can engage in to help prevent infection by spyware or other viruses?
3. Discuss the advantages and disadvantages of a wireless network to organizations such as Lakehead University.

an unauthorized user might be able to intrude into the network. The intruder can then obtain a free Internet connection and possibly gain access to important data and other resources.

Eavesdropping refers to efforts by unauthorized users to access data that are travelling over wireless networks. Finally, in *radio-frequency (RF) jamming*, a person or a device intentionally or unintentionally interferes with your wireless network transmissions.

In Technology Guide 3, we discuss a variety of techniques and technologies that you should implement to help you avoid these threats.

BEFORE YOU GO ON ...
1. Describe the four major threats to the security of wireless networks.
2. Which of these threats is the most dangerous for a business? Which is the most dangerous for an individual? Support your answers.

WHAT'S IN IT FOR ME?

FOR THE ACCOUNTING MAJOR

Wireless applications help accountants to count and audit inventory. They also expedite the flow of information for cost control. Price management, inventory control, and other accounting-related activities can be improved by use of wireless technologies.

FOR THE FINANCE MAJOR

Wireless services can provide banks and other financial institutions with a competitive advantage. For example, wireless electronic payments, including micropayments, are more convenient (any place, any time) than traditional means of payment, and they are also less expensive. Electronic bill payment from mobile devices is becoming more popular, increasing security and accuracy, expediting cycle time, and reducing processing costs.

FOR THE MARKETING MAJOR

Imagine a whole new world of marketing, advertising, and selling, with the potential to increase sales dramatically. Such is the promise of mobile computing. Of special interest for marketing are location-based advertising as well as the new opportunities resulting from pervasive computing and RFIDs. Finally, wireless technology also provides new opportunities in sales force automation (SFA), enabling faster and better communications with both customers (CRM) and corporate services.

FOR THE PRODUCTION/OPERATIONS MANAGEMENT MAJOR

Wireless technologies offer many opportunities to support mobile employees of all kinds. Wearable computers enable off-site employees and repair personnel working in the field to service customers faster, better, and less expensively. Wireless devices can also increase productivity within factories by enhancing communication and collaboration as well as managerial planning and control. In addition, mobile computing technologies can improve safety by providing quicker warning signs and instant messaging to isolated employees.

FOR THE HUMAN RESOURCES MANAGEMENT MAJOR

Mobile computing can improve human resources training and extend it to any place at any time. Payroll notices can be delivered as SMSs. Finally, wireless devices can make it even more convenient for employees to select their own benefits and update their personal data.

FOR THE MANAGEMENT INFORMATION SYSTEM MAJOR

Management information systems (MIS) personnel provide the wireless infrastructure that enables all organizational employees to compute and communicate at any time, anywhere. This convenience provides exciting, creative new applications for organizations to cut costs and improve the efficiency and effectiveness of operations (for example, to gain transparency in supply chains). Unfortunately, as we discussed earlier, wireless applications are inherently insecure. This lack of security is a serious problem that MIS personnel must deal with.

SUMMARY

1. **Discuss today's wireless devices and wireless transmission media.**

   In the past, we have discussed these devices in separate categories, such as pagers, e-mail handhelds, personal digital assistants (PDAs), cellular telephones, and smart phones. Today, however, new devices, generally called *smart phones*, combine the functions of these devices. The capabilities of these new devices include cellular telephony, Bluetooth, Wi-Fi, a digital camera, global positioning system (GPS), an organizer, a scheduler, an address book, a calculator, access to e-mail and short message service, instant messaging, text messaging, an MP3 music player, a video player, Internet access with a full-function browser, and a QWERTY keyboard.

Microwave transmission systems are widely used for high-volume, long-distance, point-to-point communication. Communication *satellites* are used in satellite transmission systems. The three types of satellite are geostationary earth orbit (GEO), medium earth orbit (MEO), and low earth orbit (LEO). *Radio* transmission uses radio-wave frequencies to send data directly between transmitters and receivers. *Infrared* light is red light not commonly visible to human eyes. The most common application of infrared light is in remote-control units for televisions and VCRs. Infrared transceivers are being used for short-distance connections between computers and peripheral equipment and LANs. Many portable PCs have infrared ports, which are handy when cable connections with peripheral equipment are not practical.

2. **Describe wireless networks according to their effective distance.**
Wireless networks can be grouped by their effective distance: short range, medium range, and wide area. Short-range wireless networks simplify the task of connecting one device to another, eliminating wires and enabling users to move around while they use the devices. In general, short-range wireless networks have a range of 30 metres or less, and include Bluetooth, ultra-wideband (UWB), and near-field communications (NFC).

Medium-range wireless networks are the familiar wireless local area networks (WLANs). The most common type of medium-range wireless network is wireless fidelity or Wi-Fi. Another type of medium-range wireless network is the mesh network, which uses multiple Wi-Fi access points to create a wide-area network. Mesh networks are essentially a series of interconnected local area networks.

Wide-area wireless networks connect users to the Internet over geographically dispersed territory. These networks typically operate over the licensed spectrum. That is, they use portions of the wireless spectrum that are regulated by the government. In contrast, Bluetooth and Wi-Fi operate over the unlicensed spectrum and therefore are more prone to interference and security problems. In general, wide-area wireless network technologies include cellular radio and wireless broadband, or WiMAX.

3. **Define mobile computing and mobile commerce and describe m-commerce applications.**
Mobile computing is a computing model designed for people who travel frequently. *Mobile commerce (m-commerce)* is any e-commerce conducted in a wireless environment, especially via the Internet.

Mobile financial applications include banking, wireless payments and micropayments, wireless wallets, and bill payment services. Job dispatch is a major intrabusiness application. *Voice portals* and *mobile portals* provide access to information. Location-based applications include retail shopping, advertising, and customer service. Other major m-commerce applications include wireless *telemedicine and telemetry.*

4. **Define pervasive computing and its underlying technologies.**
Pervasive computing is invisible everywhere computing that is embedded in the objects around us. Two technologies provide the infrastructure for pervasive computing: *radio-frequency identification (RFID)* and *wireless sensor networks (WSNs).*

RFID is the term for technologies that use radio waves to automatically identify the location of individual items equipped with tags that contain embedded microchips. WSNs are networks of interconnected, battery-powered, wireless devices placed in the physical environment to collect data from many points over an extended space.

5. **Examine threats to wireless networks.**
The four major threats unique to wireless networks are rogue access points, war driving, eavesdropping, and radio-frequency jamming. A rogue access point is an unauthorized access point to a

wireless network. War driving is the act of locating WLANs while driving around a city or elsewhere. Eavesdropping refers to efforts by unauthorized users to access data that are travelling over wireless networks. Radio-frequency jamming occurs when a person or a device intentionally or unintentionally interferes with wireless network transmissions. Wireless network users should also remember to retain security that is used by other types of networks to prevent unauthorized access.

KEY TERMS

Bluetooth, 215
cellular telephones
  (cell phones), 218
digital radio, 214
global positioning system
  (GPS), 213
hotspot, 216
infrared, 214
location-based commerce
  (l-commerce), 224
mesh network, 218
microbrowser, 208
microwave transmission, 211
mobile commerce
  (m-commerce), 207

mobile computing, 207
mobile portal, 224
mobile wallet, 223
near-field communications
  (NFC), 215
personal area network, 215
pervasive computing, 207
propagation delay, 212
radio-frequency identification
  (RFID) technology, 226
radio transmission, 214
satellite radio, 214
satellite transmission, 211
short message service
  (SMS), 209

telemetry, 226
ubiquitous computing, 207
ultra-wideband (UWB), 215
voice portal, 224
wireless, 207
wireless access point, 216
wireless application
  protocol (WAP), 208
wireless fidelity (Wi-Fi), 216
wireless local area network
  (WLAN), 216
wireless network interface
  card (NIC), 216
wireless sensor network
  (WSN), 228

DISCUSSION QUESTIONS

1. Discuss how mobile computing can solve some of the problems of the digital divide.
2. You can use location-based tools to help you find your car or the closest gas station. However, some people see location-based tools as an invasion of privacy. Discuss the pros and cons of location-based tools.
3. Some experts say that Wi-Fi is winning the battle with 3G cellular service. Others disagree. Discuss both sides of the argument and support each one.
4. Discuss how m-commerce can expand the reach of e-business.
5. List three to four major advantages of wireless commerce to consumers and explain what benefits they provide to consumers.
6. Discuss the ways Wi-Fi is being used to support mobile computing and m-commerce. Describe the ways Wi-Fi is affecting the use of cellular phones for m-commerce.
7. Discuss the benefits of telemetry in health care for the elderly.
8. Which of the applications of pervasive computing do you think are likely to gain the greatest market acceptance over the next few years? Why?
9. Explain how security threats could affect organizational networks.

PROBLEM-SOLVING ACTIVITIES

1. Enter *www.kyocera-wireless.com* and view the demos. What is a smart phone? What are its capabilities? How does it differ from a regular cell phone?

2. Explore *www.nokia.com*. Prepare a summary of the types of mobile services and applications Nokia currently supports and plans to support in the future.

3. Enter *www.packetvideo.com*. Examine the demos and products and list their capabilities.

4. Access *www.bluetooth.com*. Examine the types of products being enhanced with Bluetooth technology. Present two of these products to the class and explain how they are enhanced by Bluetooth technology.

5. Research the status of 3G and 4G cellular service by visiting *www.itu.int*, *www.4g.co.uk*, and *www.3gnewsroom.com*. Prepare a report on the status of 3G and 4G service based on your findings.

6. Enter *www.pbinsight.com*,go to MapInfo Professional and look for location-based services demos. Try all the demos. Find all of the wireless services. Summarize your findings.

7. Enter *www.ibm.com*. Search for wireless e-business. Research the resulting stories to determine the types of wireless capabilities and applications that IBM's software and hardware supports. Describe some of the ways these applications have helped specific businesses and industries.

8. Investigate commercial applications of voice portals. Visit several vendors (e.g., *www.tellme.com*, *www.nuance.com*, and others). What capabilities and applications do these vendors offer?

9. Investigate commercial uses of GPS. Start with *http://gpshome.ssc.nasa.gov*; then go to *www.neigps.com*. Can some of the consumer-oriented products be used in industry? Prepare a report on your findings.

10. Enter *www.onstar.com*. What types of fleet services does OnStar provide? Are these any different from the services OnStar provides to individual car owners? (Play the movie.)

11. Access *www.itu.int/osg/spu/publications/internetofthings/InternetofThings_summary.pdf*. Read about the Internet of Things. What is it? What types of technologies are necessary to support it? Why is it important?

12. Examine how new data capture devices such as RFID tags help organizations accurately identify and segment their customers for activities such as targeted marketing. Browse the Web and develop five potential new applications for RFID technology not listed in this chapter. What issues would arise if a country's laws mandated that such devices be embedded in everyone's body as a national identification system?

13. Using a search engine, try to determine whether there are any commercial Wi-Fi hotspots in your area. (Hint: Access *www.hotspot-locations.com*.) Enter *www.wardriving.com*. Based on information provided at this site, what sorts of equipment and procedures could you use to locate hotspots in your area?

TEAM ASSIGNMENTS

1. Each team should examine a major vendor of mobile devices (Nokia, Kyocera, Motorola, Palm, BlackBerry, and so on). Each team will research the capabilities and prices of the devices offered by each company and then make a class presentation, the objective of which is to convince the rest of the class that they should buy that company's products.

2. Each team should explore the commercial applications of m-commerce in one of the following areas: financial services, including banking, stocks, and insurance; marketing and advertising; manufacturing; travel and transportation; human resources management; public services; and health care. Each team will present a report to the class based on their findings. (Start at *www.mobiforum.org*.)

3. Each team should take one of the following areas—homes, cars, appliances, or other consumer goods such as clothing—and investigate how embedded microprocessors are currently being used and will be used in the future to support consumer-centric services. Each team will present a report to the class based on their findings

HATS OFF TO TOP HAT FOR LEARNING

THE BUSINESS PROBLEM

There are many different types of software and hardware available that all converge in the classroom. Students come with different types of devices, such as notebooks, laptops, and cellular telephones, from many suppliers, with different capabilities.

Students like to search the Internet for materials and work with different products or reference material. Sometimes a single textbook for a course does not provide the right content. Instead, the instructor may use multiple textbooks or provide a course reader package on paper that provides material from different sources.

Universities, colleges, and other educational organizations have fixed budgets for education, and are looking at ways to further engage their students. Teaching faculty use videos, web-based media, as well as other types of material in the classroom. Some schools have purchased specialty "clickers" for students to answer multiple choice or true-false questions and have the responses automatically tracked. Yet such clickers are only useful at that institution, for the courses that organize themselves to use the technology.

How can the schools take advantage of the existing technology in use by their students, without investing in further hardware and software themselves?

THE IT SOLUTION

In 2009, a group of students, faculty, and other technology experts at the University of Waterloo in Waterloo, Ontario founded an organization called Top Hat Monocle (*www.tophatmonocle.com*). The team has a broad base of experience from the academic world as well as in technology. The company's objective was to create a learning platform that would facilitate the use of technology by students.

The software enables the fixed and mobile devices (such as smart phones or touch pads) to be used for typical in-classroom use, such as collecting answers for quizzes, asking students questions (and obtaining the answers), as well as sending mini-lectures or other material to these devices. By requiring every student to have a reader or smart phone, these interactive products could be enabled.

The new product is called monocleCAT (computer assisted teaching) and was initially field tested in January 2010.

Another Canadian organization, a Toronto-based corporation called Symtext (*www.symtext.com*), decided that it would provide a more fluid capability to books, so the company called its product Liquid Textbooks. This service enables users to request portions of a variety of books, and have them placed into an e-book format.

THE RESULTS

It is still too early to tell the impact of monocleCAT and Liquid Textbooks—perhaps you can get your school to field test these products. However, these products may be useful at schools such as Blyth Academy, a Toronto-based school that has decided to use readers rather than textbooks. Commencing in September 2009, the school provided students with Kindle readers from Amazon. The school also purchased licences for textbooks so that students could access the textbooks from the school's central server. It (and other schools) could also purchase licences for customized on-line texts such as those provided by Symtext. This would result in less use of paper, more tailored educational products, and the ability to use both readers and smart phones that already belong to students.

Sources: Compiled from N. Carniol, "Turning the Page," *Toronto Star*, May 24, 2010, pp. B1 and B2; K. Rushowy, "End of the Textbook," *Toronto Star*, November 18, 2009, p. A4; Top Hat Monacle website (*www.tophatmonocle.com*).

QUESTIONS

1. Think about the last few courses that you have taken and the type of work that you completed. How could it have been done using your smart phone, laptop, or an e-book reader?
2. What underlying infrastructure, hardware, and software would be needed to effectively use monocleCat or Liquid Textbooks?

Web Resources

Student Website www.wiley.com/canada/rainer

- Web quizzes
- Lecture slides in PowerPoint

- Author podcasts
- Interactive Case: Ruby's Club assignments

ALL OF THE ABOVE AND...

- E-book
- Manager videos
- Vocabulary flash cards

- Pre- and post-lecture quizzes
- Microsoft Office 2007 lab manual and projects

DEVELOPING WIRELESS SOLUTIONS FOR RUBY'S CLUB

Go to the Ruby's Club link at the Student Companion website or WileyPLUS for information about your current internship assignment. You will investigate applications of wireless computing that will enhance Ruby's customer experience, and you'll prepare a summary report for Ruby's managers.

ORGANIZATIONAL INFORMATION SYSTEMS

LEARNING OBJECTIVES

1. Describe transaction processing systems.

2. Describe functional area information systems and the support they provide for each functional area of the organization.

3. Describe enterprise resource planning systems, their benefits, and limitations.

THE BREADTH OF INFORMATION TECHNOLOGY APPLICATIONS AT UPS

The Canadian Press/John Bazemore

THE BUSINESS PROBLEM

Founded in 1907 as a messenger company in the United States, UPS (*www.ups.com*) has grown into a $45-billion corporation by focusing on the goal of enabling commerce around the globe. Of course, like most business organizations, UPS is not impervious to recessions. As of mid-2010, the entire express shipping industry, including UPS, was experiencing the effects of the economic downturn. Despite its problems, however, UPS plans not only to survive the difficult times but to emerge from them in better shape than its competitors. In fact, the company is positioning itself for rapid growth as the economy improves. To achieve this vision, UPS is adhering to its long-term commitment to information technology investments.

THE IT SOLUTIONS

UPS has made effective use of information technology early on and has maintained this policy to the present. Despite the difficult economy, the company budgeted $1 billion for IT in 2008. It currently has several IT initiatives underway to enhance its status as a global enterprise.

As one example, in 2008, for the first time, the number of kilometres flown internationally by UPS cargo planes surpassed the distance flown domestically. To help handle that kind of growth, UPS is stepping up its IT projects. One international initiative is the development of translation software for Eastern European languages to facilitate UPS business operations in those countries.

Another new application is a live chat feature for certain clients in the United States who process international shipments. Not only can they get their questions answered quickly when a transaction is complex, but they can also get improved documentation needed to process the shipments as they cross borders.

Another major UPS initiative is Worldport, a highly automated sorting facility located in Louisville, Kentucky. Every day, about 100 planes and 160 trucks move through this 370,000-square-metre (4 million-square-foot) facility. Software tracks and directs the UPS planes on the ground, while other applications combine these data with what's happening on the planes themselves, such as sensing when the cargo door is locked and therefore loaded and ready to take off. This technology reduces time spent taxiing and waiting on the runway, saving an estimated 885,000 litres of fuel annually.

How exactly does Worldport operate? When a package arrives at the facility, it is loaded onto a conveyor, where its barcode is scanned. A UPS application then uses the barcode data to determine where the package is going and what plane it should depart on that night. Another application activates automated sorters to send the package down the correct path through 110 miles (177 kilometres) of conveyor belts and delivers it for loading onto the correct plane. In the peak holiday season, Worldport handles about 2.5 million packages within a three-and-a-half hour period. To manage this volume, the network must process about 100 million messages per night. In addition, all Worldport applications must be able to handle problems, from routing around mechanical breakdowns in the sorting facility to adjusting plane routes for weather delays.

UPS is keen on developing technology customized to its needs. For example, it teamed up with Hewlett-Packard to create a futuristic device for its warehouse workers: a wearable ink-jet printer. Instead of having to carry boxes to a scanner-printer to print and apply a label to each one, employees can spray sorting instructions directly onto packages. The wearable printer has a barcode reader and Wi-Fi capability, which enable it to generate the necessary information. Creating the device presented several challenges, such as ink visibility, ergonomics, durability, and battery life.

By 2009, UPS was marking 1.5 million packages per day with these printers. The company predicted that number would double in 2010. The cost savings are tremendous. It can reduce the number of warehouse employees to do the task from six to five people, saving an estimated $30 million over the next five years. It can expect another $12 million in savings for stationary label printers. The wearable printers will also save

1,300 tonnes of paper per year. In addition to reducing costs, the last benefit is also a "green" measure that will contribute to conservation.

Although UPS makes extensive use of IT, it does not implement all potential IT applications. For example, it could adopt high-end videoconferencing to cut travel costs, but the price tag is too high. Instead, to minimize travel expenses, the company owns no corporate jets, and it requires all of its executives, including the CEO, to fly economy class.

WHAT DO YOU THINK?

1. Take a look at the UPS website at *www.ups.com*. What types of information systems does UPS use with its customers? What are some additional information systems that the company could use?

2. What type of security should UPS have over its systems? Why is security and privacy important for a company like UPS?

Sources: Compiled from C. Murphy, "UPS: Positioned for the Long Haul," *InformationWeek*, January 17, 2009; M. Hamblen, "UPS Is Testing a Tool to Keep Track of Truck Data," *Computerworld*, October 13, 2008; P. Thibodeau, "Pentagon Looks to UPS, FedEx, Others for IT Advice," *CIO*, July 28, 2008; R. Mitchell, "Project Delivers Savings for UPS," *Computerworld*, April 21, 2008; W. Gardner, "New UPS Technologies Aim to Speed Worldwide Package Delivery," *InformationWeek*, March 20, 2007; B. Brewin, "Sidebar: FedEx vs. UPS: The Technology Arms Race," *Computerworld*, April 19, 2004; UPS website (*www.ups.com*), accessed March 29, 2009.

Chapter Preview

The opening case illustrates many of the information systems that we discuss in detail in this chapter and introduced in Chapter 2. UPS continues to develop information systems to support its global operations. In fact, UPS has implemented many different information systems and integrated them successfully, with outstanding corporate results.

In this chapter we discuss the various systems that support organizations. Such systems are so important that they need to be well managed and properly protected with security and other management controls, discussed in Chapter 3. We begin this chapter by considering transaction processing systems (TPSs), the most fundamental information systems within organizations. We continue our discussion by following a progression from information systems that support part of an organization (the functional area management information systems) to those that support an entire organization (enterprise resource planning systems). In Chapter 9 we continue this progression by examining customer relationship management systems, which also support an entire organization. Finally, in

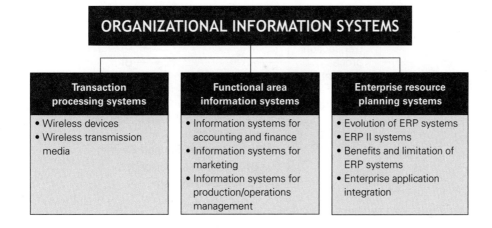

Chapter 10 we turn our attention to information systems that span multiple organizations, particularly supply chain management systems and the technologies that support them.

8.1 Transaction Processing Systems

Millions (sometimes billions) of transactions occur in every organization every day. A **transaction** is any business event that generates data worthy of being captured and stored in a database. Examples of transactions are a product manufactured, a service sold, a person hired, and a payroll cheque generated. When you check out at Walmart, every time one of your purchases is swiped over the bar code reader, that is one transaction.

Transaction processing systems (TPSs) monitor, collect, store, and process data generated from all business transactions. These data are inputs to the organization's database. In the modern business world, they also are inputs to the functional area information systems, decision support systems, customer relationship management, knowledge management, and e-commerce. TPSs have to handle both high volume and large variations in volume (for example, during peak times) efficiently. They must avoid errors and downtime, record results accurately and securely, and maintain privacy and security. Avoiding errors is particularly critical, because data from the TPSs are input into the organization's database and must be correct (remember: "garbage in, garbage out"). Figure 8.1 shows how TPSs manage data.

Regardless of the specific data processed by a TPS, the actual process tends to be standard, whether it occurs in a manufacturing firm, a service firm, or a government organization. First, data are collected by people or sensors and are entered into the computer via an input device. Generally speaking, organizations try to automate the TPS data entry as much as possible because of the large volume involved, a process called *source data automation*.

Next, the system processes data in one of two basic ways: batch processing or on-line processing. In **batch processing**, the firm collects data from transactions as they occur, placing them in groups or batches. The system then prepares and processes the batches periodically (say, every night).

In **real-time transaction processing** (also called *on-line transaction processing*), business transactions are processed on-line as soon as they occur. For example, when you pay for an item at a store, the system records the sale by reducing the inventory on hand by a unit, increasing the store's cash position by the amount you paid, and increasing sales figures for the item by one unit—by means of on-line technologies and in real time.

Transaction processing systems are strategically important to all organizations. IT's About Business 8.1 illustrates how important TPSs are at financial services company Elavon.

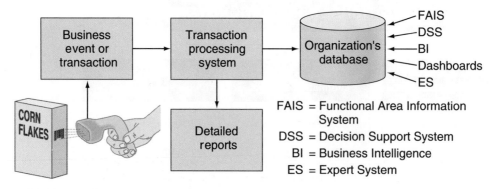

FIGURE 8.1 How transaction processing systems manage data.

IT'S ABOUT BUSINESS 8.1
TRANSACTION PROCESSING SYSTEMS AT ELAVON

The financial services company Elavon (*www.elavon. com/acquiring/canada/*) provides secure payment services to 1 million locations in 30 countries across the globe. In fact, the company is the third largest merchant acquirer in North America. A merchant acquirer is an organization that: (1) recruits merchants who will accept bank-generated credit cards and (2) underwrites those merchants. Elavon's customers include restaurants, stores, hotels, mail-order businesses, and government agencies. The company processes millions of transactions every day on behalf of its merchant customers. Consumers can pay for goods and services using cheques, debit cards, credit cards, and prepaid gift cards. Elavon supplies the hardware, such as cash registers, gas pump terminals, and printers, along with the software needed to operate these terminals.

For Elavon to continue to grow, it must provide consistently high-quality customer service, including processing customer transactions as quickly as possible. To provide optimum levels of service, the company's transaction processing systems (TPSs) must be resilient, reliable, always available, and scalable. Above all else, merchants expect the systems to be always available, with no unexpected interruptions of service.

Elavon's TPSs are at the heart of the company's daily operations and are critical to its success. For this reason, Elavon has tightly coupled its TPSs with its business strategies and its customers' expectations. As a result, the company must pay close attention to software and hardware issues that impact its TPSs.

Software. Elavon manages millions of lines of source code in its TPSs. Because the amount of code is so huge, the TPSs can require as many as 500 source code updates, changes, and error "fixes" per month.

Hardware. The greater the number of transactions Elavon's TPSs can process, the more cost-effective the system becomes. The company turned to server virtualization to increase performance while decreasing costs. (You will see in Technology Guide 1 that server virtualization creates multiple virtual servers on a single physical server). Using virtualization,

Elavon has been able to consolidate hundreds of physical servers into just a few virtualized servers, thus saving money and increasing performance. Another benefit of virtualization is redundancy, meaning that if one partition in a server fails, another automatically handles its operation.

The desire to improve customer service is one reason to effectively manage TPS hardware and software, but so is the need to meet required standards. Elavon must adhere to the Payment Card Industry (PCI) Data Security Standards, which prescribe procedures for processing transactions. If it doesn't follow these rules, it could be barred from processing transactions.

The PCI standards also require companies like Elavon to demonstrate a separation of duties among employees responsible for performing various tasks in the process, which can help reduce errors and fraud. For example, companies must not combine roles such as depositing cash and reconciling bank statements or approving time cards and having custody of paycheques. This means that Elavon must keep an electronic or paper trail to show the flow of transactions, or what is called an audit trail, for any changes to its TPSs, both in hardware or software.

Elavon's attention to its TPSs has helped the company control costs, simplify regulatory compliance and audits, rapidly and accurately process 1 billion customer payments per year, and maintain consistently high levels of customer service. The bottom line? Elavon's TPSs are providing a strategic advantage for the firm in the competitive financial services industry.

Sources: Compiled from D. Brattain, "Transforming IT at Elavon," *Baseline Magazine*, March 6, 2009; "Elavon Teams with CA for Enterprise IT Transformation, Wins InfoWorld 100 Award," *MSN Money*, January 7, 2009; "2008 InfoWorld 100 Awards," *InfoWorld*, November 17, 2008; C. Babcock, "Virtualization Comes to the Big Four Management Vendors," *InformationWeek*, October 11, 2008; Elavon website (*www.elavon.com*), accessed March 31, 2009.

QUESTIONS
1. Explain why TPSs are essential to Elavon.
2. How do Elavon's TPSs help the firm adhere to PCI standards?

BEFORE YOU GO ON ...

1. Define TPS.
2. List the key objectives of a TPS.

8.2 Functional Area Information Systems

As we discussed in Chapter 2, functional area information systems (FAISs) provide information primarily to lower- and middle-level managers in the various functional areas. Managers use this information to help plan, organize, and control operations. The information is provided in a variety of reports, which we describe later in this section. As shown in Figure 8.1, the FAISs access data from the corporate databases.

Traditionally, information systems were designed within each functional area. Their purpose was to support the area by increasing its internal effectiveness and efficiency. Typical function-specific systems are accounting and finance, marketing, production/operations (POM), and human resources management. In the next sections, we discuss the support that management information systems provide for these functional areas.

Information Systems for Accounting and Finance

A primary mission of the accounting and finance functional areas is to manage money flows into, within, and out of organizations. This mission is very broad because money is involved in all functions of an organization. As a result, accounting and finance information systems are very diverse and comprehensive. In this section we focus on certain selected activities of the accounting/finance functional area.

Financial Planning and Budgeting

Appropriate management of financial assets is a major task in financial planning and budgeting. Managers must plan for both the acquisition of resources and their use.

- **Financial and Economic Forecasting.** Knowledge about the availability and cost of money is a key ingredient for successful financial planning. Cash flow projections are particularly important, because they tell organizations what funds they need and when, and how they will acquire them.

  Funds for operating organizations come from multiple sources, including shareholders' investments, bond sales, bank loans, sales of products and services, and income from investments. Decisions about sources of funds for financing ongoing operations and for capital investment can be supported by decision support systems, business intelligence applications, and expert systems, which we discuss in Chapter 11. In addition, numerous software packages for conducting economic and financial forecasting are available. Many of these packages can be downloaded from the Internet, some of them for free.

- **Budgeting.** An essential part of the accounting/finance function is the annual budget, which allocates the organization's financial resources among participants and activities. The budget allows management to distribute resources in the way that best supports the organization's mission and goals.

  Several software packages are available to support budget preparation and control and to facilitate communication among participants in the budget process. These packages can reduce the time involved in the budget process. Further, they can automatically monitor exceptions for patterns and trends.

Managing Financial Transactions

Many accounting/finance software packages are integrated with other functional areas. For example, Peachtree by Sage (*www.peachtree.com*) offers a sales ledger, purchase ledger, cash book, sales order processing, invoicing, inventory control, fixed assets register, and more. Canadian payroll software is available (*www.canadianpayroll.com/peachtree.asp*) for the Sage Peachtree software.

Companies involved in electronic commerce need to access customers' financial data (e.g., credit line), inventory levels, and manufacturing databases (to see available capacity, to place orders). For example, Microsoft Dynamics (formerly Great Plains Software; *www.microsoft.com/dynamics/en/ca/default.aspx*) offers 50 modules that meet the most common financial, project, distribution, manufacturing, and e-business needs. Other e-commerce financial transactions include global stock exchanges, managing multiple currencies, the virtual close, and expense management automation. We discuss each of these applications next.

- **Global Stock Exchanges.** Financial markets operate in global, 24/7/365, distributed electronic stock exchanges that use the Internet both to buy and sell stocks and to broadcast real-time stock prices.
- **Managing Multiple Currencies.** Global trade involves financial transactions in different currencies. Conversion ratios of these currencies change very quickly. Financial/accounting systems take financial data from different countries and convert the currencies from and to any other currency in seconds. Reports based on these data, which used to take days to generate, now take seconds. These systems manage multiple languages as well.
- **Virtual Close.** Companies traditionally closed their books (accounting records) quarterly, usually to meet regulatory requirements. Today, many companies want to be able to close their books at any time, on very short notice. The ability to close the books quickly, called a virtual close, provides almost real-time information on the organization's financial health.
- **Expense Management Automation.** Expense management automation (EMA) refers to systems that automate the data entry and processing of travel and entertainment expenses. EMA systems are web-based applications that enable companies quickly and consistently to collect expense information, enforce company policies and contracts, and reduce unplanned purchases or travel expenses. They also allow companies to reimburse their employees more quickly, because expense approvals are not delayed by poor documentation.

Investment Management

Organizations invest large amounts of money in shares, bonds, real estate, and other assets. Managing these investments is a complex task for several reasons. First, there are literally thousands of investment alternatives, and they are dispersed throughout the world. In addition, these investments are subject to complex regulations and tax laws, which vary from one location to another.

Investment decisions require managers to evaluate financial and economic reports provided by diverse institutions, including federal and provincial agencies, universities, research institutions, and financial services firms. In addition, thousands of websites provide financial data, many of them for free.

To monitor, interpret, and analyze the huge amounts of on-line financial data, financial analysts employ two major types of IT tools: (1) Internet search engines and (2) business intelligence and decision support software.

Control and Auditing

One major reason that organizations go out of business is their inability to forecast and/or secure sufficient cash flow. Underestimating expenses, overspending, engaging in fraud, and mismanaging financial records can lead to disaster. Consequently, it is essential that organizations effectively control their finances and financial statements. We discuss several forms of financial control next.

- **Budgetary control.** Once an organization has decided on its annual budget, it divides those amounts into monthly allocations. Managers at various levels monitor departmental expenditures and compare them against the budget and the operational progress of the corporate plans.

- **Internal auditing.** The Institute of Internal Auditors (*www.theiia.org*) explains that internal auditors should be independent of management by reporting to the audit committee of the board of directors. Then, these internal auditors can evaluate the controls at the organization and evaluate the organization's risk assessment and governance processes. These employees can also prepare for periodic external audits by outside public accounting firms.
- **Financial ratio analysis.** Another major accounting/finance function is to monitor the company's financial health by assessing a set of financial ratios. Included here are liquidity ratios (the availability of cash to pay debt); activity ratios (how quickly a firm converts non-cash assets to cash assets); debt ratios (the firm's ability to repay long-term debt); and profitability ratios (the firm's use of its assets and control of its expenses to generate an acceptable rate of return).

Information Systems for Marketing

It is impossible to overestimate the importance of customers to any organization. Therefore, any successful organization must understand its customers' needs and wants, and then develop its marketing and advertising strategies around them. Information systems provide numerous types of support to the marketing function. In fact, customer-centric organizations are so important that we devote Chapter 9 (Customer Relationship Management) to this topic.

Information Systems for Production/Operations Management

The production and operations management (POM) function in an organization is responsible for the processes that transform inputs into useful outputs and for the operation of the business. Because of the breadth and variety of POM functions, we present only four here: in-house logistics and materials management, planning production and operation, computer-integrated manufacturing (CIM), and product life cycle management (PLM).

The POM function is also responsible for managing the organization's supply chain. Because supply chain management is vital to the success of modern organizations, we devote Chapter 10 to this topic.

In-House Logistics and Materials Management

Logistics management deals with ordering, purchasing, inbound logistics (receiving), and outbound logistics (shipping) activities. Related activities include inventory management and quality control.

Inventory Management. Inventory management determines how much inventory to keep available for manufacturing or for sale to customers. Overstocking can be expensive, due to storage costs and the costs of spoilage and obsolescence. However, keeping insufficient inventory is also expensive (due to last-minute orders and lost sales).

Operations personnel make two basic decisions: when to order and how much to order. Inventory models, such as the economic order quantity (EOQ) model, support these decisions. A large number of commercial inventory software packages are available that automate the application of these inventory models.

Many large companies allow their suppliers to monitor their inventory levels and ship products as they are needed. This strategy, called vendor-managed inventory (VMI), eliminates the need for the company to submit purchase orders.

Quality Control. Quality-control systems used by manufacturing units provide information about the quality of incoming material and parts, as well as the quality of in-process semi-finished products and final finished products. Such systems record the results of all inspections and compare the actual results with established metrics. These systems also generate periodic reports containing information about quality (e.g., percentage of defects, percentage of rework needed). Quality-control data may be collected by web-based sensors and interpreted in real time, or they can be stored in a database for future analysis.

Planning Production and Operations

In many firms, POM planning is supported by IT. POM planning has evolved from material requirements planning (MRP), to manufacturing resource planning (MRP II), to enterprise resource planning (ERP). We briefly discuss MRP and MRP II here, and we address ERP later in this chapter.

Inventory systems that use an EOQ approach are designed for those individual items for which demand is completely independent (for example, the number of identical personal computers a computer manufacturer will sell). However, in manufacturing operations, the demand for some items will be interdependent. For example, a company may make three types of chairs that all use the same screws and bolts. Therefore, the demand for screws and bolts depends on the total demand for all three types of chairs and their shipment schedules. The planning process that integrates production, purchasing, and inventory management of interdependent items is called *material requirements planning* (MRP).

MRP deals only with production scheduling and inventories. More complex planning also involves allocating related resources (e.g., money and labour). In such a case, more complex, integrated software, called *manufacturing resource planning* (MRP II), is available. MRP II integrates a firm's production, inventory management, purchasing, financing, and labour activities. Thus, MRP II adds functions to a regular MRP system. In fact, MRP II has evolved into enterprise resource planning (ERP), which we discuss later in this chapter.

Computer-Integrated Manufacturing

Computer-integrated manufacturing (CIM; also called *digital manufacturing*) is an approach that integrates various automated factory systems. CIM has three basic goals: (1) to simplify manufacturing technologies and techniques, (2) to automate as many of the manufacturing processes as possible, and (3) to integrate and coordinate design, manufacturing, and related functions via computer systems. IT's About Business 8.2 shows how Tata Motors used CIM to build the world's cheapest car, the Nano.

Product Life Cycle Management

Even within a single organization, product design and development can be expensive and time-consuming. When multiple organizations are involved, the process can become very complex. Product life cycle management (PLM) is a business strategy that enables manufacturers to share product-related data to support product design and development and supply chain operations. PLM applies web-based collaborative technologies to product development. By integrating formerly disparate functions, such as a manufacturing process and the logistics that support it, PLM enables these functions to collaborate, essentially forming a single team that manages the product from its inception through its completion.

Information Systems for Human Resource Management

Initial human resource information system (HRIS) applications dealt primarily with transaction processing, such as managing benefits and keeping records of vacation days. As organizational systems have moved to intranets and the Web, however, so have HRIS applications.

Many HRIS applications are delivered via an HR portal. For example, numerous organizations use their web portals to advertise job openings and conduct on-line hiring and training. In this section,

IT'S ABOUT BUSINESS 8.2
THE WORLD'S CHEAPEST CAR

Tata Motors (*www.tatamotors.com*), India's largest commercial vehicle manufacturer, flourished for decades because of a lack of competition. Because the company had more demand than it could handle, it did not need to concern itself with customer desires. In 1991, however, the Indian government implemented reforms that opened its economy to greater competition. As more competitors began to enter the market, however, Tata truck and bus sales dropped by 40 percent. In 2000 alone the company lost $110 million. This loss was Tata's first since the company was founded in 1945.

Tata made dump trucks, cement mixers, ambulances, and buses. But it spotted a market it needed to capitalize on in order to regain market share: it would start making passenger cars. In India, there are only 7 cars for every 1,000 people; in 2007, only 1.3 million passenger vehicles were sold, in a country with more than 1 billion people. There are lots of motorcycles, though—in 2007, some 7 million scooters and motorcycles were sold in India, costing between $675 and $1,600. In order to sell cars, Tata executives felt they needed to be priced not much more than motorcycles. Its goal was to develop a car to sell for $2,500 and still meet requirements for low emissions, fuel efficiency, and performance.

Making a safe and affordable car would not be easy, so Tata relied on CIM technology from Dassault Systems called the Digital Enterprise Lean Manufacturing Interactive Application (DELMIA). The software allowed Tata to not only design the cars, but to design the processes for building them and even the layouts of the plants. Using existing production lines, the software can simulate what new techniques will do. A computer model can also simulate the products and make changes at the click of a button, eliminating the previous process of making expensive physical models.

Since Tata implemented DELMIA, plant efficiency has improved drastically. Changing a die on the passenger car assembly line now takes between 12 and 15 minutes, down from 2 hours in 2000. Further, the company's capacity utilization is one of the best in the entire global automotive industry. Tata also uses electronic procurement to obtain its inbound products. The company saved an average of 7 percent on its supplies—everything from car parts to food in the employee cafeteria—by holding 750 reverse auctions (discussed in Chapter 6) on Ariba (*www.ariba.com*) in 2007.

Tata is taking vehicle manufacturing one step further, using the CIM technology to design its new Nano car modularly. Like flat-pack furniture, the Nano components can come in a kit and be shipped to any location, to be assembled by local entrepreneurs. Tata's chairman wants to "share the wealth" of his company's success by turning entrepreneurs across India and the rest of the world into assemblers and associates.

Sources: Compiled from E. Kinetz, "Tata Nano Finally Goes on Sale Across India," Associated Press, April 10, 2009; "Tata Motors to Produce Up to 80,000 Units of the Nano by March 2010," *India Automotive*, January 20, 2009; M. Kripalani, "Inside the Tata Nano Factory," *BusinessWeek*, May 9, 2008; J. Hagel and J. Brown, "Learning from Tata's Nano," *BusinessWeek*, February 27, 2008; "Tata's Little Car Makes Big Impact," *The Times* (UK), February 6, 2008; R. Meredith, "The Next People's Car," *Forbes*, April 16, 2007; Tata Motors website (*www.tatamotors.com*), accessed March 29, 2009.

QUESTIONS

1. Describe how computer-integrated manufacturing technology enabled Tata to produce the world's cheapest car.
2. The company's chairman plans to produce the Nano as a kit and encourage entrepreneurs throughout India to assemble and service the car. Discuss the advantages and disadvantages of this policy, first from the perspective of the company and then from the perspective of a prospective entrepreneur. Would you consider setting up a Nano dealership in Canada? Why or why not?

we consider how organizations are using IT to perform some key HR functions: recruitment, HR maintenance and development, and HR planning and management.

Recruitment

Recruitment involves finding potential employees, evaluating them, and deciding which ones to hire. Some companies are flooded with viable applicants, while others have difficulty finding the right people. IT can be helpful in both cases. In addition, IT can help in related activities such as testing and screening job applicants.

With millions of resumés available on-line, it is not surprising that companies are trying to find appropriate candidates on the Web, usually with the help of specialized search engines. Companies also advertise hundreds of thousands of jobs on the Web. On-line recruiting can reach more candidates, which may bring in better applicants. In addition, the costs of on-line recruitment are usually lower than traditional recruiting methods such as advertising in newspapers or in trade journals.

Human Resources Maintenance and Development

After employees are recruited, they become part of the corporate human resources pool, which means they must be evaluated, maintained, and developed. IT provides support for these activities.

Most employees are periodically evaluated by their immediate supervisors. Peers or subordinates may also evaluate other employees. Evaluations are typically digitized and are used to support many decisions, ranging from rewards, to transfers, to layoffs.

IT also plays an important role in training and retraining. Some of the most innovative developments are taking place in the areas of intelligent computer-aided instruction and the application of multimedia support for instructional activities. For example, corporate training is delivered over the company's intranet or via the Web.

Human Resources Planning and Management

Managing human resources in large organizations requires extensive planning and detailed strategy. Here we discuss three areas where IT can provide support.

- **Payroll and employees' records.** The HR department is responsible for payroll preparation. This process is typically automated with paycheques being printed or money being transferred electronically into employees' bank accounts.
- **Benefits administration.** Employees' work contributions to their organizations are rewarded by wages, bonuses, and other benefits. Benefits include expanded health and dental care, pension contributions, fitness programs, and child care centres.
- **Employee relationship management.** In their efforts to better manage employees, companies are developing employee relationship management (ERM) applications. A typical ERM application is a call centre for employees' problems.

Table 8.1 provides an overview of the activities that the functional area information systems support. Figure 8.2 (*see* p. 249) diagrams many of the information systems that support these five functional areas.

Functional Area Information Systems Reports

As we just discussed, each functional area information system, or FAIS, generates reports in its functional area. The FAIS also sends information to the corporate data warehouse and can be used for decision support. An FAIS produces primarily three types of reports: routine, ad-hoc (on-demand), and exception. We examine each type below.

Routine reports are produced at scheduled intervals. They range from hourly quality control reports to daily reports on absenteeism rates. Although routine reports are extremely valuable to an organization, managers frequently need special information that is not included in these reports.

TABLE 8.1
ACTIVITIES SUPPORTED BY FUNCTIONAL AREA INFORMATION SYSTEMS

Accounting and Finance

Financial planning—availability and cost of money

Budgeting—allocating financial resources among participants and activities

Capital budgeting—financing of asset acquisitions

Managing financial transactions

Handling multiple currencies

Virtual close—ability to close books at any time on short notice

Investment management—managing organizational investments in shares, bonds, real estate, and other investments

Budgetary control—monitoring expenditures and comparing against budget

Auditing—evaluating controls and corporate governance

Payroll—processing paycheques

Marketing and Sales

Customer relations—knowing who customers are and treating them like royalty

Customer profiles and preferences

Sales force automation—using software to automate the business tasks of sales, thereby improving the productivity of salespeople

Production/Operations and Logistics

Inventory management—knowing how much inventory to order, how much inventory to keep, and when to order new inventory

Quality control—controlling for defects in incoming material and defects in goods produced

Materials requirements planning—planning process that integrates production, purchasing, and inventory management of interdependent items (MRP)

Manufacturing resource planning—planning process that integrates an enterprise's production, inventory management, purchasing, financing, and labour activities (MRP II)

Just-in-time systems—principle of production and inventory control in which materials and parts arrive precisely when and where needed for production (JIT)

Computer-integrated manufacturing—manufacturing approach that integrates several computerized systems, such as computer-assisted design (CAD), computer-assisted manufacturing (CAM), MRP, and JIT

Product life cycle management—business strategy that enables manufacturers to collaborate on product design and development efforts, using the Web

Human Resource Management

Recruitment—finding employees, testing them, and deciding which ones to hire

Performance evaluation—periodic evaluation by superiors

Training

Employee records

Benefits administration—medical, retirement, disability, unemployment, and others

Other times they need the information but at different times ("I need the report today, for the last three days, not for one week"). Such out-of-the routine reports are called **ad-hoc (on-demand) reports.** Ad-hoc reports also can include requests for the following types of information:

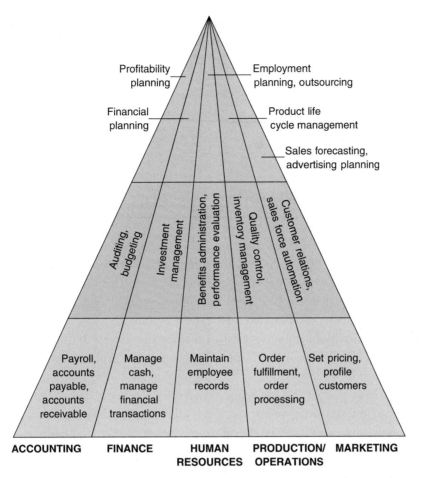

FIGURE 8.2 Examples of information systems supporting the functional areas.

- **Drill-down reports** show a greater level of detail. For example, a manager might examine sales by region and decide to "drill down to more detail" to look at sales by store and then sales by salesperson.
- **Key-indicator reports** summarize the performance of critical activities. For example, a chief financial officer might want to monitor cash flow and cash on hand.
- **Comparative reports** compare, for example, performances of different business units or during different time periods.

Finally, some managers prefer **exception reports**. Exception reports include only information that falls outside certain threshold standards. To implement management by exception, management first creates performance standards. The company then sets up systems to monitor performance (via the incoming data about business transactions such as expenditures), compare actual performance with the standards, and identify predefined exceptions. Managers are alerted to the exceptions via exception reports.

Let's use sales as an example. First, management establishes sales quotas. The company then implements an FAIS that collects and analyzes all sales data. An exception report would identify only those cases where sales fell outside an established threshold; for example, more than 20 percent short of the quota. It would not report sales that fell within the accepted range of standards. By leaving out all "acceptable" performances, exception reports save managers' time and help them focus on problem areas.

BEFORE YOU GO ON ...

1. What is a functional area information system? List its major characteristics.
2. How do information systems benefit the finance and accounting functional area?
3. Explain how POM personnel use information systems to perform their jobs more effectively and efficiently.
4. What are the most important HRIS applications?
5. How does an FAIS support management by exception? How does it support on-demand reports?

8.3 Enterprise Resource Planning Systems

Historically, functional area information systems were developed independently of one another, resulting in "information silos." These silos did not communicate with one another, and this lack of communication and integration made organizations less efficient. This inefficiency was particularly evident in business processes that involved more than one functional area. For example, developing new products involves all functional areas. To understand this point, consider an automobile manufacturer. Developing a new automobile involves design, engineering, production/operations, marketing, finance, accounting, and human resources. To solve their integration problems, companies developed enterprise resource planning systems.

Enterprise resource planning (ERP) systems take a business process view of the overall organization to integrate the planning, management, and use of all of an organization's resources, employing a common software platform and database. Recall from Chapter 1 that a business process is a set of related steps or procedures designed to produce a specific outcome. Business processes can be located entirely within one functional area, such as approving a credit card application or hiring a new employee. They can also span multiple functional areas, such as fulfilling a large order from a new customer.

The major objectives of ERP systems are to tightly integrate the functional areas of the organization and to enable information to flow seamlessly across the functional areas. Tight integration means that changes in one functional area are immediately reflected in all other pertinent functional areas. In essence, ERP systems provide the information necessary to control the business processes of the organization.

Although some companies have developed their own ERP systems, most organizations use commercially available ERP software. The leading ERP software vendor is SAP (*www.sap.com*), with its SAP R/3 package. Other systems include Oracle and PeopleSoft both provided by Oracle (*www.oracle.com*). With more than 700 customers, PeopleSoft is the market leader in higher education. For up-to-date information on ERP software, visit *http://erp.ittoolbox.com*. Small business ERP systems are also available, such as Sage Accpac ERP (*www.sageaccpac.com*).

Evolution of ERP Systems

ERP systems were originally deployed to facilitate manufacturing business processes, such as raw materials management, inventory control, order entry, and distribution. However, these early ERP systems did not extend to other functional areas of the organization, such as sales and marketing. They also did not include any customer relationship management (CRM) capabilities that would allow organizations to capture customer-specific information. Further, they did not provide web-enabled customer service or order fulfillment.

Over time, ERP systems evolved to include administrative, sales, marketing, and human resources processes. Companies now employ an enterprise-wide approach to ERP that uses the Web and connects all facets of the value chain. These systems are called ERP II.

ERP II Systems

ERP II systems are interorganizational ERP systems that provide web-enabled links between a company's key business systems (such as inventory and production) and its customers, suppliers, distributors, and others. These links integrate internal-facing ERP applications with the external-focused applications of supply chain management and customer relationship management. Figure 8.3 illustrates the organization and functions of an ERP II system.

ERP II systems functions are now delivered as e-business suites. The major ERP vendors have developed modular, web-enabled software suites that integrate ERP, customer relationship management, supply chain management, procurement, decision support, enterprise portals, and other business applications and functions. Examples are Oracle's e-Business Suite and SAP's mySAP. The goal of these systems is to enable companies to operate most of their business processes using a single web-enabled system of integrated software rather than a variety of separate e-business applications.

ERP II systems include a variety of modules, which are divided into core ERP modules (financial management, operations management, and human resource management) and extended ERP modules (customer relationship management, supply chain management, business intelligence, and e-business). Table 8.2 describes each of these modules.

Benefits and Limitation of ERP Systems

ERP systems can generate significant business benefits for an organization. The major benefits fall into the following categories:

- **Organizational flexibility and agility.** As we have discussed, ERP systems break down many former departmental and functional silos of business processes, information systems, and information resources. In this way they enable organizations to be more flexible, agile, and adaptive. The organizations can therefore react quickly to changing business conditions and also capitalize on new business opportunities.

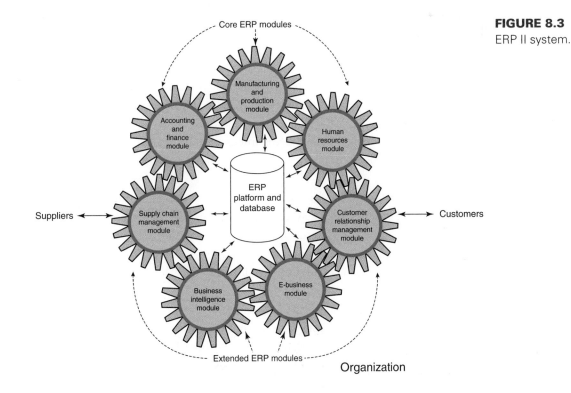

FIGURE 8.3
ERP II system.

TABLE 8.2
CORE ERP MODULES

Financial Management. These modules support accounting, financial reporting, performance management, and corporate governance. They manage accounting data and financial processes such as general ledger, accounts payable, accounts receivable, fixed assets, cash management and forecasting, product-cost accounting, cost-centre accounting, asset accounting, tax accounting, credit management, budgeting, and asset management.

Operations Management. These modules manage the various aspects of production planning and execution, such as demand forecasting, procurement, inventory management, materials purchasing, shipping, production planning, production scheduling, materials requirements planning, quality control, distribution, transportation, and plant and equipment maintenance.

Human Resource Management. These modules support personnel administration (including workforce planning, employee recruitment, assignment tracking, personnel planning and development, and performance management and reviews), time accounting, payroll, compensation, benefits accounting, and regulatory requirements.

Extended ERP Modules

Customer Relationship Management. These modules support all aspects of a customer's relationship with the organization. They help the organization to increase customer loyalty and retention, and thus improve its profitability. They also provide an integrated view of customer data and interactions, enabling organizations to be more responsive to customer needs.

Supply Chain Management. These modules manage the information flows between and among stages in a supply chain to maximize supply chain efficiency and effectiveness. They help organizations plan, schedule, control, and optimize the supply chain from the acquisition of raw materials to the receipt of finished goods by customers.

Business Intelligence. These modules collect information used throughout the organization, organize it, and apply analytical tools to assist managers with decision making.

E-Business. Customers and suppliers demand access to ERP information including order status, inventory levels, and invoice reconciliation. Further, they want this information in a simplified format available through the Web. As a result, these modules provide two channels of access into ERP system information: one channel for customers (B2C) and one for suppliers and partners (B2B).

- **Decision support.** ERP systems provide essential information on business performance across functional areas. This information significantly improves managers' ability to make better, more timely decisions.
- **Quality and efficiency.** ERP systems integrate and improve an organization's business processes, resulting in significant improvements in the quality and efficiency of customer service, production, and distribution.
- **Decreased costs.** ERP systems can reduce transaction costs, and hardware and software costs. In addition, the integrated ERP system requires a smaller IT support staff than did the previous non-integrated information systems.

The advantages of an ERP system are illustrated with the case of the World Bank in IT's About Business 8.3.

Despite all of their benefits, ERP systems have drawbacks. The business processes in ERP software are often predefined by the best practices that the ERP vendor has developed. **Best practices** are the most successful solutions or problem-solving methods for achieving a business objective. As a result, companies may need to change existing business processes to fit the predefined business processes of the software. For companies with well-established procedures, this requirement can be a huge

IT'S ABOUT BUSINESS 8.3
THE WORLD BANK UNDERGOES A TRANSFORMATION

The World Bank (*www.worldbank.org*) is an international financial institution that provides financial and technical assistance to developing countries for development programs with the stated goal of reducing poverty. The bank is owned by its members—185 countries. It employs about 10,000 people, two thirds of whom work in the World Bank headquarters in Washington, D.C. The rest work in field offices throughout 80 member countries. The bank loans out about $20 billion annually, making it one of the world's largest sources of development assistance.

The World Bank has transformed itself from a hierarchical source of low-interest loans to a decentralized organization that uses knowledge-sharing technologies to fight poverty and disease in developing nations that are often technologically disenfranchised. Its ambitious goal is to share tools and knowledge with its clients to not only improve their lives but their economies. To accomplish these goals, the bank had to completely overhaul its IT infrastructure and its global communications network.

The bank's existing IT infrastructure consisted of disparate and disconnected IT systems located throughout the organization. There were 90 business processes, 65 software programs or systems, and 100 databases. Field offices were responsible for their own IT systems and often could not communicate electronically with other offices or with headquarters. They would rely on couriers, which took weeks sometimes, as in the case of filing mission reports from the field offices to headquarters.

The severity of the problem was illustrated by the creation of the bank's annual report. This report was prepared by the staff in the president's office, who relied on data from the organization's financial database, which they believed was the bank's master data source. Actually, the numbers in the financial database came from the cost accounting system, which in turn came from various sectors across the bank. The numbers in the annual report were premature because the final amounts had not yet been transferred to the financial database.

The Enterprise Resource Planning System. The bank selected the enterprise resource planning product from SAP (*www.sap.com*), called SAP R/3. The bank consolidated its various administrative systems to standardize procedures at headquarters and in the field offices. The bank implemented eight SAP modules to improve its procurement, materials management, project management, and financial reporting processes.

While the bank put all its business transactions into SAP, it selected Oracle (*www.oracle.com*) for its databases. All the bank's millions of official reports, records, e-mails, and audio and video resources—including historical records going back 60 years and written in dozens of languages—went into its Record Integrated Information System (RIIS), which is based on the Oracle databases.

The Document Management System. In the next phase of its IT overhaul, the bank selected Teragram (*www.teragram.com*), now a division of SAS, to help it access the documents stored in its RIIS. Teragram is the market-leading, multilingual natural language technology company that uses the meaning of text to distill relevant information from vast amounts of data.

The bank's document management system, also based on the Oracle databases, allow bank employees to transmit documents to be stored. The Teragram software then automatically analyzes the contents of these documents and classifies and categorizes them for quick retrieval.

IT Initiatives Working in East and South African Countries. While the World Bank is developing its own sophisticated IT structures, it's helping developing nations meet more basic needs with technology. It's focusing on 25 countries in east and southern Africa where the only way to make a phone call is with expensive satellites. Lacking fibre-optic broadband, these countries are slated to get regional and national terrestrial networks that will bring high-speed services to Kenya, Burundi, and Madagascar. Such fibre-optic networks will not only help with local infrastructure, but will also assist the World Bank in receiving its own information more rapidly.

Sources: Compiled from M. Farrell, "Saving the World, One Loan at a Time," *Forbes*, March 26, 2009; L. Laurent, "Eastern Europe Gets a Helping Hand," *Forbes*, February 27, 2009; "World Bank to 'Fast Track' Financial Aid," CNN.com, December 10, 2008; J. McCormick, "Knowledge Management: 5 Big Companies that Got It Right," *Baseline Magazine*, October 4, 2007; M. Pommier, "How the World Bank Launched a Knowledge Management Program," KnowledgePoint, 2007; L. McCartney and B. Watson, "World Bank: Behind the I.T. Transformation," *Baseline Magazine*, August 5, 2007; "World Bank Profile: Best Practices in Knowledge Management," American Productivity and Quality Center, January 2003; World Bank website (*www.worldbank.org*), accessed April 3, 2009.

QUESTIONS

1. Why did the World Bank deploy an ERP system before the other information systems?
2. Was the World Bank's transformation primarily a result of strategic vision or the effective implementation of information technology? Support your answer.
3. Provide examples of different types of transaction processing that could be completed by the World Bank's ERP systems.

problem. In addition, ERP systems can be extremely complex, expensive, and time-consuming to implement.

In fact, the costs and risks of failure in implementing a new ERP system are substantial. Quite a few companies have experienced costly ERP implementation failures. Large losses in revenue, profits, and market share have resulted when core business processes and information systems failed or did not work properly. In many cases, orders and shipments were lost, inventory changes were not recorded correctly, and unreliable inventory levels caused major stock outs (unavailability of inventory) to occur. Companies such as Hershey Foods, Nike, A-DEC, and Connecticut General Life Insurance Company sustained losses in amounts up to hundreds of millions of dollars. In the case of FoxMeyer Drugs, a $5 billion pharmaceutical wholesaler, a failed ERP implementation caused the company to file for bankruptcy protection.

In almost every ERP implementation failure, the company's business managers and IT professionals underestimated the complexity of the planning, development, and training that were required to prepare for a new ERP system that would fundamentally change their business processes and information systems. Causes of failed implementations include:

- Failure to involve affected employees in the planning and development phases and in change management processes
- Trying to do too much too fast in the conversion process
- Insufficient training in the new work tasks required by the ERP system
- Failure to perform proper data conversion and testing for the new system

Enterprise Application Integration

For some organizations, ERP systems are not appropriate. This is particularly true for non-manufacturing companies as well as manufacturing companies that find the process of converting from their existing system too difficult, time-consuming, or expensive.

Such companies, however, may still have isolated information systems that need to be connected with one another. To accomplish this task some of these companies use enterprise application integration. An **enterprise application integration (EAI) system** integrates existing systems by providing layers of software that connect applications together. In essence, the EAI system enables existing applications to communicate and share data, thereby enabling organizations to use existing applications while eliminating many of the problems caused by isolated information systems.

BEFORE YOU GO ON ...

1. Define ERP and describe its functionalities.
2. What are ERP II systems?
3. Differentiate between core ERP modules and extended ERP modules.
4. List some drawbacks of ERP software.

WHAT'S IN IT FOR ME?

FOR THE ACCOUNTING MAJOR

Understanding the functions and outputs of TPSs effectively is a major concern of any accountant. It is also necessary to understand the various activities of all functional areas and how they are interconnected. Accounting information systems are a central component in any ERP package. In fact, all large accounting firms actively consult with clients on ERP implementations, using specially trained accounting majors. Also, many supply chain issues, ranging from inventory management to risk analysis, fall within the realm of accounting.

FOR THE FINANCE MAJOR

IT helps financial analysts and managers perform their tasks better. Of particular importance is analyzing cash flows and securing the financing required for smooth operations. In addition, financial applications can support such activities as risk analysis, investment management, and global transactions involving different currencies and fiscal regulations.

Finance activities and modelling are key components of ERP systems. Flows of funds (payments), at the core of most supply chains, must be done efficiently and effectively. Financial arrangements are especially important along global supply chains, where currency translation and financial regulations must be considered.

FOR THE MARKETING MAJOR

Marketing and sales expenses are usually targets in a cost-reduction program. Also, sales force automation not only improves salespeople's productivity (and thus reduces costs), but it also improves customer service.

FOR THE PRODUCTION/OPERATIONS MANAGEMENT MAJOR

Managing production tasks, materials handling, and inventories in short time intervals, at a low cost, and with high quality is critical for competitiveness. These activities can be achieved only if they are properly supported by IT. In addition, IT can greatly enhance interaction with other functional areas, especially sales. Collaboration in design, manufacturing, and logistics requires knowledge of how modern information systems can be connected.

FOR THE HUMAN RESOURCES MANAGEMENT MAJOR

Human resources managers can increase their efficiency and effectiveness by using IT for some of their routine functions. Human resources personnel need to understand how information flows between the HR department and other functional areas. Finally, the integration of functional areas via ERP systems has a major impact on skill requirements and scarcity of employees, which are related to the tasks performed by the HR department.

FOR THE MIS MAJOR

The MIS function is responsible for the most fundamental information systems in organizations, the transaction processing systems. The TPSs provide the data for the databases. In turn, all other information systems use these data. MIS personnel develop applications that support all levels of the organization (from clerical to executive) and all functional areas. The applications also enable the firm to do business with its partners.

SUMMARY

1. **Describe transaction processing systems.**

   The backbone of most information systems applications is the transaction processing system. TPSs monitor, store, collect, and process data generated from all business transactions. These data provide the inputs into the organization's database.

2. **Describe functional area information systems and the support they provide for each functional area of the organization.**

   The major business functional areas are production/operations management, marketing, accounting/finance, and human resources management. A functional area information system (FAIS) is designed to support lower- and mid-level managers in functional areas. FAISs generate reports (routine, ad-hoc, and exception) and provide information to managers regardless of their functional areas. Table 8.1 provides an overview of the many activities in each functional area supported by FAISs.

3. **Describe enterprise resource planning systems, their benefits, and limitations.**

   Enterprise resource planning (ERP) systems integrate the planning, management, and use of all of the organization's resources. The major objective of ERP systems is to tightly integrate the functional areas of the organization. This integration enables information to flow seamlessly across the various functional areas. ERP software includes a set of interdependent software modules, linked to a common database, that provide support for internal business processes.

KEY TERMS

ad-hoc (on-demand) reports, 248

batch processing, 240

best practices, 252

comparative reports, 249

computer-integrated manufacturing (CIM), 245

drill-down reports, 249

enterprise application integration (EAI) system, 254

enterprise resource planning (ERP) system, 250

ERP II systems, 251

exception reports, 249

functional area information systems (FAISs), 242

key-indicator reports, 249

real-time transaction processing, 240

routine reports, 247

transaction, 240

DISCUSSION QUESTIONS

1. Describe the role of a TPS in a service organization.
2. Describe the relationship between TPS and FAIS.
3. Discuss how IT facilitates the budgeting process.
4. How can the Internet support investment decisions?
5. Why is it logical to organize IT applications by functional areas?
6. Discuss the role that IT plays in support of auditing.
7. Investigate the role of the Web in human resources management.
8. Describe the benefits of integrated accounting software packages.
9. What is the relationship between information silos and enterprise resource planning?

PROBLEM-SOLVING ACTIVITIES

1. Examine the capabilities of the following (and similar) financial software packages: Financial Analyzer (from Oracle) and CFO Vision (from SAS Institute). Prepare a report comparing the capabilities of the software packages.

2. Surf the Net and find three free accounting software packages (try *www.shareware.com*, *www.rkom.com*, *www.tucows.com*, and *www.passtheshareware.com*). Download the software and try it. Compare the ease of use and usefulness of each software package.

3. Examine the capabilities of the following financial software packages: TekPortal (from *www.teknowledge.com*), Financial Analyzer (from *www.oracle.com*), and Financial Management (from *www.sas.com*) Prepare a report comparing the capabilities of the software packages.

4. Find Simply Accounting from Sage Software (*www.simplyaccounting.com/productsServices/accounting_solutions/*) and select the link for First Step. Why is this product recommended for small businesses?

5. Enter *www.iemployee.com* and find the support it provides to human resources management activities. View the demos and prepare a report on the capabilities of the products.

6. Enter *www.microsoft.com/dynamics/sl/product/demos.mspx*. View three of the demos in different functional areas of your choice. Prepare a report on each product's capabilities.

7. Enter *www.sas.com* and access revenue optimization there. Explain how the software helps in optimizing prices.

8. Go to *www.caplus.com/articles.aspx?aid=160* and read the success stories. What type of financial software are these organizations implementing? What are the advantages and disadvantages of the software?

TEAM ASSIGNMENTS

1. The class is divided into groups. Each group member represents a major functional area: accounting/finance, sales/marketing, production/operations management, and human resources. Find and describe several examples of processes that require the integration of functional information systems in a company of your choice. Each group will also show the interfaces to the other functional areas.

2. Each group is to investigate an HRM software vendor (Oracle, Peoplesoft [now owned by Oracle], SAP, Lawson Software, and others). The group should prepare a list of all HRM functionalities supported by the software. Then each of the groups makes a presentation to convince the class that its vendor is the best.

3. Each group in the class will be assigned to a major ERP vendor such as SAP, Oracle, Lawson Software, and others. Members of the groups will investigate topics such as: (a) web connections, (b) use of business intelligence tools, (c) relationship to CRM and to EC, and (d) major capabilities by the specific vendor. Each group will prepare a presentation for the class, trying to convince the class why the group's software is best for a local company known to the students (for example, a supermarket chain).

THE NO-FLY ZONE

THE PROBLEM

In the weeks following the attacks of September 11, 2001, the U.S. government sought ways to increase the amount of intelligence data accessible to all agents and key agencies in the form of meaningful reports. For example, in a now-famous memo from an FBI field office in Phoenix, Arizona, an agent reported suspicions about Middle Eastern men training in Arizona flight schools prior to September 2001. Unfortunately, the agent's superiors never acted on this information. These men turned out to be among the 9/11 hijackers. The government's objectives were to prevent such lapses in the future and to foresee future attacks by consolidating and sharing data among intelligence and law-enforcement agencies, including the CIA, the FBI, the State Department, the Defense Department, the National Security Agency, the Transportation Security Agency (TSA), the Department of Homeland Security (DHS), U.S. Customs and Border Protection, the Secret Service, the U.S. Marshals Service, and the White House.

THE IT SOLUTION

The Bush administration established the National Counterterrorism Center (NCTC) to organize and standardize information about suspected terrorists from multiple government agencies into a single database. As a result, the NCTC faced one of the most complex database challenges ever encountered.

The NCTC feeds data to the FBI's Terrorist Screening Center (TSC), which is responsible for maintaining a database of suspected terrorists. The NCTC data contain information on individuals suspected of having ties to international terrorism. Such individuals appear on a report called the watch list. In turn, the FBI provides

the watch list to the TSC concerning individuals with ties to domestic terrorism. As of mid-2009, the watch list contained more than 1 million names, and it was growing at the rate of 20,000 names per month.

Information from the watch list is distributed to many government agencies in the United States and around the world, among them the TSA. Airlines use data supplied by the TSA system in their No-Fly and Selectee lists for prescreening passengers. No-Fly passengers are not allowed on the plane. Selectee passengers can fly, but they are subject to extra searches and possible additional questioning. Canada also created its own no-fly list in 2005, which has far fewer names, numbering in the thousands.

THE RESULTS

James Robinson is a retired Air National Guard brigadier general and a commercial pilot for a major airline. He has even been certified by the TSA to carry a weapon into the cockpit as part of the government's defence program should a terrorist try to commandeer a plane. However, he has trouble even getting to his plane because his name is on the government's terrorist watch list. This means that he cannot use an airport kiosk to check in, he cannot check in on-line, and he cannot check in curbside. Instead, like thousands of Americans whose names match a name or an alias used by a suspected terrorist on the list, he must go to the ticket counter and have an agent verify that he is James Robinson, the pilot, and not James Robinson, the terrorist. Canadian problems also occurred, and in one high-profile case, Maher Arar was deported by the United States because he was on a watch list and ended up in Syria, where he was in jail for over a year, abused and tortured.

Canadians and Americans have demanded that the TSC and the TSA fix the problems with the list that are making travel so difficult for people on these lists. People are considered "misidentified" if they are matched in the databases and then, upon further examination, are found not to match. They are usually misidentified because they have the same name as someone in the database. Misidentifications typically lead to delays, intensive questioning and searches, and missed flights.

More than 30,000 airline passengers who have been misidentified in the United States have asked the TSA to have their names cleared from the watch list. The problem has become so severe that the DHS developed the Traveler Redress Inquiry Program, or TRIP. The purpose of this program is to clear people who are routinely subjected to extra airport security screening and even detention simply because their names are confused with those on the watch list.

Unfortunately, the number of requests to TRIP is more than 2,000 names per month. That number is so high that the DHS has been unable to meet its goal of resolving cases in 30 days.

Sources: Compiled from "Critics Alarmed by Canada's No-fly List," CBC News, June 18, 2007; P. Eisler, "Terrorist Watch List Hits 1 Million," *USA Today*, March 10, 2009; D. Griffin and K. Johnston, "Airline Captain, Lawyer, Child on Terror 'Watch List'," CNN.com, August 19, 2008; R. Singel, "U.S. Terror Watch List Surpasses 900,000 Names, ACLU Estimates," *Wired*, February 27, 2008; M. Hall, "15,000 Want Off the U.S. Terror Watch List," *USA Today*, November 6, 2007; M. Hall, "Terror Watch List Swells to More Than 755,000," *USA Today*, October 23, 2007; R. Singel, "700,000 Name Terror Watch List Still Riddled with False Information," *Wired*, September 7, 2007; "Justice Department Report Tells of Flaws in Terrorist Watch List," CNN.com, September 6, 2007; T. Claburn, "TSA to Clean Up 'No Fly List'," *InformationWeek*, January 19, 2007; B. Helm, "The Terror Watch List's Tangle," *BusinessWeek*, May 11, 2005.

QUESTIONS

1. Is the watch list program a success or a failure? Support your answer.
2. Are the problems with the watch list the result of technology? If so, how? If not, what is the cause of the problems with the watch list? Support your answer.

CASE 8.2

Web Resources

Student website www.wiley.com/canada/rainer

- Web quizzes
- Lecture slides in PowerPoint

- Author podcasts
- Interactive Case: Ruby's Club assignments

WILEY PLUS

ALL OF THE ABOVE AND...

- E-book
- Manager videos
- Vocabulary flash cards

- Pre- and post-lecture quizzes
- Microsoft Office 2007 lab manual and projects

260

IMPROVING TRANSACTION PROCESSING FOR RUBY'S CLUB

Go to the Ruby's Club link at the Student Companion website or WileyPLUS for information about your current internship assignment. You will outline a plan to help Ruby's managers effectively collect and analyze their organizational data.

9 CUSTOMER RELATIONSHIP MANAGEMENT

LEARNING OBJECTIVES

1. Define customer relationship management (CRM) and discuss the objectives of CRM.
2. Describe operational CRM and its major components.
3. Describe analytical CRM.
4. Discuss mobile CRM, on-demand CRM, and open-source CRM.

HARRY ROSEN GOES WITH CRM SOLUTION

Courtesy Harry Rosen

THE BUSINESS PROBLEM

Harry Rosen Inc. (*www.harryrosen.com*) is a retail chain store that sells high-end men's clothing. Its first store was opened in 1954 in Cabbagetown in Toronto, and since then, Harry Rosen has been growing steadily. It now has stores in most of Canada's major cities and accounts for nearly 40 percent of the fine menswear market in Canada, selling such labels as Armani, Brioni, Hugo Boss, Dolce & Gabbana, and Ermenegildo Zegna.

Since its beginnings, Harry Rosen has been committed to providing excellent customer service. In order to do so, the company relies on a one-on-one sales approach where customers are encouraged to book an appointment with a sales associate who will help them make purchasing decisions. Once the appointment is scheduled, the sales associate prepares for the meeting by consulting any customer information that they already collected such as the customer's body measurements and purchase history. However, this system suffered from a number of problems. For example, sometimes during the appointment with the customer, the sales associate would have to leave the customer to access the information on a workstation at the other end of the store. Also, sales associates were not able to help customers by locating merchandise in another store, showing them what other patterns or fabrics were available to order, or letting them know when particular merchandise would be available in the store. In addition, the system would not work with customers who did not make an appointment.

It was clear that for top-notch customer service, some changes needed to be made, starting with sales associates being able to access real-time information from other stores as well as a new way to assist customers who did not make an appointment.

THE IT SOLUTION

Harry Rosen realized that customer relationship management software could help solve some of its problems. After researching several options, the company selected SalesLogix CRM system from software vendor Sage. The solution combined applications for web deployment, mobile devices, and system integration capabilities.

The solution included the acquisition of new mobile devices and the development of a customized application on pocket PCs to provide sales associates with quick access to customer data and product preferences, such as how often a customer shops, average purchase price, and brands most often purchased. The devices also allow them to look up inventory across the company's 16 retail locations in real time, know when a new shipment of merchandise will arrive, and schedule tasks such as suit tailoring—all while still on the sales floor.

In addition, the new CRM system is integrated with the point-of-sale system, allowing managers at Harry Rosen to develop marketing campaigns that target individual customers based on purchasing preferences. For example, when a store hosts an event to display the latest patterns and fabrics from a specific designer, the system would look at the customers' purchase history and identify those customers who most often buy clothes from that designer.

Sources: "Menswear Retailer Harry Rosen Boosts Sales by 10% with HP CRM Solution," HP customer case study, October 2007; V. Himmelsbach, "Harry Rosen Gets Tailored Solution," *Computer Dealer News*, Vol. 22, No. 14, October 13, 2006; "Sage CRM SalesLogix for Harry Rosen," *www.erpko.com*, April 27, 2010.

WHAT DO YOU THINK?

1. What are the possible implications for Harry Rosen Inc. if sales associates don't have easy access to customer, sales, and inventory data?
2. What are the potential benefits for the company of implementing the new CRM system?
3. How could managers benefit from the CRM system at Harry Rosen?

Chapter Preview

The chapter-opening case provides a specific example of the evolving nature of the business–customer relationship. Before the supermarket, the mall, and the automobile, people went to their neighbourhood store to purchase goods. The owner and employees recognized customers by name and knew their preferences and wants. For their part, customers remained loyal to the store and made repeated purchases. Over time, however, this personal customer relationship became impersonal as people moved from farms to cities, consumers became mobile, and supermarkets and department stores were established to achieve economies of scale through mass marketing efforts. Although prices were lower and products were more uniform in quality, the relationship with customers became nameless and impersonal.

In response to this situation, organizations are emphasizing a customer-centric approach to their business practices because they know that sustainable value is found in long-term customer relationships that extend beyond today's business transaction. This customer-centric approach is known in businesses as customer relationship management (CRM).

Clearly, CRM is critical to the success of modern businesses. However, you may be asking yourself: Why should I learn about CRM? As we will see in the chapter, customers are supremely important to all organizations. Regardless of the particular job you perform, you will have either a direct or an indirect impact on your firm's customers. Therefore, it is important that you have a working knowledge of CRM.

In this chapter, we discuss the various aspects of building long-term customer relationships through CRM. We first define the CRM concept and then turn our attention to the two major aspects of CRM: operational CRM and analytical CRM. We conclude the chapter with a look at additional types of CRM, which include mobile CRM, on-demand CRM, and open-source CRM.

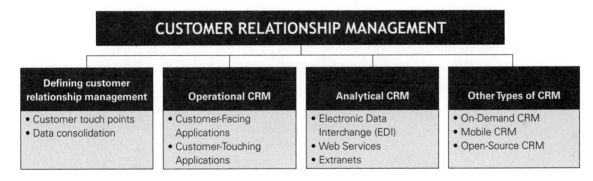

9.1 Defining Customer Relationship Management

The customer relationship has become even more impersonal with the rapid growth of the Internet and the World Wide Web. In today's hypercompetitive marketplace, customers are increasingly powerful. If they are dissatisfied with a product and/or a service from one organization, a competitor is often just one mouse click away. Further, as more and more customers shop on the web, an enterprise does not even have the opportunity to make a good first impression in person.

Customer relationship management returns to personal marketing. Rather than market to a mass of people or companies, businesses market to each customer individually. With this approach, businesses can use information about each customer (for example, previous purchases, needs, and wants) to create offers that customers are more likely to accept. The CRM approach is designed to achieve customer intimacy and is enabled by information technology.

CRM is an organizational strategy that is customer-focused and customer-driven. That is, organizations concentrate on satisfying customers by assessing their requirements for products and services, and then providing high-quality, responsive service. CRM is not a process or a technology per se;

rather, it is a way of thinking and acting in a customer-centric fashion. The focus of organizations today has shifted from conducting business transactions to managing customer relationships. In general, organizations recognize that customers are the core of a successful enterprise, and success depends on effectively managing relationships with them.

CRM builds sustainable long-term customer relationships that create value for the company as well as for the customer. CRM helps companies acquire new customers, retain existing profitable customers, and grow the relationships with existing customers. This last CRM function is particularly important because repeat customers are the largest generator of revenue for an enterprise. Also, organizations have long known that getting a customer back after he or she has switched to a competitor is vastly more expensive than keeping that customer satisfied in the first place.

Figure 9.1 depicts the CRM process. The process begins with marketing efforts, where the organization solicits prospects from a target population of potential customers. A certain number of prospects will make a purchase, thus becoming customers. Of the organization's customers, a certain number will become repeat customers. The organization then segments its repeat customers into low-value and high-value repeat customers.

The organization will lose a certain percentage of customers, a process called customer churn. The optimal result of an organization's CRM efforts is to maximize the number of high-value repeat customers while minimizing customer churn.

CRM is basically a simple idea: Treat different customers differently, because their needs differ and their value to the company also may differ. Successful CRM implementations not only have improved customer satisfaction, but they have made the company's sales and service employees more productive, which in turn has led to increased profits. In fact, researchers at the National Quality Research Center at the University of Michigan found that a 1 percent increase in customer satisfaction can lead to as much as a 300 percent increase in a company's market capitalization (the number of shares of the company's stock outstanding multiplied by the price per share of the stock).

There are many examples of organizations that have gone beyond what is merely expected in their efforts to be customer centric. IT's About Business 9.1 illustrates how US Airways took the customer-centric concept to the limit.

FIGURE 9.1
The customer relationship management process.

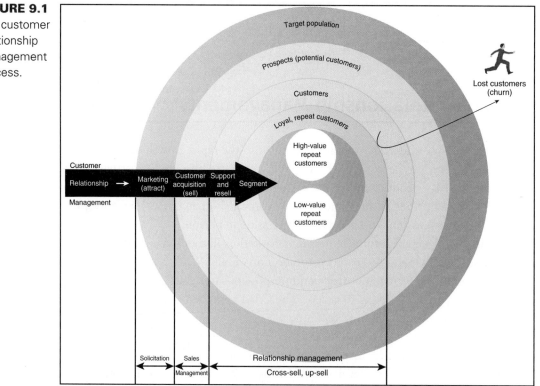

IT'S ABOUT BUSINESS 9.1
THE AFTERMATH OF THE "MIRACLE ON THE HUDSON"

On January 15, 2009, all 155 passengers and crew of US Airways Flight 1549 survived a forced landing on the Hudson River in New York City, after their plane struck a flight of Canada geese. The airline's handling of the near-disaster provides an outstanding example of customer relationship management in a crisis.

Airlines prepare for such emergencies by holding regular drills. At every airport it flies into, US Airways stages a mock emergency at least three times a year. Designated employees are trained to act as "Care Team" members in an emergency and are on standby to be sent to the scene of an emergency.

When the news broke of Flight 1549, US Airways set up a toll-free number for families to call, and it flew more than 100 employees from headquarters in Tempe, Arizona, to New York. One of these employees was Scott Stewart, managing director for corporate finance, who handed out cash for passengers and credit cards for employees to replace any needed personal items that passengers may have lost, such as medicines and toiletries.

Other employees arrived with prepaid cell phones and dry clothes. US Airways arranged for passengers' accommodation, transportation, and meals—whether staying in a New York hotel, taking another flight, renting a car or taking the train, or accessing all-hours buffets. Further, the airline contacted executives at Hertz and Amtrak to make certain that passengers who had lost their driver's licences did not have any trouble renting a car or purchasing a train ticket. For keyless passengers who lived in the New York area, the airline hired locksmiths so they could get into their homes and cars.

Significantly, US Airways' customer relationship efforts did not end after the passengers were rescued and attended to. Rather, these efforts have been ongoing. For example, the company has communicated by letter to passengers with regular updates, refunded the cost of their original ticket, and issued a $5,000 cheque to each passenger to cover the loss of their possessions. The airline has also processed claims of more than $5,000 from some passengers, and did not put a caveat on the compensation that passengers had to waive their legal rights to sue, something that some observers said was "an unprecedented exception to the industry norm."

Finally, US Airways upgraded all passengers on board Flight 1549 to "Chairman's Preferred" status, entitling them to automatic upgrades, exemptions from baggage fees, and bonus miles for a year. This status is normally reserved for passengers who fly more than 100,000 miles annually on US Airways.

The real test of CRM in this crisis is how many customers come back. US Airways claims that, as of April 2009, one third of the 150 passengers on Flight 1549 have already flown the airline again. It appears that the CRM efforts of US Airways were very successful.

Sources: Compiled from D. Foust, "U.S. Airways: After the 'Miracle on the Hudson'," *BusinessWeek*, March 2, 2009; M. Phillips, "Air Crash Law Firm Contacted by U.S. Airways 1549 Passengers," *The Wall Street Journal*, February 26, 2009; C. Cooper, "Flight 1549: The Importance of Good Public Relations," *America's Best Companies*, January 19, 2009; R. Goldman, R. Esposito, and E. Friedman, "Passengers: First Engine on Fire, Then Frigid Water," ABC News, January 16, 2009; *www.usair.com*, accessed March 22, 2009.

QUESTIONS

1. Describe the various CRM aspects of US Airways' response to the Flight 1549 incident. Could the airline have done anything else? If so, what?
2. Do you think that the US Airways' responses to the incident will be sufficient to forestall any lawsuits arising from Flight 1549's emergency landing? Why or why not?

Although CRM varies according to circumstances, all successful CRM policies share two basic elements. First, the company must identify the many types of customer touch points. Second, it needs to consolidate data about each customer. Let's examine these two elements in more detail.

Customer Touch Points

Organizations must recognize the numerous and diverse interactions that they have with their customers. These various types of interactions are referred to as **customer touch points**. Traditional customer touch points include telephone contact, direct mailings, and actual physical interactions with customers during visits to a store. However, organizational CRM must manage many additional customer touch points that occur through the use of popular personal technologies. These touch points include e-mail, websites, and communications via smart phones (see Figure 9.2).

FIGURE 9.2
Customer
touch points.

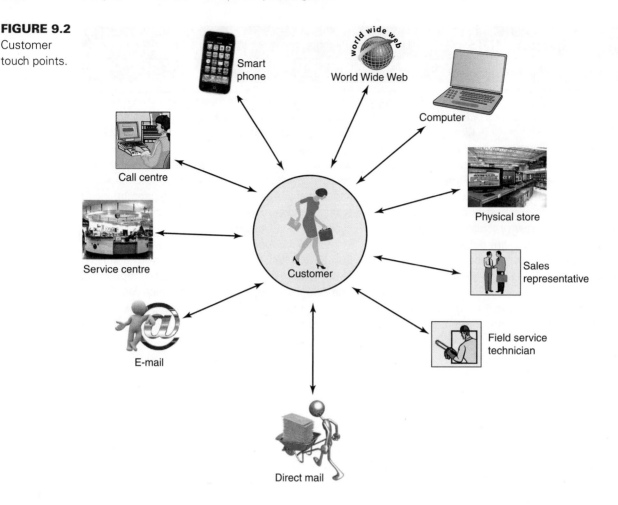

Data Consolidation

Data consolidation is also critically important to an organization's CRM efforts. In the past, customer data were located in isolated systems in functional areas across the business. For example, it was not uncommon to find customer data stored in separate databases in the finance, sales, logistics, and marketing departments. Even though all of these data related to the same customer, it was difficult to share the data across the various functional areas.

As we discussed in Chapter 8, modern, interconnected systems built around a data warehouse now make all customer-related data available to every unit of the business. This complete data set on each customer is called a *360-degree view* of that customer. By accessing this 360-degree view, a company can enhance its relationship with its customers and ultimately make more productive and profitable decisions.

Data consolidation and the 360-degree view of the customer enable the organization's functional areas to readily share information about customers. This sharing of customer information leads to collaborative CRM. **Collaborative CRM** systems provide effective and efficient interactive communication with the customer throughout the entire organization. That is, collaborative CRM integrates communications between the organization and its customers in all aspects of marketing, sales, and customer support processes. Collaborative CRM also enables customers to provide direct feedback to the organization. As we discussed in Chapter 5, Web 2.0 applications such as blogs and wikis are very important to companies that value customer input into their product and service offerings, as well as into new product development. The following example shows how an Indian bank, YES Bank, developed its own collaborative CRM.

EXAMPLE 9.1

YES Bank (*www.yesbank.in*) was founded in 2004 and is one of the youngest banks in India. Until recently the company managed customer relations using Excel spreadsheets, which created a number of problems. For example, new sales leads were sometimes duplicated or had missing information. In addition, the company had no way of capturing customer feedback, which was critical to growing the business.

YES Bank developed a CRM tool called YES Bank Collaborative CRM (YCCRM) to encourage collaboration among employees and capture customer feedback at every step of serving a customer. The new YCCRM comes with such collaborative tools as chat, messaging, discussion boards, and access to the most popular web search engines all embedded into a dashboard in order to facilitate searching information about a sales lead. Employees can also enter the leads in text format in order to make it quick and easy to enter data into the CRM system while dealing with a customer.

YES Bank also created blogs for its employees so customer information could be made available across all branches in a quick, interactive way. These blogs include ideas and suggestions about a particular piece of data or a key metric. Blogs are useful to regularly post information on a website and to invite comments. This information can later be used to customize existing products or develop new ones.

Sources: S. Karjatkar, "Bank Boosts Customer Service 60 per cent with Open Source Tool," itbusiness.ca, October 8, 2009; "YES Bank Launches a New CRM Solution," *www.cio.in*, accessed May 26, 2010.

A CRM system in an organization contains two major components: operational CRM and analytical CRM. We discuss these components in the next two sections.

BEFORE YOU GO ON …

1. What is the definition of customer relationship management?
2. Why is CRM so important to any organization?
3. Define and give examples of customer touch points.

9.2 Operational CRM

Operational CRM is the component of CRM that supports the front-office business processes. These processes are those that directly interact with customers; that is, sales, marketing, and service. The two major components of operational CRM are customer-facing applications and customer-touching applications.

Customer-Facing Applications

Customer-facing CRM applications are those applications where an organization's sales, field service, and customer interaction centre representatives actually interact with customers. These applications include customer service and support, sales force automation, marketing, and campaign management.

Customer Service and Support

Customer service and support refers to systems that automate service requests, complaints, product returns, and requests for information. Today, organizations have implemented **customer interaction centres (CIC)**, where organizational representatives use multiple communication channels such as the web, telephone, fax, and face-to-face interactions to support the communication preferences of customers. The CIC manages several different types of customer interaction.

Customer service centres use multiple communication channels to support the communication preferences of customers.

Organizations use the CIC to create a call list for the sales team, whose members contact sales prospects. This type of interaction is called *outbound telesales*. In these interactions, the customer and the sales team collaborate in discussions of products and services that can satisfy customers' needs and generate sales.

Customers can communicate directly with the CIC if they wish to initiate a sales order, inquire about products and services before placing an order, or obtain information about a transaction that they have already made. These interactions are referred to as *inbound teleservice*. Teleservice representatives respond to requests either by using service instructions found in an organizational knowledge base or by noting incidents that cannot be handled through the CIC, but must be addressed by field service technicians.

The CIC also provides the Information Help Desk. The Help Desk assists customers with their questions concerning products or services and also processes customer complaints. Complaints generate follow-up activities such as quality-control checks, delivery of replacement parts or products, service calls, generation of credit memos, and product returns.

New technologies are extending the functionality of the traditional CIC to include e-mail and web interaction. For example, Epicor (*www.epicor.com*) provides software solutions that combine web channels, such as automated e-mail reply, and web knowledge bases, and make the information they provide available to CIC representatives or field service personnel. Another new technology, live chat, allows customers to connect to a company representative and conduct an instant messaging session. The advantage of live chat over a telephone conversation is the ability to show documents and photos (see *www.livechatinc.com* and *www.websitealive.com*). Some companies conduct the chat with a computer rather than a real person using natural language processing (discussed in Chapter 11).

Because customer service and support are essential to a successful business, organizations must place a great deal of emphasis on the CRM process. Amazon even includes vendors that sell on its website in its customer service policy, as we see in IT's About Business 9.2.

Amazon's CRM policies were so successful that the company maintained its sales volume even during the economic downturn.

IT'S ABOUT BUSINESS 9.2
AMAZON EXTENDS THE CUSTOMER EXPERIENCE TO VENDORS

The CEO of the world's largest on-line retailer, Amazon (*www.amazon.com*), Jeff Bezos, makes a distinction between customer service and customer experience. At Amazon, customer service is a component of customer experience.

Customer experience includes offering both the lowest price and the fastest delivery. In addition, the entire process must be so reliable that customers do not need to contact an actual person. Customer service involves direct interactions between customer and Amazon employees, and Bezos wants those situations to be the exception rather than the rule. That is, Amazon limits customer service to truly unusual situations, such as a customer receiving a book with missing pages.

In addition to providing enhanced customer experience, Amazon has gone the extra mile by doing something that no other retailer has done. It's trying to ensure that third-party suppliers provide the same customer experience level as Amazon does itself.

For some time, Amazon has allowed other retailers to sell through its website to broaden the selection of products that it offers. However, these companies and individuals can pose a problem if they do not have the commitment to the customer experience that Amazon has.

As a result, Amazon has instituted many internal safeguards to ensure enhanced customer service. First, Amazon's customers can rate their experience with merchants. Second, customers have to be able to communicate with outside merchants through an e-mail service on the Amazon website so that Amazon can track the correspondence. Third, Amazon tracks how many problems merchants have, such as how many customer complaints are received and how often orders are cancelled because of stock-outs. If more than 1 percent of a supplier's orders have problems, they can be removed from the website.

Another effort by Amazon to improve the customer experience is what it calls Fulfillment. In this process, Amazon receives shipments of products from the merchants and then uses its usual order fulfillment system: it takes on-line orders, packages the merchandise, communicates with customers, and handles any product returns. During the last quarter of 2008, Amazon shipped 3 million Fulfillment orders from its partners, an increase of 600 percent from 500,000 in the last quarter of 2007.

Amazon takes a cut from the Fulfillment orders, but the service is not about the revenue from its outside merchants. "The service does not make Amazon much money," explains Bezos. "It is important because it improves the customer experience markedly."

Policies such as Fulfillment allow Amazon to be more hands-on with the customer experience, ensuring its quality and reliability. Ensuring a positive customer experience will encourage more people to use the on-line retailer and spend more money. It appears that Amazon's CRM policies are successful, as the company has maintained its sales volume even in the recession.

Sources: Compiled from L. Dignan, "Piper Jaffray Upgrades Amazon on Customer Satisfaction; Kindle; iPhone Apps," ZDNet, March 9, 2009; H. Green, "How Amazon Aims to Keep You Clicking," *BusinessWeek*, March 2, 2009; "Overstock, Amazon, Near Top of Best Customer Service Survey," Seeking Alpha, January 14, 2009; *www.amazonservices.com*, accessed March 22, 2009.

QUESTIONS
1. Describe the distinction between customer service and the customer experience at Amazon.
2. Discuss how Amazon rates customer service by its outside vendors.

Sales Force Automation

Sales force automation (SFA) is the component of an operational CRM system that automatically records all the aspects in a sales transaction process. SFA systems include a *contact management system*, which tracks all contact that has been made with a customer, the purpose of the contact, and any follow-up that might be necessary. This system eliminates duplicated contacts and redundancy, which reduces the risk of irritating customers. SFA also includes a *sales lead tracking system*, which lists potential customers or customers who have purchased related products. Other elements of an SFA system can include a *sales forecasting system*, which is a mathematical technique for estimating future sales, and a *product knowledge system*, which is a comprehensive source of information regarding products and services. More-developed SFA systems have on-line product-building features (called *configurators*) that enable customers to model the product to meet their specific needs. In just one example, you can customize your own running shoe at NikeID (*http://nikeid.nike.com*). Finally, many of the current SFA systems provide for remote connectivity for the salesperson in the field via web-based interfaces that can be displayed on smart phones.

Marketing

Thus far we have focused primarily on how sales and customer service personnel can benefit from CRM. However, CRM has many important applications for an organization's marketing department as well. For example, it enables marketers to identify and target their best customers, manage marketing campaigns, and generate quality leads for the sales teams. Additionally, CRM marketing applications provide opportunities to sift through volumes of customer data—a process known as data mining—and develop purchasing profiles—a snapshot of a consumer's buying habits—that may lead to additional sales through cross-selling, up-selling, and bundling. (We discuss data mining in Chapter 11.)

Cross-selling is the practice of marketing additional related products to customers based on a previous purchase. This sales approach has been used very successfully by Amazon. For example, if you have purchased several books on Amazon, the next time you visit the site, it will recommend other books you might like to purchase.

Up-selling is a sales strategy in which the business person will give customers the opportunity to purchase higher-value related products or services as opposed to or along with the consumer's initial product or service selection. For example, if a customer goes into an electronics store to buy a new television, a salesperson may show him a 1080i High Definition LCD next to a non-HD TV in the hope of selling the more expensive set, if the customer is willing to pay the extra cost for a sharper picture. Other common examples of up-selling are warranties on electronics purchases and the purchase of a carwash after you bought gas at the gas station.

Finally, **bundling** is a form of cross-selling in which a business sells a group of products or services together at a price that is lower than the combined individual prices of the products. For example, your cable company might offer a bundle price that includes basic cable TV, broadband Internet access, and local telephone service at a lower price than if you acquired each service separately.

Campaign Management

Campaign management applications help organizations plan campaigns so that the right messages are sent to the right people through the right channels. Organizations manage their customers very carefully to avoid targeting people who have opted out of receiving marketing communications. Further, companies use these applications to personalize individual messages for each particular customer.

Customer-Touching Applications

Corporations have used manual CRM for many years. The term electronic CRM (or e-CRM) appeared in the mid-1990s, when organizations began using the Internet, the Web, and other electronic touch points (e.g., e-mail, point-of-sale terminals) to manage customer relationships. Customers interact directly with these technologies and applications rather than with a company representative as is the case with customer-facing applications. Such applications are called **customer-touching CRM applications** or **electronic CRM (e-CRM) applications**. Using these applications, customers typically are able to help themselves. There are many types of e-CRM applications. We discuss some of the major applications in this section.

Search and Comparison Capabilities

With the vast array of products and services available on the Web, it is often difficult for customers to find what they want. To assist customers, many on-line stores and malls offer search and comparison capabilities, as do independent comparison websites (see *www.mysimon.com*).

Technical and Other Information and Services

Many organizations offer personalized experiences to induce a customer to make a purchase or to remain loyal. For example, websites often allow customers to download product manuals. One example is General Electric's website (*www.ge.com*), which provides detailed technical and maintenance information and sells replacement parts for discontinued models for customers who need to repair outdated home appliances. Another example is Goodyear's website (*www.goodyear.com*), which provides information about tires and their use.

Customized Products and Services

Another customer-touching service that many on-line vendors use is mass customization, a process in which customers can configure their own products. For example, Dell Computer (*www.dell.ca*) allows customers to configure their own computer systems. The Gap (*www.gap.com*) allows customers to "mix and match" an entire wardrobe. Websites such as Hitsquad (*www.hitsquad.com*) and Surprise (*www.surprise.com*) allow customers to pick individual music titles from a library and customize a CD, a feature that traditional music stores do not offer.

In addition, customers can now view their account balances or check the shipping status of their orders at any time from their computers or smart phones. If you order books from Amazon, for example, you can look up the anticipated arrival date. Many other companies follow this model and provide similar services (see *www.fedex.ca* and *www.ups.ca*).

Personalized Web Pages

Many organizations permit their customers to create their own personalized web pages. Customers use these pages to record purchases and preferences, as well as problems and requests. For example, American Airlines generates personalized web pages for each of its approximately 800,000 registered travel-planning customers.

FAQs

Frequently asked questions (FAQs) are a simple tool for answering repetitive customer queries. Customers who find the information they need by using this tool do not need to communicate with an actual person.

E-mail and Automated Response

The most popular tool for customer service is e-mail. Inexpensive and fast, e-mail is used not only to answer inquiries from customers but also to disseminate information, send alerts and product information, and conduct correspondence regarding any topic.

Loyalty Programs

Loyalty programs recognize customers who repeatedly use a vendor's products or services. Perhaps the best-known loyalty programs are the airlines' frequent flyer programs. In addition, casinos use their players' clubs to reward their frequent players, and supermarkets use similar programs to reward frequent shoppers. Loyalty programs use a database or data warehouse to keep a record of the points (or miles) a customer has accrued and the rewards to which he or she is entitled. The programs then use analytical tools to mine the data and learn about customer behaviour.

Loyalty programs have proved to be very valuable for various organizations. However, some loyalty programs have experienced problems, as IT's About Business 9.3 shows.

IT'S ABOUT BUSINESS 9.3
FRAUD AT SUBWAY LEADS TO NEW LOYALTY PROGRAM

For years, Subway restaurants (*www.subway.com*) attracted and held on to customers through a reward system known as the Sub Club. How did this system work? Basically, Subway gave its patrons business-sized cards with tiny stamps on them. Every time a card filled up with stamps, the patron earned a free meal. Unfortunately, Subway had to discontinue the Sub Club, much to the dismay of its loyal customers. The reason? Fraud.

The availability of cheaper home laser printers and multimedia personal computers has made counterfeiting increasingly easy. Using materials available at any office supply store, people with some knowledge of photo-editing software could duplicate the Subway reward cards and the stamps. In fact, fraudulent Subway cards and stamps were even being sold on eBay.

This fraud hurt Subway owners, all of whom are franchisees. At the same time, however, customers loved the program. To resolve this dilemma, the huge restaurant chain (30,000 restaurants and $9 billion revenue in 2008) instituted a new loyalty program. This program uses a card with a magnetic stripe. Each card has a unique 16-digit identification number. Customers can use this card to make payments, access instant loyalty rewards, and track highly targeted promotions. At the same time, the card enables Subway to gather data on customers from its point-of-sale (POS) terminals to its CRM applications. One Subway executive called this program "the single largest integrated cash card program in the world." Subway says its new card is unique because of its wide range of capabilities and also because it was deployed over such a huge number of restaurants.

Subway rolled out the new card to more than 20,000 stores and integrated the card into its existing POS software. This integration was difficult for Subway's IT group. Since all the restaurants are owned by franchisees, Subway has greater IT challenges than global chains of a similar size. In many cases, the Subway IT group can only recommend that its individual stores follow a particular IT

strategy. The rollout of the new card was mandatory for all stores in North America. By requiring that all of its North American stores adopt the new card, Subway management accumulated far more data to analyze than it had previously. However, the company's POS software enabled it to standardize the information technology on a common platform across the stores.

Subway's CRM system (its new card plus the POS software) can target the behaviour of consumers in a particular geographic area, as well as customers in an individual store, and can entice and reward that behaviour.

One example of an application of the CRM system is a cookie promotion. First, Subway can target all customers who visit once a month or less. When these customers next buy something, their receipt doubles as a coupon for a free cookie if they come back within a week.

This new CRM program has been successful in attracting new customers and in influencing existing customers to visit the restaurants more often. The new card has proven to be many times more successful than traditional coupon promotions.

Sources: Compiled from "CRM Delivers Value Chain Improvements for Subway Restaurant Owners," PRLog, June 20, 2007; "Subway: Payment, Loyalty, and Vouchering All in One Card," *Internet Retailing*, August 17, 2006; E. Schuman, "Subway Merges Payment, Loyalty, and CRM Programs," *Baseline Magazine*, August 10, 2006; J. Ogles, "Fraud Sinks Subway's Sub Club," *Wired*, September 21, 2005; "Fraud Stamps Out Subway Sandwich Promo," Associated Press, June 2, 2005; *www.subway.com*, accessed March 25, 2009.

QUESTIONS
1. Discuss the advantages of Subway's new loyalty card versus its old loyalty program.
2. Will Subway's new loyalty card provide the restaurant chain with a sustainable competitive advantage? Why or why not? If not, then what other steps could Subway take in the area of CRM to achieve and maintain a competitive advantage?

Operational CRM provides the following benefits:

- Efficient, personalized marketing, sales, and service;
- A 360-degree view of each customer;
- Ability of sales and service employees to access a complete history of customer interaction with the organization, regardless of the touch point.

Another example of operational CRM involves Caterpillar, Inc. (*www.cat.com*), an international manufacturer of industrial equipment. Caterpillar uses its CRM tools to accomplish the following:

- Assist the organization in improving sales and account management by optimizing the information shared by multiple employees, and streamlining existing processes (for example, taking orders using mobile devices).
- Form individualized relationships with customers, with the aim of improving customer satisfaction and maximizing profits.
- Identify the most profitable customers, and provide them the highest level of service.
- Provide employees with the information and processes necessary to know their customers.
- Understand and identify customer needs, and effectively build relationships among the company, its customer base, and its distribution partners.

9.3 Analytical CRM

Whereas operational CRM supports front-office business processes, **analytical CRM** systems analyze customer behaviour and perceptions in order to provide actionable business intelligence. For example, analytical CRM systems typically provide information on customer requests and transactions, as well as on customer responses to an organization's marketing, sales, and service initiatives. These systems also create statistical models of customer behaviour and the value of customer relationships over time, as well as forecasts of customer acquisition, retention, and loss. Figure 9.3 illustrates the relationship between operational CRM and analytical CRM.

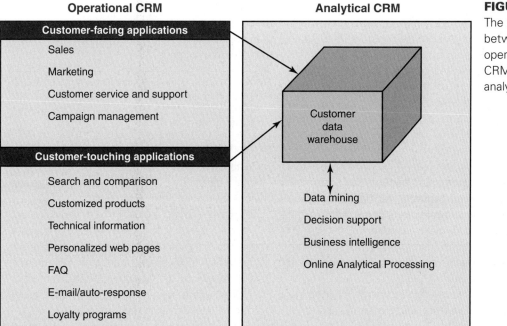

FIGURE 9.3
The relationship between operational CRM and analytical CRM.

Important technologies in analytical CRM systems include data warehouses, data mining, decision support, and other business intelligence technologies (discussed in Chapter 11). Once the various analyses are complete, information is delivered to the organization in the form of reports and digital dashboards. IT's About Business 9.4 illustrates the example of how commercial airlines are using analytical CRM to know their customers better.

Analytical CRM analyzes customer data for a variety of purposes, including:

- Designing and executing targeted marketing campaigns
- Increasing customer acquisition, cross-selling, and up-selling
- Providing input into decisions relating to products and services (e.g., pricing, and product development)
- Providing financial forecasting and customer profitability analysis

Soon staff at airport check-in counters will have access to a customer's travel history, allowing them to offer customers a more personalized travel experience.

IT'S ABOUT BUSINESS 9.4
AIRLINES TRY TO KNOW THEIR CUSTOMERS BETTER

Luxury hotels track customer preferences and on-line retailers pitch products based on their customers' buying histories. For their part, airlines have rewarded their best customers through perks tied to frequent-flyer programs. "Elite" flyers receive upgrades, priority boarding, and sometimes access to special security lines. In addition, the airlines have deployed self-service kiosks, electronic boarding passes on handheld devices, and automatic flight-alert systems to make flying less of a hassle. However, the airlines want to learn more about their customers to retain them during a declining economy and to differentiate themselves from their competitors.

In contrast to other industries, airlines have made only limited use of data mining to learn more about their customers. The airlines maintain that they have been slow to implement such applications because they have multiple legacy systems that do not share information well.

At airports today, airline agents can find a traveller's itinerary and frequent-flyer status. However, they do not have information about past complaints, delays, baggage problems, cancelled flights, or missed connections. In addition, they generally do not have information about how much money you spend with the airline.

To address these shortcomings, airlines are developing data warehouses to integrate customer data currently located in their legacy systems and are implementing data-mining tools to analyze these data. Data-mining tools will enable the airlines to calculate the value of each customer. Further, these tools will provide airport agents with the customer's ticket-buying and travel history, flag key customers to flight attendants, and offer sales targeted to flyers' vacation patterns. If flight attendants know key passengers, they can offer them extra services (for example, free drinks or meals) or, when necessary, they can offer personalized apologies (say, for missed flights or lost baggage).

Sources: Compiled from M. Betts, "Airlines Working on CRM Systems to Pamper the Elites," *Computerworld*, March 30, 2009; S. McCartney, "Your Airline Wants to Get to Know You," *The Wall Street Journal*, March 24, 2009.

QUESTIONS
1. Customer surveys have found that customers really want a hassle-free flight rather than the extra services discussed here. If you were an airline chief information officer, would the survey findings affect the resources that you were planning to allocate to a data warehouse and data-mining tools? If so, where would you spend your scarce resources?
2. In addition to the ones mentioned here, what other extra services could the airlines provide to make your flying experience more enjoyable?

BEFORE YOU GO ON ...

1. What is the main objective of analytical CRM?
2. What is the relationship between operational CRM and analytical CRM?

9.4 Other Types of CRM

Now that we have examined operational and analytical CRM, we turn our focus to other types of CRM systems. Three exciting developments in CRM are on-demand CRM, mobile CRM, and open-source CRM. We discuss these types of CRM in this section.

On-Demand CRM

Customer relationship management systems may be implemented as either on-premise or on-demand. Traditionally, organizations utilized on-premise CRM systems, meaning that they purchased the systems and installed them on site. This arrangement was expensive, time-consuming, and inflexible. Some organizations, particularly smaller ones, could not justify the cost.

On-demand CRM became a solution for the drawbacks of on-premise CRM. **On-demand CRM** is a CRM system that is hosted by an external vendor in the vendor's data centre. This arrangement spares the organization the costs associated with purchasing the system. In addition, because the vendor creates and maintains the system, the organization's employees need to know only how to access and use it. The concept of on-demand is also known as utility computing (see Technology Guide 1) or software-as-a-service (SaaS; see Technology Guide 2).

Despite its benefits, on-demand CRM does have potential problems. First, the vendor could prove to be unreliable, in which case the company would have no CRM functionality at all. Second, hosted software is difficult or impossible to modify, and only the vendor can upgrade it. Third, it may be difficult to integrate vendor-hosted CRM software with the organization's existing software. Finally, giving strategic customer data to vendors carries risk.

Mobile CRM

Mobile CRM is an interactive CRM system that enables an organization to conduct communications related to sales, marketing, and customer service activities through a mobile medium for the purpose of building and maintaining relationships with its customers. Put simply, mobile CRM involves interacting directly with consumers through their own portable devices such as smart phones. Many forward-thinking companies believe mobile CRM holds tremendous promise as an avenue to create a personalized customer relationship that may be accessed anywhere and at any time. In fact, the potential opportunities provided through mobile marketing appear so rich that a host of companies have already identified mobile CRM as a cornerstone of their future marketing activities.

The chapter-opening case provides an excellent example of mobile CRM. In IT's About Business 9.5, we see that Disney has implemented a different flavour of mobile CRM in its theme parks.

Open-Source CRM

As we discuss in Technology Guide 2, the source code for open-source software is available at no cost to developers or users. **Open-source CRM**, therefore, is CRM software whose source code is available to developers and users.

IT'S ABOUT BUSINESS 9.5
DISNEY REDEFINES ITS CRM EFFORT

Disney, through its theme parks, sells "the Disney experience of fantasy." As such, Disney has long been a leader in customer relationship management. However, the Disney brand is losing its lustre among the children of the digital age. In recent years, park attendance has declined by almost 15 percent. Many of the same complaints that have plagued Disney for years—unmanageable lines for concessions, long wait times for rides and events, and disorganized traffic patterns within the park—have been cited as deterrents for attendance. As revenue continues to fall, Disney Inc. has launched an ambitious, next-generation CRM strategy that is based on mobile, real-time interfaces with customers.

Disney has created a CRM strategy designed to help Walt Disney World restore the shine of its aging brand, increase efficiencies, and improve attendance and the bottom line. This strategy integrates global positioning satellites, smart sensors, and wireless technology into a 25-cm tall stuffed doll called Pal Mickey. The goal is to reinvent the customer experience, influence visitor behaviour, and ease over-crowding throughout the parks.

With a powerful infrared sensor in its nose, Pal Mickey acts as a virtual tour guide, providing tips on which rides have the shortest lines and information on events. How does Pal Mickey work? A zipper in its fur conceals a central processing unit, an internal clock, small speakers, and a tiny infrared sensor. When the doll is carried into the park, the sensor receives a wireless data upload from one of the 500 infrared beacons concealed in park lampposts, rooftops, and bushes, which transmit information from a Disney data centre.

Pal Mickey provides families with relevant information during their park experience, and it entertains children during the down time between rides and events. With a squeeze of Pal Mickey's hand, families receive real-time updates regarding which rides have the shortest wait times.

Pal Mickey is not the only technology-based CRM initiative under development at Disney. Another initiative, Destination Disney, is a customer-centric program that allows park-goers to pre-plan activities during their visit to Disney theme parks. Using the interactive website, visitors can schedule a complete day before they arrive. Once inside the park, Destination Disney members will use their smart phones to receive messages regarding their scheduled activities for the day. The real value of Destination Disney becomes apparent for those customers who plan to visit more than one Disney park during their trip. They can use Destination Disney to pre-arrange travel accommodations from event to event and park to park and thus avoid long walks between various activities.

Disney hopes that its emphasis on CRM will provide a richer and more enjoyable experience for its customers. The major challenge that Disney faces is knowing when to rely on technology and when to employ the human-to-human personal touch that many people associate with Disney's theme parks.

QUESTIONS
1. Discuss the advantage of Pal Mickey for visitors to Disney theme parks.
2. Discuss possible disadvantages of using Pal Mickey as a CRM tool.

Open-source CRM does not provide more or fewer features or functions than other CRM software, and it may be implemented either on-premise or on-demand. Leading open-source CRM vendors include SugarCRM (*www.sugarcrm.com*), Concursive (*www.concursive.com*), and vtiger (*www.vtiger.com*).

The benefits of open-source CRM include favourable pricing and a wide variety of applications. In addition, open-source CRM is very easy to customize, an attractive feature for organizations that need CRM software designed for their specific needs. Updates and bug (software error) fixes occur rapidly, and extensive support information is available free of charge.

Like all software, however, open-source CRM does have risks. The biggest risk involves quality control. Because open-source CRM is created by a large community of unpaid developers, there may be a lack of central authority that is responsible for overseeing the quality of the product. Further, for best results, companies must have the same information technology platform in place as the platform on which the open-source CRM was developed.

WHAT'S IN IT FOR ME?

FOR ACCOUNTING AND FINANCE MAJORS

CRM systems can help companies establish controls for financial reporting related to interactions with customers in order to support compliance with legislation. For example, Sarbanes-Oxley requires companies to establish and maintain an adequate set of controls for accurate financial reporting that can be audited by a third party. Other sections (302 and 401[b]) have implications for customer activities, including the requirements that sales figures reported for the prior year are correct. Section 409 requires companies to report material changes to financial conditions, such as the loss of a strategic customer or significant customer claims about product quality.

CRM systems can track document flow from a sales opportunity, to a sales order, to an invoice, to an accounting document, thus enabling finance and accounting managers to monitor the entire flow. CRM systems that track sales quotes and orders can be used to incorporate process controls that identify questionable sales transactions. CRM systems can provide exception-alert capabilities to identify instances outside defined parameters that put companies at risk.

CRM systems allow companies to track marketing expenses, collecting appropriate costs for each individual marketing campaign. These costs can then be matched to corporate initiatives and financial objectives, demonstrating the financial impact of the marketing campaign.

Pricing is another key area that impacts financial reporting. For example, what discounts are available? When can a price be overridden? Who approves discounts? CRM systems can put controls into place for these issues.

FOR THE MARKETING MAJOR

Customer relationship management systems are an integral part of every marketing professional's work activities. CRM systems contain the consolidated customer data that provide the foundation for making informed marketing decisions. Using these data, marketers develop well-timed and targeted sales campaigns with customized product mixes and established price points that enhance potential sales opportunities and therefore increase revenue. CRM systems also support the development of forecasting models for future sales to existing clients through the use of historical data captured from previous transactions.

FOR THE PRODUCTION/OPERATIONS MANAGEMENT MAJOR

Production is heavily involved in the acquisition of raw materials, conversion, and distribution of finished goods. However, all of these activities are driven by sales. Increases or decreases in demand for goods results in a corresponding increase or decrease in a company's need for raw materials. Integral to a company's demand is forecasting future sales, an important part of CRM systems. Sales forecasts are created through the use of historical data stored in CRM systems.

This information is critically important to a production manager who is placing orders for manufacturing processes. Without an accurate future sales forecast, production managers may face one of two dilemmas. First, an unforeseen increase in demand may result in an inability for a production manager to provide retailers with enough products to avoid stock-outs. This situation costs both the retailer and the manufacturer revenue in the form of lost sales. Conversely, if a production manager fails to decrease the acquisition of materials and subsequent production with falling demand, he or she runs the risk of incurring unnecessary costs in the form of carrying expense for excess inventory. Again, this reduces profitability. In both these situations, the use of CRM systems for production and operational support is critical to efficiently managing company resources.

FOR THE HUMAN RESOURCES MANAGEMENT MAJOR

As companies try to enhance their customer relationships, they must recognize that employees who interact with customers are critical to the success of CRM strategies. Essentially, CRM will be successful based on the employees' desire and ability to promote the company and its CRM initiatives. In fact, research analysts have found that customer loyalty is largely based on employees' capabilities and their commitment to the company.

As a result, human resource managers know that if their company desires valued customer relationships, then it needs valued relationships with its employees. Therefore, HR managers are implementing programs to increase employee satisfaction and are providing training for employees so that they can execute CRM strategies.

FOR THE MIS MAJOR

The IT function in the enterprise is responsible for the corporate databases and data warehouse, and the correctness and completeness of the data in them. The IT function is also responsible for the business intelligence tools and applications used to analyze data in the data warehouse. Further, IT personnel provide the technologies underlying the customer interaction centre.

SUMMARY

1. **Define customer relationship management (CRM) and discuss the objectives of CRM.**
   CRM is a customer-focused and customer-driven organizational strategy with the following objectives:

   - Market to each customer individually.
   - Treat different customers differently.
   - Satisfy customers by assessing their requirements for products and services, and then by providing high-quality, responsive services.
   - Build long-term, sustainable customer relationships that create value for the company and the customer.
   - Help companies acquire new customers, retain existing profitable customers, and grow relationships with existing customers.

2. **Describe operational CRM and its major components.**
   Operational CRM is that part of an overall CRM effort in an organization that supports the front-office business processes that directly interact with customers; i.e., sales, marketing, and service. The two major components of operational CRM are customer-facing applications and customer-touching applications.

   Customer-facing CRM applications are the areas where customers directly interact with the enterprise. These areas include customer service and support, sales force automation, marketing, and campaign management.

   Customer-touching applications (also called electronic CRM applications) include those technologies with which customers interact and typically help themselves. These applications include search and comparison capabilities, technical and other information and services, customized products and services, personalized web pages, FAQs, e-mail and automated response, and loyalty programs.

3. **Describe analytical CRM.**
   Analytical CRM systems analyze customer behaviour and perceptions in order to provide actionable business intelligence. Important technologies in analytical CRM systems include data warehouses, data mining, and decision support.

4. **Discuss on-demand CRM, mobile CRM, and open-source CRM.**
   On-demand CRM is a CRM system that is hosted by an external vendor in the vendor's data centre. Mobile CRM is an interactive CRM system where communications related to sales, marketing, and customer service activities are conducted through a mobile medium for the purpose of building and maintaining customer relationships between an organization and its customers. Open-source CRM is CRM software whose source code is available to developers and users.

KEY TERMS

analytical CRM, 273
bundling, 270
campaign management applications, 270
collaborative CRM, 266
cross-selling, 270
customer-facing CRM
   applications, 267
customer interaction
   centre (CIC), 267
customer relationship management, 263

customer-touching CRM applications
   (electronic CRM or e-CRM), 270
customer touch point, 265
loyalty program, 271
mobile CRM, 275
on-demand CRM, 275
open-source CRM, 275
operational CRM, 267
sales force automation (SFA), 269
up-selling, 270

DISCUSSION QUESTIONS

1. How do customer relationship management systems help organizations achieve customer intimacy?
2. What is the relationship between data consolidation and CRM?
3. Discuss the relationship between CRM and customer privacy.
4. Distinguish between operational CRM and analytical CRM.
5. Differentiate between customer-facing CRM applications and customer-touching CRM applications.
6. Explain why web-based customer interaction centres are critical for successful CRM.
7. Why are companies so interested in e-CRM applications?
8. Discuss why it is difficult to justify CRM applications.
9. You are the CIO of a small company with a rapidly growing customer base. Which CRM system would you use: on-premise CRM system, on-demand CRM system, or open-source CRM system? Remember that open-source CRM systems may be implemented either on-premise or on-demand. Discuss the pros and cons of each type of CRM system for your business.

PROBLEM-SOLVING ACTIVITIES

1. Access *www.ups.ca* and *www.fedex.ca*. Examine some of the IT-supported customer services and tools provided by the two companies. Compare and contrast the customer support provided on the two companies' websites.
2. Enter *www.holtrenfrew.com*, *www.hermes.com*, and *www.tiffany.com*. Compare and contrast the customer service activities offered by these companies on their websites. Do you see marked similarities? Differences?
3. Access your college or university's website. Investigate how it provides for customer relationship management. Hint: First decide who your institution's customers are.
4. Enter *www.livechatinc.com* and *www.websitealive.com* and view their demos. Write a report about how live chat works. Be sure to discuss all the available features.
5. Access *www.infor.com* and view the demo (registration required). Prepare a report on the demo to the class.

6. Access *www.sugarcrm.com* and take the interactive tour. Prepare a report on SugarCRM's functionality to the class.

7. Enter the Teradata website (*http://www.teradata.com/*) and search for "Customer Relationship Management case studies." Choose one of the case studies and prepare a presentation outlining the business problem, the IT solution, and the results. Complete the case study by searching for additional information about the same company and their use of CRM.

TEAM ASSIGNMENTS

1. Each group will be assigned to an open-source CRM vendor. Each group should examine the vendor, its products, and the capabilities of those products. Each group will make a presentation to the class detailing how its vendor product is superior to the other on-demand CRM products. See SugarCRM (*www.sugarcrm.com*), Concursive (*www.concursive.com*), vtiger (*www.vtiger.com*), SplendidCRM Software (*www. splendidcrm.com*), Compiere (*www.compiere.com*), and openCRX (*www.opencrx.com*).

2. Each group will be assigned to an on-demand CRM vendor. Each group should examine the vendor, its products, and the capabilities of those products. Each group will make a presentation to the class detailing how its vendor product is superior to the other on-demand CRM products. See Salesforce (*www.salesforce.com*), Oracle (*http://crmondemand.oracle.com*), Aplicor (*www.aplicor.com*), NetSuite (*www.netsuite.com*), SalesNexus (*www.salesnexus.com*), SageCRM (*www.sagecrm.com*), and Commence (*www.commence.com*).

3. Create groups to investigate the major CRM applications and their vendors.

   - Sales force automation (Microsoft Dynamics, Oracle, FrontRange Solutions, RightNow Technologies, Maximizer Software)
   - Call centres (LivePerson, Cisco, Oracle)
   - Marketing automation (SalesNexus, Marketo, Chordiant, Infor, Consona, Pivotal, Oracle)
   - Customer service (Oracle, Amazon, Dell)

   Start with *http://searchcrm.techtarget.com/* and *www.customerthink.com* (to ask questions about CRM solutions). Each group will present arguments to convince the class members to use the product(s) the group investigated.

TESCO RETURNS TO THE CORNER SHOPS OF ENGLAND'S PAST

Courtesy David Wright

THE BUSINESS PROBLEM

Tesco (*www.tesco.com*) was not always the United Kingdom's largest grocer. In fact, at one time the grocer struggled to maintain its position as the number two grocery chain in England. Deteriorating same-store sales and poor customer retention had eroded the company's market position and profitability. Tesco's business problem was apparent. How could the grocery chain improve its sales, market share, and profitability? In an attempt to improve sagging sales in many of its stores, Tesco implemented a loyalty program, called the Tesco Club Card.

THE IT SOLUTION

Tesco's information systems, like those of many other retailers, were designed around a product-based cost approach. Specifically, most stores maintain their profit margins through managing the cost of products sold and negotiating partnerships with suppliers. Tesco found that this cost-based type of system would not support the customer-centric approach that it felt was needed to rejuvenate its business.

Tesco addressed this issue by implementing an enterprise-wide CRM system called the Club Card program. The system enables Tesco to collect, store, and analyze the data generated by Tesco Club Card customers and other customers as well. Specifically, it places each customer into one of three categories: cost-conscious, mid-market, and up-market. These segments are further divided into shopping tendencies such as healthy, gourmet, convenient, family living, and others. Tesco then targets communications to

each customer segment. Tailoring communications according to customers' individual behaviours, needs, and desires helps Tesco reach the right person in the right way with an appropriate message.

Tesco hired dunnhumby (*www.dunnhumby.com*) to help it analyze these data. Dunnhumby is a British marketing research firm that mines data from credit card transactions and customer loyalty programs to uncover hidden and potentially lucrative facts about its clients' current customers. For example, dunnhumby can identify customers who might be interested in a particular sale or who will not go back to a store if it does not offer a particular product.

Dunnhumby analyzes three types of data: customer data (e.g., from a loyalty card program), sales data (e.g., from electronic point-of-sale), and traditional market research data. These analyses provide company managers and analysts with valuable insights into customer behaviour. Dunnhumby then uses these insights to create customer-driven action plans, which are strategies to build a client's business by better matching all aspects of the client's retail operations with the customers' needs and aspirations. In this case, Tesco used the insights provided by dunnhumby to help shape its Club Card program.

THE RESULTS

Some 10 million households are holders of Tesco's Club Card. Tesco's CRM system can segment customers on several dimensions and tailor communication to each household's particular buying patterns. Recently, Tesco printed and mailed 4 million unique quarterly club mailings with coupons targeted toward very specific customer segments. To Tesco customers this is proof that they can count on their "local grocer" to know what they want and need.

An unusually high percentage of coupons—between 20 and 40 percent—are redeemed, and the cost to Tesco for each redemption has been falling. Sales were boosted by 52 percent five years after the club was launched, and sales growth is consistently higher than the industry average. Tesco's floor space has more than doubled, thanks to new store openings and expansions of existing locations.

Tesco has experienced rapid growth in revenue, proof that the company truly accomplished its customer focus. Tesco's customers began to feel appreciated and in return they developed a tremendous affinity for the company. Interestingly, the company's success has extended to the Web as well. Tesco's website (*www.tesco.com*) boasts 500,000 transactions weekly, totalling nearly £2 billion in sales each year.

CASE 9.2

The in-depth understanding of its customers changed the company's way of thinking about both the customers and the business. The company moved away from thinking about an "average customer" and began viewing each customer as an individual. Therefore, the Tesco motto became "changing the way they think about us." Tesco's Chairman, Sir Terry Leahy, placed this mission statement in the centre of one of the company's annual reports: "Continually increasing value for customers to earn their lifetime loyalty."

Tesco's new way of thinking about its customers caused the grocer to go back 40 years in time to England's "corner grocers," where the proprietors knew their customers' preferences, wants, and needs, and customers remained loyal to the store.

Sources: Compiled from M. Duff, "Dunnhumby Complicates Outlook for Tesco, Kroger, Wal-Mart," BNET Retail Insights, January 13, 2009; N. McElhatton, "DM Media Digest: Dunnhumby Gains Fame in the US," Brand Republic, January 8, 2009; B. Helm, "Getting Inside the Customer's Mind," *BusinessWeek*, September 22, 2008; J. Hall,

"Tesco's Clubcard Company to Check Out Macy's," Telegraph.co.uk, August 22, 2008; S. Johnson, "Macy's Hands Dunnhumby Its Data Account," MarketingDirect, August 14, 2008; "Tesco Has Links With the Corner Shops of England's Past," *www.loyalty.vg*, 2005; *www.tesco.com*, accessed March 17, 2009; *www.dunnhumby.com*, accessed March 20, 2009.

QUESTIONS

1. Explain what a customer-driven action plan is. Are such plans designed to keep existing customers or to attract new customers? Support your answer.
2. Describe how dunnhumby helps its client companies achieve greater customer intimacy. Is dunnhumby invading customers' privacy? Support your answer.
3. Will Tesco's CRM strategy allow the grocer to achieve a sustainable competitive advantage? Why or why not?
4. Based on Tesco's experience, what managerial and organizational factors are necessary for a CRM system to be successful?

Web Resources

Student website www.wiley.com/canada/rainer

- Web quizzes
- Lecture slides in PowerPoint
- Author podcasts
- Interactive Case: Ruby's Club assignments

ALL OF THE ABOVE AND...

- E-book
- Manager videos
- Vocabulary flash cards
- Pre- and post-lecture quizzes
- Microsoft Office 2007 lab manual and projects

PLANNING CRM SOLUTIONS FOR RUBY'S CLUB

Go to the Ruby's Club link at the Student Companion website or WileyPLUS for information about your current internship assignment. You will investigate how CRM can help retain customers at Ruby's Club.

10

SUPPLY CHAIN MANAGEMENT

LEARNING OBJECTIVES

1. Describe the structure of a supply chain.
2. Identify various problems that can occur along supply chains and possible solutions to them.
3. Explain what a supply chain management system and related technologies are.

3M CANADA REDUCES INVENTORY WITH SUPPLY CHAIN MANAGEMENT SYSTEM

AP Photo/The Canadian Press/Seth Perlman

THE BUSINESS PROBLEM

3M Canada is one of the largest adhesives and sealants manufacturers in the country with eight manufacturing facilities in three provinces: Ontario, Manitoba, and Quebec. Back in the early 1980s, 3M Canada invested in a new materials resource planning (MRP) system in order to plan production more accurately and reduce inventory. However, as the company grew, it became more difficult to plan orders and it was forced to keep large inventory of products in order to satisfy customer demand.

3M Canada quickly realized that the inventory problems were not only due to the obsolete MRP system but to the entire supply chain. The company bet that it could gain significant incremental savings by focusing on the entire supply chain. If it could improve its supply chain, then customer service would improve, which would result in sales growth.

THE IT SOLUTION

3M Canada responded to the problem by implementing a supply chain management (SCM) system from i2 Technologies. The new system would provide managers with complete and accurate inventory of products and production information across all of its manufacturing facilities. The software would also allow production managers to collaboratively coordinate forecasting, planning, and executing activities.

The new i2 SCM system has allowed managers to better predict future requirements, rapidly identify shifts in customer demand, and evaluate the effect of new promotions on customer demand. Since implementing the new i2 SCM system, 3M Canada's planning and scheduling productivity has increased by 20 percent, customer service levels went from 92 percent to 98 percent, and inventory has decreased by 23 percent. As a result, 3M Canada's sales are up as well as its bottom line and cash flow.

Sources: Compiled from "Replacing Inventory with Information at 3M Canada," i2 customer success story, i2 website *(www.i2.com)*, accessed May 3, 2010; 3M website *(www.3m.com)*, accessed May 3, 2010.

WHAT DO YOU THINK?

1. What is it so important for managers to have accurate demand forecasting?
2. How can the accuracy of forecasts be increased?
3. What is the role of other supply chain members (i.e., customers, suppliers) in producing accurate forecasts?
4. How could information technology be used to enable the participation of extended supply chain members in producing accurate forecasts?

Chapter Preview

Modern organizations are increasingly concentrating on their core competencies and on becoming more flexible and agile. To accomplish these objectives, they are relying on other companies to supply necessary goods and services, rather than owning these companies themselves. Organizations recognize that these suppliers can perform these activities more efficiently and effectively than they can. This trend toward relying on an increasing number of suppliers has led to the supply chain concept.

Supply chains have become a vital component of the overall strategies of many modern organizations. To utilize supply chains efficiently, a business must become tightly integrated with its suppliers, business partners, distributors, and customers. One of the most critical aspects of this integration is the use of information systems to facilitate the exchange of information among the participants in the supply chain.

You might ask, why do I need to study supply chain management? The answer is that supply chains are critical to organizations. Therefore, regardless of your position in an organization, you will be involved with some aspect of your company's supply chain. We start the chapter by discussing the concept of supply chain and its main components. We then examine some of the major problems in supply chains and the role of supply chain management. We conclude the chapter by discussing the main technologies supporting supply chain management.

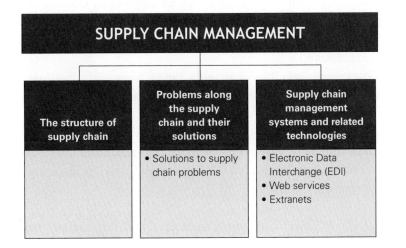

10.1 The Structure of Supply Chains

The term *supply chain* comes from a picture of how the partnering organizations are linked together. A supply chain refers to the flow of materials, information, money, and services from raw material suppliers, through factories and warehouses, to the end customers. A supply chain also includes the *organizations* and *processes* that create and deliver products, information, and services to end customers.

A typical supply chain, which links a company with its suppliers and its distributors and customers, is illustrated in Figure 10.1. Recall that Figure 2.2 (see p. 43) also illustrated a supply chain in a slightly different way. Note that the supply chain involves three segments:

1. *Upstream*, where sourcing or procurement from external suppliers occurs. In this segment, supply chain (SC) managers select suppliers to deliver the goods and services the company needs to produce its product or service. Further, SC managers develop the pricing, delivery, and payment processes between a company and its suppliers. Included here are processes for managing

FIGURE 10.1
Generic supply chain.

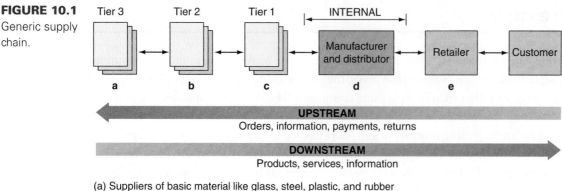

(a) Suppliers of basic material like glass, steel, plastic, and rubber
(b) Suppliers of windshields, tires, plastic mouldings, etc.
(c) Suppliers of integrated components such as dashboards
(d) Manufacturer and distributor
(e) Car dealership affiliated with an automobile manufacturer

inventory, receiving and verifying shipments, transferring goods to manufacturing facilities, and authorizing payments to suppliers.

If you look closely at Figure 10.1, you will notice that there are several tiers of suppliers. As the diagram shows, a supplier may have one or more sub-suppliers, and the sub-supplier may have its own sub-supplier(s), and so on. For example, with an automobile manufacturer, Tier 3 suppliers produce basic products such as glass, plastic, and rubber. Tier 2 suppliers use these inputs to make windshields, tires, and plastic mouldings. Tier 1 suppliers produce integrated components such as dashboards and seat assemblies.

2. *Internal*, where packaging, assembly, or manufacturing takes place. SC managers schedule the activities necessary for production, testing, packaging, and preparing goods for delivery. SC managers also monitor quality levels, production output, and worker productivity.

3. *Downstream*, where distribution takes place, frequently by external distributors. In this segment, SC managers coordinate the receipt of orders from customers, develop a network of warehouses, select carriers to deliver their products to customers, and develop invoicing systems to receive payments from customers.

There are typically three flows in the supply chain: materials, information, and financial. *Material flows* are the physical products, raw materials, supplies, and so forth that flow along the chain. Material flows also include *reverse* flows (or reverse logistics)—returned products, recycled products, and disposal of materials or products. A supply chain thus involves a *product life cycle* approach, from "dirt to dust."

Information flows consist of data that are related to demand, shipments, orders, returns, and schedules, as well as changes in any of these data. Finally, *financial flows* involve money transfers, payments, credit card information and authorization, payment schedules, e-payments, and credit-related data.

The flow of information and goods can be bidirectional. For example, damaged or unwanted products can be returned, a process known as *reverse logistics*. Using the retail clothing industry as an example, reverse logistics would involve clothing that customers return, either because the item had defects or because the customer did not like the item after all.

All supply chains do not have the same number and types of flows. For example, in service industries there may be no physical flow of materials, but frequently there is a flow of information, often in the form of documents (physical or electronic copies). In fact, the digitization of software, music, and other content may create a supply chain without any physical flow. Notice, however, that in such a case, there are two types of information flows: one that replaces materials flow (for example, digitized software) and one that provides the supporting information (orders, billing, and so on).

To manage the supply chain an organization must coordinate all of the above flows among all of the parties involved in the chain. IT's About Business 10.1 illustrates the example of the Walt Disney Studios supply chain, components, and flows.

Next time you're at the movies, spare a thought to the complicated supply chain that brings each movie to your local theatre.

IT'S ABOUT BUSINESS 10.1
DISNEY GOES DIGITAL

Producing and distributing a film is a huge undertaking involving hundreds of contributors and a major budget. Therefore, for a Hollywood studio, the transition from traditional film making to digital shooting, storage, and distribution is an enormously complex process. Like most of its competitors, Walt Disney Studios (*http://studioservices.go.com*) is updating from traditional to digital movie making. This shift requires massive changes to three elements of Disney's supply chain: production (filming), storage, and distribution.

Production. Most film directors have used traditional film-based cameras for their entire careers. The transition to filmless digital cameras (called *electronic cinematography*) creates huge amounts of data. Multiple digital cameras produce multiple data streams. A single Hollywood movie typically totals about 200 hours of raw footage. This footage translates into several hundred terabytes of raw data, which increases with each edit.

Storage and Post-Production. These data flow from each camera at 2 gigabits per second into RAID storage devices (discussed in Technology Guide 1) located in a data repository. This process

ensures that the data are reliable, which is essential on movie sets, particularly in situations in which scenes cannot be easily reproduced. Further, this process requires extremely high-speed, fibre optic communications and huge amounts of fast-access, secure data storage.

Once the data are stored in the repository, Disney technicians produce the *digital intermediate* that Disney artists use to create effects. These intermediates must be available for use in collaborative efforts involving effects supervisors, digital artists, film and sound editors, and archivists. Digital intermediates are held in storage for many months or even years. If they are lost, a director would have to recreate an entire movie set, actors included.

Distribution. Digital film making enables Disney to distribute its films digitally. After the digital intermediates are archived and post-production is finished, the studio prepares the movies for distribution. Most movies are currently sent to theatres on encrypted hard disks. In the future, they will be delivered over very high-speed communication channels directly to theatres and eventually to homes. Transmitting several hundred terabytes of data is a

(Continued on next page)

challenge, especially considering that the studio has to send these huge files to many different locations simultaneously.

The initial result of digital movie making has been lower costs, tighter integration of filming and post-production, improved workflow processes, and improved quality of the final product. Consumers should also benefit as movie quality increases, prices decrease, and the public's favourite movies are made available in theatres even sooner.

Sources: Compiled from D. Chmielewski, "Major Studios in Deal to Convert to Digital Movie Projection," *Los Angeles Times*, October 2, 2008; J. Brandon, "Disney Fast-Forwards into the Digital Age," *Baseline Magazine*, June 26, 2008; S. Kirsner, "Studios Shift to Digital Movies, But Not Without Resistance," *New York Times*,

July 24, 2006; L. Sullivan, "Hollywood Promos Digital Movies with Games, Live Events," *InformationWeek*, March 10, 2006; J. Borland, "Top Theaters on Path to Digital Films," CNET News, December 2005; "Disney to Finance Digital Movie Distribution," *Audio Visual News*, September 19, 2005; D. Lieberman, "Top Hollywood Studios Agree on Standards for Digital Films," *USA Today*, July 27, 2005; Walt Disney Studios website (*http://studioservices.go.com*), accessed April 2, 2009.

QUESTIONS
1. Draw the supply chain for Disney and identify the different upstream, internal, and downstream components, including its supply chain flows.
2. What are the differences between a supply chain for digital products versus a supply chain for physical goods?

The purpose of the supply chain concept is to improve trust and collaboration among supply chain partners, thus improving supply chain visibility and inventory velocity. **Supply chain visibility** is the ability for all organizations in a supply chain to access or view relevant data on purchased materials as these materials move through their suppliers' production processes and transportation networks to their receiving docks. In addition, organizations can access or view relevant data on outbound goods as they are manufactured, assembled, or stored in inventory, and then shipped through their transportation networks to their customers' receiving docks. **Inventory velocity** is the time between the receipt of incoming goods and the dispatch of finished, outbound products. In general, the greater your inventory velocity, the more quickly you can deliver your products and services, which in turn increases customer satisfaction.

BEFORE YOU GO ON...

1. Describe the three segments of a supply chain.
2. Describe the flows in the supply chain.

10.2 Problems along the Supply Chain and their Solutions

One major consequence of ineffective supply chains is poor customer service. In some cases, supply chains do not deliver products or services when and where customers—either individuals or businesses—need them. In other cases the supply chain provides poor-quality products. Other problems are high inventory costs and loss of revenues.

The problems along the supply chain stem primarily from two sources: (1) uncertainties, and (2) the need to coordinate several activities, internal units, and business partners. A major source of supply chain uncertainties is the *demand forecast*. Demand for a product can be influenced by numerous factors such as competition, prices, weather conditions, technological developments, economic

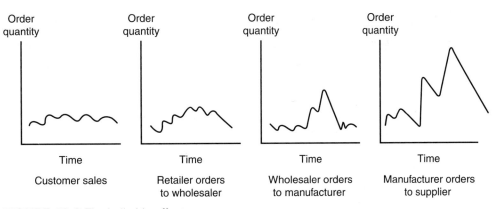

FIGURE 10.2 The bullwhip effect.

conditions, and customers' general confidence. Another uncertainty is delivery times, which depend on factors ranging from production machine failures to road construction and traffic jams. In addition, quality problems in materials and parts can create production delays, which also lead to supply chain problems.

One of the major challenges that managers face in setting accurate inventory levels throughout the supply chain is known as the bullwhip effect. The **bullwhip effect** refers to erratic shifts in orders up and down the supply chain (see Figure 10.2). Basically, the variables that affect customer demand can become magnified when they are viewed through the eyes of managers at each link in the supply chain. If each distinct entity that makes ordering and inventory decisions places its interests above those of the chain, then stockpiling can occur at as many as seven or eight locations along the chain. Research has shown that in some cases such hoarding has led to as much as a 100-day supply of inventory that is waiting "just in case" (versus 10–20 days under normal circumstances).

Very often the bullwhip effect is due to the use of the push production model in the supply chain. In the **push model** (also known as *make-to-stock*), the production process begins with a forecast, which is simply an educated guess as to customer demand. The forecast must predict which products customers will want as well as the quantity of each product. The company then produces the amount of products in the forecast, typically by using mass production, and sells, or "pushes," those products to consumers.

Unfortunately, these forecasts are often incorrect. Consider, for example, an automobile manufacturer that wants to produce a new car. Marketing managers do extensive research (customer surveys, analyses of competitors' cars) and provide the results to forecasters. If the forecasters are too high in their prediction—that is, they predict that sales of the new car will be 200,000 and actual customer demand turns out to be 150,000—then the automaker has 50,000 cars in inventory and will incur large carrying costs. Further, the company will probably have to sell the excess cars at a discount.

From the opposite perspective, if the forecasters are too low in their prediction—that is, they predict that sales of the new car will be 150,000 and actual customer demand turns out to be 200,000—then the automaker will probably have to run extra shifts to meet the demand and thus will incur large overtime costs. Further, the company risks losing customers to competitors if the car they want is not available.

Another problem that can adversely affect supply chains is implementing an incorrect business model. IT's About Business 10.2 shows how OfficeMax gained valuable benefits from its supply chain by redefining its business model.

IT'S ABOUT BUSINESS 10.2
OFFICEMAX GETS A HANDLE ON ITS INVENTORY

OfficeMax (*www.officemax.com*) is a leading retailer in the office products market, selling office supplies and equipment to both businesses and consumers. The company operates superstores in the United States and in Latin America and employs more than 30,000 full- and part-time workers.

OfficeMax executives realize that there are many office supply stores where customers can shop and there is intense competition based on service, selection, and other factors. The company was forced to re-examine its business operations after the economic slowdown and changing tastes and products in the computer and office supply market.

This analysis revealed that the company's business model was faulty. OfficeMax had established supply chain processes where its individual retail stores ordered products from suppliers, and the suppliers shipped products directly to the stores. This process, known as the direct-to-store environment, required individual stores to place orders based on the suppliers' minimum quantities and not the store's needs. The direct-to-store environment created a situation in which actual inventory levels were too high for low-turnover items and too low for high-turnover items. Thus, OfficeMax regularly experienced shortages of high-demand items, which caused customer dissatisfaction to rise to unacceptable levels. Additionally, the company had very high inventory carrying costs.

There were many other problems with the direct-to-store environment. The company had no intermediate distribution points, so its entire inventory had to be located in its stores. This problem was so acute that it affected store layouts. Stores had inventory stacked up to the ceiling, blocking much of the lighting. Not only did customers not like the dimness, but they complained that they had difficulty navigating through the store once they entered the "big valleys."

In addition, associates in the stores had to manage inbound shipments rather than spending time with customers. These shipments could number in the hundreds each week, and some stores had to wait more than a month to receive their goods. Not only were goods delayed, but they were more costly because individual stores did not order enough products to qualify for quantity discounts. The suppliers were not satisfied either, because they had to ship to thousands of places, a very inefficient and expensive process.

To help overcome these numerous problems, OfficeMax created a new supply chain that revolves around three large distribution centres that receive goods and then distribute them to individual stores.

Today, these distribution centres supply more than 95 percent of each OfficeMax store with its inventory. This new arrangement has benefited the company in many ways. First, the distribution centres can handle bulk orders from suppliers and have substantially reduced the number of deliveries to each store. Also, the replenishment cycle time for OfficeMax stores has improved from 35 days to 8 days. Finally, the company has reduced $400 million in inventory.

Sources: Compiled from "mySAP Supply Chain Management at OfficeMax," SAP Case Study, *www.sap.com*, accessed April 4, 2009; OfficeMax website (*www.officemax.com*), accessed March 15, 2009.

QUESTIONS
1. Discuss the importance of analyzing a company's business model before analyzing its supply chain.
2. Describe the problems that OfficeMax experienced with its direct-to-store supply chain model.
3. Explain how the new supply chain model has benefited OfficeMax.

Solutions to Supply Chain Problems

Supply chain problems can be very costly. Therefore, organizations are motivated to find innovative solutions. During the oil crises of the 1970s, for example, Ryder Systems, a large trucking company, purchased a refinery to control the upstream part of the supply chain and to make certain it would have enough gasoline for its trucks. Ryder's decision to purchase a refinery is an example of vertical integration. **Vertical integration** is a business strategy in which a company buys its upstream suppliers to ensure that its essential supplies are available as soon as they are needed. Ryder later sold the refinery because it could not manage a business it did not know and because oil became more plentiful.

Ryder's decision to vertically integrate was not the optimal method to manage its supply chain. In the remainder of this section, we will look at some other possible solutions to supply chain problems, many of which are supported by IT.

Using Inventories to Solve Supply Chain Problems

Undoubtedly, the most common solution to supply chain problems is *building inventories* as insurance against supply chain uncertainties. The major problem with this approach is that it is very difficult to correctly determine inventory levels for each product and part. If inventory levels are set too high, the costs of keeping the inventory will greatly increase. (Also, as we have seen, excessive inventories at multiple points in the supply chain can result in the bullwhip effect.) If the inventory is too low, there is no insurance against high demand or slow delivery times. In such cases, customers don't receive what they want, when they want or need it. The result is lost customers and lost revenues. In either event, the total cost—including the costs of maintaining inventories, the costs of lost sales opportunities, and the costs of developing a bad reputation—can be very high. Thus, companies make major attempts to optimize and control inventories.

A well-known initiative to optimize and control inventories is the **just-in-time (JIT) inventory system**, which attempts to minimize inventories. That is, in a manufacturing process, JIT systems deliver the precise number of parts, called *work-in-process* inventory, to be assembled into a finished product at precisely the right time.

Sharing Information

Another common way to solve supply chain problems, and especially to improve demand forecasts, is *sharing information* along the supply chain. In addition, information sharing enables a company to implement a **pull model**, also known as *make-to-order*. In a pull production model the production process begins with a customer order. Therefore, companies make only what customers want, a process closely aligned with mass customization.

A prominent example of a company that uses the pull model is Dell Computer. Dell's production process begins with a customer order. This order not only specifies the type of computer the customer wants, but it also alerts each Dell supplier as to the parts of the order for which that supplier is responsible. In that way, Dell's suppliers ship only the parts Dell needs to produce the computer.

Another notable example of information sharing across the supply chain occurs between Walmart and Procter & Gamble (P&G). Walmart provides P&G access to daily sales information from every store for every item P&G makes for Walmart. This access enables P&G to manage the inventory replenishment for Walmart's stores, something generally called in business a **vendor-managed inventory** strategy. By monitoring inventory levels, P&G knows when inventories fall below the threshold for each product at any Walmart store. These data trigger an immediate shipment. The benefit for P&G of this information sharing agreement with Walmart is accurate and timely information on consumer demand for its products. Thus, P&G can plan production more accurately, minimizing the bullwhip effect.

Information sharing can be facilitated by the use of supply chain management systems and related technologies, such as EDI, extranets, and portals. We will discuss these systems next.

BEFORE YOU GO ON ...

1. Describe various problems that can occur along the supply chain.
2. Discuss possible solutions to problems along the supply chain.

10.3 Supply Chain Management Systems and Related Technologies

The function of **supply chain management (SCM)** consists in planning, organizing, and optimizing the various activities performed along the supply chain. As such, supply chain management systems provide support to SCM using information technology.

SCM systems are a type of inter-organizational information system. An **inter-organizational information system (IOS)** involves information flows among two or more organizations. By connecting the information systems of business partners, IOSs enable the partners to perform a number of tasks and receive a number of benefits:

- Reduce the costs of routine business transactions
- Improve the quality of the information flow by reducing or eliminating errors
- Compress the cycle time involved in fulfilling business transactions
- Eliminate paper processing and its associated inefficiencies and costs
- Make the transfer and processing of information easier for users

The goal of SCM systems is to reduce the problems, or friction, along the supply chain. Friction can involve increased time, costs, and inventories as well as decreased customer satisfaction. SCM systems, then, reduce uncertainty and risks by decreasing inventory levels and cycle time and improving business processes and customer service. All of these benefits make the organization more profitable and competitive. IT's About Business 10.3 illustrates these advantages as they apply to the supply chain of the Inditex Corporation.

IT'S ABOUT BUSINESS 10.3
SUPPLY CHAIN MANAGEMENT DRIVES THE SUCCESS OF INDITEX

Spain's $14-billion Inditex Corporation (*www.inditex.com*) is the world's second-largest clothing retailer, behind only The Gap. Inditex has more than 4,200 stores in 73 countries, with eight well-known brands: Zara (*www.zara.com*), Pull and Bear (*www.pullandbear.com*), Massimo Dutti (*www.massimodutti.com*), Bershka (*www.bershka.com*), Stradivarius (*www.e-stradivarius.com*), Oysho (*www.oysho.com*), Zara Home (*www.zarahome.com*), and Uterque (*www.uterque.es*). The Inditex Group is composed of more than 100 companies associated with the business of textile design, manufacturing, and distribution. The mission of Inditex is to produce creative and quality designs coupled with a rapid response to market demands.

Since 2000, Inditex sales, profits, and locations have increased by nearly 400 percent. What is the company's secret? Besides selling relatively inexpensive yet trendy clothes, the company closely monitors every link in its supply chain. As a result, Inditex can put new clothes on the rack in as little as two weeks from the first conception. Other retailers have borrowed this strategy, including fellow Spanish chain Mango (*www.mango.com*), the American firm Forever 21 (*www.forever21.com*), and Britain's Topshop (*www.topshop.com*).

Inditex has spent more than 30 years fine-tuning its strategy. Designers drive the clothing in most fashion companies. In contrast, Inditex starts on the sales floor, as store managers monitor daily sales. Managers have great incentive to respond to trends quickly and correctly because almost three quarters of their compensation is commission. They keep an eye on what customers ask for and what they buy, and they send this information to the company's design team, which numbers 300. The designers can create clothes to fill demand almost immediately.

Most clothing firms aren't in the manufacturing business and outsource to factories in Asia. Inditex not only produces half of its items in-house, but it keeps production close to home, with factories in Spain, Portugal, and Morocco. It only outsources basic items such as T-shirts. Inditex also pays higher wages than its competitors. For example, its Spanish factory workers earn an average of $1,650 per month,

(Continued on next page)

IT'S ABOUT BUSINESS 10.3 *(Continued)*
SUPPLY CHAIN MANAGEMENT DRIVES THE SUCCESS OF INDITEX

more than eight times the earnings of a typical factory worker in China's Guangdong Province, where many apparel companies have located their factories. Inditex achieves savings of both time and money because its plants are closer to the stores, and they use just-in-time systems (discussed later in this chapter) to control inventory.

All the Inditex warehouses are in Spain, from where it can supply its European stores within a day. It can supply its stores in the Americas and Asia within two days because it ships by commercial airliners, which is more expensive than using ocean freighters but there's a business case for it. Inditex products are made in smaller batches, resulting in a higher turnover of items and greater demand from customers who want something exclusive and want to see a steady stream of new designs. This means that, unlike its competitors, its stores aren't saddled with racks of mass items that have to be marked down drastically to get rid of this overstock. Because Inditex has the latest styles in stock, it can typically charge more than its competitors while reducing its fashion risk.

Sources: Compiled from K. Capell, "Zara Thrives By Breaking All the Rules," *BusinessWeek*, October 20, 2008; "Spain's Inditex Breaks All the Supply Chain Rules," *WorldTrade Magazine*, October 11, 2008; "Fashion Goes 3D," *Fortune*, September 26, 2008; J. Reingold, "The British (Retail) Invasion," *Fortune*, July 3, 2008; "Zara's Supply Chain Innovation," Kaleidoscope (*www.kascope.com*), December 3, 2007; T. Claburn, "Math Whizzes Turbocharge an Online Retailer's Sales," *InformationWeek*, October 5, 2007; "Merchants of Innovation," Crossroads 2007: Supply Chain Innovation Summit (MIT Center for Transportation and Logistics), March, 2007; K. Anderson and J. Lovejoy, "The Speeding Bullet: Zara's Apparel Supply Chain," *TechExchange*, March, 2007; "Zara Shows Supply Chain Future," BNET.com, October 20, 2005; Inditex website (*www.inditex.com*), accessed January 20, 2009.

QUESTIONS
1. Describe the "fast fashion" process at Inditex. How do supply chain management systems enable this process?
2. Do you anticipate that other apparel firms will adopt similar SCM systems to Inditex? Why or why not?
3. Why does Inditex not have to drastically cut prices to sell out-of-season stock?

Clearly, SCM systems are essential to the successful operation of many businesses. As we discussed, these systems—and IOSs in general—rely on various forms of IT to resolve problems. Three technologies in particular provide support for IOSs and SCM systems: electronic data interchange, extranets, and web services.

Electronic Data Interchange (EDI)

Electronic data interchange (EDI) is a communication standard that enables business partners to exchange routine documents, such as purchasing orders, electronically. EDI formats these documents according to agreed-upon standards (for example, data formats). It then transmits messages using a converter, called a *translator*. The message travels over a communications network, typically either a value-added network (VAN; see Technology Guide 4) or the Internet.

EDI provides many benefits compared with a manual delivery system (see Figure 10.3). To begin with, it minimizes data entry errors, because each entry is checked by the computer. In addition, the length of the message can be shorter, and the messages are secured. EDI also reduces cycle time, increases productivity, enhances customer service, and minimizes paper usage and storage.

Despite all of the advantages of EDI, several factors have prevented it from being more widely used. To begin with, implementing an EDI system involves a significant initial investment. In addition, the ongoing operating costs also are high, due to the use of expensive, private VANs. Another major issue for some companies is that the traditional EDI system is inflexible. For example, it is difficult to make quick changes, such as adding business partners. In addition, an EDI system requires a long start-up period. Further, business processes must sometimes be restructured to fit EDI requirements. Finally, there are many EDI standards in use today. As a result, one company might have to use several standards in order to communicate with different business partners.

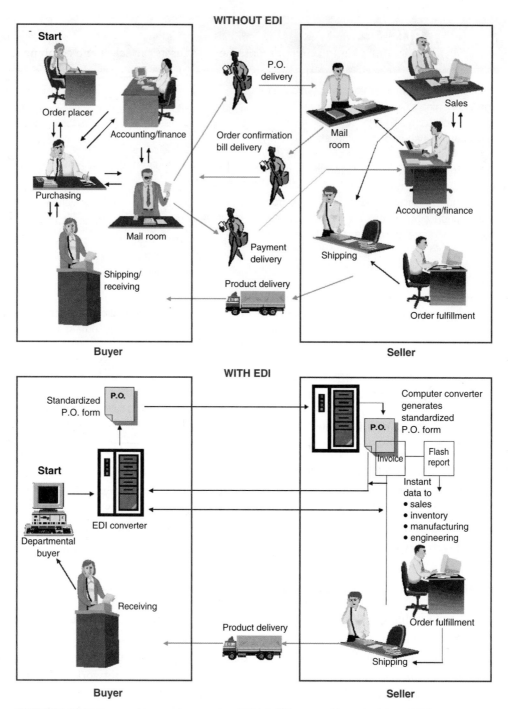

FIGURE 10.3 Comparing purchase order (P.O.) fulfillment with and without EDI.
Source: Drawn by E. Turban.

EDI is especially problematic for small businesses, for several reasons. First, many EDI systems require support from specialized IT experts who spend an inordinate amount of time fine-tuning the data-exchange process. This requirement places the costs of implementing EDI beyond the reach of many smaller organizations. Another problem for smaller organizations arises if their larger supply chain partners mandated that all participants in their supply chains invest in and use EDI technology. Thus, smaller organizations must either adopt EDI technology, regardless of the cost, or lose significant business partners.

Despite these complications, EDI remains popular, particularly among major business partners, though it is being replaced by XML-based web services.

Web Services

Web services are applications, delivered over the Internet, that users can select and combine through almost any device, from personal computers to mobile phones. By using a set of shared protocols and standards, these applications permit different systems to "talk" with one another—that is, share data and services—without requiring human beings to translate the conversations.

Web services have great potential because they can be used in a variety of environments: over the Internet, on an intranet inside a corporate firewall, or on an extranet set up by business partners. Web services perform a wide variety of tasks, from automating business processes to integrating components of an enterprise-wide system to streamlining on-line buying and selling.

Closely related to web services is the concept of **service-oriented architecture (SOA)**, which is an IT architecture that makes it possible to construct business applications using web services. The web services can be reused across an organization in other applications and with business partners. The following example shows the value of web services and SOA at Sears Canada.

EXAMPLE 10.1

Sears Canada is a $6-billion firm with 33,000 employees, 122 company-owned stores, 176 dealer stores, 64 home improvement showrooms, over 1,800 catalogue merchandise pick-up locations, 106 Sears Travel offices, and a nationwide maintenance, repair, and installation network. Sears department stores sell a broad range of merchandise from apparel and home fashions to appliances. In addition to the traditional brick-and-mortar stores, Sears also sells through catalogue and Internet ordering.

Since the arrival of the Internet, the retail market for consumer goods has undergone tremendous changes. As a result, consumers have higher expectations than ever before for high quality merchandise, a broad selection of brands, and good deals, no matter where they shop. To be successful, Sears Canada needed to ensure that all of its sales channels—stores, catalogue, and on-line—were fully stocked with the right mix of merchandise. Thus, the exchange of information across all of the company's business partners and suppliers was of critical importance to the business.

Specifically, the company needed to exchange product information such as sizes, colours, and other product attributes between its 3,000 suppliers and its internal database systems. However, this task presented a number of challenges for its existing information systems infrastructure. Sears Canada operated a combination of legacy systems and multiple applications running across several operating systems that caused unnecessary complexity, duplicated the development of applications, and posed an obstacle to the company's ability to respond quickly to customers' needs and tastes. The company wanted to develop a more efficient and cost-effective approach by developing software that could be reused in other parts of the business.

Sears Canada wanted to avoid developing a new and distinctive network connection for each supplier the company needed to exchange product information with. Instead, the organization restructured its existing information systems into its new service-oriented architecture (SOA) so it could integrate its internal and external business systems and respond more quickly to customers' needs.

Sears Canada selected the IBM WebSphere software product as the basis for its new supplier network web service application. The initial plan was to pilot the new supplier web service application with one supplier and roll it out to the rest of the network once it was clear that it could deliver the product information needed, when needed, and in the format needed at a reasonable cost.

The first benefit for Sears was the time saved spent in retyping and scanning the data each time information was updated and, with a network of over 3,000 suppliers, this was one of the most attractive cost savings. Sears estimated that between 5 to 15 percent of its software code was suitable for reuse and calculated that the effort would deliver an attractive payback even at a seemingly low 5 percent level of reuse. A new connection with a supplier can now be set up in a matter of minutes. Overall, Sears Canada estimates a payback period for the new infrastructure as between two to three years.

Sources: Compiled from "Sears Canada Increases Code Reuse by 5%–15% with SOA solution," IBM case study, April 30, 2009; "SOA Helps Sears Canada Keep Pace with Change," IBM case study, December 18, 2009; Sears Canada website (*www.sears.ca*), accessed February 10, 2010.

FIGURE 10.4
The structure of
an extranet.

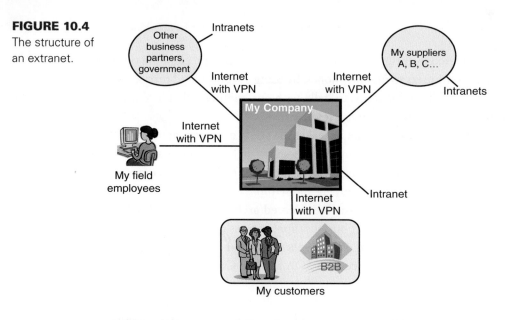

FIGURE 10.4
The structure of an extranet.

Extranets

To implement IOSs and SCM systems, a company must connect the intranets of its various business partners to create extranets. As we have discussed in previous chapters, extranets link business partners to one another over the Internet by providing access to certain areas of one another's corporate intranets (see Figure 10.4).

The primary goal of extranets is to foster collaboration between and among business partners. An extranet is open to selected B2B suppliers, customers, and other business partners. These individuals access the extranet through the Internet. Extranets enable people who are located outside a company to work together with the company's internally located employees. An extranet also allows external business partners to enter the corporate intranet, via the Internet, to access data, place orders, check the status of those orders, communicate, and collaborate. It also enables partners to perform self-service activities such as checking inventory levels.

Extranets use virtual private network (VPN) technology to make communication over the Internet more secure. The Internet-based extranet is far less costly than proprietary networks. It is a non-proprietary technical tool that can support the rapid evolution of electronic communication and commerce. The major benefits of extranets are faster processes and information flow, improved order entry and customer service, lower costs (for example, for communications, travel, and administrative overhead), and an overall improvement in business effectiveness.

Types of Extranets

There are three major types of extranets. Companies choose a particular type depending on the business partners involved and the purpose of the supply chain. We discuss each type below, along with its major business applications.

A Company and Its Dealers, Customers, or Suppliers. This type of extranet is centred around a single company. An example is the FedEx extranet that allows customers to track the status of a delivery. To do so, customers use the Internet to access a database on the FedEx intranet. By enabling a customer to check the location of a package, FedEx saves the cost of having a human operator perform that task over the phone.

An Industry's Extranet. Just as a single company can set up an extranet, the major players in an industry can team up to create an extranet that will benefit all of them. IT's About Business 10.4 relates the case of the GS1 Canada web portal (*www.gs1ca.org*), which enables companies to collaborate effectively in the case of a product recall through a network that provides a secure medium for B2B information exchange.

IT'S ABOUT BUSINESS 10.4
EXTRANET FOR PRODUCT RECALLS HELPS CANADIAN MANUFACTURERS AND RETAILERS

In August 2008, Maple Leaf Foods Ltd. had to recall some of its products after they were linked to a listeriosis outbreak in one of its manufacturing plants. One of the challenges that Maple Leaf Foods had at that time was identifying which retailers had bought contaminated products and how to communicate with them to handle the product recall.

In response to this and other recent product recall events, GS1 Canada, a not-for-profit supply chain standards organization, launched in 2010 a pilot web-based product recall system to allow manufacturers to inform retailers any time there is a health or safety issue with one of its products.

The web-based system, available at first to retailers on a trial basis, will provide retailers with rapid access to important information regarding manufacturers' product recalls, such as how to handle defective or contaminated products and how they would get reimbursed from manufacturers. The bilingual system allows both manufacturers and retailers to interact and communicate in the event of a product recall.

The system is not designed to replace the current Canadian Food Inspection Agency product notification process, but it is intended to complement it by providing retailers with detailed information and instructions about how to go about the product recall. Specifically, in the case of a product recall, a manufacturer would first need to authenticate and

then fill out an on-line form with product information and the reason for the recall. Then a screenshot of the form would be sent by e-mail to all retailers carrying that product. Retailers can also access the system and report back to the manufacturer as to how many potential harmful products they had and how many have been taken from the shelves. Manufacturers can also view a report of how many e-mailed retailers have read the recall e-mail, giving them a sense of the status of the product recall process.

Sources: Compiled from K. Lau, "GS1 Canada Web Portal to Hasten Product Recall," *ComputerWorld Canada*, November 3, 2009; K. Owram, "Meat Scandal Fallout Eases for Maple Leaf Foods," *Toronto Star*, February 24, 2009; GS1 Canada website (*www.gs1ca.org*), accessed May 4, 2010.

QUESTIONS
1. Why is it so important for manufacturers to trace their products in the supply chain?
2. Could upstream members in the supply chain such as suppliers of meat manufacturers benefit from the GS1 Canada product recall website? Why or why not?
3. Why do you think GS1 Canada selected the use of web technology for its product recall service?
4. Do more research about product traceability and find out what other information technology innovations are used to trace products along the supply chain.

Joint Ventures and Other Business Partnerships. In this type of extranet, the partners in a joint venture use the extranet as a vehicle for communications and collaboration. An example is the Bank of America's extranet for commercial loans. The partners involved in making these loans include a lender, a loan broker, and a title company. The extranet connects lenders, loan applicants, and the loan organizer, the Bank of America. A similar example is Lending Tree (*www.lendingtree.com*), a company that provides mortgage quotes for your home and also sells mortgages on-line. Lending Tree uses an extranet for its business partners (for example, the lenders).

BEFORE YOU GO ON...

1. Define EDI, and list its major benefits and limitations.
2. Explain how web services contribute to supply chain management.
3. Define an extranet, and explain its infrastructure.
4. List and briefly define the major types of extranets.

WHAT'S IN IT FOR ME?

FOR THE ACCOUNTING MAJOR

The cost accountant will play an important role in developing and monitoring the financial accounting information associated with inventory and cost of goods sold. In a supply chain, much of the data for these accounting requirements will flow into the organization from various partners within the chain. It is up to the chief accountant, the comptroller, or CFO to prepare and review these data.

Going further, accounting rules and regulations and the cross-border transfer of data are critical for global trade. IOSs can facilitate such trade. Other issues that are important for accountants are taxation and government reports. In addition, creating information systems that rely on EDI requires the attention of accountants. Finally, fraud detection in global settings (for example, transfers of funds) can be facilitated by appropriate controls and auditing.

FOR THE FINANCE MAJOR

In a supply chain, the finance major will be responsible for analyzing the data created and shared among supply chain partners. In many instances, the financial analyst will assume the responsibility for recommending actions to improve supply chain efficiencies and cash flow. This may benefit all the partners in the chain. These recommendations will be based on the development of financial models that incorporate key assumptions such as supply chain partner agreements for pricing. Through the use of extensive financial modelling, the financial analyst helps to manage liquidity in the supply chain.

Many finance-related issues exist in implementing IOSs. For one thing, establishing EDI and extranet relationships involves structuring payment agreements. Global supply chains may involve complex financial arrangements, which may have legal implications.

FOR THE MARKETING MAJOR

A tremendous amount of useful sales information can be derived from supply chain partners through the supporting information systems. For example, many of the customer support activities take place in the downstream portion of the supply chain. For the marketing manager, an understanding of how the downstream activities of the supply chain relate to prior chain operations is critical.

Furthermore, tremendous amounts of data are fed from the supply-chain–supporting information systems into the CRM systems that are used by marketers. The information and a complete understanding of its genesis is vital for mixed-model marketing programs.

FOR THE PRODUCTION/OPERATIONS MANAGEMENT MAJOR

The production/operations management major plays a crucial role in the supply chain development process. In many organizations, the production/operations management staff may even lead the supply chain integration process because of their extensive knowledge of the manufacturing components of the organization. Because they are in charge of the procurement, production, materials control, and logistical handling, a comprehensive understanding of the techniques of SCM is vital for the production/operations staff.

The downstream segment of supply chains is where marketing, distribution channels, and customer service are conducted. An understanding of how downstream activities are related to the other segments is critical. Supply chain problems can reduce customer satisfaction and negate marketing efforts. It is essential, then, that marketing professionals understand the nature of such problems and their solutions. Also, learning about CRM, its options, and its implementation is important for designing effective customer services and advertising.

As competition intensifies globally, finding new global markets becomes critical. Use of IOSs provides an opportunity to improve marketing and sales. Understanding the capabilities of these technologies and their implementation issues will enable the marketing department to excel.

FOR THE HUMAN RESOURCES MANAGEMENT MAJOR

Supply chains require interactions among employees from partners in the chain. These interactions are the responsibility of the human resources manager. The HR manager must be able to address supply chain issues that relate to staffing, job descriptions, job rotations, and accountability. All of these areas are complex within a supply chain and require the HR function to understand the relationship among partners as well as the movement of resources.

Preparing and training employees to work with business partners (frequently in foreign countries) requires knowledge about how IOSs operate. Sensitivity to cultural differences and extensive communication and collaboration can be facilitated with IT.

FOR THE MIS MAJOR

The MIS staff will be instrumental in the design and support of information systems—both internal and inter-organizational—to underpin the business processes that are part of the supply chain. In this capacity, the MIS staff must have a concise knowledge of the business, the systems, and points of intersection between the two.

SUMMARY

1. **Describe the structure of a supply chain.**
   A supply chain refers to the flow of materials, information, money, and services from raw material suppliers, through factories and warehouses, to the end customers. A supply chain involves three segments: upstream, where sourcing or procurement from external suppliers occurs; internal, where packaging, assembly, or manufacturing takes place; and downstream, where distribution takes place, frequently by external distributors.

2. **Identify various problems that can occur along supply chains and possible solutions to them.**
   Friction can develop within a supply chain. The consequences of friction include poor customer service, late deliveries of products and services, poor-quality products and services, high inventory costs, and loss of revenues. Another problem with supply chains is the bullwhip effect, which refers to erratic shifts in orders up and down the supply chain. Finally, incorrect business models can cause problems with supply chains.

3. **Explain what a supply chain management system and related technologies are.**
   Supply chain management (SCM) systems support the activities of planning, organizing, and optimizing the activities performed along the supply chain. SCM-related technologies include electronic data interchange (EDI), web services, and extranets. EDI is a communication standard that enables the electronic transfer of routine documents, such as purchasing orders, between business partners. Web services are self-contained, self-describing applications, delivered over the Internet, that users can select and combine through almost any device (from personal computers to mobile phones). Extranets are networks that link business partners to one another over the Internet by providing access to certain areas of one another's corporate intranets.

KEY TERMS

DISCUSSION QUESTIONS

1. List and explain the important components of a supply chain.
2. Refer to IT's About Business 10.2 about OfficeMax. Draw the supply chain for OfficeMax. Label the upstream, internal, and downstream components.
3. Explain how a supply chain approach may be part of a company's overall strategy.
4. Explain the role that information systems play in supporting a supply chain strategy.
5. Would Rolls-Royce Motorcars (*www.rolls-roycemotorcars.com*) use a push model or a pull model in its supply chain? Support your answer.
6. Why is planning so important in supply chain management?
7. Differentiate between EDI and extranets.

PROBLEM-SOLVING ACTIVITIES

1. Go to a bank and find out the process and steps of obtaining a mortgage for a house. Draw the supply chain.

2. GXS (*www.gxs.com*) is one of the largest providers of EDI services worldwide. Review what EDI products it provides and prepare a report. Would a small company be able to implement these solutions? Prepare a report with your analysis.

3. Enter Teradata University Network (*http://academicprograms.teradata.com/tun/*) and find the podcasts that deal with supply chains (by Jill Dyche). Identify the benefits cited in the podcasts.

4. Access *www.ups.com* and *www.fedex.com*. Examine some of the IT-supported customer services and tools provided by the two companies. Write a report on how the two companies contribute to supply chain improvements.

5. Enter *http://supply-chain.org, www.cio.com, www.findarticles.com*, and *www.google.com* and search for recent information on supply chain management.

TEAM ASSIGNMENTS

1. Each group in the class will be assigned to a major supply chain management vendor, such as SAP, Oracle, i2, and IBM. Each group will investigate topics such as: (a) the products; (b) major capabilities; (c) relationship to customer relationship management; and (d) customer success stories. Each group will prepare a presentation for the class, trying to convince the class why that group's software product is best.

2. Have each team locate several organizations that use IOSs, including one with a global reach. Students should contact the companies to find what IOS technology support they use (for example, an EDI, extranet, web services). Then find out what issues they faced in implementation. Prepare a report.

CHRYSLER BENEFITS FROM WEB-BASED EDI

The Canadian Press/Frank Gunn

THE BUSINESS PROBLEM

Chrysler Group, one of the largest auto manufacturers in the world, began in 1925 in Detroit, Michigan. Today, Chrysler counts assembly factories in all five continents and has almost 60,000 employees worldwide.

Chrysler has a longstanding commitment to using information technologies to communicate with its business partners, especially with suppliers. For example, in the 1990s Chrysler made it mandatory for high-volume suppliers (those that submitted more than 30 invoices a month) to use electronic data interchange (EDI) to send purchase orders and invoices. The initiative turned out to be a success and it contributed to reducing the amount of time that it took to process purchase orders with high-volume suppliers.

However, most of Chrysler's suppliers are small and medium enterprises with low volume transactions, which could not afford the set-up costs of EDI. Thus, processing purchase orders and invoices from small suppliers was still a paper-based and mail process that took several weeks. For example, it used to take a document sent by mail two weeks to reach the Chrysler Group's Canadian suppliers. Chrysler had to find a solution that could accommodate the company's needs and be affordable enough that it would ensure adoption by small suppliers.

THE IT SOLUTION

Chrysler found a solution by developing a web-based exchange portal in partnership with GXS, a company that specializes in providing IT solutions to trading partners. The new web-based system would allow Chrysler's low-volume suppliers to send their purchase orders, invoices, and other business documents using EDI technology. Chrysler's small suppliers would only be required to have a personal computer and an Internet connection to access the GXS portal.

THE RESULTS

Chrysler has benefited greatly since it introduced the exchange portal for small suppliers. The company has saved millions of dollars each year in costs related to the processing of purchase orders, invoices, and other trading documents. Invoices and purchase orders can now be transmitted in a matter of minutes instead of several weeks if the partner was located in a different country. The new system has also improved the accuracy of information.

Suppliers have also benefited from the new technology. For example, payments from the Chrysler Group are now processed within one month instead of several months, and the follow-up time of invoices with errors (incorrect number of parts, wrong account number, etc.) has been reduced. All of this has contributed to improve the relationship between Chrysler and its suppliers.

Sources: Compiled from the Chrysler Group website (*www.chryslergroupllc.com*), accessed May 7, 2010; "Chrysler Group, LLC," GXS case studies, *www.gxs.com*, accessed May 7, 2010.

QUESTIONS

1. Should a company ensure connectivity with larger supply chain partners at the risk of losing connectivity with smaller supply chain partners? Support your answer.
2. Sometimes the use of communication technologies between trading partners is imposed by the larger partner. Discuss this situation from the perspective of the supplier and the manufacturer.
3. What other business documents could be transferred using EDI? Indicate the types of business documents and business partners (e.g., supplier, government agency, customer).

CASE 10.2

Web Resources

Student website www.wiley.com/canada/rainer

- Web quizzes
- Lecture slides in PowerPoint

- Author podcasts
- Interactive Case: Ruby's Club assignments

ALL OF THE ABOVE AND...

- E-book
- Manager videos
- Vocabulary flash cards

- Pre- and post-lecture quizzes
- Microsoft Office 2007 lab manual and projects

CREATING SUPPLY CHAIN MANAGEMENT SOLUTIONS FOR RUBY'S CLUB

ruby's club

Go to the Ruby's Club link at the Student Companion website or WileyPLUS for information about your current internship assignment. You will help Ruby's managers build a better forecast for purchasing food and drinks using past data.

11

MANAGERIAL SUPPORT SYSTEMS

LEARNING OBJECTIVES

1. Describe the concepts of management, decision making, and computerized support for decision making.

2. Describe business intelligence systems, including multi-dimensional data analysis, data mining, and decision support systems and digital dashboards.

3. Describe data visualization, including geographical information systems and virtual reality.

4. Describe artificial intelligence, including expert systems, natural language processing, and neural networks.

BLUE MOUNTAIN RESORTS PUT BUSINESS INTELLIGENCE TO WORK

CASE 11.1

THE BUSINESS PROBLEM

Canada's third-busiest ski resort, and Ontario's largest mountain resort, is Blue Mountain Resorts (*www. bluemountain.ca*), located near Collingwood. More than a million people visit each winter. Open year-round, Blue Mountain also has a conference centre, mountain-biking trails, gondolas, tennis courts, and a golf course. It has more than 1,000 employees.

In 1999, Blue Mountain became part of the large Intrawest (*www.intrawest.com*) resort chain when the Vancouver-based publicly held company bought a 50 percent interest in Blue Mountain. The new owners wanted improved financial information for the resort's 13 lines of business, including accommodations, restaurants, call centres, and ticketing.

Previously, Blue Mountain used a spreadsheet to keep track of financial information, but the system was not keeping up. Further, the information technology (IT) department consisted of only three people, none of whom was responsible for updating and maintaining the old system. The IT department had to wait for each business segment to report its own information because the financial system was not automated.

To achieve the necessary efficiency in reporting, Blue Mountain implemented a business intelligence and financial performance management system. The system had to be able to analyze labour costs and revenue with minimal effort. To perform this task, it needed to collect and integrate data from different sources and types of applications. In addition, because Blue Mountain had only three IT people, the new system had to be very easy to install and maintain.

THE IT SOLUTION

Blue Mountain investigated several business intelligence and performance management systems and chose IBM Cognos TM1. The resort uses the software's standard features for budgeting, forecasting, planning, reporting, and analysis, as well as modules designed specifically for the hospitality industry. Thus, it required minimal customization, making it quick and cost-effective to implement. The package also has on-line analytical processing (OLAP) capability, explained in Section 11.2.

Blue Mountain implemented the system separately in each particular seasonal business as that business opened. Because the resort attracts large numbers of guests during peak seasons, it deployed the system first in its lodging division. The IT staff could use data in the old system to build the new one. A new data warehouse contains historical data, reservation information, weather information, and staff schedules so managers can do a thorough analysis. Once Blue Mountain concluded that the installation had been successful, it implemented the system across the hospitality, retail, ski, golf, and food and beverage departments as well.

Sources: Compiled from "Blue Mountain Resort Scales Large Amounts of Data for Better Customer Service to Resort Guests," *Financial Services Technology*, January 13, 2009; "Blue Mountain," IBM Success Case Study, *www.ibm.com*, November 24, 2008; J. Gowers, "Ski Resort Gets a Life from Business Intelligence," *Baseline Magazine*, July 30, 2008; "ROI Case Study: IBM Cognos TM1—Blue Mountain Resorts," Nucleus Research case study, May 2008; L. Tucci, "Business Intelligence Lifts Revenue at Ontario Ski Resort," SearchCIO.com, February 20, 2007; Blue Mountain website (*www.bluemountain.ca*), accessed January 15, 2009.

WHAT DO YOU THINK?

1. Why is it neccessary for businesses to measure and track their performance?
2. How important is data management for business intelligence applications? Explain your answer.
3. What areas of a business can business intelligence software be applied to?
4. What type of business problems can business intelligence software assist with?

Chapter Preview

The Blue Mountain Resorts case illustrates the importance and far-reaching nature of business intelligence (BI) applications. BI applications enable decision makers to quickly ascertain the status of a business enterprise by looking at key performance indicators. Blue Mountain managers needed current, timely, and accurate information that they were not receiving from their old system. Implementing the BI applications produced significant benefits throughout the company, supporting important decisions across Blue Mountain's lines of business.

This chapter describes information systems that support managerial decision makers. We begin by reviewing the manager's job and the nature of today's decisions. This discussion will help you to understand why managers need computerized support. We follow by presenting the concepts of business intelligence for supporting individuals, groups, and entire organizations. Next we turn our attention to data visualization technologies, which help decision makers make sense out of vast amounts of data. Finally, we conclude the chapter by examining several types of intelligent systems and their role in supporting managerial decision making.

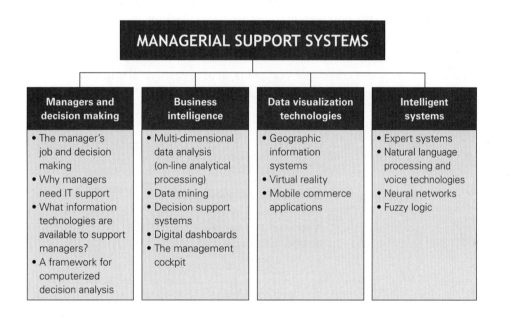

11.1 Managers and Decision Making

Management is a process by which an organization achieves its goals through the use of resources (people, money, energy, materials, information, space, and time). These resources are considered *inputs*. Achieving the organization's goals is the *output* of the process. Managers oversee this process in an attempt to optimize it. A manager's success is often measured by the ratio between inputs and outputs for which he or she is responsible. This ratio is an indication of the organization's **productivity**.

The Manager's Job and Decision Making

To appreciate how information systems support managers, we must first understand the manager's job. Managers do many things, depending on their position in the organization, the type and size of the organization, organizational policies and culture, and the personalities of the managers themselves.

Despite this variety, all managers have three basic roles (according to Canadian academic Henry Mintzberg):

1. *Interpersonal roles*: figurehead, leader, liaison
2. *Informational roles*: monitor, disseminator, spokesperson, analyzer
3. *Decisional roles*: entrepreneur, disturbance handler, resource allocator, negotiator

Early information systems primarily supported the informational roles. In recent years, information systems have been developed that support all three roles. In this chapter, we focus on the support that IT can provide for decisional roles.

A *decision* refers to a choice that individuals and groups make among two or more alternatives. Decisions are diverse and are made continuously. Decision making is a systematic process. Economist Herbert Simon described (in 1977) the process as being composed of three major phases: *intelligence*, *design*, and *choice*. Figure 11.1 illustrates this three-stage process, indicating which tasks are included in each phase. Note that there is a continuous flow of information from intelligence to design to choice (bold lines), but at any phase there may be a return to a previous phase (broken lines).

The decision-making process starts with the *intelligence phase*, in which managers examine a situation and identify and define the problem. In the *design phase*, decision makers construct a **model** that simplifies the problem. They do this by making assumptions that simplify reality and by expressing the relationships among all the relevant variables. Managers then validate the model by using test data. Finally, decision makers set criteria for evaluating all of the potential solutions that are proposed. The *choice phase* involves selecting a solution, which is tested "on paper." Once this proposed solution

FIGURE 11.1
The process and phases in decision making.

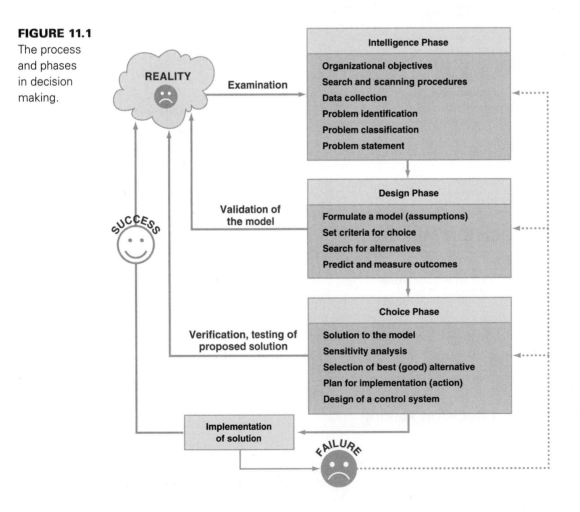

seems to be feasible, the decision is implemented. Implementation is successful if the proposed solution actually resolves the problem. If the solution fails, the process returns to the previous phases. Computer-based decision support attempts to automate several tasks in the decision-making process, in which modelling is the core.

Why Managers Need IT Support

It is difficult to make good decisions without valid and relevant information. Information is vital for each phase and activity in the decision-making process. Despite the widespread availability of information, making decisions is becoming increasingly difficult due to the following trends:

- The *number of alternatives* to be considered is constantly *increasing*, due to innovations in technology, improved communications, the development of global markets, and the use of the Internet and e-business. A key to good decision making is to explore and compare many relevant alternatives. The more alternatives that exist, the more a decision maker needs computer-assisted search and comparisons.
- Most decisions must be made *under time pressure*. It is often not possible to process information manually fast enough to be effective.
- Due to increased uncertainty in the decision environment, decisions are becoming more complex. It is usually necessary to *conduct a sophisticated analysis* in order to make a good decision. Such analysis requires the use of modelling.
- It is often necessary to rapidly access remote information, consult with experts, or conduct a group decision-making session, all without incurring large expenses. Both decision makers and information can be in different locations. Bringing them all together quickly and inexpensively can be a difficult task.

The following example also provides some insight into why good managers still make bad decisions.

EXAMPLE 11.1

Why is it that good leaders make bad decisions? Why did Daimler-Benz CEO Jürgen Schrempp decide to merge Chrysler and Daimler and then sell it for almost nothing nine years later? Why did top government officials in the United States decide not to react to the Hurricane Katrina disaster even when reports alerted them of the vast destruction happening? These are just two examples of top executives highly qualified for their positions but who end up making the wrong decisions.

In 2009, Andrew Campbell and co-authors Jo Whitehead and Sydney Finkelstein wrote an article in *Harvard Business Review* analyzing why managers may end up making bad decisions. The heart of the matter, according to the authors, lies in a few key factors. The first one is pattern recognition. Managers could make bad decisions because they assign the same cause to a similar problem. For example, if an IT executive is trying to resolve some problem that

happened before and software was the source of it, he will again see the software as the problem if the same or similar symptoms are around. There is likely to be a bias.

The second factor for making bad decisions is what the authors call "emotional tagging." This means that a manager's experiences and thoughts are engraved in their memory alongside with the emotions they experienced. For example, if an IT manager had a very good experience with a new enterprise resource planning (ERP) project, then he will have a strong emotional tag toward ERP systems.

In addition, managers should also consider three "red flag" conditions—self-interest, distorting attachments, and misleading memories—and implement checks and balances in the decision-making process. For example, consider the case of an IT manager who has championed a project for six months but the project has now lost its attractiveness to the organization

(Continued on next page)

EXAMPLE *(Continued)*

and she is considering abandoning it. All three red flag conditions are present as she makes her decision. Because of her commitment to the project, the IT manager has misleading memories because in the past she decided the project was a good idea, and she also has a distorting attachment and potential interest because of the negative consequences for

her and those dependant on her of this decision; for example, the loss of jobs and reputation.

Sources: Compiled from A. Campbell, J. Whitehead, and S. Finkelstein, "Why Good Leaders Make Bad Decisions," *Harvard Business Review*, February 2009, Volume 87, issue 2, pp. 60–66; K. Melymuka, "Why Good Leaders Make Bad Decisions," *Computerworld*, February 16, 2009.

These trends and factors create major difficulties for decision makers. Fortunately, as we will see throughout this chapter, a computerized analysis can be of enormous help.

What Information Technologies Are Available to Support Managers?

In addition to discovery, communication, and collaboration tools (Chapter 5) that provide indirect support to decision making, several other information technologies have been successfully used to support managers. As we noted earlier, these technologies are collectively referred to as **business intelligence (BI) systems** and intelligent systems. These systems and their variants can be used independently, or they can be combined, with each one providing a different capability. They are frequently related to data warehousing (discussed in Chapter 4). We now address additional aspects of decision making to put our discussion of these systems in context. We look first at the different types of decisions that managers face.

A Framework for Computerized Decision Analysis

To better understand BI and intelligent systems, we classify decisions along two major dimensions: problem structure and the nature of the decision (according to the 1971 work of A. Gorry and M. S. Scott Morton). Figure 11.2 provides an overview of decision making along these two dimensions.

Type of Decision	Operational Control	Management Control	Strategic Planning	Support Needed
Structured	Accounts receivable, order entry [1]	Budget analysis, short-term forecasting, personnel reports, make-or-buy analysis [2]	Financial management (investment), warehouse location, distribution systems [3]	MIS, management science models, financial and statistical models
Semistructured	Production scheduling, inventory control [4]	Credit evaluation, budget preparation, plant layout, project scheduling, reward systems design [5]	Building new plant, mergers and acquisitions, new product planning, compensation planning, quality assurance planning [6]	Decision support systems (DSS)
Unstructured	Selecting a cover for a magazine, buying software, approving loans [7]	Negotiating, recruiting an executive, buying hardware, lobbying [8]	R & D planning, new technology development, social responsibility planning [9]	DSS Expert systems (ES) neural networks
Support Needed	MIS, management science	Management science, DSS, business intelligence (BI), ES	BI, ES, neural networks	

FIGURE 11.2 Decision support framework. Technology is used to support the decisions shown in the column at the far right and in the bottom row.

Problem Structure

The first dimension is *problem structure.* Decision-making processes fall along a continuum ranging from highly structured to highly unstructured decisions (see the left column in Figure 11.2.). *Structured decisions* involve routine and repetitive problems for which standard solutions exist, such as inventory control. In a structured problem, the three phases of the decision process—intelligence, design, and choice—are laid out in a particular sequence, and the procedures for obtaining the best (or at least a good enough) solution are known. Two basic criteria that are used to evaluate proposed solutions are minimizing costs and maximizing profits.

A factory worker with a bar code reader maintaining stocks of finished products in a warehouse.

At the other extreme of problem complexity are *unstructured decisions.* These are "fuzzy," complex problems for which there are no cut-and-dried solutions. An unstructured problem is one in which intelligence, design, and choice are not organized in a particular sequence. In such a problem, human intuition often plays an important role in making the decision. Typical unstructured problems include planning new service offerings, hiring an executive, and choosing a set of research and development (R&D) projects for the coming year.

Located between structured and unstructured problems are *semistructured* problems, in which only some of the decision process phases are structured. Semistructured problems require a combination of standard solution procedures and individual judgement. Examples of semistructured problems are evaluating employees, setting marketing budgets for consumer products, performing capital acquisition analysis, and trading bonds.

The Nature of Decisions

The second dimension of decision support deals with the *nature of decisions.* We can define three broad categories that encompass all managerial decisions:

1. *Operational control*—executing specific tasks efficiently and effectively
2. *Management control*—acquiring and using resources efficiently in accomplishing organizational goals
3. *Strategic planning*—the long-range goals and policies for growth and resource allocation

These categories are shown along the top row of Figure 11.2.

The Decision Matrix

The three primary classes of problem structure and the three broad categories of the nature of decisions can be combined in a decision-support matrix that consists of nine cells, as shown in Figure 11.2. Lower-level managers usually perform the structured and operational control-oriented tasks (cells 1, 2, and 4). The tasks in cells 3, 5, and 7 are usually the responsibility of middle managers and professional staff. Finally, tasks in cells 6, 8, and 9 are generally carried out by senior executives.

Computer Support for Structured Decisions

Computer support for the nine cells in the matrix is shown in the right-hand column and the bottom row of Figure 11.2. Structured and some semistructured decisions, especially of the operational and management control type, have been supported by computers since the 1950s. Decisions of this type are made in all functional areas, but particularly in finance and operations management.

Problems that lower-level managers encounter on a regular basis typically have a high level of structure. Examples are capital budgeting (for example, replacement of equipment), allocating resources, distributing merchandise, and controlling inventory. For each type of structured decision, prescribed solutions have been developed through the use of mathematical formulas. This approach is called *management science* or *operations research*, and it is also executed with the aid of computers.

As we have noted, business intelligence systems support managerial decision making. There is a variety of business intelligence systems and we discuss them in detail in the next section.

BEFORE YOU GO ON ...

1. Describe the decision-making process proposed by Simon.
2. Why do managers need IT support?
3. Describe the decision matrix.

11.2 Business Intelligence

Once an organization has captured data and organized them into databases, data warehouses, and data marts, it can use the data for further analysis (see Figure 11.3). **Business intelligence (BI)** refers to applications and technologies for consolidating, analyzing, and providing access to vast amounts of data to help users make better business and strategic decisions. BI applications provide historical, current, and predictive views of business operations.

Many vendors offer integrated packages of these tools under the overall name of business intelligence software. Major BI software packages include SAS (*www.sas.com*), Hyperion (*www.oracle.com/hyperion/index.html*), SAP Business Objects (*www.businessobjects.com*), IBM Cognos (*www-01.ibm.com/software/data/cognos/*), and SPSS Inc. (*www.spss.com*).

In an overall sense, organizations are using BI applications to improve their performance in a number of different ways. For example, in our opening case the IBM Cognos TM1 system benefited Blue Mountain across all lines of business, particularly customer service, retail, hospitality, and lodging. The resort enters data in the same way for each line of business. Managers can then use real-time analytics to compare and analyze reports and view each department's performance. The system thus improved reporting by transforming disparate pieces of data into actionable business information.

IBM Cognos TM1 also enabled Blue Mountain to streamline its budgeting process and move away from its legacy spreadsheet model. The marketing team can now view historical data and perform "what-if" analyses against daily revenue reports. For example, if a particular room type is not selling as well in 2010 as it did in 2009, managers can compare the variables that have remained consistent over the years with those variables that have changed. This way they can determine which variables have likely led to decreased sales and why they have done so. They can then use this information to decide whether to update room rates, lower them to last year's rates, or implement a new marketing campaign to give the affected area greater visibility.

As in any resort, staffing accounts for a large part of the resort's operating budget, and managing this line item is essential to the resort's success. Here again, Blue Mountain has benefited from the new

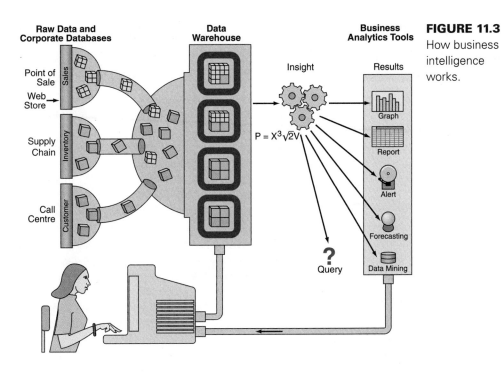

Raw Data and Corporate Databases

Point of Sale

Web Store

Supply Chain

Call Centre

Sales

Inventory

Customer

Data Warehouse

Insight

$P = X^3 \sqrt{2V}$

?
Query

Business Analytics Tools

Results

Graph

Report

Alert

Forecasting

Data Mining

FIGURE 11.3
How business intelligence works.

system. Although the staffing level is set during the budgeting process, the IBM Cognos TM1 system enables managers to adjust the actual staffing levels daily, depending on the weather, the number of presold tickets, the number of arrivals and departures, major conferences, and historic business patterns. If staffing levels exceed budget constraints, overstaffing must be cleared with an area director. This process helps the resort maximize its profits.

Blue Mountain also uses the new system to maintain inventories in its rental shops. For example, the system combines the data from the application that runs the equipment rental shop with the expected number of skiers in a given year to calculate how many boots in each size the resort needs to order.

One final critical area is customer service, which must be responsive and helpful. The guests' first interaction with the resort is through its call centre. With the new system, managers can calculate the number of inbound calls they will receive based on a number of factors, including the time of year, the time of day, proximity to a holiday, and current resort promotions. They then use this information to ensure that the call centre is appropriately staffed every day.

The bottom line for Blue Mountain's new system? The resort is saving $2.5 million per year in labour costs. Even more impressive, the resort maintains that the return on investment for the new system is an amazing 1,829 percent. Finally, it took Blue Mountain only one month to recoup all of the money it spent to acquire and implement the new system.

One specific use of BI applications consists in monitoring and managing an organization's performance according to key performace indicators such as revenue, return on investment, overhead, and operational costs. This area of BI is often called **corporate performance management**. For on-line businesses, corporate performance management includes additional factors such as the number of page views, server load, network traffic, and transactions per second. BI applications allow managers and analysts to analyze data to obtain valuable information and insights concerning the organization's key performace indicators. IT's About Business 11.1 shows how performance management software helps managers at Sharp Corporation.

There are two basic types of business intelligence applications: (1) those that provide data analysis tools (multi-dimensional data analysis, data mining, and decision support systems), and (2) those that provide easily accessible information in a structured format (digital dashboards).

IT'S ABOUT BUSINESS 11.1
CORPORATE PERFORMANCE MANAGEMENT AT SHARP CORPORATION

Founded in Japan by Tokuji Hayakawa in 1912, Sharp Corporation is a leading company employing 55,000 people worldwide and sales of over $29 billion annually. Sharp manufactures a wide range of electronics such as LCD and plasma TVs, 3G phones, computer monitors, and calculators, both for consumers and businesses.

Innovation is the single most important factor for businesses like Sharp to remain competitive in the electronics market. One of the ways for Sharp to quickly respond to market changes is by continuously providing managers with current and on-time information. Until recently, managers at Sharp had to sort through mountains of tabulated data they were given on manufacturing, sales, and inventory in a spreadsheet form, which sometimes were already a month old. This way of performance measurement was very inefficient and ineffective to identify current changes in customer preferences and trends.

In order to improve the way information was getting to managers, Sharp implemented a new data warehouse and IBM's Business Warehouse Accelerator solution. As a consequence, database search times have been drastically reduced and are now running as much as 30 times faster and query processing speed is now a thousand times faster. This has meant up-to-date information for managers instead of the month-old data they were used to.

Sharp also wanted the data to be presented to management in a way that was meaningful, especially to senior management. Therefore, Sharp installed large LCD screens in the president's room and the directors' office. The screens track key performance indicators in critical business areas such as sales, production, and inventory, and the data are updated daily at 7:00 am. This new "management cockpit" (explained in the section The Management Cockpit below) also has an alert system to immediately warn management when key performance indicators reach a certain level; for example, if sales drop below a certain value or if inventory costs exceed a set limit. Currently, the cockpit rooms can be accessed by 130 managers and 100 staff and are intended to provide them, using a simple graphical user interface, with quick current and reliable information for decision making.

Sources: "Sharp Brings Daily Reports to Life with IBM Systems Solution for SAP NetWeaver BW Accelerator," IBM case study, November 19, 2009; Sharp website (*http://sharp-world.com*), accessed May 11, 2010.

QUESTIONS

1. What characteristcs should business intelligence technology have if it is to be used in corporate performance management? Discuss issues around data, technology, and management.
2. Visit the websites of some of the leading business intelligence software applications and prepare a table listing the benefits that they offer to an organization.

Multi-dimensional Data Analysis (On-line Analytical Processing)

Multi-dimensional data analysis or on-line analytical processing (OLAP) is the process of performing complex, multi-dimensional analyses of data stored in a database or data warehouse (recall our discussion of data warehouses in Chapter 4), typically using graphical software tools. Multi-dimensional analysis provides users with an excellent view of what is happening or what has happened. To accomplish this task, multi-dimensional analysis tools allow users to "slice and dice" the data in any desired way. In the data warehouse, relational tables can be linked, forming multi-dimensional data structures, or *cubes*. These cubes can then be "rotated" so that users can view them from different perspectives. Statistical tools provide users with mathematical models that they can apply to the data to gain answers to their queries.

Figure 11.4 uses Figure 4.10 in Chapter 4 to illustrate an example of multi-dimensional data analysis. Assume that a business has organized its sales force by regions—say East, West, and Central. These three regions might then be broken down into provinces. The VP of sales could slice and dice the data cube to see the sales figures for each region (that is, the sales of nuts, screws, bolts, and washers). The VP might then want to see the East region broken down by province so she could evaluate the performance of individual provincial sales managers.

The power of multi-dimensional analysis lies in its ability to analyze the data in such a way that allows users to quickly answer business questions. "How many bolts were sold in the East region in

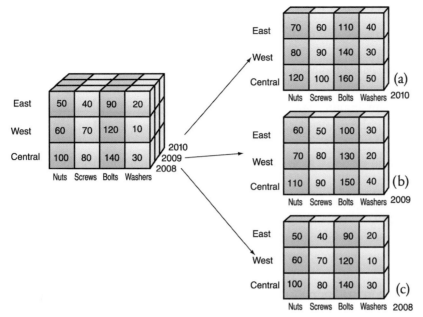

FIGURE 11.4
Multi-dimensional data analysis.

2009?" "What is the trend in the sales of washers in the West region over the past three years?" "Are any of the four products typically purchased together? If so, which ones?"

Data Mining

While multi-dimensional analysis provides users with a view of what is happening, data mining helps to explain why it is happening and it helps to predict what will happen in the future. **Data mining** refers to the process of searching for valuable business information in a large database, data warehouse, or data mart with the intent of identifying a business opportunity in order to create a sustainable competitive advantage. Therefore, data mining can perform two basic operations: (1) predicting trends and behaviours, and (2) identifying previously unknown patterns.

Regarding the first operation, data mining automates the process of finding predictive information in large databases. Questions that traditionally required extensive hands-on analysis can now be answered directly and quickly from the data. A typical example of a predictive problem is *targeted marketing*. Data mining can use data from past promotional mailings to identify people who are most likely to respond favourably to future mailings. Another example of a predictive problem is forecasting bankruptcy and other forms of default.

Data mining can also identify previously hidden patterns. For example, it can analyze retail sales data to discover seemingly unrelated products that are often purchased together.

One interesting pattern-discovery problem is detecting fraudulent credit card transactions. After you use your credit card for a time, a pattern emerges of the typical ways you use your card (for example, where use your card, the amount you spend, and so on). If your card is stolen and used fraudulently, this usage is often different from your pattern of use. Data mining tools can distinguish the difference in the two patterns of use and bring this issue to your attention.

Numerous data mining applications are used in business and in other fields. According to a Gartner, Inc. report (*www.gartner.com*), most of the Fortune 1000 companies worldwide currently use data mining, as the following examples from various industries and fields illustrate.

- *Retailing and sales*: Predicting sales, preventing theft and fraud, and determining correct inventory levels and distribution schedules among outlets.

- *Banking*: Forecasting levels of bad loans and fraudulent credit card use, predicting credit card spending by new customers, and determining which kinds of customers will best respond to (and qualify for) new loan offers.
- *Manufacturing and production*: Predicting machinery failures, and finding key factors that help optimize manufacturing capacity.
- *Insurance*: Forecasting claim amounts and medical coverage costs, classifying the most important elements that affect medical coverage, and predicting which customers will buy new insurance policies.
- *Police work*: Tracking crime patterns, locations, and criminal behaviour; identifying attributes to assist in solving criminal cases.
- *Health care*: Correlating patients' demographics with critical illnesses, and developing better insights on how to identify and treat symptoms and their causes.
- *Marketing*: Classifying customer demographics that can be used to predict which customers will respond to a mailing or buy a particular product.

We can see that there are myriad opportunities to use data mining in organizations.

Decision Support Systems

Decision support systems (DSS) combine models and data in an attempt to solve semistructured and some unstructured problems. As such, DSS are designed to enable business managers and analysts to access data interactively, to manipulate these data, and to conduct appropriate analyses.

DSS can support decisions made by one individual and also decisions that need to be made by a group. Electronic support for a decision-making group is referred to as a *group decision support system (GDSS)* and an *organizational decision support system (ODSS)*. In contrast to a GDSS, which assists a particular group within an organization, an organizational decision support system (ODSS) focuses on an *organizational* task or activity that involves a *sequence* of operations and decision makers. Examples of organizational tasks are capital budgeting and developing a divisional marketing plan. To complete an organizational task successfully, each individual's activities must mesh closely with other people's work. In these tasks, computer support serves primarily as a vehicle for improving communication, coordination, and problem solving.

Decision support systems can contribute to all levels of decision making and typically require extensive involvement on the part of the user. They can also perform a wide range of analyses including sensitivity analysis, what-if analysis, and goal-seeking analysis, which we discuss next.

Sensitivity Analysis

Sensitivity analysis is the study of the impact that changes in one (or more) parts of a decision-making model have on other parts. Most sensitivity analyses examine the impact that changes in input variables have on output variables.

Sensitivity analysis is extremely valuable because it enables the system to adapt to changing conditions and to the varying requirements of different decision-making situations. It provides a better understanding of the model and the problem it purports to describe. It may also increase the users' confidence in the model, especially if it indicates that the model is not very sensitive to changes. A *sensitive model* means that small changes in conditions dictate a different solution. In a *nonsensitive model*, changes in conditions do not significantly change the recommended solution. For this reason the chances for a solution to succeed are much higher in a nonsensitive model than a sensitive one.

What-If Analysis

What-if analysis attempts to predict the impact of a change in the assumptions (input data) on the proposed solution. For example, what will happen to the total inventory cost *if* the originally assumed cost of carrying inventories is not 10 percent but 12 percent? In a well-designed BI system, managers themselves can interactively ask the computer these types of questions as many times as they need to.

Goal-Seeking Analysis

Goal-seeking analysis represents a "backward" solution approach. It attempts to find the value of the inputs necessary to achieve a desired level of output. For example, let's say that an initial solution of a BI system yielded a profit of $2 million. Management may want to know what sales volume and additional advertising would be necessary to generate a profit of $3 million. To find out they would perform a goal-seeking analysis.

Digital Dashboards

Digital dashboards evolved from executive information systems, which were information systems designed specifically for the information needs of top executives. Today, however, all employees, business partners, and customers can use digital dashboards.

A **digital dashboard** (also called an executive dashboard or a management cockpit) provides rapid access to timely information and direct access to management reports. It is very user-friendly and is supported by graphics. Of special importance, it enables managers to examine exception reports and drill-down reports (discussed in Chapter 8). Table 11.1 summarizes capabilities common to many digital dashboards.

TABLE 11.1
THE CAPABILITIES OF DIGITAL DASHBOARDS

CAPABILITY	DESCRIPTION
Drill-down	The ability to go to details, at several levels; can be done by a series of menus or by direct queries (using intelligent agents and natural language processing).
Critical success factor (CSF)	Calculates the factors most critical for the success of business. These can be organizational, industry, departmental, etc.
Key performance indicator (KPI)	Calculates the specific measures of CSFs.
Status access	The latest data available on KPI or some other metric, ideally in real time.
Trend analysis	Short-, medium-, and long-term trend of KPIs or metrics, which are projected using forecasting methods.
Ad-hoc analysis	Analyses made any time, upon demand, and with any desired factors and relationships.
Exception reporting	Reports that highlight deviations larger than certain thresholds. Reports may include only deviations.

In addition, some of the capabilities discussed in this section are now part of many business intelligence products, an example of which is shown in Figure 11.5.

FIGURE 11.5
Sample
performance
dashboard.
Source: Image
courtesy of
Dundas Data
Visualization,
www.dundas.com.

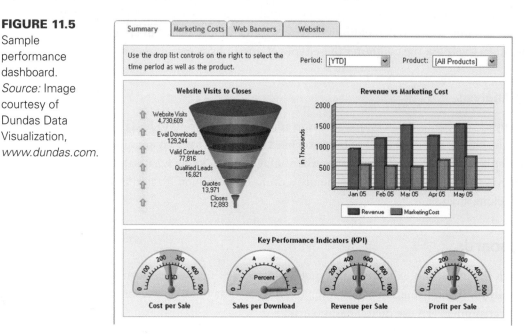

One outstanding example of a digital dashboard is the "Bloomberg." Bloomberg LP (*www.bloomberg.com*), a privately held company, provides a subscription service that sells financial data, software to analyze these data, trading tools, and news (electronic, print, TV, and radio). All of this information is accessible through a colour-coded Bloomberg keyboard that displays the desired information on a computer screen, either your own or one that Bloomberg provides. Users can also set up their own computers to use the service without a Bloomberg keyboard. The subscription service plus the keyboard is called the "Bloomberg" and it represents a do-it-yourself digital dashboard, because users can customize their information feeds as well as the look and feel of those feeds. See Figure 11.6.

FIGURE 11.6
A Bloomberg
terminal.
Source: Carlos
Osorio/Toronto
Star/Zuma Press.

The Management Cockpit

One important application of digital dashboards to support the informational needs of executives is the management cockpit. Essentially, a management cockpit is a strategic management room containing an elaborate set of digital dashboards that enables top-level decision makers to pilot their businesses better. The aim is to create an environment that encourages more efficient management meetings and boosts team performance via effective communication. To help achieve this goal, key performance indicators and information relating to critical success factors are displayed graphically on the walls of a meeting room, called the management cockpit room (see Figure 11.7). The cockpit-like arrangement of instrument panels and displays helps managers grasp how all the different factors in the business interrelate.

FIGURE 11.7
Management Cockpit. The Management Cockpit is a registered trademark of SAP, created by Professor Patrick M. Georges.

Courtesy MAsolutions *(www.ma-solutions.co.uk)*

Within the room, the four walls are designated by colour: black, red, blue, and white. The black wall shows the principal success factors and financial indicators. The red wall measures market performance. The blue wall projects the performance of internal processes and employees. Finally, the white wall indicates the status of strategic projects. The flight deck, a six-screen, high-end PC, enables executives to drill down to detailed information. External information needed for competitive analysis can easily be imported into the room.

Board members and other executives hold meetings in the cockpit room. Managers also meet there with the comptroller to discuss current business issues. For this purpose, the management cockpit can implement various what-if scenarios. It also provides a common basis for information and communication. Finally, it supports efforts to translate a corporate strategy into concrete activities by identifying performance indicators.

BEFORE YOU GO ON …

1. Describe the capabilities of data mining.
2. What are the major differences between a GDSS and an ODSS?
3. What are some of the capabilities of digital dashboards?
4. What is a management cockpit?

11.3 Data Visualization Technologies

After data have been processed, they can be presented to users in visual formats such as text, graphics, and tables. This process, known as data visualization, makes IT applications more attractive and understandable to users. Data visualization is becoming more and more popular on the Web not only for entertainment but also for decision support. A variety of visualization methods and software packages that support decision making are available. The most popular technologies include geographic information systems and virtual reality.

Geographic Information Systems

A **geographic information system (GIS)** is a computer-based system for capturing, integrating, manipulating, and displaying data using digitized maps. Its most distinguishing characteristic is that every record or digital object has an identified geographical location. This process, called *geocoding*, enables users to generate information for planning, problem solving, and decision making. In addition, the graphical format makes it easy for managers to visualize the data.

In 1962, Dr. Roger Tomlinson led the development of the first operational GIS for the Canadian government, called the Canada Geographic Information System (CGIS). The system was used until the 1990s to map rural land use in Canada and to create an inventory of information about land use (for instance, the types of soil, wildlife, and agriculture). Tomlinson spearheaded the use of spatial analysis and complex data analysis for the whole database. The system was mainframe-based and used by Canada's federal and provincial governments.

Today, relatively inexpensive, fully functional PC-based GIS packages are readily available. Representative GIS software vendors are ESRI (*www.esri.com*), Intergraph Corporation (*www.intergraph.com*), and MapInfo (*www.pbinsight.com/welcome/mapinfo/*). GIS data are available from a wide variety of sources. Both government sources and private vendors provide diversified commercial data. Some packages are free; for example, downloadable material from *http://data.geocomm.com*.

There are countless applications of GISs to improve decision making in the public and private sectors. IT's About Business 11.2 illustrates a GIS application at Sears.

IT'S ABOUT BUSINESS 11.2
ENTERPRISE GIS MAKES SEARS MORE EFFICIENT

Sears Holding Corporation (*www.sears.com*) has a huge presence in the United States, with almost 900 stores carrying the full line and another 1,100 selling specialty items. In all, more than 48 million U.S. households are Sears customers.

The company also services more items than any other in the United States, operating one of the largest home-appliance repair businesses in the world. Every year, its more than 10,000 technicians make approximately 11 million service visits in homes throughout the United States. Such an operation must work like clockwork, and Sears turned to geographic information system (GIS) technology for help. In short, GIS applications can consider more routing options than a dispatcher can, such as finding the optimal (though not necessarily the shortest) path between stops.

To fulfill its promise of "Satisfaction Guaranteed or Your Money Back," Sears looked to ESRI (*www.esri.com*) for a GIS solution to its huge routing application. Sears and ESRI developed the Capacity Area Management System (CAMS) and the Computer-Aided Routing System (CARS). CAMS tracks and manages the availability and whereabouts of technicians working in a certain geographic area. By providing street-level geocoding, CARS helps Sears technicians choose the best routes for their calls. CARS also helps technicians navigate in their vehicles to find the homes and reduce travel time.

Before Sears implemented the GIS solution, it managed the large number of calls it received manually and then routed the technicians by hand. CARS's computer routing system has shaved about four minutes off the time to travel to an average call, boosting productivity by more than 10 percent per technician, who can add another one-half completed call per day.

Productivity has risen in other ways. For example, CARS enables Sears dispatchers to manage three to five times more technicians than they were able to handle previously. As a result, Sears was able to reduce the number of dispatchers by 75 percent. It has also increased the size of the district territories, thereby eliminating more support positions. The CAMS and CARS systems have more than paid for themselves through the cost savings. Most important, Sears is experiencing increased customer retention through improved service levels.

Sources: Compiled from "Sears Product Repair Services," ESRI Case Study, *www.esri.com*, accessed February 17, 2009; "Sears Holding Corporation Deploys GIS Navigation and Mapping System," ESRI news release, *www.geotecnologias.com*, accessed February 18, 2009; "Enterprise GIS Improves Product Repair Services and Home Delivery," *Aerospace Online*, January 8, 2007; ESRI website (*www.esri.com*) and Sears website (*www.sears.com*), accessed February 20, 2009.

QUESTIONS

1. Discuss the benefits of geographical information systems to Sears. Discuss additional GIS applications that could benefit Sears.
2. Are there drawbacks to the CAMS and CARS systems from the perspective of Sears? From the perspective of the company's employees? Support your answer.

Virtual Reality

There is no standard definition of virtual reality. The most common definitions usually describe **virtual reality (VR)** as interactive, computer-generated, three-dimensional graphics delivered to the user through a head-mounted display. In VR, a person "believes" that what she is doing is real even though it is artificially created.

More than one person and even a large group can share and interact in the same artificial environment. For this reason, VR can be a powerful medium for communication, entertainment, and learning. Instead of looking at a flat computer screen, the VR user interacts with a three-dimensional, computer-generated environment. To see and hear the environment, the user wears stereo goggles and a headset. To interact with the environment, control objects in it, or move around within it, the user wears a computerized display and hand-position sensors (gloves). VR displays achieve the illusion of a surrounding medium by updating the display in real time. The user can grasp and move virtual objects. Table 11.2 provides examples of the many different types of VR applications, and the following example illustrates one popular application.

TABLE 11.2
EXAMPLES OF VIRTUAL REALITY APPLICATIONS

APPLICATIONS IN MANUFACTURING	APPLICATIONS IN BUSINESS
Training	Real estate presentation and evaluation
Design testing and the interpretation of results	Advertising
Safety analysis	Presentations in e-commerce
Virtual prototyping	Presentation of financial data
Engineering analysis	
Ergonomic analysis	
Virtual simulation of assembly, production, and maintenance	

APPLICATIONS IN MEDICINE	APPLICATIONS IN RESEARCH AND EDUCATION
Training of surgeons (with simulators)	Virtual physics lab
Interpretation of medical data	Representation of complex mathematics
Planning of surgeries	Galaxy configurations
Physical therapy	
Psychotherapy	

APPLICATIONS IN AMUSEMENT	APPLICATIONS IN ARCHITECTURE
Virtual museums	Design of buildings and other structures
Three-dimensional racecar games (on PCs)	
Air combat simulation (on PCs)	
Virtual reality arcades and parks	

EXAMPLE 11.2

In 2009 a neurosurgeon in Halifax developed a virtual reality simulator to allow doctors to practise their surgeries before they actually do it. The system, inspired by advanced flight-simulator technology, is designed to build a replica of the brain to be operated on using data from MRIs, photos, and other patient data.

The simulator looks as if the doctor were in the operating room and the virtual brain looks and feels and behaves as it would do in real life. For example, the brain pulsates and moves as it would in real life and the surgeon can feel the resistance from tumour tissue and see the differences in colour as he or she would in real life.

Virtual reality is also being used by organizations to perform virtual meetings where managers use avatars in a virtual reality room. Universities are not foreign either to the use of virtual reality in the classroom. One professor at York University is using the Second Life simulation software to get students to manage emergency situations such as the response to a massive propane explosion in a densely populated area or to a pandemic situation of swine flu. However, because of the costs developing and maintaining these systems, only a small proportion of organizations use virtual reality.

Sources: Compiled from The Canadian Press, "Halifax Surgeon Removes Brain Tumour Using Virtual Reality Simulator," *The Globe and Mail*, August 20, 2009; M. Wente, "For God's Sake, Get a Second Life (or Not)," August 14, 2009; J. Hall, "Taking a Dry Run at Brain Surgery," *The Toronto Star*, August 20, 2009; E. Shein, "Avatars Add Sizzle to 'Immersive Learning'," *Computerworld*, April 9, 2010.

BEFORE YOU GO ON ...

1. Why is data visualization important?
2. What is a geographical information system?
3. What is virtual reality, and how does it contribute to data visualization?

11.4 Intelligent Systems

In the first three sections of this chapter, we have discussed a variety of information systems that support managerial decision making. In this section, we turn our attention to information systems that can make a decision themselves. These systems are called intelligent systems.

Intelligent system is a term that describes the various commercial applications of artificial intelligence. **Artificial intelligence (AI)** is a subfield of computer science that is concerned with studying the thought processes of humans and recreating the effects of those processes via machines, such as computers and robots.

One well-publicized definition of AI is "behaviour by a machine that, if performed by a human being, would be considered *intelligent.*" This definition raises the question: What is *intelligent behaviour*? The following capabilities are considered to be signs of intelligence: learning or understanding from experience, making sense of ambiguous or contradictory messages, and responding quickly and successfully to new situations. The following example relates the case of a new AI system designed to detect insider trading cases.

EXAMPLE 11.3

Insider trading has long plagued the capital markets and some statistics have suggested that in the United States, up to 40 percent of deals might be affected by insider trading. Insider trading is defined as trading shares using information that is not yet available to other investors and the public in general.

The University of Sunderland in the UK is working on a new artificial intelligence system that detects suspicious trading of shares. The system is nicknamed Cassandra, or Computerized Analysis of Stocks and Shares for Novelty Detection of Radical Activities and it will analyze share trading

(Continued on next page)

EXAMPLE (*Continued*)

data and news headlines from organizations such as Bloomberg, Reuters, and the Associated Press, along with information about internal changes in the company, and changes in government regulation. After analyzing all these data, the Cassandra system would then produce a time series that would serve as the base to detect unusual trading behaviours. If the system detects a change in a time series that cannot be explained by the data collected, then there is a high chance that insider trading has happened.

Cassandra will use modelling techniques to find out what is normal activity for a particular company. It will also use adaptive learning algorithms that can learn about a time series and then make

generalizations of what should happen when new data are introduced. The algorithms will also remember over time what they've learned before.

The system is still in its infancy and the main researchers plan to have a working prototype that will be focused on data and headline analysis exclusively. Once the system is proven to work and there is sufficient demand for this type of service from the business community, a more sophisticated development project will be undertaken, which could take as long as three to five years.

Sources: Compiled from D. Addison, "Artificial Intelligence in the C-Suite," *National Post*, July 7, 2009; J. Kirk, "Software System Sniffs Out Insider Trading," *Computerworld*, April 27, 2009.

AI's ultimate goal is to build machines that will mimic human intelligence. An interesting test to determine whether a computer exhibits intelligent behaviour was designed by Alan Turing, a British AI pioneer. The **Turing test** proposes that a person and a computer both pretend to be human, and the human interviewer has to decide which is which. Based on this standard, the intelligent systems exemplified in commercial AI products are far from exhibiting any significant intelligence. The potential value of AI can be better understood by contrasting it with natural (human) intelligence. AI has several important commercial advantages over natural intelligence, but it also has some limitations, as shown in Table 11.3.

TABLE 11.3
COMPARISON OF THE CAPABILITIES OF NATURAL VS. ARTIFICIAL INTELLIGENCE

CAPABILITIES	NATURAL INTELLIGENCE	ARTIFICIAL INTELLIGENCE
Preservation of knowledge	Perishable from an organizational point of view	Permanent
Duplication and dissemination of knowledge	Difficult, expensive, takes time	Easy, fast, and inexpensive once in a computer
Total cost of knowledge	Can be erratic and inconsistent, incomplete at times	Consistent and as thorough as the collection process
Documentability of process and knowledge	Difficult, expensive	Requires a structured process and well-trained staff; can be costly
Creativity	Can be very high	Low, uninspired
Use of sensory experiences	Direct and rich in possibilities	Must be interpreted first; limited
Recognition of patterns and relationships	Fast, easy to explain	Machine learning is still not as good as people in most cases, but in some cases can do better than people
Reasoning	Makes use of a wide context of experiences	Good only in narrow, focused, and stable domains

The major intelligent systems are: expert systems, natural language processing, speech recognition, and artificial neural networks. We discuss each of these systems in this section. In addition, two or more of these systems can be combined into a *hybrid* intelligent system. We conclude this section by discussing fuzzy logic, a branch of mathematics that is often useful in AI applications.

Expert Systems

When an organization has a complex decision to make or a problem to solve, it often turns to experts for advice. These experts have specific knowledge and experience in the problem area. They can offer alternative solutions and predict how likely the proposed solutions are to succeed. At the same time, they can calculate the costs that the organization may incur if it does not resolve the problem. Companies engage experts for advice on such matters as mergers and acquisitions, advertising strategy, and purchasing equipment. The more unstructured the situation, the more specialized and expensive is the advice.

Expertise refers to the extensive, task-specific knowledge acquired from training, reading, and experience. This knowledge enables experts to make better and faster decisions than non-experts in solving complex problems. Expertise takes a long time (often many years) to acquire, and it is distributed across organizations in an uneven manner.

An **expert system (ES)** is a computer system that attempts to mimic human experts by applying expertise in a specific domain. Expert systems (ESs) can either *support* decision makers or completely *replace* them. They are the most widely applied and commercially successful AI technology.

Typically, an ES is decision-making software that can reach a level of performance comparable to a human expert in certain specialized problem areas. Essentially, an ES transfers expertise from an expert (or other source) to the computer to be stored there. Users can consult the computer for specific advice as needed. The computer can make inferences and arrive at conclusions. Then, like a human expert, it offers advice or recommendations. In addition, it can explain the logic behind the advice. Because expert systems can integrate and manipulate so much data, they sometimes perform better than any single expert can. Let's now look at some applications and benefits of expert systems.

Applications, and Benefits, of Expert Systems

Today, expert systems are found in all types of organizations. They are especially useful in 10 generic categories, displayed in Table 11.4.

TABLE 11.4	
TEN GENERIC CATEGORIES OF EXPERT SYSTEMS	
CATEGORY	**PROBLEM ADDRESSED**
Interpretation	Inferring situation descriptions from observations.
Prediction	Inferring likely consequences of given situations.
Diagnosis	Inferring system malfunctions from observations.
Design	Configuring objects under constraints.
Planning	Developing plans to achieve goals.
Monitoring	Comparing observations to plans, and flagging exceptions.
Debugging	Prescribing remedies for malfunctions.

(Continued on next page)

TABLE 11.4 *(Continued)*	
Repair	Executing a plan to administer a prescribed remedy.
Instruction	Diagnosing, debugging, and correcting student performance.
Control	Interpreting, predicting, repairing, and monitoring systems behaviour.

During the past few years, thousands of organizations worldwide have successfully applied ES technology to problems ranging from AIDS research to analyzing dust in mines. Why have expert systems become so popular? The answer is because they provide a large number of capabilities and benefits, as can be seen in Table 11.5.

TABLE 11.5
BENEFITS OF EXPERT SYSTEMS

BENEFIT	DESCRIPTION
Increased output and productivity	ESs can configure components for each custom order, increasing production capabilities.
Increased quality	ESs can provide consistent advice and reduce error rates.
Capture and dissemination of scarce expertise	Expertise from anywhere in the world can be obtained and used.
Operation in hazardous environments	Sensors can collect information that an ES interprets, enabling human workers to avoid hot, humid, or toxic environments.
Accessibility to knowledge and help desks	ESs can increase the productivity of help-desk employees, or even automate this function.
Reliability	ESs do not become tired or bored, call in sick, or go on strike. They consistently pay attention to details.
Ability to work with incomplete or uncertain information	Even with an answer of "don't know," an ES can produce an answer, although it may not be a definitive one.
Provision of training	The explanation facility of an ES can serve as a teaching device and knowledge base for novices.
Enhancement of decision-making and problem-solving capabilities	ESs allow the integration of expert judgement into analysis (for example, diagnosis of machine- and problem-malfunction and even medical diagnoses).
Decreased decision-making time	ESs usually can make faster decisions than humans working alone.
Reduced downtime	ESs can quickly diagnose machine malfunctions and prescribe repairs.

Natural Language Processing and Voice Technologies

Intelligent systems such as expert systems require users to communicate with computers. **Natural language processing (NLP)** means communicating with a computer in the user's native language. To understand a natural language inquiry, a computer must have the knowledge to analyze and then interpret the input. This knowledge may include linguistic knowledge about words, domain knowledge (knowledge of a narrowly defined, specific area, such as student registration or air travel), commonsense knowledge, and even knowledge about the users and their goals. Once the computer understands the input, it can perform the desired action.

In this section we briefly discuss two types of NLP: natural language (NL) understanding and natural language (NL) generation. NL understanding is the input side of NLP, and NL generation is the output side.

Natural Language Understanding

Natural language understanding, or **speech (voice) recognition**, allows a computer to comprehend spoken instructions given in the user's everyday language. Speech recognition is deployed today in wireless smart phones as well as in many applications in stores and warehouses.

Natural language understanding offers several advantages. First, it is easy to use. Many more people can speak than can type. As long as communication with a computer depends on typing skills, many people will not be able to use computers effectively. In addition, voice recognition is faster than typing. Even the most competent typists can speak more quickly than they can type. It is estimated that the average person can speak twice as quickly as a proficient typist can type.

A final advantage is manual freedom. Obviously, communicating with a computer through typing occupies your hands. There are many situations in which computers might be useful to people whose hands are otherwise engaged, such as product assemblers, airplane pilots, busy executives, and drivers. Speech recognition also enables people with hand-related physical disabilities to use computers.

However, NL understanding also has limitations that restrict its use. The major limitation is its inability to recognize long sentences. Also, the better the system is at speech recognition, the higher its cost.

Natural Language Generation

Natural language generation, or **voice synthesis**, is a technology that enables computers to produce everyday languages—either by "voice" or on a screen—so people can understand computers more easily. As the term *synthesis* implies, sounds that make up words and phrases are electronically constructed from basic sound components. Significantly, these sounds can be made to form any desired voice pattern.

The current quality of synthesized voice is very good, but the technology remains somewhat expensive. Anticipated lower costs and improved performance should encourage more widespread commercial *interactive voice response* (IVR) applications, especially on the Web. Theoretically, IVR can be used in almost all applications that can provide an automated response to a user, such as inquiries by employees pertaining to payroll and benefits. A number of banks and credit card companies already offer voice service to their customers to provide information on balances, payments, and so on. For a list of other voice synthesis and voice recognition applications, see Table 11.6.

Neural Networks

A **neural network** is a system of programs and data structures that simulates the underlying concepts of the human brain. A neural network usually involves a large number of processors operating in parallel, each with its own small sphere of knowledge and access to data in its local memory (see Figure 11.8). Typically, a neural network is initially "trained" or fed large amounts of data and rules about data relationships.

Neural networks are particularly good at recognizing subtle, hidden, and newly emerging patterns within complex data, as well as interpreting incomplete inputs. Neural networks can help users solve a wide range of problems, from airline security to infectious disease control. They have become the

TABLE 11.6
EXAMPLES OF VOICE TECHNOLOGY APPLICATIONS

TYPES OF APPLICATIONS	COMPANIES	DEVICES USED
Answering inquiries about reservations, schedules, lost baggage, etc.	Scandinavian Airlines, other airlines	Output
Informing credit card holders about balances and credits, providing bank account balances and other information to customers	Royal Bank, many other banks	Output
Verifying coverage information	London Life Insurance	Output
Requesting pickups, ordering supplies	Federal Express	Input
Giving information about services, receiving orders	Bell Canada, other telephone companies	Output and Input
Enabling stores to order supplies, providing price information	Domino's Pizza	Output and Input
Allowing inspectors to report results of quality assurance tests	General Electric, Rockwell International, Eastman Kodak	Input
Allowing receivers of shipments to report weights and inventory levels of various meats and cheeses	Cara Donna Provisions	Input
Conducting market research and telemarketing	Carlar Hospitality Consultants, Ipsos Canada	Input
Notifying people of emergencies detected by sensors	U.S. Department of Energy, Idaho National Engineering Lab, Honeywell	Output
Notifying parents about the cancellation of classes and about where students are	Toronto District School Board	Output
Activating radios, heaters, etc. by voice	Car manufacturers	Input
Logging in and out to payroll department by voice; status reports	Qatalys Software Technologies	Input and Output
Prompting doctors in the emergency room to conduct all necessary tests, reporting of results by doctors	St. Elizabeth's Hospital Washington, D.C.	Output and Input

FIGURE 11.8
Neural
network.

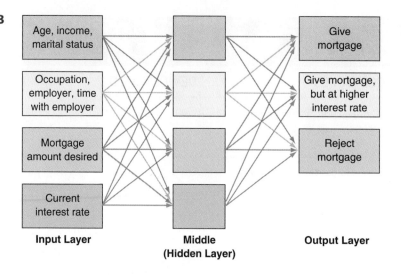

standard for combatting fraud in the credit card, health care, and telecommunications industries, and they are playing an increasingly important role in today's stepped-up international efforts to prevent money laundering.

Figure 11.8 illustrates how a neural network would process a typical mortgage application. Note that the network has three levels of interconnected nodes (similar to the human brain): an input layer, a middle or hidden layer, and an output layer. As you train the neural network, the strengths (or weights) of the connections change. In our example, the input nodes are age, income, occupation, marital status, employer, length of time with that employer, amount of mortgage desired, and current interest rate. The neural network has already been trained with data input from many successful and unsuccessful mortgage applications. That is, the neural network has established a pattern as to which input variables are necessary for a successful mortgage application. Interestingly, the neural network can adjust as mortgage amounts increase or decrease and interest rates increase or decrease.

Fuzzy Logic

Fuzzy logic is a branch of mathematics that deals with uncertainties by simulating the process of human reasoning. The rationale behind fuzzy logic is that decision making is not always a matter of black and white, true or false. It often involves grey areas where the term *maybe* is more appropriate.

A computer programmed to use fuzzy logic precisely handles subjective concepts that humans do not define precisely. A term such as "warm" is related, via precisely defined formulas, to an imprecise concept. For example, where the concept is "income," "high" could have values ranging over $200,000 per year and "moderate" could have values ranging from $75,000 to $150,000 per year. A loan officer at a bank might use fuzzy values such as high and moderate when considering a loan application.

Fuzzy logic has also been used in financial analysis and the manufacture of antilock brakes. In accounting and finance, fuzzy logic allows you to analyze information with imprecise values, such as intangible assets like goodwill.

BEFORE YOU GO ON …

1. Describe what is meant by intelligent behaviour.
2. Compare artificial and natural intelligence.
3. What are the benefits of expert systems?
4. What are the advantages and disadvantages of natural language processing?
5. What are the advantages and disadvantages of artificial neural networks?
6. What is fuzzy logic?

WHAT'S IN IT FOR ME?

FOR THE ACCOUNTING MAJOR

BI systems, dashboards, and intelligent systems are used extensively in auditing to uncover irregularities. They are also used to uncover and prevent fraud. Today's public accountants use BI and intelligent systems for many of their duties, ranging from risk analysis to cost control. Accounting personnel also use intelligent agents for several mundane tasks such as managing accounts and monitoring employees' Internet use.

FOR THE FINANCE MAJOR

People have been using computers for decades to solve financial problems. Innovative BI applications exist for activities such as making stock market decisions, refinancing bonds, assessing debt risks, analyzing financial conditions, predicting business failures, forecasting financial trends, and investing in global markets. In many cases, intelligent systems can facilitate the use of spreadsheets and other computerized systems used in finance. Finally, intelligent systems can help to reduce fraud in credit cards, stocks, and other financial services.

FOR THE MARKETING MAJOR

Marketing personnel use BI systems and dashboards in many applications, from allocating advertising budgets to evaluating alternative routings of salespeople. New marketing approaches such as targeted marketing and marketing transaction databases are heavily dependent on IT in general and on intelligent systems in particular. Intelligent systems are particularly useful in mining customer databases and predicting customer behaviour. Successful applications are visible in almost every area of marketing and sales, from analyzing the success of one-to-one advertising to supporting customer help desks. With the increased importance of customer service, the use of intelligent agents is becoming critical for providing fast response.

FOR THE PRODUCTION/OPERATIONS MANAGEMENT MAJOR

BI systems and dashboards support complex operations and production decisions, from inventory to production planning. Many of the early expert systems (ESs) were developed in the production/operations management field for tasks ranging from diagnosis of machine failures and prescription of repairs to complex production scheduling and inventory control. Some companies, such as DuPont and Kodak, have deployed hundreds of ESs in the planning, organizing, and control of their operational systems.

FOR THE HUMAN RESOURCES MANAGEMENT MAJOR

Human resources personnel use BI systems, dashboards, and intelligent systems for many applications. For example, these systems can find resumés of applicants posted on the Web and sort them to match needed skills. Expert systems are used in evaluating candidates (tests, interviews). Intelligent systems are used to facilitate training and to support self-management of fringe benefits. Neural computing is used to predict employee performance on the job as well as to predict labour needs. Voice recognition systems provide benefits information to employees.

FOR THE MIS MAJOR

The MIS function provides the data and models that managers use in BI systems and the structured information used in dashboards. MIS personnel are also responsible for the information on each screen of digital dashboards. MIS employees have the difficult task of interacting with subject-area experts to develop expert systems.

SUMMARY

1. **Describe the concepts of management, decision making, and computerized support for decision making.**

   Management is a process by which organizations achieve their goals through the use of resources (people, money, energy, materials, space, time). Managers have three basic roles: interpersonal, informational, and decisional. When making a decision, either organizational or personal, the decision maker goes through a three-step process: intelligence, design, and choice. When the choice is made, the decision is implemented. Several information technologies have been successfully used to directly support managers. Collectively, they are referred to as business intelligence information systems and intelligent systems.

2. **Describe business intelligence systems, including multi-dimensional data analysis, data mining, and decision support systems and digital dashboards.**

   Multi-dimensional data analysis provides users with a view of what is happening or what has happened by allowing users to "slice and dice" data in any desired way. Data mining searches for valuable business information in a large database, data warehouse, or data mart. Data mining can perform two basic operations: (1) predicting trends and behaviours, and (2) identifying previously unknown patterns. Decision support systems (DSS) combine models and data in an attempt to solve semistructured and some unstructured problems. DSS can support decisions made by one individual and also decisions that need to be made by a group. Digital dashboards provide rapid access to timely, structured information and direct access to management reports. Digital dashboards are user-friendly, supported by graphics, and allow users to examine various structured reports.

3. **Describe data visualization, including geographical information systems and virtual reality.**

   Data visualization involves presenting data by technologies such as geographical information systems and virtual reality. A geographical information system (GIS) is a computer-based system for manipulating and displaying data using digitized maps. Virtual reality refers to interactive, computer-generated, three-dimensional graphics delivered to the user through a head-mounted display.

4. **Describe artificial intelligence, including expert systems, natural language processing, and neural networks.**

   Artificial intelligence (AI) involves studying the thought processes of humans and attempting to represent those processes in machines (computers, robots, and so on). AI's ultimate goal is to build machines that will mimic human intelligence. Expert systems (ESs) are an attempt to mimic the reasoning abilities of human experts. An ES is decision-making software that can reach a level of performance comparable to a human expert in some specialized and usually narrow problem area. Natural language understanding or speech (voice) recognition allows certain applications to comprehend instructions given in ordinary language. Natural language generation or voice synthesis strives to allow computer applications to produce ordinary language, on the screen or by voice, so people can understand computers more easily. A neural network is a system of programs and data structures that approximates the operation of the human brain. A neural network usually involves a large number of processors operating in parallel, each with its own small sphere of knowledge and access to data in its local memory. Typically, a neural network is initially "trained" or fed large amounts of data and rules about data relationships.

KEY TERMS

DISCUSSION QUESTIONS

1. Your company is considering opening a new factory in China. List several typical activities involved in each phase of the decision (intelligence, design, choice, and implementation).
2. Your company announced that it was interested in acquiring a U.S. company in the health maintenance organization (HMO) field. Two decisions were involved in this act: (1) the decision to acquire an HMO, and (2) the decision of which HMO to acquire. How can your company use BI systems, expert systems, and digital dashboards to assist in this endeavour?
3. A major difference between a conventional BI system and an expert system is that the former can explain a *how* question whereas the latter can also explain a *why* question. Discuss the implications of this statement.
4. Discuss the strategic benefits of BI systems.
5. Will BI systems replace business analysts? (Hint: See W. McKnight, "Building Business Intelligence: Will Business Intelligence Replace the Business Analyst?" *DMReview*, February 2005).
6. Why is the combination of GIS and GPS becoming so popular? Examine some applications of GIS/GPS combinations related to data management.

PROBLEM-SOLVING ACTIVITIES

1. The City of London, England, charges an entrance fee for automobiles and trucks into the city centre. About 1,000 digital cameras photograph the licence plate of every vehicle passing by. Computers read the plate numbers and match them against records in a database of cars for which the fee has been paid for that day. If the computer does not find a match, the car owner receives a citation (ticket) by mail. Examine the issues pertaining to how this process is accomplished, the mistakes it can make, and the consequences of those mistakes. Also examine how well the system is working by checking news reports. Finally, relate the process to business intelligence.

2. Enter the site for Cognos BI and FPm at *http://www-01.ibm.com/software/data/cognos/* and visit the demos on the right side of the page. Prepare a report on the various features shown in each demo.

3. Enter *www.fico.com* and find products for fraud detection and risk analysis. Prepare a report.

4. Visit *www.dwexplorer.com/products/producttour/default.aspx* and work through the DataWarehouse Explorer information. Answer the following questions:
   a. What are the different functions provided by the DataWarehouse Explorer?
   b. What strategic advantages could be realized when implementing this product for inventory management?
   c. Did you find the product self-explanatory? What type of training would be required when implementing this type of product?

5. Go to *www.ibm.com/us/en/* and do a search for the "Business Intelligence Tutorial." Open the first link in the list of results and answer the following questions:
   a. What technology components are required to implement business intelligence systems?
   b. Who are the potential users of BI at TBC, The Beverage Company? What would each type of user attempt to achieve?
   c. What type of training would be required for the employees involved in implementing and testing the business intelligence systems at TBC?

6. Access *www.ted.com/index.php/talks/view/id/92* to find the video of Hans Rosling's fascinating presentation. Comment on his data visualization techniques.

7. Access *http://businessintelligence.ittoolbox.com*. Identify all types of business intelligence software. Join a discussion group about topics discussed in this chapter. Prepare a report.

8. Visit the sites of some GIS vendors (such as *www.pbinsight.com/welcome/mapinfo/*, *www.esri.com*, *www.autodesk.com*). Join a newsgroup and discuss new applications in marketing, banking, and transportation. Download a demo. What are some of the most important capabilities and applications?

9. Analyze Microsoft Bing Maps (*www.microsoft.com/maps/*) as a business intelligence tool. (Hint: Access *www.microsoft.com/Industry/government/solutions/virtual_earth/demo/ps_gbi.html*). What are the business intelligence features of this product?

10. Visit *www.kdnuggets.com/education/usa-canada.html* and select three courses or programs on data mining. Compare the programs. Which would you take if you had the choice? Why?

11. Enter *www.visualmining.com*. Explore the relationship between visualization and business intelligence. See how business intelligence is related to dashboards.

TEAM ASSIGNMENTS

1. Access *www.dmreview.com/more/product_reviews*. Examine the list of products, and identify software with analytical capabilities. Each group will prepare a report on five companies. Use Google to find combined GIS/GPS applications. Also, look at various vendor sites to find success stories. For GPS vendors, look at *http://biz.yahoo.com* (directory) and Google. Each group will make a presentation of five applications and their benefits.

2. Each group will access a leading business intelligence vendor's website (for example, MicroStrategy, Oracle, Microsoft, SAS, SPSS, IBM Cognos, and Business Objects). Each group will present a report on a vendor, highlighting each vendor's BI.

BUSINESS INTELLIGENCE AT DOREL

THE BUSINESS PROBLEM

Dorel Industries (*www.dorel.com*) is the leading marketer of juvenile products and bicycles in North America and it is headquartered in Montreal. Dorel employs 4,600 people in 15 countries across North America and Europe and has annual sales over $2 billion. The company sells its products under a suite of brands, including Cosco, Eddie Bauer, Schwinn, Mongoose, and Maxi-Cosi in over 60 countries worldwide.

The company is organized in several operating divisions and subsidiaries in three market segments: juvenile, recreational/leisure, and home furnishings. Dorel's Juvenile segment manufactures and distributes infant car seats, strollers, high chairs, toddler beds, cribs, infant health and safety aids, feeding aids, play-yards, and juvenile accessories. Dorel's Recreational/Leisure segment assembles and distributes bicycles and other recreational products. The Home Furnishings segment manufactures and sells a wide variety of ready-to-assemble furniture for home and office use as well as metal folding furniture, futons, step stools, ladders, and a vast array of imported furniture items. Each of these business segments and the business units within each segment operates independently although the organization strives to maximize cross-selling, cross-marketing, procurement, and other complementary opportunities.

Until recently the company had struggled with a common problem across the board that was putting into jeopardy the company's major strengths: innovation, product quality, and strong brands. The company was generating too much data without timely or consistent

access to them. For example, the main reporting tool was the use of spreadsheets and legacy applications and, although there were only three main reports to be produced every month, the number of variations was so great that it made the process very inefficient. In addition, there was the problem of obtaining consistent financial and non-financial data across subsidiaries, especially those located in different countries. There were too many ad-hoc requests by different people in different formats, which made comparisons by year or by business unit not reliable.

THE IT SOLUTION

In order to find a solution to its problem, the company conducted a number of interviews with managers across the majority of the North American and European subsidiaries in order to understand the information needs across the business. The idea behind the project was to select an IT solution that would address the needs of the whole group and not just one subsidiary.

As a consequence the company decided to implement the IBM Cognos business intelligence (BI) suite. The new BI software provided financial integration for all the business units and subsidiaries worldwide and helped Dorel with its reporting, scorecarding, and performance monitoring processes. Performance management was further enabled through the implementation of a worldwide portal where managers can access financial and non-financial reports and through the use of digital dashboards.

THE RESULTS

The implementation of BI has helped Dorel in several ways. It has improved the access to data across the business regardless of where a unit is located and what currency it uses. For example, executives at headquarters can instantly drill down into a business unit's figures and identify what is happening. Previously, if sales revenue had dropped in one of the units in Europe, say the French unit, managers had no way of identifying if the problem was due to a sales drop in France, Spain, or Portugal. Now they have access to all this detailed information. Consequently, senior managers at Dorel have gained a much better understanding of the company's global operations. One senior executive in procurement was impressed with the dashboard application since it had helped him to make the connection between the group total daily sales and the amount of goods and services his department has to buy to support the business.

Another key benefit of the new BI software has been the improved effectiveness and flexibility in generating business reports. For example, managers are now provided with a year-to-date sales report for all its units, by country, by customer, and by stock keeping unit (SKU). Before, the same information would have had to be prepared by someone else and it would take days to prepare. Managers were not sure if they were getting what they asked for.

Another of the tangible benefits of the BI system is that operations and finance managers now spend more time analyzing data trends and less time collecting data. Managers can also use the forecasting capabilities of the BI application to get a better idea of how much product they should order and how many workers they should schedule, which improves the overall efficiency of operations.

Managers have also indicated that the use of dashboards has been of great help. The new BI software provides them with instant access to up-to-date information, which makes them more confident when delivering a presentation or reporting to senior management because they are backed up by data.

Sources: Compiled from "From Data and Integration to Smarter Operations: Performance Management at Dorel," IBM case study, September 14, 2009; Dorel website (*www.dorel.com*), accessed May 12, 2010.

QUESTIONS

1. Describe the various benefits that Dorel is seeing from its business intelligence system.
2. Discuss additional analyses that Dorel managers and analysts could run that would benefit the company and its business units and provide competitive advantage.
3. How could visualization technologies be used to support Dorel's senior managers' decision-making process?
4. Identify different ways in which intelligent systems could be used at Dorel. Build a table identifying the type of intelligent system, how it would work, and the benefits for the company.

Web Resources

Student website www.wiley.com/canada/rainer

- Web quizzes
- Lecture slides in PowerPoint
- Author podcasts
- Interactive Case: Ruby's Club assignments

ALL OF THE ABOVE AND...

- E-book
- Manager videos
- Vocabulary flash cards
- Pre- and post-lecture quizzes
- Microsoft Office 2007 lab manual and projects

DEVELOPING INFORMATION SECURITY MEASURES FOR RUBY'S CLUB

Go to the Ruby's Club link at the Student Companion website or WileyPLUS for information about your current internship assignment. You will analyze and recommend managerial support systems to help the club's managers better understand their monthly goals and how to achieve them.

12 ACQUIRING INFORMATION SYSTEMS AND APPLICATIONS

LEARNING OBJECTIVES

1. Define project management and describe how projects should be managed and controlled.

2. Provide alternatives for justifying IT investments.

3. Identify and describe the advantages and disadvantages of the major alternative strategies for acquiring information systems.

4. Describe the SDLC (systems development life cycle) approach.

5. Explain how the IT development process can been modified and why.

6. Describe the process for vendor and software selection.

THE LEUKEMIA & LYMPHOMA SOCIETY MAKES IT EASIER TO DONATE

Source: Courtesy The Leukemia & Lymphoma Society

THE BUSINESS PROBLEM

The Leukemia & Lymphoma Society (LLS, *www.lls.org*, *www.leukemia-lymphoma.org/all_chap* in Canada) is the largest charity in the world that works in the area of blood cancer research, education, and patient services. The society aims to cure leukemia, lymphoma, Hodgkin's disease, and myeloma, as well as improve the quality of life for patients and their families.

To achieve its goals, the organization depends on donations. LLS has developed creative methods to raise money, particularly through event-oriented fundraising activities. Programs such as Team in Training, Light the Night, and the Leukemia Cup Regatta are especially noteworthy. Team in Training (*www.TeamInTraining. org*) is the charity's largest fundraiser. This innovative program works with amateur endurance athletes to build their skills and improve their fitness. In exchange, the athletes participate in fundraising events such as marathons and triathlons. Since the program started in 1988, its participants have raised more than $850 million. Team in Training has grown to be the world's largest sports-endurance training program.

LLS has employed a combination of promotion and word of mouth to dramatically increase participation in Team in Training. At the same time, the organization has shifted a large percentage of its fundraising from traditional channels to on-line channels, thanks to improved fundraising and e-commerce technology. The increased emphasis on Team in Training and on-line strategies has strained LLS's existing fundraising systems, prompting the organization to develop a new IT infrastructure.

In the past, LLS outsourced its fundraising to an on-line donation service, which provided a website for contributors. For a fee, the service provider collected these donations and transmitted the funds at the end of each month to LLS. However, the service provider could not manage the increase in donations experienced by LLS and technical problems resulted. For example, donation transactions often failed or were mistakenly duplicated. These problems burdened the LLS IT group with having to manage customer calls, which distracted them from their actual IT functions.

The application had a financial effect on LLS as the fees it paid to the service provider eventually reached 7 percent of every on-line donation, because the agreement called for fees to increase along with the percentage of donations coming from the website. LLS also missed out on interest revenue because the service provider turned over donations at the end of every month.

THE IT SOLUTION

LLS decided to redesign its IT functions from scratch and take back control of its information systems. It turned over the job to its in-house specialists, giving them just three months to come up with new systems. To accomplish this challenging feat, the society based its development on service-oriented architecture (SOA). As we discussed in Chapter 10, SOA is an IT architecture that allows an organization to make its applications and computing resources, such as databases, available as services that can be called upon when necessary. A service is a set of processes and activities that make up a business function. To determine what services it needed to include, LLS first defined its business functions, one of which was Manage Donations. It then broke down each function into services, such as Create Donation, Process Donation, Acknowledge Donation, Apply Donation, and so on.

LLS started with the front end of its IT function—what the users would see and use. For example, participants in society programs would visit the website and sign up for various fundraising events and manage their own pledges and donations. Other users include the Team in Training chapters, which can use new tools on the IT system to manage their local organizations. Using the SOA framework, LLS then worked on the back end of its IT system—the various applications and databases working behind the scenes to power the front-end experience. Back-end services ensure the local Team in Training chapters can manage their donations, for example.

Developing and managing its IT function in-house has paid off dramatically for LLS. Website performance and user satisfaction have improved enormously, as have fundraising costs. The society has slashed the cost of donations from a 7 percent fee to just 2 percent per transaction to pay for IT overhead—freeing up more money to put into research and patient services. In the first two months of operation, the new system brought in more than $10 million in donations.

Since the new system went live, it has yet to experience a failure. This frees up the IT department to focus on innovation—with plans to add more features such as blogs, discussion groups, and on-line forums—instead of being a help desk to deal with technical problems.

WHAT DO YOU THINK?

1. Should LLS have handled its technology development on its own or done the outsourcing? Why or why not?
2. Take a look at the LLS website. Are the services well-designed? What changes would you make?

Sources: Compiled from "Leukemia & Lymphoma on the 200 Largest U.S. Charities," *Forbes*, November 19, 2008; "Mule-Source Helps the Leukemia & Lymphoma Society Raise $10 Million in Two Months," Reuters, September 23, 2008; O. Mazhar, "Fundraising on the Fast Track," *Baseline Magazine*, April 10, 2009; The Leukemia & Lymphoma Society website (*www.lls.org*) and the Team in Training website (*www.TeamInTraining.org*), accessed April 13, 2009.

CASE 12.1

Chapter Preview

The Leukemia & Lymphoma Society (LLS) case first illustrates how outsourcing can cause problems for an organization. The LLS case also demonstrates that organizations can successfully develop new information systems in-house, with excellent results.

Competitive organizations move as quickly as they can to acquire new information technologies (or modify existing ones) when they need to improve efficiencies and gain strategic advantage. Today, however, acquisition goes beyond building new systems in-house, and IT resources go beyond software and hardware. The old model in which firms built their own systems is being replaced with a broader perspective of IT resource acquisition that provides companies with a number of options.

ACQUIRING INFORMATION SYSTEMS AND APPLICATIONS

Information technology project management	Justifying IT applications	Strategies for acquiring IT applications	The traditional systems development life cycle	Alternative methods and tools for systems development	Vendor and software selection
• The project management process • Project management failure	• Evaluating and justifying IT investment: benefits, costs, and issues	• Buy the applications (off-the-shelf approach) • Lease the applications • Use software-as-a-service • Use open-source software • Outsource • Develop the applications in-house	• Systems investigation • Systems analysis • Systems design • Programming and testing • Implementation • Operation and maintenance	• Prototyping • Joint application design • Integrated computer-assisted software engineering tools • Rapid application development • Agile development • End-user development • Component-based development • Object-oriented development	

Thus, companies now must decide which IT tasks will remain in-house, and even whether the entire IT resource should be provided and managed by outside organizations. Regardless of which approach an organization chooses, however, it must be able to manage IT projects adeptly.

In this chapter we describe the elements of IT project management and the process of acquiring IT resources from a managerial perspective. This means from your perspective, because you will be closely involved in all aspects of acquiring information systems and applications in your organization. In fact, when we mention "users" in this chapter, we are talking about you. We pay special attention to the available options for acquiring IT resources and how to evaluate the options. We also take a close look at planning and justifying the acquisition of new information systems.

12.1 Information Technology Project Management

Projects are short-term efforts to create a specific business-related outcome. These outcomes may take the form of products or services. In the context of information systems (IS), many of the resource investments made by organizations are in the form of projects. For example, Home Depot (*www.homedepot.ca*) recently engaged in an IS project to develop an inventory management system. The objectives of the project were to improve inventory turnover, reduce product stock outs, and integrate more tightly with supply chain partners. The outcome was to lower company-wide costs by carrying less physical inventory.

Almost every organization that uses information technology to support business processes engages in some form of IS project management. **IS project management** is a directed effort to plan, organize, and manage resources to bring about the successful achievement of specific IS goals. All projects, whether they are IS projects or not, are constrained by the same three factors, known as the **triple constraints of project management**: time, cost, and scope. *Time* refers to the window of opportunity in which a project must be completed to provide a benefit to the organization. Cost is the actual amount of resources, including cash and labour, that an organization can commit to completing a project. Finally, scope refers to the processes that ensure that the project includes all the work required—and only the work required—to complete the project successfully. For an IS project to be successful, the organization must allow an adequate amount of time, provide an appropriate amount of resources, and carefully define what is and is not included in the project. Throughout the project, the organization should also have effective security over its data and programs to prevent unauthorized changes or access to programs and data. IT's About Business 12.1 illustrates how a problem with information systems project completion can have far-reaching effects.

IT'S ABOUT BUSINESS 12.1
WESTJET CUSTOMERS WAIT, AND WAIT, AND WAIT …

WestJet (*www.westjet.com*) is Canada's second-largest airline, in business since 1996. WestJet wanted to improve its ability to serve its customers, including adding capability to have its seats booked by other carriers. The airline spent close to four years and about $38 million working with a software supplier to develop a new airline reservation system. The systems were never delivered, never completed. WestJet cancelled the contract, and wrote off the amounts invested in the new system.

Instead, in fall 2009, WestJet purchased and implemented the fully functioning and well-known SabreSonic reservation system from Sabre Holdings (*www.sabre.com*). Part of a group of products, SabreSonic provides transaction processing for passengers, ticketing, Internet bookings, as well as other products (for example, loyalty card processing and inventory management). The new SabreSonic systems were supposed to upgrade WestJet's customer service.

(Continued on next page)

IT'S ABOUT BUSINESS 12.1 *(Continued)*
WESTJET CUSTOMERS WAIT, AND WAIT, AND WAIT …

However, the new system had problems with about half a million reservations made prior to the conversion date of October 16, 2009. One of the features of implementing a new system is the transfer of old data – if old systems are not fully understood, such transfer of data may be impossible or very difficult, which is not a fault of the new system. The SabreSonic system was very slow in accessing the old information, and airline employees seemed unable to process these transactions. As a result, travellers spent hours and days trying to confirm their reservations. In addition, new services, such as the loyalty program and sharing with other airlines, were not implemented, and were delayed into 2010 and 2011 due to reasons not disclosed by WestJet. The airline advised customers to call after midnight or before 6 a.m. if they wanted a rapid response to their queries—a rather difficult time to call!

In addition to the writedown costs of the software that was never implemented, WestJet paid for the SabreSonic software, and had lower than expected bookings after the new reservation systems were put in place, reducing profits for the final quarter of 2009.

Sources: B. Evans, "WestJet's IT Nightmare and the Power Of Customers," *InformationWeek: Global CIO*, April 16, 2010; J. Monchuk, The Canadian Press, "WestJet's New Reservation System Again Delayed," AirportBusiness.com, July 7, 2008; E. Roseman, "Reservation Overhaul Leaves Customers Up in the Air," *Toronto Star*, December 1, 2009.

QUESTIONS
1. Why might WestJet have initially attempted to obtain its software as a new, custom-developed system?
2. What are the disadvantages of going with a new vendor of software? Of going with an existing vendor?

The Project Management Process

The WestJet case illustrates the pitfalls of information systems projects. Such projects need to be carefully managed by organizations, with decisions and approvals required frequently throughout the project (called project milestones). The traditional approach to project management divides every project into five distinct phases: initiation, planning, execution, monitoring and control, and completion. These phases are sequential and we discuss them in order.

Project Initiation

The first phase in the management of a process is to clearly define the problem that the project is intended to solve and the goals that it is to achieve. In this phase, it is also necessary to identify and secure the resources needed for the project, analyze the costs and benefits of the project, and identify potential risks. It is important that future users be involved, to ensure that their needs are properly identified. The users should also be part of the approval process before moving to the next phase. As we will discuss later in this chapter, the initiation phase is the equivalent of the systems investigation phase of the systems development life cycle.

Project Planning

As the term *planning* suggests, in this phase, every project objective and every activity associated with that objective must be identified and sequenced. Many tools assist developers in sequencing these activities, including dependence diagrams, program evaluation and review technique (PERT), critical path method (CPM), and a timeline diagram called the Gantt chart. Project managers use these tools to ensure that activities are performed in a logical sequence and to determine how long each activity—and, ultimately the entire project—will take. As the project progresses, project managers also employ these tools to evaluate whether the project is on schedule and if not, where the delays are occurring and what they must do to correct them. With each logical sequence, it may also be necessary to review project viability. For example, if WestJet had decided earlier that its new systems might not be completed, the company would not have lost as much money.

Project Execution

In this phase, the work defined in the project management plan is performed to accomplish the project's requirements. Execution coordinates people and resources, and it integrates and performs project activities in accordance with the plan.

Project Monitoring and Control

The purpose of monitoring and control is to determine whether the project is progressing as planned. This phase consists of three steps: (1) monitoring ongoing project activities (where we are); (2) comparing project variables (cost, effort, time, resources, etc.) with the actual plan (where we should be); and (3) identifying corrective actions (how do we get on track again). Any changes should be approved by user management. Major changes should trigger reviews of project viability.

Project Completion

The project is completed when it is formally accepted by the organization. All activities are finalized, and all contracts are fulfilled and settled. In addition, all files are archived and all lessons learned are documented.

Project Management Failure

Many times IT projects fail to achieve their desired results. In fact, analysts have found that only 29 percent of all IS projects are completed on time, within budget, and with all the features and functions originally specified. Further, between 30–40 percent of all IS software development projects are *runaway projects*, meaning they are so far over budget and past deadline that they must be abandoned, typically with large monetary loss, as illustrated by our WestJet case. There are a number of reasons why IS projects do not deliver their potential value, including:

- Lack of sufficient planning at the start of a project
- Difficulties with technology compatibility (that is, new technology may not work with existing technology)
- Lack of commitment by management in providing the necessary resources
- Poorly defined project scope
- Lack of sufficient time to complete the project

BEFORE YOU GO ON ...

1. What are the triple constraints of any project?
2. Describe the phases of a project.
3. What is a runaway project?

12.2 Justifying IT Applications

In Chapter 1, we explained that it is important to carefully plan IT acquisitions. This includes being sure that new IT applications are consistent with the organization's IT strategic plan and the overall organization's strategic plan. Once an organization identifies a potential IT application, it then proceeds to the next step of evaluating and justifying the application.

Evaluating and Justifying IT Investment: Benefits, Costs, and Issues

As we already discussed, developing an IT plan is the first step in the acquisition process. All companies have a limited amount of resources available to them. For this reason they must justify investing resources in some areas, including IT, rather than in others. Essentially, justifying IT investment involves assessing the costs, assessing the benefits (values), and comparing the two. This comparison is frequently referred to as cost-benefit analysis. Cost-benefit analysis can be complex.

Assessing the Costs

Placing a dollar value on the cost of IT investments may not be as simple as it sounds. One of the major challenges that companies face is to allocate fixed costs among different IT projects. *Fixed costs* are those costs that remain the same regardless of any change in the activity level. For IT, fixed costs include infrastructure cost, cost of IT services, and IT management cost. For example, the salary of the IT director is fixed, and adding one more application will not change it.

Another complication is that the cost of a system does not end when the system is installed. Costs for maintaining, debugging, and improving the system can accumulate over many years. In some cases the company does not even anticipate these costs when it makes the investment.

A dramatic example of unanticipated expenses was the Year 2000 (Y2K) reprogramming projects, which cost organizations worldwide billions of dollars at the end of the twentieth century. In the 1960s, computer memory was very expensive. To save money, programmers coded the "year" in the date field 19_ _, instead of _ _ _ _. With the "1" and the "9" hard-coded in the computer program, only the last two digits varied, so computer programs needed less memory. However, this process meant that when we reached the year 2000, computers would have 1900 as the year instead of 2000. This programming technique could have caused serious problems with, for example, financial applications, insurance applications, and so on.

Other unanticipated changes to systems can include tax changes. For example, effective July 2010, two provinces changed their sales tax system, combining the provincial sales tax with the federal GST (goods and services tax). This meant that systems that process sales transactions needed to be changed for that date.

Assessing the Benefits

Evaluating the benefits of IT projects is typically even more complex than calculating their costs. Benefits may be harder to quantify, especially because many of them are intangible (for example, improved customer or partner relations or improved decision making). You will probably be asked for input about the intangible benefits that an information system provides for you.

The fact that organizations use IT for many different purposes further complicates benefit analysis. In addition, to obtain a return from an IT investment, the company must implement the technology successfully. In reality, many systems are not implemented on time, within budget, or with all the features originally envisioned for them. Finally, the proposed system may be "cutting edge." In these cases there may be no previous evidence of what sort of financial payback the company can expect.

Conducting Cost-Benefit Analysis

After a company has assessed the costs and benefits of IT investments, it must compare the two. There is no uniform strategy to conduct this analysis. Rather, it can be performed in several ways. Here we discuss four common approaches: net present value, return on investment, break-even analysis, and the business case approach.

1. Using the *net present value (NPV)* method, analysts convert future values of benefits to their present-value equivalent by "discounting" them at the organization's cost of funds. They can then compare the present value of the future benefits to the cost required to achieve those benefits to determine whether the benefits exceed the costs. NPV analysis works well in situations where the costs and benefits are well defined or "tangible" enough to be converted into monetary values.

2. *Return on investment (ROI)* measures management's effectiveness in generating profits with its available assets. ROI is calculated by dividing net income attributable to a project by the average assets invested in the project. ROI is a percentage, and the higher the percentage return, the better. The greater the value of ROI, the more likely the company is to approve the investment.

3. *Break-even analysis* determines the point at which the cumulative dollar value of the benefits from a project equals the investment made in the project. Break-even analysis is attractive for its simplicity, but is flawed because it ignores the value of system benefits after the break-even point.

4. In the *business case approach*, system developers write a business case to justify funding one or more specific applications or projects. You will be a major source of input when business cases are developed because these cases describe what you do, how you do it, and how a new system could better support you. The business case helps to clarify how the organization can best use its resources to accomplish its IT strategy. It helps the organization to concentrate on justifying the investment. It also focuses on risk management and on how an IT project corresponds with the organization's mission.

BEFORE YOU GO ON …

1. What are some problems associated with assessing the costs of IT?
2. What difficulties accompany the intangible benefits from IT?
3. Describe the NPV, ROI, break-even analysis, and business case approaches.

12.3 Strategies for Acquiring IT Applications

If a company has successfully justified an IT investment, it must then decide how to pursue it. Companies have several options for acquiring IT applications. Six common options are to (1) buy standard applications, (2) lease them, (3) use software-as-a-service, (4) use open-source software, (5) outsource them, and (6) develop them in-house.

Buy the Applications (Off-the-Shelf Approach)

The standard features required by IT applications can be found in many commercial software packages. Buying an existing package can be a cost-effective and time-saving strategy compared with developing the application in-house. Nevertheless, a company should carefully consider and plan the buy option to ensure that the selected package contains all of the features necessary to address the company's current and future needs. Otherwise these packages can quickly become obsolete. Before a company can perform this process, it must decide which features a selected package must have to be suitable.

In reality, a single software package can rarely satisfy all of an organization's needs. For this reason a company sometimes must purchase multiple packages to fulfill different needs. It then must integrate these packages with one another as well as with its existing software.

TABLE 12.1
ADVANTAGES AND LIMITATIONS OF THE "BUY" OPTION OF STANDARD SOFTWARE

ADVANTAGES	DISADVANTAGES
Many different types of off-the-shelf software are available.	Software may not exactly meet the company's needs.
Software can be tried out before purchase.	Software may be difficult or impossible to modify, or it may require huge business process changes to implement.
Much time can be saved by buying rather than building.	The company will not have control over software improvements and new versions.
The company can know what it is getting before it invests in the product.	Purchased software can be difficult to integrate with existing systems.
The company is not the first and only user, so software has been tested.	Vendors may drop a product or go out of business.
Purchased software may avoid the need to hire personnel specifically dedicated to a project.	Software is controlled by another company with its own priorities and business considerations.
	There is a lack of intimate knowledge in the purchasing company about how the software works and why it works that way.

The buy option is especially attractive if the software vendor allows the company to modify the technology to meet its needs. However, this option is less attractive in cases where customization is the only method of providing the necessary flexibility to address the company's needs, since the software will need to be customized every time the package is upgraded. It also may be a poor strategy when the software is either very expensive or is likely to become obsolete in a short time. Table 12.1 summarizes the advantages and limitations of the buy option. When the buy option is not appropriate, organizations frequently consider leasing.

Lease the Applications

Compared with the buy option and the option to develop applications in-house, the "lease" option can save a company both time and money. Of course, leased packages (like purchased packages) may not exactly fit the company's application requirements. However, vendor software generally includes the features that are most commonly needed by organizations in a given industry. Again, the company will decide which features are necessary.

It is common for interested companies to apply the 80/20 rule when evaluating vendor software. Put simply, if the software meets 80 percent of the company's needs, then the company should seriously consider changing its business processes so it can use the remaining 20 percent. Many times this is a better long-term solution than modifying the vendor software. Otherwise, the company will have to customize the software every time the vendor releases an updated version.

Leasing can be especially attractive to small to medium-sized enterprises (SMEs) that cannot afford major investments in IT software. Large companies may also prefer to lease packages in order to test potential IT solutions before committing to heavy investments. Also, a company with a shortage of IT personnel with appropriate skills for developing custom IT applications may choose to lease instead of developing software in-house. Even those companies that employ in-house experts may not be able to afford the long wait for strategic applications to be developed in-house. Therefore, they lease (or buy) applications from external resources to establish a quicker presence in the market.

Leasing can be done in one of three ways. The first way is to lease the application from a software developer and install it on the company's premises. The vendor can help with the installation and frequently will offer to contract for the support and maintenance of the system. Many conventional applications are leased this way. The second way is to use an application service provider (ASP). The third way is to use software-as-a-service.

FIGURE 12.1
Operation of an application service provider (ASP).

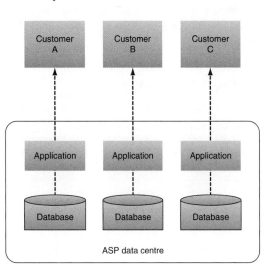

An **application service provider** is an agent or a vendor that assembles the software needed by enterprises and packages the software with services such as development, operations, and maintenance. The customer then accesses these applications via the Internet. Figure 12.1 shows the operation of an ASP. Note that the ASP hosts an application and database for each customer.

Use Software-as-a-Service

Software-as-a-service (SaaS) is a method of delivering software in which a vendor hosts the applications and provides them as a service to customers over a network, typically the Internet. Customers do not own the software; rather, they pay for using it. SaaS makes it unnecessary for customers to install and run the application on their own computers. Therefore, SaaS customers save the expense (money, time, IT staff) of buying, operating, and maintaining the software. For example, Salesforce (*www.salesforce.com*), a well-known SaaS provider for customer relationship management software solutions, provides these advantages for its customers. Figure 12.2 shows the operation of an SaaS vendor. Note that the SaaS vendor hosts an application that many customers can use. Further, the vendor hosts a database that is partitioned for each customer to protect the privacy and security of each customer's data.

Use Open-Source Software

Organizations can use open-source software (which we discuss in Technology Guide 2) to develop applications in-house. Organizations obtain a licence to employ an open-source software product and either use it as-is, or customize it, to develop applications.

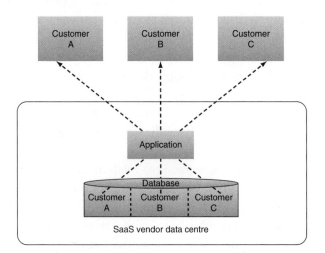

FIGURE 12.2 Operation of a software-as-a-service (SaaS) vendor.

Outsource

Small or medium-sized companies with few IT staff and limited budgets are best served by outside contractors. Acquiring IT applications from outside contractors or external organizations is called outsourcing. Large companies may also choose this strategy in certain circumstances. For example, they might want to experiment with new IT technologies without making a substantial up-front investment. They also might use outsourcing to protect their internal networks and to gain access to outside experts. One disadvantage of outsourcing is that a company's valuable corporate data may be under the control of the outsourcing vendor. IT's About Business 12.2 shows how DuPont has used outsourcing as part of its strategy to focus on its core competencies.

IT'S ABOUT BUSINESS 12.2
DUPONT'S FOCUS: CHEMICALS, NOT INFORMATION TECHNOLOGY

Organizations that outsource their entire IT function tend to be small and medium-sized businesses. But don't tell that to DuPont (*www.dupont.com*), the second-largest chemical conglomerate in the world, behind only BASF, the German chemical giant (*www.basf.com*). With more than $26 billion in revenue in 2009, and some 58,000 employees operating in 80 countries, DuPont might seem an unlikely candidate to give control of its information technology to another company.

But that's exactly what happened with DuPont, creators of household names and materials like nylon, Teflon, Kevlar, Lycra, and Corian. DuPont, whose core competencies are chemical research and development, saw itself as a science company, not an IT company. Its decision to outsource its entire IT function initially raised some eyebrows, but the results have proved sceptics wrong.

Instead of contracting out to multiple vendors to provide specialized IT services, DuPont chose Computer Science Corporation (*www.csc.com*) to be the single IT services provider. So complete was the handover of the IT function that 2,600 DuPont IT workers became employees of CSC.

Under the 10-year, $40-billion contract, CSC was responsible for everything from engineering to administration—the whole IT life cycle—in 40 countries where DuPont operates. This included everything from e-mail to the enterprise resource planning system; from more than 55,000 desktop computers to mainframe computers; and from help desk support to network support.

Outsourcing often benefits organizations by allowing them to focus on their business instead of IT. Not only has DuPont done this, but it's saved money as well. Its IT costs were reduced by 6–8 percent more than was originally forecast when the contract with CSC was signed. User satisfaction has increased significantly as well. DuPont is so satisfied with the arrangement that it extended CSC's contract for another seven years, valued at nearly an additional $2 billion.

Sources: Compiled from B. Violino, "Outsourcing Governance: A Success Story," The Outsourcing Institute, March 21, 2008; P. McDougall, "DuPont Set to Hand CSC $1.9 billion Outsourcing Extension," *InformationWeek*, July 2005; "DuPont: IT Outsourcing Provides the Flexibility for Change," CSC Case Study, *www.csc.com*, accessed April 9, 2009; "DuPont Takes a Strategic Move Towards Outsourcing to Achieve Performance Success," *ZDNet*, January 1, 2003; DuPont website (*www.dupont.com*), accessed July 8, 2010.

QUESTIONS
1. Why do you think more organizations have not adopted the model of outsourcing IT functions that DuPont has?
2. What disadvantages do you see with this type of outsourcing agreement?

Several types of vendors offer services for creating and operating IT systems including e-commerce applications. Many software companies, from IBM to Oracle, offer a range of outsourcing services for developing, operating, and maintaining IT applications. IT outsourcers, such as EDS, offer a variety of services. Also, the large public accounting companies and management consultants (for example, Accenture) offer some outsourcing services. As the trend to outsource is rising, so is the trend to relocate these operations offshore, particularly in India and China. *Offshoring* can save money, but it includes risks as well, such as sending sensitive corporate data overseas.

Develop the Applications In-House

A third development strategy is to build applications in-house. Although this approach is usually more time-consuming and more costly than buying or leasing, it often results in a better fit with the organization's specific requirements.

In-house development can make use of various methodologies. The basic, backbone methodology is the systems development life cycle (SDLC), which we discuss in the next section. In Section 12.5, we examine the methodologies that complement the SDLC: prototyping, joint application development, integrated computer-assisted systems development tools, and rapid application development. We also consider four other methodologies: agile development, end-user development, component-based development, and object-oriented development.

BEFORE YOU GO ON ...

1. Describe the advantages and disadvantages of acquiring or leasing standard software.
2. Define ASPs, and discuss the advantages to companies using them.
3. Explain the advantages of outsourcing IT services.

12.4 The Traditional Systems Development Life Cycle

The **systems development life cycle (SDLC)** is the traditional systems development method that organizations use for large-scale IT projects. The SDLC is a structured framework that consists of sequential processes by which information systems are developed (see Figure 12.3; the processes and terms shown will be discussed throughout the chapter). For our purposes we identify six processes:

- systems investigation
- systems analysis
- systems design
- programming and testing
- implementation
- operation and maintenance.

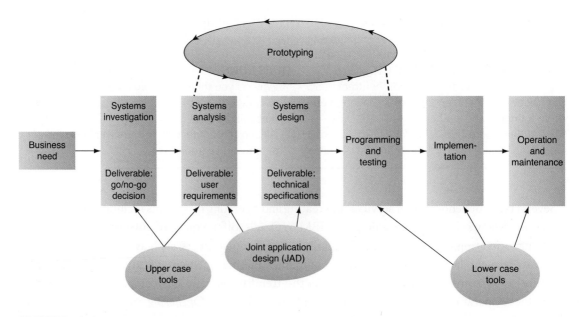

FIGURE 12.3 A six-stage systems development life cycle (SDLC) with supporting tools.

Each process in turn consists of well-defined tasks.

Other models for the SDLC contain more or fewer than the six stages we present here. The flow of tasks, however, remains largely the same. When problems occur in any phase of the SDLC, developers must often go back to previous phases.

Systems development projects produce desired results through team efforts. Development teams typically include users, systems analysts, programmers, and technical specialists. *Users* are employees from all functional areas and levels of the organization who interact with the system, either directly or indirectly. **Systems analysts** are IS professionals who specialize in analyzing and designing information systems. **Programmers** are IS professionals who modify existing computer programs or write new computer programs to satisfy user requirements. **Technical specialists** are experts on a certain type of technology, such as databases or telecommunications. Finally, the **systems stakeholders** include everyone who is affected by changes in a company's information systems (users and managers, for example). All stakeholders are typically involved at various times and in varying degrees in systems development. Table 12.2 discusses the advantages and disadvantages of the SDLC.

TABLE 12.2
ADVANTAGES AND DISADVANTAGES OF SYSTEM ACQUISITION METHODS

	ADVANTAGES	DISADVANTAGES
Traditional Systems Development (SDLC)	• Forces staff to systematically go through every step in a structured process. • Enforces quality by maintaining standards. • Has lower probability of missing important issues in collecting user requirements.	• Users may be unwilling or unable to study the specifications they approve. • Takes too long to go from the original ideas to a working system. • Users have trouble describing requirements for a proposed system. • Systems may be error prone and poorly tested.
Prototyping	• Helps clarify user requirements. • Helps verify the feasibility of the design. • Promotes genuine user participation. • Promotes close working relationship between systems developers and users. • Works well for ill-defined problems. • May produce part of the final system.	• May encourage inadequate problem analysis. • Not practical with large number of users. • Users may not give up the prototype when the system is completed. • May generate confusion about whether the system is complete and maintainable. • System may be built quickly, which may result in lower quality.
Joint Application Design (JAD)	• Involves many users in the development process. • Saves time. • There is greater user support for new system.	• Difficult to get all users to attend JAD meeting. • JAD approach has all the problems associated with any group meeting.

(Continued on next page)

TABLE 12.2 (Continued)		
	• The quality of the new system is improved. • New system easier to implement. • New system has lower training costs.	
Integrated Computer-Assisted Software Engineering (ICASE)	• Can produce systems with a longer effective operational life. • Can produce systems that closely meet user requirements. • Can speed up the development process. • Can produce systems that are more flexible and adaptable to changing business conditions. • Can produce excellent documentation.	• Systems are often more expensive to build and maintain. • Requires more extensive and accurate definition of user requirements. • Difficult to customize.
Rapid Application Development (RAD)	• Can speed up systems development. • Users intensively involved from the start. • Improves the process of rewriting legacy applications.	• Produces functional components of final systems, but not final systems.
End-User Development	• Bypasses the IS department and avoids delays. • User controls the application and can change it as needed. • Directly meets user requirements. • There is increased user acceptance of new system. • Frees up IT resources.	• May eventually require maintenance from IS department. • Documentation may be inadequate. • Poor quality control. • System may not have adequate interfaces to existing systems. • May create lower-quality systems.
Object-Oriented Development	• Objects model real-world entities. • May be able to reuse some computer code.	• Works best with systems of more limited scope; i.e., with systems that do not have huge numbers of objects.

Systems Investigation

The initial stage in a traditional SDLC is systems investigation. Systems development professionals agree that the more time they invest in (a) understanding the business problem to be solved, (b) specifying the technical options for systems, and (c) anticipating the problems that are likely to occur during development, the greater the chances of success. For these reasons, systems investigation addresses *the business problem* (or business opportunity) by means of the feasibility study.

The main task in the systems investigation stage is the feasibility study. Organizations have three basic solutions to any business problem relating to an information system: (1) do nothing and continue to use the existing system unchanged, (2) modify or enhance the existing system, or (3) develop a new system. The **feasibility study** analyzes which of these three solutions best fits the particular business problem. It also provides a rough assessment of the project's technical, economic, and behavioural feasibility, as we discuss next.

- *Technical feasibility* determines if the hardware, software, and communications components can be developed and/or acquired to solve the business problem. Technical feasibility also determines whether the organization can use its existing technology to achieve the project's performance objectives.
- *Economic feasibility* determines if the project is an acceptable financial risk, and if so, whether the organization has the necessary time and money to successfully complete the project. We have already discussed the commonly used methods to determine economic feasibility: NPV, ROI, break-even analysis, and the business case approach.
- *Behavioural feasibility* addresses the human issues of the systems development project. Clearly, you will be heavily involved in this aspect of the feasibility study.

After the feasibility analysis is completed, a "Go/No-Go" decision is reached by the **IT steering committee**, if there is one, or by top management in the absence of a committee. The Go/No-Go decision does not depend solely on the feasibility analysis. Organizations often have more feasible projects than they can fund. Therefore, the firm must prioritize the feasible projects, pursuing those with the highest priority. Unfunded feasible projects may not be presented to the IT department at all. These projects therefore contribute to the *hidden backlog*, which are projects that the IT department is not aware of.

If the decision is "No-Go," then the project either is put on the shelf until conditions are more favourable, or it is discarded. If the decision is "Go," then the project proceeds, and the systems analysis phase begins.

Systems Analysis

Once a development project has the necessary approvals from all participants, the systems analysis stage begins. **Systems analysis** is the examination of the business problem that the organization plans to solve with an information system.

The main purpose of the systems analysis stage is to gather information about the existing system in order to determine the requirements for an enhanced system or a new system. The end product of this stage, known as the "deliverable," is a set of *system requirements*.

Arguably the most difficult task in systems analysis is to identify the specific requirements that the system must satisfy. These requirements are often called *user requirements*, because users (meaning you) provide them. You can see that you will have a great deal of input into these processes. The closer your involvement, the better the chance that you will get an information system or application that meets your needs. When the systems developers have accumulated the user requirements for the new system, they proceed to the systems design stage.

Systems Design

Systems design describes how the system will resolve the business problem. The deliverable of the systems design phase is the set of *technical system specifications*, which specifies the following:

- System outputs, inputs, and user interfaces
- Hardware, software, databases, telecommunications, personnel, and procedures
- A blueprint of how these components are integrated

When the system specifications are approved by all participants, they are "frozen." That is, once the specifications are agreed upon, they should not be changed. Adding functions after the project has been initiated causes **scope creep**, which endangers the budget and schedule of a project. Scope creep occurs during development when users add to or change the information requirements of a system after those requirements have been "frozen." Because scope creep is expensive, successful project managers place controls on changes requested by users. These controls help to prevent runaway projects.

Programming and Testing

If the organization decides to construct the software in-house, then programming begins. **Programming** involves translating the design specifications into computer code. This process can be lengthy and time-consuming, because writing computer code is as much an art as a science. Large systems development projects can require hundreds of thousands of lines of computer code and hundreds of computer programmers. These large-scale projects employ programming and testing teams. These teams often include functional area users, who help the programmers focus on the business problem and assist with the testing.

Thorough and continuous testing occurs throughout the programming stage. Testing is the process that checks to see if the computer code will produce the expected and desired results and is designed to detect errors, or bugs, in the computer code.

Implementation

Implementation (or *deployment*) is the process of converting from the old system to the new system. Organizations use three major conversion strategies: direct, pilot, and phased.

In a **direct conversion**, the old system is cut off and the new system is turned on at a certain point in time. This type of conversion is the least expensive. It is also the most risky if the new system does not work as planned, because there is no support from the old system. Because of these risks, few systems are implemented using direct conversion.

A **pilot conversion** introduces the new system in one part of the organization, such as in one plant or in one functional area. The new system runs for a period of time and is then assessed. If the assessment confirms that the system is working properly, then it is introduced in other parts of the organization.

A **phased conversion** introduces components of the new system, such as individual modules, in stages. Each module is assessed. If it works properly, then other modules are introduced until the entire new system is operational.

A fourth strategy, parallel conversion, where the old and new systems operate simultaneously for a time, is hardly used today. For example, parallel conversion is totally impractical when both the old and new systems are on-line. Imagine that you are finishing an order on Amazon.com, only to be told, "Before your order can be entered here, you must provide all the same information again, in a different form, and on a different set of screens." The results would be disastrous for Amazon. A variation, called a "historic parallel," is used in which real transactions are run through the new system and the results compared before the new systems are moved in for live usage.

All of these tasks are done by programmers. IT's About Business 12.3 illustrates the importance of tracking work done by programmers, and of testing that work.

IT'S ABOUT BUSINESS 12.3
WHAT IS YOUR PROGRAMMER DOING?

In addition to preparing invoices, calculating paycheque amounts, and sending money via e-commerce, software programs are involved in sending many routine reports or documentation to customers, clients, or suppliers. Let's look at what might be a least favourite topic for many people: income taxes. Most people pay income taxes, and some people get distributions such as tax credit payments. Software programs calculate whether someone is eligible for these tax credit

(Continued on next page)

payments, and sends payments or forms to individuals for completion.

In the United Kingdom, the department that handles income taxes and customs and excise taxes is called HM Revenue and Customs (HMRC; *www.hmrc.gov.uk*). In May 2010, HMRC sent tax forms to 50,000 people with income information and banking information so that these forms could be completed and people could receive their tax credit. The problem was that the addresses and private information were mixed up. People received someone else's private information, including income information and portions of bank account numbers. Only a computer programming error could account for this size of error!

Unfortunately, this was not the first time that HMRC had problems managing its systems. Apparently about 1,600 information requests about dependents were also sent to the wrong families in February 2010.

Both of the above examples indicate some kind of problem with testing—perhaps selection criteria for creating the data to circulate were incorrectly established. Alternatively, a program that matched data from customers with mailing data was incorrectly done.

Another instance where closer tabs should have been kept on programmers occurred at Goldman Sachs (*www2.goldmansachs.com/worldwide/canada/*), the worldwide investment banking service organization, with locations in 32 countries. Goldman Sachs uses custom developed software as part of its operations to differentiate the company from its competition. In July 2009, the company charged a former employee with stealing computer software and allegedly selling this software to a competing firm. Goldman Sachs had electronic logs (data files that tracked the key strokes of its employees, including copying and erasing attempts) that the company claimed supported its charges.

It is routine for programmers at organizations to have access to software for development and testing purposes. Goldman Sachs needed to entrust its software development to trustworthy people so that it could continue to provide services to its customers.

Sources: Compiled from G. Gilmore, "Revenue Sends Wrong Private Information to 50,000 People," Timesonline.co.uk, May 27, 2010; D. Glovin, C. Harper, and S. Kishan, "Goldman May Lose Millions from Ex-worker's Code Theft," Bloomberg, July 7, 2009; G. Keizer, "Senior Developer Arrested for 'Stealing' Stock Trading Code," itbusiness.ca, July 9, 2009; May 27, 2010, "Taxman Sends Wrong Personal Details to 50,000," ThisIsMoney.co.uk, May 27, 2010.

QUESTIONS

1. Provide examples of methods that HMRC could use to test its data or programs before sending it to individuals.
2. What can organizations such as Goldman Sachs do to protect their proprietary software?
3. Why would Goldman Sachs have custom-developed software rather than packaged software?

Operation and Maintenance

After the new system is implemented, it will operate for a period of time, until (like the old system it replaced) it no longer meets its objectives. Once the new system's operations are stabilized, the company performs *audits* to assess the system's capabilities and to determine if it is being used correctly.

Systems need several types of maintenance. The first type is *debugging* the program, a process that continues throughout the life of the system. The second type is *updating* the system to accommodate changes in business conditions. An example is adjusting to new governmental regulations, such as the general change in the GST tax rate in Canada on January 1, 2008, from six percent to five percent. These corrections and upgrades usually do not add any new functions. Instead, they simply help the system to continue meeting its objectives. In contrast, the third type of maintenance *adds new functions* to the existing system without disturbing its operation.

BEFORE YOU GO ON ...

1. Describe the feasibility study.
2. What is the difference between systems analysis and systems design?
3. Describe structured programming.
4. What are the four conversion methods?

12.5 Alternative Methods and Tools for Systems Development

There are a number of tools that are used in conjunction with the traditional systems development life cycle (SDLC). The first four tools that we discuss in this section are designed to supplement the SDLC and make various functions of the SDLC easier and faster to perform. These tools are prototyping, joint application design, computer-aided software engineering, and rapid application development.

We then shift our focus to alternative methods of developing systems that are used instead of the SDLC. These methods include agile development, end-user development, component-based development, and object-oriented development.

Prototyping

The **prototyping** approach defines an initial list of user requirements, builds a model of the system, and then improves the system in several iterations based on users' feedback. Developers do not try to obtain a complete set of user specifications for the system at the outset, and they do not plan to develop the system all at once. Instead, they quickly develop a smaller working version of the system known as a *prototype*. A **prototype** can take two forms. In some cases it contains only the components of the new system that are of most interest to the users. In other cases it is a small-scale working model of the entire system.

Users make suggestions for improving the prototype, based on their experiences with it. The developers then review the prototype with the users and use their suggestions to refine the prototype. This process continues through several iterations until the users approve the system or it becomes apparent that the system cannot meet the users' needs. If the system is viable, then the developers can use the prototype to build the full system. Figure 12.3 shows how this relates to the traditional systems development life cycle. One typical use of prototyping is to develop screens that a user will see and interact with. Table 12.2 describes the advantages and disadvantages of the prototyping approach.

Prototyping also has disadvantages. The first disadvantage is that users, seeing screens that appear to behave like the completed system, will not realize the amount of work that still must be done behind the scenes to provide an operational system with a database, error checking, security precautions, and all the other functions that a prototype does not have (and does not need).

Joint Application Design

Joint application design (JAD) is a group-based tool for collecting user requirements and creating system designs (see Figure 12.3). JAD is most often used within the systems analysis and systems design stages of the SDLC. JAD involves a group meeting attended by the analysts and all of the users. It is basically a group decision-making process that can be conducted manually or via the computer. During this meeting, all users jointly define and agree on the system requirements. This process saves a tremendous amount of time. Table 12.2 lists the advantages and disadvantages of the JAD process.

Among the JAD approach's disadvantages is that it is very difficult to get all users to attend the JAD meeting. For example, in large organizations the users might be scattered all over the world. Second, the JAD approach has all the problems associated with any group process (for example, one person can dominate the meeting, some participants may not contribute in a group setting, and so on). To alleviate these problems, JAD sessions usually have a facilitator who is skilled in systems analysis and design as well as in managing group meetings and processes. Also, the use of groupware (such as GDSS, group decision support system, discussed in Chapter 11) can help facilitate the meeting.

Integrated Computer-Assisted Software Engineering Tools

Computer-aided software engineering (CASE) is a development approach that uses specialized tools to automate many of the tasks in the SDLC. The tools used to automate the early stages of the SDLC (systems investigation, analysis, and design) are called *upper CASE tools* (see Figure 12.3). The tools used to automate later stages in the SDLC (programming, testing, implementation, operation, and maintenance) are called *lower CASE tools* (see Figure 12.3). CASE tools that provide links between upper CASE and lower CASE tools are called integrated CASE (ICASE) tools. Table 12.2 lists the advantages and disadvantages of ICASE tools.

CASE tools provide advantages for systems developers. These tools can produce systems with a longer effective operational life and that more closely meet user requirements. They can also speed up the development process. Further, they help produce systems that are more flexible and adaptable to changing business conditions. Finally, systems produced using CASE tools typically have excellent documentation.

At the same time, however, initial systems produced by CASE tools are often more expensive to build and maintain. In addition, CASE tools require more extensive and accurate definitions of user needs and requirements. Finally, CASE tools are difficult to customize. For this reason, they are sometimes difficult to use with existing systems.

Rapid Application Development

Rapid application development (RAD) is a systems development method that can combine JAD, prototyping, and ICASE tools to rapidly produce a high-quality system. In the first RAD stage, developers use JAD sessions to collect system requirements, ensuring that users are intensively involved early on. The development process in RAD is iterative, similar to prototyping. That is, requirements, designs, and the system itself are developed and then undergo a series, or sequence, of improvements. RAD uses ICASE tools to quickly structure requirements and develop prototypes. As the prototypes are developed and refined, users review them in additional JAD sessions. RAD produces functional components of a final system, rather than limited-scale versions. To understand how RAD functions and how it differs from SDLC, see Figure 12.4. Table 12.2 shows the advantages and disadvantages of the RAD process.

RAD methodologies and tools make it possible to develop systems faster, especially systems where the user interface is an important component. RAD can also improve the process of rewriting legacy applications.

Agile Development

Agile development is a software development methodology that delivers functionality in rapid iterations, which are usually measured in weeks. To be successful, this methodology requires frequent

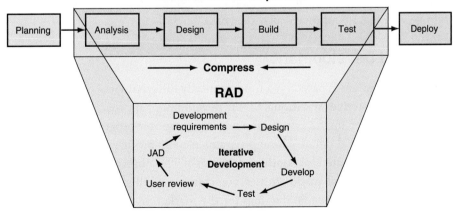

FIGURE 12.4 A rapid prototyping development process versus the traditional SDLC development approach.
Source: datawarehouse-training.com/Methodologies/rapid-application-development.

communication, development, testing, and delivery. Agile development focuses on rapid development and frequent user contact to create software that addresses the needs of business users. This software does not have to include every possible feature the user will require. Rather, it must meet only the user's more important and immediate needs. It can be updated later to introduce additional functions as they become necessary. The core tenet of agile development is to do only what you have to do to be successful right now.

Agile development uses small (five- to nine-person) teams, which are located with users and are cross-functional. The teams deliver project features about every two to four weeks. They schedule a demonstration with users in order to receive feedback. After each demo, the development team meets to decide which aspects of the project are going well and which aspects need improvement. The team then selects the next three top priorities and adjusts the upcoming schedule accordingly.

A "very present" user is critical to the success of agile development. For example, consider a system with an initial requirement to handle electronic payments. The development team discovers that using PayPal will be much easier than trying to write new computer code to integrate with credit card processors. If the user agrees that PayPal is sufficient, then the development team can quickly implement the solution.

End-User Development

End-user development refers to an organization's end users developing their own applications with little or no formal assistance from the IT department. Table 12.2 shows the advantages and disadvantages of end-user development. Beneficial as end-user development is to both workers and the organization as a whole, it has some limitations. To begin with, end users may not be skilled enough in application development. This lack of skill can jeopardize quality and cost unless the organization installs proper controls. Also, many end users do not take enough time to document their work. In addition, they sometimes fail to take proper security measures. Finally, users often develop databases that cannot efficiently manage all of their production data.

Component-Based Development

Component-based development uses standard components to build applications. Components are reusable applications that generally have one specific function, such as a shopping cart, user authentication, or a catalogue. Component-based development is closely linked with the idea of web services and service-oriented architectures, which we discussed in Chapter 10.

Many start-up companies are pursuing the idea of component-based application development, or less programming and more assembly. An example is Ning (*www.ning.com*), which allows you to create, customize, and share your own social network.

Object-Oriented Development

Object-oriented development is based on a fundamentally different view of computer systems than the perception that characterizes traditional SDLC development approaches. Traditional approaches provide specific step-by-step instructions in the form of computer programs, in which programmers must specify every procedural detail. These programs usually produce a system that performs the original task but may not be suited for handling other tasks. This observation applies even when these other tasks involve the same real-world entities. For example, a billing system will handle billing but probably cannot be adapted to handle mailings for the marketing department or generate leads for the sales force. This is true even though the billing, marketing, and sales functions all use similar data, including customer names, addresses, and purchases. In contrast, an *object-oriented (OO) system* begins not with the task to be performed, but with the aspects of the real world that must be modelled to perform that task. Therefore, in the example above, if the firm has a good model of its customers and its interactions with them, this model can be used equally well for billings, mailings, and sales leads.

The development process for an object-oriented system begins with a feasibility study and an analysis of the existing system, like other types of developments. Systems developers identify the *objects* in the new system—the fundamental elements in OO analysis and design. Each object represents a tangible, real-world entity, such as a customer, bank account, student, or course. Objects have *properties*, or *data values*. For example, a customer has an identification number, name, address, account number(s), and so on. Objects also contain the *operations* that can be performed on their properties. For example, customer objects' operations may include obtain-account-balance, open-account, withdraw-funds, and so on. Operations are also referred to as *behaviours*.

In this way, object-oriented analysts define all the relevant objects needed for the new system, including their properties and operations. They then model how the objects interact to meet the objectives of the new system. In some cases, analysts can reuse existing objects from other applications (or from a library of objects) in the new system. This process saves the analysts the time they otherwise would spend coding these objects. In most cases, however, even with object reuse, some coding will be necessary to customize the objects and their interactions for the new system. The major disadvantages of object-oriented programming is that it becomes very complex as the number of objects increase, which can slow down processing. Table 12.2 summarizes the advantages and disadvantages of object-oriented development.

We have discussed many methods that can be used to acquire new systems. Table 12.2 provides an overview of the advantages and disadvantages of these methods.

BEFORE YOU GO ON ...

1. Describe the tools that augment the traditional SDLC.
2. Describe the alternate methods that can be used for systems development, other than the traditional SDLC.

12.6 Vendor and Software Selection

Few organizations, especially SMEs (small and medium enterprises), have the time, financial resources, or technical expertise required to develop today's complex IT or e-business systems. As a result, business firms are increasingly relying on outside vendors to provide software, hardware, and technical expertise. For example, packaged accounting software is available from TSM Newviews (*http://nv2accounting.com/nv2_evaluation.aspx*), Intuit Quickbooks (*http://quickbooks.intuit.ca/accounting-software/index.jsp*) and Simply Accounting (*http://www.simplyaccounting.com/*).

Selecting and managing these vendors and their software offerings has become a major aspect of acquiring an IT application. The following six steps for selecting a software vendor and an application package are useful.

Step 1: Identify Potential Vendors. Companies can identify potential software application vendors through various sources:

- Software catalogues
- Lists provided by hardware vendors
- Technical and trade journals
- Consultants and industry analysts experienced in the application area
- Peers in other companies
- Web searches

These sources often yield so many vendors and packages that the company must use some evaluation criteria to eliminate all but the most promising ones from further consideration. For example, it can eliminate vendors that are too small or have a questionable reputation. Also, it can eliminate packages that do not have the required features or are not compatible with the company's existing hardware and/or software.

Step 2: Determine the Evaluation Criteria. The most difficult and crucial task in evaluating a vendor and a software package is to select a detailed set of evaluation criteria. Some areas in which a customer should develop detailed criteria are:

- Characteristics of the vendor
- Functional requirements of the system
- Technical requirements that the software must satisfy
- Amount and quality of documentation provided
- Vendor support of the package

These criteria should be set out in a **request for proposal (RFP)**. An RFP is a document that is sent to potential vendors inviting them to submit a proposal that describes their software package and explains how it would meet the company's needs. The RFP provides the vendors with information about the objectives and requirements of the system. Specifically, it describes the environment in which the system will be used, the general criteria that the company will use to evaluate the proposals, and the conditions for submitting proposals. The RFP may also request a list of current users of the package whom the company may contact. Finally, it can require the vendor to demonstrate the package at the company's facilities using specified inputs and data files.

Step 3: Evaluate Vendors and Packages. The responses to an RFP generate massive volumes of information that the company must evaluate. The goal of this evaluation is to determine the gaps between the company's needs (as specified by the requirements) and the capabilities of the vendors and their application packages. Often, the company gives the vendors and packages an overall score by (1) assigning an importance weight to each of the criteria, (2) ranking the vendors on each of the weighted criteria (say 1 to 10), and then (3) multiplying the ranks by the associated weights. The company can then shorten the list of potential suppliers to include only those vendors who achieved the highest overall scores.

Step 4: Choose the Vendor and Package. Once the company has shortened the list of potential suppliers, it can begin negotiations with these vendors to determine how their packages might be modified to remove any discrepancies with the company's IT needs. Thus, one of the most important factors in the decision is the additional development effort that may be required to tailor the system to the company's needs or to integrate it into the company's computing environment. The company must also consider the opinions of both the users and the IT personnel who will have to support the system.

Several software selection methods exist. For a list of general criteria, see Table 12.3.

Step 5: Negotiate a Contract. The contract with the software vendor is very important. It specifies both the price of the software and the type and amount of support that the vendor agrees to provide. The contract will be the only recourse if either the system or the vendor does not perform as expected. It is essential, then, that the contract directly reference the proposal, because this is the method that the vendor used to document the functionality supported in its system. Furthermore, if the vendor is modifying the software to tailor it to the company's needs, the contract must include detailed specifications (essentially the requirements) of the modifications. Finally, the contract should describe in detail the acceptance tests that the software package must pass.

Contracts are legal documents, and they can be quite tricky. For this reason, companies might need the services of experienced contract negotiators and lawyers. Many organizations employ

The contract outlines all the services provided by the software vendor.

TABLE 12.3
CRITERIA FOR SELECTING A SOFTWARE APPLICATION PACKAGE

Functionality (Does the package do what the organization needs?)	Availability and quality of documentation Necessary hardware and networking resources
Cost and financial terms	Required training (check if provided by vendor)
Upgrade policy and cost	Quality of security
Vendor's reputation and availability for help	Learning (speed of) for developers and users
Vendor's success stories (visit their website, contact clients)	Quality of graphical presentation
System flexibility	Data handling capabilities
Ease of Internet interface	Nature of system-required hardware

software-purchasing specialists who assist in negotiations and write or approve the contract. These specialists should be involved in the selection process from the start.

Step 6: Establish a Service Level Agreement. **Service level agreements (SLAs)** are formal agreements that specify how work is to be divided between the company and its vendors. These divisions are based on a set of agreed-upon milestones, quality checks, and what-if situations. They describe how quality checks will be made and what is to be done in case of disputes. SLAs accomplish these goals by (1) defining the responsibilities of both partners, (2) providing a framework for designing support services, and (3) allowing the company to retain as much control as possible over its own systems. SLAs include such issues as performance, availability, backup and recovery, upgrades, and hardware and software ownership. For example, the SLA might specify that the ASP have its system available to the customer 99.9 percent of the time.

BEFORE YOU GO ON ...

1. List the major steps in selecting a vendor and a software package.
2. Describe a request for proposal (RFP).
3. Explain why SLAs play an important role in systems development.

WHAT'S IN IT FOR ME?

FOR THE ACCOUNTING MAJOR

Accounting personnel help perform the cost-benefit analyses on proposed projects. They may also monitor ongoing project costs to keep them within budget. Accounting personnel undoubtedly will find themselves involved with systems development at various points throughout their careers.

FOR THE FINANCE MAJOR

Finance personnel are frequently involved with the financial issues that accompany any large-scale systems development project (for example, budgeting). They also are involved in cost-benefit and risk analyses. To perform these tasks they need to stay abreast of the emerging techniques used to determine project costs and ROI. Finally, because they must manage vast amounts of information, finance departments are also common recipients of new systems.

FOR THE MARKETING MAJOR

In most organizations, marketing, like finance, involves massive amounts of data and information. Like finance, then, marketing is also a hotbed of systems development. Marketing personnel will increasingly find themselves participating in systems development teams. Such involvement increasingly means helping to develop systems, especially web-based systems that reach out directly from the organization to its customers.

FOR THE PRODUCTION/OPERATIONS MANAGEMENT MAJOR

Participation on development teams is also a common role for production/operations people. Manufacturing is becoming increasingly computerized and integrated with other allied systems, from design to logistics to customer support. Production systems interface frequently with marketing, finance, and human resources. In addition, they may be part of a larger, enterprise-wide system. Also, many end users in POM either develop their own systems or collaborate with IT personnel on specific applications.

FOR THE HUMAN RESOURCES MANAGEMENT MAJOR

The human resources department is closely involved with several aspects of the systems acquisitions process. Acquiring new systems may require hiring new employees, changing job descriptions, or terminating employees. Human resources performs all of these tasks. Further, if the organization hires consultants for the development project or outsources it, the human resources department may handle the contracts with these suppliers.

FOR THE MIS MAJOR

Regardless of the approach that the organization adopts for acquiring new systems, the MIS department spearheads it. If the organization chooses either to buy or to lease the application, the MIS department leads in examining the offerings of the various vendors and in negotiating with the vendors. If the organization chooses to develop the application in-house, then the process falls to the MIS department. MIS analysts work closely with users to develop their information requirements. MIS programmers then write the computer code, test it, and implement the new system.

SUMMARY

1. **Define project management and describe how projects should be managed and controlled.**

   IS project management is a directed effort to plan, organize, and manage resources to bring about the successful achievement of a specific systems-related goal and its associated results. Projects should match business needs and be effectively approved at all phases. All projects, whether they are IS projects or not, are constrained by the same three factors, known as the triple constraints of project management: time, cost, and scope. *Time* refers to the window of opportunity in which a project may be completed to provide a benefit to the organization. *Cost* is the actual amount of resources, including cash and labour, which an organization can commit to completing a project. *Scope* is the processes required to ensure that the project includes all the work required, and only the work required, to complete the project successfully.

2. **Provide alternatives for justifying IT investments.**

   The justification process is basically a comparison of the expected costs versus the benefits of each application. Although measuring costs generally is not complex, measuring benefits is, due to the many intangible benefits involved. Several methodologies exist for evaluating costs and benefits, including net present value, return on investment, break-even analysis, and the business case approach.

3. **Identify and describe the advantages and disadvantages of the major alternative strategies for acquiring information systems.**

   Companies have several options for acquiring IT applications. Six common options are to (1) buy standard applications, (2) lease them, (3) use software-as-a-service, (4) use open-source software, (5) outsource them, and (6) develop them in-house.

4. **Describe the SDLC (systems development life cycle) approach.**

   The systems development life cycle (SDLC) is the traditional method used by most organizations today. The SDLC is a structured framework that consists of distinct sequential processes: systems investigation, systems analysis, systems design, programming, testing, implementation, operation, and maintenance. These processes, in turn, consist of well-defined tasks. Some of these tasks are present in most projects, and others are present in only certain types of projects. That is, smaller development projects may require only a subset of tasks, whereas large projects typically require all tasks. Using the SDLC guarantees quality and security, but it is slow and expensive.

5. **Explain how the IT development process can been modified and why.**

   The major options for developing IT are buy, lease, and build (develop in-house). Building in-house can be done by using the SDLC, prototyping, or other methodologies. It can be done by outsourcers, hosting vendors, the IS department employees, or end users (individually or together).

   The more common alternative for the SDLC is quick prototyping, which helps to test systems. Useful prototyping tools for SDLC are joint application design (for finding information needs) and rapid application development (which uses CASE tools). For smaller and rapidly needed applications, designers can use agile development, component-based development, and object-oriented development tools, which are popular in web-based applications. These alternative methods are used to lower SDLC costs and speed the process.

6. **Describe the process for vendor and software selection.**

   The process of vendor and software selection is composed of six steps: identify potential vendors, determine evaluation criteria, evaluate vendors and packages, choose the vendor and package, negotiate a contract, and establish service level agreements.

KEY TERMS

DISCUSSION QUESTIONS

1. Describe the phases of project management and how they can be applied to the acquisition of information systems technology.
2. ABC Company is considering implementing a software system that costs about $25,000. Describe the methods that can be used to justify spending this sum.
3. Discuss the advantages of an information systems acquisition as a lease option versus a buy option.
4. Why is it important for everyone in business organizations to have a basic understanding of the systems development process?
5. Discuss the various types of feasibility studies. Why are they all needed?
6. Discuss the issue of assessing intangible benefits and the proposed solutions.
7. Should prototyping be used on every systems development project? Why or why not?
8. Discuss the reasons why end-user-developed information systems can be of poor quality. What can be done to improve this situation?
9. Why are ASPs becoming so increasingly attractive?
10. You have been asked to find a suitable customer relationship management software for your employer's small business, a company that installs and repairs air conditioners and furnaces. What considerations should you keep in mind while conducting your analysis of available suppliers?

PROBLEM-SOLVING ACTIVITIES

1. Your company is thinking of implementing new local area network software (purchase of an upgraded office suite with accounting software). Using the phases of project management, describe how this project should be managed.

2. In addition to saving money, what are some of the additional benefits that organizations would achieve from implementing a new customer relationship management system?

3. Your organization is thinking of switching from using its own in-house payroll system to using a payroll service by another organization. Describe how this change would be justified.

4. Rather than purchasing software for its accounting system, your company is thinking of using an ASP (application service provider). What are the advantages and disadvantages of purchasing versus using an application service provider?

5. Enter the websites of Gartner, Inc. (*www.gartnergroup.com*), the Yankee Group (*www.yankeegroup.com*), and CIO (*www.cio.com*). Search for recent material about ASPs and outsourcing, and prepare a report on your findings.

6. Enter *www.ibm.com/software*. Find its WebSphere product. Read recent customers' success stories. What makes this software so popular? What would be the advantages of acquiring this software versus developing your own software?

7. Access *www.ecommerce-guide.com*. Find the product review area. Read reviews of three software payment solutions. Assess them as possible components within a major systems development process. State the advantages of using these components.

8. Use an Internet search engine to obtain information on CASE and ICASE tools. Select several vendors and compare and contrast their offerings.

TEAM ASSIGNMENTS

1. Assessing the functionality of an application is a part of the planning process (Step 1) of acquiring software. Select three to five websites catering to the same type of buyer (for instance, several websites that offer CDs or computer hardware), and divide the sites among the teams. Each team will assess the functionality of its assigned website by preparing an analysis of the different sorts of functions provided by the sites. In addition, the team should compare the strong and weak points of each site from the buyer's perspective.

2. Divide into groups, with each group visiting a local company (include your university or college). At each organization, study the systems acquisition process. Find out the methodology or methodologies used by each organization and the type of application each methodology applies to. Prepare a report and present it to the class.

3. As a group, design an information system for a start-up business of your choice. Describe your chosen IT resource acquisition strategy, and justify your choices of hardware, software, telecommunications support, and other aspects of a proposed system.

CANADA REVENUE AGENCY: IMPROVING SYSTEMS DEVELOPMENT

Courtesy Canada Revenue Agency

THE BUSINESS PROBLEM

Try to save money and reduce costs as you process as many as three million transactions per hour. Be sure to process transactions accurately, and send tax refunds promptly! These are admirable goals, and part of the mandate of the Canada Revenue Agency (CRA, *www.cra-arc.gc.ca*). Employing about 4,000 information technology professionals and with over $500 million in its annual information technology budget, the CRA has been challenged to replace aging systems and reduce costs while doing so. The CRA has many tasks; it collects taxes, analyzes tax returns (personal, corporate, sales and excise taxes), as well as processes collections for other departments within the government (such as pension and unemployment insurance).

In 2006 the Office of the Auditor General of Canada (OAG, *www.oag-bvg.gc.ca*) reported that the federal government had invested $7.1 billion in information technology over a three-year period, with $431 million going to the Canada Revenue Agency. The OAG then found that governance of the projects was inadequate, including poor preparation of business cases.

In 2008, the OAG took a closer look at the management of information technology projects at the CRA. It found improvements, but also found that six of eight projects audited in detail did not meet the agency's own project management guidelines. For example, business cases did not contain sufficient detail, and one project was not accepted by the area that was supposed to use it. These deficiencies were particularly important because the CRA was in the process of preparing a catalogue of its systems to decide which ones needed to be updated.

The CRA stated that it had about 450 applications used nationally, and that about 141 of these needed to be updated in the next few years because they were no longer supported or because they used programming languages or software platforms that were being phased out. There were also hundreds of "local applications" that were used by one or more local offices. The agency did not know how all of these applications fit into the national systems and how they would be affected as the older systems were upgraded.

The key issue is that the CRA's information technology budget could not grow substantially; $500 million per year was likely to be the limit, and priorities needed to be established and a better method found to decide on which projects would be implemented and how they would be implemented.

THE IT SOLUTION

The CRA used an integrated risk management framework, which identifies risks and considers their likelihood and impact. The CRA completed its inventory of its information systems, and assessed the fit of the systems into the organization. It developed a multi-year strategic investment plan that considered its business needs and information needs. These included the replacement of a data centre and requirements for supporting its IT infrastructure. (In 2008 that infrastructure included 1,200 servers, 6 mainframe computer systems operating from two data centres, and almost 56,000 user stations.)

Management involvement in the planning process was high, making sure that teams from multiple functional units were involved in the planning, as well as meeting twice per year to consider short-term and long-term business requirements and priorities. Senior management met once per year to review the work that had been done as well as to evaluate the strategies developed.

THE RESULTS

In 2010, the OAG assessed how five government organizations, including the CRA, were dealing with aging information technology systems, and found that the CRA was the only agency that was most effectively identifying its risks and managing and monitoring those risks. Based upon that risk analysis, the CRA was the only one of the five government organizations that had looked at its needs strategically over a period of years rather than simply asking for funds on a project-by-project basis.

Sources: Compiled from: *2006 November Report of the Auditor General of Canada*, "Chapter 3—Large Information Technology Projects";

2008 December Report of the Auditor General of Canada, "Chapter 5—Managing Information Technology Investments: Canada Revenue Agency"; *2010 Spring Report of the Auditor General of Canada*, "Chapter 1—Aging Information Technology Systems."

QUESTIONS

1. What are some other ways that the Canada Revenue Agency can improve the process of managing the development of its information systems?
2. Provide examples of some uses of technology that you think would be suitable for the CRA to implement.

Web Resources

Student website www.wiley.com/canada/rainer

- Web quizzes
- Lecture slides in PowerPoint
- Author podcasts
- Interactive Case: Ruby's Club assignments

ALL OF THE ABOVE AND... WILEY ⊕ PLUS

- E-book
- Manager videos
- Vocabulary flash cards
- Pre- and post-lecture quizzes
- Microsoft Office 2007 lab manual and projects

ACQUIRING SYSTEMS FOR RUBY'S CLUB

Go to the Ruby's Club link at the Student Companion website or WileyPLUS for information about your current internship assignment. You will help the club's managers make decisions about purchasing, outsourcing, or building new systems for Ruby's.

TECHNOLOGY GUIDE 1
COMPUTER HARDWARE

LEARNING OBJECTIVES

1. Identify the major hardware components of a computer system.
2. Discuss strategic issues that link hardware design to business strategy.
3. Discuss the innovations in hardware utilization.
4. Describe the hierarchy of computers according to power and their respective roles.
5. Differentiate the various types of input and output technologies and their uses.
6. Describe the design and functioning of the central processing unit, and the relationship between memory and performance.
7. Discuss the relationships between microprocessor component designs, storage systems, and performance.

Technology Guide Overview

Decisions about hardware focus on three interrelated factors: appropriateness for the task, speed, and cost. The incredibly rapid rate of innovation in the computer industry complicates hardware decisions, because computer technologies become obsolete more quickly than other organizational technologies.

The overall trends in hardware are that it becomes smaller, faster, cheaper, and more powerful over time. In fact, these trends are so rapid that they make it difficult to know when to purchase (or upgrade) hardware. This difficulty lies in the fact that companies that delay hardware purchases will, more than likely, be able to buy more powerful hardware for the same amount of money in the future.

This technology guide will help you better understand the computer hardware decisions your organization must make as well as your personal computing decisions. Many of the design principles presented here apply to computers of all sizes, from an enterprise-wide system to your home computer. In addition, the dynamics of innovation and cost that we discuss can affect personal as well as corporate hardware decisions.

You might be wondering: Why do I have to know anything about hardware? There are several reasons why it is advantageous to know hardware basics. First, regardless of your major (and future functional area in an organization), you will be using hardware throughout your career. Second, you will have input concerning the hardware you are using. In this capacity you will be required to answer many questions, such as "Is it performing adequately for your needs? If not, what types of problems are you experiencing?" Third, you will also have input into decisions when your functional area or organization upgrades or replaces its hardware. MIS employees will act as advisors, but you will provide important input into such decisions. Finally, in some organizations, the budget for hardware is allocated to functional areas or departments. In such cases, you might be making hardware decisions (at least locally) yourself.

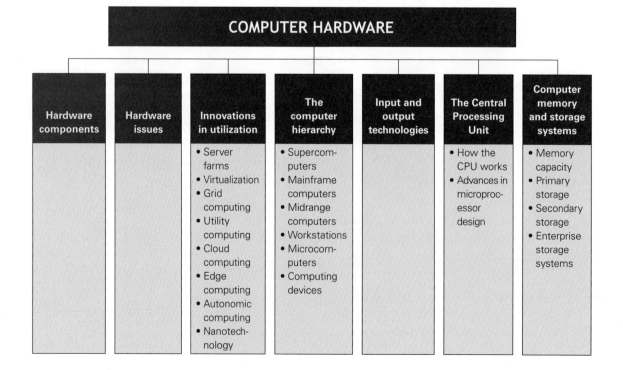

TG1.1 Introducing Hardware Components

As we noted in Chapter 1, *hardware* refers to the physical equipment used for the input, processing, output, and storage activities of a computer system. It consists of the following:

- *Central processing unit (CPU).* Manipulates the data and controls the tasks performed by the other components.
- *Primary storage.* Temporarily stores data and program instructions during processing.
- *Secondary storage.* External to the CPU; stores data and programs for future use.
- *Input technologies.* Accept data and instructions and convert them to a form that the computer can understand.
- *Output technologies.* Present data and information in a form people can understand.
- *Communication technologies.* Provide for the flow of data from external computer networks (e.g., the Internet and intranets) to the CPU, and from the CPU to computer networks.

The next two sections discuss broad hardware issues: strategic hardware issues and hardware innovations. The following sections address the various types of computers, input and output technologies, and storage methods.

BEFORE YOU GO ON ...

1. Decisions about hardware focus on what three factors?
2. What are the overall trends in hardware?
3. Define hardware, and list the major hardware components.

TG1.2 Strategic Hardware Issues

For many businesspeople the most important hardware issues are what the hardware enables, how it is advancing, and how rapidly it is advancing. In many industries, exploiting computer hardware is a key to achieving competitive advantage. Successful hardware exploitation comes from thoughtful consideration of the following questions:

- How do organizations keep up with the rapid price and performance advancements in hardware? For example, how often should an organization upgrade its computers and storage systems? Will upgrades increase personal and organizational productivity? How can organizations measure such increases?
- How should organizations determine the need for the new hardware infrastructures, such as server farms, virtualization, grid computing, and utility computing?
- Portable computers and advanced communications technologies have enabled employees to work from home or from anywhere. Will these new work styles benefit employees and the organization? How do organizations manage such new work styles?

One strategic consideration when choosing hardware is the cost and ease of use of the software that goes with it. Suppliers are taking steps to make that decision easier for clients, as the following example shows.

BEFORE YOU GO ON …

1. How do you think the various types of computer hardware affect personal productivity? Organizational productivity?

TG1.3 Innovations in Hardware Utilization

To fully understand hardware, we should have an idea of current innovations in hardware. In this section we discuss how companies are using their hardware resources in innovative ways, including server farms, virtualization, grid computing, utility computing, cloud computing, edge computing, autonomic computing, and nanotechnology.

Server Farms

Many companies are finding that they do not have enough computer processing power to meet their needs. In particular, they are experiencing an increasing shortage of facilities needed to manage, transmit, and store the data flowing from web-based applications. To address this problem they are building massive data centres called **server farms**, which contain hundreds of thousands of networked computer servers (see Figure TG1.1). As we discuss later in this technology guide, a *server* is a computer that supports networks, enabling users to share files, software, and other network devices.

The huge number of servers in a server farm provides redundancy and fault tolerance in case one or more servers fail. Server farms require massive amounts of electrical power, air conditioning, backup generators, security, and money. They also need to be located fairly closely to fibre optic communications links.

FIGURE TG1.1
Server farm.

Locations satisfying these requirements are difficult to find. For example, Yahoo and Microsoft constructed huge server farms in Quincy, Washington to take advantage of cheap, local hydroelectric power. Google built a massive server farm in Oregon for the same reason.

Virtualization

According to Gartner Inc. (*www.gartner.com*), a research firm, utilization rates on servers range from 5–10 percent. That is, most of the time, organizations are using only a small percentage of their total computing capacity. One reason for this low rate is that most organizations buy a new server every time they implement a new application. CIOs tolerate this inefficiency in order to make certain that they can supply enough computing resources to users when they are needed. Also, server prices have dropped more than 80 percent in the last decade, making it easier and cheaper to buy another server than to increase the utilization of the servers the company already has. However, virtualization has changed this situation.

Virtualization means that servers no longer have to be dedicated to a particular task. **Server virtualization** uses software-based partitions to create multiple virtual servers (called *virtual machines*) on a single physical server. Therefore, multiple applications can run on a single physical server, with each application running within its own software environment. Many benefits accrue to organizations using virtualization, including the following:

- a lower number of physical servers leads to cost savings in equipment, energy, space in the data centre, cooling, personnel, and maintenance
- enhanced organizational agility, as virtualization enables organizations to quickly modify their systems to respond to changing demands
- the focus of the information technology department can shift from the technology itself to the services that the technology can provide.

The following example illustrates the benefits of virtualization at the 407 Express Toll Route.

EXAMPLE TG1.2

The 407 Express Toll Route (407 ETR, see *www.407etr.com*) is a toll highway that runs 108 kilometres across the top of Toronto. This toll route uses automation (wireless devices) to charge for its tolls. The company that manages the highway, 407 ETR Concession Company Limited, employs about 500 people for billing and collections, as well as highway and information systems maintenance. The company wanted to use less physical space for its servers, improve response time for adding servers, and save money on electricity. It decided that one way to do so was to implement server virtualization using VMware (*www.vmware.com*) with the help of a Canadian outsourcing organization called Scalar Decisions Inc. (*www.scalar.ca*).

The company was able to almost immediately reduce the number of servers it had from 148 to 108. This was done by implementing 65 virtual servers. The software and hardware acquired by 407 ETR will enable it to add another 60 servers, with implementation times of less than an hour per server, which is substantially less time than what it would take to implement physical servers. The company expects to save about 24,000 kilowatt hours of electricity per year, which it says is equivalent to driving 28 cars.

Sources: Compiled from B. Jackson, "407 Expressway's Tech Team Cuts Costs, Saves Time with Server Virtualization," itbusiness.ca, March 29, 2010; S. Ward, "Virtualization," VMware website (*www.vmware.com*), accessed June 15, 2010.

Grid Computing

Grid computing applies the unused processing resources of many geographically dispersed computers in a network to form a virtual supercomputer. Target problems are usually scientific or technical in nature and require a great number of computer processing cycles or access to large amounts of data.

EXAMPLE TG1.3

Acxiom (*www.acxiom.com*) is an international data aggregator, which is an organization that compiles information from databases on individuals and sells that information to others. Acxiom gathers data on consumers and their habits, analyzing billions of pieces of data monthly. The company wanted to find a faster and cheaper method to process increasingly large volumes of information.

Acxiom previously used mainframes for data processing (discussed later in this technology guide). This method proved very expensive. Therefore, in 2000 the company started developing its grid computing environment. With its grid, Acxiom spread its applications (computer programs designed to satisfy a business need) over multiple computers instead of several mainframes.

The company has seen significant improvements due to the grid, including a 77 percent increase in the speed with which it can deliver information to clients. As an example, Acxiom reduced processing time for one application from 30 days with a mainframe to just one day with the grid. Its hardware costs also fell by 86 percent.

Sources: Compiled from M. Pratt, "Acxiom Corps' Homegrown Grid," *Computerworld*, August 14, 2007; R. Whiting, "True Grid: Acxiom Outgrows Symmetric Multiprocessing," *InformationWeek*, October 25, 2004.

Utility Computing

In **utility computing**, a service provider makes computing resources and infrastructure management available to a customer as needed. The provider then charges the customer for specific usage rather than a flat rate. Utility computing is also called *subscription computing* and *on-demand computing*. Utility computing enables companies to efficiently meet fluctuating demands for computing power by lowering the cost of owning hardware infrastructure.

Utility computing also provides fault tolerance, redundancy, and scalability. That is, if one server fails, another takes it place. Scalability means that if an application requires additional servers, they can easily be added as they are needed.

Cloud Computing

Every year, companies spend billions of dollars on information technology infrastructure and expert staffs to build and maintain complex information systems. Software licensing (discussed in Technology Guide 2), hardware integration, power and cooling, and staff training and salaries add up to a large amount of money for an infrastructure that may or may not be used to its full capacity. Enter cloud computing.

In **cloud computing**, tasks are performed by computers physically removed from the user and accessed over a network, in particular the Internet. The "cloud" is composed of the computers, the software on those computers, and the network connections among those computers. The computers in the cloud are typically located in data centres, or server farms, which can be located anywhere in the world and accessed from anywhere in the world (see Figure TG1.2).

Although some experts differentiate among the concepts, cloud computing simply incorporates the characteristics of grid computing and utility computing on a global basis. That is, the cloud supplies as many computers as are needed for a particular task (grid computing) and users pay for the amount of actual processing and storage used (utility computing). The advantages of cloud computing include much lower infrastructure costs, and the disadvantages consist of privacy, security, and reliability concerns.

Amazon (*www.amazon.com*) is a leading company in cloud computing with its Elastic Compute Cloud (EC2) and Simple Storage Service (S3). The next example demonstrates how Amazon's cloud helped the *New York Times*.

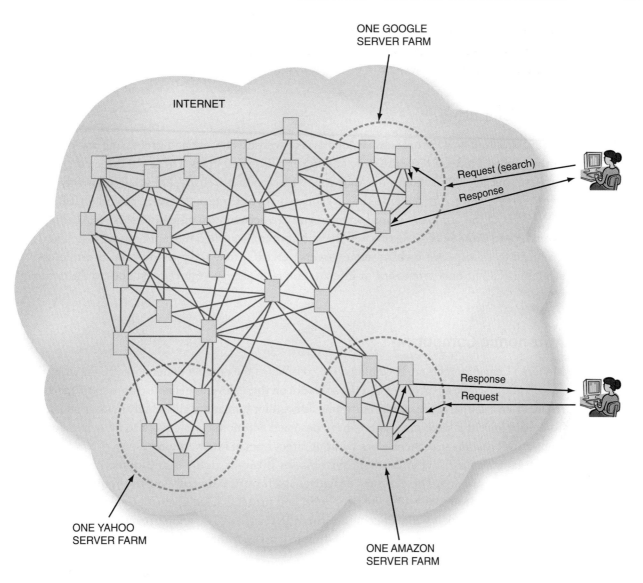

FIGURE TG1.2 Organizational server farms in relation to the Internet.

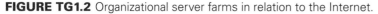

EXAMPLE TG1.4

Imagine digitizing back issues from one of the biggest newspapers in the world, and one of the oldest in the United States. When the *New York Times* decided to make its archives from 1851–1922 available in a web-friendly format, it turned to cloud computing to handle the vast amounts of data. The paper chose Amazon's Simple Storage Service to create the TimesMachine (*http://timesmachine.nytimes.com*). Users can view an image of the actual pages and zoom in on particular articles, photographs, and even advertisements. What seems like an expensive undertaking cost just $1,500, plus a small monthly fee based on how much traffic the TimesMachine generates.

Sources: Compiled from T. Kontzer, "Cloud Computing: Anything as a Service," *CIO Insight*, August 5, 2008; E. Larkin, "New TimesMachine from the Gray Lady," *PC World*, May 23, 2008; "New York Times' TimesMachine Offers Paper's Impressive Backcatalog," AppScout. com, February 25, 2008.

The *New York Times* is an example of a large organization using cloud computing. However, cloud computing can be used effectively by small businesses and entrepreneurs as well. These companies can avoid the costs of an IT infrastructure and IT staff by renting as much computing and storage capacity that they need, and paying for only what they use. Continuing with our example, Amazon charges from $0.10 to $0.20 per hour on one server for computing capacity (the Amazon EC2). Similarly, Amazon charges from $0.15 to $0.20 per gigabyte for storage (the Amazon S3).

Edge Computing

Edge computing is the process by which parts of website content and processing are located close to the user to decrease response time and lower processing costs. There are three components in edge computing: (1) the computer that you use to access a website; (2) small, relatively inexpensive servers—called *edge servers*—that are located at your Internet service provider (ISP); and (3) the servers of the company whose website you are accessing. Companies such as Akamai (*www.akamai.com*) provide edge servers, where web content is cached for rapid access. When you make a request to a company's website, edge servers process it first and provide your information if it is available. If additional processing or information is necessary, your request goes to the company's servers.

Autonomic Computing

Modern IT environments are becoming more complex as the number of networked computing devices (wireline and wireless) increases and the software on these devices becomes more sophisticated. As a result, IT environments are rapidly becoming difficult for humans to adequately manage and maintain. To help resolve this problem, experts have designed **autonomic systems** (also known as **autonomic computing**) that manage themselves without direct human intervention.

Organizations using autonomic systems set business policies and objectives for the self-management process. The system configures itself optimally to meet the requirements, finds and repairs hardware and software problems, and protects itself against attacks and failures. For example, much work is being done in information security to develop proactive defences to automatically detect malicious software and disable it, even if that software has not been seen before (see Chapter 3).

Nanotechnology

Finally, **nanotechnology** refers to the creation of materials, devices, and systems at a scale of 1 to 100 nanometres (billionths of a metre). In the near future, still-experimental computers will be constructed on a nanotechnology scale and could be used literally anywhere. They will require very little power, yet they will have huge storage capacities. In an interesting application, one company, Nano Tex, incorporates nanotechnology into its fabrics to make them wrinkle free and stain resistant. For a demonstration, see *www.nanotex.com*. Another application is the WaterStick from Seldon Technologies (*www.seldontechnologies.com*). The WaterStick uses carbon nanomaterials to absorb contaminants from water. Applications abound for campers, hikers, and travellers. Nanotechnology can be especially beneficial in many areas of the developing world, where clean drinking water is in critically short supply.

BEFORE YOU GO ON ...

1. What are server farms? Virtualization? Grid computing? Utility computing? Cloud computing? Edge computing? Autonomic computing?
2. What is nanotechnology? Provide an example of a practical use for nanotechnology.

TG1.4 The Computer Hierarchy

Computer hardware has evolved through five stages, or generations, of technology: vacuum tubes, transistors, integrated circuits, ultra-large-scale integrated circuits, and massively parallel processing. Each generation has provided increased processing power and storage capacity while simultaneously decreasing costs.

The traditional way of comparing classes of computers is by their processing power. Analysts typically divide computers—called the *hardware platform* in the computer industry—into six categories: supercomputers, mainframes, midrange computers (minicomputers and servers), workstations, microcomputers, and computing devices. Recently, the lines among these categories have become blurred. This section presents each class of computers, beginning with the most powerful and ending with the least powerful. It describes both the computers and their roles in modern organizations.

Supercomputers

The term **supercomputer** does not refer to a specific technology. Rather, it indicates the fastest computing engines available at any given time. At the time of this writing (mid-2010), the fastest supercomputers had speeds exceeding one petaflop (one petaflop is 1,000 trillion floating point operations per second). A floating point operation is an arithmetic operation involving decimals.

People generally use supercomputers for computationally demanding tasks involving very large data sets. Rather than transaction processing and business applications—the forte of mainframes and other multiprocessing platforms—supercomputers typically run military and scientific applications. Although they cost millions of dollars, they are being used for commercial applications where huge amounts of data must be analyzed. For example, large banks use supercomputers to calculate the risks and returns of various investment strategies and health-care organizations use them to analyze giant databases of patient data to determine optimal treatments for various diseases.

Mainframe Computers

Although mainframe computers are increasingly viewed as just another type of server, albeit at the high end of the performance and reliability scales, they remain a distinct class of systems differentiated by hardware and software features. **Mainframes** remain popular in large enterprises for extensive computing applications that are accessed by thousands of users at one time. Examples of mainframe applications are airline reservation systems, corporate payroll programs, website transaction processing systems (e.g., for Amazon and eBay), and student grade calculation and reporting.

Mainframes are less powerful and generally less expensive than supercomputers. A mainframe system can have terabytes of primary storage. Secondary storage (see the discussion of enterprise storage systems) may use high-capacity magnetic and optical storage media with capacities of many terabytes. Typically, thousands of on-line computers can be linked to a single mainframe. Today's most advanced mainframes perform at teraflop (trillions of floating point operations per second) speeds and can handle billions of transactions per day.

Some large organizations that moved away from mainframes toward distributed systems now are moving back to mainframes because of their centralized administration, high reliability, and increasing flexibility. This process is called *recentralization*. This shift has occurred for several reasons, including the following:

- Supporting the high transaction levels associated with e-commerce
- Reducing the total cost of ownership of distributed systems
- Simplifying administration

- Reducing support-personnel requirements
- Improving system performance

In addition, mainframe computing provides a secure, robust environment in which to run strategic, mission-critical applications.

Midrange Computers

Larger midrange computers, called **minicomputers**, are relatively small, inexpensive, and compact computers that perform the same functions as mainframe computers, but to a more limited extent. In fact, the lines between minicomputers and mainframes have blurred in both price and performance. Minicomputers are a type of **server**; that is, a computer that supports computer networks and enables users to share files, software, peripheral devices, and other resources. Note that mainframes are a type of server as well, because they provide support for entire enterprise networks.

Minicomputers can provide flexibility to organizations that do not want to spend IT dollars on mainframes, which are less scalable. Scalable computers are inexpensive enough so that adding more computers of that type is not prohibitive. Because mainframes are so expensive, we say that they are not very scalable.

Organizations with heavy transaction-processing requirements often use multiple servers in *server farms*. As companies pack greater numbers of servers in their server farms, they increasingly use pizza-box-sized servers called *rack servers* that can be stacked in racks. These computers run cooler and thus can be packed more closely, requiring less space. To further increase density, companies use a server design called a blade. A *blade* is a card about the size of a paperback book on which the memory, processor, and hard drives are mounted.

Workstations

Computer vendors originally developed desktop engineering workstations, or workstations for short, to provide the high levels of performance demanded by engineers. That is, **workstations** run computationally intensive scientific, engineering, and financial applications. Workstations provide both very high-speed calculations and high-resolution graphic displays. These computers are widely used within the scientific and business communities. Workstation applications include electronic and mechanical design, medical imaging, scientific visualization, 3-D animation, and video editing. Today, the distinction between workstations and personal computers is negligible.

Microcomputers

Microcomputers—also called *micros, personal computers*, or *PCs*—are the smallest and least expensive category of general-purpose computers. It is important to point out that people frequently define a PC as a computer that uses the Microsoft Windows operating system. In fact, there are a variety of PCs available, many of which do not use Windows. One well-known example is the Apple Macintosh, which uses the Macintosh OS X operating system.

The major categories of microcomputers are desktops, thin clients, laptops and notebooks, ultramobile PCs, and netbooks.

Desktop PCs

The *desktop personal computer* has become the dominant method of accessing workgroup and enterprise-wide applications. It is the typical, familiar microcomputer system that has become a standard tool for business and the home. It typically has a central processing unit (CPU)—which we discuss later—and a separate but connected monitor and keyboard. In general, modern micro-computers have gigabytes of primary storage, a rewriteable CD-ROM and a DVD drive, and several terabytes of secondary storage.

Thin-Client Systems

Before we discuss thin-client systems, we need to differentiate between clients and servers. Recall that servers are computers that provide a variety of services for clients, including running networks, processing websites, processing e-mail, and many other functions. *Clients* are typically computers on which users perform their tasks, such as word processing, spreadsheets, and others. (See Technology Guide 4 for a discussion of client/server computing.)

Thin-client systems are desktop computer systems that do not offer the full functionality of a PC. Compared with a PC, or **fat client**, thin clients are less complex, particularly because they lack locally installed software due to an absence of disk drive storage. That is, a thin client would not have Microsoft Office installed on it but would instead access software from a network. Thus, thin clients are easier and less expensive to operate and support than PCs. The benefits of thin clients include fast application deployment, centralized management, lower cost of ownership, and easier installation, management, maintenance, and support. The main disadvantage of thin clients is that if the network fails, then users can do very little on their computers. In contrast, if users have fat clients and the network fails, they can still perform their jobs because Microsoft Office is installed on their computers.

Laptop and Notebook Computers

As computers have become much smaller and vastly more powerful, they also have become portable. **Laptop and notebook computers** are small, easily transportable, lightweight microcomputers that fit easily into a briefcase. In general, notebook computers are smaller than laptops. Notebooks and laptops are designed to be as convenient and easy to transport as possible. Just as importantly, they also provide users with access to processing power and data outside an office environment. At the same time, they cost more than desktops for similar functionality.

As laptop and notebook computers become smaller in size and price, their popularity has exploded, to the point where they're a familiar sight in public places like coffee shops, as the following example shows.

EXAMPLE TG1.5

In June 2010, Starbucks announced that Wi-Fi access would be free at its U.S. locations (in Canada there are 650 Starbucks locations, where Wi-Fi is free for up to two hours for customers). This means that Starbucks needs to have the Wi-Fi communications infrastructure available at its stores. If free Wi-Fi means that more customers will use the Wi-Fi (a strategic decision on the part of Starbucks), then Starbucks will need to purchase more Wi-Fi capacity.

As a user, you would decide what type of equipment you will bring to your Starbucks coffee experience. Will you bring a Dell Vostro Laptop (*www.dell.com/ca*), with a 14-inch screen and a media card reader to transfer pictures, or will you take your iPad (*www.apple.com/ipad*), which happens to also have high-speed browsing capability? Your decision with respect to the hardware you purchase will be based upon the speed of processing you required (which is affected by your CPU and the type of storage), the type of screen that you would like (one of the outputs of your machine), and the way that you will be transferring information to and from your machine (input and output).

Sources: Compiled from T. Wailgum, "Starbucks Brews Free WiFi, Other Deals to Entice Patrons," itbusiness.ca, June 17, 2010; Apple website (*www.apple.com/ipad*), accessed June 17, 2010.

FIGURE TG1.3 The netbook is a small and portable computer made for browsing websites and getting emails.

Ultra-mobile PCs

Ultra-mobile PCs are small, mobile computers that run various mobile operating systems. Ultra-mobile PCs have the full functionality of a desktop computer, but they are smaller and lighter than traditional laptop and notebook computers. These computers have multiple input methods, including touch screen, stylus, speech, and Bluetooth or traditional keyboard. Figure TG1.3 shows an ultra-mobile PC.

Netbooks

A **netbook** is a very small, lightweight, low-cost, energy-efficient, portable computer. Netbooks are generally optimized for Internet-based services such as web browsing and e-mailing.

Computing Devices

Improved computer technology has led to the development of improved, ever-smaller computing and communication devices. Technologies such as wearable computing and communication devices are now common. This section briefly looks at some of these new devices.

Wearable computers (wearable devices) are designed to be worn and used on the body. Industrial applications of wearable computers include systems for factory automation, warehouse management, and performance support, such as viewing technical manuals and diagrams while building or repairing something. This technology is already widely used in such diverse industries as freight delivery (e.g., the electronic tablet that your UPS courier carries), aerospace, securities trading, law enforcement, and the military.

Embedded computers are placed inside other products to add features and capabilities. For example, the average mid-sized automobile has more than 3,000 embedded computers, called *controllers*, that monitor every function from braking to engine performance to seat controls with memory.

BEFORE YOU GO ON ...

1. Describe the computer hierarchy from the largest to the smallest computers.
2. Differentiate between laptop computers and ultra-mobile PCs.
3. Contrast the uses of supercomputers with the uses of mainframe computers.

TG1.5 Input and Output Technologies

Input technologies allow people and other technologies to put data into a computer. The two main types of input devices are human data-entry devices and source-data automation devices. As their name implies, *human data-entry* devices require a certain amount of human effort to input data. Examples are keyboard, mouse, pointing stick, trackball, joystick, touchscreen, stylus, and voice recognition.

An interesting development in keyboard technology is the Bluetooth laser virtual keyboard (see Figure TG1.4). This device, only 9 centimetres high, uses a laser to project a full QWERTY keyboard on any flat surface. (QWERTY are the first six alphabetic keys, from left to right, on a standard keyboard.) The device connects to smart phones and computers using Bluetooth (discussed in Chapter 7).

In contrast, *source-data automation* devices input data with minimal human intervention. These technologies speed up data collection, reduce errors, and gather data at the source of a transaction or other event. Barcode readers are an example of source-data automation. Table TG1.1 describes the various input devices.

FIGURE TG1.4
Bluetooth laser virtual keyboard. *Source:* WENN Photos/ NewsCom.

TABLE TG1.1 INPUT DEVICES	
Human Data-Entry Devices	
Keyboards	Most common input device (for text and numerical data).
Mouse	Hand-held device used to point cursor at point on screen, such as an icon; user clicks button on mouse instructing computer to take some action.
Optical mouse	Mouse not connected to computer by a cable; mouse uses camera chip to take images of surface it passes over, comparing successive images to determine its position.
Trackball	Ball built into top of device that user rotates to move cursor (rather than moving entire device such as a mouse).
Pointing stick	Small button-like device; cursor moves in the direction of the pressure you place on the stick.
Touchpad	Sensitized pad that user slides finger across to move the cursor. User then can tap pad when cursor is in desired position to instruct computer to take action (also called *glide-and-tap pad*).
Graphics tablet	Device that can be used in place of, or in conjunction with, a mouse or trackball; has a flat surface for drawing and a pen or stylus that is programmed to work with the tablet.
Joystick	Device that moves cursor to desired place on screen; commonly used in workstations that display dynamic graphics and in video games.
Touch screen	Screen by which users instruct computer to take some action by touching a particular part of the screen; commonly used in information kiosks such as ATM machines. Touch screens now have gesture controls for browsing through photographs, moving objects around on a screen, flicking to turn the page of a book, and playing video games. For example, see the Apple iPhone.

(Continued on next page)

TABLE TG1.1 *(Continued)*

Stylus	Pen-style device that allows user either to touch parts of a predetermined menu of options or to handwrite information into the computer (as with some PDAs); works with touch-sensitive screens.
Digital pen	Mobile device that digitally captures everything you write; built-in screen confirms what you write has been saved; also captures sketches, figures, etc, with on-board flash memory.
Wii	Video game console by Nintendo. A distinguishing feature of the Wii is its wireless controller, which can be used as a hand-held pointing device and can detect movement in three dimensions.
Web camera (webcam)	Real-time video camera whose images can be accessed via the Web or instant messaging.
Voice recognition	Software that converts voice wave sounds into digital input for computer; critical technology for physically challenged people who cannot use other input devices.

Source-Data Automation Input Devices

Automated teller machine	Device that includes source-data automation input in the form of a magnetic stripe reader; human input via a keyboard; and output via a monitor, printer, and cash dispenser.
Magnetic stripe reader	Device that reads data from a magnetic stripe, usually on the back of a plastic card (for example, credit or debit cards).
Point-of-sale terminals	Computerized cash registers that also may incorporate touchscreen technology and barcode scanners (see below) to input data such as item sold and price.
Barcode scanners	Devices that scan black-and-white barcode lines printed on merchandise labels.
Optical mark reader	Scanner for detecting presence of dark marks on predetermined grid, such as multiple-choice test answer sheets.
Magnetic ink character reader	Device that reads magnetic ink printed on cheques that identify the bank, chequing account, and cheque number.
Optical character recognition sensors	Software that converts text into digital form for input into computer. Collect data directly from the environment and input data directly into computer; examples include your car's airbag activation sensor and radio frequency identification (RFID) tags.
Cameras	Digital devices that capture images and convert them into digital files.
Heads-up displays	Transparent display that presents data without requiring that the user look away from his or her usual viewpoint; for example, see Microvision (*www.microvision.com*).
Radio frequency identification (RFID)	Active or passive tags (transmitters) that wirelessly transmit product information to electronic readers.

The output generated by a computer can be transmitted to the user via several output devices and media. These devices include monitors, printers, plotters, and voice. Table TG1.2 describes the various output devices.

TABLE TG1.2
OUTPUT DEVICES

Monitors

Cathode ray tubes	Video screens on which an electron beam illuminates pixels on display screen.
Liquid crystal display (LCDs)	Flat displays that have liquid crystals between two polarizers to form characters and images on a backlit screen.
Flexible displays	Thin, plastic, bendable computer screens.
Organic light-emitting diodes (OLEDs)	Displays that are brighter, thinner, lighter, cheaper, faster, and take less power to run than LCDs.
Retinal scanning displays	Displays that project image directly onto a viewer's retina; used in medicine, air traffic control, and controlling industrial machines.

Printers

Laser	Printer that uses laser beams to write information on photosensitive drums; produce high-resolution text and graphics.
Inkjet	Printer that shoots fine streams of coloured ink onto paper; usually less expensive to buy than laser printers, but can be more expensive to operate; can offer resolution quality equal to laser printers.
Plotters	Printer that uses computer-directed pens for creating high-quality images, blueprints, schematics, drawing of new products, etc.

Voice Output	Speaker/headset that can output sounds of any type; voice output is a software function that uses this equipment.
Electronic Book Reader	Wireless, portable reading device with access to books, blogs, newspapers, and magazines. On-board storage holds hundreds of books.
Pocket Projector	Projector in a hand-held device that provides an alternative display method to alleviate the problem of tiny display screens in hand-held devices. Pocket projectors will project digital images onto any viewing surface.

Multimedia technology is the computer-based integration of text, sound, still images, animation, and digitized motion video. It merges the capabilities of computers with televisions, VCRs, CD players, DVD players, video and audio recording equipment, and music and gaming technologies. Multimedia usually represents a collection of various input and output technologies. High-quality multimedia processing requires powerful microprocessors and extensive memory capacity, including both primary and secondary storage.

BEFORE YOU GO ON …

1. Distinguish between human data-input devices and source-data automation.
2. What are the differences among various types of monitors?
3. What are the main types of printers? How do they work?
4. Describe the concept of multimedia, and give an example of a multimedia system.

TG1.6 The Central Processing Unit

The **central processing unit (CPU)** performs the actual computation or "number crunching" inside any computer. The CPU is a **microprocessor** (for example, a Nehalem chip by Intel) made up of millions of microscopic transistors embedded in a circuit on a silicon wafer or *chip*. Hence, microprocessors are commonly referred to as chips.

How the CPU Works

As shown in Figure TG1.5, the microprocessor has different parts, which perform different functions. The **control unit** sequentially accesses program instructions, decodes them, and controls the flow of data to and from the ALU, the registers, the caches, primary storage, secondary storage, and various output devices. The **arithmetic-logic unit (ALU)** performs the mathematic calculations and makes logical comparisons. The **registers** are high-speed storage areas that store very small amounts of data and instructions for short periods of time.

In the CPU, inputs enter and are stored until they are needed. At that point, they are retrieved and processed, and the output is stored and then delivered somewhere.

FIGURE TG1.5
Parts of a microprocessor.

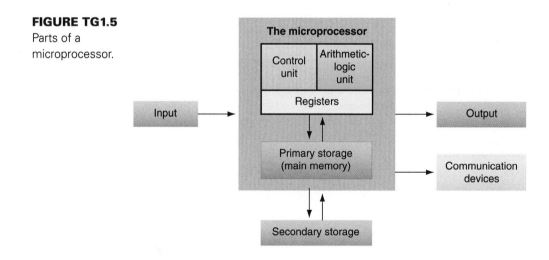

Advances in Microprocessor Design

Innovations in chip designs are coming at a faster and faster rate, as described by **Moore's Law**. In 1965, Gordon Moore, a co-founder of Intel Corporation, predicted that microprocessor complexity would double approximately every two years. His prediction has been amazingly accurate.

The advances predicted from Moore's Law arise mainly from the following changes:

- Producing increasingly miniaturized transistors.
- Making the physical layout of the chip's components as compact and efficient as possible; that is, decreasing line width.
- Using materials for the chip that improve the *conductivity* (flow) of electricity. Chips traditionally have been made of silicon, which is a semiconductor of electricity; that is, electrons can flow through it, but only at a certain rate. Newer materials such as gallium arsenide and silicon germanium allow even faster electron travel, although they are more expensive.

- Placing multiple processors on a single chip. Chips with more than one processor are called *multicore* chips. For example, the Cell chip, produced by a consortium of Sony, Toshiba, and IBM, contains nine processors. Computers using the Cell chip display very rich graphics. The chip is also used in TV sets and home theatres that can download and show large numbers of high-definition programs. Intel (*www.intel.com*) and AMD (*www.amd.com*) have chips with four processors, called quad-core chips. In addition, Intel is developing a chip with 80 processors that will be able to perform more than 1 trillion floating point operations per second, or 1 *teraflop*.

In addition to increased speeds and performance, Moore's Law has had an impact on costs, as we can see in Table TG1.3.

TABLE TG1.3
COMPARISON OF PERSONAL COMPUTER COMPONENTS AND COST OVER TIME

YEAR	CHIP	RAM	HARD DRIVE	MONITOR	COST
1997	Pentium II	64 megabytes	4 gigabytes	17-inch	$4,000
2007	Dual-core	1 gigabyte	250 gigabytes	19-inch	$1,700
2010	Quad-core	6 gigabytes	1 terabyte	24-inch	$1,500

Although organizations certainly benefit from microprocessors that are faster, they also benefit from chips that are less powerful but are smaller and less expensive. These chips, known as **microcontrollers**, are embedded in countless products and technologies, from cellular telephones, to toys, to automobile sensors. Microprocessors and microcontrollers are similar except that microcontrollers usually cost less and work in less-demanding applications.

BEFORE YOU GO ON ...

1. Briefly describe the components of the CPU.
2. How are microprocessor designs advancing?

TG1.7 Computer Memory and Storage Systems

The amount and type of memory that a computer possesses has a great deal to do with its general utility. A computer's memory can affect the types of programs it can run, the work it can do, its speed, the cost of the machine, and the cost of processing data. There are two basic categories of computer memory. The first is *primary storage*. It is called "primary" because it stores small amounts of data and information that will be used immediately by the CPU. The second is *secondary storage*, which stores much larger amounts of data and information (an entire software program, for example) for extended periods of time.

Memory Capacity

CPUs process only **binary** units—0s and 1s—which are translated through computer languages (covered in Technology Guide 2) into **bits**. A particular combination of bits represents a certain alphanumeric character or a simple mathematical operation. Normally, eight bits are needed to represent any one of these characters. This 8-bit string is known as a byte. The storage capacity of a computer is measured in bytes. Bits typically are used as units of measure only for telecommunications capacity, as in how many million bits per second can be sent through a particular medium.

The hierarchy of terms used to describe memory capacity is as follows:

- *Kilobyte. Kilo* means 1 thousand, so a kilobyte (KB) is approximately 1,000 bytes. Actually, a kilobyte is 1,024 bytes.
- *Megabyte. Mega* means 1 million, so a megabyte (MB) is approximately 1 million bytes. Most personal computers have hundreds of megabytes of RAM memory (a type of primary storage, discussed later).
- *Gigabyte. Giga* means 1 billion, so a gigabyte (GB) is approximately 1 billion bytes. The storage capacity of a hard drive (a type of secondary storage, discussed shortly) in modern personal computers is hundreds of gigabytes.
- *Terabyte.* A terabyte is approximately 1 trillion bytes.
- *Petabyte.* A petabyte is approximately 1,000 terabytes.
- *Exabyte.* An exabyte is approximately 1,000 petabytes.
- *Zettabyte.* A zettabyte is approximately 1,000 exabytes.

To get a feel for these amounts, consider the following example: If your computer has one terabyte of storage capacity on its hard drive (a type of secondary storage), it can store approximately 1 trillion bytes of data. If the average page of text contains about 2,000 bytes, then your hard drive could store approximately 10 percent of the entire print collections of the Library of Congress.

Primary Storage

Primary storage, or **main memory** as it is sometimes called, stores three types of information for very brief periods of time: (1) data to be processed by the CPU, (2) instructions for the CPU as to how to process the data, and (3) operating system programs that manage various aspects of the computer's operation. Primary storage takes place in chips mounted on the computer's main circuit board, called the *motherboard*, which is located as close as physically possible to the CPU chip (see Figure TG1.6). As with the CPU, all the data and instructions in primary storage have been translated into binary code.

There are four main types of primary storage: (1) register, (2) random access memory (RAM), (3) cache memory, and (4) read-only memory (ROM). The logic of primary storage is that those components that will be used immediately are stored in very small amounts as close to the CPU as possible. Remember that, as with CPU chip design, the shorter the distance the electrical impulses (data) have to travel, the faster they can be transported and processed. The four types of primary storage, which follow this logic, are described next.

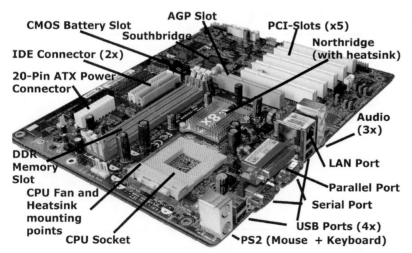

CMOS Battery Slot
AGP Slot
Southbridge
PCI-Slots (x5)
IDE Connector (2x)
Northridge (with heatsink)
20-Pin ATX Power Connector
Audio (3x)
DDR Memory Slot
LAN Port
CPU Fan and Heatsink mounting points
Parallel Port
Serial Port
CPU Socket
USB Ports (4x)
PS2 (Mouse + Keyboard)

FIGURE TG1.6 Internal workings of a common personal computer.
Source: www.computer-hardware-explained.com / Nathanael Vanderkolk

Registers

Registers are part of the CPU. They have the least capacity, storing extremely limited amounts of instructions and data only immediately before and after processing.

Random Access Memory

Random access memory (RAM) is the part of primary storage that holds a software program and small amounts of data for processing. When you start most software programs on your computer (such as Microsoft Word), the entire program is brought from secondary storage into RAM. As you use the program, small parts of the program's instructions and data are sent into the registers and then to the CPU. Compared with the registers, RAM stores more information and is located farther away from the CPU. However, compared with secondary storage, RAM stores less information and is much closer to the CPU. Again, getting the data and instructions as close to the CPU as possible is vital to the computer's speed. Also vital is the fact that RAM is a type of microprocessor chip. As we shall discuss later, microprocessor chips are much faster (and more costly) than secondary storage devices. It is easy and inexpensive to add RAM to a computer system. As of mid-2010, 1 gigabyte of RAM cost less than $100.

RAM is temporary and, in most cases, *volatile*. That is, RAM chips lose their contents if the current is lost or turned off, as in a power surge, brownout, or electrical noise generated by lightning or nearby machines. However, there are nonvolatile RAM technologies, such as magnetic RAM, which we discuss below. RAM chips are located directly on the motherboard or in other chips located on peripheral cards that plug into the main circuit board.

The two main types of RAM are *dynamic RAM (DRAM)* and *static RAM (SRAM)*. DRAM memory chips offer the greatest capacities and the lowest cost per bit, but they are relatively slow. SRAM costs more than DRAM, but it is faster. For this reason, SRAM is the preferred choice for performance-sensitive applications.

An emerging technology is *magnetic RAM (MRAM)*. As its name suggests, MRAM uses magnetism, rather than electricity, to store data. One major advantage of MRAM over DRAM and SRAM is that it is nonvolatile, which means that it retains data when the power is shut off. In addition, whereas DRAM wastes a lot of electricity because it needs to be supplied with a constant current to store data, MRAM requires only a tiny amount of electricity. In essence, MRAM combines the high speed of SRAM, the storage capacity of DRAM, and the nonvolatility of flash memory (discussed later in this technology guide).

Cache Memory

Cache memory is a type of high-speed memory that enables the computer to temporarily store blocks of data that are used more often and that a processor can access more rapidly than main memory (RAM). It augments RAM in the following way: Many modern computer applications (Microsoft Windows Vista, for example) are very complex and have huge numbers of instructions. It takes considerable RAM capacity (usually a minimum of 512 megabytes) to store the entire instruction set. Also, many applications might exceed your RAM. In either case, your processor must go to secondary storage to retrieve the necessary instructions. To alleviate this problem, software is often written in smaller blocks of instructions. As these blocks are needed, they can be brought from secondary storage into RAM. This process is still slow, however.

Cache memory is physically located closer to the CPU than RAM where the computer can temporarily store those blocks of instructions that are used most often. Blocks used less often remain in RAM until they are transferred to cache; blocks used infrequently remain in secondary storage. Cache memory is faster than RAM because the instructions travel a shorter distance to the CPU.

Read-only Memory

Most of us have lost data at one time or another due to a computer "crash" or a power failure. What is usually lost is whatever is in RAM, cache, or the registers at the time, because these types of memory are volatile. Therefore, we need greater security when we are storing certain types of critical data or instructions. Cautious computer users frequently save data to nonvolatile memory (secondary storage). In addition, most modern software applications have autosave functions. Programs stored in secondary storage, even though they are temporarily copied into RAM when they are being used, remain intact because only the copy is lost, not the original.

Read-only memory (ROM) is the place—actually, a type of chip—where certain critical instructions are safeguarded. ROM is nonvolatile, so it retains these instructions when the power to the computer is turned off. The read-only designation means that these instructions can only be read by the computer and cannot be changed by the user. An example of ROM is the instructions needed to start or "boot" the computer after it has been shut off.

Secondary Storage

Secondary storage is designed to store very large amounts of data for extended periods of time. Secondary storage can have memory capacity of several terabytes or more. Significantly, only small portions of those data are placed in primary storage at any one time. Secondary storage has the following characteristics:

- It is nonvolatile.
- It takes more time to retrieve data from secondary storage than it does from RAM.
- It is cheaper than primary storage (see Figure TG1.7).
- It can take place on a variety of media, each with its own technology, as we discuss next. The overall trends in secondary storage are toward more direct-access methods, higher capacity with lower costs, and increased portability.

Magnetic Media

Magnetic tape is kept on a large open reel or in a smaller cartridge or cassette. Although this is an old technology, it remains popular because it is the cheapest storage medium, and it can handle enormous amounts of data. The downside is that it is the slowest method for retrieving data, because all the data are placed on the tape sequentially. **Sequential access** means that the system might have to run through the majority of the tape before it comes to the desired piece of data.

Organizations often use magnetic tape storage for information that they must maintain but use only rarely or do not need immediate access to. Industries with huge numbers of files (e.g., insurance companies) use magnetic tape systems. Modern versions of magnetic tape systems use cartridges and often a robotic system that selects and loads the appropriate cartridge automatically. There are also some tape systems, like digital audio tapes (DAT), for smaller applications such as storing copies of all the contents of a personal computer's secondary storage ("backing up" the storage).

FIGURE TG1.7
Primary memory compared with secondary storage.

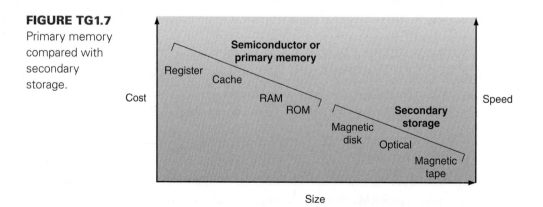

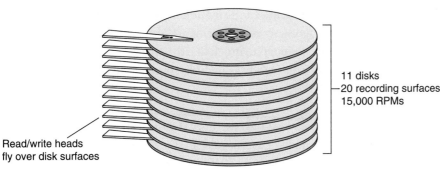

FIGURE TG1.8
Read/write heads.

11 disks
20 recording surfaces
15,000 RPMs

Read/write heads
fly over disk surfaces

Magnetic disks are a form of secondary storage on a magnetized disk that is divided into tracks and sectors that provide addresses for various pieces of data. These disks come in a variety of styles and are popular because they allow much more rapid access to the data than magnetic tape does. Magnetic disks, called **hard drives** or fixed disk drives, are the most commonly used mass storage devices because of their low cost, high speed, and large storage capacity. Hard disk drives read from, and write to, stacks of rotating (at up to 15,000 rotations per minute or RPM) magnetic disk platters mounted in rigid enclosures and sealed against environmental and atmospheric contamination. These disks are permanently mounted in a unit that may be internal or external to the computer.

Hard drives store data on platters that are divided into concentric tracks. Each track is further divided into segments called *sectors*. To access a given sector, a read/write head pivots across the rotating disks to locate the right track, which is calculated from an index table. The head then waits as the disk rotates until the right sector is underneath it (see Figure TG1.8). Because the head floats just above the surface of the disk (less than 25 microns), any bit of dust or contamination can disrupt the device. When this happens, it is called a *disk crash*, and it usually results in catastrophic loss of data since the medium is physically destroyed. For this reason, hard drives are hermetically sealed when they are manufactured.

Every piece of data has an address attached to it, corresponding to a particular track and sector. Any piece of desired data can be retrieved in a nonsequential manner, by direct access. This is why hard disk drives are sometimes called *direct access storage devices*. The read/write heads use the data's address to quickly find and read the data (see Figure TG1.8). Unlike magnetic tape, the system does not have to read through all the data to find what it wants.

Modern personal computers typically have internal hard drives with storage capacity ranging from hundreds of gigabytes to several terabytes. Data access is very fast, measured in milliseconds, though still much slower than RAM. Because they are somewhat susceptible to mechanical failure and because users may need to take all their hard drive's contents to another location, many users back up their hard drive's contents with either a portable hard disk drive system or thumb drives (discussed later in this technology guide).

To take advantage of the new, faster technologies, disk drive interfaces must also be faster. Most PCs and workstations use one of two high-performance disk interface standards: *Enhanced Integrated Drive Electronics (EIDE)* or *Small Computer Systems Interface (SCSI)*. EIDE offers good performance, is inexpensive, and supports up to four disks, tapes, or CD-ROM drives. In contrast, SCSI drives are more expensive than EIDE drives, but they offer a faster interface and support more devices. SCSI interfaces are therefore used for graphics workstations, server-based storage, and large databases.

Optical Storage Devices

Unlike magnetic media, **optical storage devices** do not store data via magnetism. Rather, a laser reads the surface of a reflective plastic platter. Optical disk drives are slower than magnetic hard drives, but they are less susceptible to damage from contamination and they are less fragile.

In addition, optical disks can store a great deal of information, both on a routine basis and also when combined into storage systems. Optical disk storage systems are often implemented in the form of optical jukeboxes, which store many disks and operate much like the automated phonograph record changers for which they are named. Types of optical disks include **compact disk read-only memory (CD-ROM)** and **digital video disk (DVD)**.

Compact Disk, Read-Only Memory. Compact disk, read-only memory (CD-ROM) storage devices feature high capacity, low cost, and high durability. However, because a CD-ROM is a read-only medium, it cannot be written on. Compact disk, rewritable (CD-RW) adds rewritability to the recordable compact disk market.

Digital Video Disk. The digital video disk (DVD) is a disk the same physical size as a CD-ROM but with the capacity to store about 135 minutes of digital video. DVDs provide sharp detail, true colour, no flicker, and no snow. DVDs can also perform as computer storage disks, providing storage capabilities of 17 gigabytes. DVD players can read current CD-ROMs, but current CD-ROM players cannot read DVDs. The access speed of a DVD drive is faster than that of a typical CD-ROM drive.

Two standards, which did not work together, were competing to replace the standard DVD: Blu-ray and High-Density DVD (HD DVD). On January 4, 2008, Warner Bros., the only major studio still releasing movies in both HD DVD and Blu-ray format, announced it would release only in Blu-ray disk after May 2008. Following this announcement, major U.S. retailers such as Best Buy and Walmart dropped HD DVD in their stores. In addition, Netflix and Blockbuster stopped carrying HD DVDs. On February 19, 2008, Toshiba—the main company supporting HD DVD—announced that it would no longer develop, manufacture, or market HD DVD players and recorders. Almost all other HD DVD companies followed suit, effectively ending the competition between the two formats.

A dual-layer Blu-ray disk can store 50 gigabytes, almost six times the capacity of a dual-layer DVD. Development of the Blu-ray technology is ongoing, with 10-layered Blu-ray discs being tested.

Holographic Memory. Holographic memory is an optical technology that uses a three-dimensional medium to store data. InPhase Technologies (*www.inphase-technologies.com*) has produced a write-once, read-many (WORM) optical disk that stores 300 gigabytes. Each disk has 63 times the capacity of a DVD and can store more than 35 hours of broadcast-quality video.

Flash Memory Devices. Flash memory is nonvolatile computer memory that can be electrically erased and reprogrammed. This technology can be built into a system or installed on a personal computer card.

Flash memory devices (or *memory cards*) are electronic storage devices that contain no moving parts and use 30 times less battery power than hard drives. Flash devices are also smaller and more durable than hard drives. The trade-offs are that flash devices store less information than hard drives.

There are many different types of flash devices, and they are used in many different places. For example, flash devices are used with digital cameras, hand-held and laptop computers, telephones, music players, and video game consoles. Apple (*www.apple.com*) replaced the micro hard-drive-based iPod Mini with the flash-based iPod Nano for four reasons: (1) rapid improvements in the storage capacity of flash memory chips, (2) rapid decreases in cost, (3) much longer battery life, and (4) smaller size.

One popular flash memory device is the **thumb drive** (also called *memory stick, jump drive*, or *flash drive*). These devices fit into universal serial bus (USB) ports on personal computers and other devices, and they can store many gigabytes. Thumb drives have replaced magnetic floppy disks for portable storage (see Figure TG1.9).

Enterprise Storage Systems

To deal with ever-expanding volumes of information, companies employ enterprise storage systems. An **enterprise storage system** is an independent, external system that includes two or more storage devices. Enterprise storage systems provide large amounts of storage, high-performance data transfer, a high degree of availability, protection against data loss, and sophisticated management tools.

The performance of enterprise storage system hardware has improved very rapidly. In 1956, the first disk storage unit was the size of two refrigera-

FIGURE TG1.9 Thumb drive.

tors and it stored 5 megabytes of information. Current disk storage units are half that size and they store 320 terabytes. There are three major types of enterprise storage systems: redundant arrays of independent disks, storage area networks, and network-attached storage.

Redundant Arrays of Independent Disks

Hard drives in all computer systems are susceptible to failures caused by temperature variations, head crashes, motor failure, and changing voltage conditions. To improve reliability and to protect the data in their enterprise storage systems, many organizations use **redundant arrays of independent disks (RAID)** storage products. RAID links groups of standard hard drives to a specialized microcontroller. The microcontroller coordinates the drives so they appear as a single logical drive, but they take advantage of the multiple physical drives by storing data redundantly, meaning data that are duplicated in multiple places. This arrangement protects against data loss due to the failure of any single drive.

Storage Area Network

A **storage area network (SAN)** is an architecture for building special, dedicated networks that allow rapid and reliable access to storage devices by multiple servers. **Storage over IP**, sometimes called *IP over SCSI* or *iSCSI*, is a technology that uses the Internet protocol to transport stored data among devices within an SAN. SANs employ **storage visualization software** to graphically plot an entire network and allow storage administrators to monitor all networked storage devices from a single console.

Network-Attached Storage

A **network-attached storage (NAS)** device is a special-purpose server that provides file storage to users who access the device over a network. The NAS server is simple to install (i.e., plug-and-play) and works exactly like a general-purpose file server, so no user retraining or special software is needed.

Table TG1.4 compares the advantages and disadvantages of the various secondary storage media.

TABLE TG1.4
SECONDARY STORAGE

TYPE	ADVANTAGES	DISADVANTAGES	APPLICATION
Magnetic Storage Devices			
Magnetic tape	Lowest cost per unit stored	Sequential access means slow retrieval speeds	Corporate data archiving
Hard drive	Relatively high capacity and fast retrieval speed	Fragile; high cost per unit stored	Personal computers through mainframes
RAID	High capacity; designed for fault tolerance and reduced risk of data loss; low cost per unit stored	Expensive, semi-permanent installation	Corporate data storage that requires frequent, rapid access
SAN	High capacity; designed for large amounts of enterprise data	Expensive	Corporate data storage that requires frequent, rapid access
NAS	High capacity; designed for large amounts of enterprise data	Expensive	Corporate data storage that requires frequent, rapid access
Memory cards	Portable; easy to use; less failure-prone than hard drives	Expensive	Personal and laptop computers
Thumb drives	Extremely portable and easy to use	More volatile than other types of storage, easily lost and damaged	Consumer electronic devices; moving files from portable devices to desktop computers
Optical Storage Devices			
CD-ROM	Moderate capacity; moderate cost per unit stored; high durability	Slower retrieval speeds than hard drives; only certain types can be rewritten	Personal computers through corporate data storage
DVD	Moderate capacity; moderate cost per unit stored	Slower retrieval speeds than hard drives	Personal computers through corporate data storage

BEFORE YOU GO ON ...

1. Describe the four main types of primary storage.
2. Describe different types of secondary storage.
3. How does primary storage differ from secondary storage in terms of speed, cost, and capacity?
4. Describe the three types of enterprise storage systems.

WHAT'S IN IT FOR ME?

FOR ALL BUSINESS MAJORS

Practically all professional jobs in business today require computer literacy and skills for personal productivity. Going further, all industries use computer technology for one form of competitive advantage or another.

Clearly, the design of computer hardware has profound impacts for business people. It is also clear that personal and organizational success can depend on an understanding of hardware design and a commitment to knowing where it is going and what opportunities and challenges innovations will bring. Because these innovations are occurring so rapidly, hardware decisions at both the individual level and at the organizational level are difficult.

At the *individual level*, most people who have a home or office computer system and want to upgrade it, or people who are contemplating their first computer purchase, are faced with the decision of *when* to buy as much as *what* to buy and at what cost. At the *organizational level*, these same issues plague IS professionals. However, there they are more complex and more costly. Most organizations have many different computer systems in place at the same time. Innovations may come to different classes of computers at different times or rates. Therefore, managers must decide when old *legacy systems* still have a productive role in the IS architecture and when they should be replaced. A legacy system is an old computer system or application that continues to be used, typically because it still functions for the users' needs, even though newer technology is available.

IS management at the corporate level is one of the most challenging careers today, due in no small part to the constant innovation in computer hardware. That may not be your career objective, but you will benefit from becoming familiar with this field. After all, the people who keep you equipped with the right computing hardware, as you can now see, are very important allies in your success.

SUMMARY

1. **Identify the major hardware components of a computer system.**
   Today's computer systems have six major components: the central processing unit (CPU), primary storage, secondary storage, input technologies, output technologies, and communications technologies.

2. **Discuss strategic issues that link hardware design to business strategy.**
   Strategic issues linking hardware design to business strategy include: How do organizations keep up with the rapid price/performance advancements in hardware? How often should an organization upgrade its computers and storage systems? How can organizations measure benefits gained from price/performance improvements in hardware?

3. **Discuss the innovations in hardware utilization.**
   Server farms contain hundreds of thousands of networked computer servers, which provide redundancy, fault tolerance, and automatic roll-over in case one or more servers fail. Server virtualization means that multiple applications can run on a single physical server. Grid computing applies the unused processing resources of many geographically dispersed computers in a network to form a virtual supercomputer. In utility computing, a service provider makes computing resources

and infrastructure management available to a customer as needed. In cloud computing, tasks are performed by computers physically removed from the user and accessed over a network. Edge computing locates parts of website content and processing close to the user to increase response time and lower technology costs. Autonomic systems are designed to manage themselves without direct human intervention. Nanotechnology refers to the creation of materials, devices, and systems at a scale of 1 to 100 nanometres (billionths of a metre).

4. **Describe the hierarchy of computers according to power and their respective roles.**
Supercomputers are the most powerful computers, designed to handle the maximum computational demands of science and the military. Mainframes are not as powerful as supercomputers, but they are powerful enough for large organizations to use for centralized data processing and large databases. Minicomputers are smaller and less-powerful versions of mainframes that are often devoted to handling specific subsystems. Workstations fall in between minicomputers and personal computers in speed, capacity, and graphics capability. Desktop personal computers (PCs) are the most common personal and business computers. Laptop or notebook computers are small, easily transportable PCs. Wearable computers free their users' movements. Embedded computers are placed inside other products to add features and capabilities.

5. **Differentiate the various types of input and output technologies and their uses.**
Principal human data-entry input technologies include the keyboard, mouse, optical mouse, trackball, touchpad, joystick, touchscreen, stylus, and voice-recognition systems. Principal source-data automation input devices are ATMs, point-of-sale terminals, barcode scanners, optical mark readers, magnetic ink character readers, optical character readers, sensors, cameras, radio frequency identification, and retinal scanning displays. Common output technologies include various types of monitors, printers, plotters, and voice output.

6. **Describe the design and functioning of the central processing unit, and the relationship between memory and performance.**
The CPU is made up of the arithmetic-logic unit (ALU), which performs the calculations; the registers, which store minute amounts of data and instructions immediately before and after processing; and the control unit, which controls the flow of information on the microprocessor chip. After processing, the data in their original form and the instructions are sent back to a storage place outside the chip. Increased amounts of memory allow for faster processing, and for processing of more complex software.

7. **Discuss the relationships between microprocessor component designs, storage systems, and performance.**
Microprocessor designs aim to increase processing speed by minimizing the physical distance that the data (as electrical impulses) must travel and by increasing the capacity of the chip. There are four types of primary storage: registers, random access memory (RAM), cache memory, and read-only memory (ROM). All are direct-access memory; only ROM is nonvolatile. Secondary storage includes magnetic media (tapes, hard drives, and thumb, or flash, drives) and optical media (CD-ROM, DVD, and optical jukeboxes).

Primary storage has much less capacity than secondary storage, and it is faster and more expensive per byte stored. It is located much closer to the CPU than is secondary storage. Sequential-access secondary storage media such as magnetic tapes are much slower and less expensive than direct-access media (for example, hard drives, optical media).

An enterprise storage system is an independent, external system with intelligence that includes two or more storage devices. There are three major types of enterprise storage subsystems:

redundant arrays of independent disks (RAIDs), storage area networks (SANs), and network-attached storage (NAS). RAID links groups of standard hard drives to a specialized microcontroller. SAN is an architecture for building special, dedicated networks that allow access to storage devices by multiple servers. An NAS device is a special-purpose server that provides file storage to users who access the device over a network.

KEY TERMS

arithmetic-logic unit (ALU), 378

autonomic systems (autonomic computing), 370

binary, 379

bits, 379

cache memory, 381

central processing unit (CPU), 378

cloud computing, 368

compact disk read-only memory (CD-ROM), 384

control unit, 378

digital video disk, 384

edge computing, 370

enterprise storage system, 385

fat client, 373

flash memory, 384

flash memory devices, 384

grid computing, 367

hard drive, 383

holographic memory, 384

laptop and notebook computers, 373

magnetic disks, 383

magnetic tape, 382

mainframe, 371

microcomputers, 372

microcontrollers, 379

microprocessor, 378

minicomputers, 372

Moore's Law, 378

multimedia technology, 377

nanotechnology, 370

netbook, 374

network-attached storage (NAS), 385

optical storage devices, 383

primary storage (main memory), 380

random access memory (RAM), 381

read-only memory (ROM), 382

redundant arrays of independent disks (RAID), 385

registers, 378

secondary storage, 382

sequential access, 382

server, 372

server farm, 366

server virtualization, 367

storage area network (SAN), 385

storage over IP, 385

storage visualization software, 385

supercomputer, 371

thin-client systems, 373

thumb drive, 384

ultramobile PC, 374

utility computing, 368

workstations, 372

DISCUSSION QUESTIONS

1. Describe the hardware components included in a typical desktop computer.
2. What is the value of server farms and virtualization to any large organization?
3. If you were the chief information officer (CIO) of a firm, how would you explain the workings, benefits, and limitations of cloud computing?
4. What is the value of cloud computing to a small organization?
5. Where might you find embedded computers at home, at school, and/or at work?
6. What are some of the input and output technologies that would be used by a typical retail organization? Describe how the technology would be used.
7. What factors affect the speed of a microprocessor?
8. If you were the CIO of a firm, what factors would you consider when selecting secondary storage media for your company's records (files)?

9. Given that Moore's Law has proved itself over the past two decades, speculate on what chip capabilities will be in 10 years. What might your desktop PC be able to do?

10. If you were the CIO of a firm, how would you explain the workings, benefits, and limitations of using thin clients as opposed to fat clients?

11. Describe how and why a large organization, such as a bank, would use storage systems.

PROBLEM-SOLVING ACTIVITIES

1. Access the websites of the major chip manufacturers, for example Intel (*www.intel.com*), Motorola (*www.motorola.com*), and Advanced Micro Devices (*www.amd.com*), and obtain the latest information regarding new and planned chips. Compare performance and costs across these vendors. Prepare a report for your class.

2. Access The Journey Inside on Intel's website (*http://educate.intel.com/en/thejourneyinside/*). Select one of the lessons that interest you and prepare a summary for your classmates.

3. Investigate the status of cloud computing by having each person research the offerings of one of these leading vendors. Note any inhibitors to cloud computing. Compare your notes and prepare a presentation for your class.
   * Dell (see *www.dell.com/cloudcomputing*)
   * Oracle (see *www.oracle.com/technetwork/topics/cloud/whatsnew/index.html*)
   * IBM (see *www.ibm.com/ibm/cloud*)
   * Amazon (see *http://aws.amazon.com*)
   * Microsoft (see *www.microsoft.com/azure/default.mspx*)
   * Google (see e.g., *www.technologyreview.com/biztech/19785/?a=f*)

TECHNOLOGY GUIDE 2
COMPUTER SOFTWARE

LEARNING OBJECTIVES

1. Define software and differentiate between system and application software.
2. Describe the general functions of the operating system.
3. Describe the major types of application software.
4. Discuss the advantages and disadvantages of open-source software.
5. Explain how software has evolved, and consider trends for the future.

Technology Guide Overview

Software has become an everyday feature of our business and personal lives. Regardless of your major, you will be using many different types of software throughout your career. In addition, you will provide input about the current types of software you use, such as: Does the software help you do your job? Is it easy to use? Do you need more functionality and if so, what functionality would be helpful to you? In your functional area, MIS employees will act as your advisors, but you will have definitive input into the software needed to do your job. In some organizations, the budget for software is allocated to functional areas or departments, meaning that you might be making software decisions (at least locally) yourself. Finally, when your functional area or organization considers acquiring new applications (discussed in Chapter 12), you will again have input into these decisions.

In Technology Guide 2 we begin by discussing the importance of software and some of the most relevant software issues of today. We will continue with an introduction to system software and its main characteristics, followed by an explanation of application software. We will conclude this technology guide with a brief discussion of some of the most relevant programming languages.

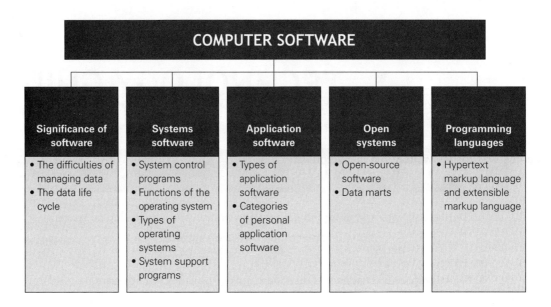

TG2.1 Significance of Software

Computer hardware is only as effective as the instructions we give it, and those instructions are contained in **software**. The importance of computer software cannot be overestimated. The first software applications of computers in business were developed in the early 1950s. Software was less costly in computer systems then. Today, software makes up a much larger percentage of the cost of modern computer systems because the price of hardware has dramatically decreased, while the complexity and the price of software have dramatically increased.

We will begin our examination of software by defining some fundamental concepts. Software consists of **computer programs**, which are sequences of instructions for the computer.

Unlike the hardwired computers of the 1950s, modern software uses the **stored program concept**, in which software programs are stored in the computer's hardware. These programs are accessed and their instructions are executed (followed) in the computer's CPU. Once the program has finished executing, a new program is loaded into the main memory, and the computer hardware addresses another task.

Computer programs include **documentation**, which is a written description of the functions of the program. Documentation helps the user operate the computer system and it helps other programmers understand what the program does and how it accomplishes its purpose. Documentation is vital to the business organization. Without it, if a key programmer or user leaves, the knowledge of how to use the program or how it is designed may be lost as well.

All too often, computer program code is inefficient, poorly designed, and riddled with errors. The Software Engineering Institute at Carnegie Mellon University in Pittsburgh defines good software as usable, reliable, defect free, cost effective, and maintainable. As we become increasingly dependent on computers and networks, the risks associated with software defects are getting worse. This is evident in the following example of a faulty McAfee virus update.

EXAMPLE TG2.1

On April 21, 2010, the popular antivirus software maker McAfee released a virus update with a software glitch. According to a company spokesperson, the flawed software occurred with the 5958 virus definition file, which flagged a core system file on Windows PCs as a malware threat. The affected PCs displayed a shutdown error or blue error screen and went into an endless cycle of rebooting.

According to company officials, the flawed update could significantly reduce performance on systems running Windows XP Service Pack 3 but not PCs running Vista or Windows 7. As soon as McAfee was made aware of the faulty software, the company stopped making it available on their servers and prepared an emergency file that was posted on its forum site with detailed instructions on how to fix the problem. However, the McAfee forum site was so overwhelmed with customer visits that it had to be taken off-line to prevent it from crashing. In the meantime, McAfee developers had been working on developing a new virus update definition file, which was made available the same day and gave users detailed instructions to recover affected systems.

Sources: G. Keizer, "Flawed McAfee Update Paralyzes Corporate PCs," *Computerworld*, April 22, 2010; T. Bradley, "Recovering From the Flawed McAfee Update," *PC World*, April 22, 2010.

According to Watts Humphrey, on average, professional programmers make about 100 errors in every 1,000 lines of code they write. Fortunately, the software industry recognizes this problem. Unfortunately, however, the problem is enormous and the industry is taking only initial steps to resolve it. One critical step is better design and planning at the beginning of the development process (discussed in Chapter 12).

The computer is able to do nothing until it is instructed by software. Although computer hardware is, by design, general purpose, software enables the user to instruct a computer system to perform specific functions that provide business value. There are two major types of software: systems software and application software. The relationship among hardware, systems software, and application software is illustrated in Figure TG2.1.

Systems software is a set of instructions that serves primarily as an intermediary between computer hardware and application programs. Systems software provides important self-regulatory functions for computer systems, such as loading itself when the computer is first turned on and providing commonly used sets of instructions for all applications. *Systems programming* refers to both the creation and the maintenance of systems software.

Application software is a set of computer instructions that provides more specific functionality to a user. That functionality may be broad, such as general word processing, or narrow, such as

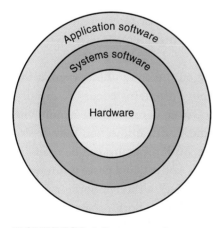

FIGURE TG2.1 Systems software services as intermediary between hardware and functional applications.

an organization's payroll program. Essentially, an application program applies a computer to a certain need. *Application programming* refers to both the creation and the modification and improvement of application software. Application software may be proprietary or off-the-shelf. As we shall see, there are many different software applications that are used by organizations today.

BEFORE YOU GO ON …

1. What is the importance of software in a computer system?
2. What is the significance of software defects in computer systems?
3. What are the differences between systems software and application software?

TG2.2 Systems Software

As we discussed earlier, systems software is the class of programs that controls and supports the computer system and its information-processing activities. Systems software also facilitates the programming, testing, and debugging of computer programs. Systems software programs support application software by directing the basic functions of the computer. For example, when the computer is turned on, the initialization program (a systems program) prepares and readies all devices for processing. Systems software can be grouped into two major functional categories: system control programs and system support programs.

System Control Programs

System control programs control the use of the hardware, software, and data resources of a computer system. The main system control program is the operating system. The **operating system (OS)** supervises the overall operation of the computer. One of its key functions is to monitor the computer's status and scheduling operations, including the input and output processes. In addition, the operating system allocates CPU time and main memory to programs running on the computer. It also provides an interface between the user and the hardware. This interface hides the complexity of the hardware from the user. That is, you do not have to know how the hardware actually operates. You simply have to know what the hardware will do and what you need to do to obtain desired results.

Functions of the Operating System

The operating system manages the program or programs (also called *jobs* or *tasks*) running on the processor at a given time. Operating systems provide various types of program management, such as multi-tasking, multi-threading, and multiprocessing.

The management of two or more tasks, or programs, running on the computer system at the same time is called **multi-tasking**. Because switching among these programs occurs so rapidly, all of the programs appear to be executing at the same time. However, because there is only one processor, only one program is actually executing at any one time. For example, you may create a graph with Microsoft Excel and insert it into a Word document. Both programs can be open on your screen in separate windows, enabling you to create your graph, copy it, and paste it into your Word document, without having to exit Excel and start Word. However, although both programs are open, at any given moment you are working in either Excel or Word. Both programs cannot execute at the same time.

Multi-threading is a form of multi-tasking that involves running multiple tasks, or threads, within a single application simultaneously. For example, a word processor application may edit one document while spell-checking another. **Multiprocessing** occurs when a computer system with two or more processors can run more than one program at a given time by assigning them to different processors.

In addition to managing programs executing on computer hardware, operating systems must also manage main memory and secondary storage. Operating systems enable a process called **virtual memory**, which simulates more main memory than actually exists in the computer system. Virtual memory allows a program to behave as if it had access to the full storage capacity of a computer rather than access only to the amount of primary storage installed on the computer. Virtual memory divides an application program or module into fixed-length portions called *pages*. The system executes some pages of instructions while pulling others from secondary storage. In effect, virtual memory allows users to write programs as if primary storage was larger than it actually is.

The ease or difficulty of the interaction between the user and the computer is determined to a large extent by the *interface design*. Older, text-based interfaces like DOS (disk operating system) required the user to type in cryptic commands. In an effort to make computers more user friendly, programmers developed the graphical user interface. The **graphical user interface** (GUI, pronounced "gooey") allows users to exercise direct control of visible objects (such as icons) and actions that replace complex commands. The GUI was developed by researchers at Xerox Palo Alto Research Center (PARC) and then popularized by the Apple Macintosh computer. Microsoft soon introduced its GUI-based Windows operating system for IBM-style PCs.

The next generation of GUI technology will incorporate features such as virtual reality, head-mounted displays, speech input (user commands) and output, pen and gesture recognition, animation, multimedia, artificial intelligence, and cellular/wireless communication capabilities. The new interfaces, called *natural user interfaces (NUIs)*, will combine social interfaces, haptic interfaces, touch-enabled gesture-control interfaces, and spatial operating environments.

A **social interface** is a user interface that guides the user through computer applications by using cartoon-like characters, graphics, animation, and voice commands. The cartoon-like characters can be cast as puppets, narrators, guides, inhabitants, or avatars (computer-generated humanlike figures).

A **haptic interface** is one that allows the user to feel a sense of touch by applying forces, vibrations, and/or motions to the user. The Wii video game console by Nintendo is a good example of a haptic interface.

Touch-enabled gesture-control interfaces enable users to browse through photos, "toss" objects around a screen, "flick" to turn the pages of a book, play video games, and watch movies. Examples of this type of interface are Microsoft Surface and the Apple iPhone.

A **spatial operating environment** is a user interface where the user stands or sits in front of one or more computer screens, and gestures with gloved hands to move images around, touch virtual objects, trace shapes, and navigate complex data. For example, Oblong Industries (*http://oblong.com*) has developed the g-speak spatial operating environment. Oblong claims that g-speak makes computers more intuitive and logical to the human brain. G-speak is being used at many Fortune 500 companies, government agencies, and universities.

Types of Operating Systems

As we previously discussed, operating systems are necessary in order for computer hardware to function. **Operating environments** are sets of computer programs that add features that enable system developers to create applications without directly accessing the operating system; they function only *with* an operating system. That is, operating environments are not operating systems, but they work only with an operating system. For example, the early versions of Windows were operating environments that provided a graphical user interface and were functional only with MS-DOS.

Operating systems are classified into different types depending on the type of computer on which they run and the number of users they support. *Operating systems for mobile devices* are designed to support a single person using a mobile, hand-held device or information appliance. Small computer operating systems (*notebooks, laptops, desktops,* and *workstations*) are designed to support a single user or a small workgroup of users. Large computer operating systems (*midrange computers* and *mainframes*) typically support between a few dozen and thousands of concurrent users. Large computer operating systems offer greater functionality than the other types, including reliability, backup, security, fault tolerance, and rapid processing speeds. One important exception to this generalization is the user interface, which is most sophisticated on desktop operating systems and least sophisticated on large computer operating systems.

We are most familiar with small computer operating systems, because we use them daily. Examples are Windows XP and Vista, the Apple operating system (Mac OS X), and Linux. The Windows family of operating systems is the dominant small computer operating system. Various versions run on laptops, notebooks, desktops, and servers. In the future, operating systems might be able to run in a web browser and be available for free (see, for example, the XIOS Operating System by Swedish vendor Xcerion; *www.xcerion.com*). The following example illustrates the implementation of the new Windows 7 operating system.

EXAMPLE TG2.2

Students and teachers at Meadow Green Academy in Mississauga, Ontario used to take an average of 30 minutes to log on and open the program that manages the printing of documents in the school's network. This is not a story from the early 90s but rather a story of a private school of the twenty-first century in one of the more technologically advanced countries in the world.

Luckily, a good IT Samaritan, IT consultant Mitch Garvis, volunteered his time to fix the computer problems at his son's school. The work started by carefully evaluating the school's computer infrastructure. The school had 30 computers distributed among administration, classrooms, and computer lab, that served 20 staff and 130 students from kindergarten to Grade 8. Most of the computers were four-year-old Dell Pentium desktops with 256 MB of RAM and old video cards. Even though the computers were a bit old they were in perfect condition. Even more, the problem was not so much the technology as a lack of management and maintenance. For example, the school lack centralized tools to control virus infections.

The computer facelift consisted of switching the operating system from Windows XP to the newly released Windows 7 operating system. The main reason for the move was the increased security and the fact that it was easier to manage centrally. For example, now if a computer gets infected by a virus, it only takes the press of a couple of buttons and the system does everything automatically, reducing the need for human intervention to about three minutes. Teachers and students are very pleased with the overhaul that Mitch Garvis performed and they all thank him for that.

Sources: Compiled from J. Kavur, "Dad Performs IT Makeover at Son's School," *ComputerWorld Canada*, March 10, 2010; G. Keizer, "Windows 7 Steals Big Share from XP," *ComputerWorld*, December 1, 2009.

Today's desktop operating systems use GUIs with icons to provide instant access to common tasks and plug-and-play capabilities. **Plug-and-play** is a feature that can automate the installation of new hardware by enabling the operating system to recognize new hardware and then automatically install the necessary software, called *device drivers*. These operating systems also provide transparent, three-dimensional windows to make it easier to see files and other windows on your monitor. Your screen itself can be a movie or an animated image. Plug-and-play provides you with an area of your screen where you can put mini-applications such as clocks, stock tickers, calendars, and RSS readers (discussed in Chapter 5). You can view all open windows in a fanned-out, playing card view, and you have a GUI for finding and organizing directories, folders, and files.

Current desktop operating systems allow your computer to become a digital hub. For example, you can easily store and wirelessly transmit pictures from your computer to digital picture frames placed around your house as well as to other computers. In addition, you can easily listen to your digital music and wirelessly stream your tunes to speakers located around your home. You can also view videos (including movies) on your computer.

System Support Programs

The second major category of systems software, system support programs, supports the operations, management, and users of a computer system by providing a variety of support services. Examples of system support programs are system utility programs, performance monitors, and security monitors.

System utilities are programs that have been written to accomplish common tasks such as sorting records and creating directories and subdirectories. These programs also restore accidentally erased files, locate files within the directory structure, and manage memory usage. System performance monitors are programs that monitor the processing of jobs on a computer system. They monitor performance in areas such as processor time, memory space, input/output devices, and system and application programs. System security monitors are programs that monitor the use of a computer system to protect it and its resources from unauthorized use, fraud, and destruction.

BEFORE YOU GO ON ...

1. What are the two main types of systems software?
2. What are the major differences among mobile device, desktop, and mainframe operating systems?

TG2.3 Application Software

As we discussed earlier, application software consists of instructions that direct a computer system to perform specific information-processing activities and that provide functionality for users. Because there are so many different uses for computers, there are a correspondingly large number of application software programs.

Types of Application Software

Application software includes both proprietary and off-the-shelf software. Proprietary application software addresses a specific or unique business need for a company. This type of software may be developed in-house by the organization's information systems personnel, or it may be commissioned from a software vendor. Specific software programs developed for a particular company by a vendor are called contract software.

Alternatively, off-the-shelf application software can be purchased, leased, or rented from a vendor that develops programs and sells them to many organizations. Off-the-shelf software may be a standard package, or it may be customizable. Special-purpose programs or "packages" can be tailored for a specific purpose, such as inventory control or payroll. The word package is a commonly used term for a computer program (or group of programs) that has been developed by a vendor and is available for purchase in a prepackaged form. We discuss the methodology involved in acquiring application software, whether proprietary or off-the-shelf, in Chapter 12.

Categories of Personal Application Software

General-purpose, off-the-shelf application programs designed to help individual users increase their productivity are referred to as **personal application software**. Some of the major types of personal application software are listed in Table TG2.1. *Software suites* combine some of these packages and integrate their functions. Microsoft Office is a well-known example of a software suite.

Speech recognition software is an input technology, rather than strictly an application, that can feed systems software and application software. **Speech recognition software**, also called *voice recognition*, recognizes and interprets human speech, either one word at a time (discrete speech), or in a conversational stream (continuous speech). Advances in processing power, new software algorithms, and better microphones have enabled developers to design extremely accurate voice recognition

TABLE TG2.1
PERSONAL APPLICATION SOFTWARE

CATEGORY OF PERSONAL APPLICATION SOFTWARE	MAJOR FUNCTIONS	EXAMPLES
Spreadsheets	Uses rows and columns to manipulate primarily numerical data; useful for analyzing financial information, and for what-if and goal-seeking analyses.	Microsoft Excel Corel Quattro Pro
Word processing	Allows users to manipulate primarily text with many writing and editing features.	Microsoft Word Corel WordPerfect
Desktop publishing	Extends word processing software to allow the production of finished, camera-ready documents, which may contain photographs, diagrams, and other images combined with text in different fonts.	Microsoft Publisher QuarkXPress
Data management	Allows users to store, retrieve, and manipulate related data.	Microsoft Access FileMaker Pro
Presentation	Allows users to create and edit graphically rich information to appear on electronic slides.	Microsoft PowerPoint Corel Presentations
Graphics	Allows users to create, store, and display or print charts, graphs, maps, and drawings.	Adobe Photoshop Corel DRAW
Personal information management	Allows users to create and maintain calendars, appointments, to-do lists, and business contacts.	IBM Lotus Notes Microsoft Outlook
Personal finance	Allows users to maintain chequebooks, track investments, monitor credit cards, and bank and pay bills electronically.	Quicken Microsoft Money
Web authoring	Allows users to design websites and publish them on the Web.	Microsoft FrontPage Macromedia Dreamweaver
Communications	Allows users to communicate with other people over any distance.	Novell Groupwise Internet Explorer Messenger

software. Experts predict that, in the near future, voice-recognition systems will likely be built into almost every device, appliance, and machine that people use. Applications for voice recognition technology abound. Consider these examples:

- Call centres are using the technology. The average call-centre call costs $5 if it is handled by an employee, but only $0.50 with a self-service, speech-enabled system. Bell Canada, for example, uses voice recognition software to route customer calls.
- IBM's Embedded ViaVoice software (*http://www-306.ibm.com/software/voice/viavoice/*) powers GM's OnStar and other dashboard command systems, such as music players and navigational systems.
- Apple's Macintosh OS X and Microsoft's Vista operating system come with built-in voice technology.
- Nuance's Dragon NaturallySpeaking (*www.nuance.com*) allows for accurate voice-to-text and e-mail dictation.
- Vocera Communications (*www.vocera.com*) has developed a communicator badge that combines voice recognition with wireless technologies. Among its first customers were medical workers, who use the badge to search through hospital directories by voice and find the right person to help with a patient problem or to find medical records.
- Vox-Tec's (*www.voxtec.com*) Phraselator, a hand-held device about the size of a chequebook, listens to a request for a phrase and then delivers a translation in any of 41 specified languages. The Phraselator is helping an Alberta First Nation, the Siksika, and other Aboriginal groups across North America preserve their languages.

BEFORE YOU GO ON ...

1. Which classes of personal application software are essential for the productivity of a business or other organization with which you are familiar? Which are non-essential?
2. What do you see as the advantages of speech recognition software? Disadvantages?

TG2.4 Open Systems

The concept of open systems refers to a model of computing products that work together. Achieving this goal is possible through the use of the same operating system with compatible software on all the different computers that would interact with one another in an organization. A complementary approach is to produce application software that will run across all computer platforms. If hardware, operating systems, and application software are designed as open systems, the user will be able to purchase the best software for the job, called *best of breed*, without worrying whether it will run on particular hardware.

Open-Source Software

There is a trend within the software industry away from proprietary software toward open-source software. Proprietary software is software that has been developed by a company and has restrictions on its use, copying, and modification. The company developing such software spends money and time on research and development of its software product, and then sells it in the marketplace. The proprietary nature of the software means that the company keeps the source code—the actual computer instructions—private (as Coca-Cola does with its formula).

In contrast, the source code for **open-source software** is available at no cost to developers or users. Open-source software is not shareware or freeware. Shareware typically allows no access to the underlying source code. Freeware is copyrighted software that is made available to the user free of charge for an unlimited time. In contrast, open-source software is copyrighted and distributed with license terms ensuring that the source code will always be available.

Open-source software products have worldwide "communities" of developers who write and maintain the code. Inside each community, however, only a small group of developers, called *core developers*, is allowed to modify or submit changes to the code. Other developers submit code to the core developers.

There are advantages and disadvantages to implementing open-source software in an organization. According to The Open Source Initiative (*www.opensource.org*), open-source development produces high-quality, reliable, flexible (code can be changed to meet the needs of the user), low-cost software. In many cases, open-source software is more reliable than commercial software. Because the code is available to many developers, more bugs are discovered early and quickly and are fixed immediately. Support for open-source software is also available from firms that provide products derived from the software. An example is Red Hat for Linux (*www.redhat.com*). These firms provide education, training, and technical support for the software for a fee.

However, open-source software also has disadvantages. To begin with, organizations that do not have in-house technical experts will have to buy maintenance-support contracts from a third party. In addition, questions have arisen concerning the ease of use of open-source software, the amount of time and expense needed to train users, and the compatibility with existing systems or with the systems of business partners.

There are many examples of open-source software, including the suite of software called GNU (which stands for GNU's Not UNIX, *www.gnu.org*) developed by the Free Software Foundation Inc. (*www.fsf.org*); the Linux operating system (*www.linuxhq.com*); Apache web server (*www.apache.org*); sendmail SMTP (Send Mail Transport Protocol) e-mail server (*www.sendmail.org*); the Perl programming language (*www.perl.org*); the Firefox browser from Mozilla (*www.mozilla.com*); and the Oracle Open Office applications suite (*www.oracle.com/us/products/applications/open-office/index.html*). In fact, there are about 140,000 open-source projects under way on SourceForge (*http://sourceforge.net*), the popular open-source hosting site.

Linux and Apache are excellent examples of how open-source software is moving to the mainstream. Linux was initially developed by Linus Torvalds in 1991 as an alternative to Windows and the more expensive UNIX systems. Linux is gaining market share in servers, now running on approximately one quarter of all servers, whereas Microsoft runs on about two thirds of all servers. Further, almost two thirds of the world's web servers now run Apache, compared with one third for Microsoft.

Many major companies use open-source software. For example, Japan's Shinsei Bank (*www.shinseibank.com*) uses Linux on its servers, SugarCRM (*www.sugarcrm.com*) for certain customer relationship management tasks, and MySQL (*www.mysql.com*) open-source database management software. Further, the *Los Angeles Times* uses Alfresco (*www.alfresco.com*) to manage some of the images and video for the newspaper's website. The following example shows the economics of using an open-source product from the perspectives of both the purchaser and the vendor.

EXAMPLE TG2.3

Ogihara America Corporation (*www.ogihara.com*) is part of Japan's Ogihara Group, which is a global Japanese tool and die company for the automotive industry. Ogihara America stamps autobody parts for Canadian and U.S. car manufacturers. The company has been downsizing in response to troubles in the Canadian and U.S. automotive industry, eliminating two thirds of its workforce over the last several years.

When the going gets tough, the tough keep going. Despite the economic downturn, Ogihara

(Continued on next page)

EXAMPLE (Continued)

was determined to continue with a product lifecycle management (PLM) initiative using open-source software from Aras Corporation (*www.aras.com*). The Aras software includes modules that support developing, engineering, and refining products and all the materials that go into a product.

Ogihara's agreement with Aras is that a contract to support the software is optional. That means if Aras wanted the contract, it had to be flexible when Ogihara's business waned. The two firms negotiated a reduced yearly rate of $15,000 for software support, versus the usual $85,000. The price will increase as Ogihara's business bounces back.

When Aras moved to open-source, the company gave up licensing revenue. It radically changed its business model, eliminating its sales department in favour of selling the product on-line. Some manufacturers download the software for free and even get free support by getting advice from other users

on the Aras website. Other manufacturers prefer to pay Aras for a formal support contract.

Traditional software support contracts are based on the customer's characteristics, such as the number of users, servers, and modules installed. But with the open-source model, the cost of the support contract has nothing to do with these quantitative factors. Customers such as Ogihara like it this way because they can roll out the modules incrementally as their needs—and revenues—change.

Sources: Compiled from D. Carr, "Open Source Saves the Day," *CIO Insight*, January 21, 2009; M. McGee, "CIO Prescription: How IT Is Riding Out the Recession," *InformationWeek*, January 17, 2009; R. King, "Cost-Conscious Companies Turn to Open-Source Software," *BusinessWeek*, December 1, 2008; N. Rouse-Talley, "Open-Source PLM," *Desktop Engineering*, August 13, 2007; "Ogihara Implements Aras Microsoft-Based Enterprise Open Source Solutions for Quality Compliance," The Free Library, April 10, 2007; Ogihara website (*www.ogihara.com*), accessed January 17, 2009.

BEFORE YOU GO ON ...

1. What is the difference between open-source software and open systems?
2. What are the advantages and disadvantages of open-source software?

TG2.5 Programming Languages

Programming languages allow people to write instructions that tell computers what to do. They are the means by which all systems and application software are developed. Because computers do exactly what they are told, programming languages require a high degree of precision and completeness. Also, digital computers only understand 0s and 1s, or binary digits. Therefore, all computer languages, except machine language, must be translated into binary digits for processing. This process is accomplished by a type of systems software called a **compiler**. Table TG2.2 provides a description of common categories of programming languages.

It would be unusual for most businesspeople to write computer programs at work using the programming languages in Table TG2.2, or in object-oriented programming languages. (MIS majors may not do much programming either.) However, you should have a basic knowledge of these languages because your organization's computer programmers will use some of them to develop the applications that you will use.

Object-oriented languages work differently than the languages in Table TG2.2. **Object-oriented languages** are based on the idea of taking a small amount of data and the instructions about what to do with that data, which are called **methods**, and combining them into what is called an **object**. When the object is selected or activated, the computer has the desired data and takes the desired action. This is what happens when you click on an icon on your GUI-equipped computer screen. For example, when you click on the Internet Explorer (IE) icon on your desktop (which is an object), the IE window will open. The IE icon object contains the program code for opening a window.

TABLE TG2.2
PROGRAMMING LANGUAGES

CATEGORY	CHARACTERISTICS
First Generation Language (Machine)	Consists of 0s and 1s; extremely difficult to use by programmers.
Second Generation Language (Assembly)	More user-friendly than machine language; uses mnemonics for people to use, such as ADD for add, SUB for subtract, and MOV for move.
Third Generation Language (Procedural)	Requires the programmer to specify, step by step, exactly how the computer must accomplish a task. Examples include C, Basic, FORTRAN, and COBOL.
Fourth Generation Language (Non-procedural)	Allows the user to specify the desired result without having to specify step-by-step procedures; simplifies and accelerates the programming process. Examples include SAS, SPSS, and APL.
Visual Programming Language	Employed within a graphical environment and uses a mouse, icons, symbols on the screen, or pull-down menus to make programming easier. An example is Visual Basic.

Object-oriented languages also have a **reusability feature**, which means that objects created for one purpose can be used in a different object-oriented program if desired. For example, a student object in a university system can be used for applications ranging from grades to fees to applications for graduation. Java is a powerful and popular object-oriented language, and we look at it here in more detail.

Java is an object-oriented language, developed by Sun Microsystems, which enables programmers to develop applications that work across the Internet. Java can handle text, data, graphics, sound, and video, all within one program. Java is used to develop small applications, called **applets**, which can be included in an HTML page on the Internet. When an individual uses a Java-compatible browser to view a page that contains a Java applet, the applet's code is transferred to the user's system and is executed by the user's browser.

Applications written in Java can be stored on Internet servers, downloaded as needed, and then erased from the local computer when the processing is completed. This feature means that users no longer need to store copies of the application on the hard drive of their PC.

Hypertext Markup Language and Extensible Markup Language

Hypertext markup language and extensible markup language are programming languages that are used to build rich multimedia web pages, websites, and web-based applications. For example, you can use these languages to build your own web page.

Hypertext markup language (HTML) is used for creating and formatting documents on the World Wide Web. HTML gives users the option of controlling visual elements such as fonts, font size, and paragraph spacing without changing the original information.

Hypertext is an approach to document management in which documents are stored in a network of nodes connected by links, which are called **hyperlinks**. Users access data through an interactive browsing system. The combination of nodes, links, and supporting indexes for any particular topic constitutes a **hypertext document**. A hypertext document may contain text, images, and other types of information such as data files, audio, video, and executable computer programs.

English Text	HTML	XML
MNGT 3070 Introduction to MIS 3 semester hours Professor Smith	<TITLE>MNGT 3070</TITLE> <BODY> <UL> <LI>Introduction to MIS <LI>3 semester hours <LI>Professor Smith </UL></BODY>	<Department and course="MNGT 3070"> <COURSE TITLE>Introduction to MIS<COURSE> <HOURS UNIT="Semester">3</NUMBER OF HOURS> <INSTRUCTOR>Professor Smith<INSTRUCTOR>

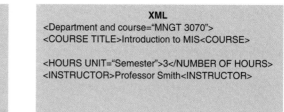

FIGURE TG2.2 Comparison of HTML and XML.

Extensible markup language (XML) improves the functionality of web documents by describing what the data in documents actually mean, and identifying the business purpose of the documents themselves. As a result, XML improves the compatibility among the disparate systems of business partners by allowing XML documents to be moved to any format on any platform without the elements losing their meaning. Consequently, the same information can be published to a web browser, a PDA, or a smart phone, and each device would use the information appropriately.

A programmer showing the XML structure on a whiteboard.

XML and HTML are not the same. The purpose of HTML is to help build web pages and display data on web pages. The purpose of XML is to describe data and information. It does not say *how* the data will be displayed (which HTML does). XML can be used to send complex messages that include different files (and HTML cannot).

Figure TG2.2 compares HTML and XML. Notice that HTML describes only where an item appears on a page, whereas XML describes what the item is. For example, HTML shows only that "Introduction to MIS" appears on line 1, where XML shows that "Introduction to MIS" is the Course Title.

BEFORE YOU GO ON ...

1. Differentiate between HTML and XML.
2. What are the strategic advantages of using an object-oriented programming language?

WHAT'S IN IT FOR ME?

FOR THE ACCOUNTING MAJOR

Accounting application software performs the organization's accounting functions, which are repetitive and high volume. Each business transaction (a person hired, a paycheque produced, an item sold) produces data that must be captured. After accounting applications capture the data, they manipulate them as necessary. Accounting applications adhere to relatively standardized procedures, handle detailed data, and have a historical focus (in other words, they deal with what happened in the past).

FOR THE FINANCE MAJOR

Financial application software provides information about the firm's financial status to people and groups inside and outside the firm. Financial applications include forecasting, funds management, and control applications. Forecasting applications predict and project the firm's future activity in the economic environment. Funds management applications use cash flow models to analyze expected cash flows. Control applications enable managers to monitor their financial performance, typically by providing information about the budgeting process and performance ratios.

FOR THE MARKETING MAJOR

Marketing application software helps management solve problems that involve marketing the firm's products. Marketing software includes marketing research and marketing intelligence applications. Marketing applications provide information about the firm's products and competitors, its distribution system, its advertising and personal selling activities, and its pricing strategies. Overall, marketing applications help managers develop strategies that combine the four major elements of marketing: product, promotion, place, and price.

FOR THE PRODUCTION/OPERATIONS MANAGEMENT MAJOR

Managers use production/operations management applications software for production planning and as part of the physical production system. POM applications include production, inventory, quality, and cost software. These applications help management operate manufacturing facilities and logistics. Materials requirements planning (MRP) software is also widely used in manufacturing. This software identifies which materials will be needed, how much will be needed, and the dates on which they will be needed. This information enables managers to be proactive.

FOR THE HUMAN RESOURCES MANAGEMENT MAJOR

Human resources management application software provides information concerning recruiting and hiring, education and training, maintaining the employee database, termination, and administering benefits. HRM applications include workforce planning, recruiting, workforce management, compensation, benefits, and environmental reporting subsystems (employment equity records and analysis, union enrolment, toxic substances, and grievances).

FOR THE MIS MAJOR

If your company decides to develop software itself, the MIS function is responsible for managing this activity. If the company decides to buy software, the MIS function deals with software vendors in analyzing their products. The MIS function is also responsible for upgrading software as vendors release new versions.

SUMMARY

1. **Define software and differentiate between system and application software.**

   Software consists of computer programs (coded instructions) that control the functions of computer hardware. Software itself is becoming much more complex, expensive, and time-consuming to develop, with computer program code often containing errors. There are two main categories of software: systems software and application software. Systems software manages the hardware resources of the computer system; it functions between the hardware and the application software. Systems software includes the system control programs (operating systems) and system support programs. Application software enables users to perform specific tasks and information-processing activities. Application software may be proprietary or off-the-shelf.

2. **Describe the general functions of the operating system.**

   Operating systems manage the actual computer resources (in other words, the hardware). They schedule and process applications (jobs), manage and protect memory, manage the input and output functions and hardware, manage data and files, and provide clustering support, security, fault tolerance, graphical user interfaces, and the opening of programs in on-screen windows.

3. **Describe the major types of application software.**

   The major types of application software are spreadsheet, data management, word processing, desktop publishing, graphics, multimedia, communications, speech recognition, and groupware. Software suites combine several types of application software (for instance, word processing, spreadsheet, and data management) into an integrated package.

4. **Discuss the advantages and disadvantages of open-source software.**

   Advantages of open-source software include high quality, reliability, flexibility (code can be changed to meet the needs of the user), and low cost. Open-source software can be more reliable than commercial software. Because the code is available to many developers, more bugs are discovered early and quickly and are fixed immediately. Disadvantages include the relatively high cost of maintenance support contracts, the difficulty of use, the amount of time and expense needed to train users, and incompatibility with existing systems or with the systems of business partners.

5. **Explain how software has evolved, and consider trends for the future.**

   Software and programming languages continue to become more user-oriented. Programming languages have evolved from the first generation of machine languages, which is directly understandable to the CPU, to higher levels that use more natural language and do not require users to specify the detailed procedures for achieving desired results.

KEY TERMS

applet, 402

application software, 393

compiler, 401

computer program, 392

contract software, 397

documentation, 393

extensible markup language (XML), 403

graphical user interface (GUI), 395

haptic interface, 395

hyperlink, 402

hypertext, 402

hypertext document, 402

hypertext markup language (HTML), 402

Java, 402

method, 401

multiprocessing, 395

multi-tasking, 394

multi-threading, 394

DISCUSSION QUESTIONS

1. You are the CIO of your company and you have to develop an application of strategic importance to your firm. What are the advantages and disadvantages of using open-source software?

2. You have to take a programming course, or maybe more than one, in your MIS program. Which programming language(s) would you choose to study? Why? Should you even have to learn a programming language? Why or why not?

3. What type of personal application software would a university student require? What type of application software does a professor need to teach a class?

PROBLEM-SOLVING ACTIVITIES

1. A great deal of software is available free over the Internet. Go to *www.pcmag.com* and look at all the software that is available for free. Choose one software program and download it to your computer. Prepare a brief discussion about the software for your class.

2. Enter the IBM website (*www.ibm.com*) and search for "software." Click on the drop box for Products, and notice how many software products IBM provides. Is IBM only a hardware company?

3. Compare the following proprietary software packages with their open-source software counterparts. Prepare your comparison for the class.

Proprietary	Open Source
Microsoft Office	Google Docs, Oracle Open Office
Adobe Photoshop	Picnik.com, Google Picasa

4. Compare the Microsoft Surface interface (*www.microsoft.com/surface/*) with Oblong Industries' g-speak spatial operating environment *(http://oblong.com/)*. Demonstrate examples of each to the class. What are the advantages and disadvantages of each interface?

TECHNOLOGY GUIDE 3 PROTECTING YOUR INFORMATION ASSETS

LEARNING OBJECTIVES

1. Identify the various behavioural actions you can take to protect your information assets based upon your risk assessment of information asset risks.

2. Identify the various computer-based actions you can take to protect your information assets based upon your information asset risks.

Technology Guide Overview

We travel in our work, we work from home, and we access the Internet from home for personal reasons (for example, shopping, ordering products, planning trips, gathering information, staying in touch with friends and family via e-mail). Therefore, in this technology guide we discuss how to protect your information assets when you are computing at home or while you are travelling. The level of protection needs to be geared toward the type of information that is being stored or transported. Your term paper requires a different level of protection from your banking records and identification information. Information that you are a custodian of (such as your employer's customers' data) requires a high level of protection, while other information, such as pictures of your cat, requires less security.

It is important to note that when you are at work or when you access your university's network from home or on the road, you hopefully have the advantage of "industrial-strength" information security that your university's information systems department has implemented. In all other cases, though, you are on your own, and it is your responsibility to protect yourself. Protecting yourself is becoming even more critical because organized crime increasingly is turning its attention to home users. As businesses improve their information security, consumers become the next logical target. According to Symantec (*www.symantec.com*), which manufactures the Norton Internet security products, if you connected an unprotected personal computer to the Internet in 2003, it would be attacked within 15 minutes. Today, that same computer will be attacked within seconds.

The first step to any security actions you take is to make an inventory of the types of information you are using, storing, or accessing. Then, you need to consider what could go wrong if the information were to be copied or stolen. That will be your guide as to the level of protection you need to put in place.

You can take two types of actions to protect your information assets: behavioural actions and computer-based actions. Behavioural actions are those actions that do not specifically involve a computer. Computer-based actions relate to safe computing. If you take both types of action, you will protect your information and greatly reduce your exposure to fraud and identity theft.

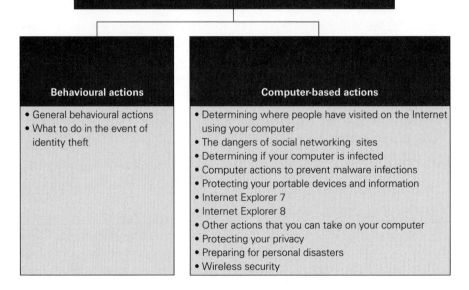

PROTECTING YOUR INFORMATION ASSETS

Behavioural actions	Computer-based actions
• General behavioural actions • What to do in the event of identity theft	• Determining where people have visited on the Internet using your computer • The dangers of social networking sites • Determining if your computer is infected • Computer actions to prevent malware infections • Protecting your portable devices and information • Internet Explorer 7 • Internet Explorer 8 • Other actions that you can take on your computer • Protecting your privacy • Preparing for personal disasters • Wireless security

TG3.1 Behavioural Actions

There are a number of behavioural actions that you should take to protect your information assets. We discuss these actions in this section.

General Behavioural Actions

You should not provide personal information to strangers in any format (physical, verbal, or electronic). As we discussed in Chapter 3, you will face social engineering attacks at home as well as at work. It is important that you know who you are communicating with when assessing the type of information you will provide. For example, verify that you are talking to authorized personnel before you provide personal information over the telephone. To accomplish this, you should hang up and call the person or company back. If you have a caller-ID telephone, check the display for the company name that is shown.

A critically important behavioural action that you can take is to protect your social insurance number. Unfortunately, far too many organizations use your social insurance number to uniquely identify you. When you are asked to provide this number, ask if there is other information that can be used as unique identification, such as your telephone number or address. If the person asking for your social insurance number, for example your physician's clerk, is not responsive, ask to speak with a supervisor. There is a movement underway to avoid using social insurance numbers everywhere for identification. If this movement is successful, then you might have to remember many more identifiers. However, your information security would improve. Remember, you have to take the initiative.

Another critical consideration involves your use of credit cards. Securing your credit cards is important because fraudulent credit card use is so widespread. Where available, use credit cards with your picture on them. Although cashiers probably cannot read your signature on the back of your card, they can certainly compare your picture to your face. For example, in the United States, the Bank of America will place a customer's picture on several of its credit cards for free. To view this service, visit *www.bankofamerica.com/creditcards* and click on the Security Features link. Since credit cards with photo identification are not available in Canada, it might be an easier alternative to not sign your credit card, and place the words "ask for photo identification" in the signature space. This means that every time that you use your credit card, you will need to provide photo identification. While this may be cumbersome, it makes your credit card harder to use by an unauthorized person if it is lost.

You may also want to use virtual credit cards, which offer you the option of shopping on-line with a disposable credit card number. For no extra charge, you sign up at your credit card's website and typically download software onto your computer. When you are ready to shop, you receive a randomly generated substitute 16-digit number that you can use at the on-line store. The number can be used once or, in some cases, repeated at the same store. The card number can also be used to buy goods and services over the phone and through the mail, although it cannot be used for in-store purchases that require a traditional plastic card. Two card issuers that offer virtual cards are Citibank and Discover (recall our discussion of electronic credit cards in Chapter 6).

Pay close attention to your credit card billing cycles. You should know, to within a day or two, when your credit card bills are due. If a bill does not arrive when expected, call your credit card company immediately. If your credit card is stolen and is being used fraudulently, the first thing the thief does is change the address on the account so that you do not receive the bill or statement. Finally, when you write cheques to pay any of your accounts, particularly your credit card accounts, do not write your complete card number on the "For" line of your cheque. Instead, write only the last four digits.

Another important action is to limit your use of debit cards. Debit cards are linked to your bank account, meaning that a person who steals your debit card and personal identification number (PIN) can clean out your bank account. With proof of identity theft, your bank will return the funds, but it could take weeks or months. In contrast, your liability with credit cards is usually zero (or a small amount). Your credit card company bears the liability for fraudulent charges, provided that you notify the company within 60 days of the theft. However, it is good practice to notify them as soon as you are aware of anything unusual happening with your account. One way to limit your risk is to reduce the number of different credit cards you have, and hold only a relatively small credit limit, such as $500 to $2,000, on each credit card. If you want to spend more, you can always prepay prior to a large purchase.

It is important to be aware of what is happening with your financial accounts, as the source of identity theft could be someone hacking into the places where you bank or conduct your transactions. For example, in April 2006 a breach was reported in the Bank of Canada accounts that handle automatic payroll deductions for Canada Savings Bonds.

Depending on the type of traffic in the area where you live, you might choose to avoid using a personal mailbox at your home or apartment for anything other than catalogues and magazines. You could use a private mailbox or a Post Office box. It is far too easy for thieves to steal mail from home mailboxes when there is no one at home for much of the day. Think about the wealth of information that could be stolen from your mailbox: credit card statements, bank statements, investment statements, and so on.

Care should be taken when discarding mail and old records.

When you discard mail or old records, use a cross-cut, or confetti, shredder to cut them up. Recall our discussion of dumpster diving in Chapter 3. A single-cut shredder is not sufficient because, with enough time, a thief can reassemble the strips.

As you take these actions, consider your financial exposure. Do you live in a rental unit and regularly have more than $500 in the bank? What if someone took out a student loan in your name? What is the value of your assets that could be mortgaged, or used as collateral? If you live in a home that is worth several hundred thousand dollars without a mortgage, someone could place a mortgage on your home. This could be protected by title insurance at a relatively low cost per month. Do you have stocks and bonds? How much are they worth? As you decide the actions you are going to take to protect yourself, the context should be the amount of money you could lose, or the amount you would have to pay in legal fees to recover your assets if they were stolen by someone else assuming your identity.

Another security option is to sign up with a company that provides proactive protection of your personal information. Examples of such companies are LifeLock (*www.lifelock.com*), TrustedID (*www.trustedid.com*), and CardCops (*www.cardcops.com*).

LifeLock and TrustedID state that they enable customers to lock their credit files so that new lines of credit cannot be opened unless customers first unlock their existing files. Locking credit files means that merchants and banks must have verbal or written permission from customers before opening new credit in their names. Ordinarily, the locking process involves sending registered mail to each of the two major credit agencies every 90 days. These agencies are Equifax Canada Inc. (*www.equifax.com/EFX_Canada/*) and TransUnion (*www.transunion.ca*).

Security protection organizations claim to monitor your various credit files. They also may provide an early warning service that notifies you that the company has found your personal information circulating on the Internet. They may collect compromised data on the Internet and make them available to their customers and to merchants. Be sure to check the quality of the organization that you want to sign up with first.

What to Do in the Event of Identity Theft

According to PhoneBusters (*www.phonebusters.com*), which tracks telephone and mail marketing fraud as well as identity theft frauds, there were about 11,125 Canadian victims of identity theft in 2009, and 11,540 in 2008. There were almost 10 million victims in the United States in 2008, a 22 percent increase over 2007. If you follow the behavioural and computer-based action recommendations in this technology guide, you will greatly reduce, but

Approximately 11,125 Canadians were victims of identity theft in 2009.

not eliminate, the chances that your identity will be stolen. If your identity is stolen despite these precautions, the actions you take depend upon what assets or credit have been compromised. Listed are some of the steps you may need to take to recover.

- If your social insurance number has been compromised, you would contact Service Canada; in the event of passport theft you would contact your local passport office.
- If you believe your mail is being diverted, contact your local Canada Post office.
- Cancel all affected credit cards and obtain new credit card numbers.
- Consult a lawyer for the type of paperwork that may be required to deal with disputes with financial institutions or credit-granting organizations.
- Get organized. Keep a file with all your paperwork, including the names, addresses, and phone numbers of everyone you contact about this crime.
- File a detailed police report. Send copies of the report to creditors and other agencies or organizations that may require proof of the crime.
- Get the name and phone number of your police investigator, and give it to your creditors.
- In all communications about the crime, use certified, return-receipt mail. Report that you are the victim of identity theft to the fraud divisions of both credit reporting agencies: Equifax and TransUnion. Due to the increased incidence of identity theft, federal law now gives you the right to have one free credit report per year. If you request your free annual credit report from both of the agencies, you will receive one free report every six months.
- Be sure to get your unique case number from each credit agency, and ask each agency to send you your credit report.
- Tell each agency to issue a fraud alert. The fraud alert requires mortgage brokers, car dealers, credit card companies, and other lenders to scrutinize anyone who opens an account in your name for 90 days.

- Get the document that you need to file a long-term fraud alert, which lasts for seven years and can be cancelled at any time.
- Ask the credit agencies for the names and phone numbers of lenders with whom recent accounts have been opened in the affected time frame, so you can identify fraudulent accounts that have been opened.
- Point out all entries generated due to fraud to each agency. Ask each agency to remove the specified fraudulent entries.
- Tell each agency to notify anyone who received your report in the last six months (or the affected time frame) that you are disputing the information.
- You may be able to order a "credit freeze" with all three major credit agencies. This freeze requires lenders, retailers, utilities, and other businesses to get special access to your credit report through a PIN-based system. It also helps prevent anyone from getting any new loans or credit in your name.
- Be alert for change-of-address forms in your mail. The post office must send notifications to your old and new addresses. If someone tries to change your mailing address, it is a major indication that you have been victimized.
- If debt collectors demand payment of fraudulent accounts, write down the name of the company as well as the collector's name, address, and phone number. Tell the collector that you are the victim of identity theft. Send the collection agency a registered letter with a completed police report. If this does not work, refer the agency to your lawyer.

In addition to these behavioural actions, the computer-based actions we discuss in the next section will further help you protect yourself.

BEFORE YOU GO ON ...

1. Why is it so important for you to protect your information assets?
2. Describe behavioural actions you can take to protect your information assets.

TG3.2 Computer-Based Actions

There are many computer-based actions that you can take to help you increase the security of your information. We first discuss how to determine where persons who may be using your computer have visited on the Internet. Next, we touch briefly on being careful of social networking sites.

We will look at how to determine if your computer is infected with malicious software (malware) and what actions to take to prevent such infections. We then discuss how to protect your portable devices (for example, laptops, flash drives) and the information on them. We follow with discussions of other computer-based actions to take, how to protect your privacy when using the Internet and e-mail, how to recover from a disaster, and how to protect yourself when computing wirelessly. Note that we thoroughly discuss Microsoft Windows XP. We also provide a section on Microsoft's Internet Explorer 7, because this browser has added security features. We do not discuss other operating systems and browsers due to space limitations.

Determining Where People Have Visited on the Internet Using Your Computer

At home, you may have a single computer or several computers connected to a network. Although you may practise "safe computing," not everyone using your computer may do the same. For example, you might have roommates who use your computer. Their friends could be using your computer as well.

You can check to see where anyone who may have used your computer has visited on the Internet. To accomplish this, you check the Browser history by following these steps in Internet Explorer:

- Click on Tools in the menu bar
- Click on Internet Options
- Under the section Browsing History, click on Settings
- Click on View Files
- If the Browser History is empty, it means that someone has either (1) not been surfing the Internet at all or (2) has erased the browser history.
- If you now check the Recycle Bin and it is also empty, this means that someone has also emptied the Recycle Bin. At this time, you should consider installing monitoring software on your computer (discussed later).

The Dangers of Social Networking Sites

You should never post personal information about yourself or your family in chat rooms or on social networking sites. In fact, you should access these websites and review any entries that you have made. One reason for these precautions is that potential employers are now searching these websites for information about you. Well-known social networking sites include MySpace, Friendster, Xanga, YouTube, Facebook, and Flickr.

The good news is that social networking websites have added features to give us more control over our information. The bad news is that the privacy settings are not always easy to find and use. Your first decision is whether to make your profile publicly available or to keep it more private. More than 33 percent of adult users allow everyone to see their profiles. In contrast, some 60 percent restrict access in some way.

All the major social networking sites give you control over public accessibility, but they provide different ways for you to control access. The full profiles of MySpace users aged 18 and over are available to everyone on the Internet by default. You can make your profile private by following these steps:

- Go to My Account
- Click on Privacy
- Now, customize who gets to see what on your profile

On Facebook, the default is a private profile, where users decide what is publicly available. To make privacy adjustments on Facebook, follow these steps:

- Click on your name to take you to your wall
- Scroll to the left side of the screen
- Click on Account
- Click on Settings
- Click on Privacy Settings
- Work with the options here

If you want to keep a low profile on Facebook, it is a good idea to look at the "Applications" section in Privacy Settings. You may have shielded parts of your profile, but that does not mean that you have done the same for Facebook applications that have access to much of your same data by default.

On LinkedIn, most people want public profiles and that is the default. The information that LinkedIn users share tends to be professional credentials, not details of their social lives, so there is less need for privacy. If you want additional privacy on LinkedIn, follow these steps:

- Click on Profile
- Click on Edit Public Profile Settings
- Scroll down to Public Profile and adjust your privacy settings

One company, Reputation Defender (*www.reputationdefender.com*), states that its goal is to search out all information about you on the Internet and present it to you in the form of a report. Then, at your command, the company states that it will "destroy all inaccurate, inappropriate, hurtful, and slanderous information about you."

Determining If Your Computer Is Infected

Your first action is to determine if your computer system is infected with malicious software. Here are the signs to look for:

- Your computer shuts down unexpectedly by itself.
- Your computer refuses to start normally.
- Running the DOS CHKDSK (**CHECK DISK**) command shows that less than 655,360 (640 kilobytes) bytes are available. To run the CHKDSK command, follow these steps:
  - Click on Start
  - Click on Programs
  - Click on Accessories
  - Click on Command Prompt
  - Type in CHKDSK and hit Enter
- Your computer shows erratic behaviour, exhibiting some or all of these characteristics:
  - Your system unexpectedly runs out of memory on your computer's hard drive.
  - Your system continually runs out of main memory (RAM).
  - Programs take longer to load than normal.
  - Programs act erratically.
  - Your monitor displays strange graphics or messages.
  - Your system displays an unusually high number of error messages.
  - Your e-mail program sends messages to all the contacts in your address book without your knowledge or permission.

If you note any or all of these signs, then your computer might be infected with malware. You can then take the computer-based actions discussed later in this technology guide to rid your computer of this software. However, if you take the actions discussed in the next section, it will reduce your chances of getting such an infection in the first place.

Computer Actions to Prevent Malware Infections

Many of the actions we discuss in this section are common sense, but surprisingly large numbers of people do not pay attention to them. Taking these steps will help you prevent a malware infection of your computer system.

We begin by considering actions that you must *never* do with your computer. Never open unrequested attachments to e-mail files, even those from people you know and trust. Their computers may have been compromised without their knowledge, in which case the e-mail could be a phishing attack.

Never open attachments or web links in e-mails from people you do not know. These attachments can infect your system with a worm or virus. Similarly, these web links can be a phishing attack that can infect your system with a Trojan horse, turning your computer into a zombie, or bot (short for robot). As we saw in Chapter 3, when this occurs your computer is no longer under your control.

Never accept files transferred to you during Internet chat or instant messaging sessions. These files are usually not from people you know, and they can infect your system with malware.

Never download any files or software over the Internet from websites that you do not know. Never download files or software that you have not requested.

Test Your System

It is a good idea to test your system. Several websites provide free security tests. These tests send different types of messages to your computer to evaluate how well your system is protected from a variety of attacks. Free testing websites include HackerWhacker (*www.hackerwhacker.com*), Shields Up! (*www.grc.com*), Symantec Security Check (*http://security.norton.com*), McAfee MySecurity Status (*http://us.mcafee.com/MySecurityStatus/*), and AuditMyPC (*www.auditmypc.com*).

Microsoft provides a scanning tool called the Microsoft Baseline Analyzer. This useful tool scans Windows-based computers for common security problems and generates individual security reports for each computer that it scans. The Baseline Analyzer is a free download available at this website: *http://technet.microsoft.com/en-ca/security/cc184924.aspx*.

You can also run free malware scans on your computer. Several companies will scan your computer to identify viruses, worms, and other malware, and also offer suggestions about how to clean your system if it is infected. These companies include:

- Trend Micro (*http://housecall.trendmicro.com*)
- McAfee (*http://us.mcafee.com/root/mfs/default.asp*)
- Panda Software (*www.pandasoftware.com/activescan/com/activescan_principal.htm*)

Install a Security Suite on Your Computer

Security suites are software packages that contain a variety of security products, such as anti-malware software, spam protection, e-mail fraud protection, spyware detection, intrusion detection, monitoring software, and others. As you can see, these suites provide a great deal of functionality in one package. There is a question whether the individual functions in a security suite can match the combined functions of a group of individual products. Therefore, we discuss individual products in the next sections.

Well-known security suites include the following, but there are many others:

- ZoneAlarm Security Suite (*www.zonelabs.com*)
- McAfee Internet Security Suite (*www.mcafee.com*)
- Norton Internet Security (*www.symantec.com*)
- PC-cillin Internet Security (*www.trendmicro.com*)

Install an Anti-Malware Product on Your Computer

You should install an anti-malware product on your computer and use it, ideally at least once per week. Remember that every time you scan your computer for malware with your anti-malware product, you must update your malware definitions before you scan. Typically, anti-malware product vendors automatically update your malware definitions over the Web.

There are free anti-malware products and commercial anti-malware products. In general, the free products are adequate, but the commercial products offer more functionality. Thefreecountry. com is an excellent resource offering a great deal of information on free anti-malware products, as well as many other security products. For free anti-malware products, see *www.thefreecountry.com/ security/antivirus.shtml*.

Well-known commercial anti-malware products include the following, but there are many others: Norton Anti-malware (*www.symantec.com*), PC-cillin (*www.trendmicro.com*), and VirusScan (*www. mcafee.com*).

Install a Firewall on Your Computer

A personal firewall is software installed on your home computer that controls communications to and from your computer by permitting or denying communications based on your security settings. A personal firewall will not usually protect any more than the computer on which the software is installed. Nevertheless, firewalls perform essential functions.

Essentially, firewalls should make your computer invisible. This means that your firewall should not respond to Internet requests to ports—that is, communications links to your computer—that are not used for common Internet use. In effect, your computer operates in stealth mode on the Internet.

Firewalls also should alert you to suspicious behaviour. They should tell you when a program or connection is attempting to do something unwanted, such as download software or run a program such as ActiveX.

ActiveX (by Microsoft), which can execute programs downloaded from Internet Explorer, can be exploited by attackers trying to compromise your computer. To manage ActiveX in Internet Explorer, follow these steps:

- Click on Tools
- Click on Internet Options
- Click on the Security tab
- Click on the button that says "Custom level. . . ."
- Scroll down and choose the following:
    - the button for Prompt "Download signed ActiveX controls"
    - the button for Disable "Download unsigned ActiveX controls"

Finally, firewalls should block outbound connections that you do not initiate. Your firewall should not let your computer access the Internet on its own. If your computer tries to access the Internet by itself, this is a sure sign that it is infected with malware.

As with anti-malware programs, there are both free firewall products and commercial firewall products. Again, the free products are adequate, but the commercial products offer more functionality. For a list of free firewall software visit: *http://netsecurity.about.com/od/personalfirewalls/a/ aafreefirewall.htm*.

Because Microsoft Windows XP is in such wide use, we briefly discuss its personal firewall here. Microsoft Windows XP Service Pack 2 includes the Windows Security Center and free firewall software. However, this product protects against only unwanted inbound connections. It does not stop existing malware on your computer from making outbound connections. (Note: Microsoft's Internet Explorer 7 has added a security feature to its firewall that blocks outbound connections.)

Many companies offer commercial firewall software. Some of the best-known commercial firewall products are:

- ZoneAlarm Security Suite (*www.zonelabs.com*)
- Norton Internet Security (*www.symantec.com*)
- PC-cillin Internet Security (*www.trendmicro.com*)
- McAfee Internet Security (*www.mcafee.com*)
- F-Secure Internet Security (*www.f-secure.com*)
- Panda Platinum Internet Security (*www.pandasoftware.com*)

It is a good idea to test your firewall. However, it is best to use only those websites that are run by actual firewall or security software companies. A good firewall test site is the McAfee Hackerwatch site at *www.hackerwatch.org/probe/*. The Hackerwatch site allows you to do a basic probe test on your computer to see if your firewall is blocking ports that may be vulnerable.

Install an Antispyware Product on Your Computer

As with anti-malware products and firewalls, free antispyware products are adequate, but commercial antispyware products offer more functionality. Free antispyware products include Ad-Aware SE Personal (*www.lavasoft.com*) and Spybot Search&Destroy (*www.safer-networking.org*).

Well-known commercial antispyware products include the following, but there are many others: CounterSpy (*www.sunbeltsoftware.com*), Spy Sweeper (*www.webroot.com*), Ad-Aware (*www.lavasoft.com*), SpyCatcher (*www.tenebril.com*), and Spyware Eliminator (*www.aluriasoftware.com*).

Several companies offer free spyware scans. Take a look at Spy Audit (*www.webroot.com*), Zonelabs (*www.zonelabs.com*), and Norton (*www.symantec.com*).

Install Monitoring Software on Your Computer

Monitoring software logs keystrokes, e-mails, applications, windows, websites, Internet connections, passwords, chat conversations, webcams, and even screenshots. Companies that offer monitoring software include SpyAgent (*www.spytech-web.com*), SpyBuddy (*www.exploreanywhere.com*), WinSpy (*www.win-spy.com*), and SpectorSoft (*www.spectorsoft.com*). Monitoring software is used by employers to track employee productivity, and as explained in Chapter 3, it can also be used by hackers in a virus to lock your keystrokes and trap your passwords. You can use such software for yourself to backup the action that you have done on your computer, and also to determine whether someone else has been using your computer.

Install Content Filtering Software on Your Computer

Content filtering software performs many functions. It can block access to undesirable websites, and record and view all websites visited. It can also record both sides of chat conversations from AOL Instant Messenger (AIM and AIM Triton), Yahoo Messenger, and MSN Messenger.

This software provides many filter categories, enabling you to selectively filter content. Companies that offer content filtering software include Cybersitter (*www.cybersitter.com*), NetNanny (*www.netnanny.com*), and CyberSpy (*www.cyberspyware.com*). In addition, a free content filtering software product may be found at *www.web-locker.com*.

Internet Explorer's Content Advisor utility allows you to block access to websites that meet specified criteria and to set your own tolerance levels for various types of Internet content. To activate and configure Content Advisor, follow these steps:

- Open Internet Explorer
- Click on Tools

- Click on Internet Options
- When the Internet Options dialog box appears, select the Content Tab
- Click on the Enable button
- You will see four categories: language, nudity, sex, violence. For each category, you can move the slide bar for increased restriction
- After you have set the slide bar for each category, click OK

You can also block selected websites. To accomplish this, follow these steps:

- Open Internet Explorer
- Click on Tools
- Click on Internet Options
- When the Internet Options dialog box appears, select the Content Tab
- Click on the Enable button
- Click the Approved Sites tab
- Enter the websites you wish to block, and click Never
- Click OK

Install Anti-spam Software on Your Computer

Anti-spam software helps you to control spam. Well-known commercial anti-spam products include the following, but there are many others:

- Cloudmark (*www.cloudmark.com*)
- SonicWALL (*www.sonicwall.com*)
- SpamKiller (*www.mcafee.com*)
- Norton Antispam (*www.symantec.com*)
- SpamGourmet (*www.spamgourmet.com*)
- SpamAssassin (*http://spamassassin.apache.org/*)

You might also want to set up multiple free e-mail accounts, such as accounts on Hotmail and Gmail. Then, as you surf the Internet and are asked for your e-mail address, you use one of these accounts and not your home or business e-mail account. When your free e-mail accounts are full of spam, you can close them and open new accounts.

Install Proactive Intrusion Detection and Prevention Software on Your Computer

As we have discussed, anti-malware software is reactive in nature, leaving you vulnerable to zero-day attacks (discussed in Chapter 3). For this reason, it is important to add proactive intrusion detection and prevention software to your defences. One such product is Prevx (*www.prevx.com*). You can download and install Prevx for free, and it will scan your computer for malicious software. If it finds any, it will activate a free 30-day clean-up account and remove the malware from your computer. Once this period runs out, Prevx will continue to scan incoming programs and protect your computer from them. However, if you subsequently get infected and want to continue using Prevx, you must pay for one year of protection.

Manage Patches

You should download and install all patches immediately (for example, patches for Windows). Software patches are typically released to repair security problems. As soon as patches are announced and released, hackers use zero-day attacks to exploit them before unwary users react. Therefore, if you do not download and install patches quickly, your computer will be extremely vulnerable to attack.

Microsoft provides an automatic method that checks for, and downloads, any new patches. To enable Automatic Update in Windows XP, follow these steps:

- Right click on Start
- Click on Explore
- Scroll down and click on Control Panel
- Click on System
- Click on the Automatic Updates tab at the top of the box
- You can now configure when you want to download and install updates

To open the Microsoft Update window in Windows XP, follow these steps:

- Click on Start
- Click on All Programs
- Click on Windows Update

If you click the Express button, your system will be scanned, and you will be notified if any new updates are available. You can then review suggested updates and install them.

Use a Browser Other Than Internet Explorer

You might want to use a browser other than Internet Explorer, such as Firefox (*www.mozilla.org*), Opera (*www.opera.com*), or Safari from Apple (*www.apple.com/safari/*). These browsers are not impregnable, but they are less prominent and hackers, at least so far, have paid less attention to them. Even if you decide to use a browser other than Internet Explorer, however, you should still implement all of the security measures discussed.

You should also keep your browser updated. For browser updates of Internet Explorer 6, see this site: *www.microsoft.com/windows/ie/ie6/downloads/default.mspx*. Microsoft released Internet Explorer 7 (IE7) in October 2006, and Internet Explorer 8 (IE8) in March 2009. As we discuss later in this technology guide, both IE7 and IE8 have added security features.

Use an Operating System Other Than Windows

The two main alternatives to Windows XP, Vista, and Windows 7 are Apple's Mac OS X and Linux. These two operating systems are not invulnerable but they are both based on UNIX, which makes them inherently more secure than any version of Windows. (UNIX is an operating system developed by AT&T in the 1960s and 1970s that usually runs on servers rather than desktops.) In addition, Linux and Mac OS X have much smaller market shares than Windows and thus are less attractive targets for malware.

Protecting Your Portable Devices and Information

Theft or loss of laptops, notebook computers, personal digital assistants, BlackBerrys, and thumb drives, as well as the data on these devices, is a significant problem. There are many proactive steps that you can take to protect portable devices and the data on them, including preventing their theft, using two-factor authentication and encrypting your data. You can also take reactive steps after a theft or loss. We cover all of these actions in this section.

Before we discuss these steps, there are two common-sense precautions that many people forget. First, keep your laptop in an inconspicuous container. Laptop cases with your company logo simply draw the attention of thieves. Second, do not leave your laptop unattended in plain view (for example, in the back seat of your car where it can be seen). You should lock it in the trunk.

Take steps to protect portable devices like laptops and PDAs.

To prevent theft of a portable device, you can use alarms. Laptop security systems operate by detecting motion, analyzing it to determine whether a threat exists, and implementing responses. They are battery-powered, they are independent of the computer operating system, and they operate whether the laptop is on or off. If a laptop armed with a security system is carried beyond a perimeter specified by the user, the alarm assumes the laptop is being stolen. It can then prevent access to the operating system, secure passwords and encryption keys, and sound an audible alarm. One company that provides laptop security systems is Caveo (*www.caveo.com*).

Two-factor authentication means that you must have two forms of identification to access your laptop or notebook. The first authentication factor uses a token or biometrics. The second factor is your personal password.

A token generates a one-time password that you must enter within a specified time limit. This password typically consists of six digits, which appear on the token's LCD screen. Companies offering tokens for two-factor authentication include Authenex (*www.authenex.com*), Kensington (*www.kensington.com*), and SecuriKey (*www.securikey.com*).

Fingerprints are the biometric used for two-factor authentication, by incorporating fingerprint readers into the laptop itself. See IBM (*www.ibm.com*) and Microsoft (*www.microsoft.com*). You can also use fingerprint authentication on your thumb drive with the SanDisk Cruzer (*www.sandisk.com*), the Lexar JumpDrive TouchGuard (*www.lexar.com*), the Sony MicroVault (*www.sony.net*), and the Kanguru Bio Slider (*www.kanguru.com*).

Data encryption provides additional protection by turning data into meaningless symbols, decipherable only by an authorized person. You can encrypt some or all of the data on your computer by using Windows XP's built-in encryption, folder-based encryption, or full-disk encryption.

Windows XP's Encrypting File System allows you to encrypt files or folders. Follow these steps:

- Right click on the file or folder
- Click on Properties
- Click the General tab at the top
- Click the Advanced tab
- Check the box labelled Encrypt Contents to Secure Data
- Click OK

Beachhead Solutions (*www.beachheadsolutions.com*) and Credant (*www.credant.com*) also provide applications that allow you to encrypt files and folders.

Another step you can take to improve your security is to encrypt your entire hard drive, including your applications. See Mobile Armor (*www.mobilearmor.com*), the Kanguru Wizard (*www.kanguru. com*), and the PCKey (*www.kensington.com*).

If your laptop is lost or stolen, you can use laptop tracing tools or device reset/remote kill tools. For example, the XTool Computer Tracker (*www.computersecurity.com*), PC PhoneHome (*www. pcphonehome.com*), and LaptopLocate (*www.laptoplocate.net*) provide transmitters that secretly send a signal to their respective company control centres via telephone or the Internet. This signal enables the company, with the help of the local authorities, Internet service providers, and telephone companies, to track your computer's location.

You can also use device reset/remote kill tools to automatically eliminate specified data on a lost or stolen laptop to prevent it from being compromised or misused. The solution works even when other security software or encryption methods fail. Examples of companies providing these solutions are Trust Digital (*www.trustdigital.com*), Intellisync (*http://tourmalinenetworks.com/*), and Beachhead Solutions (*www.beachheadsolutions.com*).

Internet Explorer 7

Internet Explorer 7 (IE7) offers multiple, interrelated security features to help defend your computer against malicious software as well as safeguards to help ensure that your personal information does not fall into the hands of fraudulent or deceptive websites. Together with Windows Defender, the security features in IE7 are an improvement over the security features of Windows XP alone. IE7 has been improved so that it limits the amount of damage that malware can do if it is able to penetrate your system. Further, IE7 includes several features designed to prevent attackers' efforts to trick you into entering personal data on websites when you should not. We discuss these features in this section.

Protected Mode

In Protected Mode, IE7 (running in Windows Vista) cannot modify any of your files and settings without your consent. Protected Mode requires you to confirm any activity that tries to place any software on your computer or start another program. This feature also makes you aware of what a website is trying to do, giving you a chance to stop it and check the trustworthiness of the site.

ActiveX Opt-In

ActiveX Opt-In automatically disables all but a small group of well known, pre-approved controls. Therefore, if a website tries to use an ActiveX control that you have not used before, IE7 displays a notice in the Information Bar. This notification enables you to permit or deny access when you are viewing unfamiliar websites.

Fix My Settings

Because most users install and use applications with their default settings, IE7 is shipped to you with security settings that provide the maximum level of usability while maintaining strict security control. Fix My Settings is a feature that alerts you when you might be browsing with unsafe settings on your computer. The new feature reminds you about these unsafe settings with a warning displayed in the Information Bar as long as your settings remain unsafe. You can quickly reset your security settings to the Medium-High default level by clicking the Fix My Settings option in the Information Bar. If you close your browser and it reopens with unsafe settings, you will see a notification page reminding you to correct your settings before you can visit any websites.

Windows Defender

Windows Defender protects you against spyware and thus helps prevent malware from penetrating your system via piggyback download on spyware. Spyware that has malware piggybacked on it is a common mechanism by which malware is distributed and installed silently on your system.

Personal Data Safeguards

IE7 provides the Security Status Bar, located next to the Address Bar, which helps you quickly differentiate authentic websites from suspicious or malicious ones. This feature enhances your access to digital certificate information that helps you validate the trustworthiness of websites.

The Security Status Bar gives you prominent, check-coded visual cues indicating the safety and trustworthiness of a website. Earlier versions of Internet Explorer placed a gold padlock icon in the lower right corner of your browser window to designate the trust and security level of the website. IE7 displays the padlock more prominently. You can also view a website's digital certificate information with a single click on the padlock icon. To give you a visual cue to recognize questionable websites, the padlock icon appears on a red background if IE7 detects any irregularities in the website's certificate information.

The Security Status Bar also supports new Extended Validation (EV) certificates that offer stronger identification of secure websites such as banking sites. These sites have undergone a comprehensive verification to ensure that their identity is that of the real business entity. IE7 highlights these validated websites with a green-shaded address bar and prominently displays the associated business's name.

IE7 also provides an Address Bar in every window. This requirement helps ensure that you will be able to learn more about the true source of any information that you are seeing.

Phishing Filter

The Phishing Filter is an opt-in feature that maintains a list of websites that should be blocked by scanning for suspicious website characteristics. Known phishing websites are denoted by turning the Address Bar red. Users are navigated away from that page and a warning message is displayed about the potential for a phishing attack. Suspicious websites—where a page has certain suspicious characteristics—display a yellow Address Bar, and acceptable websites display the standard white Address Bar.

Delete Browsing History

IE7 provides a Delete Browsing History option for one-click cleanup so that you can easily and quickly erase all personal information stored in the browser. This feature is particularly important when you use a friend's computer, or computers in public environments such as libraries, schools, conference centres, and hotel business centres.

Internet Explorer 8

Microsoft's Internet Explorer 8 (IE8) has a new security application called InPrivate, which features InPrivate Browsing and InPrivate Blocking. *InPrivate Browsing* helps prevent your browser from retaining your browsing history, temporary Internet files, cookies, and user names and passwords, thus leaving no evidence of your browsing or search history.

Today, websites increasingly access content from multiple sources, providing tremendous value to consumers. However, users may not be aware that some content, images, and advertisements are being provided from third-party websites, or that these sites can potentially track their behaviour.

InPrivate Blocking enables users to block the information that third-party websites can potentially use to track their browsing history.

Other Actions That You Can Take on Your Computer

There are other actions that you can take on your computer for added protection. These actions consist of detecting worms and Trojan horses, turning off peer-to-peer file sharing, looking for new and unusual files, detecting spoofed (fake) websites, and adjusting the privacy settings on your computer.

How to Detect a Worm

Worms are malicious programs that perform unwanted actions on your computer (see Chapter 3). They exhibit several characteristics that you can watch for.

- Your system exhibits unexplained hard disk activity.
- Your system connects to the Internet by itself without any action on your part.
- Your system seems to be short on available memory.
- Your family, friends, or colleagues notify you that they have received an odd e-mail message from you, that they are sure you did not send.

Ordinarily, your anti-malware software should detect and remove worms. However, if your computer is currently infected with a worm, you may not be able to delete that file. In this case, you will have to reboot (start up) your system from a bootable disk and then delete the worm file from the Command Prompt. (Follow the steps for How to Look for New and Unusual Files, discussed below, to find the worm file.) Normally, when you reboot your system, the worm file should no longer be present.

How to Detect a Trojan Horse

Trojan horses are malicious programs disguised as, or embedded within, legitimate software (see Chapter 3). The steps listed below describe one method of determining whether your computer is infected with a Trojan horse. These steps will enable you to see if your computer is "listening" for instructions from another computer. You will be using the DOS-based utility program called Netstat (part of Windows).

- Close all running applications and reboot your computer.
- When your computer restarts, do NOT establish a dial-up Internet connection. It is OK to let your computer access the Internet via a broadband connection (for example, cable modem or DSL).
- Open the DOS window:
  - Click on Start
  - Click on Programs
  - Click on Accessories
  - Click on Command Prompt
- In the DOS window, type the following and press Enter:
  netstat.exe –an>>c:\netstat.txt
- Wait for the root directory to appear
- Close the DOS window and:
  - Click on Start
  - Click on All Programs
  - Click on Accessories
  - Click on Notepad

- In Notepad, click on File and then on Open.
- Type in c:\netstat.txt in the box provided.
- You will see a number of active connections in a Listening state. Each active connection will have a local address. The local address will be in a form like this:
    0.0.0.0.xxxxx (where the x's refer to a sequence of numbers)
- If a Trojan horse is present, your system will be listening for one of the addresses listed here. Netstat addresses for a few common Trojans:
    - Back Orifice 0.0.0.0.31337 or 0.0.0.0.31338
    - Deep Throat 0.0.0.0.2140 or 0.0.0.0.3150
    - NetBus 0.0.0.0.12345 or 0.0.0.0.12346
    - Remote Grab 0.0.0.0.7000
- Symantec provides a list of recent threats and risks, which includes Trojan horses. When you click on the name of the virus and follow through to the CVE (Common Vulnerabilities and Exposures) description you can learn more about the viruses and Trojan horses. If you find any viruses like this on your machine, you should immediately update your anti-virus software and run the anti-virus software. If the Trojan is still there after you have run the anti-virus software, contact the anti-virus software supplier for further assistance.

How to Turn Off Peer-to-Peer (P2P) File Sharing

Peer-to-peer (P2P) networks do not use central file servers. Instead, the computers on P2P networks act as both clients and servers. These networks, such as Kazaa, Limewire, Ares, and Gnutella, are very poorly protected from viruses, and various types of malware spread through them quite easily.

When you join a P2P file-sharing network, you are no longer an anonymous computer on the Internet. Attackers often focus on P2P networks because computers on these networks can be easy targets. Therefore, you may find it advisable to turn off P2P file sharing on your computer. To do so, follow these steps in Windows 7:

- First, you must have Administrator privileges (which you will likely have at home).
- Click on My Computer
- Click on Control Panel
- Click on Network and Sharing Center
- Click on Local Area Connection
- Click on Properties in the Local Area Connection Status box
- Click on File and Printer Sharing for Microsoft Networks
- Click Uninstall

How to Look for New and Unusual Files

When an attacker compromises your computer, he or she leaves one or more new files somewhere on your hard drive. In Windows XP, you can use the Search Companion utility to look for newly created files. Follow these steps in Windows XP:

- Right click on Start
- Click on Search
- When the Search window opens, select All Files and Folders
- When the Search Companion window appears, enter *.* in the All or Part of the File Name blank field
- Click the When Was It Modified button, and select Within the Last Week

- Click on the Search button
- Windows will return a list of files modified any time within the last week. Study this list for any files that look suspicious

How to Detect Fake Websites

A fake website is typically created to look like a well-known, legitimate site with a slightly different or confusing URL. The attacker tries to trick people into going to the spoofed site by sending out e-mail messages (known as phishing, described in Chapter 3), hoping that some users will not notice the incorrect URL and give away important information. Examples of products that help detect fake websites are the Verification Engine, and McAfee's SiteAdvisor. These products are not definitive solutions, but they are helpful.

The Verification Engine (*www.vengine.com*) allows you to verify that the site you are visiting or are directed to via e-mail can be trusted. If you mouse to the logo brand or image you want to verify, the Verification Engine will authenticate the trust credentials of the site you are surfing. In addition, during a secure communications session with Internet Explorer, you can mouse over the padlock to verify that: (1) the padlock is genuine and not a fraudulent graphic and (2) the site uses a secure socket layer (SSL) certificate (discussed in Chapter 3) containing the correct information about the company to which you are connected.

McAfee's SiteAdvisor (*www.siteadvisor.com*) sticks a green, yellow, or red safety logo next to search results on Google, Yahoo, and MSN. The product puts a check-coded button in the Internet Explorer toolbar. Mousing over the button displays details explaining why the website is good or bad. SiteAdvisor also scores websites on excessive use of pop-up advertisements, how much spam the website will generate if you reveal your e-mail address, and whether the website spreads spyware and adware.

Protecting Your Privacy

In today's hostile Internet environment, you must use strong passwords (discussed in Chapter 3) and adjust the privacy settings on your computer. You may also wish to protect your privacy by surfing the Web and e-mailing anonymously. In this section we discuss these actions.

Use Strong Passwords

You can use the Secure Password Generator at PCTools (*www.pctools.com/guides/password*) to create strong passwords. The Generator lets you select the number and type of characters in your password.

Remembering multiple passwords is difficult. You can use free software such as Password Safe (*http://passwordsafe.sourceforge.net/*) or Roboform (*www.roboform.com*) to help you remember your passwords and maintain them securely.

How to Adjust Your Privacy Settings on Your Computer

Internet Explorer allows you to select the level of privacy that you want when using your computer. Here are the steps to follow to adjust your privacy settings:

- Click on Tools
- Click on Internet Options
- Click on the Privacy tab at the top
- Manipulate the slide bar to determine the level of privacy you desire

- You will see an explanation of what each level means as you use the slide bar
- The levels of privacy and their meanings are:
  - Lowest (Accept All Cookies)
    - All cookies will be saved on this computer
    - Existing cookies on this computer can be read by the websites that created them
  - Low
    - Restricts third-party cookies that do not have a compact privacy policy (*http://compact privacypolicy.org/* explains that this is a framework that enables the privacy policy to be transmitted in machine language so that it can be analyzed by your browser);
    - Restricts third-party cookies that use personally identifiable information without your implicit consent
  - Medium
    - Blocks third-party cookies that do not have a compact privacy policy
    - Blocks third-party cookies that use personally identifiable information without your implicit consent
    - Restricts first-party cookies that use personally identifiable information without your implicit consent
  - Medium High
    - Blocks third-party cookies that do not have a compact privacy policy
    - Blocks third-party cookies that use personally identifiable information without your explicit consent
    - Blocks first-party cookies that use personally identifiable information without your explicit consent
  - High
    - Blocks cookies that do not have a compact privacy policy
    - Blocks cookies that use personally identifiable information without your explicit consent
  - Very High (Block All Cookies)
    - Cookies from all websites will be blocked
    - Existing cookies on your computer cannot be read by websites

Note: A first-party cookie either originates on, or is sent to, the website you are currently viewing. These cookies are commonly used to store information, such as your preferences when visiting that site. In contrast, a third-party cookie either originates on, or is sent to, a different website from the one you are currently viewing. Third-party websites usually provide some content on the website you are viewing. For example, many sites use advertising from third-party websites, and those third-party websites may use cookies. A common use for this type of cookie is to track your web page use for advertising or other marketing purposes.

How to Surf the Web Anonymously

Many users worry that knowledge of their IP addresses is enough for outsiders to connect their on-line activities to their "real-world" identities. Depending on his or her technical, physical, and legal access, a determined party (such as a government prosecutor) may be able to do so, especially if he or she is assisted by the records of the ISP that has assigned the IP address. As a result, many people surf the Web and e-mail anonymously.

Surfing the Web anonymously means that you do not make your IP (Internet protocol) address or any other personally identifiable information available to the websites that you are visiting. There are two ways to go about surfing the Web anonymously: you can use an anonymizer website as a proxy server, or you can use an anonymizer as a permanent proxy server in your web browser.

A proxy server is a computer to which you connect, that in turn connects to the website you wish to visit. You remain anonymous because only the information on the proxy server is visible to outsiders.

For example, consider Anonymouse (*http://anonymouse.org*). When you access this site, after selecting your language, you can click on a link called "Your calling card without Anonymouse." You will see the information that is available to any website you visit when you surf normally.

If you want to surf anonymously, enter the URL of the site you want to visit on the Anonymouse website where it says "Enter URL." For example, suppose you wish to visit *www.amazon.com*. You enter Amazon's URL where indicated on the Anonymouse website. When the Amazon website opens on your computer, the URL will look like this:

http://anonymouse.org/cgi-bin/anon-www.cgi/http://www.amazon.com

You are now anonymous at Amazon because Anonymouse is a proxy server for you and Amazon sees only the information from Anonymouse. Keep in mind that although anonymous surfing is more secure than regular surfing, it is also typically slower.

Other anonymizers include Anonymize (*www.anonymize.net*), IDZap (*www.idzap.com*), Ultimate Anonymity (*www.ultimate-anonymity.com*), The Cloak (*www.the-cloak.com*), and GhostSurf Platinum (*www.tenebril.com/consumer*).

Another way to surf the Web anonymously is to use an anonymizer as a permanent proxy server on your computer. Here are the steps to do this:

- Open Internet Explorer
- Click on Tools
- Click on Internet Options
- Select the Connections tab
- Click on LAN Settings
- When the Local Area Network (LAN) Settings dialog box opens, check the Use A Proxy Server for Your LAN option
- Enter the anonymizer's web address in the Address field (it is your choice of which anonymizer you wish to use)
- Enter 8080 in the Port box
- Click on OK

How to E-Mail Anonymously

The reasons for anonymous e-mail are the same as those for surfing the Web anonymously. Basically, you want to protect your privacy. Anonymous e-mail means that your e-mail messages cannot be tracked back to you personally, to your location, or to your computer. That is, your e-mail messages are sent through another server belonging to a company—known as a re-mailer—that provides anonymous e-mail services. The recipient of your e-mail sees only the re-mailer's header on your e-mail. In addition, your e-mail messages are encrypted so that if they are intercepted, they cannot be read. If you do use a re-mailer, it is possible that your intended recipient will not open your e-mail because he or she will not know it is from you.

Leading commercial re-mailers include CryptoHeaven (*www.cryptoheaven.com*), Ultimate Anonymity (*www.ultimate-anonymity.com*), and Hushmail (*www.hushmail.com*). The commercial version of Pretty Good Privacy (PGP) is available at *www.pgp.com*.

There are free products for anonymous e-mailing and encryption that are widely available. For example, the free, open source version of Pretty Good Privacy, called Open PGP, is available at *www.pgpi.org*. For a list of these free products and a discussion of each one, visit *http://netsecurity.about.com/cs/hackertools/a/aafreecrypt.htm*.

The Outlook e-mail that comes with Microsoft Office also allows you to encrypt outgoing e-mail messages. This product is based on public key technology (discussed in Chapter 3), so you must download and purchase a digital certificate. The first time you send an encrypted message, Microsoft takes you through the steps necessary to obtain your digital certificate.

The steps necessary to use e-mail encryption in Outlook are as follows:

- Open Outlook and compose your message
- Click on the Options tab
- Select the dialog box launcher icon beside More Options
- Click on the Security Settings button
- The Security Properties window now opens
- Check the Encrypt message contents and attachments checkbox
- For the time being, you should not check the Add digital signature to this message checkbox, because you first need to install a digital certificate
- Click on OK in the Security Properties dialog box
- You should now be returned to your message
- Choose an address to send the message to
- Click on the Send button
- You see the Welcome to Secure E-mail window
- Click on the Get Digital ID. . . . button
- You now are taken to a Microsoft website with links to two digital certificate providers: GeoTrust and VeriSign
- You have to register for the digital certificate at each provider; you need access to your e-mail (and your telephone for GeoTrust)
- After the registration process, you click an installation button to install the digital certificate
- When you start the installation, Microsoft may display a Potential Scripting Violation warning; click on Yes to continue
- Once you get the digital certificate installed, you can click on the Send button in Microsoft Outlook
- You may encounter problems if the people you are sending encrypted messages to do not have digital certificates; also, some e-mail systems may not accept encrypted messages because anti-virus scanners cannot scan encrypted e-mail

Thawte offers a free personal digital e-mail certificate. See *www.thawte.com/secure-email/personal-email-certificates/index.html*.

It is a good idea to periodically check the trusted certificate authorities that are configured in your browser and verify that those companies can be trusted. In Internet Explorer, follow these steps:

- Right click on Start
- Right click on Explore
- Click on Control Panel
- Click on Security Center
- Click on Internet Options
- Click on the Content tab
- Click on the Certificates button
- Click on the Intermediate Certification Authorities tab and check that the companies listed can be trusted
- Click on the Trusted Publishers tab and check that the companies listed can be trusted

The StealthSurfer II ID Protect

The StealthSurfer II ID Protect (*www.stealthsurfer.biz*) is a thumb drive that allows you to surf the Web with anonymity from any computer, even if you use a wireless (Wi-Fi) connection. Using the device's integrated web browser, you surf in an encrypted mode that masks your IP address and secures your data from interception by outsiders. The device is ideal for frequent coffee shop surfers, airport travellers, Internet café goers, or anyone who uses his or her laptop wirelessly in a public "hotspot."

When you use StealthSurfer, all your sensitive Internet files such as cookies, Internet history, and cache are stored on the device instead of your computer. Should your StealthSurfer fall into unwanted hands, password protection maintains your data's privacy and security. StealthSurfer helps stop identity theft by concealing your web surfing habits, files, and visited websites from anyone who has physical access to your computer.

Remember to surf in an encrypted mode when using your laptop wirelessly in a public "hotspot."

Small enough to carry on a keychain, the thumb drive plugs into the USB port of your computer. The device contains a comprehensive privacy solution, which includes the following packages already integrated on the device:

- Firefox Internet browser (*www.mozilla.com/firefox*)
- MojoPac: MojoPac (*www.mojopac.com*) is a software virtualization product that turns any USB 2.0 storage device, such as iPods, USB flash drives, portable hard drives, USB-enabled smart phones, and USB-enabled digital cameras, into a portable computing environment.
- Tor software: Tor (*www.torproject.org*) provides for anonymous web surfing by bouncing your communications around a distributed network of servers run by volunteers around the world. Tor software prevents an attacker from observing your Internet connection and learning what websites you visit. Further, the software prevents websites that you visit from learning your physical location.
- RoboForm: This Internet privacy product simplifies the process of filling out on-line forms by storing your user identity, including name, address, phone number, and other important information. It securely stores confidential data such as passwords, bank accounts, and credit card numbers using strong encryption.
- Thunderbird: This product allows for portable, secure e-mail access.
- Hushmail: Discussed above in the section How to E-Mail Anonymously.

Erasing Your Google Search History

If you have signed up for Google's Personalized Search, you can follow these steps to erase your search history. First you sign in to your Google account at *www.google.com/psearch*. You can examine the Search History page and choose days on the calendar to see every search you have made since you created your Google account. Click on the Remove Items button. Remember, however, that even after you remove items from your computer, logs and backups will still exist on Google's servers. To prevent Google from collecting this information in the future, select items such as Web, Images, and News about which you do not want data collected, and then click the Pause button.

Preparing for Personal Disasters

As with a business, you can experience a disaster at home (for example, fires and floods). There are steps you should take to protect your information assets, whether they are stored on your computer (digital form) or in another form (hard copy). First and foremost, you should have a safety deposit box at your bank for your important papers. You should also have a fireproof safe at home where you can store other important papers. You should keep your operating system installation CD and the installation CDs for all your programs in this safe. In addition, you should make a regular backup of your key files and keep these backups in the safe as well. You might also want to encrypt your backup files if they contain sensitive information.

Restoring Backup Files

You can use the Windows Backup utility to restore the backup copies to your hard disk. In Windows XP, you launch Backup following these steps:

- Click on Start
- Click on Programs
- Click on Accessories
- Click on System Tools
- Click on Backup

Windows XP has a utility called Windows System Restore. This utility automatically restores key system files to the state they were in before you had problems. System Restore creates a "mirror" of key system files and settings—called a restore point—every 10 hours, whenever you install a new piece of software, or whenever you manually indicate. When your system encounters a problem, such as being infected with a virus or worm, you can revert to a restore point from before the problem occurred, thereby putting your system back in working order.

To use System Restore:

- Click on Start
- Click on Programs
- Click on Accessories
- Click on System Tools
- Click on System Restore
- When the System Restore window opens, choose the Restore My Computer To An Earlier Time option
- Click on Next
- When the Select A Restore Point screen appears, you will see a calendar showing the current month. Any date highlighted in bold contains a restore point. Select a restore point from before the problem appeared, and click on the Next button
- When the confirmation screen appears, click on Next

Wireless Security

Many home users have implemented a wireless local area network. The security considerations for wireless networks are greater than those for a wired home network. The reason for this is simple. If you are wirelessly computing and communicating, then you are broadcasting, and therefore, by definition, you are non-secure. The most common reason for intruders to connect to a non-secure wireless network is to gain access to the Internet. Intruders might also connect in order to use your network as a base for spamming or for other unethical or illegal activities. Finally, they may do so to gain access to your sensitive personal information.

Unfortunately, recent studies have shown that three-fourths of all home wireless users have not activated any security features to protect their information. Unless you take the steps we discuss here, your information assets are extremely vulnerable.

Hide Your Service Set Identifier (SSID)

Your wireless router, which connects your home network with your ISP, comes with a default SSID that is the same for thousands or millions of routers made by the manufacturer. Therefore, an attacker can search for wireless networks by looking for a relatively small number of default SSIDs. For this reason, you should change your default SSID to a unique SSID and tell your wireless home network to stop broadcasting its SSID. A step-by-step guide to perform these security measures is available here: *http://netsecurity.about.com/od/stepbystep/ss/change_ssid.htm.*

Use Encryption

To avoid broadcasting in the clear, you must use encryption with your wireless home network. Wireless equivalent protocol (WEP) is an old protocol that is now very easy to crack and should not be used. Instead, you should use Wi-Fi Protected Access (WPA2), which is the second generation of WPA. WPA2 is much stronger than WEP and will strengthen your encryption from attackers trying to crack it. Note: Your wireless router must support WPA2. Otherwise, use WPA rather than WEP. In addition, you should use a strong pass phrase of at least 20 random characters on your router.

Filter Out Media Access Control (MAC) Addresses

Every piece of networking hardware has a unique identification number called a media access control (MAC) address that looks like this: 00-00-00-00-00-00. (Note that this MAC address is only an example.) You should get the MAC address of all computers on your home wireless network. Then, instruct your router to connect only with these computers and deny access to all other computers attempting to connect with your network.

- To find the MAC address of your computer, follow these steps:
  - Click on Start
  - Click on Programs
  - Click on Accessories
  - Click on Command Prompt
  - At the cursor, type ipconfig/all
  - Hit Enter
  - The MAC address will be the Physical Address

Limit Internet Protocol (IP) Addresses

You should instruct your router to allow only a certain number of IP addresses to connect to your network. Ideally, the number of IP addresses will be the same as the number of computers on your network.

Sniff Out Intruders

A variety of wireless intrusion detection systems will monitor your wireless network for intruders, tell you they are on your network, show their IP addresses and their activity, and even tell them you know that they are there. Commercial products include the Internet Security Systems (*www.iss.net*) wireless scanner and AirDefense Personal (*www.airdefense.net*). AirSnare is a free wireless intrusion detection system (see *http://home.comcast.net/~jay.deboer/airsnare*).

Using a Public Hotspot

When you travel, keep in mind that most public wireless providers and hotspots employ no security measures at all. As a result, everything you send and receive is in the clear and has no encryption. Many intruders go to public hotspots and listen in on wireless computing and communications taking place there. If you must use a computer wirelessly at a public hotspot, here are several things you should do before you connect.

- Use virtual private networking (VPN) technology to connect to your organization's network (discussed in Chapter 3).
- Use Remote Desktop to connect to a computer that is running at your home.
- Configure the Windows firewall to be "on with no exceptions."
- Only use websites that use secure socket layer (SSL) for any financial or personal transactions.

Other Good Information

Microsoft provides excellent resources for wireless networking and wireless security. For an explanation of the Wireless Network Setup Wizard in Windows XP Service Pack 2, see *www.microsoft.com/technet/community/columns/cableguy/cg0604.mspx*. This overview provides the background for applying the security measures we discussed previously. For an overview of WPA Wireless Security for Home Networks, see *www.microsoft.com/windowsxp/using/networking/expert/bowman_03july28.mspx*.

After you have finished all the steps necessary to protect your wireless home network, it is a good idea to test the network for vulnerabilities. eEye has created a free Wi-Fi vulnerability scanner that you can download here: *www.eeye.com/html/resources/downloads/wifi/RetinaWiFi.html*. This tool is a comprehensive scanner that scans your vicinity looking for wireless devices to test. When you run it, it generates a detailed report outlining all the security problems it finds.

Wireless Security Software

For extra security, you can buy wireless security programs. Trend Micro (*www.trendmicro.com*) has added Wi-Fi Intrusion Detection to PC-cillin, which also includes a personal firewall, anti-virus software, and anti-spyware software. The software warns you when an unknown user tries to access your wireless network. Zonelabs (*www.zonelabs.com*) has a product called ZoneAlarm Wireless Security. This software automatically detects wireless networks and helps secure them.

McAfee (*www.mcafee.com*) provides a free scan to check the security of the wireless network connection that you are using. The scan works only with Internet Explorer. For the scan, go to *www.mcafee.com*, click the section for home users, and look under Free Services for McAfee Wi-Fi scan.

BEFORE YOU GO ON ...

1. Identify problems that can arise on your computer due to hackers, viruses, or worms.
2. Describe the computer-based actions that you can take to mitigate the likelihood of the problems you described.

SUMMARY

1. **Identify the various behavioural actions you can take to protect your information assets based upon your risk assessment of information asset risks.**

   - Do not provide personal information to strangers in any format (physical, verbal, or electronic).
   - Protect your social insurance number.
   - Where available, use credit cards with your picture on them.
   - Do not sign the back of your credit cards. Instead, write "Photo ID Required."
   - Pay very close attention to your credit card billing cycles.
   - Limit your use of debit cards.
   - Do not use a personal mailbox at your home for anything other than catalogues and magazines.
   - Use a cross-cut, or confetti, shredder.
   - Sign up with a reputable company that provides proactive protection of your personal information.

2. **Identify the various computer-based actions you can take to protect your information assets based upon your information asset risks.**

   - Check to see where anyone who may have used your computer has visited on the Internet.
   - Never post personal information about yourself or your family in chat rooms or on social networking sites. Use the privacy features provided by social networking sites to limit public access to your profile.
   - Never open unrequested attachments to e-mail files, even those from people you know and trust.
   - Never open attachments or web links in e-mails from people you do not know.
   - Never accept files transferred to you during Internet chat or instant messaging sessions.
   - Never download any files or software over the Internet from websites that you do not know.
   - Never download files or software that you have not requested.
   - Test your system.
   - Run free malware scans on your computer.
   - Have an anti-malware product on your computer and use it (ideally at least once per week).
   - Have a firewall on your computer.
   - Have an anti-spyware product on your computer.
   - Have monitoring software on your computer.
   - Have content filtering software on your computer.
   - Have anti-spam software on your computer.
   - Have proactive intrusion detection and prevention software on your computer.
   - Manage patches.
   - Use a browser other than Internet Explorer.
   - Use a laptop security system.
   - Use two-factor authentication.
   - Use encryption.
   - Use laptop tracing tools or device reset/remote kill tools.
   - Turn off peer-to-peer (P2P) file sharing.
   - Look for new and unusual files.
   - Detect fake websites.
   - Use strong passwords.
   - Surf the Web anonymously.

- E-mail anonymously.
- Adjust the privacy settings on your computer.
- Erase your Google search history.
- Personal disaster preparation: backup, backup, backup!
- Wireless security:
  - Hide your Service Set Identifier (SSID).
  - Use encryption.
  - Filter out media access control (MAC) addresses.
  - Limit Internet protocol (IP) addresses.
  - Sniff out intruders.
  - Change the default administrator password on your wireless router to something not easily guessed.
  - Use virtual private networking (VPN) technology to connect to your organization's network.
  - Use Remote Desktop to connect to a computer that is running at your home.
  - Configure Windows firewall to be "on with no exceptions."
  - Only use websites that use secure socket layer (SSL) for any financial or personal transactions (discussed in Chapter 3).
  - Use wireless security programs.

DISCUSSION QUESTIONS

1. Why is it so important for you to protect your information assets? Can you assume that your organization's MIS department will do it for you?

2. Discuss the differences between behavioural actions that you should take to protect your information assets and computer-based actions that you should take.

PROBLEM-SOLVING ACTIVITIES

1. Using one product suggested in this technology guide or a product you find, do the following:
   - Test or scan your computer for malware.
   - Test your firewall.
   - Scan your computer for spyware.

2. Follow the steps in this technology guide to see if you have a Trojan horse on your computer.

TECHNOLOGY GUIDE 4 TELECOMMUNICATIONS, NETWORKS, AND THE WORLD WIDE WEB

LEARNING OBJECTIVES

1. Understand the basics of telecommunications systems including the main types of wired communications media and transmission technologies.

2. Differentiate between local area network and wide area network.

3. Describe the main network protocols and processing.

4. Explain how the Internet works and how it can be accessed.

5. Differentiate between the Internet and the World Wide Web.

Technology Guide Overview

Networks support new ways of doing business, from marketing and supply chain management to customer service and human resources management. In particular, the Internet and its private organizational counterpart, intranets, have an enormous impact on our lives, both professionally and personally. In fact, for all organizations, having an Internet strategy is no longer a competitive advantage. Rather, it is necessary for survival.

In Technology Guide 4, we discuss how networks function. First, we describe the basic telecommunications system. Understanding this system is important because it is the way all networks function, regardless of their size. We also discuss the various types of networks, followed by a look at network protocols and types of network processing. We then discuss the basics of the Internet and the World Wide Web, describing how we can access the Internet followed by a definition of the World Wide Web and its differences from the Internet.

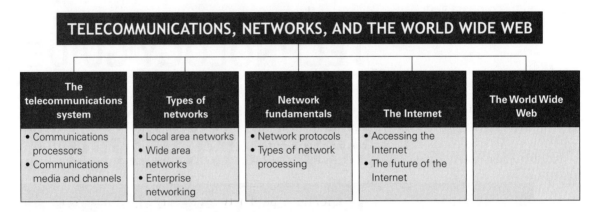

The telecommunications system	Types of networks	Network fundamentals	The Internet	The World Wide Web
• Communications processors • Communications media and channels	• Local area networks • Wide area networks • Enterprise networking	• Network protocols • Types of network processing	• Accessing the Internet • The future of the Internet	

(Chart heading: TELECOMMUNICATIONS, NETWORKS, AND THE WORLD WIDE WEB)

TG4.1 The Telecommunications System

A **telecommunications system** consists of hardware and software that transmit information from one location to another. These systems can transmit text, data, graphics, voice, documents, or full-motion video information. They transmit this information with two basic types of signals: analog and digital. **Analog signals** are continuous waves that transmit information by altering the characteristics of the waves. Analog signals have two parameters: amplitude and frequency. For example, all sounds are analog, travelling to human ears in the form of waves. The greater the height (or amplitude) of the waves, the louder the sound; the more closely packed the waves, the higher the frequency or pitch.

In contrast, **digital signals** are discrete pulses that are either on or off, representing a series of **bits** (0s and 1s). This quality allows them to convey information in a binary form that can be clearly interpreted by computers. Figure TG4.1 illustrates both analog and digital signals.

FIGURE TG4.1
Analog and digital signals.

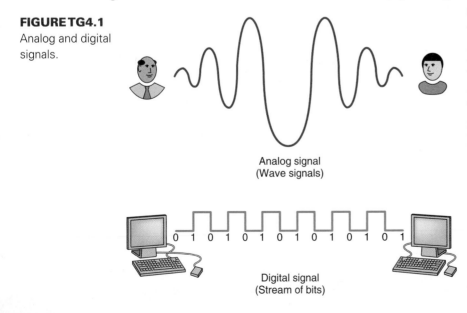

Analog signal
(Wave signals)

Digital signal
(Stream of bits)

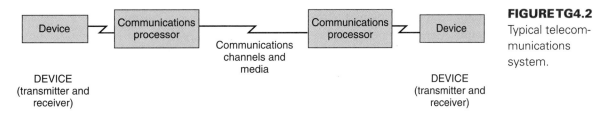

FIGURE TG4.2
Typical telecommunications system.

The basic components of a telecommunications system are devices, communications processors, communications channels and media, and networking software. Devices include all types of hardware, from smart phones to supercomputers. Figure TG4.2 shows a typical telecommunications system. Note that these systems communicate in both directions, so devices serve as both transmitters and receivers.

Communications Processors

Communications processors are hardware devices that support data transmission and reception across a telecommunications system. These devices include modems, multiplexers, and front-end processors.

Modems

The function of **modems** is to convert digital signals to analog signals, a process called *modulation*, and analog signals to digital signals, a process called *demodulation*. Modems are used in pairs. The modem at the sending end converts a computer's digital information into analog signals for transmission over analog lines (for example, telephone lines). At the receiving end, another modem converts the analog signal back into digital signals for the receiving computer. There are three types of modems: dial-up modems, DSL modems, and cable modems.

Most public telephone systems were originally designed as an analog network to carry voice signals or sounds in an analog wave format. In order for this type of network to carry digital information, that information must be converted into an analog wave pattern by a dial-up modem. Dial-up modems have transmission speeds of up to 56 Kbps.

Cable modems are modems that operate over coaxial cable (for example, cable TV). They offer high-speed access to the Internet or corporate intranets. Cable modems use a shared line. Therefore, when large numbers of users access the same modem, they can slow down the access speed.

DSL (*digital subscriber line*, discussed later in this technology guide) modems operate on the same lines as voice telephones and dial-up modems, but DSL signals do not interfere with voice service. Also, DSL modems always maintain a connection, so an Internet connection is immediately available.

Multiplexer

A **multiplexer** is an electronic device that allows a single communications channel to carry data transmissions simultaneously from many sources. Multiplexing can be accomplished by dividing a high-speed channel into multiple channels of slower speeds or by assigning each transmission source a very small amount of time for using the high-speed channel. Multiplexers lower communication costs by allowing devices to share communications channels. Multiplexing thus makes more efficient use of these channels by merging the transmissions of several computers (for example, personal computers) at one end of the channel, while a similar unit separates the individual transmissions at the receiving end (for example, a mainframe).

Front-End Processor

With most mainframes and minicomputers, the central processing unit (CPU) must communicate with multiple computers at the same time. Routine communication tasks can absorb a large proportion of the CPU's processing time, leading to degraded performance on more important jobs. In order not to waste valuable CPU time, many computer systems have a small secondary computer dedicated solely to communication. Known as a **front-end processor**, this specialized computer manages all routing communications with peripheral devices.

Communications Media and Channels

For data to be communicated from one location to another, some form of pathway or medium must be used. These pathways are called **communications channels**. The communications channels are listed below. Note that they are divided into two types of media: cable (twisted-pair wire, coaxial cable, and fibre-optic cable) and broadcast (microwave, satellite, radio, and infrared).

Cable or **wireline media** use physical wires or cables to transmit data and information. Twisted-pair wire and coaxial cable are made of copper, and fibre-optic cable is made of glass. The alternative is communication over **broadcast** or **wireless media**. The key to mobile communications in today's rapidly moving society is data transmissions over electromagnetic media—the "airwaves." In this section we discuss the three wireline channels. Table TG4.1 summarizes the advantages and disadvantages of each of these channels. We discussed wireless media in Chapter 7.

Twisted-Pair Wire

Twisted-pair wire is the most prevalent form of communications wiring; it is used for almost all business telephone wiring. Twisted-pair wire consists of strands of copper wire twisted in pairs (see Figure TG4.3). It is relatively inexpensive to purchase, widely available, and easy to work with. It can be made relatively unobtrusive by running it inside walls, floors, and above ceilings. However, twisted-pair wire has some significant disadvantages. It is relatively slow for transmitting data, it is subject to interference from other electrical sources, and it can be easily tapped by unintended receivers for gaining unauthorized access to data.

FIGURE TG4.3
Twisted-pair wire.

Coaxial Cable

Coaxial cable (Figure TG4.4) consists of insulated copper wire. It is much less susceptible to electrical interference than is twisted-pair wire, and it

TABLE TG4.1
ADVANTAGES AND DISADVANTAGES OF WIRELINE COMMUNICATIONS CHANNELS

CHANNEL	ADVANTAGES	DISADVANTAGES
Twisted-pair wire	Inexpensive Widely available Easy to work with Unobtrusive	Slow (low bandwidth) Subject to interference Easily tapped (low security)
Coaxial cable	Higher bandwidth than twisted-pair Less susceptible to electromagnetic interference	Relatively expensive and inflexible Easily tapped (low to medium security) Somewhat difficult to work with
Fibre-optic cable	Very high bandwidth Relatively inexpensive Difficult to tap (good security)	Difficult to work with (difficult to splice)

can carry much more data. For these reasons, it is commonly used to carry high-speed data traffic as well as television signals (thus the term "cable TV"). However, coaxial cable is more expensive and more difficult to work with than twisted-pair wire. It is also somewhat inflexible.

FIGURE TG4.4
Coaxial cable.

Fibre Optics

Fibre-optic cables (Figure TG4.5) consist of thousands of very thin filaments of glass fibres that transmit information via light pulses generated by lasers. The fibre-optic cable is surrounded by cladding, a coating that prevents the light from leaking out of the fibre.

Fibre-optic cables are significantly smaller and lighter than traditional cable media. They also can transmit far more data, and they provide greater security from interference and tapping. As of mid-2009, optical fibre had reached data transmission rates of more than 40 trillion bits (terabits) per second in laboratory experiments. Fibre-optic cable is typically used as the backbone for a network, whereas twisted-pair wire and coaxial cable connect the backbone to individual devices on the network. One example of the use of fibre-optic cable as the backbone is The Ontario Research and Innovation Optical Network (ORION), which recently added 1,500 km of fibre-optic cable to connect urban and rural communities in Ontario to its network. The network supports transmission speeds of 1 to 10 Gbps using DWDM technology (dense wavelength division multiplexing).

FIGURE TG4.5
Fibre-optic cable.

One problem associated with fibre optics is *attenuation*, the reduction in the strength of a signal. Attenuation occurs for both analog and digital signals. To resolve attenuation problems, manufacturers must install equipment to receive the weakened or distorted signals, amplify them to their original strength, and then send them out to the intended receiver.

Transmission Speed

Bandwidth refers to the range of frequencies available in any communications channel. Bandwidth is a very important concept in communications because the transmission capacity of any channel (stated in bits per second or bps) is largely dependent on its bandwidth. In general, the greater the bandwidth, the greater the channel capacity.

Narrowband channels typically provide low-speed transmission speeds up to 64 Kbps, although some now reach speeds of up to 2 Mbps. **Broadband** channels provide high-speed transmission rates ranging from 256 Kbps up to several terabits per second.

The speeds of particular communications channels are as follows:

- Twisted-pair wire: up to 1 Gbps (one billion bits per second)
- Microwave: up to 600 Mbps
- Satellite: up to 600 Mbps
- Coaxial cable: up to 1 Gbps
- Fibre-optic cable: more than 40 Tbps (one trillion bits per second)

Transmission Technologies

A number of telecommunications technologies enable users to transmit high-volume data quickly and accurately over any type of network. We address these technologies in this section.

Integrated Services Digital Network

Integrated services digital network (ISDN) is an older international telephone standard for network access that uses existing telephone lines and allows users to transfer voice, video, image, and data simultaneously.

Digital Subscriber Line

Digital subscriber lines (DSL) provide high-speed, digital data transmission from homes and businesses over existing telephone lines. Because the existing lines are analog and the transmission is digital, you need DSL modems.

Asynchronous Transfer Mode

Asynchronous transfer mode (ATM) networks allow for almost unlimited bandwidth on demand. ATM offers several advantages. It makes possible large increases in bandwidth. It provides support for data, video, and voice transmissions on a single communications line. ATM currently requires fibre-optic cable, but it can transmit up to 2.5 gigabits per second. On the downside, ATM is more expensive than ISDN and DSL.

Synchronous Optical Network

Synchronous optical network (SONET) is an interface standard for transporting digital signals over fibre-optic lines that allows users to integrate transmissions from multiple vendors. SONET defines optical line rates, known as optical carrier (OC) signals. The base rate is 51.84 Mbps (OC-1), and higher rates are direct multiples of the base rate. For example, OC-3 runs at 155.52 Mbps, or three times the rate of OC-1.

T-Carrier System

The **T-carrier system** is a digital transmission system that defines circuits that operate at different rates, all of which are multiples of the basic 64 Kbps used to transport a single voice call. These circuits include T1 (1.544 Mbps, equivalent to 24 channels); T2 (6.312 Mbps, equivalent to 96 channels); T3 (44.736 Mbps, equivalent to 672 channels); and T4 (274.176 Mbps, equivalent to 4,032 channels).

The following example provides an illustration of how different types of communications media and transmission technologies can coexist in the same computer network.

EXAMPLE TG4.1

"The value of high-speed Internet to a child's education in today's information-rich society can never be understated," says Joseph DiFrancesco, Principal of Notre Dame Catholic School in Caledonia. The school is part of the Brant Haldimand Norfolk Catholic District School Board in southwestern Ontario. The board manages 10,500 students, 32 elementary schools, and three secondary schools and covers an area of almost 4,000 square kilometres, much of it rural.

The board's network used to be unreliable and slow and e-mail access and Internet connection was affected on a regular basis. The problem was even more acute in rural schools, which sometimes would have Internet speeds of less than 50 or 100 Kbps. Sometimes schools would go without Internet access for weeks.

In order to provide a reliable high-speed Internet connection for teachers, students, and staff, the school board developed a solution based on its existing network infrastructure. Schools already had a closed-circuit TV (CCTV) infrastructure in place, making the choice of a cable network attractive. And even though the board had to invest in new network technology, the monthly cost of maintaining the new network would be approximately the same as what it was paying before. Another alternative was to set up a fibre optic network in every school; however, this option would have cost millions of dollars.

(Continued on next page)

EXAMPLE (*Continued*)

After several alternatives were considered, the board decided to install a network using a hybrid of fibre optics and coaxial cable. This was one of the first hybrid networks of its kind in Canada and combined Brantford Hydro Inc.'s NetOptiks fibre optics infrastructure and Rogers Cable's coaxial-ADSL (asymmetric digital subscriber line) infrastructure to provide high-speed Internet access and other IT applications to all of the board's schools.

One of the main benefits of the new hybrid network is its reliability and speed. Some of the rural schools were accustomed to little service, and sometimes no service at all. The new network ensures an always-on connection with consistent high-speed access. Before the new network was implemented, a rural school may have gotten 100 Kbps Internet speed, but now it gets the same access speeds as those in the city: up to 5 Mbps. Another benefit of the new network is the ability for teachers, students, and staff to send and receive voice, video, and data over a single network. Students can download information in a fraction of the time that it used to take them and they regularly e-mail their projects to their teachers.

Sources: Compiled from D. Webb, "Hybrid Network Overcomes Geographic Challenges," *Network World*, July 5 2007; Media release, Yahoo! Finance: "NetOptiks and Rogers Partner to Bring Brant Haldimand Norfolk Catholic Schools into the High-Speed Information Age," June 26, 2007; *www.netoptiks.com*, accessed August 22, 2007.

BEFORE YOU GO ON …

1. Describe the basic components of a telecommunications system.
2. Compare and contrast the three wireline communications channels.
3. Describe the various technologies that enable users to send high-volume data over any network.
4. Compare and contrast the ATM, SONET, and T-carrier systems.

TG4.2 Types of Networks

A **computer network** is a system that connects computers via communications media so that data can be transmitted among them. Computer networks are essential to modern organizations for many reasons. First, networked computer systems enable organizations to be more flexible so they can adapt to rapidly changing business conditions. Second, networks enable companies to share hardware, computer applications, and data across the organization and among different organizations. Third, networks make it possible for geographically dispersed employees and work groups to share documents, ideas, and creative insights. This sharing encourages teamwork, innovation, and more efficient and effective interactions. Finally, networks are a critical link between businesses and their customers.

There are various types of computer networks, ranging from small to worldwide. Types of networks include (from smallest to largest) personal area networks (PANs), local area networks (LANs), metropolitan area networks (MANs), wide area networks (WANs), and the Internet. PANs are short-range networks (typically a few metres) used for communication among devices close to one person. PANs can be wired or wireless. We discussed wireless PANs in Chapter 7. MANs are relatively large computer networks that cover a metropolitan area. MANs fall between LANs and WANs in size. In this section, we discuss local area and wide area networks. We consider the basics of the Internet in Section TG4.5.

Local Area Networks

A **local area network (LAN)** connects two or more devices in a limited geographical region, usually within the same building, so that every device on the network can communicate with every other device. Figure TG4.6 shows a LAN with four computers and a printer that connect via a **switch**, which is a special-purpose computer that allows the devices in a LAN to communicate directly with each other. Every device in a LAN has a **network interface card (NIC)** that allows the device to physically connect to the LAN's communications medium. This medium is typically unshielded twisted-pair wire (UTP).

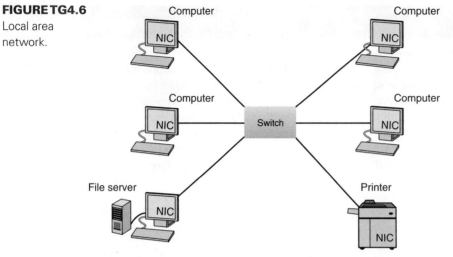

Although not required, many LANs have a **file server** or **network server**. File servers are often powerful microcomputers with large, fast-access hard drives. The server typically contains various software and data for the network. It also houses the LAN's network operating system, which manages the server and routes and manages communications on the network.

The network gateway connects the LAN to external networks—either public or corporate—so that the LAN can exchange information with them. A **gateway** is a communications processor that connects dissimilar networks by translating from one set of protocols (rules that govern the functioning of a network) to another. In contrast, a communications processor that connects two networks of the same type is called a **bridge**. A **router** is a communications processor that routes messages through several connected LANs or across a wide area network such as the Internet.

As we mentioned earlier, because a LAN is restricted to a small area, the nodes can be connected either through cables or via wireless technologies. **Wireless local area networks (WLANs)** provide LAN connectivity over short distances, typically less than 150 metres. We discussed WLANs and other wireless technologies in Chapter 7.

Wide Area Networks

When businesses have to transmit and receive data beyond the confines of the LAN, they use wide area networks. **Wide area networks (WANs)** are networks that cover large geographic areas. WANs typically connect multiple LANs. WANs generally are provided by common carriers such as telephone companies and the international networks of global communications services providers. WANs have large capacity, and they typically combine multiple channels (for example, fibre-optic cables, microwave, and satellite). The Internet, which we discuss in the next section, is an example of a WAN.

One important type of WAN is the **value-added network (VAN)**. VANs are private, data-only networks managed by outside third parties that provide telecommunication and computing services to multiple organizations. Many companies use VANs to avoid the expenses of creating and managing their own networks.

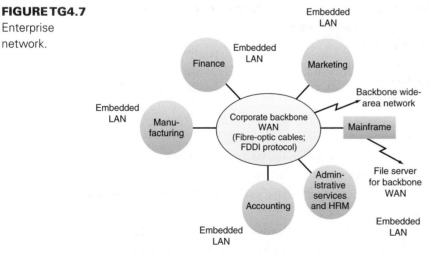

Enterprise Networking

Organizations today have multiple LANs and may have multiple WANs, which are interconnected to form an **enterprise network**. Figure TG4.7 shows a model of enterprise computing. Note that the enterprise network in the figure has a backbone network composed of fibre-optic cable. Corporate **backbone networks** are high-speed central networks to which multiple smaller networks (such as LANs and smaller WANs) connect. The LANs are called *embedded LANs* because they connect to the backbone WAN.

BEFORE YOU GO ON ...

1. What are the main business reasons for using networks?
2. What is the difference between LANs and WANs?
3. Describe an enterprise network.

TG4.3 Network Fundamentals

We now turn our attention to the fundamentals of networks. This section addresses network protocols and types of network processing. These topics describe how networks actually transmit and process data and information over the basic telecommunications system.

Network Protocols

Computing devices that are connected to the network access and share the network to transmit and receive data. These components are often referred to as "nodes" of the network. They work together by adhering to a common set of rules that enables them to communicate with one another. This set of rules and procedures that govern transmission across a network is a **protocol**. In this section we discuss two major network protocols: Ethernet and TCP/IP.

Ethernet

A common LAN protocol is **Ethernet**. Most large corporations use 10 gigabit Ethernet in which the network provides data transmission speeds of 10 billion bits per second. However, 100-gigabit Ethernet is becoming the standard (100 billion bits per second).

Transmission Control Protocol/Internet Protocol

The **transmission control protocol/Internet protocol (TCP/IP)** is the protocol of the Internet. TCP/IP uses a suite of protocols, the main ones being the transmission control protocol (TCP) and the Internet protocol (IP). The TCP performs three basic functions: (1) it manages the movement of packets (discussed next) between computers by establishing a connection between the computers, (2) it sequences the transfer of packets, and (3) it acknowledges the packets that have been transmitted. The **Internet protocol (IP)** is responsible for disassembling, delivering, and reassembling the data during transmission, a process we discuss next.

Before data are transmitted over the Internet, they are broken down into small, fixed bundles of data called packets. The transmission technology that breaks up blocks of text into packets is called **packet switching**. Each packet carries the information that will help it reach its destination—the sender's Internet protocol (IP) address (discussed in Section TG4.4), the intended receiver's IP address, the number of packets in this message, and the number of this particular packet within the message. Each packet travels independently across the network and can be routed through different paths in the network. When the packets reach their destination, they are reassembled into the original message. The packets use TCP/IP to carry their data.

TCP/IP functions in four layers (see Figure TG4.8). We now take a look at each layer. The *application layer* enables client application programs to access the other layers and defines the protocols that

FIGURE TG4.8
The four layers
of the TCP/IP
reference model.

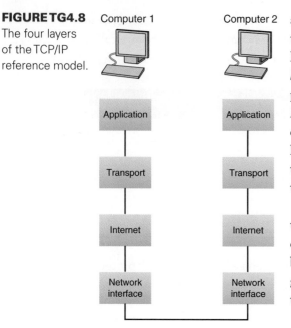

Computer 1   Computer 2

Application   Application

Transport   Transport

Internet   Internet

Network interface   Network interface

applications use to exchange data. One of these application protocols is the **hypertext transfer protocol (HTTP)**, which defines how messages are formulated and transmitted. The *transport layer* provides the application layer with communication and packet services. This layer includes TCP and other protocols. The *Internet layer* is responsible for addressing, routing, and packaging data packets. The Internet protocol is one of the protocols in this layer. The *network interface layer* places packets on and receives them from the network medium, which could be any networking technology.

Two computers using TCP/IP can communicate even if they use different hardware and software. Data sent from one computer to another proceed downward through all four layers, beginning with the sending computer's application layer and going through its network interface layer. After the data reach the receiving computer, they travel up the layers.

TCP/IP enables users to send data across sometimes-unreliable networks with assurance that the data will arrive in uncorrupted form. TCP/IP is very popular with business organizations due to its reliability and the ease with which it can support intranets and related functions.

Let's look at an example of packet switching across the Internet. Figure TG4.9 illustrates a message being sent from Toronto to Calgary over a packet-switching network. Note that the different coloured packets travel by different routes to reach their destination in Calgary, where they are reassembled into the complete message.

Types of Network Processing

Organizations typically use multiple computer systems across the firm. **Distributed processing** divides processing work among two or more computers. This process enables computers in different locations to communicate with one another via telecommunications links. A common type of distributed processing is client/server processing. A special type of client/server processing is peer-to-peer processing.

Client/Server Computing

Client/server computing links two or more computers in an arrangement in which some machines (called **servers**) provide computing services for user PCs (called **clients**). Usually, an organization does the bulk of its processing or application/data storage on suitably powerful servers that can be

FIGURE TG4.9
Packet switching.

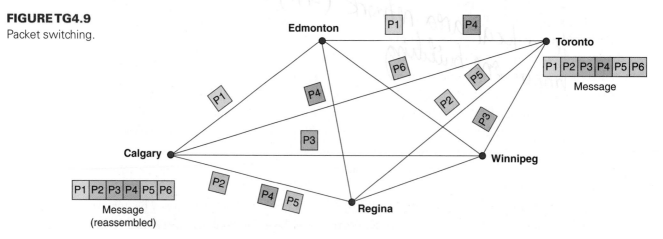

accessed by less powerful client machines. The client requests applications, data, or processing from the server, which acts on these requests by "serving" the desired commodity.

Client/server computing leads to the ideas of "fat" clients and "thin" clients. As we discussed in Technology Guide 1, *fat clients* have large storage and processing power and therefore can run local programs (for example, Microsoft Office) if the network is down. In contrast, *thin clients* may have no local storage and limited processing power. Thus, they must depend on the network to run applications and are of little value when the network is not functioning.

Peer-to-Peer Processing

Peer-to-peer (P2P) processing is a type of client/server distributed processing in which each computer acts as *both* a client and a server. Each computer can access (as assigned for security or integrity purposes) all files on all other computers.

There are three basic types of peer-to-peer processing. The first accesses unused CPU power among networked computers. A well-known application of this type is SETI@home (*http://setiathome. ssl.berkeley.edu*), which is a scientific experiment using Internet-connected computers to search for extraterrestrial intelligence (Figure TG4.10). These applications are from open-source projects and can be downloaded at no cost.

The second form of peer-to-peer is real-time, person-to-person collaboration, such as Google Talk. Companies such as Microsoft have P2P collaborative applications (SharePoint Workspace; *http://office.com/en-gb/sharepoint-workspace/*) that use buddy lists to establish a connection and allow real-time collaboration within the application.

The third peer-to-peer category is advanced search and file sharing. This category is characterized by natural-language searches of millions of peer systems and lets users discover other users, not just data and web pages. One example of this is BitTorrent.

BitTorrent (*www.bittorrent.com*) is an open-source, free, peer-to-peer file-sharing application that is able to simplify the problem of sharing large files by dividing them into tiny pieces, or "torrents." BitTorrent addresses two of the biggest problems of file sharing: (1) downloading bogs down when many people access a file at once; and (2) some people leech, downloading content but refusing to share. BitTorrent eliminates the bottleneck by having everyone share little pieces of a file at the same time—a process called *swarming*. The program prevents leeching because users must upload a file while they download it. This means that the more popular the content, the more efficiently it zips over a network.

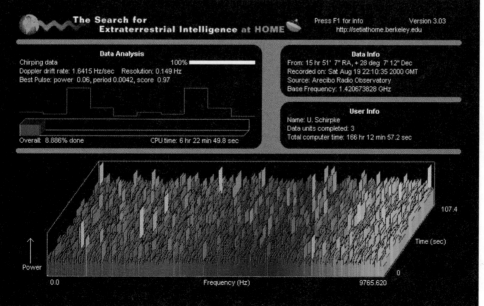

FIGURE TG4.10
SETI@home.

TG4.4 The Internet

The **Internet ("the net")** is a global WAN that connects approximately one million organizational computer networks in more than 200 countries on all continents, including Antarctica, and features in the daily routine of almost 2 billion people. Participating computer systems, called nodes, include smart phones, PCs, LANs, databases, and mainframes.

The computers and organizational nodes on the Internet can be of different types and makes. They are connected to one another by data communications lines of different speeds. The main network connections and telecommunications lines that link the nodes are referred to as the back-bone. For the Internet, the backbone is a fibre-optic network that is operated primarily by large telecommunications companies.

As a network of networks, the Internet enables people to access data in other organizations and to communicate, collaborate, and exchange information seamlessly around the world, quickly and inexpensively. Thus, the Internet has become a necessity in the conduct of modern business.

The Internet grew out of an experimental project of the Advanced Research Project Agency (ARPA, now known as the Defense Advanced Research Project Agency, or DARPA) of the U.S. Department of Defense. The project began in 1969 as the *ARPANET*. Its purpose was to test the feasibility of a WAN over which researchers, educators, military personnel, and government agencies could share data, exchange messages, and transfer files. Today, Internet technologies are being used both within and among organizations. An **intranet** is a network designed to serve the internal informational needs of a single organization. Intranets support discovery (easy and inexpensive browsing and search), communication, and collaboration. For example, Petro-Canada provides on-line training for business owners and service attendants through its corporate intranet and it also allows employees to consult policies and procedures. For the numerous uses of intranets, see *www.intranetjournal.com*.

In contrast, an **extranet** connects parts of the intranets of different organizations and allows secure communications among business partners over the Internet using virtual private networks. Extranets offer limited accessibility to the intranets of participating companies, as well as necessary inter-organizational communications. They are widely used in the areas of business-to-business (B2B) electronic commerce (see Chapter 6) and supply chain management (SCM; see Chapter 10).

Darknets are private networks that run on the Internet but are open only to users who belong to the network. Typically, relatively few people or organizations have access to a darknet, due to security concerns. These users swap passwords or digital keys so they can communicate securely with one another. The data flowing between computers are often encrypted, making darknets more secure than typical corporate intranets, because companies usually do not encrypt data located inside corporate firewalls. There are three major uses for darknets: (1) they contribute to freedom of speech in countries that practise strict censorship; (2) they enable companies to create highly secure networks to protect sensitive data; and (3) they allow people to illegally share music, movies, and software that are protected by copyrights.

No central agency manages the Internet. Instead, the cost of its operation is shared among hundreds of thousands of nodes. Thus, the cost for any one organization is small. Organizations must pay a small fee if they wish to register their names, and they need to have their own hardware and software to operate their internal networks. The organizations are obliged to move any data or information that enters their organizational network, regardless of their source, to their destination, at no charge to the senders. The senders, of course, pay the telephone bills for using either the backbone or regular telephone lines.

Accessing the Internet

There are several ways to access the Internet. From your place of work or your university, you can access the Internet via your organization's LAN. A campus or company backbone connects all the various LANs and servers in the organization to the Internet. You can also log on to the Internet from your home or on the road, using either wireline or wireless connections.

Connecting via an On-line Service

You can also access the Internet by opening an account with an Internet service provider. An **Internet service provider (ISP)** is a company that offers Internet connections for a fee. Large ISPs include Bell Sympatico (*http://bell.ca/home/*), RogersYahoo! (*www.rogers.com*), TekSavvy (*www.teksavvy.com*), and Telus (*www.telus.com*). In addition, many telephone providers and cable companies sell Internet access, as do computer companies such as Microsoft. To use this service you need a modem and standard communications software. To find a local ISP, access *www.canadianisp.com*. There, you can search by your province and city for an ISP that services your area.

ISPs connect to one another through **network access points (NAPs)**. NAPs are exchange points for Internet traffic. They determine how traffic is routed. NAPs are key components of the Internet backbone.

Connecting via Other Means

There have been several attempts to make access to the Internet cheaper, faster, and easier. For example, terminals known as **Internet kiosks** have been located in public places such as libraries and airports (and even in convenience stores in some countries) for use by people who do not have their own computers. Accessing the Internet from cell phones is also becoming more common, as is fibre-to-the-home (FTTH). FTTH involves placing fibre-optic cable directly in individual homes. In practice, this is usually done only in new residential developments, but it is rapidly spreading. Table TG4.2 summarizes the various means that you can use to connect to the Internet.

TABLE TG4.2
INTERNET CONNECTION METHODS

SERVICE	CHARACTERISTICS
Dial-up	Still used where broadband is not available
ISDN	More expensive than broadband connections
DSL	Broadband access via telephone companies
Cable modem	Access over your cable TV coaxial cable. Can have degraded performance if many of your neighbours are accessing the Internet at once.
Satellite	Access where cable and DSL are not available
Wireless	Very convenient and WiMAX will increase the use of broadband wireless
Fibre-to-the-home (FTTH)	Expensive and usually only placed in new housing developments

Addresses on the Internet

Each computer on the Internet has an assigned address, called the **Internet protocol (IP) address**, that distinguishes it from all other computers. The IP address consists of numbers, in four parts, separated by dots. For example, the IP address of one computer might be 135.62.128.91. You can access a website by typing this number in the address bar of your browser.

IP addresses must be unique so computers on the Internet know where to find each other. The Internet Corporation for Assigned Names (ICANN) (*www.icann.org*) coordinates these unique addresses throughout the world. Without that coordination, we would not have one global Internet.

Because the numeric IP addresses are difficult to remember, most computers have names as well. ICANN accredits certain companies called registrars to register these names, which are derived from a system called the **domain name system (DNS)**.

Domain names consist of multiple parts, separated by dots, which are read from right to left. For example, consider the domain name "software.ibm.com". The rightmost part of an Internet name is its **top-level domain (TLD)**. The letters "com" in software.ibm.com indicate that this is a commercial site. Popular TLDs are:

.com	commercial sites
.edu	educational sites
.mil	military government sites
.gov	civilian government sites
.org	organizations

To finish our domain name example, "ibm" is the name of the company (IBM), and "software" is the name of the particular machine (computer) within the company to which the message is being sent.

In countries other than the United States, the country name or designator is often the TLD. The use of TLDs within a country is up to that country. Canada uses the TLD ".ca." For further examples, "de" stands for Germany, "it" for Italy, and "ru" for Russia. In essence, every country decides for itself whether to use TLDs. Moreover, those countries that use TLDs may or may not necessarily follow the generic TLD system. For example, the United Kingdom uses ".co" where the United States uses ".com," and uses ".ac" (for academic) where the United States uses ".edu." Many websites around the world do use generic TLDs, especially ".com."

IP Addressing Schemes

Currently, there are two IP addressing schemes. The first scheme, IPv4 (Internet Protocol version 4), is the most predominant. IP addresses using IPv4 consist of 32 bits, meaning that there are 2^{32} possibilities for IP addresses (or 4,294,967,295 distinct addresses). When IPv4 was developed, there were not as many computers that needed addresses as there are today. Therefore, a new IP addressing scheme has been developed, called IPv6 (Internet Protocol version 6).

IP addresses using IPv6 consist of 128 bits, meaning that there are 2^{128} possibilities for distinct IP addresses, which is an unimaginably large number. IPv6, which is replacing IPv4, will accommodate the rapidly increasing number of devices that need IP addresses, such as smart phones.

EXAMPLE TG4.2

Canadian organizations and Internet service providers aren't moving fast enough to prepare for the next generation of Internet Protocol, IPv6, says Andree Toonk, the network architect for BCNet, a broadband network for British Columbia university researchers. According to his estimates only seven per cent of organizations with IPv4 addresses are sending out IPv6 prefixes now and a recent report

(Continued on next page)

EXAMPLE *(Continued)*

from the Organization of Economic Co-operation and Development (OECD) said that at the beginning of 2010 there were only 5.5 percent of networks capable of handling IPv6.

The move from IPv4 to IPv6 is being driven by the need for additional IP addresses as we run out of IPv4 web addresses. According to some recent estimates in 2012 there will be no more IPv4 addresses to assign. When IPv4 was first developed, it had a little more than four billion Internet Protocol addresses. That amount of IP addresses was sufficient for the Advanced Research Projects Agency Network. However, this number is insufficient for today when more and more devices such as wireless phones and consumer appliances need IP addresses.

It is important to understand that when we run out of IPv4 addresses, the Internet is not going to fall apart or fail. Websites, IP telephony and technology supported by IP addresses will continue to work just fine. The implications will be that there will be no new IP addresses for new growth on the Internet.

In contrast, when the new IPv6 comes into effect, there will be an almost unlimited number of IP addresses available; IPv6 has the capability for 340 billion billion billion billion – with an extra 282,000 million billion billion left over. However, organizations should be making sure their network equipment is IPv6-ready, as soon as possible.

Sources: G. Meckbach, "IPv6 upgrade needs work: Experts," Network World Canada, April 20, 2010; H. Solomon, "Canadians lagging in IPv6 readiness, says expert," Network World Canada, April 11, 2010.

The Future of the Internet

Consumer demand for content delivered over the Internet is increasing at 60 percent per year. In mid-2009, monthly traffic across the Internet was about eight exabytes (one exabyte is equivalent to 50,000 years of DVD-quality data). With more people working on-line, the soaring popularity of websites such as YouTube that require large amounts of bandwidth, and the demand for high-definition television delivered over the Internet, there is concern that Internet users will experience regular "brownouts." These brownouts will initially lead to computers going off-line for several minutes at a time. Researchers assert that if Internet bandwidth is not improved rapidly, then by 2012 the Internet will only be able to function at a much reduced speed.

Therefore, in some cases the Internet is too slow for data-intensive applications. Examples of such applications are full-motion video files (movies) or large medical files (X-rays). In addition, the Internet is unreliable and is not secure. As a result, research networks in different countries are working toward developing new technologies to support the growing needs of the Internet. In Canada, CANARIE Inc. (*www.canarie.ca*) is a not-for-profit organization supported by the government and the private sector with the goal of doing research and implementing advanced communication networks. CAnet 4 is CANARIE's most advanced network and interconnects provincial research networks, universities, research centres, government research laboratories, and schools. CANARIE develops and deploys advanced network applications essential for national and international collaboration, such as remote medical diagnosis, digital libraries, distance education, on-line simulation, and virtual laboratories. **Internet2** is the equivalent of CANARIE in the United States and is designed to be fast, always on, everywhere, natural, intelligent, easy, and trusted. It allows the deployment of advanced applications such as remote medical diagnosis, digital libraries, distance education, on-line simulation, and virtual laboratories. Internet2 is not a separate physical network from the Internet. For more details, see *www.internet2.edu*.

BEFORE YOU GO ON ...

1. Describe the evolution of the Internet, and describe Internet2.
2. Describe the various ways you can connect to the Internet.
3. Describe the parts of an Internet address.

TG4.5 The World Wide Web

Many people equate the Internet with the World Wide Web. However, they are not the same thing. The Internet functions as a transport mechanism, whereas the World Wide Web is an application that uses those transport functions. Other applications, such as e-mail, also run on the Internet.

The World Wide Web (the Web, WWW, or W3) is a system of universally accepted standards for storing, retrieving, formatting, and displaying information via a client/server architecture. The Web handles all types of digital information, including text, hypermedia, graphics, and sound. It uses graphical user interfaces, so it is very easy to navigate.

Organizations that wish to offer information through the Web must establish a home page, which is a text and graphical screen display that usually welcomes the user and explains the organization that has established the page. In most cases, the home page will lead users to other pages. All the pages of a particular company or individual are collectively known as a website. Most web pages provide a way to contact the organization or the individual. The person in charge of an organization's website is its webmaster (note: the term "webmaster" is not gender-specific).

To access a website, the user must specify a uniform resource locator (URL), which points to the address of a specific resource on the Web. For instance, the URL for Microsoft is "http://www.microsoft.com". HTTP stands for hypertext transport protocol, which we discussed in Section TG4.3. (Note that throughout this textbook, to save space, when citing web addresses, the "http://" has been left off the beginning of URLs that start with "www.") The remaining letters in this URL—"www.microsoft.com"—indicate the domain name that identifies the web server storing the website.

Users access the Web primarily through software applications called browsers. Browsers provide a graphical front end that enables users to point and click their way across the Web, a process called surfing. Web browsers became a means of universal access because they deliver the same interface on any operating system under which they run. Leading browsers include Internet Explorer from Microsoft, Firefox from Mozilla, and Safari from Apple.

BEFORE YOU GO ON ...

1. What are the roles of browsers?
2. Describe the difference between the Internet and the World Wide Web.
3. What is a URL?

SUMMARY

1. **Understand the basics of telecommunications systems including the main types of wired communications media and transmission technologies.**

   Telecommunications systems are composed of computers, which act as transmitters and receivers of information; communications processors (for example, modems, multiplexers, and front-end processors); communications channels and media; and networking software.

   The main communications wired media include twisted-pair wire, coaxial cable, and fibre-optic cable. The main transmission media include *integrated services digital network (ISDN)*, *digital subscriber lines (DSL)*, *asynchronous transfer mode (ATM)*, *synchronous optical network (SONET)* and the *T-carrier system*.

2. **Differentiate between local area network and wide area network.**

   The two major types of networks are local area networks (LANs) and wide area networks (WANs). LANs encompass a limited geographic area and are usually composed of one communications medium. In contrast, WANs encompass a broad geographical area and are usually composed of multiple communications media.

3. **Describe the main network protocols and processing.**

   A common LAN protocol is *Ethernet*. Large corporations typically use gigabit Ethernet, which provides data transmission speeds of one billion bits per second. The *transmission control protocol/ Internet protocol (TCP/IP)* is a file transfer, packet-switching protocol that can send large files of information with the assurance that the data will arrive in uncorrupted form. Client/server architecture divides processing between clients and servers. Both are on the network, but each processor is assigned those functions it is best suited to perform. Peer-to-peer processing is a type of client/server distributed processing that allows two or more computers to pool their resources, so that each computer acts as both a client and a server.

4. **Explain how the Internet works and how it can be accessed.**

   The Internet is a global wide area network using a common communications protocol, TCP/IP. The set of rules used to send and receive packets from one machine to another over the Internet is known as the Internet protocol (IP). Other protocols are used in connection with IP. The best-known of these is the *transmission control protocol (TCP)*. The IP and TCP protocols are so commonly used together that they are referred to as the *TCP/IP protocol*.

   The Internet can be accessed through a number of different ways including Dial-up, ISDN, DSL, cable modem, satellite, wireless, and Fibre-to-the-home(FTTH).

5. **Differentiate between the Internet and the World Wide Web.**

   The Internet is a global network of computer networks, using a common communications protocol, TCP/IP. The *World Wide Web* is a system that stores, retrieves, formats, and displays information accessible through a browser.

KEY TERMS

analog signals, 436

asynchronous transfer mode (ATM), 440

backbone network, 443

bandwidth, 439

bits, 436

bridge, 442

broadband, 439

broadcast media, 438

browsers, 450

cable media, **438**

cable modem, 437

clients, 444

client/server computing, 444

coaxial cable, 438

communications channels, 438

communications processors, 437

DISCUSSION QUESTIONS

1. What are the implications of having fibre-optic cable in everyone's home?
2. What are the implications of peer-to-peer computing for the music industry? For the motion picture industry?
3. Discuss the pros and cons of P2P networks.
4. Should the Internet be regulated? If so, by whom?
5. Discuss the pros and cons of delivering this book over the Internet.
6. Explain how the Internet works. Assume you are talking with someone who has no knowledge of information technology (in other words, keep it very simple).
7. Do some web pages take longer to download than others? If so, why? Explain your answer.
8. Draw a chart of your university's campuses and faculties and indicate where it would use LANs and WANs.
9. Visit the World Wide Web Consortium (*www.w3.org*) and prepare a presentation explaining what it does and its role in developing the world wide web.

PROBLEM-SOLVING ACTIVITIES

1. Access several P2P applications, such as SETI@home. Describe the purpose of each and which ones you would like to join.

2. Access *www.ipv6.com* and learn about more advantages of IPv6.

3. Access *www.icann.org* and learn more about this important organization.

4. You want to set up your own website using your name for the domain name (for example, KellyRainer).
   a. Explain the process for registering a domain.
   b. Which top-level domain will you use and why?
   c. Access *www.icann.org* and obtain the name of an agency or company that can register a domain for the TLD that you selected.

   Access the website for that agency or company to learn the process that you must use. How much will it initially cost to register your domain name? How much will it cost to maintain that name in the future?

GLOSSARY

access controls Controls that restrict unauthorized individuals from using information resources and that are concerned with user identification.

accountability The taking of responsibility for actions that were taken.

ad-hoc (on-demand) reports Non-routine reports that often contain special information that is not included in routine reports.

adware Alien software designed to help pop-up advertisements appear on your screen.

affinity portal Website offering a single point of entry to an entire community of people with affiliated interests.

aggregator Website that provides collections of content from the Web.

agile development A software development methodology that delivers functionality in rapid iterations, measured in weeks, requiring frequent communication, development, testing, and delivery.

AJAX (asynchronous Java script and XML) Web development technique that allows portions of web pages to reload with fresh data instead of requiring the entire web page to reload.

alien software Clandestine software that is installed on your computer through duplicitous methods.

analog signals Continuous waves that transmit information by altering the amplitude and frequency of the waves.

analytical CRM Customer relationship management systems that analyze customer behaviour and perceptions in order to provide actionable business intelligence.

anti-malware systems (antivirus software) Software packages that attempt to identify and eliminate viruses, worms, and other malicious software.

applet A small Java application that can be included in an HTML page on the Internet.

application controls Controls that protect specific applications.

application portfolio A prioritized list of existing and potential IT systems, organized by application.

application program (also called **program**) A computer program designed to support a specific task or business process.

application service provider (ASP) An agent or vendor who assembles the software needed by enterprises and packages them with outsourced development, operations, maintenance, and other services.

application software The class of computer instructions that directs a computer system to perform specific processing activities and provide functionality for users.

arithmetic-logic unit (ALU) Portion of the CPU that performs the mathematic calculations and makes logical comparisons.

artificial intelligence (AI) A subfield of computer science concerned with studying the thought processes of humans and representing the effects of those processes via machines.

asymmetric encryption (see **public key encryption**)

asynchronous transfer mode (ATM) Data transmission technology that uses packet switching and allows for almost unlimited bandwidth on demand.

attribute (also called **field**) Characteristic or quality of a particular entity.

auction Competitive process in which either a seller solicits consecutive bids from buyers or a buyer solicits bids from sellers.

audit The accumulation and evaluation of evidence that is used to prepare a report about the information or controls that are being examined, using established criteria and standards.

authentication A process that determines the identity of the person requiring access.

authorization A process that determines which actions, rights, or privileges the person has, based on verified identity.

autonomic systems (also called **autonomic computing**) Computer systems designed to manage themselves without human intervention.

backbone network The main fibre-optic network that links the nodes of a network.

back door Typically a password, known only to the attacker, that allows the attacker to access the system without having to go through any security procedures.

bandwidth The range of frequencies available in a communications channel, stated in bits per second.

banner Electronic billboard on a website. These typically contain a short text or graphical message to promote a product or a vendor.

batch processing The use of a transaction processing system to process data in batches at fixed periodic intervals.

best practices The most successful solutions or problem-solving methods for achieving a business outcome.

binary The form in which data and instructions can be read by the CPU—only 0s and 1s.

biometrics The science and technology of authentication (i.e., establishing the identity of an individual) by measuring the subject's physiologic or behavioural characteristics.

bits Binary digit (0s and 1s), the only data that a CPU can process.

blacklisting A process in which a company identifies certain types of software that are not allowed to run in the company environment.

blog (also called **weblog**) Personal website, open to the public, in which the site creator expresses his or her feelings or opinions.

blogosphere Collection of the millions of blogs on the Web.

Bluetooth Chip technology that enables short-range connection (data and voice) between wireless devices.

bricks-and-mortar organization Purely physical organizations.

bridge A communications processor that connects two networks of the same type.

broadband A transmission speed ranging from 256 Kbps up to several terabits per second.

broadcast media (also called **wireless media**) Communications channels that use electromagnetic media (the "airwaves") to transmit data.

browsers Software applications through which users primarily access the World Wide Web.

brute force attack A password attack that uses massive computing resources to try every possible combination of password options to uncover a password.

buddy mining (see **social data mining**)

bullwhip effect Erratic shifts in orders from customers, manufacturers, and suppliers in a supply chain.

bundling A form of cross-selling where an enterprise sells a group of products or services together at a lower price than the combined individual price of the products.

business intelligence (BI) systems Information systems that provide computer-based support for complex, non-routine decisions, primarily for middle managers and knowledge workers.

business model Method by which a company generates revenue to sustain itself.

business process A collection of related activities that produce a product or a service of value to the organization, its business partners, and/or its customers.

business process management (BPM) A management technique that includes methods and tools to support the design, analysis, implementation, management, and optimization of business processes.

business-to-business electronic commerce (B2B) Electronic transactions where both the sellers and the buyers are organizations.

business-to-consumer electronic commerce (B2C) Electronic transactions where the sellers are organizations and the buyers are individuals.

business-to-employee electronic commerce (B2E) The provision of information and services from an organization to its employees via electronic means.

buy-side marketplace Electronic business model in which organizations attempt to buy needed products or services from other organizations electronically.

byte Group of eight bits.

cable media (also called **wireline media**) Communications channels that use physical wires or cables to transmit data and information.

cache memory A type of primary storage where the computer can temporarily store blocks of data used more often and that a processor can access more rapidly than main memory (RAM).

cable modem A modem that operates over coaxial cable and offers high-speed access to the Internet or corporate intranets.

campaign management applications Customer relationship management applications that help organizations plan marketing campaigns so that the right messages are sent to the right people through the right channels.

cellular telephones (also called **cellphones**) Telephones that use radio waves to provide two-way communication.

central processing unit (CPU) Hardware that performs the actual computation or "number crunching" inside any computer.

certificate authority A third party that acts as a trusted intermediary between computers (and companies) by issuing digital certificates and verifying the worth and integrity of the certificates.

channel conflict Problem in electronic retailing where different distribution channels compete for the same customer.

chat room Virtual meeting place where groups of regulars communicate.

chief information officer (CIO) The executive in charge of the information systems department in an organization.

clicks-and-mortar organization An organization that conducts some e-commerce activities over the Internet, yet its primary business is conducted in the physical world.

clickstream data Data that visitors and customers produce when they visit a website and click on hyperlinks.

clients A computer, such as a user's personal computer, that uses any of the services provided by servers.

client/server computing Form of distributed processing in which some machines (servers) perform computing functions for end-user PCs (clients).

cloud computing A type of computing where tasks are performed by computers physically removed from the user and accessed over a network.

coaxial cable Insulated copper wire; used to carry high-speed data traffic and television signals.

code of ethics A collection of principles that are intended to guide decision making by members of an organization.

cold site A backup location that provides only rudimentary services and facilities.

collaboration Efforts by two or more entities (individuals, teams, groups, or organizations) who work together to accomplish certain tasks.

collaborative CRM A function of customer relationship management systems where communications between the organization and its customers are integrated across all aspects of marketing, sales, and customer support processes.

commercial (public) portal A website that offers fairly routine content for diverse audiences; offers customization only at the user interface.

communications channel Pathway for communicating data from one location to another.

communications controls (also called **network controls**) Controls that deal with the movement of data across networks.

communications processor Hardware device that supports data transmission and reception across a telecommunications system.

compact disk read-only memory (CD-ROM) An optical disk that can be written once and then read repeatedly.

comparative reports Reports that compare performances of different business units or time periods.

competitive advantage An advantage over competitors in some measure such as cost, quality, or speed; leads to control of a market and to larger-than-average profits.

competitive forces model A business framework devised by Michael Porter that analyzes competitiveness by recognizing five major forces that could endanger a company's position.

compiler A type of systems software that converts other computer languages into machine language.

component-based development A software development methodology that uses standard components to build applications.

computer-aided software engineering (CASE) Development approach that uses specialized tools to automate many of the tasks in the systems development life cycle; upper CASE tools automate the early stages of the life cycle, and lower CASE tools automate the later stages.

computer-based information system (CBIS) An information system that uses computer technology to perform some or all of its intended tasks.

computer-integrated manufacturing (CIM) An information system that integrates various automated factory systems.

computer network A system connecting communications media, hardware, and software needed by two or more computer systems and/or devices.

computer program The sequence of instructions for the computer that make up software.

consumer-to-consumer electronic commerce (C2C) The selling of products or services between individuals.

contract software A specific software program developed for a particular company by a vendor.

control environment Management attitudes toward controls, as evidenced by management actions, as well as stated policies and procedures that address ethical issues and the quality of supervision.

control unit Part of the microprocessor in the central processing unit that sequentially accesses program instructions, decodes them, and controls the flow of data to and from the arithmetic-logic unit, the registers, the caches, primary storage, secondary storage, and attached output devices.

controls (also called **countermeasures**) Actions or measures implemented by management to prevent or detect risks or hazards, or mitigate problems.

controls evaluation A process in which the organization identifies security deficiencies and calculates the costs of implementing adequate control measures.

cookie Small amounts of information that websites store on your computer, temporarily or more or less permanently.

copyright A grant that provides the creator of intellectual property with ownership of it for the life of the creator plus 50 years.

corporate performance management The monitoring and managing of an organization's performance according to key performance indicators such as revenue, return on investment, overhead, and operational costs.

corporate portal Personalized, single point of access through a web browser to critical business information located inside and outside of an organization.

cross-selling The practice of marketing additional related products to customers based on a previous purchase.

customer-facing CRM applications Areas where customers directly interact with the organization, including customer service and support, sales force automation, marketing, and campaign management.

customer interaction centre (CIC) A customer relationship management operation where organizational representatives use multiple communication channels to interact with customers in functions such as inbound teleservice and outbound telesales.

customer relationship management (CRM) A customer-focused and customer-driven organizational strategy that concentrates on satisfying customers by addressing their requirements for products and services, and then by providing high-quality, responsive service.

customer-touching CRM applications (also called **electronic CRM** or **e-CRM**) Applications and technologies with which customers interact and typically help themselves.

customer touch point Any interaction between a customer and an organization.

cyberbanking Conducting various banking activities from home, at a place of business, or on the road instead of at a physical bank location.

cyber-crime Illegal activities executed on the Internet.

cybersquatting Registering or using domain names for the purpose of profiting from the goodwill or trademark belonging to someone else.

cyber-terrorism A premeditated, politically motivated attack against information, computer systems, computer programs, and data that results in violence against non-combatant targets by sub-national groups or clandestine agents.

cyber-warfare War in which a country's information systems could be paralyzed from a massive attack by destructive software.

darknet A private network that runs on the Internet but is open only to users who belong to it.

dashboard (also called **digital dashboard**) Information systems that support all managers of the organization by providing rapid access to timely information and direct access to structured information in the form of reports.

database A collection of related files or tables containing data.

database management system (DBMS) Set of programs that provides users with tools to add, delete, access, and analyze data stored in one location.

data dictionary Central repository that defines the format necessary to enter the data into the database.

data items An elementary description of things, events, activities, and transactions that are recorded, classified, and stored but are not organized to convey any specific meaning.

data governance Approach to managing information across an entire organization.

data mart Small data warehouse that is designed for the end user's needs in a strategic business unit (SBU) or a department.

data mining The process of searching for valuable business information in a large database, data warehouse, or data mart.

data model Diagram that represents entities in the database and their relationships.

data warehouse Repository of historical data organized by subject to support decision makers in the organization.

decision support system (DSS) System that combines models and data in an attempt to solve semi-structured and some unstructured problems.

demilitarized zone (DMZ) A separate organizational local area network that is located between an organization's internal network and an external network, usually the Internet.

denial-of-service attack A cyber-attack in which an attacker sends a flood of data packets to the target computer with the aim of overloading its resources.

dictionary attack A password attack that tries combinations of letters and numbers that are most likely to succeed in breaching security, such as all words from a dictionary.

digital certificate An electronic document attached to a file certifying that the file is from the organization it claims to be from and has not been modified from its original format or content.

digital dashboard (see **dashboard**)

digital divide The gap between those who have access to information and communications technology and those who do not.

digital dossier An electronic description of a user and his or her habits.

digital radio (see **satellite radio**)

digital signal A discrete pulse, either on or off, that conveys information in a binary form.

digital subscriber line (DSL) A high-speed, digital data-transmission technology using existing analog telephone lines.

digital video disk An optical storage device used to record digital video.

digital wallet (also called **e-wallet**) Software mechanisms that provide security measures, combined with convenience, to electronic commerce purchasing.

direct conversion Implementation process in which the old system is cut off and the new system is turned on at a certain point in time.

disintermediation Process of eliminating intermediaries ("middle men") when conducting business transactions.

distance learning (DL) Learning situation in which instructors and students do not meet face-to-face.

distributed denial-of-service (DDoS) A denial-of-service attack that sends a flood of data packets from many compromised computers simultaneously.

distributed processing Network architecture that divides processing work between two or more computers, linked together in a network.

documentation A written description of the functions of a software program.

domain name The name assigned to an Internet site, consisting of multiple parts, separated by dots, which are translated from right to left.

domain name system (DNS) The system administered by the Internet Corporation for Assigned Names and Numbers (ICANN) that assigns names to each site on the Internet.

drill-down reports Reports that show a greater level of detail than is included in routine reports.

e-business The electronic servicing of customers, collaboration with business partners, and performance of transactions within an organization.

edge computing The process by which parts of website content and processing are located close to the user to decrease response time and lower processing costs.

e-government The government's use of Internet technology in general and e-commerce in particular to deliver information and public services to citizens and business partners and suppliers.

e-learning Learning supported by the Web.

electronic commerce (EC or e-commerce) Process of buying, selling, transferring, or exchanging products, services, or information via computer networks, including the Internet.

electronic commerce systems A type of interorganizational information system that enables organizations to conduct transactions with other businesses and with customers.

electronic CRM (e-CRM) (see **customer-touching CRM applications**)

electronic data interchange (EDI) Communication standard that enables business partners to exchange routine documents, such as purchasing orders, electronically.

electronic mall Collection of individual shops under one Internet address.

electronic marketplace Central virtual market space on the Web where many buyers and many sellers can conduct electronic commerce and electronic business activities.

electronic payment system System for paying for goods and services through electronic means.

electronic retailing (e-tailing) Direct sale of products and services through electronic storefronts or electronic malls.

electronic storefront Website that represents a single store.

electronic surveillance Monitoring or tracking people's activities with the aid of computers.

employee monitoring systems Systems that monitor employees' computers, e-mail activities, and Internet surfing activities.

encryption The process of converting an original message into a form that cannot be read by anyone except the intended receiver.

end-user development The development by an organization's end users of their own applications with little or no formal assistance from the IT department.

enterprise application integration (EAI) system A system that integrates existing systems by providing layers of software that connect applications together.

enterprise network A network composed of interconnected multiple LANs and WANs.

enterprise resource planning (ERP) system Information system that takes a business process view of the overall organization to integrate the planning, management, and use of all of an organization's resources, employing a common software platform and database.

enterprise storage system An independent, external storage system that includes two or more storage devices.

entity (see **record**)

entity classes Groupings of entities of a given type.

entity-relationship (ER) diagram Graphical representation of a database consisting of entities, attributes, and relationships.

entity-relationship (ER) modelling The planning and developing of a database.

entry barrier Product or service feature that customers expect from organizations in a certain industry; an organization trying to enter this market must provide this product or service at a minimum to be able to compete.

e-procurement The purchasing of goods and services using electronic means.

ergonomics The science of adapting machines and work environments to people, focusing on creating an environment that is safe, well lit, and comfortable.

ERP II systems Interorganizational ERP systems that provide web-enabled links between key business systems (such as inventory and production) of a company and its customers, suppliers, distributors, and others.

Ethernet A common local area network protocol.

ethics The principles of right and wrong that individuals use to make choices to guide their behaviours.

e-wallet (see **digital wallet**)

exception reports Reports that include only information that exceeds certain threshold standards.

exchange (see **public exchange**)

expert systems (ES) Information systems that attempt to duplicate the work of human experts by applying reasoning capabilities, knowledge, and expertise within a specific domain.

explicit knowledge Codified (documented) knowledge in a form that can be distributed to others or transformed into a process or strategy.

exposure The harm, loss, or damage that can result if a threat compromises an information resource.

extensible markup language (XML) A programming language designed to improve the functionality of web documents by providing more flexible and adaptable data identification.

extranet A network that connects parts of the intranets of different organizations.

fat client A standard computing system such as a personal computer with hard disk and memory, attached to a network.

feasibility study Investigation that gauges the probability of success of a proposed project and provides a rough assessment of the project's feasibility.

fibre-optic cables Thousands of very thin filaments of glass fibres, surrounded by cladding, that transmit information via light pulses generated by lasers.

field (see **attribute**)

file (also called **table**) Logical grouping of related records.

file server (also called **network server**) A computer that contains various software and data files for a local area network, and contains the network operating system.

firewall A system (either hardware, software, or a combination of both) that prevents a specific type of information from moving between untrusted networks, such as the Internet, and private networks, such as a company's network.

flash memory Non-volatile computer memory that can be electronically erased and reprogrammed.

flash memory devices Electronic storage devices that contain no moving parts, use flash memory, and use 30 times less battery power than hard drives.

forward auction An auction selling goods or services where buyers bid continuously for them.

front-end processor A small secondary computer, dedicated solely to communication, that manages all routing communications with peripheral devices.

functional area information systems (FAISs) A system that provides information to managers (usually mid-level) in the functional areas, in order to support managerial tasks of planning, organizing, and controlling operations.

functional exchange Website where services such as temporary help or extra office space are traded on an "as-needed" basis.

gateway A communications processor that connects dissimilar networks by translating from one set of protocols to another.

general controls Controls that apply to more than one functional or application area.

geographic information system (GIS) A computer-based system for capturing, integrating, manipulating, and displaying data using digitized maps.

global positioning system (GPS) A wireless system that uses satellites to enable users to determine their position anywhere on earth.

globalization The integration and interdependence of economic, social, cultural, and ecological facets of life, enabled by rapid advances in information technology.

goal-seeking analysis Study that attempts to find the value of the inputs necessary to achieve a desired level of output.

graphical user interface (GUI) System software that allows users to have direct control of visible objects (such as icons) and actions, which replace command syntax.

grid computing A process that applies the unused processing resources of many geographically dispersed computers in a network to form a virtual supercomputer.

group purchasing The combining of orders by multiple buyers so that they constitute a large volume and therefore attract more seller attention.

haptic interface An interface that allows the user to feel a sense of touch by applying forces, vibrations, and/or motions to the user.

hard drive (also called **magnetic disk**) A form of secondary storage on a magnetized disk that is divided into tracks and sectors that provide addresses for various pieces of data.

hardware A set of devices (e.g., processor, monitor, keyboard, printer) that together accept data and information, process them, and display them.

holographic memory An optical technology that uses a three-dimensional medium to store data.

home page A text and graphical screen display that welcomes users and describes the organization that has established the web page.

horizontal exchange Website connecting buyers and sellers across many industries, used mainly for maintenance, repair, and operations materials.

hot site A fully configured computer facility, with all information resources and services, communications links, and physical plant operations, that duplicate a company's computing resources and provide near real-time recovery of IT operations.

hotspot A small geographical perimeter within which a wireless access point provides service to a number of users.

hyperlink A link that connects document nodes in hypertext.

hypertext An approach to document management in which documents are stored in a network of nodes connected by links and are accessed through interactive browsing.

hypertext document The combination of nodes, links, and supporting indexes for any particular topic in hypertext.

hypertext markup language (HTML) The standard programming language used on the Web to create and recognize hypertext documents.

hypertext transfer protocol (HTTP) The communications standard used to transfer pages across the Web portion of the Internet; defines how messages are formulated and transmitted.

identifier (see **primary key**)

identity theft Crime in which someone uses the personal information of others to create a false identity and then uses it for fraud.

implementation The process of converting from an old computer system to a new one.

individual social responsibility (see **organizational social responsibility**)

industry-wide portal Web portal serving an entire industry.

information Data that have been organized so that they have meaning and value to the recipient.

information systems (IS) (see **management information systems**)

information systems controls The procedures, devices, or software aimed at preventing a compromise to a system.

information technology (IT) Any computer-based tool that people use to work with information and support the information and information-processing needs of an organization.

information technology (IT) architecture A high-level map or plan of the information assets in an organization.

information technology (IT) infrastructure The physical facilities, IT components, IT services, and IT personnel that support an entire organization.

information technology (IT) steering committee A committee composed of a group of managers or staff whose purpose is to establish IT priorities and to ensure that the management information systems function is meeting the needs of the organization.

information technology (IT) strategic plan A set of long-range goals that describe the IT infrastructure and identify the major IT initiatives needed to achieve the organization's goals.

infrared A type of wireless transmission that uses red light not commonly visible to human eyes.

instance Representation of one particular entity.

integrated CASE (ICASE) tools Computer-aided software engineering (CASE) tools that provide links between upper CASE and lower CASE tools.

integrated services digital network (ISDN) A high-speed technology that allows users to transfer voice, video, image, and data simultaneously, over existing telephone lines.

intellectual capital (or **intellectual asset**; see **knowledge**)

intellectual property The intangible property created by individuals or corporations that is protected under trade secret, patent, and copyright laws.

intelligent system The various commercial applications of artificial intelligence.

Internet ("the net") The massive network that connects computer networks of businesses, organizations, government agencies, and schools around the world, quickly, seamlessly, and inexpensively.

Internet kiosk A terminal for public Internet access.

Internet protocol (IP) A set of rules responsible for disassembling, delivering, and reassembling packets over the Internet.

Internet protocol (IP) address An assigned address that uniquely identifies a computer on the Internet.

Internet service provider (ISP) A company that provides Internet connections for a fee.

Internet telephony (see **voice over Internet protocol**)

Internet2 A new, faster telecommunications network that deploys advanced network applications such as remote medical diagnosis, digital libraries, distance education, on-line simulation, and virtual laboratories.

interorganizational information system (IOS) Information system involving information flows among two or more organizations.

intranet A private network that uses Internet software and TCP/IP protocols.

intrusion detection system A system designed to detect malicious network traffic and computer usage that cannot be detected by a firewall.

inventory velocity Time between the receipt of incoming goods and the dispatch of finished, outbound products.

IS project management A directed effort to plan, organize, and manage resources to bring about the successful achievement of specific information systems goals.

IT governance A structure of relationships and processes to direct and control an enterprise in order to achieve the enterprise's goals by adding value while balancing risk versus return over IT and its processes.

IT steering committee A committee, composed of a group of managers and staff representing various organizational units, set up to establish IT priorities and to ensure that the management information systems function is meeting the needs of the enterprise.

Java Object-oriented programming language, developed by Sun Microsystems, that gives programmers the ability to develop applications that work across the Internet.

joint application design (JAD) A group-based tool for collecting user requirements and creating system designs.

just-in-time (JIT) inventory system The replenishment of inventory on an as-needed basis, reducing the overall inventory in stock.

key-indicator reports Reports that summarize the performance of critical activities.

keystroke loggers (keyloggers) Hardware or software that can record all keystrokes made on a compromised computer.

knowledge (also called **intellectual capital** and **intellectual asset**) Data and/or information that have been organized and processed to convey understanding, experience, accumulated learning, and expertise as they apply to a current problem or activity.

knowledge management (KM) Process that helps organizations manipulate important knowledge that is part of the organization's memory, usually in an unstructured format.

knowledge management system (KMS) Use of modern information technologies—the Internet, intranets, extranets, groupware, and data warehouses—to systematize, enhance, and expedite intrafirm and interfirm knowledge management.

knowledge workers Professional employees who are experts in a particular subject area and create information and knowledge.

least privilege A principle that users be granted the privilege for an activity only if there is a justifiable need to grant this authorization.

laptop and notebook computers Small, easily transportable, lightweight microcomputers.

liability The legal right that individuals have to recover the damages done to them by other individuals, organizations, or systems.

local area network (LAN) A network that connects communications devices in a limited geographical region (e.g., a building), so that every user device on the network can communicate with every other device.

location-based commerce (l-commerce) Mobile commerce transactions targeted to individuals in specific locations at specific times.

logic bombs Segments of computer code embedded within an organization's existing computer programs.

logical controls Controls that are implemented by software.

loyalty program A program that recognizes customers who repeatedly use the products or services offered by a vendor.

magnetic disk (see **hard drive**)

magnetic tape A secondary storage medium on a large open reel or in a smaller cartridge or cassette.

mainframe Relatively large computers used in large enterprises for extensive computing applications that are accessed by thousands of users.

main memory (see **primary storage**)

make-to-order (see **pull model**)

malware Malicious software such as viruses and worms.

management A process by which organizational goals are achieved through the use of resources.

management information systems (MIS) (also called **information systems**) The planning, development, management, and use of information technology tools to help people perform all tasks related to information processing and management.

mashup Website that takes different content from a number of other websites and mixes them together to create a new kind of content.

mass customization A production process in which items are produced in large quantities but are customized to fit the desires of each customer.

master data Set of core data, such as customer, product, employee, vendor, geographic location, and so on, that span the enterprise information systems.

master data management Process of storing, maintaining, exchanging, and synchronizing consistent, accurate, and timely core master data that spans all organizational business processes and applications.

mesh network Multiple Wi-Fi access points used to create a wide area network; a series of interconnected LANs.

metasearch engine Type of search engine that searches several engines at once and integrates the various findings to answer queries posted by users.

method In object-oriented programming, an instruction about what to do with encapsulated data objects.

microbrowser Internet browsers with a small file size that can work within the low-memory constraints of wireless devices and the low bandwidths of wireless networks.

microcomputers The smallest and least expensive category of general-purpose computers; also called micros, personal computers, or PCs.

microcontrollers Embedded computer chips that usually cost less and work in less-demanding applications than microprocessors.

microprocessor The central processing unit, made up of millions of transistors embedded in a circuit on a silicon wafer or chip.

microwave transmission A wireless system that uses microwaves for high-volume, long-distance, point-to-point communication.

minicomputers Relatively small, inexpensive, and compact midrange computers that perform the same functions as mainframe computers, but to a more limited extent.

mobile commerce (m-commerce) Buying and selling goods that is conducted entirely in a wireless environment.

mobile computing A real-time wireless connection between a mobile device and other computing environments, such as the Internet or an intranet.

mobile CRM An interactive customer relationship management system where communications related to sales, marketing, and customer service activities are conducted through a mobile medium for the purpose of building and maintaining customer relationships between an organization and its customers.

mobile portal A portal that aggregates and provides content and services for mobile users.

mobile wallet A technology that allows users to make purchases with a single click from their mobile devices.

model In decision making, a simplified representation, or abstraction, of reality.

modem Device that converts signals from analog to digital and vice versa.

Moore's Law Prediction by Gordon Moore, an Intel co-founder, that microprocessor complexity would double approximately every two years.

multi-channelling Integrating a company's on-line and traditional selling channels.

multi-dimensional structure Process in data warehouses of storing and representing data in more than two dimensions.

multimedia technology Computer-based integration of text, sound, still images, animation, and digitized full-motion video.

multiplexer Electronic device that allows a single communications channel to carry data transmissions simultaneously from many sources.

multiprocessing Simultaneously processing more than one program by assigning them to different processors (multiple CPUs).

multi-tasking The management of two or more tasks, or programs, running concurrently on the computer system (one CPU).

multi-threading A form of multi-tasking that runs multiple tasks within a single application, simultaneously.

nanotechnology The creation of materials, devices, and systems at a size of 1 to 100 nanometres (billionths of a metre).

narrowband A transmission speed up to 64 Kbps that can now reach speeds of up to 2 Mbps.

natural language generation (also called **voice synthesis**) Technology that enables computers to produce ordinary language, by "voice" or on a screen, so people can understand computers more easily.

natural language processing (NLP) Communicating with a computer in the user's native language.

natural language understanding (also called **speech** or **voice recognition**) The ability of a computer to comprehend instructions given in ordinary language, via the keyboard or by voice.

near-field communications (NFC) The smallest of the short-range wireless networks that is designed to be embedded in mobile devices such as cellphones and credit cards.

netbook A very small, lightweight, low-cost, energy-efficient, portable computer, typically optimized for Internet-based services such as web browsing and e-mailing.

network A connecting system (wireline or wireless) that permits different computers to share their information.

network access point (NAP) A computer that acts as an exchange point for Internet traffic and determines how traffic is routed.

network-attached storage (NAS) An enterprise storage system in which a special-purpose server provides file storage to users who access the device over a network.

network controls (see **communications controls**)

network interface card (NIC) A type of computer hardware that allows devices in a local area network to physically connect to the LAN's communications medium.

network server (see **file server**)

neural network A system of programs and data structures that approximates the operation of the human brain.

normalization Analyzing and reducing a relational database to its most streamlined form for minimum redundancy, maximum data integrity, and best processing performance.

object In object-oriented programming, the combination of a small amount of data with instructions about what to do with the data.

object-oriented development A systems development methodology that begins with aspects of the real world that must be modelled to perform a task.

object-oriented language A programming language that encapsulates a small amount of data with instructions about what to do with the data.

office automation systems (OASs) Information systems that typically support clerical staff, lower and middle managers, and knowledge workers.

off-the-shelf application software Software purchased, leased, or rented from a vendor that develops programs and sells them to many organizations; can be standard or customizable.

off-site data storage A service that allows companies to store valuable data in a secure location geographically distant from the company's data centre.

on-demand CRM A customer relationship management system that is hosted by an external vendor in the vendor's data centre.

on-line analytical processing (OLAP) Performing complex, multi-dimensional analyses of data stored in a database or data warehouse.

on-line transaction processing (OLTP) Processing of business transactions electronically in real time.

open-source CRM Customer relationship management software whose source code is available to developers and users.

open-source software Software made available in source code form at no cost to developers.

open system A model of computing products that work together by use of the same operating system with compatible software on all the different computers that would interact with one another in an organization.

operating environment A set of computer programs that adds features that enable developers to create applications without directly accessing the operating system; functions only with an operating system.

operating system (OS) The main system control program, which supervises the overall operations of the computer, allocates CPU time and main memory to programs, and provides an interface between the user and the hardware.

operational CRM The component of customer relationship management that supports the front-office business processes that directly interact with customers; i.e., sales, marketing, and service.

optical storage devices A form of secondary storage in which a laser reads the surface of a reflective plastic platter.

opt-in model A model of informed consent in which a business is prohibited from collecting any personal information unless the customer specifically authorizes it.

opt-out model A model of informed consent that permits a company to collect personal information until the customer specifically requests that the data not be collected.

organizational decision support system (ODSS) A decision support system that focuses on an organizational task or activity involving a sequence of operations and decision makers.

organizational social responsibility (also called **individual social responsibility**) Efforts by organizations to solve various social problems.

outsourcing Use of outside contractors or external organizations to acquire IT services.

package A computer program developed by a vendor and available for purchase in pre-packaged form.

packet switching The transmission technology that breaks up blocks of text into packets.

pass phrase A series of characters that is longer than a password but can be memorized easily.

password A private combination of characters that only the user should know.

password attack (see **brute force attack** and **dictionary attack**)

patent A document that grants the holder exclusive rights on an invention or process for 20 years.

peer-to-peer (P2P) processing A type of client/server distributed processing that allows two or more computers to pool their resources, making each computer both a client and a server.

penetration test A method of evaluating the security of an information system by simulating an attack by a malicious perpetrator.

people Those individuals who use hardware and software, interface with it, or use its output.

permission marketing Asking consumers to give their permission to voluntarily accept marketing tools such as on-line advertising and e-mail.

person-to-person payment Form of e-cash that enables two individuals or an individual and a business to transfer funds without using a credit card.

personal application software General-purpose, off-the-shelf application program that supports general types of processing, rather than being linked to any specific business function.

personal area network A computer network used for communication among computer devices close to one person.

pervasive computing (also called **ubiquitous computing**) A computer environment in which virtually every object has processing power with wireless or wired connections to a global network.

phased conversion Implementation process that introduces components of the new system in stages, until the entire new system is operational.

phishing attack An attack that uses deception to fraudulently acquire sensitive personal information by masquerading as an official-looking e-mail.

physical controls Controls that restrict unauthorized individuals from gaining physical access to a company's computer facilities.

pilot conversion Implementation process that introduces the new system in one part of the organization on a trial basis; when the new system is working properly, it is introduced in other parts of the organization.

piracy Copying a software program without making payment to the owner.

plug-and-play A feature that enables the operating system to recognize new hardware and install any necessary software (called device drivers) automatically.

podcast Digital audio file that is distributed over the Web using really simple syndication for playback on portable media players and personal computers.

pop-under ad Website advertisement that appears underneath the active browser window.

pop-up ad Website advertisement that appears in front of the active browser window.

portal Web-based, personalized gateway to information and knowledge that provides relevant information from different IT systems and the Internet using advanced search and indexing techniques.

primary activities Those business activities related to the production and distribution of the firm's products and services, thus creating value.

primary key (also called **identifier**) Attribute or field that uniquely identifies a record so that it can be retrieved, updated, and sorted.

primary storage (also called **main memory**) High-speed storage located directly on the motherboard that stores data to be processed by the CPU, instructions telling the CPU how to process the data, and operating systems programs.

privacy The right to be left alone and to be free of unreasonable personal intrusion.

privacy codes (see **privacy policies**)

privacy policies (also called **privacy codes**) An organization's guidelines with respect to protecting the privacy of customers, clients, and employees.

privilege A collection of related computer system operations that can be performed by users of the system.

procedures The set of instructions about how to combine components of information systems in order to process information and generate the desired output.

productivity The ratio between the inputs to a process and the outputs from that process.

profiling The process of compiling a digital dossier on a person.

program (see **application program**)

programmers IS professionals who modify existing computer programs or write new computer programs to satisfy user requirements.

programming The translation of a system's design specifications into computer code.

project A targeted effort to create a specific business-related outcome.

propagation delay The one-quarter second transmission delay in communication to and from geostationary earth orbit satellites.

proprietary application software Software that addresses a specific or unique business need for a company; it may be developed in-house or commissioned from a software vendor.

protocol The set of rules and procedures governing transmission across a network.

prototype A small-scale working model of an entire system or a model that contains only the components of the new system that are of most interest to the users.

prototyping An approach that defines an initial list of user requirements, builds a prototype system, and then improves the system in several iterations based on users' feedback.

public exchange (also called **exchange**) E-marketplace in which there are many sellers and many buyers.

public key encryption (also called **asymmetric encryption**) A type of encryption that uses two different keys, a public key and a private key.

pull model (also called **make-to-order**) Production process beginning with a customer order.

push model Production process beginning with a customer demand forecast.

query by example (QBE) Language to find information in a database where the user fills out a grid or template to construct a sample or description of the data wanted.

radio-frequency identification (RFID) technology A wireless technology that allows manufacturers to attach tags with antennas and computer chips on goods and then track their movement through radio signals.

radio transmission Transmission that uses radio-wave frequencies to send data directly between transmitters and receivers.

random access memory (RAM) The part of primary storage that holds a software program and small amounts of data when they are brought from secondary storage.

rapid application development (RAD) A development method that uses special tools and an iterative approach to rapidly produce a high-quality system.

read-only memory (ROM) Type of primary storage where certain critical instructions are safeguarded; the storage is non-volatile and retains the instructions when the power to the computer is turned off.

really simple syndication (RSS) Web technology allowing users to receive the information they want (customized information), when they want it, without having to visit a website.

real-time transaction processing Processing where transactions are processed on-line as soon as they occur.

record (also called **entity**) Person, place, thing, or event—such as a customer, an employee, or a product—about which information is maintained.

redundant arrays of independent disks (RAID) An enterprise storage system that links groups of standard hard drives to a specialized microcontroller that coordinates the drives so they appear as a single logical drive.

registers High-speed storage areas in the CPU that store very small amounts of data and instructions for short periods of time.

regular ID card An identification card that typically has the person's picture and often his or her signature.

relational database model The storage of data in two-dimensional tables where tables are related and each one contains entities (as records listed in rows) and attributes (as fields listed in columns).

request for proposal (RFP) Document that is sent to potential vendors inviting them to submit a proposal describing their software package and how it would meet the company's needs.

responsibility The acceptance of the consequences of one's decisions and actions.

reusability feature Feature of object-oriented languages that allows objects created for one purpose to be used in a different object-oriented program if desired.

reverse auction An auction selling goods or services where the supplying firms place bids for them.

reverse social engineering A type of attack in which employees approach the attacker.

risk The likelihood that a threat will occur.

risk acceptance A strategy in which an organization accepts potential risk, continues to operate with few or no controls, and absorbs any damages that occur.

risk analysis The process by which an organization assesses the value of each asset being protected, estimates the probability that each asset might be compromised, and compares the probable costs of each being compromised with the costs of protecting it.

risk limitation A strategy in which the organization limits its risk by implementing controls that minimize the impact of a threat.

risk management A process that identifies, controls, and minimizes the impact of threats in an effort to reduce risk to manageable levels.

risk mitigation A process whereby the organization takes concrete actions against risks, such as implementing controls and developing a disaster recovery plan.

risk transference A process in which the organization transfers risk by using other means to compensate for a loss, such as purchasing insurance.

router A communications processor that routes messages through several connected LANs or to a wide area network.

routine reports Reports produced at scheduled intervals.

sales force automation (SFA) The component of an operational customer relationship management system that automatically records all the aspects in a sales transaction process.

satellite radio (also called **digital radio**) A wireless system that offers uninterrupted, near CD-quality music that is beamed to radios from satellites.

satellite transmission A wireless transmission system that uses satellites for broadcast communications.

scope creep The addition of functions to an information system after the project has begun.

screen scraper Software that records a continuous "movie" of a screen's contents rather than simply recording keystrokes.

search engine Computer program that searches for specific information, by keywords, and reports the results.

secondary keys Fields that have some identifying information but typically do not identify the record or entity with complete accuracy.

secondary storage Technology that can store very large amounts of data for extended periods of time.

secure socket layer (SSL) (also called **transport layer security**) An encryption standard used for secure transactions such as credit card purchases and on-line banking.

sell-side marketplace The selling of products or services to other organizations electronically from a company's own private e-marketplace website and/or from a third-party website.

sensitivity analysis The study of the impact that changes in one (or more) parts of a model have on other parts.

sequential access Data access in which the computer system must run through data in sequence in order to locate a particular piece.

server Smaller mid-range computers that support networks, enabling users to share files, software, and other network devices.

server farm Massive data centre containing thousands of servers.

server virtualization The use of software to partition a server into separately operating virtual machines.

service level agreements (SLAs) Formal agreements regarding the division of work between a company and its vendors.

service-oriented architecture The building of business applications using web services.

short message service (SMS) A service provided to digital cellphones that can send and receive short text messages (up to 160 characters in length).

signature recognition The process by which a user signs his or her name and the system matches this signature with one previously recorded under controlled, monitored conditions.

smart card (or **smart ID card**) Card containing an embedded chip with pertinent information about the user.

social data mining (also called **buddy mining**) An attack that occurs when perpetrators seek to learn who knows whom in an organization, and how, in order to target specific individuals.

social engineering The process of getting around security systems by tricking computer users inside a company into revealing sensitive information or gaining unauthorized access privileges.

social interface A user interface that guides the user through computer applications by using cartoon-like characters, graphics, animation, and voice commands.

social networking The uploading of content on the Web in the form of text (e.g., blogs), voice (e.g., podcasts), images, and videos (e.g., videocasts) in order to share it with other users.

software A set of programs that enables the hardware to process data.

software-as-a-service (SaaS) A software delivery method in which a vendor hosts the applications and provides them as a service to customers over the Internet.

spam Unsolicited e-mail.

spamming Indiscriminate distribution of electronic ads without the permission of the receiver.

spamware Alien software that uses a computer as a launch platform for spammers.

spatial operating environment A user interface where the user stands or sits in front of one or more computer screens, gesturing with gloved hands to move images around, touch virtual objects, trace shapes, and navigate complex data.

speech recognition software Software that recognizes and interprets human speech, either one word at a time (discrete speech) or in a stream (continuous speech).

spyware Alien software that can record a user's keystrokes and/or capture passwords.

storage area network (SAN) An enterprise storage system architecture for building special, dedicated networks that allow rapid and reliable access to storage devices by multiple servers.

storage over IP Technology that uses the Internet protocol to transport stored data between devices within a storage area network; sometimes called IP over SCSI or iSCSI.

storage visualization software Software used with storage area networks to graphically plot an entire network and allow storage administrators to monitor all devices from a single console.

stored program concept Modern hardware architecture in which stored software programs are accessed and their instructions are executed (followed) in the computer's CPU, one after another.

stored-value money card Card the size of a credit card that stores a fixed amount of prepaid money.

strategic information systems (SISs) Systems that help an organization gain a competitive advantage by supporting its strategic goals and/or increasing performance and productivity.

strong passwords A password that is difficult to guess; is longer rather than shorter; contains upper- and lowercase letters, numbers, and special characters; and is not a recognizable word or string of numbers.

structured query language (SQL) Database language used to manage data in a relational database management system.

supercomputer Computers with the most processing power available; used primarily in scientific and military work for computationally demanding tasks on very large data sets.

supply chain The flow of materials, information, money, and services from raw material suppliers through factories and warehouses to the end customers.

supply chain management (SCM) The planning, organizing, and optimizing of the various activities performed along the supply chain.

supply chain visibility Ability for all organizations in a supply chain to access or view relevant data on purchased materials as these materials move through their suppliers' production processes and transportation networks to their receiving docks.

support activities Business activities that do not add value directly to a firm's product or service under consideration but support the primary activities that do add value.

surfing The process of navigating around the Web by pointing and clicking a web browser.

switch A special-purpose computer that allows devices in a local area network to communicate directly with each other.

synchronous optical network (SONET) An interface standard for transporting digital signals over fibre-optic lines; allows the integration of transmissions from multiple vendors.

system control program A software program that controls the use of the hardware, software, and data resources of a computer system.

system performance monitor A program that monitors the processing of jobs on a computer system and monitors system performance in areas such as processor time, memory space, and application programs.

system security monitor A program that monitors a computer system to protect it and its resources from unauthorized use, fraud, or destruction.

system support program Software that supports the operations, management, and users of a computer system by providing a variety of support services. Examples include system utility programs, performance monitors, and security monitors.

system utility A program that accomplishes common tasks such as sorting records, creating directories and subdirectories, locating files, and managing memory usage.

systems analysis The examination of the business problem that the organization plans to solve with an information system.

systems analysts IS professionals who specialize in analyzing and designing information systems.

systems design Specifications that describe how the new system will provide a solution to the business problem.

systems development life cycle (SDLC) Traditional structured framework, used for large IT projects, that consists of sequential processes by which information systems are developed.

systems software The class of computer instructions that serves primarily as an intermediary between computer hardware and application programs; provides important self-regulatory functions for computer systems.

systems stakeholders All people who are affected by changes in information systems.

table (see **file**)

tacit knowledge Cumulative store of subjective or experiential learning (an organization's experiences, insights, expertise, know-how, trade secrets, skill sets, understanding, and learning).

tag Keyword or term that describes a piece of information (e.g., a blog, a picture, an article, or a video clip).

T-carrier system A digital transmission system that defines circuits that operate at different rates, all of which are multiples of the basic 64 Kbps used to transport a single voice call.

technical specialists Experts on a certain type of technology, such as databases or telecommunications.

telecommunications system The hardware and software that transmit information from one location to another.

telecommuting Ability to work from anywhere and at any time enabled by information technology.

teleconferencing The use of electronic communication that allows two or more people at different locations to have a simultaneous conference.

telemetry The wireless transmission and receipt of data gathered from remote sensors.

thin-client systems Desktop computer systems that do not offer the full functionality of a PC.

threat Any danger to which an information resource may be exposed.

thumb drive Storage device that fits into the USB port of a personal computer and is used for portable storage.

token Device with embedded chip and a digital display that presents a log-in number that employees use to access the organization's network.

top-level domain (TLD) The rightmost part of an Internet name, indicating the type of organization that owns the site.

trade secret Intellectual work, such as a business plan, that is a company secret and is not based on public information.

transaction Any business event that generates data worth capturing and storing in a database.

transaction processing system (TPS) An information system that supports the monitoring, collection, storage, processing, and dissemination of data from the organization's basic business transactions.

transmission control protocol/Internet protocol (TCP/IP) A file transfer protocol that can send large files of information across sometimes unreliable networks with assurance that the data will arrive uncorrupted.

transport layer security (TLS) (see **secure socket layer**)

trap door (see **back door**)

triple constraint of project management Three factors—time, cost, and scope—that constrain all IS projects.

Trojan horse A software program containing a hidden function that presents a security risk.

tunnelling A process that encrypts each data packet to be sent and places each encrypted packet inside another packet.

Turing test A test for artificial intelligence in which a human interviewer, conversing with both an unseen human being and an unseen computer, cannot determine which is which; named for English mathematician Alan Turing.

twisted-pair wire Strands of copper wire twisted together in pairs.

ubiquitous computing (see **pervasive computing**)

ultramobile PC Small, mobile computer that has the full functionality of a desktop computer, but is smaller and lighter than traditional laptops and notebooks.

ultra-wideband (UWB) A high-bandwidth wireless technology with transmission speeds in excess of 100 Mbps that can be used for such applications as streaming multimedia from a personal computer to television.

unified communications Simplified and integrated forms of communications—voice, voice mail, fax, chat, e-mail, instant messaging, short message service, presence (location) services, and videoconferencing—on a common hardware and software platform.

uniform resource locator (URL) The set of letters that identifies the address of a specific resource on the Web.

up-selling A sales strategy where the organizational representative will provide to customers the opportunity to purchase higher-value related products or services as opposed to or along with the consumer's initial product or service selection.

utility computing A type of computing where a service provider makes computing resources available to a customer as needed.

value-added network (VAN) A private, data-only network that is managed by an outside third party and used by multiple organizations to obtain economies in the cost of network service and network management.

value chain model Model that shows the primary activities that sequentially add value to the profit margin; also shows the support activities.

value system A business system that includes producers, suppliers, distributors, and buyers, all with their value chains.

vendor-managed inventory Approach to inventory management where the retailer does not manage the inventory for a particular product or group of products; instead, the supplier manages the entire inventory process.

vertical exchange Website connecting buyers and sellers in a given industry.

vertical integration Business strategy in which a company buys its upstream suppliers to ensure that its essential supplies are available as soon as they are needed.

videocast Digital video file that is distributed over the Web using really simple syndication for playback on portable media players and personal computers.

videoconference Form of communication where participants in one location can see participants' documents and presentations at other locations.

viral marketing On-line "word-of-mouth" marketing.

virtual bank Bank with only an Internet presence.

virtual collaboration Using digital technologies that enable organizations or individuals to collaboratively plan, design, develop, manage, and research products, services, and innovative applications.

virtual group (team) Group members who are in different locations and connected by means of collaboration technology.

virtual memory A feature that simulates more main memory than actually exists in the computer system by extending primary storage into secondary storage.

virtual organization Company engaged only in electronic commerce.

virtual private network (VPN) A private network that uses a public network (usually the Internet) to securely connect users with encryption of the traffic.

virtual reality (VR) Interactive, computer-generated, three-dimensional graphics delivered to the user through a head-mounted display.

virtual university A university that allows students to take classes from home or at an off-site location, via the Internet.

virus Malicious software that can attach itself to (or "infect") other computer programs without the owner of the program being aware of the infection.

voice over Internet Protocol (VoIP; also called Internet telephony) Communication technology where analogue voice signals are digitized, sectioned into packets, and then sent over the Internet.

voice portal A website with an audio interface.

voice recognition A security application whereby the user speaks a phrase that has been previously recorded under controlled, monitored conditions, and the voice recognition system matches the two voice signals.

voice synthesis (see **natural language generation**)

vulnerability The possibility that an information resource will suffer harm by a threat.

vulnerability management system A system that handles security vulnerabilities on unmanaged, remote devices and, in doing so, extends the security perimeter that exists for the organization's managed devices.

warm site A site that provides many of the same services and options of the hot site but does not include the company's applications.

web services Applications delivered over the Internet using a set of shared protocols and standards, allowing different systems to "talk" with one another—that is, share data and services—without human intervention.

Web 2.0 Loose collection of information technologies and applications, and the websites that use them, that encourage user participation, social interaction, and collaboration.

weblog (see **blog**)

webmaster The person in charge of an organization's website.

website Collectively, all of the web pages of a particular company or individual.

what-if analysis The study of the impact of a change in the assumptions (input data) on the proposed solution.

whitelisting A process in which a company identifies acceptable software and permits it to run, and either prevents anything else from running or lets new software run in a quarantined environment until the company can verify its validity.

wide area networks (WANs) A network, generally provided by common carriers, that covers a wide geographic area.

wiki Website on which anyone can post material and make changes to other material.

wireless Telecommunications in which electromagnetic waves carry the signal between communicating devices.

wireless access point An antenna connecting a mobile device to a wired local area network.

wireless application protocol (WAP) The standard that enables wireless devices with tiny display screens, low-bandwidth connections, and minimal memory to access web-based information and services.

wireless fidelity (Wi-Fi) A set of standards for wireless local area networks based on the IEEE 802.11 standard.

wireless local area network (WLAN) A computer network in a limited geographical area that uses wireless transmission for communication.

wireless media (see **broadcast media**)

wireless network interface card (NIC) A device that has a built-in radio and antenna and is essential to enable a computer to have wireless communication capabilities.

wireless sensor network (WSN) Network of interconnected, battery-powered, wireless sensors (called *motes*) placed in the physical environment.

wireline media (see **cable media**)

work group Two or more individuals who act together to perform some task.

workflow Movement of information as it flows through the sequence of steps that make up an organization's work procedures.

workstations Powerful desktop-size computers that run computationally intensive scientific, engineering, and financial applications.

World Wide Web (also called **the Web, WWW,** or **W3**) A system of universally accepted standards for storing, retrieving, formatting, and displaying information via a client/server architecture; it uses the transport functions of the Internet.

worms Destructive programs that replicate themselves without requiring another program to provide a safe environment for replication.

zero-day attack An attack that takes advantage of a newly discovered, previously unknown vulnerability in a particular software product; perpetrators attack the vulnerability before the software vendor can prepare a patch for it or sometimes before the vendor is even aware of the vulnerability.

INDEX